W9-BLH-727

# CLEARING THE LAST HURDLE
## Mapping Success on the Bar Exam

## Editorial Advisors

**Rachel E. Barkow**
*Segal Family Professor of Regulatory Law and Policy*
*Faculty Director, Center on the Administration of Criminal Law*
*New York University School of Law*

**Erwin Chemerinsky**
*Dean and Distinguished Professor of Law*
*Raymond Pryke Professor of First Amendment Law*
*University of California, Irvine School of Law*

**Richard A. Epstein**
*Laurence A. Tisch Professor of Law*
*New York University School of Law*
*Peter and Kirsten Bedford Senior Fellow*
*The Hoover Institution*
*Senior Lecturer in Law*
*The University of Chicago*

**Ronald J. Gilson**
*Charles J. Meyers Professor of Law and Business*
*Stanford University*
*Marc and Eva Stern Professor of Law and Business*
*Columbia Law School*

**James E. Krier**
*Earl Warren DeLano Professor of Law*
*The University of Michigan Law School*

**Tracey L. Meares**
*Walton Hale Hamilton Professor of Law*
*Director, The Justice Collaboratory*
*Yale Law School*

**Richard K. Neumann, Jr.**
*Professor of Law*
*Maurice A. Deane School of Law at Hofstra University*

**Robert H. Sitkoff**
*John L. Gray Professor of Law*
*Harvard Law School*

**David Alan Sklansky**
*Stanley Morrison Professor of Law*
*Faculty Co-Director, Stanford Criminal Justice Center*
*Stanford Law School*

# CLEARING THE LAST HURDLE
## Mapping Success on the Bar Exam

Second Edition

Wanda M. Temm

*Clinical Professor of Law*
*Director of Bar Services*
*University of Missouri-Kansas City School of Law*

 Wolters Kluwer

Copyright © 2018 CCH Incorporated. All Rights Reserved.

Published by Wolters Kluwer in New York.

Wolters Kluwer Legal & Regulatory U.S. serves customers worldwide with CCH, Aspen Publishers, and Kluwer Law International products. (www.WKLegaledu.com)

No part of this publication may be reproduced or transmitted in any form or by any means, electronic or mechanical, including photocopy, recording, or utilized by any information storage or retrieval system, without written permission from the publisher. For information about permissions or to request permissions online, visit us at www.WKLegaledu.com, or a written request may be faxed to our permissions department at 212-771-0803.

To contact Customer Service, e-mail customer.service@wolterskluwer.com, call 1-800-234-1660, fax 1-800-901-9075, or mail correspondence to:

Wolters Kluwer
Attn: Order Department
PO Box 990
Frederick, MD 21705

Printed in the United States of America.

1 2 3 4 5 6 7 8 9 0

ISBN 978-1-4548-9225-0

Library of Congress Cataloging-in-Publication Data

Names: Temm, Wanda M., author.
Title: Clearing the last hurdle : mapping success on the bar exam / Wanda M.
    Temm, Clinical Professor of Law, Director of Bar Services, University of
    Missouri-Kansas City School of Law.
Description: Second edition. | New York : Wolters Kluwer, [2017] | Includes
    bibliographical references and index.
Identifiers: LCCN 2017029426 | ISBN 9781454892250
Subjects: LCSH: Bar examinations—United States. | Law examinations—United
    States.
Classification: LCC KF303 .T46 2017 | DDC 349.73076—dc23
LC record available at https://lccn.loc.gov/2017029426

## About Wolters Kluwer Legal & Regulatory U.S.

Wolters Kluwer Legal & Regulatory U.S. delivers expert content and solutions in the areas of law, corporate compliance, health compliance, reimbursement, and legal education. Its practical solutions help customers successfully navigate the demands of a changing environment to drive their daily activities, enhance decision quality and inspire confident outcomes.

Serving customers worldwide, its legal and regulatory portfolio includes products under the Aspen Publishers, CCH Incorporated, Kluwer Law International, ftwilliam.com and MediRegs names. They are regarded as exceptional and trusted resources for general legal and practice-specific knowledge, compliance and risk management, dynamic workflow solutions, and expert commentary.

For Katie, Carrie, and Keith—
the loves of my life,

and

For the students at the University of Missouri-Kansas City
School of Law, this is for you.

—WMT

# Summary of Contents

*Contents*                                                                  xi
*Preface and Acknowledgments*                                              xvii

CHAPTER 1
## Putting the Pieces Together                                                1

CHAPTER 2
## Understanding Memory and Mind Maps                                        11

CHAPTER 3
## Developing Your Game Plan                                                 23

CHAPTER 4
## Building Essay-Writing Skills                                             35

CHAPTER 5
## Building Multistate Performance Test Skills                               53

CHAPTER 6
## Building Multistate Bar Examination Skills                                83

CHAPTER 7
## Building Confidence with Strategies                                       93

CHAPTER 8
## Not the First Time                                                       103

CHAPTER 9
## Mapping MBE Topics—Civil Procedure                                       107

CHAPTER 10
## Mapping MBE Topics—Constitutional Law                                    125

CHAPTER 11
## Mapping MBE Topics—Contracts                                             147

CHAPTER 12
## Mapping MBE Topics—Criminal Law and Procedure                            167

CHAPTER 13
## Mapping MBE Topics—Evidence                                              189

CHAPTER 14
## Mapping MBE Topics—Real Property                                         209

CHAPTER 15
## Mapping MBE Topics—Torts                                                 233

CHAPTER 16
**Mapping Business Topics** 259

CHAPTER 17
**Mapping Trusts and Estates** 279

CHAPTER 18
**Mapping Family Law** 295

CHAPTER 19
**Mapping Secured Transactions** 309

CHAPTER 20
**Mapping Conflict of Laws** 321

APPENDIX
**Essay Score Sheets and MBE Practice Analyses** 327

# Contents

*Preface and Acknowledgments*                                    xvii

**CHAPTER 1**

## Putting the Pieces Together                                    1

   I. First Things First                                        1
  II. Developing Your Game Plan                                   2
 III. Building Confidence with Knowledge                            3
     A. Licensing Requirements                             3
     B. Character and Fitness                               5
     C. The Bar Examination                                 5
        1. Multistate Bar Examination                    5
        2. Essay Questions                               6
           a. Multistate Essay Exam                     6
           b. State-Drafted Essays                      7
        3. Performance Tests                             8
           a. Multistate Performance Test               8
           b. State Performance Tests                   8
     D. Uniform Bar Examination                             8
  IV. Maintaining Your Sanity                                    9
   V. The Next Step                                            10

**CHAPTER 2**

## Understanding Memory and Mind Maps                             11

    I. Memory: What Is It and How Does It Work?                11
   II. Importance of Encoding                                  13
  III. Forgetting                                                 15
  IV. Concentration                                              16
   V. Does Writing Impact Our Ability to Remember?             16
  VI. Improving Your Memory                                      17
 VII. Mind Maps as a Memory Tool                                   17
VIII. Creating a Mind Map                                          18

**CHAPTER 3**

## Developing Your Game Plan                                      23

  I. The Starting Gate                                           23
     A. First-Time Takers                                  23
        1. For-Credit Courses                            23
        2. Taking a Commercial Bar Preparation Course    23
        3. Self-Study Approach                           24
     B. Repeat Takers                                       24

II. **The Game Plan** ..... 25
   A. Phase One—Learn the Law ..... 25
     1. Building Your Library ..... 26
     2. Using Practice Questions to Learn the Law ..... 27
     3. Finding the Answer ..... 28
   B. Phase Two—Memorize the Law ..... 28
     1. Memory Techniques ..... 28
     2. Seek Support ..... 30
     3. Using Practice Questions to Assess Your Memorization ..... 30
   C. Phase Three—Keep It Fresh ..... 30
   D. The Exam Days ..... 32
   E. Getting Your Results ..... 34

**CHAPTER 4**

# Building Essay-Writing Skills ..... 35

  I. **Type or Handwrite?** ..... 35
  II. **Scoring** ..... 35
 III. **Think First!** ..... 36
 IV. **Proper Format** ..... 40
  V. **Autopsy Your Practice Answers** ..... 44
 VI. **Common Ways to Lose Points** ..... 49
   A. Mismanaging Time ..... 49
   B. Wasting Time Answering a Question Different from the Question Asked ..... 50
   C. Not "Showing Your Work" ..... 50
   D. Assuming the Grader Knows the Law and Not Referencing Specific Tests/Elements ..... 50
   E. Writing Lengthy Sentences and Paragraphs with Grammar Issues ..... 51
   F. And, the Biggest Point Loser—Skimming All of the Questions First! ..... 51
 VII. **Avoid Panic** ..... 52

**CHAPTER 5**

# Building Multistate Performance Test Skills ..... 53

  I. **Skills Tested** ..... 53
  II. **Game Plan for the MPT** ..... 55
 III. **Proper Format** ..... 57
 IV. **Bottom Line Is Analysis** ..... 59
  V. **Practice MPT Question** ..... 60
 VI. **Point Sheet** ..... 73
 VII. **Score Sheet** ..... 79

**CHAPTER 6**

# Building Multistate Bar Examination Skills ..... 83

  I. **Preparation** ..... 83
  II. **Go Backwards** ..... 85
 III. **Autopsy MBE Questions** ..... 88

CHAPTER 7
## Building Confidence with Strategies — 93

    I. Low-Hanging Fruit — 94
    II. 75/15/10 Strategy — 95
    III. Avoid Duping Yourself — 97
    IV. Growing Your Mindset — 98
    V. Keeping Cool—Maintaining Your Sanity — 101

CHAPTER 8
## Not the First Time — 103

    I. Insufficient Preparation — 103
      A. Time Spent — 103
      B. Detail in Memorization Materials — 104
    II. Anxiety and Mindset — 104
    III. Personal Issues — 106

CHAPTER 9
## Mapping MBE Topics—Civil Procedure — 107

    I. Mind Map — 107
    II. MBE Strategies — 117
    III. Essay Practice Question — 119
    IV. MBE Practice Questions — 120

CHAPTER 10
## Mapping MBE Topics—Constitutional Law — 125

    I. Mind Map — 125
    II. MBE Strategies — 135
    III. Essay Practice Question — 138
    IV. MBE Practice Questions — 138

CHAPTER 11
## Mapping MBE Topics—Contracts — 147

    I. Criminal Law — 147
    II. MBE Strategies — 155
    III. Essay Practice Question — 157
    IV. MBE Practice Questions — 158

CHAPTER 12
## Mapping MBE Topics—Criminal Law and Procedure — 167

    I. Criminal Law — 167
    II. Criminal Procedure — 172
    III. MBE Strategies — 177
    IV. Essay Practice Question — 179
    V. MBE Practice Questions — 180

CHAPTER 13

## Mapping MBE Topics—Evidence                                                189

   I. Mind Map                                                    189
  II. MBE Strategies                                                   200
 III. Essay Practice Question                                             201
 IV. MBE Practice Questions                                              201

CHAPTER 14

## Mapping MBE Topics—Real Property                                          209

   I. Mind Map                                                    209
  II. MBE Strategies                                                   222
 III. Essay Practice Question                                             224
 IV. MBE Practice Questions                                              224

CHAPTER 15

## Mapping MBE Topics—Torts                                                  233

   I. Mind Map                                                    233
  II. MBE Strategies                                                   249
 III. Essay Practice Question                                             250
 IV. MBE Practice Questions                                              251

CHAPTER 16

## Mapping Business Topics                                                   259

   I. Agency/Partnership                                          259
    A. Agency                                                 259
     1. Mind Map                                          259
     2. Essay Practice Question                           265
    B. Partnership                                            266
     1. Mind Map                                          266
     2. Essay Practice Question                           271
  II. Corporations                                                     272
    A. Mind Map                                               272
    B. Essay Practice Question                                278

CHAPTER 17

## Mapping Trusts and Estates                                                279

   I. Decedents' Estates                                          279
    A. Mind Map                                               279
    B. Essay Practice Question                                286
  II. Trusts                                                           287
    A. Mind Map                                               287
    B. Essay Practice Question                                292

CHAPTER 18

## Mapping Family Law                                                        295

   I. Mind Map                                                    295
  II. Essay Practice Question                                          307

CHAPTER 19
# Mapping Secured Transactions                     309

   I. Mind Map                                    309
  II. Essay Practice Question                     319


CHAPTER 20
# Mapping Conflict of Laws                          321

   I. Mind Map                                    321
     A. Recognition of Another State's Judgment    321
     B. Choice of Law                          322
        1. Torts                           324
        2. Contracts                       324
        3. Property                        324
        4. Corporations                    325
        5. Family Law                      325
  II. Essay Practice Question                     326


APPENDIX
# Essay Score Sheets and MBE Practice Analyses      327

    I. Civil Procedure                            327
   II. Constitutional Law                           337
  III. Contracts                                       353
  IV. Criminal Law and Procedure                   371
   V. Evidence                                      384
  VI. Real Property                                 398
 VII. Torts                                          414
VIII. Business Topics                                429
  IX. Trusts and Estates                           438
   X. Family Law                                    443
  XI. Secured Transactions                         447
 XII. Conflict of Laws                              450

# Preface and Acknowledgments

## Scope

Preparing to pass the bar examination is a daunting task. Intimidating and unnerving, this task is manageable by breaking your preparation into its component parts. From reviewing substantive law to memorizing rules to practicing each type of question, this book will guide you through each task involved in bar preparation and show you how to effectively structure your study. In addition, you will improve your skills by working through practice questions that include all three types of bar exam components—multiple choice questions, essay questions, and performance tests. The book's score sheets are designed to help you structure your answers to score well.

## Content

After an introductory chapter on putting the pieces together for bar preparation, the book focuses on understanding how memory works. The bottom line of bar preparation is memorizing rules so that you can recall and use the rules applied to new hypotheticals. Chapter 2 not only describes how memory works, but it offers specific suggestions for how to encode information for later recall.

Chapter 3 focuses on establishing a game plan for bar preparation study, reviewing what a bar prep student should be doing the first few weeks of study, the next weeks, and the final weeks. Most bar prep students flounder their first few weeks because they are unsure of what exactly they should be doing. This book will guide you in how to structure your study. Chapters 4 through 6 focus on the three main parts of the bar exam in most states: essay skills, MBE skills, and performance test skills. Each chapter offers guidance on improving skills in each area, showing you how to use practice questions and score sheets to the greatest advantage.

Chapter 7 focuses on building confidence. The bar exam is a high-stakes exam—often the first high-stakes exam a bar prep student has taken. As a result, anxiety runs high. This chapter will give you specific guidance on how to handle nerves and maintain sanity during the bar preparation time period.

The following chapters then focus on each topic tested by the Multistate Essay Exam (MEE) and Multistate Bar Examination (MBE). Applicants in states that do not use the MEE will find that the skill-building suggestions and strategies work just as well in any topic area. States that do not use the MEE still test most of the same topics. I have used these materials for Missouri, a Uniform Bar Examination state, and for Kansas, a state-specific essay state, as well as for other states. Each chapter includes starter mind maps.

## How to Use This Book

This book was designed to be used in a for-credit bar review course in law school. This book may also be used as a supplemental text during your bar preparation shortly before the bar examination. In a for-credit course, your professor will likely choose to cover only some of the chapters according to the goals for the course. Use the remaining chapters to supplement any commercial provider's materials during your bar preparation.

The book does not provide complete, detailed outlines of the substantive law of each topic. It does provide an initial outline of each topic that can form your initial steps in preparing your own memorization materials. As explained in Chapter 3, reviewing prepared outlines is only the first step in preparing your study materials; you will continue to supplement your materials with rules that you have missed in your practice multiple choice and essay questions.

## Author

Professor Wanda M. Temm joined the University of Missouri-Kansas City School of Law faculty in 1991 as a full-time legal writing faculty member. In the early 2000s, the UMKC School of Law faculty began studying why previous excellent bar results had taken a significant fall to 67-72%—slightly below the state average. A faculty committee ultimately concluded that a variety of factors influenced bar passage. Professor Temm co-founded the UMKC Bar Prep Program and moved the program from a few practice essays to a program that provides study strategies and tactics for all aspects of bar preparation. UMKC's current bar passage rate for students actively participating in the program is above 95%, reaching 100% on several occasions.

## Acknowledgments

This book is the product of materials developed for the UMKC Bar Prep Program. Many thanks go to the faculty who have taught in the program throughout the years, including Barbara Wilson, Judith Popper, Aaron House, and Leo Salinger, and to administrative assistants Elizabeth Couzens and Norma Karn, who have seen this manuscript in its various forms too many times. Their support has been unending and their contributions too numerous for words.

Special recognition goes to Rachel Wickstrum, the creator of the cartoons featured throughout the book. Her creativity and flair have resulted in visual representations of legal concepts that have helped many students to remember those concepts on the exam. Special thanks to research assistants Kelly Thompson and Jay Wheeler. Kelly's research on memory and her work on the essay score sheets were priceless. Jay's work creating the mind maps for the Teachers Manual was more detailed than I could have imagined. This book is better for their assistance.

Thanks as well to Dean Ellen Suni, the UMKC administration, and the UMKC law faculty and staff for their support of the UMKC Bar Prep Program over the years. That support has allowed us to provide our students a top-notch program using innovative teaching methods. This book would not have been created without their support.

Special thanks to the National Conference of Bar Examiners for working with me to ensure that bar applicants had access to authentic MBE, MEE, and MPT questions in this book. This book is better because of the NCBE's cooperation. In addition, the Mind Maps were created with iMindMap software. Mind Map is a registered trademark of the Buzan Organisation Limited 1990, www.thinkbuzan.com.

Lastly, special thanks to Professor Emeritus Edwin Hood. His request to "grade a few essays" started me down this path, helping me find my passion.

WMT
July 2017

# CLEARING THE LAST HURDLE
## Mapping Success on the Bar Exam

# CHAPTER 1

# Putting the Pieces Together

## I. FIRST THINGS FIRST

You are rounding the corner. The end of your law school education is in sight. But "it" is out there. Waiting for you. The bar exam. The last hurdle. The last obstacle to surpass to reach your goal of practicing law. The horror stories and rumors are everywhere. Students studying 80 hours a week and still failing. The top student in the class who failed. Students needing to take the exam multiple times to pass. How can you ever do this?

Relax. Take a deep breath. You can do this. You have either graduated or will soon graduate from law school. You were selected by your law school for your aptitude to succeed. Your law school received many other applications, but it chose you. You have been preparing for this exam since law school orientation. Since that day you have been developing the exact skills you need to succeed on the bar exam. That is what your law school education was all about: preparing you to be a lawyer. Law schools do that differently, and no one would argue that law schools do not need to improve. But each maintains the bottom line. The bottom line of any legal education is learning how to analyze law and how to apply that law to a new set of facts—the very skills the bar exam is assessing.

What you don't have and need to have to pass the exam are two things—a game plan and confidence. Your game plan includes the tasks that you complete to prepare to take the exam. Confidence includes confidence in your own abilities, trust in your preparation, and appreciating that you do not have to know everything to pass the bar exam.

A word about advice. Everyone will give it. Your fellow students, attorneys you know, your family, your friends—everyone has advice on taking the bar exam. Most of it will have some value. Even your parents' advice to get more sleep is good advice. For those that have actually taken the exam and succeeded, their advice to you probably helped them and may help you. But it may not be right for you. You may not learn the same way. You may not memorize the same way. So, listen to the advice and understand that it may or may not work for you.

## II. DEVELOPING YOUR GAME PLAN

Many students head into bar exam preparation assuming that completing the commercial bar course they purchased is all they need to do. They go to class or watch the video lectures at home. They fill in the lecture handout blanks. They do a few practice questions. They continue working. They take vacations. They think nothing of missing a week of lectures, as they can catch up later.

Well, later comes sooner than you think. And when it comes, it hits you that you just wasted a month doing not much of anything of the real work of bar prep.

What is the real work? First, you must learn the law you did not learn in law school. From courses you did not take to concepts you did not understand, bar prep is the time to get it done. Understand the subject matter and it goes without saying that you are on your way to succeed.

Second, you must commit that law to memory. The bar exam is not open book. In some jurisdictions, you walk in the room with nothing—not even your own pen. You may be counting on being able to recognize the correct answer on the multiple choice questions, but you have to write something down on the essay questions. Indeed, memorizing the law is actually the key to doing well on the multiple choice questions as well.

Next, you must learn the techniques to correctly answer multiple choice questions, to organize an essay to receive the highest score you can, and to understand the time pressure of every performance test.

Lastly, you need to be able to keep all the law you memorized fresh to be recalled on those two critical days.

How are you going to get this done? You should plan on approximately 500 hours of study. That includes the time spent in your commercial bar preparation class and the time you spend on your own. That also means that you will not have much free time. If you try to work while you are preparing, you will not spend the same amount of time as those who are focusing only on bar prep.

The biggest problem with working is fatigue. It's hard to put in an eight- or nine-hour work day and then spend four to six hours studying. It can be done, but it will definitely drain your energy. This book will guide you in how to spend your study time to put you in the best situation to succeed, whether working or not. Try not to work during the month of the exam or a minimum of two weeks prior to the exam.

Almost every commercial bar preparation course includes materials to use during the lecture with fill-in-the-blank sentences or spaces for short answers. You follow along filling in the blanks while the lecturer speaks. The purpose of these types of materials is to keep you engaged with the material as it is being presented. Just listening to lectures does not activate your brain in the fashion needed in order to remember the material in the long term. Likewise, just reading the materials is not enough. Engaging with the materials enables your brain to retain the information. This book includes many suggestions on how to engage with the material and how to transfer that material into your long-term memory, the essence of any game plan.

Just reading practice questions and their answers results in an insufficient engagement with the material. You should not wait to do practice questions until you have "everything" memorized. You need to use the questions as a means to help learn the level of detail you need in your rule, the level of detail you need in your application, the organization of the analysis, and the style of questions in each subject area. For example, you will find that questions testing proximate cause tend to follow similar fact patterns and similar calls of the question.

This book assists you with using practice questions as a means to ensure that you are studying the law in enough detail, that you are applying the law in enough detail in your answers, and that you are organizing your answers well. This book includes practice essay questions and score sheets that show you how a sample answer is broken down into the components of a written analysis. Yes, your first year legal writing course is on the bar exam! The written analysis on essays and on performance tests boils down to organizing by a series of analyses, each organized by Conclusion or Issue, Rule, Application, and Discussion. CRAC/IRAC lives on!

This book includes a starter "mind map" on every topic tested on the Multistate Essay Exam. Most states test the same topics or alter the list slightly. But, what is a mind map? A mind map is a way of thinking about a topic matter, working step by step through a topic to be sure that you have identified issues. Mind maps also help you take the entire subject matter and boil it down to the essential part of the topic that you must know to pass the question.

Do you need to write each step in a mind map on each essay? Not usually. The mind map is a thinking tool designed to help you identify issues and a memorization tool to help you encode the law into your memory.

Having a game plan structures your time so that you are not spinning your wheels and the time you spend is put to its best worth. Chapter 3 will give you more definite guidelines for how to spend your time during each part of bar preparation.

## III. BUILDING CONFIDENCE WITH KNOWLEDGE

Knowledge is empowering and reassuring. The more you know and understand the task ahead of you, the more directed your preparation can be and the more confidence you have because you are facing a known entity rather than an unknown one.

### A. Licensing Requirements

Your license to practice law is not a national license. Each state outlines its own requirements to obtain a license in that state. You will be licensed in just that state. States have different regulations regarding whether they will acknowledge and accept a license to practice law obtained in another state. That acknowledgment is called "reciprocity." One of your first tasks then is to understand the licensing rules for your state and for any other state in which you might wish to practice law.

Most licensing requirements have two major components: a determination of character and fitness to practice law and the passage of that state's bar examination. Character and fitness also includes passing the Multistate Professional

Responsibility Exam. Some states require new admittees to take a mandatory professionalism continuing legal education course[1] and/or a basic skills course.[2] Some states that have adopted the Uniform Bar Examination add the successful completion of a state-specific law examination to their licensing requirements.[3]

One resource to locate information about your specific jurisdiction's licensing requirements is the National Conference of Bar Examiners' (NCBE) website—www.ncbex.org. You will find links to every jurisdiction's licensing authority's website. Be sure to bookmark both the NCBE website and the website for your jurisdiction as these will be frequent reference sources for you.

Another invaluable resource is your law school's academic success faculty. These faculty usually have the information critical to your jurisdiction. The career services staff or student affairs staff are often the "go-to" folks to assist students with bar exam questions.

Take a minute and research the licensing requirements in your chosen jurisdiction. Complete this checklist to keep the requirements handy.[4]

---

**Licensing Requirements Checklist[4]**

Jurisdiction:

Educational requirements:


Law student registration required?


Due date for application to take bar examination:

Fees to take the bar examination and for character and fitness determination:


Location of bar examination:

Dates of examination:

Multistate Professional Responsibility Test passing score:

Any jurisdiction-specific additional requirements such as mandatory Continuing Legal Education (CLE) hours or passage of a state-specific exam:



Topics tested:

---

1. Ariz. R. 34(N)(1) (Arizona); C.R.C.P. 201.14(4) (Colorado).

2. West's F.S.A. Bar R. 6-12.3 (Florida); ILCS S. Ct. R. 793(C)(1) (Illinois); I.C.A. R. 41.12 (Iowa).

3. Missouri requires a mandatory open book test entitled the "Missouri Educational Component Test." Mo. Sup. Ct. R. 8.08(c). Arizona requires applicants to complete a course on Arizona law. Ariz. R. 34(j). New York requires both an online New York law course and an online New York law exam. N.Y. R. Ct. 520.9(2)-(3).

4. Denise Riebe and Michael Hunter Schwartz, *Pass the Bar!* 59-60 (Carolina Acad. Press 2006).

## B. Character and Fitness

As an attorney, you will represent clients and owe those clients a fiduciary duty. You will also be an officer of the court. The goal of a character and fitness determination is "to assure the protection of the public and safeguard the justice system."[5] To do that, the Board of Bar Examiners in each jurisdiction determines an applicant's character and fitness through an investigation.

Each jurisdiction will define "character and fitness" for itself. A typical definition is that an applicant must possess the "traits, including honesty, trustworthiness, diligence and reliability that are relevant to and have a rational connection with the applicant's present fitness to practice law."[6] Boards of bar examiners are often concerned the most with an applicant's criminal record, untreated mental illness and substance abuse, lack of candor, and irresponsibility.[7] Each board will have its own guidelines on each of these concerns. Your academic success faculty and perhaps your professional responsibility faculty may be able to answer your questions concerning personal issues.

When a Board of Bar Examiners has a concern about your character and fitness application, it may require you to appear before it to answer questions. Depending upon the concerns, you may want to engage an attorney knowledgeable about character and fitness hearings.

## C. The Bar Examination

The actual exam is typically two or three days. Each state determines for itself how its examination is constructed. Typical components include multiple choice questions, essay questions, and performance tests.

### 1. Multistate Bar Examination

All states except Louisiana include multiple choice questions developed by the NCBE. In addition, Guam, Northern Mariana Islands, Palau, and the Virgin Islands have adopted these multiple choice questions. These questions are given on the same two dates across the nation in every adopting jurisdiction—the last Wednesday of February and July. This part of the bar examination is called the Multistate Bar Examination (MBE).

The MBE consists of 100 multiple choice questions in a 3-hour time period in the morning and another 100 multiple choice questions in a 3-hour time period in the afternoon. If you are down to the last five minutes and haven't answered every question, fill in the rest of the answer grid and then go back and correct if you have time. Twenty-five of the questions are being evaluated for future use. Be sure to answer all 200 questions as you will not know which questions are the test questions. There is no penalty for incorrect answers.

The subjects include Civil Procedure; Constitutional Law; Contracts, including the common law and the Uniform Commercial Code Article 2; Criminal Law

---

5. Mont. R. Pro. on Comm'n on Character and Fitness (available at https://c.ymcdn.com/sites/montanabar.site-ym.com/resource/resmgr/Admissions/Rules_for_Commission_on Char.pdf).

6. Minn. R. for Admission to the Bar 2A(6).

7. Lori E. Shaw, *What Does It Take to Satisfy Character and Fitness Requirements?*, 37 Student Lawyer, October 2009 (available at http://www.americanbar.org/publications/syllabus_home/volume_44_2012-2013/winter_2012-2013/professionalism_whatdoesittaketosatisfychracterandfitness require.html).

and Procedure; Evidence (testing the Federal Rules of Evidence); Real Property; and Torts. The NCBE provides subject matter outlines for each subject to help applicants direct their study.

The MBE is scored by the NCBE on a nation-wide basis. The 25 test questions are not included in the score. The raw score is thus determined by your correct answers to 175 of the questions minus any questions that the NCBE decides are not "good" questions. Why would a question be tossed out? Questions are tossed out when the nation-wide results show the question was ambiguous or that there truly was more than one correct answer. Your raw score is then scaled to reflect the difficulty of the exam vis-à-vis prior exams. It is that scaled score that is then used by the jurisdictions. Each jurisdiction decides how much weight to give that score. For example, Uniform Bar Examination states and California weigh the MBE scaled score at 50%.

Chapter 6 will assist you in developing your strategy for studying for the MBE and in how to attack the questions to improve your chances of selecting the correct response.

### 2. Essay Questions

No matter who drafts the essay questions or what law is applied, essays require analyzing a set of facts, recalling the rule from memory, applying that law, and then communicating your analysis in written form. Whether the question is 30 minutes or 60 minutes, contains one major issue or a dozen issues, or covers one topic or three topics, the analysis is what counts in the end.

#### a. Multistate Essay Exam

The Multistate Essay Exam (MEE) is written by the NCBE. Thirty-eight jurisdictions currently utilize MEE questions. Six 30-minute questions are offered for each administration of the exam. Jurisdictions may decide which of the questions they use. Uniform Bar Examination states must use all six. Jurisdictions also decide the relative weight given to the MEE and other scores. Uniform Bar Examination jurisdictions weight the MEE component 30%.

The NCBE considers "[t]he purpose of the MEE is to test the examinee's ability to

- identify legal issues raised by a hypothetical factual situation;
- separate material which is relevant from that which is not;
- present a reasoned analysis of the relevant issues in a clear, concise, and well-organized composition; and
- demonstrate an understanding of the fundamental legal principles relevant to the probable solution of the issues raised by the factual situation."[8]

The MEE covers the topics included in the MBE and additional topics. The following table lists these topics. Some of these topics are actually two separate topics. For example, Criminal Law has quite a different focus than Criminal Procedure. One focuses on the elements of crimes, *mens rea*, and defenses while the other focuses on the constitutional protections afforded criminal defendants.

---

8. http://www.ncbex.org/exams/mee/.

Most questions focus on only one area of law. Some questions may include more than one area of law. For example, Conflicts of Law is always paired with another topic such as Federal Civil Procedure or Family Law.

MEE questions are scored by each jurisdiction and not by the NCBE. Any questions about scoring should be directed to that jurisdiction. The raw scores are then sent to the NCBE, which takes the raw score and employs any weighting required by the jurisdiction. The NCBE determines the scaled score and returns it to the jurisdiction.

| MEE TOPICS |
| --- |
| Agency and Partnership |
| Civil Procedure |
| Conflict of Laws |
| Constitutional Law (Federal) |
| Contracts (including UCC Article 2 Sales) |
| Corporations and Limited Liability Companies |
| Criminal Law and Procedure |
| Decedents' Estates |
| Evidence |
| Family Law |
| Real Property |
| Torts |
| Trusts and Future Interests |
| Uniform Commercial Code: Secured Transactions |

### b. State-Drafted Essays

State-drafted essays are used in jurisdictions that do not use the MEE in whole. These jurisdictions may use a combination of MEE questions and state-drafted questions or rely solely on state-drafted questions. These questions are typically drafted by the members of the Board of Law Examiners themselves or by committees appointed by the board.

State-drafted essays may focus on specific aspects of that jurisdiction's law or may focus on the same topics covered in the MEE. Texas, for example, tests consumer rights, including insurance, oil and gas, and bankruptcy. Florida includes legal ethics and professionalism. Be sure to research the topics your state's bar examination covers.

State-drafted questions are scored by that jurisdiction. Different jurisdictions grade on different scales, such as 5 points, 6 points, 10 points, or 100 points. Those raw scores are then sent to the NCBE to be scaled to the same scale as the MBE with the jurisdiction's required weighting. Then, just like the MEE, that scaled score is sent back to the jurisdiction.

Chapter 4 focuses exclusively on building essay-writing skills. That chapter's focus on skill building works for MEE and for state-drafted essays. Using these specific strategies can help you have your structure set so that you can drop the rule in and apply it and keep your focus on getting enough detail in your answer.

### 3. Performance Tests

#### a. Multistate Performance Test

The Multistate Performance Test (MPT) adds another dimension to the skills tested on the bar examination. Just like the MBE and essay questions, the MPT is designed to test your analysis skills. The MPT is an assessment of "an examinee's ability to use fundamental lawyering skills in a realistic situation."[9] This is accomplished by giving the applicant a drafting "task that a beginning lawyer should be able to accomplish."[10]

Good news! The MPT does not require that you have law memorized. Instead, it gives you the law to analyze and asks you to apply that law to a set of facts. The facts are contained in a "File," which can include letters, deposition transcripts, witness interviews, invoices—basically anything that an attorney uses to gather facts. Sometimes facts are missing and part of the applicant's task is to identify those missing facts. Other facts are ambiguous or irrelevant. Your job is to recognize those situations and identify sources of additional facts.

The law is contained in a "Library." This Library includes all the law you are to analyze—statutes, excerpts from cases, administrative regulations, or rules. You are not to support your analysis with other law that you know. You analyze what is given to you.

The MPT includes a memo from a partner at your firm or from a supervising district attorney requesting that you draft a particular document. The NCBE lists the different kinds of documents that have been included in past MPTs. Most of the time, the MPT is a letter, a memo, or a brief.

MPTs are graded by the jurisdiction, usually on the same scale as an essay question. That score is then sent to the NCBE who scales it according to each jurisdiction's policies.

What is most challenging about the MPT is the time constraint. Each MPT is 90 minutes. Virtually every applicant will be time-pressured to complete the task. Time management is an essential strategy to perform well on the MPT. Chapter 5 will give you specific suggestions for developing a game plan to do well on your MPTs.

#### b. State Performance Tests

Some jurisdictions add their own performance tests. California, for example, requires that you pass one of its performance tests. It is similar to the style of the MPT, but focuses on California law.

## D. Uniform Bar Examination

In February 2011, Missouri and North Dakota were the first jurisdictions to administer the Uniform Bar Examination (UBE) developed by the National

---

9. http://www.ncbex.org/exams/mpt/.
10. *Id.*

Conference of Bar Examiners. As of the July 2018 administration, 28 jurisdictions will have adopted the examination.[11] The UBE allows your score on the bar examination to be transferred to another state, allowing licensure in more than one state without taking a second bar examination. Applicants frequently must choose a jurisdiction before they have secured employment. Once employed, they discover they are required to be licensed in a different jurisdiction. If both states have adopted the UBE, the first state's score is transferred to the second state. Thus, the applicant does not have to take two bar examinations! This increased mobility of your examination score should be more economical for an applicant. You will not have to miss work or give up weekends to study for a second bar exam. Moreover, you will not need to take another bar review course. The utility of the UBE is also seen if you do not reach a passing score in your first state. You can transfer that score to a state with a lower score cut-off if your score meets that cut-off. The second state will do its own character and fitness determination and then you become licensed to practice law after taking one bar examination. If you still desire to become licensed in your first state, you must retake the examination.

The NCBE's philosophy is that "an individual who performs to an acceptable level on a high-quality licensing test has attained valuable currency that should be accepted by other jurisdictions."[12] Each jurisdiction determines its own character and fitness requirements, sets its own passing scores, and determines how long incoming UBE scores will be accepted, among other decisions. A jurisdiction may require applicants to complete a jurisdiction-specific educational component or pass a test on jurisdiction-specific law in addition to passing the UBE.

The UBE starts with two MPT questions in the morning of the first day. The afternoon includes six 30-minute MEE questions. The second day is the MBE. The MBE is weighted 50%, the MEE 30%, and the MPT 20%. All parts of the examination are prepared by the NCBE. Jurisdictions continue to score the MEE and MPT questions themselves.

## IV. MAINTAINING YOUR SANITY

No doubt about it, the bar preparation months and examination days are a stressful time in your life. The bar examination is a high-stakes test. Failing to pass the bar exam means that you cannot practice law. While there are many things that you can do with a law degree, most graduates wish to practice law in some fashion. Additionally, most applicants either do not have employment secured following graduation or their employment requires passage of the exam. That only increases the stress.

Stress has a physical impact on your body, on your mental state, and on your thinking. If you are constantly worried and thinking about what happens after the exam, you cannot be as focused on engaging with the material and

---

11. Alabama, Alaska, Arizona, Colorado, Connecticut, District of Columbia, Idaho, Iowa, Kansas, Maine, Massachusetts, Minnesota, Missouri, Montana, Nebraska, New Hampshire, New Jersey, New Mexico, New York, North Dakota, Oregon, South Carolina, Utah, Vermont, Virgin Islands, Washington, West Virginia, and Wyoming. http://www.ncbex.org/exams/ube/.

12. http://www.ncbex.org/pdfviewer/?file=%2Fdmsdocument%2F139.

memorizing the material. Chapter 7 will give you specific suggestions for managing your stress and building your confidence in your abilities and your preparation—a key component in lessening your stress.

## V. THE NEXT STEP

Now that you have a better idea about what the bar examination actually entails, it's time to get started. Our first step is to understand how memory works. Our goal is to have as many of each bar examination topic's rules in our long-term memory as possible. How are we going to accomplish that task? Chapter 2 focuses exclusively on memory and using mind maps.

Next, you need to develop your game plan for studying and building your skills in writing essays, answering MBE questions, and writing MPTs. Chapters 4 through 6 give specific suggestions for building skills. Chapters 9 through 20 focus on specific topics and the strategies unique to each topic. Starter mind maps are included with each topic as well as practice questions. Essay score sheets and the NCBE's analysis of each MBE question are set out in the Appendix.

Lastly, you need to build your confidence. This entire book is designed to do that. Chapter 7 offers specific suggestions to build confidence. Chapter 8 focuses on specific suggestions for those repeating the exam.

Keep one thing on your mind while you prepare, whether this is your first exam or whether you have taken the exam before: You can do this!

**Finish Line**

# CHAPTER 2

# Understanding Memory and Mind Maps

Believe it or not, you have some of the law you need for the bar exam in your long-term memory. This law was not there prior to law school. Did you know what a tort was? What did you know about negligence prior to law school? Had you ever heard the phrase "proximate cause," much less known what it meant? At a minimum, you now know that to hold a defendant liable for a negligent act the defendant must have had a duty to the plaintiff and must have breached that duty. That breach must have then caused the plaintiff's damages; both actual causation and proximate causation are required. Somehow over the last three years, that information was transferred into your long-term memory. Information you did not already know. And, more importantly, you also now have the ability to recall that information effortlessly.

The more we understand about how memory works the better our chances of staying focused on encoding techniques to transfer as much information about bar-tested topics into our long-term memory.

## I. MEMORY: WHAT IS IT AND HOW DOES IT WORK?

In essence, memory is the "ability to retain information over time."[1] Our focus is on three different types of memory: sensory, short-term, and long-term. Understanding these different types of memory help us understand how they function together.

When perceived, information first enters the **sensory memory**. Our mind stores information there for very brief periods of time. Information in sensory memory will be quickly forgotten if you do not actively pay attention to it. The role of the sensory memory is two-fold: it helps filter various stimuli and prevents us from becoming overwhelmed; and it provides the opportunity to decide whether the incoming information is important. Attending to the information held in sensory memory then transfers that information to short-term memory.

**Short-term memory**, or working memory, also holds information for short periods of time. Much like sensory memory, short-term memory will dispel

---

1. Rod Plotnik, *Introduction to Psychology* 239 (6th ed. 2002).

information quickly if you do not pay attention to it. Short-term memory goes through cycles—allowing new information in, retaining it, then erasing that information and beginning again with new information.

This type of memory is characterized by two limiting features. The first is limited duration, which refers to the short period of time information remains in short-term memory—usually less than thirty seconds. Entering information quickly over-writes existing information, whether verbal or visual stimuli. Second, short-term memory can only hold about seven items simultaneously in its verbal function. Four stimuli can be held in the visual function of short-term memory at the same time as the seven verbal stimuli. Thus, "the visual function of working memory expands the number of items that students can simultaneously focus on while learning the law."[2]

Certain techniques may help overcome these limiting functions, such as maintenance rehearsal and chunking. Maintenance rehearsal refers to the act of repeating certain information in order to keep it in short-term memory for a longer period of time. Chunking aims at improving short-term memory by increasing the number of items it can hold at one time. This process consists of grouping individual pieces of information together in a larger unit to remember, called a chunk. Chunking verbal stimuli and visual stimuli together increases the number of both kinds of stimuli that can be remembered. Moreover, chunking visual and verbal stimuli leads to a better understanding and retention of the concepts than either individually.[3]

While short-term memory allows us to concentrate on relevant information, the information must be encoded in order to become permanently stored. If we do not engage the information in our short-term memory, it slips away and is forgotten. On the other hand, paying attention to the information held in short-term memory, bolstered by rehearsal techniques, allows the information to be encoded for storage in long-term memory.

**Long-term memory** is the process of storing information for extended periods of time, with the possibility of retrieving that information in the future. Information reaches long-term memory after being transferred from short-term memory through the encoding process. There are two kinds of long-term memory. Procedural, also called nondeclarative, long-term memory "involves memories for motor skills (playing tennis), some cognitive skills (learning to read), and emotional behaviors learned through classical conditioning (fear of spiders)."[4] Procedural memories are not among those we have the ability to recall. We can, however, recall and retrieve declarative memories. Declarative long-term memory "involves memories for facts or events, such as scenes, stories, words, conversations, faces, or daily events."[5] Declarative memory also consists of two different types: semantic and episodic. Semantic declarative memory refers to the knowledge of facts and concepts, while

---

2. Hillary Burgess, *Deepening the Discourse Using the Legal Mind's Eye: Lessons from Neuroscience and Psychology that Optimize Law School Learning*, 29 Quinnipiac L. Rev. 1, 27 (2011).
3. *See id.* at 29 (citing Slava Kalyuga, Paul Chandler & John Sweller, *Managing Split-Attention and Redundancy in Multimedia Instruction*, 13 Applied Cognitive Psychol. 353, 362 (1999)).
4. Plotnik, *supra* note 1, at 246.
5. *Id.*

episodic declarative memory comprises knowledge of activities, personal experience, and events.

Information stored in long-term memory remains there on a relatively permanent basis. Ideally, the information will be available for recall at a later time. Exactly what and how much we are able to recall or retrieve from long-term memory depends largely on how the information was encoded and other factors such as interference. Remember that memories are not complete and accurate copies. Our goal in bar preparation is to transfer as much information about bar-tested topics into our long-term memory. Through encoding and rehearsal, you should be able to recall the rules in detail to use in your analysis of bar questions.

| TYPES OF MEMORY | | | |
|---|---|---|---|
| | **Storage** | **Length of time** | **Attributes** |
| SENSORY | Involuntary. | Very brief; can be less than a second. | Helps us sort stimuli to not be overwhelmed. Vanishes unless we pay attention to it. |
| SHORT-TERM OR WORKING MEMORY | Focused attention moves information from sensory memory. | Short periods of time, less than 30 seconds. | Stimuli cycles in and out. Capacity is limited: 7 verbal and 4 visual stimuli. Must encode information for retention in long-term memory. |
| LONG-TERM MEMORY | Effortful encoding moves information from short-term memory. | Extended periods of time, often permanent. | Stores information for lengthy time periods with the possibility of retrieving the information in the future. |

## II. IMPORTANCE OF ENCODING

Encoding plays a central role in the ability to retrieve and recall information. The encoding process involves transferring new information from short-term memory into long-term memory by changing that information into neural codes. Two kinds of encoding can occur. Automatic encoding involves the transfer of information to long-term memory without effort. Information about personal events, skills, or habits is encoded automatically—a child's birth, your wedding day, the death of a loved one. Conversely, effortful encoding involves hard work and concentration. Usually, factual or complex information requires effort to encode. The two primary methods of effortful encoding are rehearsing/repeating the information and making associations. We will use both.

When it comes to encoding information, mere rehearsal alone proves less effective than the alternative method of forming associations. Relying solely upon repetitive rehearsal does not form a location in our memory to allow us to recall the information easily. Meanwhile, making associations or elaborative rehearsal "involves using effort to actively make meaningful associations between new information that you wish to remember and old or familiar information that is already stored in long-term memory."[6] This method of encoding provides cues as to the location of the newly stored information, thus making it more beneficial. Encoding information is much like saving information on a computer—it is necessary to have a solid system in place for labeling and filing information, otherwise retrieval will be difficult or impossible.

According to the Network or Connectionist Theory, "we store related ideas in separate categories, or files, called nodes. As we make new associations among information, we create links among thousands of nodes, which make up a gigantic interconnected network of files for storing and retrieving information."[7] Forming new associations essentially creates "mental roads" between nodes.

Another way to think about memory is to compare it to a warehouse. Better warehouse organization leads to easier recall. The most important memory improvement technique while studying is to think about what you are reading, instead of simply looking at the material—stop and reflect along the way. Echoing the significance of forming connections between new and old information, remember that "[w]hen you think about the material, you connect it to your existing knowledge, and these connections make it easier to later retrieve the material."[8]

Ultimately, remembering information boils down to how that information was encoded. The strongest system for encoding information is elaborative rehearsal, if associations are formed. Under the levels-of-processing theory, "[i]f you encode by paying attention only to basic features . . . information is encoded at a shallow level and results in poor recall. If you encode by making new associations, this information will be encoded at a deeper level, which results in better recall."[9]

Once that information is encoded by making associations, then we can use repetitive rehearsal to aid our recall. We must use the materials that we developed to form our own associations. Using someone else's outlines or a commercial provider's flash cards does not work as well because you never encoded that information by yourself first.

Doing practice bar questions is one way you will encode bar-tested topics into your long-term memory. Simply trying to answer hundreds of questions without doing something with the information you receive is an example of merely rehearsing the information. You hope by being as familiar as you can with the information that you will be able to recognize the correct answer on the exam. In essence, the information is stored on a shallow level leaving it unreliable for recall. Instead, autopsy your answers. Check that you have the same level of detail in your rule in your memorization materials. If not, then add that detail to your materials right then. If it's already there in the same detail, then highlight it. When you begin the repetitive rehearsal technique, you will recognize the rule as one you missed previously and it's encoded just a bit deeper right then.

Consider Torts. The bar examiners include topics that your first year course may not have spent much, if any, time covering. Two frequent "skipped" topics

---

6. *Id.* at 249.
7. *Id.* at 262.
8. David A. Lieberman, *Learning and Memory: An Integrative Approach* 453 (2004).
9. Plotnik, *supra* note 1, at 249.

in first year Torts are defamation and invasion of privacy. These two torts are distinct, but share some rules. Both have constitutional considerations that must be considered. For example, a public official or a public figure must prove that the tortfeasor made a defamatory statement knowing it was false or with recklessness as to its truth or falsity. This standard is "malice."[10] In an invasion of privacy action, malice applies when a plaintiff is portrayed in a false light as to a matter of public interest. It applies to any plaintiff, not just a public official or a public figure. Likewise, if the publication is newsworthy, a plaintiff cannot recover for public disclosure of private facts and no malice is required even if the plaintiff is a public official or public figure.

Is your head spinning? When is malice required in defamation action? When is malice required in an invasion of privacy action? The distinction between different levels of proof is one distinction that frequently arises on MBE questions. If all you do with MBE practice questions is read the answers, you will probably miss the distinction and decide malice is required most of the time. As a result, you are likely to be confused when faced with the same or similar question again. Only by making your own memorization materials will you be able to sort the information by tort and separate the levels of proof required for each. By doing so, you will categorize each and encode them in your memory for better issue spotting and recall on the exam.

Better memory requires better storage. Better storage requires that you make your own associations with that information, not just be familiar with the material. Encoding through making associations means that you must take the commercial provider's outlines and turn them into your own memorization materials—your library. In Chapter 3, Developing Your Game Plan, we will focus on specific techniques to help you make associations and build your library while you practice questions and review information.

## III. FORGETTING

Forgetting is the "inability to retrieve, recall, or recognize information" stored in long-term memory.[11]

Interference and poor (or changed) retrieval cues are among the most common problems when it comes to remembering.

"Retrieval . . . is initiated by the presentation of one or more retrieval cues, and the amount retrieved depends on the similarity of this retrieval cue to the stimuli present during encoding."[12]

Retrieval cues are essentially mental reminders that we generate by forming associations or mental images. Such cues might be contextual or other cues that stimulate the senses. Even if the information is stored, a missing cue may render the information irretrievable.

---

10. *New York Times v. Sullivan*, 376 U.S. 254, 279-80 (1964).
11. Plotnik, *supra* note 1, at 245.
12. Lieberman, *supra* note 8, at 425.

Interference occurs when the recall of some information is blocked by other information. "New material tends to interfere with old materials."[13] The greater the similarity between previously learned information and the information currently being learned, the greater the likelihood of confusion. Mental overcrowding is another example of interference. Other common memory problems include a negative self-concept, under-learning, disuse and lack of attention, and effort. Time can also hinder memory.

The first step to avoid forgetting is actively engaging with the material and intending to remember. Overlearning, talking about the material out loud, daily review, and practice tests are valuable tools to combat the threat of forgetting. In addition, constructing connections between ideas and getting a feel for the big picture can be quite useful. A technique called the "spacing effect" helps to prevent memory decay. The spacing effect requires eliminating cramming sessions and restructuring study habits to include studying for shorter periods over the course of several days and studying across subjects. Your game plan will take advantage of this effect by reviewing several topics a week and then going back over previously encoded topics.

## IV. CONCENTRATION

Common barriers to building concentration include fatigue, distractions, and hunger. Take care of your physical needs for sleep and food. Then, quite simply, the main solution is to build an interest in the material. Setting goals and studying in a place designated only for that purpose are also effective concentration boosters. In addition, varying the study activity, setting a time frame to study, relating learning, organizing the task, and pacing comprise several other concentration tools.

## V. DOES WRITING IMPACT OUR ABILITY TO REMEMBER?

Taking notes, writing down what we do not want to forget, seems like good common sense. But does it make a difference? At the very least, writing gives us the opportunity to clarify our thoughts. Different regions of the brain come into play. Each region of the brain processes different types of information, such as visual, auditory, or verbal communication. While each region has its own process, each communicates with the others. Writing creates spatial relationships in terms of the information being written and these spatial relationships engage different regions of the brain. Such links between regions of the brain help strengthen the process of information storage. The writer must also filter information and make decisions about which information is the most relevant or significant. Writing involves actively thinking about how to evaluate and order incoming information. This process, as opposed to the actual notes taken, is critical and helps fix ideas more firmly in our minds. The end product of what

---

13. Academic Resource Center Idea Sheet, *Forgetting*, Utah State University 1 (2006), http://www.usu.edu/arc/assistance/pdf/forgetting.pdf.

you write is far less important than the process of thinking about and analyzing the material. The thinking and analysis is the encoding.

## VI. IMPROVING YOUR MEMORY

In terms of study time, set specific goals. Identify what you need to accomplish in the time you have available. Keep your work space organized, clean, and free from distractions like your cell phone or TV. During your study session, take breaks to refocus your attention. When you complete your study session, evaluate it—identify what you can change to make the next session more productive. A wide variety of study strategies can assist you during your study session. However, some activities are more beneficial than others. Consider which methods have worked for you before and consider using other methods such as creating summaries or visual organizers.

## VII. MIND MAPS AS A MEMORY TOOL

The technique of mind mapping was developed during the 1960s. With an extensive volume of written work in the areas of learning, memory improvement, and maximizing one's mental skills; Tony Buzan is credited with, at the very least, popularizing and promoting the use of mind mapping. A mind map is essentially a diagram, or a "two-dimensional drawing or representation . . . of the critical information and concepts being discussed."[14] This type of visual diagram illustrates ideas in a "relational context, with the main topic at the center of the map, major subtopics on branches radiating from the main topic, and sub-subtopics around each subtopic," and so forth.[15] All maps start with a core idea or concept and branch outward. These maps allow us to "rapidly generate, structure, classify and visualize ideas."[16]

Mind mapping offers a variety of benefits and advantages. As opposed to traditional note-taking, the design of mind maps helps keep the big picture in mind. This technique is also more flexible than traditional outlining because it allows information to be captured and easily rearranged and enables us to step away from and return to the map without losing our place. Along the same lines, a mind map is often easier to comprehend, thus saving time and allowing us to be more productive. Because less writing is typically required to generate a mind map, reviewing the map proves much faster.

Perhaps the most significant advantage of mind mapping is the ability to see concepts in relation to each other. Because traditional, hierarchical note-taking often takes the form of listing, it is difficult to demonstrate relationships between

---

14. Nerino J. Petro, Jr., *Hate Taking Notes? Try Mind Mapping*, 27 No. 4 GPSolo 20, 21 (Feature, June 2010) (Westlaw Lawprac Index).

15. Diane Murley, *Technology for Everyone . . . Mind Mapping Complex Information*, 99 Law Libr. J. 175 (2007).

16. Dave Maxfield & Michael Deutch, *Mind Mapping for Lawyers*, 21 S.C. Law. 18, 19 (Sept. 2009).

concepts. Mind mapping provides the opportunity to "differentiate between different ideas and concepts using shapes, colors, and images" and allows us to group concepts together and show relationships between them.[17] In this sense, mind mapping engages both the creative and analytical hemispheres of the brain. The promotion of visualization plays a key role in the success of mind maps. It is often said that we think and learn in three primary ways: auditory, kinesthetic, and visual. While we each prefer one method, we use all three. "Regardless of [your] preferred learning and thinking style, visualization can simplify complex ideas, show the relationship between those ideas and help organize thoughts."[18] Mind mapping allows us to see ideas and concepts in a non-linear fashion, breaking away from more rigid forms of note-taking. Mind mapping takes advantage of our ability to hold seven stimuli in our verbal function and four stimuli in our visual function of short-term memory. Integrating these stimuli in a mind map, we are chunking the information in a manner that should lead to easier recall and open space for more integration of stimuli.

There is no one right way to create a mind map. Each is unique to the creator and for the creator's needs. It encapsulates how you envision the topic. What are its components? Are there subcomponents? Are there definitions or dates that are relevant? Numerous types of mind-mapping software are available, frequently at no cost. This listing is just a few sources that are available.

- www.thinkbuzan.com
- www.mindjet.com
- www.xmind.net
- www.mindnode.com
- www.novamind.com

There is a learning curve with any new software. Spend some time learning how to use the software before you delve into creating your maps.

## VIII. CREATING A MIND MAP

Let's create a mind map to give you an idea of how to take the mind map starters provided in each topical chapter of this book and expand them to cover what you need to know for the bar exam on that topic.

For our example, let's use a science topic in elementary school that requires understanding the different types of animals. Your goal is to memorize the characterics of each type of animal so that you can classify different animals on an upcoming exam.

The starter mind map would place each type of animal on a branch.[19]

---

17. Petro, *supra* note 14, at 22.
18. Maxfield & Deutch, *supra* note 16, at 20.
19. Laura Klappenbach, "The Basic Animal Groups," http://animals.about.com/od/animal-facts/tp/animal-groups.htm.

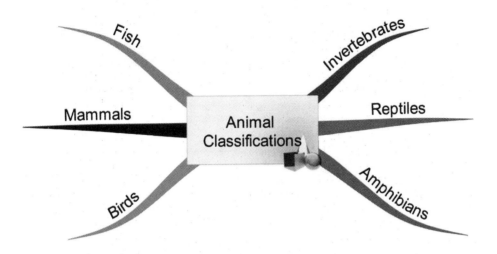

Then, based on the information you need to understand and memorize, you branch off each main component with the subcomponents. These subcomponents could be the same for each main branch. Thus, each animal type would have a branch for origins, a branch for characteristics, a branch for habitat, and a branch for food. But, they don't have to be. This mind map is for you. It doesn't have to be perfectly balanced. One animal type might need only three of the four or maybe four completely different subcomponents. It is up to you and what you need to memorize.

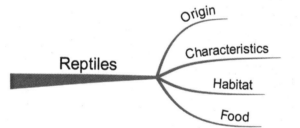

For some branches, use a text box to give a definition or explanation.

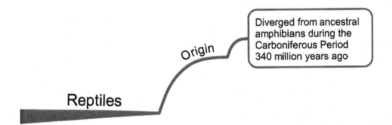

For others, use more branches for differentiation of the concepts.

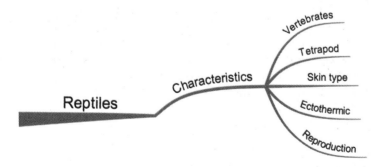

Then add more text boxes or branches as needed.

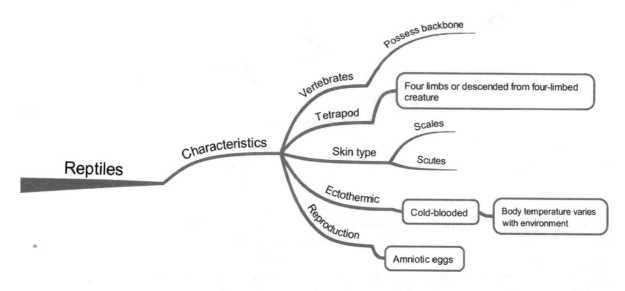

Your mind map has now grown in detail. Let's see how this branch of the map fits into the overall map.

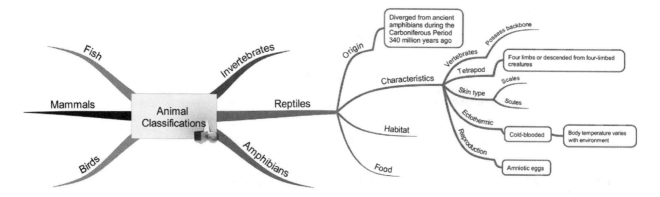

Picture doing the same thing with each branch. A mind map is not something you read left to right. Start in the middle and go out on each branch on which you are working. Then, step back and see the big picture. You will see the association between the details of the branch and the big picture.

What has been happening in your brain while you have prepared this map? While you have been sorting the information and deciding what goes where and how it should be memorialized, you have been encoding the information into your memory. This effortful encoding involves hard work and concentration and makes up a key component of the "real work" of bar preparation. You are learning the material and storing it in your mind in such a way that you will be able to recall that information when you need it on the exam. You are making associations between concepts. Now when you review the physical embodiment of your mind map before the exam, you are rehearsing and repeating the information drawing on the associations you created in the map. As an end result, the information is stored in your long-term memory and you are able to recall it when you need it.

In this book, mind mapping for the bar exam includes the visual diagramming and also serves as a method to organize your thinking about bar topics. Creating a bar topic mind map requires you to sort and prioritize information about the rules, thus analyzing and organizing the information. But you can also use the mind map on the exam itself—obviously not your written mind map, but your visualization of it. When stumped, begin at the center point of your map and follow the branches through the topics until it triggers the issue and its rule. Most of the time that will do the trick and the issue and rule will become apparent.

When should you make your mind maps? Each student will create mind maps at different times during his or her preparation. Some will immediately begin their mind maps as they conceptualize the overall topic. Others will wait until they have spent some time in the topic and feel more ready to tackle it. Either way, try to have your mind maps at least partially complete by the start of your second month of bar prep. Then, you can finish them for your needs during those last few weeks.

Remember that your ability to store rules in your long-term memory is necessary to perform well on both multiple choice questions and on the essay portions of the bar exam. This real work of bar prep takes the most significant and critical portion of your bar preparation time.

# CHAPTER 3

# Developing Your Game Plan

Your bar preparation has three phases. First, you must learn the law. Next, you must memorize the law. Lastly, you must refresh your recollection of the law in the last two weeks to be sure all the rules are fresh. How much time will this take? Approximately 500 hours. That includes time you spend in your commercial bar prep course, time you spend reviewing material, time you spend memorizing or preparing outlines, time you spend doing practice questions, even time reading this book!

## I. THE STARTING GATE

When do you start your preparation? In one sense, it started your first day of law school as you began gaining the skills you need and began learning the substance of bar topics. At the end of law school, the time is ripe to prepare for the bar exam directly.

A word of caution: Your law school may allow you to finish graduation requirements after your commencement ceremony and still certify you to take the bar exam if the jurisdiction allows it. Do not be tempted to do that. Finishing class requirements on top of starting bar prep is a recipe for failure. Just get your work done during the semester and avoid the double-work that happens if you wait.

### A. First-Time Takers

#### 1. For-Credit Courses

For first-time bar exam takers, the time to start depends upon several factors. If you are fortunate to be at a law school that offers a for-credit class in bar prep skills, that course is your best time to start. A for-credit course is frequently offered in the last semester of law school. It will help you in developing your game plan, trying out your game plan, making adjustments to your game plan as you go, reinforcing the skills you have, and attaining the skills you need.

#### 2. Taking a Commercial Bar Preparation Course

If you are not able to take a for-credit course, are graduating law school right before the exam, and are taking a commercial bar preparation course, you need to consider when your law school holds graduation and when your commercial bar preparation course begins. If possible, take some time off after graduation. Relax. Do things you enjoy. Spend time with family and friends. You just got through your finals and submitted your last papers. Bar prep can wait until your commercial bar prep course begins. That does not mean to take the first few weeks of bar prep off in order to vacation! Every week of bar prep has a purpose. If you enter bar prep planning to take a week or so off, then you need to start your bar preparation *before* the commercial prep course begins. Do not wait until you get back from vacation.

### 3. Self-Study Approach

If this is your first time taking the bar exam and you do not intend to take a commercial bar prep course, you need to consider whether you want to work at the same time. If you do not plan to work, you can still take some time off after graduation. You can begin at the same time that the commercial bar preparation courses begin. If you plan to work and study with a self-study approach, then you really do not have time for a couple of weeks off. Taking a self-study approach does not mean you can jam it all in in less time. Those 500 hours hold true for you, too. As most of your day is spent working, you will have fewer hours to devote to bar study each day. It will be necessary to start earlier and spread your study over a longer period of time.

### B. Repeat Takers

If this is not your first time taking the bar exam, the answer to when you should start is different. First, you may have significant time between the results and the next exam. You need some time to adjust to the results you received. Once the initial adjustment is over, take all that emotion and turn it around to motivate you to show the bar examiners that they should have passed you the first time!

Second, most repeat takers are employed by the time they are taking the exam again. Working 40 or more hours a week while preparing for the exam can be done, but you will be fatigued and will have little down time. If you did not do a commercial bar prep course the first time, seriously consider taking one this time. It will help you stay on track. It is a large expenditure, to be sure, but worth it.

If you did complete a commercial course the first time, you should generally start your study six to eight weeks before the first-time takers start. If you did not make your own flash cards, outlines, or flow charts the first time around, start making those for every topic. Start with the "Big Seven"—the topics tested on the MBE: Civil Procedure, Constitutional Law, Contracts, Criminal Law and Procedure, Evidence, Real Property, and Torts. Do one topic a week. Once the first-time takers begin, switch to the essay topics.

If you did make your own outlines or flash cards, two possible things happened. First, you may not have put enough detail into the rules you were memorizing. Or, you put too much detail into your rules such that you could not memorize much of them or the excessive detail kept you from focusing on what was critical. Thus, you need to supplement or cull appropriately. Chapter 8 gives repeat takers more guidance in preparing to retake the bar exam.

Whether you are taking the bar exam for the first time or retaking the exam or you are taking a commercial bar prep course or taking a self-study approach, or you are working or are spending 100% of your time on bar study, your game plan starts in the same place—learn the law.

## II. THE GAME PLAN

### A. Phase One—Learn the Law

Most commercial bar prep courses begin with the Big Seven. It makes sense to start with the Big Seven as you know they are worth half of your points in most jurisdictions. In UBE or MEE states, it also makes the most sense as you will likely have essays on the Big Seven as well.

Most law schools require these courses in the first or second year of law school; thus, they are all familiar to you. Some of the concepts you may have learned very well when you took the course, and this review will just be refreshing your recollection. Other concepts you may not have fully grasped or your professor may not have introduced in your particular course.

If you had difficulty with a course, it is tempting to save it for last. Starting with something familiar is comforting when you are under the stress of this challenge. And facing that bear of a course can be discouraging. But you do have to face it. You cannot skip a topic—particularly one of the Big Seven.

Before a lecture in your commercial bar prep course, skim the outline for that topic. You are seeking to get a big picture of the topic—how everything fits together. Start to become familiar with the buzz words or key concepts. Do not read the outline for complete understanding at this point. Just refamiliarize yourself with the topic. If you did not take a course in a particular topic, do not wait until the lecture to start learning the topic. Those are the topics in which you need to read the outline in more depth, rather than skimming the material.

During the lecture, keep engaged with the materials by filling in the blanks or doing the short answer problems. No need to bring your laptop or tablet to the lectures. Keep your phone off and out of the way. This is not the time to text friends or answer email. Facebook, Snapchat, and Twitter really can wait. Tell your family and friends not to expect immediate responses to their texts and emails during lecture. If at home, set up your environment to avoid distractions as much as you can. If possible, plan a lecture spot away from home. Take your laptop and earphones and view the lecture at your favorite coffee spot. You are less likely to be distracted by the call of undone chores.

After the lecture, review your notes. Now, you are just checking to see if you missed anything. If you did miss a concept in the lecture, ask a friend for clarification that day. Yes, that day! Even a few days later, you will forget to ask or forget why you needed to know.

A word about study groups. If you have worked with a study group in law school and found it beneficial to you, then keep working with the group during bar preparation. You can ask your questions about the law in a nonthreatening environment. Your group will support each other, even if it is just commiserating about the work involved. Study groups are a great way to learn from each other. Someone in your group may have taken a course that you did not take and can further explain concepts after the lecture if you don't understand them.

### 1. Building Your Library

Now the core of your work truly begins. In Chapter 2, we discussed the importance of memory and we discussed techniques to improve your memory. But Phase One is not about memorizing. It's about encoding—the start of the memorization process. For our purposes, it's easier to think about encoding as first getting ready to memorize and then rote repetition as actually memorizing.

Your first step is to gather your study materials and organize them in the manner in which you best memorize. How do you know what is the best manner? How have you memorized before the bar exam? Think back over your approximately 20 years of education. How did you memorize multiplication factors? You used a combination of materials from flash cards to one-minute drills. How did you memorize American history? Perhaps you made your own outline of dates and events or you read the material many times hoping the information would stick in your head. In undergraduate courses, your exams required you to show your understanding of the theories and public policies involved in historical events in an essay or a research paper, rather than memorize dates and facts.

So, which method should you use for the bar exam?

* Flash cards or note cards
* Flash card app on smartphone/tablet/computer
* Outline
* Flow chart
* PowerPoint
* Mind map

Another method may work for you. Choose the method you have had success with in the past. Some topics may work better with one method while other topics work better with a different method. Allow yourself to explore and experience different methods.

If you are not sure where to begin, start with definitions. Move to elements of causes of action and crimes. Then add detail by adding the rules for each element. Then add defenses to the causes of actions and crimes and off you go!

How much should you write on a flash card or a PowerPoint slide? For memory encoding, including full sentences may result in stimulus overload such that the key points are lost in the text. Writing out full sentences on flash cards is just showing your full outline on short pieces of paper. Instead, on one side of the card put the concept: for example, battery. On the back of the card, list the trigger phrases for the elements of that intentional tort.

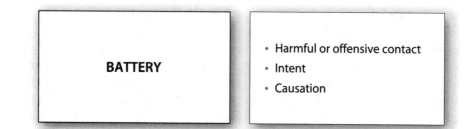

**BATTERY**

* Harmful or offensive contact
* Intent
* Causation

Then, make another flash card to set out more detail on one element.

| **Harmful or Offensive Contact** | • Reasonable person standard<br>• Includes anything connected to the person ("purse")<br>• No consent<br>• Apprehension ≠ required |

Continue with each element as needed.

You might be thinking, "Why bother? The commercial bar preparation provider provided flash cards or shortened outlines for me to use." Those materials are fine as a back-up. But it is the process of thinking and organizing the material yourself that starts the memorization process—encoding that information into your long-term memory. Reading someone else's work does not provide the same kind of encoding. Making your own library enables you to actually learn the material while you are building your own materials to memorize from in Phase Two.

Should each member of your study group make materials on a subject for you to share? That is not a wise choice. That method may have worked well for you for a final when you could rely mainly on your short-term memory. But the bar exam requires that those materials be in your long-term memory. Encoding the material over time and working with the material yourself is really the best method.

Now, how do you start building your library of materials? Do you include everything? Use the content in this book or your lecture handouts as the basis of your library. You will add to this basis throughout your bar preparation, particularly as you autopsy your answers to practice questions. Do not rely solely on the lecture handout book your commercial provider gave you. If you use it to begin your memorization materials, you still must add the more detailed rules you will find in practice questions. The autopsy is key.

### 2. Using Practice Questions to Learn the Law

Taking practice questions is an excellent way to learn material. Yes, to learn it. At this point, you are not trying to assess your memory. Instead, you are using the essays to learn the details of the rules and how they work together. As you learn the law more comprehensively, you will better understand it and it will be easier to memorize.

At this point, take practice questions open book. Spend as much time as you need. Remember, the point is to learn the material, not to assess your memory. You may wonder if spending 90 minutes doing a practice essay is worth it. It absolutely is! Those 90 minutes mean you understand that part of the law in a way that you would never have understood it if you had taken the question closed book in a limited time. Then, your answer would have been sketchy, at best. You would read the answer, but it wouldn't sink in. By practicing questions open book and with unlimited time, you are giving yourself the opportunity to really delve into the subject.

**EXAM TIP**

Do not include every single detail of the rules that are contained in the long outlines of each topic in your library. Your goal is to have 75% of the topic down cold. Chapter 7 explains this strategy.

### 3. Finding the Answer

What happens if you still don't get it? Do you give up and pray that the topic does not appear on an essay or in a multiple choice question? No. Just ask. Ask for help. Dig into the substantive outline. If that doesn't do it, email or talk with the commercial bar preparation lecturer or general office. The office will find out for you. Or, email or talk with a professor at your law school.

This is the phase to work on learning as much as you can. Don't give up on anything.

## B. Phase Two—Memorize the Law

Five weeks before the exam is the time to really start memorizing. You should have a substantial part of your library built with just a few remaining topics to complete. Start with the Big Seven. Your commercial bar prep provider will offer at least one full-day practice MBE exam. Start memorizing shortly before that exam. At the beginning of this phase, most of your time will be spent finishing your library, but adding in an hour or two of memorization per day is the way to go. As you move to the end of this phase, half of your time will be spent memorizing and half of your time will be spent on practice questions.

### 1. Memory Techniques

At this stage, the time is ripe to take your substantive material and apply memory techniques to aid your recall. By building your own library, you have already spent significant time memorizing—time well spent encoding the information into your memory. Now we want to make more new associations to achieve a deeper level of encoding.

Using various mnemonic devices can assist in making those deeper associations. Acronyms, acrostics, rhythm and song, chunking, and method of loci help to encode information by forming new associations. **Acronyms** are formed by using the first letter of each word and are particularly useful when remembering words in a specific order. Indeed, some acronyms are used more frequently than the words themselves, such as NFL (National Football League), BTUs (British Thermal Units), and Scuba (Self-Contained Underwater Breathing Apparatus).

An example for use in bar study is "A FLIP," which can assist you in remembering the four types of invasion of privacy causes of action.

***A Flip***

- **Appropriation of likeness**
- **False Light**
- **Intrusion of seclusion**
- **Publication of private facts**

**Acrostics** are similar to acronyms in that you use the first letter of each word, but you create a sentence or phrase instead of a single word. For example, the lines of a musical staff are remembered by, "Every Good Boy Does Fine." "My Dear Aunt Sally" is used to remember the mathematical order of operations—multiply and divide before you add or subtract. To remember the Dormant Commerce Clause requirements that limit state action, think:

*Nonresident Statutes Are Rude.*[1]

* **N**ondiscriminatory intent, construction, and application
* **S**ubstantial nexus between state interest and burden on nonresident
* **A**pportioned between residents and nonresidents that reflects fundamental fairness
* **R**elated to state services or resources

**Rhymes** and **songs** have been used for decades to remember information. Have you ever been in the midst of alphabetizing something and had the ABC Song float into your head? Why is that? You encoded the information through song. Indeed, for centuries rhyme, rhythm, and repetition have helped storytellers to remember a tribe's history or to remember Homer's *Odyssey*.

If you like to create, this can be a powerful tool to aid your memory. It draws upon auditory memory more than the others. A former colleague teaching Wills and Trusts began each class with her students singing parts of the intestacy rules to familiar tunes.[2] Needless to say, the students had these rules solidly memorized.

We use **chunking** regularly without thinking about it. Chunking refers to grouping information in a meaningful way to reduce the amount you need to store in your memory; thus, making it easier to remember. Telephone numbers are not a long series of numbers for a reason. The grouping of 3-3-4 is easier to remember. We can even chunk our acronyms.

*Oil Cans* are self-authenticating (self-authenticating documents).[3]

* **O**fficial publications issued by public authority
* **I**nstruments—negotiable and commercial paper
* **L**abel, tag, or trademark affixed on item in regular course of business
* **C**ertified public documents (by clerk of agency or court that had custody)
* **A**cknowledged documents signed before notary, sworn to truth, content, and execution (except wills)
* **N**ewspapers and periodicals with reasonably wide circulation
* **S**ealed documents (government certified)

**Method of loci** was also used by ancient storytellers and orators. It requires organization, visual memory, and association. Start by identifying a common path that you walk or use the set-up of a room. As you visualize your walk or the room, picture the landmarks along the way such as the door to the room or the bottom of the steps as you leave for your walk. As you picture the landmark, associate the first concept you wish to remember with that landmark. For example, defamation requires (1) defamatory language on the part of the defendant; (2) the defamatory language is of or concerning the plaintiff; (3) publication of the defamatory language to a third person; and (4) damage to the plaintiff's reputation.

Visualize "defamatory language about the plaintiff" by thinking of the word "liar" spray painted on the door (defamatory language). Then, move to the next landmark, such as the bottom of the steps leading outside. Picture the words

---

1. www.cram.com/cards/bar-exam-mnemonics-and-acrostics-mbe-and-mbee-984740.
2. Professor Julia Belian's intestacy songs are available on www.YouTube.com.
3. www.cram.com/cards/bar-exam-mnemonics-and-acrostics-mbe-and-mbee-984740.

"John is a liar" spray painted there (of or concerning the plaintiff). Then, at the next landmark picture a person whispering in the ear of another (publication to a third person). Then, picture a group of people laughing about another person (damage to reputation). At each landmark, associate the concept with the landmark. Consider how to visualize the concept with the landmark.

The best of these memory techniques are the ones you create yourself. Just by going through the process of trying to create one helps encode the information into your memory.

### 2. Seek Support

Now is the time to bring out your stack of flash cards or outlines or flowcharts and ask others to quiz you as a check on your memorization. This is a great way for the significant people in your life to help you as they all want to do. Plus, for the reluctant significant other that does not quite understand why you still can't do all the chores you used to do, it helps them see the enormity of the task you are trying to accomplish.

A 2006 family film demonstrates the power of support in learning to memorize. *Akeelah and the Bee* follows a young girl as she prepares for the National Spelling Bee. She gets her family, her friends, and her neighborhood to assist her. While you don't need to go that far and ask the cashier at your local grocery store to quiz you, enlisting others to help you not only gives you emotional support but also helps you assess your memorization status.

### 3. Using Practice Questions to Assess Your Memorization

At this point, you want to use practice questions to assess your memory of the law. If you have already written out 20 essays or more, then bullet-outline your answer. You are checking to see if you have properly identified the issues and stated the rules in enough detail. If you are still struggling with recall of the rules, dig back into straight up repetition to encode those rules a bit deeper. If you have not written out very many essays, then continue to do that in this phase. Half the points are in the application and half are in the rules.

Here, study groups can be immensely helpful. Take a practice question and have each person write out an answer. Compare your answers to the model answer and discuss why some identified certain issues and others did not. Clear up any misunderstandings of the rules. Determine why one member's rule statements worked better than yours. All of this discussion is further encoding the material into your long-term memory.

### C. Phase Three—Keep It Fresh

The last two weeks is the final push. Your goals are to continue your memorization of rules, to continue to use practice questions to assess your memory, and to keep what you have already memorized fresh to be able to recall easily. Thus, keeping track of where you are with each topic is essential. Plan these last two weeks very carefully.

One approach for the final two weeks is to review one of the Big Seven and one essay topic each day the first week. Each day, assess where you are with the previous day's topic by doing 50 MBE questions on that topic and bullet-outlining the rules for at least five essays on that topic. Still missing some of the rules? Continue to add them to your library. Continue your review of rules through the next week.

**EXAM TIP**

Remember, you must spend sufficient time on each topic. If all you study are your favorite topics and you avoid the tough ones, you are setting yourself up to fail. Your favorites may not even be on the bar exam as an essay question!

The second week, you need to review the few remaining essay topics but continue with daily MBE questions. Switch the 50 MBE questions to mixed topics. With mixed-topic question sets, you do not know the topic of each question ahead of time. This will keep you on track heading into the exam. Any additional time is spent on the topics that need more work. Then, begin reducing the number of MBE questions you do every day to avoid fatigue.

| BAR PREP CALENDAR | |
|---|---|
| Week One | Phase One—Learn the Law |
| Week Two | Phase One—Learn the Law |
| Week Three | Phase One—Learn the Law |
| Week Four | Phase One/Two—Learn/Memorize the Law |
| Week Five | Phase Two—Memorize the Law |
| Week Six | Phase Two—Memorize the Law |
| Week Seven | Phase Three—Memorize the Law/Keep It Fresh |
| Week Eight | Phase Three—Memorize the Law/Keep It Fresh |
| Exam Week | No Cramming! |

| SAMPLE SCHEDULE FOR PHASE THREE | | | | | | |
|---|---|---|---|---|---|---|
| Sunday | Monday | Tuesday | Wednesday | Thursday | Friday | Saturday |
| Finish outlines/ flash cards. MBE 50Q. on a trouble topic. Review Const. Law. | MBE Const. Law 50Q. Review Contracts, Sales, Agency/ Partnership. | MBE Contracts 50Q. Review Criminal Law/Crim. Procedure, and Corps. | MBE Criminal 50Q. Review Evidence & Secured Transactions. | MBE Evidence 50Q. Review Torts & Conflicts. | MBE Torts 50Q. Review Property & MPT samples for format. | MBE Real Property 50Q. Review Civil Procedure. |
| MBE Fed. Civ. Pro. 50Q. Review Family Law & all MBE topics. | MBE Mixed 50Q. Review Wills & Trusts. | MBE Mixed 34Q. Review any trouble topics. | MBE Mixed 34Q. Review any trouble topics. | MBE Mixed 34Q. Review all topics. | MBE Mixed 34Q. Review all topics. | MBE Mixed 34Q. Review all topics. |
| MBE Mixed 34Q. Review all topics. | Travel to exam site. Locate testing room, restrooms, etc. Get a good night's sleep! Avoid cramming. | **BAR EXAM— MPTs & Essays** | **BAR EXAM— Multistate Bar Exam** | **You Did It!!! WHEW!!!** | | |

Avoid the temptation of giving up on a topic. Giving up on a Big Seven topic is shooting yourself in the foot. Those topics will be tested. You know they will. The math simply does not work to give up on one of these topics. Not only are they a set percentage of the MBE questions, but they are also potential essay questions. That topic could also be part of the MPT question. One student "never got" Constitutional Law and gave up on it early. His bar exam included the standard number of multiple choice questions, an essay question, and the MPT—all on Constitutional Law. Without question, it was a poor judgment call to give up on that topic!

At this point in time, many students start weighing the chances of a topic appearing on an essay question to decide whether they should spend additional study time on that topic (hoping that the topics they are skipping will not be tested), or continue to study all topics. If a student decides to stop studying three topics because they never really understood them and those three topics are essay questions, they have just guaranteed a poor performance on the essay portion. Because the essay questions are worth 30% of the exam on the UBE and more in other jurisdictions, that student is risking lopping off 15% of the points or more on the exam before they start. Thus, they must perform at a high level on the rest of the exam. If one of the skipped topics is an MBE topic, they are lopping off even more.

Some students bank on excelling in one topic to make up for a poorer performance in another topic. Be careful of such an approach. Excelling on a topic at a high enough level to balance out a poor performance on another essay is very difficult to do. Reaching a high score on essay questions is difficult. Even if you did achieve a perfect score, it usually is not a mathematically sufficient margin to overcome a poor performance on another question or two.

The last weekend should be an easing off. First, you want to get plenty of sleep. The more rested your brain, the better you will perform. Second, we know that cramming does not result in long-term memory storage. And, there's too much information to keep in short-term memory to be of much good. You are better off skimming your outlines and flash cards and hitting the hay.

## D. The Exam Days

Spend the Monday before the exam traveling to the exam site. Look around and locate your testing room, the seating setup, and the restrooms. Lay off the caffeine in the evening. Set out exactly what you must and can bring into the exam including your photo identification. Get some good sleep. Set as many alarms as you can—from a hotel wake-up call, to family and friends calling you, to your travel clock, to your tablet, to your cell phone, and to the hotel's alarm clock. This is the exam you do not want to start late.

Eat breakfast with protein. Skip the donuts from the vending machine. Arrive before the exam's starting time to register and locate your seat. Once in the exam room, do not be tempted to look at your notes on your computer while you are waiting. That may result in your expulsion from the exam. Be sure to take a real break at lunch. Avoid cramming for the afternoon. Take a brief walk. Do not load up on carbohydrates. You don't want a sugar low in the middle of the afternoon.

Hopefully, on Tuesday evening some of the weight will be off your shoulders. Tuesday has the most possible topics. Tuesday evening you know the next day is only the Big Seven and that you will be tested on all of them. Spend some time

**Eat Breakfast!**

after the exam doing something to help you relieve stress—go on a run or walk, have a pedicure or massage, go to a movie, go work out in a gym—something that is designed to help you relax. Avoid alcohol. Have a decent dinner and then spend the rest of the evening relaxing, skimming the Big Seven, and getting a good night's rest. Again, set out what you need to take into the exam. Set all your alarms, once again.

If you have noticed that you are a slow starter on multiple choice questions—that is, that you need to get warmed up—then do 15 questions that morning for warm up. Then, you'll be in the groove for the actual exam. Again, take a break for lunch. The fatigue will be starting to hit. Take a walk around the block to clear your head. No cramming.

And, at last, it's over. After the exam, drive home safely. At some point, you will second guess your answers. Everyone does that; it's hard to avoid. To the extent that you can, have the attitude that you did the best you could and you could not have asked for more of yourself.

A recent successful bar taker's mother went with her to the exam site. Her mom drove, took care of setting alarms, and had lunch waiting in their room. The bar taker didn't have to think about where she was going to eat or how long the line would be. She didn't have to be around bar takers that love to talk about the questions immediately after the exam. She had someone else to talk with about other things—someone who did not put any pressure on her, but offered tons of positive support. The last day of the exam, she didn't need to worry about getting up early to pack her things to check out of the hotel on time. She slept some more. Her mom took care of packing and checking out after the bar taker started her exam. If you have a loved one who can provide practical and emotional support without pressuring you to talk or suggesting "don't you want to study more?"—then bring that person along!

**Let's Celebrate!**

The wait for the results will seem interminable. Try to keep in mind that worrying and ruminating about the results will do you no good. Your scores are out of your control at that point. If you already have a job, it is tempting to jump in and get started. If you can, take a long break or vacation. Read the book you set aside when bar prep started. Play a lot of golf. Spend time with your family and friends. Just refresh and rejuvenate before you start working.

### E. Getting Your Results

Jurisdictions differ on when they release results and how they release results. Some jurisdictions will post your individual result to an online account and others will mail letters. Some will post successful exam numbers on its website and some will post names of successful applicants. Be knowledgeable about the requirements for having your number or name posted. Some jurisdictions require that all of your character and fitness requirements are met before your name is posted, including passing the MPRE. You will have a sleepless night or two not knowing if it is character and fitness determination holding you up or if you actually failed the exam. Prevent that from happening by being sure you have all your ducks in a row for the character and fitness requirement long before the results come out.

The results are in and now you know. Celebrate sensibly. Thank your support system for all they did. Your hard work paid off!

If you were unsuccessful, it will at first seem like the end of the world. It really is not. It just means that some of your plans will be on hold until the next exam cycle. You are not the first person to be unsuccessful, nor will you be the last. Chapter 8 gives specific suggestions for those taking the exam an additional time.

# CHAPTER 4

# Building Essay-Writing Skills

## I. TYPE OR HANDWRITE?

Most jurisdictions give applicants a choice to type or handwrite their essay and MPT answers. Examiners agree that typed answers are most certainly easier to read than handwritten answers because no deciphering is required. The problem with handwriting is legibility. Bar examiners will make every effort to decode handwriting because they do not want to punish an applicant based upon poor handwriting. Yet, an irritated bar examiner is not a good thing.

Typists tend to write too much. The speed of their keyboarding skills and the ability to cut-and-paste blocks of text often means language is unnecessarily repeated, transitions are lengthy, and language is wordy. Typists' organization is often more haphazard as their ability to quickly write words means they often do not stop and think first about what they are writing. Handwritten essays tend to be shorter and more focused on the issue, resulting in better organization of the answer.

In the end, whether you type or handwrite does not affect your score on either an MPT or an essay. Both have advantages and disadvantages that may impact your score, but one does not outweigh the other as a general rule.

## II. SCORING

Essays are graded by the board of bar examiners in your state and often with the help of additional attorneys appointed for that purpose. Remember that these are busy folks. They volunteer for these positions and usually are maintaining an active law practice. As such, they appreciate the well-thought-out answer that is organized and well written.

Different jurisdictions use different scoring scales. Whether your jurisdiction uses a 5-point scale or a 100-point scale, everyone in your jurisdiction is graded along the same scale. Jurisdictions have various safeguards in place to ensure reliability of their scores. Some jurisdictions calibrate scores by more than one examiner grading the same question and the examiners exchanging exams with the other person grading the same question after a set number of answers. For example, after every 30 questions graded, they exchange their last five graded essays and grade them again to see if they receive the same score. If they don't, then they can discuss the issue and reach a decision on how to score. Jurisdictions do their reliability check in different ways, but all attempt to ensure their grading is equitable for all examinees.

Once a jurisdiction completes its essay grading, including the MPT, the raw scores are sent to the NCBE. The NCBE then scales the scores to match the 200-point scale used on the multiple choice questions.

After the NCBE completes the scaled scores, each individual jurisdiction then receives a report of all their test-takers with their scaled scores on each part of the exam and their total scaled score. Each jurisdiction decides its own cut-off score; that is, the score required to pass the exam.

When results are released, you may or may not receive your actual score. Jurisdictions differ as to how much information they reveal to their examinees when results are available. Some jurisdictions only reveal the pass/fail result. Others reveal all information given to them by the NCBE.

## III. THINK FIRST!

Begin your approach to each essay with a plan of attack. The first one-third of your time should be spent reading and planning your answer. What will you read first? What will begin your answer? How should your answer be structured?

Be sure to keep track of your time. Do *not* go over the allotted time. Each question is worth the same number of points. Perfect scores are rare, and there is no extra credit for particularly brilliant answers. Thus, deciding to spend 60 minutes on a 30-minute question is not a good idea. Even spending ten extra minutes on the first three 30-minute questions means you will have no time for the sixth question. You will not earn enough points in those extra minutes to outweigh the zero you will receive on the unanswered question.

Your plan of attack begins with **reading the call of the question**. The call of the question is a treasure trove of information. Usually, you will at least be able to determine the topic being tested. Sometimes, you will be able to narrow your focus to the more specific issue being tested. For example, the call could be as explicit as: Did Testator execute a valid will? This call not only tells us the overall topic—Wills—but also tells us the specific subtopic—formation and execution of a will. With just reading the call of the question first, you know to diligently read the facts pertaining to execution. If you read the facts first and then read the call of the question, you would need to go back and reread the facts related to execution.

Once you have determined the topic, you can let your thoughts focus on only the rules for that topic and ignore all other topics. If you are also able to identify the sub-issue, you can immediately call to mind the rule for the subtopic. You can go ahead and bullet-outline the rule.

Reading the call of the question first also prevents you from putting the analysis for part three of the question under your part one answer. You will already know how the examiners have separated the issues and how they want you to structure your answer. If you do put your answer for part three under part one, then, if handwriting, draw a simple arrow to indicate where it does belong. If typing, cut and paste your answer appropriately.

Let's try this out. Read the call of the question first.

## Call of the Question[1]

1. Was Benjamin and Susan's business relationship a general partnership, a limited partnership, or neither? Explain.
2. Does Susan have the right to end her business relationship with Benjamin? Explain.
3. Assuming Susan has the right to end the business relationship, how should Benjamin's claims be resolved? Explain.

What does the call of the question tell us? We immediately know that this question deals with partnership. We also know that the first issue involves whether this is a partnership and what kind of partnership it is. The second and third questions deal with how the relationship ended.

Bullet-outline the rules for the creation of a partnership for part one of your answer. Bullet-outline the rules for ending a partnership for part two and maybe part three of your answer. Do we need to be concerned at this point about the difference between questions two and three? Not really. The facts should help us determine the distinction.

## Bullet Outline of Rules

1. P-ship = assn of two or more persons carrying on a business as co-owners for profit.
   - General p-ship—no formalities/writing.
   - Limited p-ship—writing needed. File w/sec'y of state.
2. Can always end relationship.
   - No reason required.
   - If breaches p-ship agrmt, then liable for damages.
   - If p-ship agrmt doesn't state a specific term, then no breach.
3. Distribution of assets:
   - Costs of sale
   - Outside creditors
   - Inside creditors
   - Capital returned
   - Profits/losses split

Now, read the facts. As you read the facts, confirm the subject matter. Identify the legal relationship of the parties. Are you dealing with a buyer and seller, a tortfeasor and victim, a husband and wife? For the Wills question, is it the executor and beneficiary or two beneficiaries in the dispute? Be sure to underline any

---

1. The Multistate Bar Examination ("MBE®") questions, the Multistate Essay Examination ("MEE®") questions, and excerpts from the Multistate Performance Tests ("MPT®") have been reprinted by permission from the NCBE®. Copyright © by the National Conference of Bar Examiners. All rights reserved.

dates. Dates are given only when relevant. Rarely is a date given that is not relevant. Look for the ways any actors differ from each other. If the question is whether A is liable to B and C, look at how B and C are different. If they were the same, there would be no reason to have the call of the question ask about both. Therefore, the examiners have a reason to ask you about liability for each.

As you go through the facts, you can jot down and align the relevant facts with the parts of the rule you previously bullet-outlined. If you had not read the call of the question first, you would read all the facts then the call of the question, then determine the rule, and then probably need to reread the facts as you were not reading them with the rule for the sub-issue in mind. By reading the call of the question first, you have saved an enormous amount of time. Time is your most precious commodity in taking an exam—time that you can now spend on improving the depth and organization of your analysis.

Read the facts a second time to be sure you did not miss any legally significant facts on your first reading. Fill in your outline and prepare to write. Now that we know the facts, we can expand our outline of the rules to differentiate parts two and three. Part two deals with the dissolution of the partnership and part three deals with the distribution of the assets. Moreover, we can identify that Benjamin's claims also require us to determine if the tools and goodwill are partnership assets.

Place each legally significant fact under the rule to which it applies. Now, we are ready to write our answer.

### Facts for Sample Question

Susan is a talented furniture restorer. Benjamin is a wealthy furniture collector who enjoys buying and selling furniture. Benjamin and Susan agreed to form what they called a "limited partnership." Benjamin would be the limited partner, would contribute $50,000 for working capital, and would contribute an additional $100,000, if needed. Susan would be the general partner, with full authority to buy, restore, and sell furniture, using her own well-equipped workshop and custom tools. They would split the profits as follows: 70% to Benjamin and 30% to Susan until Benjamin received an amount equal to his $50,000 capital contribution plus interest at 11%. Thereafter, the profits would be split 50%-50%.

Benjamin and Susan did not put their agreement in writing or take any other action to formalize it. Benjamin gave Susan $50,000 for the business, and Susan purchased, restored, and sold furniture. After six months of allocating distributions under the 70%-30% formula, Benjamin was repaid his total $50,000 capital contribution and accrued interest. Thereafter, profits were split 50%-50%.

The business has now become so successful that Susan will not need any additional capital from Benjamin. The business has $8,500 in its bank account and has no outstanding debts.

Susan has told Benjamin that she wants to end their business relationship. Benjamin claims that Susan has no right to dissolve the business just as it begins to produce profits. He further claims that if Susan does end the relationship, she must pay him 50% of the cash in the bank account, his share of the goodwill, and an amount equal to 50% of the value of her tools. The tools, which were Susan's before she entered into the agreement with Benjamin, are worth $50,000, and Benjamin asserts that they are assets of the business. Susan denies that Benjamin is entitled to a share of the goodwill, if any, or to 50% of the value of the tools.

## Preparing to Write

Susan is a talented furniture restorer. Benjamin is a wealthy furniture collector who enjoys buying and selling furniture. Benjamin and Susan agreed to form what they called a "limited partnership." Benjamin would be the limited partner, would contribute $50,000 for working capital, and would contribute an additional $100,000 if needed. Susan would be the general partner, with full authority to buy, restore, and sell furniture, using her own well-equipped workshop and custom tools. They would split the profits as follows: 70% to Benjamin and 30% to Susan until Benjamin received an amount equal to his $50,000 capital contribution plus interest at 11%. Thereafter, the profits would be split 50%-50%.

Benjamin and Susan did not put their agreement in writing or take any other action to formalize it. Benjamin gave Susan $50,000 for the business, and Susan purchased, restored, and sold furniture. After six months of allocating distributions under the 70%-30% formula, Benjamin was repaid his total $50,000 capital contribution and accrued interest. Thereafter, profits were split 50%-50%.

The business has now become so successful that Susan will not need any additional capital from Benjamin. The business has $8,500 in its bank account and has no outstanding debts.

**Susan has told Benjamin that she wants to end their business relationship. Benjamin claims that Susan has no right to dissolve the business just as it begins to produce profits.** He further claims that if Susan does end the relationship, she must pay him 50% of the cash in the bank account, his share of the goodwill, and an amount equal to 50% of the value of her tools. The tools, which were Susan's before she entered into the agreement with Benjamin, are worth $50,000, and Benjamin asserts that they are assets of the business. Susan denies that Benjamin is entitled to a share of the goodwill, if any, or to 50% of the value of the tools.

1. Pship = assn of 2 or more persons carrying on a business as co-owners for profit
   - General p-shp—no formalties/ writing
   - Limited p-shp—Writing needed. File w/sec'y of state
     - called themselves a limited p-shp
     - no writing
     - profits 70/30 til capital returned, then 50/50

2. Can always end relationship
   - No reason required
   - If breaches p-shp agrmt, then liable for damages.
   - If p-shp agrmt doesn't state a specific term, then no breach
     - **no written agmt**
     - **S wants to end**

3. Claims?
   a. Bank account
      - Rule: Distribution of assets
        - Costs of sale
        - Outside creditors
        - Inside creditors
          no outstanding debts.
        - Capital returned
          Benjamin was repaid his total $50,000 capital contribution and accrued interest.
        - Profits/losses split
          split 50%-50%.
          $8,500 in bank account.
   b. Tools
      - Rule: ??
        - Susan's prior to agrmt. Used in business
   c. Goodwill
      - Rule: ??

**Sample Answer**

1. Susan and Benjamin formed a general partnership, not a limited partnership. **Under** partnership law, a partnership is an association of two or more persons to carry on as co-owners a business for profit. No written formalities are required. A limited partnership is not formed unless a certificate is filed with the secretary of state.

   **Here**, Susan and Benjamin had an agreement to form a furniture restoration business. They agreed to share profits. Although they did not put their agreement in writing, they still formed a general partnership, as no writing is required. As they did not file a certificate of limited partnership with the secretary of state, it would not be a limited partnership. **Therefore**, Susan and Benjamin formed a general partnership.

2. Susan had the right to end the partnership. **Under** partnership law, a partnership can be dissolved by a partner's refusal to carry on in the business together. If leaving violates any terms of the partnership agreement, the departing partner is in breach of the agreement and may be liable for damages.

   **Here**, the agreement is not for a set term and does not have a definite end. **Therefore**, Susan had the power and right to end the partnership and is not in violation of their agreement.

3. Benjamin is entitled to one-half of the bank account, but is not entitled to half the value of the tools. If goodwill is present, he would be entitled to half. **Under** partnership law, partnership assets are reduced to cash upon dissolution of the partnership. The proceeds are distributed first to the costs of the sale of the assets, then to outside creditors, and then to inside creditors. Capital is returned next, and any remaining funds/profits are split per the agreement.

   **Here**, the business has no debt and Benjamin's capital has already been returned with interest per their agreement. **Therefore**, any remaining assets are split 50/50.

   Cash: The $8,500 account will be split in half.

   Tools: **Under** partnership law, partnership assets are those purchased by the partnership or given to the partnership. **Here**, Susan used her own tools, but did not give them to the partnership. Even if she had, it would be her capital contribution and she would be entitled to their return. **Therefore**, Benjamin is not entitled to half of the tools' value.

   Goodwill: **Under** partnership law, goodwill is the going concern value of the business. If a value cannot be placed upon it, then it is questionable if it even exists. **Here**, it is doubtful goodwill exists as it cannot be valued. It's just Susan doing good work.

   **Therefore**, Benjamin is entitled to half of the bank account, but that is all, unless the goodwill can be valued.

## IV. PROPER FORMAT

Legal readers expect legal analysis to be written and presented in a certain manner. Bar examiners are legal readers and thus expect to read legal analysis in that same manner.

First, **use the basic structure of setting out a legal analysis in a rote manner**. Law professors use various acronyms to describe this structure—IRAC, IREAC, CRAC, CREAC, etc. Your analysis becomes a series of these structures: CRAC,

CRAC, CRAC, CRAC, CRAC, etc.; one for each issue or sub-issue. Each structure has the same underlying doctrine as its basis—it requires the drafter to set forth the rule that governs the issue before applying that rule to the facts. Rule before application. If you don't have time for the complete CRAC structure on each sub-issue when writing a particular analysis, at least do RAC, RAC, RAC, RAC; or RA, RA, RA, RA.

**Order of Analysis**

Business Records Exception to Hearsay
**Rule** = Hearsay is inadmissible without an exception.
Definition: Hearsay is an out-of-court statement offered for the truth of the matter.
**Apply** hearsay definition to facts.
**Conclude**: Hearsay?
**Rule** for business records exception.
**Apply** business records exception to facts.
**Conclude**: Business records exception apply?
If yes, then evidence is admissible.
If no, then evidence is inadmissible.

Next, start a new paragraph to start your **application** section. Don't overlook application. Just stating the rule and a conclusion will not garner the points you need. Look at any sample answer to a bar essay—half the points are in the rule and half the points are in the application. Even assuming you received every single point for every rule, that would not be enough to be successful. The key to scoring well lies within the application.

The application is not a place to retell the story or just restate the facts. It is the place where the writer connects specific legally significant facts to the specific language of the rule, often called the "phrase-that-pays" or "critical language." For example, one part of the business records exception is that the record must have been made "in the course of a regularly conducted activity of a business."[2] That phrase—"course of a regularly conducted activity of a business"—**is** the phrase that pays. That is the key language of this element of the rule that you must connect to the facts of the hypothetical.

Suppose an essay question has you representing a defendant who was sued by a plaintiff injured in a motor vehicle collision with one of your client's delivery trucks, driven by your client's employee. One of the claims is that the defendant did not properly maintain the truck. Because the defendant owns a fleet of delivery trucks, the defendant has its own maintenance department. You want to admit into evidence the maintenance records that are kept in a folder for each vehicle. You need to show that the maintenance records were made in the course of the regular activity of the business. The hypothetical states that the mechanic performing the maintenance must keep track of what service she performed, the date, and the time the work was completed. The mechanic must then sign the form.

---

2. Fed. R. Evid. 803(e).

How would you apply the rule to these facts? It would not be enough to just state that the defendant's maintenance records were kept in the course of a regularly conducted activity of a business. That is just a conclusion. You have to insert the legally significant facts and tie them to the phrase that pays to reach your conclusion.

> Defendant's maintenance records were kept in the course of a regularly conducted activity of a business as defendant had its own maintenance department and each mechanic indicated the service she performed on the maintenance folder every time maintenance was done on the vehicle.

This tying together of the legally significant facts with the phrase that pays is the heart of application and is what will garner you major points. Do this with each and every rule.

Think of application like the proof of a math problem. You need to show the examiner how you reached your answer. When you made a minor misstep in a math problem like a calculation error, the teacher would still give you partial credit. It's the same thing on the bar exam. You need to show the examiners your work—your proof of the analysis. If you make a misstep, you will get credit for the part you did do correctly. If you just state the rule and state the *incorrect* conclusion, you get no credit for the part of the application that you got correct because it stayed in your head and did not get put down on the exam. Put every step of the process you do in your head down on the paper, going step by step from the rule, through the application, to the conclusion for each issue. The examiner will not give you points for what they think you probably thought. They will only give you points for what you actually state.

Next, **use signposts**. When we drive, a signpost tells us where we are or what direction we should go. A reader needs signposts to keep track of where they are and where they are going. As the writer, it is your responsibility to make the reader's job effortless. Signposts help you do that. Moreover, ritualistically using signposts helps you keep track of where you are and what you need to do next.

The first signpost to use is **UNDER**. "Under" begins the sentence where you state a rule. Follow "under" with the general source of the rule. "Under the Uniform Commercial Code. . . ." "Under the Federal Rules of Civil Procedure. . . ." "Under Torts law. . . ." This signpost immediately tells the reader that this sentence will be the rule. It helps you to be sure that you state the source of the rule and that you clearly separate the rule from the application and conclusion sections.

The signpost that signals the reader that the writer has moved to application is **HERE** or **IN THIS CASE**. "Here, the husband supported the wife throughout law school." "In this case, the plaintiff filed its complaint on. . . ." "Here, the directors held a meeting without giving notice to. . . ." Using "here" cues your reader that you are starting the application. It is also your clue that you need to make those connections between the facts and the critical language.

**THEREFORE** signals the reader that you are now concluding this part of the analysis. There should be a conclusion—a "therefore" sentence—at the end of each sub-issue and then again at the end of each answer to a call of the question. "Therefore, the maintenance records are admissible under the business records exception to the hearsay rule." "Therefore, the petition was filed out-of-time under the statute of limitations," etc.

If thinking about your analysis using an IRAC or CRAC doesn't come easily, then always do **Under-Here-Therefore; Under-Here-Therefore; Under-Here-Therefore, etc.**, and you won't go wrong!

Next, if the question has **multiple parts**, your answer should have the same number of parts and be in the same order. Do not be tempted to collapse the parts into one analysis or analyze the parts in a different order. Remember, the examiners designed the question to have multiple parts and had a reason to do so. The examiners are addressing different issues in each part of the question. If you can't identify the separate issues, then look carefully at how the actors differ such that the analysis differs.

Use headings to separate the different parts. If you do not like to use headings, leave a space between each part and number each part to match the call of the question, at a minimum. If there is only one call of the question, there will still be multiple parts. Bar essay questions usually contain more than one issue. If it does appear to be only one issue, then do a separate IRAC or CRAC for its multiple sub-issues. Be sure to analyze each issue and sub-issue separately.

Next, **discuss any general rules before you discuss any exceptions**. It may be clear that the call of the question is asking about an exception. But you need to lay the foundation of the general rule before you reach the exception. For example, a question involving the business records exception to the hearsay requirement may be clear-cut from the call of the question. But before you address the particulars of the rule for the business records exception, the examiner needs to first know that it actually is hearsay. Thus, analyze the general rule about hearsay before you discuss the business records exception.

Finally, **use definitions** immediately after your rule for any parts of the rule that are at issue. Don't assume the reader knows what you are talking about. Explain the rule as you would to a client, not to someone whom you believe knows the rule. For example, stating the rule that hearsay is inadmissible without an exception[3] is not enough. Hearsay must be defined—an out-of-court statement offered for the truth of the matter.[4] Then, apply that rule to your facts and conclude whether the evidence is hearsay and thus inadmissible. Then, give the rule for the business records exception and apply it to the facts. Only then have you given the examiners a complete analysis of the call of the question. Note that you do not give the rule for hearsay and its exception at the same time to create one large rule. They are separate sub-issues that must be analyzed separately.

Check the table of the Order of Analysis for the Business Records Exception discussed previously to see how definitions fit into rule statements, how the general rule is analyzed before the exception, and how each sub-issue—is this hearsay and is this admissible under the business records exception—is set out with separate CRACs.

---

3. Fed. R. Evid. 802.
4. Fed. R. Evid. 801(c).

## V. AUTOPSY YOUR PRACTICE ANSWERS

An integral part of your game plan is doing practice essay questions. During Phase One, you are using your practice to help learn the law. In Phase Two, the goal is to assess your memorization of the law. During both phases, doing an autopsy of your practice answer is critical to your game plan's success.

Only you are in your head when you write the essay answer. Only you know why you did or did not state something. Did you not know that rule? Did you not remember the rule, although you did know it? Did you not see that issue? Did you do a cursory application? Did you misread the facts? Only you can determine the underlying reasons why your answer was incomplete or inaccurate.

Examining or performing an autopsy of your answer includes looking at everything you wrote and classifying it as rule, application, or conclusion. Then, analyze the model answer and identify the rules, applications, and conclusions. The score sheets utilized in this text already do that for you.

Lay them side by side. What was in the model answer, but not in your answer? Was it a rule? If yes, then add that rule to your flash cards/outlines/flowcharts you are making on each topic. Was that rule already in your flash cards/outlines/flowcharts? Then, highlight it. The next time you review your materials your brain will pause on the highlighted area and that will remind you that you missed it once before, and pausing will also encode that rule deeper into your long-term memory. Was it application? Take note of how the examiners tie the facts to the critical language or phrase that pays of the rule for each issue. As you do more practice essays, strive to include the same level of application in your answers.

Also, check your organization. Did you lay out the rule before you applied it to the facts? Did you lump all the rules together and then try one big application? Note how the sample answer has a conclusion-rule-application-conclusion for each and every issue and sub-issue. Did your organization follow the same pattern? Take note of the order that the examiners laid out the different issues and sub-issues. Are your issues in a similar order? Consider why you did not lay them out in the same order.

Be brutally honest in assessing your answer. Your rule needs to match the stated rule with the same level of detail. Do the critical language, phrase that pays, or buzz words match? While some variation is allowed in sentence structure, the gist must be the same. For example, your answer states that hearsay is a statement made by someone not at the trial. The rule is both that hearsay is an out-of-court statement offered for the truth of the matter and that hearsay is inadmissible without an exception. You cheat yourself if you see those two statements as the same.

Consider this autopsy as a part of your learning and memorization process. Each review of the law encodes it into your memory. If all you do is read the answer, it does not encode the rules at a deep enough level. The tough autopsy does that.

Let's work through an autopsy by analyzing the model answer to identify rule-application-conclusion on each issue. Then, we want to lay our answer beside it to see what we missed and what we could articulate in a clearer manner. Highlight the model answer with what you missed. Then, to pinpoint the areas we need to improve, use a score sheet that you can incorporate into your flash cards or outline. Lastly, add what was missing to your outline or flash cards. If that rule is already there, then highlight it. Remember, while you are doing this autopsy, you are actually encoding the rules further into your long-term memory. Thus, it is time well spent.

Highlight the portions of the Model Answer that are not in the Sample Answer of our sample question. Then, do the same thing with the Score Sheet.

Now check your outline/flash cards/etc. to be sure these rules missing in your answer are there and in the same detail. Add them or highlight them to help you remember the next time.

## SAMPLE ANSWER

1. Susan and Benjamin formed a general partnership, not a limited partnership. **Under** partnership law, a partnership is an association of two or more persons to carry on as co-owners a business for profit. No written formalities are required. A limited partnership is not formed unless a certificate is filed with the secretary of state.

   **Here**, Susan and Benjamin had an agreement to form a furniture restoration business. They agreed to share profits. Although they did not put their agreement in writing, they still formed a general partnership as no writing is required. As they did not file a certificate of limited partnership with the secretary of state, it would not be a limited partnership. **Therefore**, Susan and Benjamin formed a general partnership.

2. Susan had the right to end the partnership. **Under** partnership law, a partnership can be dissolved by a partner's refusal to carry on in the business together. If leaving violates any terms of the partnership agreement, the departing partner is in breach of the agreement and may be liable for damages.

   **Here**, the agreement is not for a set term and does not have a definite end. **Therefore**, Susan had the power and right to end the partnership and is not in violation of their agreement.

3. Benjamin is entitled to one-half of the bank account, but is not entitled to half the value of the tools. If goodwill is present, he would be entitled to half. **Under** partnership law, partnership assets are reduced to cash upon dissolution of the partnership. The proceeds are distributed first to the costs of the sale of the assets, then to outside creditors, and then to inside creditors. Capital is returned next, and any remaining funds/profits are split per the agreement.

   **Here**, the business has no debt and Benjamin's capital has already been returned with interest per their agreement. **Therefore**, any remaining assets are split 50/50.

   Cash: The $8,500 account will be split in half.

   Tools: **Under** partnership law, partnership assets are those purchased by the partnership or given to the partnership. **Here**, Susan used her own tools, but did not give them to the partnership. Even if she had, it would be her capital contribution and she would be entitled to their return. **Therefore**, Benjamin is not entitled to half of the tools' value.

   Goodwill: **Under** partnership law, goodwill is the going concern value of the business. If a value cannot be placed upon it, then it is questionable if it even exists. **Here**, it is doubtful goodwill exists as it cannot be valued. It's just Susan doing good work.

   **Therefore**, Benjamin is entitled to half of the bank account, but that is all, unless the goodwill can be valued.

## MODEL ANSWER

1. The business relationship between Benjamin and Susan was a general partnership. Although Benjamin and Susan agreed to form a limited partnership, a limited partnership was not created because a limited partnership may only be created under specific statutory authority. The Revised Uniform Limited Partnership Act requires, among other things, that a certificate of limited partnership be filed with the secretary of state. Here, the facts indicate that Benjamin and Susan did not put their agreement in writing or take any other action to formalize it. Thus, Benjamin and Susan's relationship was not a limited partnership.

   Notwithstanding the fact that Benjamin and Susan did not create a limited partnership, they did create a general partnership. A partnership is an association of two or more persons to carry on as co-owners a business for profit. No formal agreement is required to create a partnership, and it is generally not necessary for a partnership agreement to be in writing. In this case, it is clear that Benjamin and Susan created a partnership, although they did not evidence such a relationship in writing. Benjamin and Susan agreed to operate a furniture business with Benjamin providing the working capital and Susan having full authority to operate the business. They further agreed that they would split the profits of the business. The Uniform Partnership Act provides that the receipt by a person of a share of the profits is prima facie evidence that he is a partner in the business (and under the Revised Uniform Partnership Act, a person who receives a share of the profits is presumed to be a partner). Here, the profits would initially be split 70% to Benjamin and 30% to Susan until Benjamin was repaid his capital contribution, and later they would be split 50%-50%. Consequently, a partnership was established between Benjamin and Susan.

2. Susan has the right to end the business relationship with Benjamin. As noted above, the relationship between Benjamin and Susan was a partnership. When no definite term or particular undertaking is specified for a partnership, a partnership at will is created. A partnership at will may be dissolved by the express will of any partner at any time without penalty to the partner dissolving the partnership. Because Benjamin and Susan did not specify a term or particular undertaking for their partnership, Susan has the right to end the business relationship.

3. Benjamin is entitled to 50% of the cash in the bank account and may be entitled to his share of the goodwill of the business, but he is not entitled to 50% of the value of Susan's tools. Dissolution gives to each partner the right to have the business wound up and her share of the surplus paid in cash. Here, Susan has rightfully terminated the partnership and is entitled to have the business liquidated. Because there are no partnership liabilities and Benjamin has been repaid his capital contribution, Benjamin and Susan will split the partnership assets equally per their agreement.

   Benjamin is not, however, entitled to receive 50% of the value of Susan's tools because the tools are not partnership property. The controlling factor in determining if property is partnership property is the intent of the partners. Although Benjamin and Susan agreed that Susan would use her tools in conducting partnership business, they did not agree that Susan would make a contribution of the tools to the partnership. . . .

## SCORE SHEET

| Stated | Implied | |
|---|---|---|
| __√__ | _____ | **1. Creation (40%-50%)**<br><br>**Conclusion/Issue:** Benjamin and Susan formed a general partnership, not a limited partnership. |
| _____ | __√__ | **Rule:** Under the uniform acts regarding partnership law, |
| __√__ | _____ | Creation of a partnership is function of the intent of the putative partners to establish "an association of two or more persons to carry on as co-owners a business for profit." |
| _____ | _____ | Receipt of a share of the profits is prima facie evidence of partnership. |
| __√__ | _____ | No writing requirement needed for a general partnership. |
| __√__ | _____ | To form a limited p-ship, a written certificate of limited p-ship must be executed and filed with the secretary of state. |
| _____ | _____ | Subjective belief of the parties is not relevant. |
| __√__ | _____ | **Application:** Here, |
| __√__ | _____ | B & S intended to operate their furniture restoration business as co-owners for profit, even though they were legally mistaken in calling the venture a limited p-ship. |
| _____ | _____ | Profits first divided 70%-30% then 50%-50%. |
| __√__ | _____ | Relationship was not memorialized in writing of any kind and there was no filing with the secretary of state. |
| __√__ | _____ | **Conclusion:** Therefore, Benjamin and Susan formed a general partnership. |
| __√__ | _____ | **2. Dissolution (5%-10%)**<br><br>**Conclusion:** Susan has the legal right to terminate the partnership. |
| _____ | __√__ | **Rule:** A partner always has the right to dissolve the p-ship. |
| _____ | _____ | Partner is not required to have a reason to dissolve. |
| __√__ | _____ | Partner is liable for damages if the dissolution contravenes the partnership agreement. |
| _____ | __√__ | Where partnership agreement does not specify a definite term or objective for the p-ship to achieve, then dissolution does not contravene the partnership agreement. |
| __√__ | _____ | **Application:** Here, |
| __√__ | _____ | Agreement does not specify any term. |
| _____ | _____ | Purpose of p-ship is to restore and sell furniture, which is a continuous activity that does not constitute a particular undertaking. |
| _____ | __√__ | **Conclusion:** Thus, this is a partnership at will and Susan has the power and the legal right to dissolve the partnership. |
| __√__ | _____ | **3. Winding Up (40%-50%)**<br><br>**Conclusion:** Benjamin is entitled to one-half of the cash and one-half of any goodwill (if it exists). |

*continued on next page*

| Stated | Implied | |
|:---:|:---:|---|
| ____ | __√__ | **Rule dividing assets:** When not a wrongful dissolution, p-ship property is applied to discharge the p-ship's liabilities, and the surplus is paid to the partners. |
| ____ | ____ | If no contrary agreement of the parties, surplus split 50%-50%. |
| __√__ | ____ | **Application:** Here, |
| __√__ | ____ | No liabilities. No outside or inside creditors as B has already been paid. Need only to split up partnership property. |
| __√__ | ____ | **Rule on partnership property:** All property brought into the partnership or subsequently acquired is p-ship property. |
| __√__ | ____ | **Application:** Here, |
| __√__ | ____ | Cash on hand is p-ship asset. |
| __√__ | ____ | Facts state S "would use her own" well-equipped workshop and custom tools for the p-ship's operations. |
| __√__ | ____ | S did not contribute ownership of tools to p-ship, but made them available for use by the p-ship. |
| __√__ | ____ | Somewhat like B's $50,000 contribution as of equivalent amounts. |
| ____ | ____ | Although not like $50,000 as B was repaid with interest and no similar provision for the tools. |
| ____ | ____ | No evidence that the parties treated tools as p-ship property. |
| __√__ | ____ | **Conclusion:** Probably not p-ship property. |
| __√__ | ____ | Even if tools considered p-ship property, their contribution was a "capital contribution" by S. |
| ____ | __√__ | She is entitled to return of capital contribution prior to distribution of profits. |
| __√__ | ____ | Goodwill is the "going concern" value. |
| __√__ | ____ | **Application:** Here, |
| ____ | __√__ | S will argue that because she is a professional there is no goodwill attributable to the business, but instead her personal reputation and individual skill. Thus, no goodwill to divide. |
| ____ | __√__ | **Conclusion:** As no wrongful dissolution, goodwill is valued and divided, if recognized. |
| __√__ | ____ | **Overall conclusion:** B entitled to receive one-half of the $8,500 bank account and one-half of any goodwill, if recognized. |

## VI. COMMON WAYS TO LOSE POINTS

### A. Mismanaging Time

Multistate Essay Examination questions are 30 minutes each. You will have six of them in a three-hour period in an MEE or UBE jurisdiction and you must keep track of your own time. Other jurisdictions' essays have longer or shorter time periods. Some jurisdictions prohibit watches, and all prohibit cell phones. As soon as you are registered and locate your seat, make note of each clock in the room so you can look up quickly. Limit yourself to the time limit for each question. Even if you feel just 10 more minutes would push your score to new heights, avoid the temptation. The numbers just don't work for that to happen. Rarely is that time worth it, because it means 10 minutes must be taken off another question. Do that on the first three 30 minute questions and you now have 60 minutes for the three remaining questions that need 90 minutes. They are worth the same number of points as the ones you spent more time on, and you just short-circuited the number of points you could possibly receive.

### B. Wasting Time Answering a Question Different from the Question Asked

Every hypothetical raises several issues. If the call of the question is very general, such as "discuss" or "explain the causes of action," then you are free to discuss them all. More likely, however, the call of the question will not be that broad and will focus on two or more issues or one issue that has several sub-issues.

You may be tempted to show the examiner how much you know by addressing other possible issues. Indeed, one of those issues may be so appealing to you that you decide to focus most of your time on it. But then, that is not what the examiner asked. Indeed, that is exactly what the examiner chose not to ask. The points are assigned to the questions asked; no bonus points are left over. Thus, failing to analyze the questions asked and answering something else is not a strong strategy. Indeed, no matter how brilliant that other answer is, it cannot make up for the points lost by not answering the questions asked.

### C. Not "Showing Your Work"

The examiner does not get to speculate. He may only give you points for what is written down. He cannot guess at what you meant to put down or what you thought about before you began writing. Your written answer must stand on its own. Thus, show every step of your analysis for every issue—rule, including definitions; application; and conclusion. Lead the examiner step by step through your thinking process so that there is no doubt that your analysis is proven. When you make a mistake in that analysis and reach the wrong conclusion, the examiner can still give you points for how you got there. The examiner can only do that if you show your work.

### D. Assuming the Grader Knows the Law and Not Referencing Specific Tests/Elements

As a law student, you are accustomed to writing final exam essays that you know will be read and graded by your professor. You may use a shorthand method of referring to certain rules that your professor used in class. You know the professor knows the rule, so you may feel no need to explain it.

Your bar essays are to be written to your client. Not another lawyer, a client. You must assume that your reader knows nothing about the rules. You must explain everything to the reader. Define every term of art. Lay out every element of a rule and then define each. Apply every single element. Don't skip a single step of the process.

Remember, your goal is not to tell the examiners every single thing you know about a topic. The examiners only want to know about the specific issues in the call of the question. Thus, don't spend time discussing how to create a partnership when the facts explicitly state that the partners entered into a valid partnership agreement. Likewise, don't list all possible hearsay exceptions when only one or two are at issue.

Likewise, don't repeat all the facts. The examiner already knows them. Stick to CRAC with all discussion of the facts tied to the critical language of the "phrase that pays" of the rule.

### E. Writing Lengthy Sentences and Paragraphs with Grammar Issues

Listen up, typists. The "Enter" key is your friend. Use it. There is nothing worse as a grader than getting a wall of typed words without a single paragraph to break it up. It's reading a stream of consciousness rather than an organized analysis. Separate issues deserve separate paragraphs. Indeed, in a lengthy issue, put the rule and application in separate paragraphs.

Everyone needs to use periods. Frequently. Short sentences serve you better. Your analysis will be easier to read and to understand. In a lengthy sentence, your main point may be buried in the middle or saved until the end when the reader has given up trying to understand what you were trying to say. Now, you don't have to go the route of "See Jane. Run Jane. Look Jane." Shorter sentences do not mean you must be laconic in your writing. Just don't make them 50 words long! As a rule of thumb, avoid having a sentence that runs more than three lines of typed text.

Avoid using the shorthand abbreviations you use to take notes. Use only recognized abbreviations after you have first identified them. Thus, the first time state "Uniform Commercial Code (UCC)," and the next time you can just state UCC.

Do your best to use correct spelling and proper grammar. Some errors will be overlooked, but an essay riddled with errors will not impress an examiner and make her want to bring you into the fold. That's not to say you need polished, perfect writing. You don't. But constant sentence fragments and misspelled words make the examiner doubt your ability.

### F. And, the Biggest Point Loser—Skimming All of the Questions First!

It's so tempting. You are handed the essay questions in a group and are given the signal to begin. You just want to take a peek at them to make sure that your dreaded topic isn't there and that your favorite topic is there. Going through each question enough to be sure about their topics takes time. Doing that with all of the questions takes a significant amount of time. And, what's the end result? Peace of mind? Nope. Panic.

You'll see that your favorite topic is not there and your least favorite topic is there instead. You begin to dread what is coming up. You can't focus on the first question, because you know number two is the worst topic. All you can think about is number two. You end up doing poorly on the first question even though it is a topic with which you are fairly comfortable. You skip number two and move on to three, another comfortable topic. Except, now you are still thinking about number two and how on earth you are ever going to be able to answer it. And on it goes.

Avoid this temptation. Answer each question in the order that it is given to you. Spend the allotted time and then move on. If you don't spend all of the time on a topic, then you'll have time to go back later. You have to attempt the dreaded topics when they come. Apply your mind map and do your best. Then move on. If something comes to you later, you can go back and add it. This approach helps to avoid the panic that sets in when you skim them all first.

## VII. AVOID PANIC

One common fear of applicants is having a question that they will have no idea how to answer. Let's put that fear at ease right now. You will. You will have a question that you do not immediately have any idea how to answer. So, no need to panic that it might happen, as we know it will happen.

What are you going to do when that happens? Hyperventilate? You might have if you didn't know that it was actually going to happen. Because you do know, you can plan what to do. Bring to mind your mind map of how to tackle questions in that topic area. Go through the topic step by step and it will come to you.

What if nothing comes to you? Your mind is a complete blank. Then, guess. Yes, guess. It's an educated guess, but making a guess may garner you a point while leaving it blank is worth zero points.

For example, a groom demands his bride sign a pre-nuptial agreement the morning of their wedding without talking about it beforehand. It states that she agrees to no property provision if they divorce within five years. One year later, the couple is now divorcing and she discovers that he had hidden assets, is worth several million dollars, and is not a penniless law student after all.

The issue is whether the pre-nuptial agreement is valid. You did not take Family Law in law school and you did not study it very much in your bar preparation. First, take a deep breath. Get as much oxygen flowing to your brain as you can. Then, pause and consider—what do you know? An "agreement" indicates it's a contract. You do know about contracts. That means there must be mutual assent. Did the bride assent? Could she fully assent when it was given to her that morning? Could she fully assent when she didn't have all the facts? What would you guess? The groom should have fully disclosed his assets and given her more time to consider. Craft a rule, put it down, apply it, and move on. If the rule comes to you later, go back and redo.

Your mindset entering the exam needs to be "I can do this," because you can do this. Have confidence in yourself. You will have studied hard for the bar exam, probably harder than anything else you have done. Take a deep breath. You will be fine.

# CHAPTER 5

# Building Multistate Performance Test Skills

## I. SKILLS TESTED

Each component of the bar exam is designed to assess your ability to apply fundamental legal principles and legal reasoning to a given fact pattern. In essence, can you identify the issues raised by a fact pattern, understand what is relevant, demonstrate an understanding of the legal principles involved, and apply the rules to the facts? The MEE does this through 30-minute essay questions. The MBE does this with 200 multiple choice questions. In both components, you must be able to recall the law on your own, closed-book.

The Multistate Performance Test (MPT) is quite different. It is designed to test the same skills, but in a more realistic situation: Can you complete a task that a beginning lawyer should be able to accomplish? "The MPT requires examinees to

- sort detailed factual materials and separate relevant from irrelevant facts;
- analyze statutory, case, and administrative materials for applicable principles of law;
- apply the relevant law to the relevant facts in a manner likely to resolve a client's problem;
- identify and resolve ethical dilemmas, when present;
- communicate effectively in writing; and
- complete a lawyering task within time constraints."[1]

The skills being assessed include the:

- ability to develop and evaluate strategies for solving a problem or accomplishing an objective, including the ability to:
  - identify and diagnose the problem;
  - generate alternative solutions and strategies;
  - develop a plan of action;
  - implement a plan of action; and
  - keep the planning process open to new information and new ideas.

---

1. www.ncbex.org/exams/mpt/preparing/.

- ability to analyze and apply legal rules and principles, including the ability to:
  - identify and formulate legal issues;
  - identify relevant legal rules within a given set of legal materials;
  - formulate relevant legal theories;
  - elaborate on legal theories;
  - evaluate legal theories; and
  - criticize and synthesize legal arguments.
- ability to analyze and use facts and to plan and direct factual investigation, including the ability to:
  - identify relevant facts within a given set of factual materials;
  - determine the need for factual investigation;
  - plan a factual investigation;
  - memorialize and organize information in an accessible form;
  - decide whether to conclude the process of fact gathering; and
  - evaluate the information that has been gathered.
- ability to communicate effectively in writing, including the ability to:
  - assess the perspective of the recipient of the communication; and
  - organize and express ideas with precision, clarity, logic, and economy.
- ability to organize and manage a legal task, including the ability to:
  - allocate time, effort, and resources efficiently; and
  - perform and complete tasks within time constraints.
- ability to represent a client consistently with applicable ethical standards, including:
  - knowledge of the nature and sources of ethical standards;
  - knowledge of the means by which ethical standards are enforced; and
  - ability to recognize and resolve ethical dilemmas.[2]

For the MPT, the examiners give you the instructions, a File, and a Library. In the past, the instructions have been identical for all MPT questions. That's not guaranteed. So, one step is to verify that the instructions have not been changed from the instructions you read during your practice questions. Just a quick skim should do it.

The File consists of documents, including a memo from the assigning attorney spelling out the task you are to accomplish. Frequently, another memorandum is included that spells out the format for the document. Read this carefully. Specific guidelines are included for specific format issues, such as headings. Note that these memos not only instruct you as to format, but also whether to use an objective or persuasive tone in the document.

Other parts of the File include fact documents such as deposition transcripts, notes from a witness interview, an invoice, a receipt, a purchase order, a contract, medical records, police reports, and letters. These are the sources for the facts, which are not summarized for you. You must extract the relevant facts from these source documents.

The Library contains the law that you are to analyze. You are not to include any law that you already know, but are to analyze only what is given in the Library. The law is set in the fictitious jurisdiction of Franklin, although the law may mirror regulations or uniform acts that you already know such as

---

2. www.ncbex.org/pdfviewer/?file=2%Fdmsdocument%2F54.

the Uniform Commercial Code. The law may include statutes, regulations, court rules, model rules, and excerpts from cases. Not all may be relevant to the issues raised. Thus, you must pull from the Library the relevant law that you will then apply to the facts.

Instead of presenting your analysis in an essay response or by answering multiple choice questions, you are to prepare a specific document. Examples include a predictive memorandum to your supervising attorney, a client letter, a persuasive brief, a statement of facts for a persuasive brief, a contract provision, a will, a proposal for settlement, a witness examination plan, a discovery plan, or a closing argument. The three documents used the most are a predictive memorandum; a letter, which can be persuasive or objective; and a persuasive brief that may include a statement of facts, point headings, and the argument. Those are not guaranteed, of course. You should be prepared to draft any of the documents listed.

Scoring the MPT is virtually identical to scoring an essay question. The same scale is used. Just like an essay question, different issues on the MPT may be worth a different number of points. Issue one may be 60% and issue two may be 40% of the total available points. Each jurisdiction decides how much weight to give the overall MPT score. Uniform Bar Examination jurisdictions weight the MPT at 20%.

## II. GAME PLAN FOR THE MPT

Your game plan for the essays and multiple choice questions has consisted of making your own materials for memorization and then using practice questions to both learn the law and memorize the law. Your game plan for the MPT is much simpler. No memorization is necessary. The examiners give you the law you need. Your preparation is twofold: practicing MPT questions and reviewing document formats.

Completing practice MPT questions is critical to your success. They cannot be taken for granted just because no memorization is involved. In many respects, they are like a closed-research writing assignment from your first year of law school; the difference is that there will be more irrelevant facts and irrelevant law. In addition, professional responsibility issues may arise. Sometimes you are asked what additional facts you need. While the format may be something with which you are very comfortable, it may not be. And, the biggest reason to do practice questions—time pressure.

No doubt about it, the MPT is a time-pressured assessment. While 90 minutes sounds like a lot of time, you will find the length of the materials you must read and analyze far exceeds the comparable time spent reading an essay question. The facts are not organized in any particular fashion.

Two schools of thought exist as to how to approach the reading. You should do sufficient practice to decide which method works best for you. The first school of thought focuses on the Library first:

- Verify that the instructions are the same as they were for the practice questions.
- Read the memo from the supervising attorney to understand the task.
- Read the memo regarding format, if included.
- Read the Library.

**EXAM TIP**

Drafting a statement of facts is more difficult than it may seem. Remember to focus on the facts relevant to that motion and not on everything that happened in the case. The examiners want to see if you know the difference.

* Analyze the law in the Library and make an outline of the rules.
* Read the File and insert the relevant facts into your outline.
* Verify the facts by a second read of the File.
* Draft the document.

The rationale behind this approach is that you will have a better analysis and save time by understanding the law before you read the facts. By understanding the law, you will more quickly see which facts are relevant. By outlining the law first, you have a jump start on the organization of the analysis. This approach is recommended for at-risk students.

The second school of thought focuses on the File first:

* Verify that the instructions are the same as they were for the practice questions.
* Read the memo from the supervising attorney to understand the task.
* Read the memo regarding format, if included.
* Read the File to better understand what happened.
* Read the Library.
* Analyze the law in the Library and make an outline of the rules.
* Read the facts a second time to identify relevant facts.
* Insert the relevant facts into your outline.
* Verify the facts by a third read of the File.
* Draft the document.

Some applicants find they must read the facts several times when they read the File first. The first time they read to understand what happened. The second time they read to identify the relevant facts. They then read a third time to verify the facts.

You will need to decide which method works best for you. The only way to do that is to do enough practice questions to know. Because this is time-pressured, you must gauge what you currently can do in that time frame. Thus, unlike your first sets of essay practice questions, you must keep to the strict time limit of 90 minutes. Then, as you practice, autopsy your answer. Your ability to analyze and draft a better document will improve.

Just like essay questions, spend your initial time reading and thinking about the issues and rules. Forty-five minutes of the 90 minutes should be spent reading and thinking. Then, the next 45 minutes are spent drafting and revising the document. Do that with each MPT if your jurisdiction requires more than one.

The Uniform Bar Examination includes two MPT questions. They are back to back, the first morning of the exam. You are given both MPT questions at the same time, and time is not called on the first MPT after 90 minutes. You must keep track of your own time. Spending too much time on the first question means you will be short on time on the second MPT. Both MPTs are worth the same numbers of points. You gain no advantage by spending more time on one than on the other. Practice taking two MPTs back to back in three hours in order to see how necessary it is to keep to the time limits. Do not read both MPTs together to decide which one to do first. You have to do both any way. Start with the first one and, at 90 minutes, switch to the second one, even if the first one is not as complete as you would like.

Just as with essay and MBE questions, reviewing your practice answer is where you will learn the most. Each MPT comes with a Point Sheet from the

NCBE. This Point Sheet outlines in detail what is expected on that MPT. Most of the time what is on the Point Sheet is more than anyone could write in 90 minutes. It is meant as a guide for the local state bar examiners to decide how to grade that MPT. It is still worth reviewing so that you can see if you properly identified all of the issues, properly synthesized the rules, organized the analysis appropriately, provided sufficient application, used the correct tone (whether objective or persuasive), and properly addressed the task recognizing any professional responsibility issues that arose.

Reviewing the bar examiners' Point Sheet also informs you about how the points are allocated. Sometimes the Point Sheet allows the grader to give credit for tangential issues not raised by the actual File and Library, for example, the canon of construction that hand-written words prevail over typewritten words in a contract. Most of the time, however, those issues are not worth the time, particularly if you focus on them to the exclusion of the main issues raised by the Library given to you. If you have a tendency to go off too much on a tangent, you need to learn what the bar examiners are really looking for to sharpen your issue-spotting skills.

## III. PROPER FORMAT

Your document needs to be in the proper format, both in substance, in form, and in tone. You can keep the form fairly basic, but it should not be in the style of an essay answer to the question. A letter should look like a letter. A brief should look like a brief. Proper citation format is not required, although you need to include some kind of attribution of authority. Just the case name, *Smith*, or the statute number, §65-210, is sufficient.

### MEMO FORMAT

**MEMORANDUM**

To:   Partner
From: Associate
Date: July 30, 2017
Re:   *Popper v. Wilson*—Intentional Interference with Contract, Jurisdiction Issues File No. 14-1234

Our client, Bonnie Wilson, was served with a complaint alleging intentional interference with contract. This dispute arises from . . . . The firm needs to decide whether to file a motion to dismiss for lack of jurisdiction.

First . . . .

[Read the memos from the partner carefully. The firm may have an established format regarding memos including the use of headings. Headings are appropriate in predictive memoranda even if not required by the supervising attorney.]

[Include your analysis here.]

## LETTER FORMAT

July 30, 2017

Dear Mr. Plate:

This letter is in response to your inquiry regarding the legal issues involved in establishing your business as a closely-held corporation.

[Again, read the memos from the partner carefully. The firm may have an established format regarding letters including the use of headings. Headings are appropriate in letters as well.]

[Include your analysis here.]

Thank you again for contacting me regarding your new business venture. Please feel free to contact me should you have further questions.

Sincerely,

[Do NOT put your name. Put your exam number, instead.]

## BRIEF FORMAT

[Sometimes called Memorandum in Support of Motion . . .
or Suggestions in Support of Motion . . . .
Do not confuse with a predictive memorandum.
It is still a persuasive brief document.]

### BRIEF IN SUPPORT OF MOTION TO SUPPRESS

#### Statement of Facts

Include only if instructions from supervising attorney require.

#### Argument

I. The Text Messages Between Plaintiff, Her Attorney, and the Investigator are Protected by Attorney-Client Privilege Because . . . and Must be Suppressed. [Check memo from supervising attorney for format.]

[Argument for first issue.]

II. Plaintiff's Facebook Posts are Irrelevant to the Issues . . . and Must be Suppressed. [Argument for second issue.]

#### Conclusion

Respectfully submitted,

[Do NOT put your name. Put your exam number, instead.]

Letters and memos usually start with at least one sentence that lays out the issues and is appropriate for that document. This should be brief. No need for a letter to start with a ton of trivial banter such as "Great to meet you," and "Thanks for meeting with us.

The second and more important part of format is the tone of the document. Memoranda are planning documents. Thus, the analysis must be objective and include the strengths and weaknesses of the client's situation. Letters can be objective or persuasive. For example, an initial settlement offer is a persuasive document to the opposing counsel as to why settlement serves both sides' best interests. A client letter, however, needs to be objective and state the strengths and weaknesses of the client's situation. A brief is always a persuasive document, but your audience is the judge. Use an advocacy tone. No need to inflate or embellish the argument, but use a strong voice.

Prepare for the MPT by reviewing formats for different documents in addition to doing practice questions. Your commercial bar preparation provider will usually provide you with several MPTs. You can also purchase additional MPTs directly from the NCBE. Use these to practice and to review format. For the MPTs you do not write out, spend time reading the MPT, bullet-outlining the law, and reviewing the format of the document.

## IV. BOTTOM LINE IS ANALYSIS

An outline of your analysis is well worth the time invested. Consider drafting a thesis at the beginning of your analysis that briefly sets out the points you want to make. If you run short on time, the examiners will at least know what you planned to do. Then, in your analysis, bullet-outline the remaining points you want to make. You will receive some credit for those, although they are not fully developed.

The organization of your analysis should be a form of CRAC, whether your writing is objective or predictive. Always put the rule before the application. Make sure you have separate CRACs for each issue or sub-issue.

Most of the authority provided to you will be binding authority. Occasionally, the examiners will include authority from another jurisdiction—persuasive authority. If they do, consider that in your analysis and be careful not to treat it as binding authority. Likewise, if secondary authority is included, do not treat it the same as primary authority. Some of the authority may be irrelevant. Your job is to analyze and decide which authority to use. Remember that your analysis is to be based only on these authorities and no others.

As you do practice MPT questions, autopsy your answer the same way you do the practice essays. Identify each rule, application, and conclusion. Note the organization of the issues and sub-issues. Be brutally honest with yourself in your critique of your answer.

Most of the points are based on the analysis. Your ultimate conclusion often does not matter. Good grammar and punctuation count. Use headings so that organization is evident. Understand the format to quickly get it out of the way so that the majority of your time and written work is on the analysis.

# V. PRACTICE MPT QUESTION

## *Wells v. Wells*[3]

### File
Memorandum from Pamela Broyles     1
Memorandum regarding persuasive briefs     2
Transcript of hearing     3

### Library
Franklin Dissolution of Marriage Act     11
*Marshall v. Marshall*, Franklin Supreme Court (2001)     12
*Feldman v. Feldman*, Franklin Court of Appeal (2002)     14

## FILE

**Broyles and Lemansky**

*Attorneys at Law*

2398 S. 25th Street

Franklin City, Franklin 33173-3209

### MEMORANDUM

**To:** Applicant
**From:** Pamela Broyles, Senior Partner
**Re:** *Wells v. Wells*
**Date:** July 29, 2004

We have just finished the evidentiary hearing in a family court proceeding in which our client, Joan Wells, petitioned the court for permission to remove her minor son, Sammy, from the State of Franklin to the State of Columbia. We ordered an expedited hearing transcript, and it is in the file.

Joan's petition is based on the assertion that she intends to relocate to Columbia to accept a new job. Sammy's father, Fred Wells, opposes the petition.

The judge has given us two days to submit concurrent briefs. This is where I need your help.

Please draft our brief in support of Joan's petition following the instructions in the Firm's memorandum on persuasive briefs. You should use all the relevant evidence as appropriate to support the arguments in the brief. Since we will not have the opportunity to present a rebuttal brief, be sure to anticipate and refute Fred's arguments.

---

3. The Multistate Bar Examination ("MBE®") questions, the Multistate Essay Examination ("MEE®") questions, and excerpts from the Multistate Performance Tests ("MPT®") have been reprinted by permission from the NCBE®. Copyright© by the National Conference of Bar Examiners. All rights reserved.

**Broyles and Lemansky**

*Attorneys at Law*

2398 S. 25th Street

Franklin City, Franklin 33173-3209

**MEMORANDUM**                                              September 8, 1999

**To:** All Lawyers

**From:** Litigation Supervisor

**Subject:** Persuasive Briefs

---

All persuasive briefs shall conform to the following guidelines:

All briefs shall include a Statement of Facts. The aim of the Statement of Facts is to persuade the tribunal that the facts support our client's position. The facts must be stated accurately, although emphasis is not improper. Select carefully the facts that are pertinent to the legal arguments. However, in a brief to a trial court, when the evidentiary hearing has just been completed, the Statement of Facts section of the brief may be abbreviated because it can be assumed that the court has the facts in mind.

The firm follows the practice of breaking the argument into its major components and writing carefully crafted subject headings that illustrate the arguments they cover. Avoid writing briefs that contain only a single broad argument heading. The argument heading should succinctly summarize the reasons the tribunal should take the position you are advocating. A heading should be a specific application of a rule of law to the facts of the case and not a bare legal or factual conclusion or a statement of an abstract principle. For example, improper: IT IS NOT IN THE CHILD'S BEST INTERESTS TO BE PLACED IN THE MOTHER'S CUSTODY. Proper: EVIDENCE THAT THE MOTHER HAS BEEN CONVICTED OF CHILD ABUSE IS SUFFICIENT TO ESTABLISH THAT IT IS NOT IN THE CHILD'S BEST INTERESTS TO BE PLACED IN THE MOTHER'S CUSTODY.

The body of each argument should analyze applicable legal authority and persuasively argue how the facts and law support our client's position. Authority supportive of our client's position should be emphasized, but contrary authority also should generally be cited, addressed in the argument, and explained or distinguished. Do not reserve arguments for reply or supplemental briefing.

The lawyer need not prepare a table of contents, a table of cases, a summary of argument, or an index. These will be prepared, when required, after the draft is approved.

## TRANSCRIPT OF HEARING
July 28, 2004

THE COURT:  This matter is here on the petition of Joan Wells for permission to remove the minor child, Sammy, from the state, specifically to Columbia. In 2002, when Joan and Fred Wells were divorced, this court awarded joint custody to the parents and designated Joan Wells primary physical custodian. Because Joan Wells indicated her intention to remove Sammy from Franklin and Fred Wells has opposed that move, this court must now decide if the custody arrangement ordered in 2002 should be modified. Present are Joan Wells, her attorney, Ms. Broyles, and Fred Wells, and his counsel, Mr. Simpson. We are ready to proceed with evidence. Ms. Broyles, call your first witness.

THE PETITIONER, Joan Wells, WAS SWORN AND IDENTIFIED.

PAMELA BROYLES: What are you asking the court to do, Ms. Wells?

JOAN WELLS:  I am asking the court to permit me to take my six-year-old son, Sammy, to Columbia City so that I can take a position as an associate professor of Irish Literature and Studies in the Irish Studies Department at Columbia State University in Columbia City, Columbia, and can better care for Sammy.

Q: Why do you wish to relocate?

A: I have just completed my doctoral degree in Irish literature. Now I can obtain a position in my field at a higher salary. This will better my life and my ability to provide for Sammy.

Q: How will Sammy be cared for if you relocate?

A: Sammy will live with me. I have found a home near campus that is a bit larger than our present home. Sammy will attend elementary school at the McAuliff Elementary School, near campus. It is a wonderful school, being staffed with so many graduates of CSU. It has an after-school program for days when I must teach late. The quality of life for children in Columbia City is great—the parks, recreational programs, youth center, great cultural opportunities in music and the other arts—Sammy will have a great life.

Q: Can you tell us anything else about the educational opportunities for Sammy?

A: CSU offers a tuition discount to children of its professors so Sammy will be able to attend college at half the cost of tuition. That will save me and Fred a lot of money.

Q: What do you propose regarding Sammy's relationship with his father?

A: I want to be sure Sammy stays in touch with his father. I would never come between him and his father. Ever since we separated, I made sure that Sammy has a photo of himself and his father by his bed. Fred can send new photos from time to time. I also have a digital camera and can send Fred photos of Sammy via e-mail. Sammy still likes to be read to. Fred can tape books and Sammy can listen to the tapes before he goes to bed. I will have Sammy send Fred a packet of school papers and art projects every week so Fred can see how Sammy is doing. I know Fred is very interested in Sammy's music and other activities so we can even record events like Sammy's school plays, concerts, and sports activities, and send a videotape to Fred.

Q: Anything else regarding Sammy and his father?

A: Fred can call him whenever he wants, and when Sammy is older, he can e-mail his father as well. Whenever Sammy wants to call Fred, I will let him, of course. If Fred wants to purchase a computer camera for himself and Sammy, I will see

*continued on next page*

that it gets hooked up at home and Sammy and Fred can see and talk with each other every day.

Q: What about visits with his father?

A: While Sammy is so young, he can fly with me to Franklin, for a week at Thanksgiving, a week in December, and a week during spring break. I would like Sammy to see my family then too, but he can spend most of the time with Fred. Of course, I will see that Sammy gets to Fred's for several weeks in the summer, preferably two weeks with Fred in June and another two weeks in July. And if Fred wants to go on vacation with Sammy for a week or two, he can do that. When Sammy is older, he can fly to see Fred. Fred is also welcome to come visit in Columbia.

Q: Tell the court what brought about this relocation.

A: Well, teaching at the university level in Irish studies has always been my dream. When Fred and I had just started dating, I told him that my goal was to get a doctoral degree in Irish literature and teach at the best university possible.

Q: Fred has suggested that you are moving to get away from him and his new wife and that you refuse to talk to Kathleen, his new wife. Can you address that?

A: I never said that I refused to talk to her. What I said was this: Kathleen and I have a past history. When Fred married her, I suggested that it would be best if Fred and I limit our discussions about Sammy to just ourselves.

Q: Are you concerned that Sammy will have trouble adjusting if you move?

A: I am concerned that we make the move as easy on Sammy as possible. That is why I want to be settled before the school year starts. But Sammy is a very resilient child. He has just finished kindergarten, so this is an ideal time for the move—before he gets really settled into school.

BROYLES: I have nothing further for this witness.

THE COURT: Cross-examination, Mr. Simpson?

THOMAS SIMPSON: Thank you, Your Honor.

Q: Right now, Fred is with Sammy almost 40 percent of the time.

A: Yes, it comes to about that.

Q: If Sammy goes with you to Columbia, Fred will have less time with Sammy, isn't that right?

A: That depends on how frequently Fred comes to Columbia.

Q: Isn't it true that Sammy has been very active in the Franklin City Children's Choir here in Franklin City, Franklin?

A: Yes.

Q: Isn't it true that Fred has been an assistant director for the choir and has been able to encourage Sammy to develop his musical talent?

A: Yes. But let's not forget Sammy is only six years old.

Q: Isn't it true that there is no comparable children's choir in Columbia City?

A: So far, I have not found one, but I will encourage Sammy's musical talents.

Q: Fred cares more about Sammy's musical talent than you do, doesn't he?

A: I think it's important to develop all of Sammy's talents.

Q: Isn't it true that Fred has been a loving father who has cared for Sammy and been very involved in his life?

A: Yes. I have never said that Fred is anything but a caring parent.

Q: Fred also goes to teacher's conferences and to doctor's visits, and generally is very involved in all aspects of Sammy's life. Is that right?

A: All true.

*continued on next page*

Q: And isn't it true that Fred has participated in every important decision about Sammy's life?

A: Yes.

Q: Haven't there been times when the two of you have disagreed about Sammy's upbringing?

A: Occasionally.

Q: On those occasions, haven't the two of you been able to resolve your differences?

A: Sure. We've talked about the issues. I respect his opinion. In fact, because he teaches children, I usually go along with him on issues involving Sammy's schooling.

SIMPSON: No further questions, Your Honor.

COURT: Call the next witness.

THE WITNESS, Michael McBryan, WAS SWORN AND IDENTIFIED.

BROYLES: How do you know Joan Wells?

McBRYAN: I am the department chair for English and Irish Literature at Franklin State University and was the committee chair for Joan's doctoral dissertation. Joan was an excellent student and shows much promise in scholarship and teaching Irish literature.

Q: Is it possible that Franklin State University will offer her a position on the faculty?

A: No. We have a policy against hiring our own graduates. Even if we did not, the position she has been offered at CSU is a very prestigious one. We cannot meet the salary. Further, they have a whole department devoted to Irish studies so she will have colleagues who will encourage her in ways that we could not. Plus, she will be eligible for raises that will make her more financially secure.

BROYLES: I have no more questions for this witness Your Honor.

THE COURT: Mr. Simpson, any cross?

SIMPSON: Yes, Your Honor. Thank you.

SIMPSON: Isn't it true that Joan Wells has tenure at the community college?

A: True.

Q: Having tenure—in essence, doesn't that mean she is ensured employment at the community college for the rest of her life?

A: In general, yes, that is what it means.

SIMPSON: That is all I have for this witness, Your Honor.

THE COURT: Ms. Broyles, any other witnesses?

BROYLES: We call the court's attention to the stipulations previously presented to the court. Sammy's physician reports that Sammy, age six, is healthy and developing normally. His teacher indicates that he did well in school during his kindergarten year and is well prepared to move into first grade. He is progressing well in school and seems emotionally and socially well adjusted. Finally, the parties have stipulated that there are four nonstop flights a day between Franklin City, Franklin, and Columbia City, Columbia, and that the airlines offer unaccompanied minor service for children flying without an adult. Petitioner rests.

THE COURT: Very well. Mr. Simpson, call your first witness.

RESPONDENT, Fred Wells, WAS SWORN AND IDENTIFIED.

SIMPSON: Tell the court about your relationship with your son, Sammy.

FRED WELLS: Ever since Joan and I separated, I have made sure that Sammy is number one in my life. I talk to him on the phone several times a week. As the court ordered in the decree, Sammy is with me every weekend and one week in the summer, and on half the major holidays. In addition to what the court ordered, at least once during the week, year round, we have dinner together, and he and I go to movies and children's

*continued on next page*

plays at least once a month. He has not yet shown much interest in sports but if he does, I will be at his games. We play T-ball in the yard when he is with me.

Q: What else do you and Sammy do when he is with you?

A: He and I play card games and board games and play trucks together. Normal father-son stuff. I put him to bed and work with him on his school projects, and help him get dressed in the morning, and prepare meals for him. When Joan and I were married, I was very involved in his day-to-day care. When he is with me on weekends, I read him several stories every night before he goes to bed.

Q: How is Sammy involved in the Franklin City Children's Choir?

A: Sammy is very musically talented. I am a music teacher and I could tell early on that he was talented. So we enrolled him in the Franklin City Children's Choir. The director loves Sammy's voice and has already given him several solos. At his age, they have practices three times a week for six weeks each fall and spring and put on two major concerts a year. In a few years, he will tour with the choir. The choir goes all over the United States and to Europe every other year. If he stays in the choir until he is 18, he will have outstanding experiences and be well prepared for a college audition, if that is what he wants. There is no children's choir like this in Columbia City.

Q: Do you think Sammy has the talent to have a career in music?

A: It is very, very possible. Talent like his is rare and needs to be cultivated if he is to have a chance at a career. Joan will not develop it like I would. Taking him to choir is just too much hassle for her. Plus, I help him with singing practice and can really be his singing mentor.

Q: Where are Sammy's grandparents, cousins, and other family located?

A: My parents live about 80 miles south of Franklin City. Joan's parents are 40 miles away in the other direction. On Joan's side of the family, Sammy has two cousins his age and on my side there are also two cousins his age, all in Franklin City. They are his most frequent playmates. Plus, he has three older cousins and one younger one, all in the area.

Q: What concerns do you have if Joan moves away with Sammy?

A: Sammy had a lot of trouble adjusting after the divorce. He was almost four at the time. He regressed to baby talk for a while and went through a period of not wanting to play with other kids or go to anyone's home. In fact, Joan and I arranged for the daycare counselor to work with him. He has gotten over all that and seems fine now. I am afraid he will regress again if he moves. I am concerned that he will lose me as a father. A child needs a mother and a father. I would never take Sammy from his mother, but it seems she wants to take him from me. As far as I know, Joan knows no one in Columbia City. Sammy knows no one there—no school pals, no cousins, no playmates. He will be lonely. He could be here with me.

Q: You have remarried. How does Sammy relate to Kathleen, your new wife?

A: Sammy gets along with my new wife. I was very careful to introduce Kathleen to Sammy early in our relationship to be sure he could get along with her. The only problem since I remarried has been Joan. Joan used to work with Kathleen at the community college, and they did not get along. Joan will not even talk to her. If Kathleen answers the phone when Joan calls for Sammy at my house, Joan immediately asks for me and will not even say hello to Kathleen. I am afraid that Joan is moving in order to avoid dealing with Kathleen. Or else she is jealous that I have moved on with my life and she has to make a bigger splash by getting a new job and moving to a new city.

*continued on next page*

Q: If Joan did move away with Sammy, how would you be able to spend time with him?

A: There is no way I could see Sammy on a regular basis if he moves to Columbia. I cannot afford to fly out there and the drive is too much for a weekend. It's more than 10 hours one way. Even if I could get there, where would I stay with Sammy? I would have no way to be with him in a home environment. He is too young to fly to Franklin by himself. Joan's proposal means that I will see Sammy about eight weeks a year—eight out of 52! Now, if you add up all the time, he currently spends about 20 weeks a year with me. I am afraid he will forget me. I won't be there for school plays and concerts and his Little League games and whatever else he does. I cannot be a father to him and children need a father.

Q: Fred, how will you be able to make decisions about Sammy's education, health, and the like if Joan moves?

A: I won't be able to. Because I will be hundreds of miles away, I won't go to school conferences, doctor appointments, etc.

Q: Then, how would you have input into these decisions?

A: I would have to rely on Joan to fill me in. I would never feel that I had firsthand information or that I was involved in the decisions.

SIMPSON: Thank you, Mr. Wells. Your Honor, I have no more questions for this witness.

THE COURT: Ms. Broyles, do you wish to cross-examine?

BROYLES: Yes. Thank you, Your Honor.

BROYLES: Isn't it true that Joan has been a good mother?

A: Yes.

Q: Isn't it true that the choir was your idea, not Sammy's?

A: I believe it was a joint decision—mine, Joan's and Sammy's.

Q: Isn't it true that Joan has never gotten in the way of your time with Sammy?

A: True.

Q: In fact, she has voluntarily agreed that you can spend significantly more time with Sammy than even what the court ordered in the divorce decree, isn't that right?

A: Yes. I guess so.

Q: You can always telephone or e-mail doctors and teachers to get information about Sammy, can't you?

A: Yes.

Q: Except for this proposed move, you and Joan have resolved disagreements about Sammy's welfare, haven't you?

A: Yes.

BROYLES: That is all I have for this witness, Your Honor.

THE COURT: Mr. Simpson, call the next witness.

THE WITNESS, Maria Niro, WAS SWORN AND IDENTIFIED.

SIMPSON: How do you know Sammy Wells?

A: I am a counselor at the day care center Sammy attended. At the time of the divorce, his parents asked me to help Sammy through the adjustment period. I am trained to work with children going through losses, like death or divorce. I do play therapy to help them express their feelings. So I worked with Sammy for about eight weeks.

Q: Was Sammy having adjustment problems?

A: Yes, the normal ones. Like any child whose parents are divorcing, Sammy directly and indirectly expressed fears about where his bed and his clothes and toys would be, who would feed him and put him to bed and take him to day care.

*continued on next page*

SIMPSON: Thank you, Ms. Niro. I have no more questions, Your Honor.

THE COURT: Ms. Broyles?

Q: You are not a licensed social worker or counselor, are you?

A: No, no, but I have been trained to work with kids experiencing divorce and death. Had I thought Sammy needed professional counseling, I would have told the Wells family to take him to a professional. But all he needed was some help through some difficult months.

Q: So, Sammy didn't exhibit an unusual level of stress as a result of his parents' divorce?

A: No. It was a relatively mild case, as these matters go.

Q: And while you were working with him, Sammy got over these fears?

A: Yes. Like most children, he adapted to the new routine.

Q: So, he has adjusted well to living separately with his mother and father?

A: Yes.

Q: And you haven't worked with Sammy in the last year?

A: That's right.

BROYLES: No further questions, Your Honor.

SIMPSON: The respondent rests, Your Honor.

THE COURT: All right. We have concluded the evidence. It's clear that, constitutionally, the court does not have the authority to prohibit Ms. Wells from moving. The sole issue, therefore, before the court is whether Joan can take Sammy with her. I want to make a decision very soon. I want both counsel to submit a post-trial brief within 48 hours. There will be no rebuttal briefs, so address all the issues in this post-trial brief. We are adjourned.

## LIBRARY

### Franklin Dissolution Of Marriage Act

**Section 30. Definitions.**

For purposes of this article, the following words shall have the following meanings:

(1) JOINT CUSTODY. Joint legal custody and joint physical custody.

(2) JOINT LEGAL CUSTODY. Both parents have equal rights and responsibilities for major decisions concerning the child, including the child's education, health care, and religious training. The court may designate one parent to have sole power to make certain decisions while both parents retain equal rights and responsibilities for other decisions.

(3) JOINT PHYSICAL CUSTODY. Physical custody is shared by the parents in a way that assures the child frequent and substantial contact with each parent. Joint physical custody does not necessarily mean physical custody of equal durations of time. The court may designate one parent as the primary physical custodian.

(4) SOLE LEGAL CUSTODY. One parent has sole right and responsibility to make major decisions concerning the child, including the child's education, health care, and religious training.

(5) SOLE PHYSICAL CUSTODY. One parent has sole physical custody and the other parent has rights of visitation except as otherwise provided by the court.

**Section 109. Removal of child.**

The court may grant leave, before or after judgment, to any party having sole legal custody or sole or primary physical custody of any minor child or children to remove such child or children from Franklin whenever such approval is in the best interests of such child or children.

**Section 402. Best interests of child.**

The court shall determine custody in accordance with the best interests of the child. The court shall consider all relevant factors including:

(1) the mental and physical health of all individuals involved;

(2) the child's adjustment to the child's home, school, and community;

(3) the interaction and interrelationship of the child with the child's parent or parents, the child's siblings, and any other person who may significantly affect the child's best interests;

(4) the wishes of the child's parent or parents as to the child's custody.

## *Marshall v. Marshall*
### Franklin Supreme Court (2001)

Sue Ellen Marshall petitioned the court for leave to remove the parties' son, Michael, from the state of Franklin to the state of Columbia. As a result of their divorce in 1998, Sue Ellen and Forest were awarded joint custody of Michael, then three years old. The court designated Sue Ellen the primary physical custodian.

The record in this case reveals on Sue Ellen's side that Sue Ellen has been offered a job in her field of nursing administration in Phillips, Columbia, at a salary significantly higher than she is currently earning and with greater career potential; and Michael has an asthma condition that will be controlled more effectively in Columbia, although it is being adequately controlled in Franklin City.

The evidence on Forest's side shows that he has been a loving and involved parent; since the divorce, he has taken full advantage of all the time he has physical custody to be with Michael; he telephones Michael twice a week, although Sue Ellen requires advance notice of the calls and limits them to five minutes each; Forest coaches Michael to develop his swimming skills and, although Sue Ellen has lodged objections with Michael's school, Forest has chaperoned school-related field trips; both sets of grandparents, whom Michael visits frequently and who are an important part of Michael's life, live within 20 miles of Franklin City; Sue Ellen has steadfastly refused to allow Forest any flexibility in the physical custody arrangements or the telephone communications. Forest has been actively involved in decisions about Michael's medical care, education, and religious upbringing through direct contact with the pediatrician, teachers, coaches, and ministers.

The only evidence presented by Sue Ellen concerning her plans for visits between Forest and Michael after the move was that Michael would spend three weeks in the summer and one week during winter break with Forest, with flights to be at Forest's expense. She also agreed to permit the twice-weekly telephone calls of five minutes' duration, also at Forest's expense.

The trial court denied the petition because it was not in Michael's best interests to be separated from his father. The appellate court reversed, holding that the trial court had failed to properly apply the judicially created presumption that a parent with sole legal custody or sole or primary physical custody may move the child from Franklin. The appellate court noted that Sue Ellen had provided a valid reason for the move. The appellate court did not address Sue Ellen's motivation or the effects of the move on Michael.

On this appeal, Forest asserts that the appellate court's interpretation of Section 109 of the Franklin Dissolution of Marriage Act failed to account for the objecting parent's relationship with the child by not requiring findings concerning the effect of Michael's separation from his father in determining the best interests of the child.

In interpreting Section 109 in the context of joint custodial situations, the court must balance the benefits derived from the parent's move, the need for finality in custody decrees, the rights of both custodial parents to make decisions for the child, the interest of the child in having a loving relationship with both parents, and the rights of both parents.

We interpret Section 109 to require the parent with primary physical custody who wishes to move with the child from this state to present a legitimate reason for the move. Once a legitimate reason has been established, a presumption is created in favor

*continued on next page*

of the parent petitioning to move. The other parent can rebut the presumption by showing that the move is not in good faith or it is not in the best interests of the child. The parent seeking to rebut the presumption has the burden of persuading the court that the move is in bad faith or is not in the best interests of the child. This standard, although fact-based, recognizes the realities of a mobile society, while also seeking to prevent the primary custodial parent from undermining a child's relationship with the other parent.

Improved employment, educational opportunities, or health of the custodial parent, the new spouse, or the child are examples of legitimate reasons for a move. A move designed primarily to interfere with the relationship between the other parent and the child does not constitute a legitimate reason. Sue Ellen has established a legitimate reason for the move—better employment for herself and improved health for Michael. There is a question, however, as to whether Forest carried his burden of persuading the court that the move is not in the best interests of Michael. Unquestionably, the move will affect the time Forest spends with Michael. The amount of time alone is not sufficient to harm the parent-child relationship, where there is a strong relationship and where the parents take other steps to encourage the relationship.

More troubling was the evidence that in the past Sue Ellen may have sought to interfere with Forest's relationship with Michael through limiting telephone calls and other measures. Based on the record, this court cannot determine whether Forest demonstrated that the move is not in the best interests of Michael. Because we cannot determine whether the trial court understood the proper test or whether the court properly considered the factors concerning best interests, we must remand to the trial court to determine whether Forest has rebutted the presumption and carried his burden of persuasion.

### *Feldman v. Feldman*
Franklin Court of Appeal (2002)

Howard and Ruth Feldman were granted joint custody of their daughters at the time of their divorce in 1998. Ruth, who is the primary physical custodian, now petitions for removal of the daughters from Franklin to Columbia.

The daughters lived with Howard between August of 2000 and December of 2001, while Ruth completed a master's degree in speech therapy, and thereafter, lived primarily with Ruth.

Ruth's new husband has recently been promoted and transferred by his company to Columbia. The daughters, who are now 13 and 15, are in good health, do well in school, and are active in tennis. Ruth has testified that the school district in Columbia has an active tennis team as well as a solid academic program.

Howard opposes the move because of its effect on his relationship with the girls. At a minimum, Howard sees the girls every weekend and has dinner with them once during the week. He regularly attends parent-teacher conferences and the girls' sports competitions, even when their mother does not. Because of the distance, if the girls move, the girls will not see their father on a regular basis. Further, Howard cannot afford to fly to Columbia to participate in their activities.

Howard concedes that, until now, he and Ruth have been able to jointly reach decisions about the girls and resolve disagreements about their care. However, he believes that Ruth is moving so far away so that the girls will develop a closer relationship with their new father that will drive a wedge between him and the girls.

Ruth proposes that the girls can fly, at her cost, to Franklin for one three-day weekend each month, September through February. She will bring the girls to Franklin for Thanksgiving, the winter break, and an extended summer break so they can spend time with their father, his family, and Ruth's family who remain in Franklin. Further, the girls have cell phones so that they can call their father regularly. She also suggests that Howard and the girls can e-mail every day to maintain contact. Finally, Ruth will arrange with the schools to send duplicate report cards to Howard.

In *Marshall v. Marshall*, our Supreme Court created a presumption that the primary custodial parent may remove the children from the state provided the parent seeking to relocate shows a legitimate reason for the move. Ruth has shown a legitimate reason for the move—improved employment of a parent or the spouse. Howard attempts to establish bad faith by presenting evidence that the move is designed to ruin his relationship with his daughters.

Howard relies on the case of *Davis v. Davis*, in which this court prohibited Mr. Davis from removing the children because he himself conceded that his reason for removing the children was to stop the mother's "bad influence." The court determined, however, that the mother was a loving parent whose influence was one of a concerned parent. Additionally, Ms. Davis presented evidence that Mr. Davis had a long history of trying to alienate the children from their mother. No such evidence was presented here, where Ruth has supported a close relationship between the girls and their father. Howard failed in his effort to show bad faith.

Howard's second contention is that the move is not in the best interests of the children. In determining "best interests," the court is guided by the factors listed in Section 402 of the Franklin Dissolution of Marriage Act. Section 402 directs the court to consider the

*continued on next page*

71

child's health, adjustment to home, school, and community, and the interaction of the child with parents and siblings.

Howard cites the case of *Lewis v. Lewis*, in which this court denied a petition for removal because of the negative effect the move would have on the health and adjustment of the child. The child was developmentally disabled and deaf. Expert testimony established that she needed very specialized care that was available in Franklin but not in Columbia, and that any change in routine, especially a relocation, would set back her progress by a year or more.

Unlike the *Lewis* case, the Feldman girls are healthy, well adjusted in their present home, and capable of adjusting to a new environment. They have visited the school they will attend if the move is permitted. Whether they remain in Franklin or move to Columbia, they will have promising careers, educationally and socially.

The children have a strong and healthy relationship with each parent. Both parents have been closely involved in the upbringing of the girls. Certainly, if the move is permitted, it will affect the time the girls spend with their father. The issue, however, is whether the move is in their best interests. It is, of course, in their best interests to have a good relationship with their father, as well as with their mother. While their relationship with Howard will be changed, we do not believe it will be destroyed. Ruth's plans for continuing contact provide Howard meaningful involvement in the children's lives.

Ruth has proposed reasonable means by which the girls can communicate with Howard on a regular, indeed daily, basis. Further, they will see Howard face to face at least once every month, during all but spring tennis season.

The trial court's order permitting the removal is affirmed.

# VI. POINT SHEET

## *I. Wells v. Wells*
### Drafters' Point Sheet[4]

In this performance test item, applicants are asked by the senior partner who represents Joan Wells to prepare a brief in support of Joan Wells' petition to remove her child from the state in order to take new employment in a neighboring state. Under the Franklin Dissolution of Marriage Act Section 109, Joan is required to submit the petition to the court because she has joint custody of the child with Fred Wells.

When Joan and Fred Wells were divorced in 2002, they were granted joint custody of their son, Sammy. Joint custody is defined as joint legal custody and joint physical custody. In Franklin, joint physical custody does not mean equal durations of time with each parent. Now Joan has the opportunity for a new position in her field, requiring her to relocate from Franklin to Columbia.

Joan wishes to move in order to accept a position as associate professor of Irish Literature and Studies at Columbia State University in Columbia City, Columbia. She wishes to take the couple's son, Sammy, with her. In anticipation of the move, Joan has arranged for Sammy's care and upbringing and for various means of maintaining a relationship with his father, Fred. Fred opposes the petition to remove the child from the state on several grounds. He argues that Sammy's development in general and especially in music will be adversely affected. Fred also claims that it will be hard for him to carry out his responsibilities as a legal custodian if Sammy is separated from him. He believes that the move is motivated by a desire to separate him from his son or by Joan's jealousy toward his new wife.

Both parties presented testimony to the court during a hearing and the senior partner ordered an expedited transcript of the testimony. At the conclusion of the testimony, the court ordered the parties to file concurrent briefs, with no rebuttal. The task for applicants is to prepare the persuasive brief that Joan will file.

The File contains the instructing memorandum from the senior partner, an office memorandum regarding persuasive briefs, and the transcript of the hearing, which includes the stipulations entered by the parties. The Library contains excerpts from the Franklin Dissolution of Marriage Act, a Franklin Supreme Court opinion, and a Franklin Court of Appeals opinion. The File does not contain evidence concerning the effect of separation of a six-year-old from his father. Nor does the Library contain any law that makes the child's wishes a factor to be considered. Applicants who discuss those issues are acting outside the materials given.

The following discussion covers all of the points the drafters intended to raise in the problem. Applicants need not cover them all to receive passing or even excellent grades. Grading is entirely within the discretion of the graders in the user jurisdictions.

---

4. The Multistate Bar Examination ("MBE®") questions, the Multistate Essay Examination ("MEE®") questions, and excerpts from the Multistate Performance Tests ("MPT®") have been reprinted by permission from the NCBE®. Copyright© by the National Conference of Bar Examiners. All rights reserved.

**I. Overview:** The office memorandum regarding persuasive briefs gives applicants the template for writing their answers in the form of a brief. Thus, it is expected that the work product will resemble a brief such as a lawyer would file with a court. Graders will have to decide how to weight the subjective components of "persuasiveness."

- There should be a statement of facts that explains the nature and essential features of the case, although, as the office memo explains, it should be abbreviated.
- The argument section should be broken down into carefully crafted headings that summarize the ensuing arguments. The arguments themselves should weave the law and the facts together into persuasive (as opposed to objective) statements of the case for the client.

Applicants are told that both sides are to file the briefs within 48 hours and that there will be no rebuttal briefs; therefore, applicants should anticipate the arguments of the opposite side and address them here.

**II. Statement of Facts:** This should include a brief recitation of the operative facts. Inasmuch as the trial judge already knows the facts, applicants should include only the key facts in the Statement of Facts and expand on them when they incorporate them into the legal argument part of the brief, but the Statement of Facts should at least describe the essence of the dispute.

- Essentially, applicants should explain that:
  - Joan and Fred Wells were divorced in 2002, and they were awarded joint custody of Sammy, now 6. Joan has primary physical custody of Sammy.
  - Joan Wells has completed her doctoral studies and has been offered a position as an associate professor in Irish Literature and Studies, her chosen field, at Columbia State University in Columbia City, Columbia.
  - She wishes to move to Columbia and take Sammy to live with her in Columbia.
  - Fred Wells, Sammy's father, opposes the move.

**III. Argument:** The argument section should reflect the steps in the legal analysis. Applicants should argue that the Franklin Supreme Court has interpreted Section 109 of the Franklin Dissolution of Marriage Act to require that the parent who has sole or primary physical custody and who seeks to remove the child from the state establish a legitimate reason for the move. *Marshall v. Marshall.* Once that parent has done so, there is a presumption that the parent may remove the child. The presumption may be rebutted by evidence from the objecting parent that the move is not being made in good faith or that it is not in the best interests of the child. *Marshall v. Marshall.*

The following headings are suggestions only and should not be taken by the graders to be the only acceptable ones.

- <u>Moving to Take a Position as Associate Professor, Which Will Improve Her Employment Opportunities and Her Financial Security Constitutes a Legitimate Reason for the Move and Entitles Joan Wells to a Presumption That the Petition Should Be Granted.</u>

The first issue is whether Joan Wells has met her burden of offering a legitimate reason for the move. Franklin Dissolution of Marriage Act Section 109; *Marshall v. Marshall.* Legitimate reasons include improvements in the education, employment, or health of the parent or child. *Marshall v. Marshall.* Joan Wells has presented evidence of a legitimate reason for the move:

- The predicate for Joan's entitlement to the judicially created presumption is that she is a parent with "primary physical custody." She meets that requirement. *See* the court's introductory statement in the transcript.
- She has been offered a position as an associate professor in Irish Literature and Studies at Columbia State University, Columbia City, Columbia.
- The position is in her field of study and offers a better career path for her than her present position at the community college, and at Columbia State University, she will have colleagues to encourage her work.
- She is not likely to be hired by Franklin State University, which has a policy against hiring its own graduates.
- The new position offers a higher salary, the promise of raises, and the potential for reduced tuition for Sammy, the child.

Thus, Joan has met her burden. She is entitled to a presumption in favor of granting her petition. *Marshall v. Marshall.*

Because the court instructed the parties that there will be no rebuttal briefs, applicants must anticipate the arguments that Fred Wells is likely to make and must address them as well.

- <u>Sammy's Ability to Maintain a Father-Son Relationship with Fred Wells and Sammy's Health and Normal Development Rebut Any Speculation About Sammy's Possible Regression, the Lack of Opportunity to Join a Children's Choir, or the Possible Harm to the Father-Son Relationship.</u>

A parent who objects to the petition to remove a child from the state may try to show that it is not in the best interests of the child. *Marshall v. Marshall.* To determine the best interests of the child, the court must consider the factors specified in Section 402 of the Franklin Dissolution of Marriage Act. *Feldman v. Feldman.* These factors include:

- The mental and physical health of all involved;
- The child's adjustment to the child's home, school, and community;
- The interaction and interrelationship of the child with the child's parents, siblings, and any other person who significantly affects the child's best interests; and
- The wishes of the child's parents as to custody.

The applicants should distinguish the *Lewis* case in which the court denied the petition to move where the *Lewis* child was deaf and developmentally disabled and in need of a routine. There, expert testimony supported the belief that the move would cause the *Lewis* child to regress by at least a year. Unlike the *Lewis* child, Sammy is developing normally and has demonstrated his ability to adjust to past changes. There is no expert testimony in this case predicting his likely regression, simply some speculation by a day care center counselor who also allowed that he is as likely to adjust well.

Fred may claim that the move is not in the best interests of Sammy. To prove that the move is not in the best interests of Sammy, Fred may assert:

* At the time of the divorce, Sammy regressed and needed assistance in dealing with the divorce;
* Sammy has no friends or family in Columbia;
* Sammy will not have the unique opportunities for developing his talent that he has with the Franklin City Children's Choir because Columbia does not have a comparable children's choir;
* Joan will not develop the talent as would Fred, who is a music teacher;
* Sammy will see his father only eight weeks a year instead of weekly as at present;
* Unlike the children in *Feldman*, Sammy is young;
* Fred will not be able to participate in Sammy's activities.

Applicants should argue, however, that Joan has effectively rebutted this evidence by showing:

* Sammy did adjust after the divorce with some limited assistance, and the counselor who worked with him at that time, a witness called by Fred, cannot predict that he will regress. The counselor had not worked with Sammy for over a year;
* Sammy is resilient as evidenced by his past ability to adapt, and the move is being made in advance of the start of the school year in order to give him a chance to adjust;
* Sammy is developing normally and is well adjusted and ready to advance in school;
* It is too early to realistically assess Sammy's musical talents but Joan will encourage the development of those talents along with others;
* As described above, Joan has a history of supporting Sammy's relationship with Fred.

Applicants should argue that the evidence taken as a whole fails to show that the move is not in the best interests of the child. In fact, the evidence shows that this move is much like that in the *Feldman* case where the court approved the petition to remove the children.

* <u>Fred Will Be Able to Carry Out His Responsibilities after the Move as a Joint Parent Through Telephone and E-mail Contact with Schools, Doctors, and Others.</u>

Fred may argue that he will be unable to carry out his responsibilities as a parent with joint legal custody (i.e., his decision-making responsibilities and his ability to maintain a loving relationship), if the move is permitted. He may suggest that the move is a ruse to set aside the court's original custody order because it will completely deprive him of joint *physical* custody. A parent, such as Fred, with joint legal custody has equal rights and responsibilities for major decisions concerning the child, including but not limited to the education of the child, health care, and religious training. *See* Section 30 of the Franklin Dissolution of Marriage Act. Fred may claim that he cannot effectively participate in decisions about Sammy because:

* He cannot effectively obtain firsthand information about Sammy and will have to rely on Joan for information about Sammy;

- He will not be able to be present for teacher-parent conferences or for doctor visits.

However, Joan has countered this evidence by testimony that:

- Fred can obtain this information through telephone or e-mail contact with the teachers and doctors;
- Joan will arrange for Sammy to regularly send packets of his schoolwork to Fred.
- Joan and Fred have a history of discussing issues that arise concerning Sammy and have been able to work out their differences in the past.

Based on this evidence, applicants should persuade the court that Fred will be able to continue to be a joint legal custodian for Sammy, even though his physical custody will be diminished.

- Evidence That Teaching Irish Literature Is a Lifelong Dream and That Joan Will Support the Father-Son Relationship Through Telephone, E-mail, and Computer Conferencing as Well as In-Person Visits Rebuts Any Suggestion of Bad Faith.

A parent objecting to the removal of the child from the state may rebut the presumption by showing that the move is in bad faith. A move is in bad faith if it is designed to interfere with the parent-child relationship. *Marshall v. Marshall; Davis v. Davis.* Applicants should distinguish *Davis*, in which the father admitted that the reason for the move was to eliminate the "bad influence" of the mother. The court determined that the mother was a loving parent and denied the father's petition.

The facts in this case are much closer to those in *Feldman* where the court permitted the move. In *Feldman*, the mother had encouraged the close relationship between the children and their father and had proposed reasonable means of sustaining it, such as regular in-person visits, regular telephone contact, and daily e-mail communications.

Fred Wells may claim that the move interferes with the parent-child relationship:

- Fred's time with Sammy will be reduced from regular weekly contacts, totaling about 20 weeks a year, to eight weeks per year;
- Sammy will not see relatives on a regular basis;
- Fred will no longer engage in activities on a weekly basis with Sammy.

But time is not the only factor courts use in assessing bad faith. The courts have permitted moves where they affect the time a parent has with the child but where the relationship can be sustained through other means. *Feldman v. Feldman.* Courts are more suspicious of the moving parent's motive where there has been a history of interference with the relationship between the objecting parent and the child. *Marshall v. Marshall; Davis v. Davis.* Unlike the situations in those cases, Joan has been supportive of the father-son relationship and has proposed means of supporting the relationship despite the distance between Fred and Sammy. Applicants should detail what Joan has done and has offered to do in support of the father-son relationship:

- Joan has kept a photo of Sammy and his father in Sammy's room ever since the separation and has not interfered in the time Sammy spends with his father.

- If the move is permitted, Joan has offered that Fred may make tapes of books for Sammy to listen to, Fred may call Sammy whenever he wants, Fred and Sammy can communicate daily by computer conferencing and later, when Sammy is older, by e-mail.
- Joan will have Sammy send his father packets of his schoolwork every week.
- She will also record Sammy's activities and send them to his father.
- She will take Sammy to visit his father in person eight weeks a year and when Sammy is older, he can fly on his own for these visits.

Fred may also claim that the move is in bad faith because it is motivated by Joan's jealousy over Fred's remarriage to someone she dislikes:

- Joan will not talk with Fred's new wife, Kathleen.
- Joan is jealous of Kathleen or of Fred's remarriage or both.

Joan will rebut this evidence by showing that her desire to move to take the position in Irish Studies is part of a lifelong dream expressed long before Fred remarried.

Applicants should argue to the court that the sort of evidence Fred introduced is insufficient to show bad faith and is rebutted by Joan's history of pursuing her career goal.

**IV. Conclusion:** Applicants should persuade the court that Joan has met her burden by offering a legitimate reason for the move and that therefore she is entitled to a presumption in favor of the petition. While Fred has attempted to rebut that presumption by offering evidence of bad faith and evidence that the move is not in the best interests of Sammy, Joan has effectively rebutted such evidence. In light of the case law in Franklin, Joan is entitled to remove Sammy.

## VII. SCORE SHEET

| Stated | Implied | |
|---|---|---|
| _____ | _____ | **FORMAT:** Should resemble a brief that would be filed with a court. A persuasive document that includes a Statement of Facts, an Argument Section with Point Headings, and a Conclusion. |
| | | **STATEMENT OF FACTS** |
| _____ | _____ | Joan and Fred Wells were divorced in 2002, and they were awarded joint custody of Sammy, now 6. |
| _____ | _____ | Joan has primary physical custody. |
| _____ | _____ | Joan Wells has completed her doctoral studies and has been offered a position as an associate professor in Irish Literature and Studies, her chosen field, at Columbia State University in Columbia City, Columbia. |
| _____ | _____ | She wishes to move to Columbia and take Sammy to live with her. |
| _____ | _____ | Fred Wells, Sammy's father, opposed the move. |
| | | **ARGUMENT** |
| _____ | _____ | Heading I: *Moving to Take a Position as an Associate Professor, Which Will Improve Her Employment Opportunities and Her Financial Security, Constitutes a Legitimate Reason for the Move and Entitles Joan Wells to a Presumption That the Petition Should Be Granted.* |
| _____ | _____ | **Rule:** Section 109 provides that parent with primary physical custody may remove the child from Franklin whenever such approval is in the best interests of the child. |
| _____ | _____ | Legitimate reasons include improvements in the education, employment, or health of the parent or child. *Marshall.* |
| _____ | _____ | Predicate is met—she has primary physical custody. |
| _____ | _____ | Offered a position as an associate professor in Irish Literature and Studies at Columbia State University in Columbia City, Columbia. |
| _____ | _____ | Position is in her field of study and offers a better career path for her than her present position at a community college, including colleagues who will encourage her work. |
| _____ | _____ | Not likely to be hired by Franklin State University due to policy against hiring own graduates. |
| _____ | _____ | The new position offers a higher salary, the promise of raises, and the potential for reduced tuition for Sammy. |
| _____ | _____ | **Conclusion:** Joan has met her burden with a legitimate reason and is entitled to a presumption to grant her petition. |
| _____ | _____ | Heading II: *Sammy's Ability to Maintain a Father-Son Relationship with Fred Wells and Sammy's Health and Normal Development Rebut Any Speculation About Sammy's Possible Regression, the Lack of Opportunity to Join a Children's Choir, or the Possible Harm to the Father-Son Relationship.* |
| _____ | _____ | **Rule:** Parent who objects to the petition to remove a child from the state may try to show that it is not in the best interests of the child. *Marshall.* |

*continued on next page*

| Stated | Implied | |
|--------|---------|---|
| _____ | _____ | Section 402 outlines factors: mental and physical health of all involved; the child's adjustment to the child's home, school, and community; the interaction and interrelationship of the child with the child's parents, siblings, and any other person who significantly affects the child's best interests, wishes of the child's parents as to custody. |
| _____ | _____ | **Application:** Fred may assert: At the time of the divorce, Sammy regressed and needed assistance in dealing with the divorce. |
| _____ | _____ | Sammy has no friends or family in Columbia. |
| _____ | _____ | Sammy will not have the unique opportunities for developing his talent that he has with the Franklin City Children's Choir because Columbia does not have a comparable children's choir. |
| _____ | _____ | Joan will not develop the talent as would Fred, who is a music teacher. |
| _____ | _____ | Sammy will see his father only eight weeks a year instead of weekly as at present. |
| _____ | _____ | Unlike the children in *Feldman*, Sammy is young. |
| _____ | _____ | Fred will not be able to participate in Sammy's activities. |
| _____ | _____ | Unlike the deaf child in *Lewis*, Sammy is developing normally and has demonstrated his ability to adjust to past changes. No expert testimony, just a day care worker who predicted his regression. |
| _____ | _____ | Joan will effectively rebut: Sammy did adjust after the divorce. Counselor has not worked with him in a year. |
| _____ | _____ | Sammy is resilient as evidenced by past ability to adapt and move being made well in advance of start of school year to give him time to adjust. |
| _____ | _____ | Sammy is developing normally and is well-adjusted. |
| _____ | _____ | Too early to realistically assess Sammy's musical talent, but Joan will encourage the development of those talents. |
| _____ | _____ | Joan has a history of supporting Sammy's relationship with Fred. |
| _____ | _____ | **Conclusion:** Evidence taken as a whole fails to show that the move is not in Sammy's best interests. |
| _____ | _____ | Like the *Feldman* case, where permission to relocate was granted. |
| _____ | _____ | **Heading III:** *Fred Will Be Able to Carry Out His Responsibilities after the Move as a Joint Parent Through Telephone and E-mail Contact with Schools, Doctors, and Others.* |
| _____ | _____ | Fred may argue that he is unable to carry out his responsibilities as a parent with joint legal custody including making decisions and maintaining a loving relationship. |
| _____ | _____ | **Rule:** Section 30 of statute provides equal rights and responsibilities for major decisions including the education of the child, health care, and religious training. |
| _____ | _____ | **Application:** Fred cannot effectively obtain firsthand information about Sammy and will have to rely on Joan for information. |
| _____ | _____ | Will not be present for teacher-parent conferences or doctor visits. |
| _____ | _____ | Joan will counter that he can obtain information through telephone and email contact with teachers/doctors |

*continued on next page*

| Stated | Implied | |
|---|---|---|
| _____ | _____ | Joan will arrange for Sammy to regularly send packets of schoolwork to Fred. |
| _____ | _____ | Joan and Fred have a history of discussing issues that arise concerning Sammy and have been able to work out their differences in the past. |
| _____ | _____ | **Conclusion:** Fred will be able to continue to be a joint legal custodian for Sammy. |
| _____ | _____ | Heading IV: *Evidence That Teaching Irish Literature Is a Lifelong Dream and That Joan Will Support the Father-Son Relationship Through Telephone, E-mail, and Computer Conferencing as Well as In-Person Visits Rebuts Any Suggestions of Bad Faith.* |
| _____ | _____ | **Rule:** A parent objecting to the removal of the child from the state may rebut the presumption by showing that the move is in bad faith. |
| _____ | _____ | A move is in bad faith if it is designed to interfere with the parent-child relationship. *Marshall; Davis.* |
| _____ | _____ | Time with child not only factor. Courts more suspicious of motive of moving parent where there has been interference already. *Marshall; Davis.* |
| _____ | _____ | **Application:** Unlike *Davis* where the move was to eliminate the mother's "bad influence and court determined mother was a loving parent"; there is no bad faith here. |
| _____ | _____ | More like *Feldman* where move allowed and relationship with parent staying was encouraged |
| _____ | _____ | Fred's time with Sammy will be reduced from regular weekly contacts, totaling about 20 weeks a year, to eight weeks per year. |
| _____ | _____ | Sammy will not see relatives on a regular basis. |
| _____ | _____ | Fred will no longer engage in activities on a weekly basis with Sammy. |
| _____ | _____ | Joan has been supportive of relationship and has proposed means of supporting the relationship long distance. |
| _____ | _____ | Photo of Sammy and his dad in Sammy's room since the separation and has never interfered in the time Sammy spends with his father. |
| _____ | _____ | Fred may make tapes of books for Sammy to listen to; Fred may call whenever he wishes; Fred and Sammy can communicate daily by computer conferencing and by email when Sammy is older. |
| _____ | _____ | Packets of schoolwork and recording of activities will be sent. |
| _____ | _____ | Joan will take Sammy to visit his father in person eight weeks a year. When Sammy is old enough, he can fly alone. |
| _____ | _____ | Joan's desire to move is based on her lifelong dream and not because she doesn't care for Fred's new wife. |
| _____ | _____ | **Conclusion:** Fred's evidence is insufficient to show move is in bad faith. |
| _____ | _____ | **Overall Conclusion:** Joan has met her burden by offering a legitimate reason for the move and therefore she is entitled to a presumption in favor of the petition. |

# CHAPTER 6

# Building Multistate Bar Examination Skills

While watching Sesame Street or in preschool, you actually took your first multiple choice assessment when you were asked, "Which of these things is different from the others?" You circled or pointed to the one out of four pictures on the page or screen that was different. A question was asked and you picked the one correct response out of several potential answers. Your elementary teachers, secondary teachers, and some undergraduate professors then continued to use multiple choice assessments throughout your education. Most of the Law School Admissions Test is set up in a multiple choice format.

The Multistate Bar Examination (MBE) is much more difficult than any other multiple choice assessment you have had for a number of reasons. First, the subject matter is more complex and more voluminous, spanning seven topics. Some law schools take two semesters just to cover one of the seven topics. In order to answer correctly, you must have detailed knowledge of each topic. A superficial understanding of the law will not suffice. You must be able to identify the issue, pull the detailed rule from your memory, and apply it correctly to the facts. Even then, more than one response can appear correct. The differences between answer responses can be subtle.

An applicant will often fall back on old test-taking strategies that worked in the past, but they will not work well on the MBE. An applicant may believe that the best way to prepare is by doing as many practice questions as possible, relying on remembering all of the answers. Unfortunately, this strategy frequently fails on the MBE. There are just too many topics. Doing hundreds of questions without autopsying the answers is a huge waste of time. Remember, in order to recall information, it must be encoded into your memory. A better preparation technique is similar to your preparation for the essay questions—focus on memorizing rules.

## I. PREPARATION

The NCBE sets the number of questions for each topic. There is no deviation from these numbers. While taking the exam, there is absolutely no need to keep track of each topic. The count breaks out as:

- Civil Procedure—25 questions
- Constitutional Law—25 questions
- Contracts and Sales—25 questions

- Criminal Law and Procedure—25 questions
- Evidence—25 questions
- Real Property—25 questions
- Torts—25 questions

Twenty-five additional questions are "test" questions. These are questions that the National Conference of Bar Examiners (NCBE) is testing for use in future examinations. They do not count in your score. Do not be concerned with identifying test questions as you take the exam. Just answer all the questions.

Your preparation to do well on MBE questions is virtually identical to your preparation for essay questions. Just like essay questions, you must have the rules memorized for all Big Seven topics. Thus, you need a library of the materials to memorize in the format that you best memorize from. Fortunately, you may use the same library for the MBE questions that you are preparing for the essay questions. No need exists for separate libraries. Why? Your memorization of the rules works for both question styles. You should do practice questions in both formats, but the memorization is the same.

Just like your practice essay questions in Phase One, take as much time as you need on the MBE questions in Phase One. Look up the rule and delve into the particular subtopic. Really try to understand it.

During Phase Two, move to doing your practice MBE questions within time limits and closed-book. Now that does not mean practice 100 questions in a three-hour block of time every day. Indeed, you should only practice in that manner—half-day practice exams—two or three times throughout your preparation.

Instead, do 17 questions in a 30-minute block of time. Why? On the bar exam, you will do 100 questions in 180 minutes—the equivalent of 1.8 minutes per question. Keeping track of the time per multiple choice question is unworkable and unrealistic. Instead, keep track in half hour or hour time periods: 17 questions in one half hour and 34 questions in one hour. For your practice, keep to 17 questions in 30 minutes.

At the end of the 30 minutes, autopsy your answers. Just like essay questions, this is critical. Practice MBE questions provide a detailed critique of the question. Read all of it. Add any misunderstood rules and lucky guesses to your library or highlight them if they are already there. One month before the exam, push your question practice to 34 questions in an hour and then 50 questions in 90 minutes. Always take the time to put the misunderstood rules and the lucky guesses in your library.

**EXAM TIP**

If you are someone that needs all the time allotted and more, use a regular #2 pencil rather than a mechanical pencil. The lead is thicker and you can fill in the circle in less time.

Initially, you will study a topic and then do practice questions in just that topic area. Once you have covered all seven topics, do a mixed-topic set of questions at least once a week.

Your commercial bar preparation provider will probably have applications for practice questions that are used on your computer and other electronic devices. While doing questions on your smartphone is not a bad idea while waiting for your table at a restaurant, doing all of your questions in this manner is not a good idea. On the exam, it is paper and pencil. You need to time yourself doing them with paper and pencil.

A greater concern over doing questions only on an electronic device is that you will be tempted to skip the autopsy of your answers. You may fall back on the old habit of thinking that you will remember all your mistakes, failing to keep in mind that you will do hundreds of practice questions in seven different topics.

Your memory will not hold rules over this length of time, in this depth, and over as many topics without conscious encoding of the material.

The last week before the exam, drop your MBE practice from 50 questions a day back to 34 questions a day. Your time is better spent working on memorizing the rules that week.

You will hear prior takers exclaim that one of the commercial provider's practice MBE questions are "more like" real MBE questions than another provider's questions. Do not believe it. No provider has any special relationship with the NCBE such that it has the inside scoop. The best test of "real" MBE questions is to take one of the NCBE online MBE exams. The NCBE offers several exams for purchase. Each exam consists of 100 questions. These are actual bar questions used in prior exams. These are the best models. No matter which commercial provider you utilize, the heart and soul of doing well on MBE questions is knowing the rules so that you can apply the rules to the facts.

**EXAM TIP**

Are you a slow starter on MBE questions? Pick out 10 to 15 questions to do the morning of the MBE before you head to the exam. Then, you'll already be in the groove.

## II. GO BACKWARDS

On the exam and in your practice, your analysis of an MBE question should be backwards. All MBE questions are set up with a hypothetical fact scenario, a call of the question, and four responses. Read the call of the question and the four responses first. You will immediately be able to pick which one of the seven topics is being tested. Reading the responses tells you the particular sub-issue that is being tested. After reading the responses, pull to mind the rule for that sub-issue. Write it down if you need to do that. Now, read the facts. Underline the facts that address that issue. Read the call and the responses again.

Do not try to pick the correct response. Instead, begin by eliminating responses you know are incorrect. Look at each response in isolation. To be correct, every aspect of the response must be accurate—its characterization of the facts, its statement of the rule, its reasoning, and its focus on the central issue. These are not easy to identify. Indeed, some calls of the question include qualifiers such as "most likely to prevail" or "what is the best argument." When you see this kind of qualifier, keep in mind that in reality only one of the responses is correct. Thus, it's not just the *best* argument; it's the *only* argument that can prevail.

At times, it may seem that you are choosing between two correct responses. Indeed, each may include correct reasoning, but one will be more precise. Even if only a snippet of the legal rule is used, the rationale of that response may be the most accurate and precise.

**EXAM TIP**

If two responses on an MBE question are the polar opposites of each other, chances are that one of them is the correct answer.

Let's try an example to see how the rationale must be accurate and precise.

Driver ran into and injured Pedestrian. Pedestrian has sued Driver alleging that Driver, while drunk, struck Pedestrian, who was in a duly marked crosswalk. Pedestrian's counsel wishes to prove that after the accident Driver went to Pedestrian and offered $1,000 to settle Pedestrian's claim.

The trial judge should rule this evidence:

A. admissible as an admission of a party.
B. admissible as an admission to show Driver's liability, provided the court gives a cautionary instruction that the statement should not be considered as bearing on the issue of damages.

C. inadmissible since it is not relevant either to the question of liability or the question of damages.

D. inadmissible because even though it is relevant and an admission, the policy of the law is to encourage settlement negotiations.

First, what do the call of the question and the responses tell us? This is an Evidence question, and some of the responses deal with admissions of a party-opponent. Others deal with relevancy. Still others deal with both. What else can we tell from reading the responses? Response A gives no reasoning and does not address relevancy. Response C addresses relevancy, but not admissions. Responses B and D appear to address both admissions and relevancy. It is likely that one of those is the correct answer because they are more precise.

Now, read the facts. What is the central issue? Looks like the central issue deals with settlement offers. What is the rule for the admissibility of settlement offers? Federal Rule of Evidence (FRE) 408(a)(1) states that evidence of "furnishing, promising, or offering . . . a valuable consideration in compromising or attempting to compromise the claim" is inadmissible.[1] FRE 408(b) gives an exception if the settlement offer is offered for another purpose such as proving a witness's bias or prejudice.[2] You need to analyze both the general rule and the exception. Under the general rule, the settlement offer is inadmissible. Under the exception, is the offer being admitted for another purpose? In all likelihood, no. It is being offered to prove liability. As a result, you know response C is incorrect. Liability is certainly relevant, but relevancy is not the reason why settlement offers are inadmissible.

But, you are not finished. Now, you have to check admission by a party-opponent. Check each step of your mind-map for hearsay. Hearsay is inadmissible without an exception.[3] Hearsay is a statement made by an out-of-court declarant that is being offered to prove the truth of the matter asserted.[4] Is the offer hearsay? It was an out-of-court statement and is being offered to prove liability. Thus, it initially would be hearsay. However, certain out-of-court statements are not hearsay. Classified as non-hearsay, an admission is a statement "offered against an opposing party and was made by the party in an individual or representative capacity."[5] Is this a statement offered against an opposing party and made by that party? Yes.

Thus, you know the offer to settle is an admission and that it is relevant, but inadmissible. Response A is correct, but does not address relevancy. Response B is incorrect. Evidence is either admissible or inadmissible. A cautionary instruction does not make the evidence admissible. Moreover, the settlement offer is being offered to prove liability, not just damages. We already excluded response C as incorrect because the settlement offer is relevant. You are left with response D. It is inadmissible, although relevant and an admission, because settlement offers are inadmissible. The reason why they are inadmissible is to encourage settlement negotiations. While response A is correct, it is not precise. Response D would be the correct answer.

---

1. Fed. R. Evid. 408(a)(1).
2. Fed. R. Evid. 408(b).
3. Fed. R. Evid. 802.
4. Fed. R. Evid. 801(c)(1)-(2).
5. Fed. R. Evid. 801(d)(2)(A).

Next, be sure to read the facts carefully. Don't skip over the details. Details matter. Ask yourself, why did the examiners include that he was an "experienced carpenter" instead of just "carpenter." Why does it matter that Tommy was four years old instead of seventeen years old? These details usually go to the core issue. In these examples, perhaps they are hinting at delegation of duty in a contract for the carpenter and witness competency for the child. Moreover, the examiners give you all the facts you need. Thus, read carefully and do not assume facts.

That's worth repeating. Try not to assume facts. For example, your impression is that the witness is a lying, cheating scumbag not to be trusted. But the response includes "if the jury believes him." Take that as fact—do not assume that it is impossible to believe him because he's a scumbag. The modifier, "if the jury believes him," takes care of that.

Let's try an example that requires careful reading of the facts.

> Painter, who has been in the painting and contracting business for ten years and has a fine reputation, contracts to paint Farmer's barn. Farmer's barn is a standard red barn with a loft. The contract has no provision regarding assignment. If Painter assigns the contract to Contractor, who has comparable experience and reputation, which of the following statements is correct?

> A. Painter is in breach of contract.
> B. Farmer may refuse to accept performance by Contractor.
> C. Farmer is required to accept performance by Contractor.
> D. There is a novation.

First, what do the call of the question and the responses tell us? First, this is a Contracts question and it deals with an assignment issue. What is the rule for assignments in contracts? One part of the rule is that an assignment cannot increase the risk that the promisee (Farmer) will not receive the promised performance. What else can we tell from reading the responses? Response A is very broad. Responses B and C are polar opposites. It is likely that one of those is the correct answer. Response D contains a term that you may not remember off the top of your head.

Now, read the facts. What is the central issue? Looks like the central issue is whether Farmer must accept the assignee's performance. What details are included in the description of the people involved? Painter has ten years' experience in the painting and contracting business and has a "fine reputation." That tells us that Painter is skilled and does good work. This is not someone that just decided to earn some money by painting. What about the assignee? Contractor has "comparable experience and reputation." Contractor's description tells us that he is also someone who is skilled and does good work.

Responses A and B state or allude to Painter having breached the contract. Responses C and D indicate that Painter has not breached the contract. Response A gives us no rationale and reasoning. It is the least precise answer and is unlikely to be correct unless all other responses are fundamentally incorrect. Response D requires that you know the term "novation." A novation requires the promisee's consent to the substitute performance. Did Farmer consent? No; thus, you can eliminate D. To determine which of the remaining three are correct, we must determine if Painter breached the contract by the assignment to Contractor.

EXAM TIP

If the response contains a Latin phrase or a rule that you have never heard, chances are that the response is incorrect. Don't assume that just because you don't recognize a concept that it must be correct.

Applying the assignment rule to the facts, did the assignment increase the risk that Farmer will not receive the promised performance—a barn painted by a skilled craftsman? As Contractor had comparable skill and experience, that answer is "no." The risk was not increased. Thus, Painter did not breach the contract and Farmer must accept the performance. Responses A and B are eliminated and response C is correct.

One fact made the difference: Contractor had comparable experience and reputation. Without that fact, a different response may have been correct. Just skimming the facts would not have highlighted that similarity.

## III. AUTOPSY MBE QUESTIONS

To get the most out of your autopsy, keep track of your elimination process as you do practice questions. Indicate which response you eliminated first, second, and third. If you are guessing, include that as well.

Then, in your autopsy, review the answers you got correct, particularly lucky guesses, to see if your reasoning matches the examiners' reasoning. For incorrect answers, assess what stumped you. Was it an issue identification problem? Did you just not remember that rule? Did you skip over a detail in the reading? Did you apply the law to the facts incorrectly? Keeping track will show patterns in your answers so that you know what to focus upon in your preparation.

Keep track of when you go back and second-guess an answer and note whether your first choice was usually correct or your changed answer was correct. This may also indicate a trend that tells you quite a bit about your test-taking skills.

The chart on page 89 is designed for you to perform this autopsy in detail.[6] Those who regularly use the chart are better prepared for the MBE portion of the exam.

Let's attack this question from the autopsy point of view using the chart.

In an automobile negligence action by Popkin against Dwyer, Juilliard testified for Popkin. Dwyer later called Watts, who testified that Julliard's reputation for truthfulness was bad.

On cross-examination of Watts, Popkin's counsel asks, "Isn't it a fact that when you bought your new car last year, you made a false affidavit to escape paying the sales tax?"

This question is

A. proper, because it will indicate Watts's standard of judgment as to reputation for truthfulness.
B. proper, because it bears on Watts's credibility.
C. improper, because character cannot be proved by specific instances of conduct.
D. improper, because one cannot impeach an impeaching witness.

Analyze and answer this question before you continue reading.

---

6. Idea originated with Denise Riebe & Michael Hunter Swartz, *Pass the Bar!* 138 (Carolina Acad. Press 2006).

If your answer was response A, this was probably a reading error. Although Watts's direct testimony was about Julliard's reputation, the cross examination had nothing to do with reputation and dealt with bad acts.

If your answer was response C, this was a result of not understanding the rule well enough. Under FRE 608(b), the general rule states that specific instances of conduct may not be proved through extrinsic evidence even for the purpose of attacking a witness's credibility.[7] An exception is that a judge may allow such evidence if it is brought out through cross-examination of the witness whose credibility is being attacked and if the bad acts are probative of truthfulness.[8] Here, Watts is being cross-examined with evidence of his own falsification of an affidavit. The act was probative of truthfulness and is being brought out on cross-examination and, thus, is proper. Therefore, response C is incorrect as it does not consider the exception to the rule.

If your answer was response D, this was a result of both an issue identification problem and not knowing the rule. There is no prohibition on impeaching an impeaching witness.

That leaves response B—the question was proper because it bore on Watts's credibility. You might have avoided this response because it seemed too straightforward. Yet, it is correct and its rationale is correct. Moreover, there is a problem with each of the other responses.

As you autopsy each practice question, fill out the chart to see if there are any common mistakes. This can tell you where to focus in your remaining preparation.

Without a doubt, focusing on memorizing rules and on autopsying your answers is the key to doing well on the MBE exam. Keep that in mind when you are tempted to just do practice questions in isolation.

| MBE PRACTICE ANALYSIS | | | | |
|---|---|---|---|---|
| Question | Order of elimination | Reason for correct answer | Reason my answer was incorrect | Type of Error [circle all that apply] |
| 1 | ____ ____ ____ ____ | | | Issue identification<br>Didn't know rule<br>Reading error<br>Application error |
| 2 | ____ ____ ____ ____ | | | Issue identification<br>Didn't know rule<br>Reading error<br>Application error |
| 3 | ____ ____ ____ ____ | | | Issue identification<br>Didn't know rule<br>Reading error<br>Application error |

---

7. Fed. R. Evid. 608(b).
8. Fed. R. Evid. 608(b)(1).

| Question | Order of elimination | Reason for correct answer | Reason my answer was incorrect | Type of Error [circle all that apply] |
|---|---|---|---|---|
| 4 | _____ | | | Issue identification<br>Didn't know rule<br>Reading error<br>Application error |
| 5 | _____ | | | Issue identification<br>Didn't know rule<br>Reading error<br>Application error |
| 6 | _____ | | | Issue identification<br>Didn't know rule<br>Reading error<br>Application error |
| 7 | _____ | | | Issue identification<br>Didn't know rule<br>Reading error<br>Application error |
| 8 | _____ | | | Issue identification<br>Didn't know rule<br>Reading error<br>Application error |
| 9 | _____ | | | Issue identification<br>Didn't know rule<br>Reading error<br>Application error |
| 10 | _____ | | | Issue identification<br>Didn't know rule<br>Reading error<br>Application error |
| 11 | _____ | | | Issue identification<br>Didn't know rule<br>Reading error<br>Application error |
| 12 | _____ | | | Issue identification<br>Didn't know rule<br>Reading error<br>Application error |
| 13 | _____ | | | Issue identification<br>Didn't know rule<br>Reading error<br>Application error |
| 14 | _____ | | | Issue identification<br>Didn't know rule<br>Reading error<br>Application error |

| Question | Order of elimination | Reason for correct answer | Reason my answer was incorrect | Type of Error [circle all that apply] |
|---|---|---|---|---|
| 15 | _____ _____ _____ _____ | | | Issue identification<br>Didn't know rule<br>Reading error<br>Application error |
| 16 | _____ _____ _____ _____ | | | Issue identification<br>Didn't know rule<br>Reading error<br>Application error |
| 17 | _____ _____ _____ _____ | | | Issue identification<br>Didn't know rule<br>Reading error<br>Application error |

# CHAPTER 7

# Building Confidence with Strategies

Throughout your third year of law school, if not all of law school, the bar exam has been the elephant in the room—always there, never moving. Most of the time we don't have to deal with it or even look at it. We know that it is in the distant future. But now, we have to tackle it. But how do we do that? Just like the old riddle that asks, "How do you eat an elephant?" The answer is, "One bite at a time."

One day, one page, one topic at a time. Step by step you will study what you need to know and practice the skills you need to pass the exam. While you need to know what the elephant looks like, you conquer the task by focusing only on what you need to be doing that day, and then what needs to be done the next day, and the day after that, and the day after that.

**Tackling the Elephant**

Bar preparation is similar to marathon training. A marathon is 26.2 miles. Yet, no marathon runner ever runs 26.2 miles in training. Instead, they follow a set schedule of shorter distances with a longer run every week. They run a certain number of miles on certain days and then they have rest days. They increase the number of miles they run as the marathon approaches.

Similarly, you will not take an entire bar exam during your bar preparation. You will tackle shorter tasks several days in a row and then accomplish a larger task on certain days. You will have rest days. You will have tasks that take a longer length of time to do, such as a one-day multiple choice practice exam and half-day essay and MPT practice exams. You will increase your preparation as the exam approaches.

The strategies included in this chapter help you to focus on the separate tasks ahead of you and to not be overwhelmed by the enormity of the overall task itself. The bar exam is the elephant. Here is your fork. One bite at a time.

## I. LOW-HANGING FRUIT

The first strategy is straightforward. Focus on the basics of each question. You may identify a minor sub-issue or tangential issue that is fascinating to you. You believe that by analyzing that difficult-to-identify issue that you have nailed the "trick" of an essay question. Except, there is no trick. The points for a difficult-to-identify sub-issue or a tangential issue that is not essential to the analysis are only a small percentage of the points available for that question. No extra credit exists. Thus, if your answer focuses exclusively on that sub-issue, you will not pass that essay or MPT question—not because your analysis was deficient on what you analyzed, but because your answer failed to analyze the bulk of the points.

The bulk of the points lies in the low-hanging fruit—the basics and foundation of each issue's rule. When stating your rule, state all the elements, including those not at issue. Apply each element, again including those not at issue. Why? The bar examiners need to know that you know all the elements and can recognize the ones at issue.

Note that the examiners do *not* want to know everything about the topic. Do not start your essay question stating everything you remember about the topic. That just shows you could not identify the issue. They do want you to state the entire rule for the specific issue identified by the call of the question. But don't get caught rule dumping about the entire topic hoping something is right.

When you don't score well on an essay, you typically have gone over all the issues in your head, decided what was at issue, decided to focus only on the disputed issue, applied the rule to the facts in your head, reached your conclusion, and then only written down the conclusion on the disputed issue. In essence, you did a complete analysis in your head, but you did not communicate that analysis to the examiner. The examiner cannot give you points for what stays in your head. They can only give you points for what is written down.

Accordingly, put down every step of that analysis. This analysis going on in your head is the low-hanging fruit—the basics of each rule and the basics of applying each rule. While phrased differently in each jurisdiction, the essence of the standard to pass the bar examination and be admitted to practice law in that jurisdiction is that the applicant has demonstrated a minimum level of

**Focus on the Low-Hanging Fruit**

competence to practice law. Not the best potential, but a minimum level. That minimum is the low-hanging fruit, not the fruit at the top of the tree.

If you sufficiently cover the low-hanging fruit on each and every topic, chances are good that you will pass the bar. There will be questions where you know more than just the low-hanging fruit and can address those mid- or high-level issues. In other questions, you don't quite get all the low-hanging fruit. The goal is an average essay score that equals 75%.

## II. 75/15/10 STRATEGY

Your commercial bar prep materials have arrived—a large box or two. As you open the boxes, the enormity of the task will hit you. Book after book, page after page of material that you are expected to know to fulfill your dream of becoming a practicing lawyer are in front of you. How on earth can the bar examiners expect you to learn and memorize all that you are provided?

They don't. You do not have to memorize 100% of the material. You must have a substantial amount of the material learned and memorized, but that doesn't equate with having it all memorized. The question becomes, which parts do you have to have memorized? That's where the 75/15/10 strategy comes into play.

The low-hanging fruit accounts for approximately 75% of the material on each topic. Having a solid handle on 75% of the material will result in a passing score. That means 75% of *each topic*. You cannot have 75% of three-fourths or one-half of the topics and hope to pass. It must be 75% of each topic. Why can't it be 75% of all the material? The reason is that you may be faced with an exam where the 25% of the topics you do not concentrate on are indeed the essay questions! You just gave yourself absolutely no chance to pass the exam as only minimal knowledge is not enough.

This begs the question—which 75% of each topic? The mind maps contained in Chapters 9 through 20 address that 75% and more. The mind maps are designed to help you sort through the material and decide where to concentrate your memorization efforts. During Phase One, you should build your library on all the material. During Phase Two, use the 75/15/10 strategy during your memorization process. Use this strategy to help you identify issues on the actual essay questions, both in practice and on the exam itself.

The next 15% is material that those having somewhat more exposure to the topic will know. If you took a class on that topic, you will have been exposed and possibly tested on this 15%. This 15% is a small cushion for that topic on the bar exam, but only for that topic. You cannot count on this cushion to pull up your 50% effort on all the other topics. First, your 15% of that topic may not be tested. Second, the math doesn't add up. If your jurisdiction scores on the 6 point scale recommended by the NCBE, you want to average 4 points to pass. That's a little less than 75% of the available points. Thus, if you count on the 5 you will receive on one question for the 15% extra knowledge, you will not pass if your other essays are all at 3. With 6 essays, your score is then 20 out of 36 or a 55.5%—a raw score that, when scaled, is still below most jurisdictions' pass point.

The last 10% is that material that delves into the far reaches of the topic. These issues are raised in the "Notes" sections after each case excerpt in your textbooks. These issues are the ones you may be able to identify if you have a special affinity for the topic. You took every course the law school offered in that area. You did extra reading on that topic. You wrote your law review article or wrote a seminar paper on that topic. The difficult-to-identify sub-issue and tangential issues are the ones that may pique your interest the most.

But this 10% of the topic is not the bulk of the points available for an essay. That issue may well be there. In fact most questions have sub-issues that deal with all three levels. The points are allocated between all the issues. The pass point does not require you to do well on every single point. You do not have to have 100% of the material memorized to pass the bar. You need a nice solid 75% of each topic.

In Chapter 2, mind maps were discussed as a tool to think about a topic in a way that helped you see the big picture of the topic and to see the relationships between ideas. The 75/15/10 strategy uses the mind map to focus on the core 75% of the material while allowing you to expand the map to include additional material. The mind map is your global positioning system (GPS) for that topic.

On any GPS, the first question it asks or determines for itself is where you are located. Similarly, as you read an essay question, the call of the question gives you your starting point. That tells you which topic's mind map to use and may tell you where on that mind map to begin. Next, you tell the GPS where you want to go. The GPS then gives you one or several routes to get where you need to go. With the call of the question as the starting point, you then use your mind map as your GPS to determine the route to take to answer the question.

That route is the 75% of the material. It includes the fundamental rules on the route you are taking. It goes step-by-step along the route. It gives signposts as to where you are going, similar to the name of the roads and whether to turn right or left on a GPS. No leap-frogging over issues or detours that are not explained. Go step by step and tell the reader how to navigate the analysis to reach the same conclusion. Note you are not discussing the entire map of the topic, but just the route for the issue.

The 15% are the additional comments provided regarding your route. It adds descriptors along the route such as restaurants and gas stations that occur at the points of turning. It doesn't just get you to the right destination. It gets you into the parking lot.

The 10% goes farther and takes you to the seat at the restaurant's table with menu in hand. The route is in full bloom with all descriptors and variants described in detail. No stone has been left unturned in order to flesh out all relevant issues and sub-issues.

Remember that focusing on that 10% is not what you need to pass. No one needs to strive to get an A on the bar exam by getting all the 10% points. It's just not needed. No one, truly no one, including an employer, cares how high you score on the bar exam as long as you have passed. The 10% issues can give you a cushion, but cannot make up for the failure to have the 75% of the material understood, memorized, and analyzed on every topic.

The 75/15/10 strategy is also helpful for issue identification on the questions themselves. When you have read the call of the question and the facts and you are still left with an unsettled feeling as to what the issue truly is, pull out your mind map to focus on the 75%. Visualize your map and peruse it going through each route. Pause at each stop along the route and ask yourself if you have any facts that would address that rule. As you go through each route, the issue will usually occur to you. This technique also works if you finish your answer and are left with doubt that you covered what you need to have covered. Run through your map to be sure you haven't missed an issue.

## III. AVOID DUPING YOURSELF

It's so easy to dupe yourself. It's a psychological defense mechanism similar to denial. If we don't think about it, we don't have to acknowledge it as an issue. So, you tell yourself that you are working harder than you ever have, because you are. You have put in 500 hours of study. You have attended or watched the commercial bar preparation lectures—all of them. You have written essay answers and done the required number of MBE questions every day.

But you skip over the fact that you have not studied all the topics. You skip over that you have spent almost all of your time on your two favorite topics and spent little to no time on your more troublesome topics. You skip over that every essay you have done has been on your favorite topics. You skip over that your MBE questions are only from three of the seven topics. You skip over that you did not make your own library but used your buddy's, as his was better organized than yours would have been. You kid yourself when you look at a sample answer and think that even though your answer is deficient, you'll do better on the actual exam now that you have read the model answer because you will remember the issue and rule. You don't add the rule to your library of materials. Indeed, you may even just skim the model answer looking for a few buzz words. You dupe yourself that you will remember, because you do nothing to truly encode the information into your memory.

As human beings, we do not like to look at the hard truths about ourselves. We do not like to admit that we have not done "everything" asked because we did the easier stuff. But you must look at the hard truths. There is no replacement for the work you must do to pass the bar exam. You can choose not to do the work and take a chance. There are lots of folks willing to join you on that chance. You will see them all again at the next sitting of the exam, because your chances of passing the first time are negligible. This is an exam you only want to take once. There is no replacement for the work that must be done.

## IV. GROWING YOUR MINDSET

What brings success? Brains and talent alone? No. A person's mindset is key. What is a mindset? In essence, your mindset is how you view your intellectual ability. Do you view yourself as someone with a fixed amount of intelligence? Or do you view yourself as someone that can cultivate your abilities through your efforts? Can anyone be the next Bill Gates or Stephen Hawking? Maybe. The limit to your intelligence is unknown.

If you believe that you have a fixed amount of intelligence, called a fixed mindset, then your view of challenges becomes a running evaluation in your head. "Will I succeed or fail? Will I look smart or dumb? Will I be accepted or rejected? Will I feel like a winner or loser?"[1] Your goal becomes proving yourself. That you are smart enough. That you are a winner. What happens when some teacher, some coach, some test tells you that you did not succeed in getting the grade, making the team, etc.? Then, your commentary on your result becomes: "I'm a total failure. I'm an idiot. I'm a loser."[2] Then, you rationalize the result. "The test wasn't like the practice tests and that's not fair." "Something was wrong with the materials I was using." "My Property professor never explained future interests clearly, so how was I supposed to know it?" The fixed mindset gives little to no recognition of the efforts involved in reaching a goal.

If you believe your efforts make a difference in your intelligence, called a growth mindset, then the commentary in your head changes to, "I need to try hard" and "I need to put forth my best efforts." With a growth mindset, what is your commentary when your goal is not achieved? "I should study harder or study in a different way for the next time." "I'll look at what went wrong on my exam and resolve to do better." The growth mindset view of your self-worth continues: "Failing this exam is not the end of my world. It is a stumbling block that I will work hard to overcome."

Individuals with both mindsets are naturally upset at not achieving their goal. But each mindset's view of why it happened and what to do next are different. Individuals with both mindsets pass the bar exam. But the fixed mindset limits achievement. Interfering thoughts disrupt your learning. It makes effort disagreeable because increased effort will probably not change the result after all, because you are probably just not smart enough any way. You study alone so others don't know how dumb you are. In contrast, individuals with the growth mindset seek allies in learning. They focus, make an all-out effort, and pull from

---

1. Carol Dweck, *Mindset: The New Psychology of Success* 6 (Random House 2012).
2. *Id.* at 8.

"a bottomless trunk of strategies."[3] That's why their abilities grow and they achieve.

Changing your mindset is possible. It takes effort and determination. When the script in your head starts on how you are not good enough and you just can't do this, focus on your past achievements including graduating from law school. Graduating from law school is a remarkable achievement. Not everyone does. But you did it. And that took a remarkable effort on your part. Keep that in mind when the doubts set in. Think of all your other achievements—riding a bicycle, learning an instrument, finishing your undergraduate degree, debate teams, sport teams, etc. You have achieved much. This is just one hurdle that you can and will get over.

Some words of wisdom from prior bar takers:

- "We have all achieved so much by the time we take the bar, but we seem to dwell on shortcomings, failure and disappointment and almost ignore our own personal victories. I tried to remember how well I perform when I put in the effort."[4]
- "What goes with 'I'm probably going to fail' is the idea that 'why even try.' 'I'm going to do it' to me means 'I'm going to do it because I'm going to study hard and smart.' To think otherwise is simply a self-defeating and, often, a self-fulfilling prophecy."[5]
- "I visualized my success and it didn't include failing the exam. I wrote a passing score on a piece of scratch paper during the exam to keep it positive."[6]
- Keep your perspective that there are bigger things in life than tests. "Find something else to focus on besides the test so you can step back and look at it with different perspective and it will eventually seem manageable."[7]
- "Even if you don't have faith in yourself, it's good to have faith in one's training."[8]
- "I told myself that it was a process I had to trust. Then I thought of all the lawyers I know, particularly some who are not very bright. I knew that if they could pass, I could pass."[9]
- "It is tempting to look at a colleague and gauge your study habits or progress based on that other individual. You may feel like someone is putting in more hours or receiving higher scores. Do not compare. Worry about yourself. The only person you need to be better than is the person you were yesterday."[10]
- "When I was really feeling sorry for myself (thank you property questions), I just thought of all of the worse things that people go through. Cancer, divorce, disability. And it really helped to keep things in perspective. In the grand scheme of life this is two days and if other people can battle through MUCH worse, then I have NO reason whatsoever to get down on

---

3. *Id.* at 67.
4. Statement from D.M. (passed bar exam the first time).
5. Statement from T.S. (passed bar exam the first time).
6. Statement from J.C. (passed bar exam the first time).
7. Statement from L.P. (passed bar exam the first time).
8. Statement from D.W. (passed bar exam the first time).
9. Statement from S.G. (passed bar exam the first time).
10. Statement from J.T. (passed bar exam the first time).

myself, complain, or think negatively. I get to take the bar. This is an opportunity, not a burden."[11]

- "I thought of all those people in years past that must have felt this way as well, but stuck with it and passed the bar exam. I also thought that if I didn't pass the bar exam and that was the biggest problem I had in my life, that I was one lucky individual who will just have to figure out another plan of attack."[12]
- "I credit my success to resting and relaxing [in the last days before the exam], but also my last-minute perceptions about the exam. The moment you understand your exam experience is subject to the lens you place between it and yourself is the moment you establish full control over your experience. In a really weird way, the time I spent away [from 10 hour study days] somehow made taking the exam 'enjoyable.'"[13]
- "When my brain hurt from all the studying and I was exhausted, I had to stop and remind myself that I did not HAVE to take the bar, I GOT to take the bar. Many people, even classmates, were not going to get that opportunity."[14]

Every morning envision yourself succeeding and what that success looks like for that particular day and what the mid-term future would look like when you succeed. Every morning, take five minutes to:

- Tell yourself that today is one more step towards being fully prepared for the bar exam.
- Envision what your perfect day would look like—"I will get my Property flash cards done. I will get through x number of MBE questions and x% of success, etc."
- Envision what you want your life to look like five years from now—"Upon success on the bar exam on my first attempt, I will be a successful lawyer in ABC practice area, and then whatever additional personal and professional goals you have."[15]

John Wooden certainly knew what it took to succeed. Coach John Wooden was the head men's basketball coach at UCLA. Coach Wooden's teams won ten NCAA championships in the 1960s and the 1970s. This dynasty is virtually unmatched. Coach Wooden's philosophy in building success is exactly the approach to take in preparing for the bar exam:

> You have to apply yourself each day to becoming a little better each and every day. Over a period of time, you will become better.

We are going to eat that elephant one day at a time, focusing on what we need to do that day and not worrying about all the days ahead.

---

11. Statement from G.T. (passed bar exam the first time).
12. Statement from J.Y. (passed bar exam the first time).
13. Statement from T.A. (passed bar exam the first time).
14. Statement from M.H. (passed bar exam the first time).
15. Process from M.W. and J.B. (both passed bar exam the first time).

## V. KEEPING COOL—MAINTAINING YOUR SANITY

Ever skipped breakfast to make it to class and then had your stomach grumble half way through the class? No doubt about it—you were hungry. At that point, your attention turned away from your Wills and Trusts class and focused on when you would get to eat and what you would have. Indeed, you may have spent several minutes focusing on lunch. Were you thinking about Wills and Trusts? No, your concentration was pulled away by hunger.

Abraham Maslow's Hierarchy of Needs theory is that we are motivated by certain needs and our motivation follows an order to achieve those needs. Our most basic needs must be met before we can seek the next level of needs. Our body's need for food, water, sleep, and warmth takes precedence. Only after those needs are met are we able to focus on the next level of needs.

One way to maintain your stress is to fulfill these needs first. You need a roof over your head, the ability to pay your utilities, and nourishing food to eat. You need sleep. Next, you need safety and security. To ensure that you have these throughout your preparation time, have your financial house in order so that you may spend the necessary time to prepare for the exam. If you are planning to fulfill these needs by working while you study, you must keep your hours at a minimum the first month of bar prep and do without working the last month of bar prep. Yes, it may be hard financially, but if you do not pass the bar the first time, you will have to go through the same financially difficult time again. Plan your finances in law school so that you are not relying on working during this time.

Avoid moving during bar preparation. Moving is more than just the physical acts of packing and unpacking possessions. Time is needed to locate a new residence. Time is needed to have utilities hooked up. Time is needed to arrange insurance, to have cars relicensed if moving to a different state, to set up new bank accounts, etc. The list is endless. Thus, you cannot just write off the few days of packing and the actual relocation. Much more time will be involved. Either move before you begin bar preparation or arrange your move after the exam.

If you are a regular exerciser, keep it up! Exercise is a great stress reducer. If you run every day, keep running. If you go to the gym regularly, keep going. You may have to reduce the time you spend running and the time you spend at the gym, but there is no need to stop it completely. If you are not a regular exerciser, consider taking walks during breaks from studying. Moving around and getting your blood flowing to your extremities can only benefit you.

A word about sleep. Get some. As much as you can. Sleep is a physical need necessary for you to think clearly. All-nighters the week before the bar exam leave you exhausted and unable to concentrate. Cramming the days and nights before the exam will leave you unable to focus. If your fears and thoughts are keeping you up at night, here are a few tips:

- Avoid caffeine in the evenings.
- Try warm milk.
- Turn off the television and electronic devices before you try to sleep.
- Take a walk in the evening.
- Keep your room just a little cooler.
- Avoid drinking lots of liquids in the evening to avoid middle of the night trips to the bathroom.

If these tips don't work, an over-the-counter sleep aid used according to directions may help. If not, see your health care provider for sleep assistance.

After your physical needs are met, your need for love, friendship, and intimacy become your focus. The important people in your life also need your time. Be sure to have a regular date night with your significant other, even if it is just watching a movie together without you having your nose in a book. Spend time with your children every day. Take regular time away from study, either a half day on the weekends or, occasionally, a full day off. You need that time with your significant other as much as they need time with you. Spend time on those days off in recreation and relaxation. The idea is to have a true break from studying, so that when you hit it again you will be rejuvenated and more motivated to keep up the pace.

Likewise, if being part of a community group is important to you, there is no need to give it up. Just don't volunteer to chair the fundraising event in the middle of bar prep! If you regularly attend worship in your faith, keep attending! We need all the help we can get and you will be less stressed if your spiritual needs have been met.

Do not be surprised when you have an overwhelming feeling that this is an impossible task and one that you are deficient on in every category. All the stress and self-doubt have been building up and they come out all at once. You have a meltdown. Good! Good? How is that possibly good? It's good because continuing to study with that stress building up will not be good study. It will be distracted studying, at best. A meltdown means you probably need to take a break for the day and pick it back up the next day. You need some time away from this process. Most folks have at least two or three meltdowns during the bar preparation process. Expect them. Everyone gets them. Nothing is wrong with you when you have one. You just need to emotionally let it all hang out.

Lastly, remember that every single bar taker is in the same boat. You have the same test. The odd questions are odd to everyone. Everyone is stressed-out and nervous. Take a deep breath. You will have studied hard and your preparation will see you through the exam. Honest. You can do this!

**All Together**

# CHAPTER 8

# Not the First Time

All of the advice in this book is not just for first-time takers, but also applies to repeat takers. If this is not your first time taking a bar exam because you were unsuccessful, know that you are not alone. Even states with a high bar passage rate still have folks who do not pass. Usually, a combination of factors led to this result:

- Insufficient preparation
  - Lack of time spent
  - Lack of details in memorization materials
- Anxiety and mindset
- Personal issues

Let's address each cause and ways to remedy these issues.

## I. INSUFFICIENT PREPARATION

### A. Time Spent

There is no getting around it. Bar preparation takes a significant amount of time. If you worked during your preparation or had family issues that took substantial time away from your study, you likely were not able to cover all the materials and do sufficient practice questions. Take the time to sit down with your significant other, family members, and employer to discuss your need to spend more time on your bar preparation. Work with your employer to take more time off to study. At a minimum, you need the entire month of the exam. A better game plan would have you take two months off.

Plan on 400-500 hours to prepare. If you took a commercial bar prep course the first time, you most likely should not need to repeat the course your second time taking the exam. If it is your third or more time taking the exam, you should consider taking another commercial bar preparation course. The lapse of time makes it more difficult to remember details. If you did not take a commercial bar prep course the first time, you should take one the second time.

Generally, insufficient time preparing means you did not review all of the topics in detail. Remember, you cannot predict which essay topics will appear on the next exam. The examiners do repeat topics twice in a row, if not more than twice. You cannot game the exam by deciding which topics are less likely to appear. You must study all topics.

If you did not make your own flash cards, outlines, or flow charts the first time around, start making those for every topic before the eight weeks of bar preparation before the exam. Start with the "Big Seven"—the topics tested on the MBE: Civil Procedure, Constitutional Law, Contracts, Criminal Law and Procedure, Evidence, Real Property, and Torts. Try to have four or more of those topics completely done prior to the start of the eight weeks. Do *not* start doing practice questions before the eight weeks. Your goal is to improve your memorization materials—to get ready to memorize. The eight weeks directly before the exam is plenty of time for practice questions.

### B. Detail in Memorization Materials

If you relied on commercial bar prep materials for your memorization, your short-cut did not work. You need to make your own outlines or flash cards. That process encodes the information much better in your memory. Just reading someone else's organization and description of the material is insufficient. Autopsy each practice question and include the information in your materials. Take this time to make your materials focus on what you need to remember. It will be worth it.

If you did make your own outlines or flash cards and were not successful, two possible things happened. First, you may not have put enough detail in the rules you were memorizing. Or, you put too much detail into your rule such that you could not memorize much of it or it kept you from focusing on what was critical. Thus, you need to supplement or cull appropriately.

Use the mind maps contained in this book to guide you in your decision making about how to supplement or cull. Always, always autopsy your answers to practice questions and include the rules in your materials.

## II. ANXIETY AND MINDSET

If you have experienced test anxiety prior to this exam, or your first bar exam was your first time with test anxiety, see a mental health professional to work on coping mechanisms. Some students with a high level of test anxiety find hypnosis beneficial.

If you have followed the advice in this book, you are more likely to pass the exam. Get to the place in your preparation where you feel that you have done your best—a positive mindset. You have done all that was asked and then some. Then, trust that preparation.

Anxiety can occur as a result of self-doubt and a mindset that you are likely to fail. Folks in the bottom of the class often feel this way. You may feel that because you did not perform in law school at the same level as the top 90% that you are more likely to fail. That mindset—"I'll probably fail"—will actually make it more likely that you will fail. In reality, folks at the bottom of the class can and do pass the exam on their first try all the time. The difference—their mindset. They maintain a growth mindset that their efforts make a difference. They then work very hard in their bar preparation. They put in their 500 hours of study. They know and feel that they have studied to the best of their abilities. Their mindset—"I can do this," "I have put forth my best effort"—carries them through the exam.

When you hear the voice in your head panic because you read a question that you don't know the answer to, immediately stop. Remember, you are not alone.

Everyone taking the exam is probably also flummoxed by this question. Everyone has their own topics they do not know as well as others and gets questions they do not immediately understand. Take a deep breath. More oxygen in the brain helps. Tell yourself—"I will do my best and this one question does not mean I will fail." Then, go through your mind map. Consider each branch and whether the facts give rise to any issue on that branch. That usually gives you something with which to begin your analysis.

If that doesn't do it, then guess. Now, it will be an educated guess and not willy-nilly. You have already gone through your mind map, but nothing jumped out at you. If you're not sure of the path, begin with the branch that is possibly related. Even if you are totally off, you will usually get a few points for the answer. Chapter 4 discusses in more detail how to guess in an intelligent manner.

Most importantly, change your mindset. Go into the exam knowing that you have done your best. Go into the exam knowing that your increased efforts will make a difference. Listen to those who had to make more than one attempt to pass successfully:

* "One word: Conquer. Owning the failure and being honest about my flaws. Embracing those flaws and conquering them on each subject. Also keeping my mind centered on the subject at hand not the overall big picture. The best thing . . . was the game plan and encouragement grounded in reality."[1]
* "After failing it once, it is really hard to convince yourself it isn't going to happen again. I know when I was studying the second time . . . and things clicked for me better . . . I would say to myself 'If I had only known that the first time I wouldn't have failed.' . . . When things made more sense the second time, it made it easier to think I was going to get it the second time."[2]
* "When I didn't pass the first time, I was very depressed. What kept me going were the words of encouragement from my professors. . . . Plus, I had to remind myself that I'd made it that far, with two very small children. If I could graduate, I could pass the stupid test."[3]
* "Am I a victim, or am I a survivor?"[4]
* "With bar passage rates declining, it has become easier to get scared of failing. But recognizing that a certain amount of microfailures are inevitable on the bar exam—a missed question, a forgotten issue—these microfailures can be incredibly generative during studying and should be embraced instead of avoided. [These microfailures] are only true failures when you don't learn from them, and with unwavering perseverance can be turned into successes. Collect the information about what questions are being answered correctly and incorrectly, why they were answered that way, and how to spot those issues on the test. Eventually you will get to a point where you know exactly how you are going to do and have the confidence from the data to back that up."[5]

---

1. Statement from S.P. (unsuccessful on first and second attempts, then passed).
2. Statement from L.H. (unsuccessful on first attempt, then passed).
3. Statement from P.R. (unsuccessful on first attempt, then passed).
4. Statement from J.R. (unsuccessful on first attempt, then passed).
5. Statement from B.W. (unsuccessful on first attempt, then passed).

- "You are smart, smarter than most people. You passed every law school exam and you didn't know all the answers then either. You are prepared, you put in the time. Focus on the question and do your best, your preparation will take over."[6]

## III. PERSONAL ISSUES

Life happens. It's unpredictable and unavoidable. Few things are under your control. Some of these were mentioned in Chapter 7: avoid working, avoid moving, etc. But most of life is not under your control. In February 2013, the test site of the Missouri bar exam was hit with a major snow storm. Being in the middle of the country, we can usually see our weather coming, and this would be a big one. Our applicants were told to travel the weekend before rather than the day before. All made it safely.

Then, during the exam, the power went out. Came on and went out again. The afternoon session was delayed. The applicants started and it went out again. When they finally started, the exam software failed. All the typists had to handwrite. The exam was not over until the early evening instead of the afternoon. They were hungry, anxious, and tired. All the applicants that worked with the plan in this book passed. They gave credit to their preparation and that they were not as exhausted as other takers. They had listened to the advice in this book and were ready.

On the other hand, on another prior testing date, an applicant's hotel had a fire in the middle of the night. The guests were all displaced to another hotel. That applicant did not fare well. He needed to still study the night before. He had not taken the advice to heart.

Another applicant's wife asked for a divorce ten days before the bar. Talk about sabotage! She had graduated two years earlier and was an anxious test taker herself. She was working at the firm where he had accepted an offer. She insisted he look for a different job right then and move out of their residence ASAP. And, she was keeping their dog. His whole life was turned around. It was a very tough time, emotionally. But, he persevered. He refused to move out and refused to renege on his employment with the firm. He had been running his game plan and was well prepared prior to her announcement. The bar actually motivated him to show her. He passed. And, he kept his dog.

Sometimes when life happens, it is a time to reevaluate your priorities. There will always be another test date. Spending time with a loved one who is terminally ill is more important than an exam. Most employers understand if you need to postpone. It is truly not the end of the world if you must postpone. Some states limit the number of times you can take the exam. Don't waste a try by letting a personal issue interfere; better to postpone.

As one applicant said, "[T]he bar exam is a test of how you handle real world situations, so relax and just do it one step at a time."[7]

---

6. Statement from T.M. (successful on first attempt, unsuccessful on first attempt in a second state, then passed the second state).

7. Statement from J.C. (overheard from another applicant during the snowed-in exam in February 2013).

# CHAPTER 9

# Mapping MBE Topics—Civil Procedure

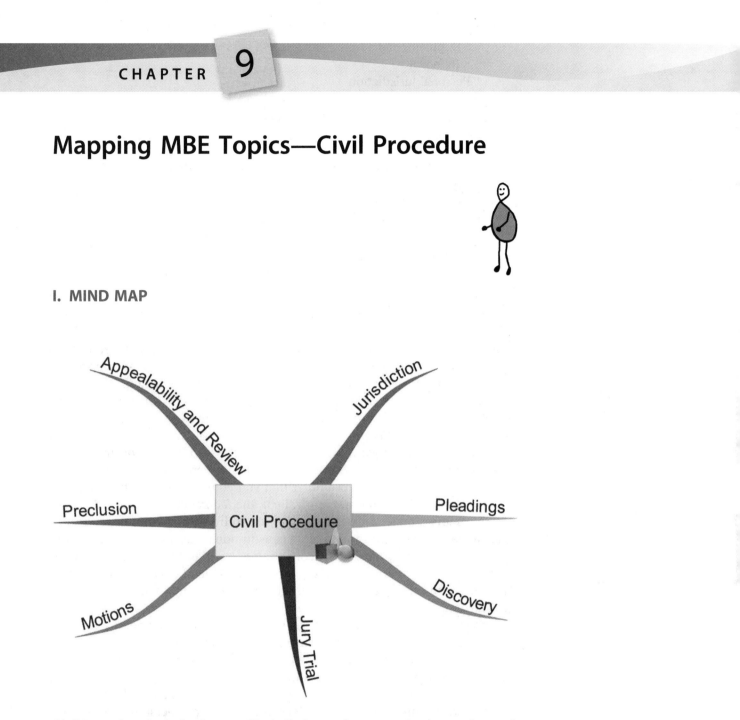

## I. MIND MAP

Civil Procedure includes issues of jurisdiction and process. Statutes, rules, and case law serve as its foundation. Jurisdiction is laid out by statutes. The Federal Rules of Civil Procedure govern most issues regarding process. Case law further develops and interprets both.

The mind map moves chronologically through the decision-making process from bringing a lawsuit to its conclusion. Essentially, the same mind map can be used for federal and state civil procedure:

- Jurisdiction and preliminary matters
  - Subject-matter jurisdiction
    - Original

- Supplemental
- Removal
  - Personal jurisdiction
  - Service of process
  - Venue v. transfer
- Pleadings
  - Joinder of claims
  - Joinder of parties
  - Amendments
- Discovery
- Jury trial
- Motions
- Preclusion
- Appealability and review

For civil procedure, **jurisdiction** means the power of the court. A court must have jurisdiction over the subject matter and jurisdiction over the person in order for any judgment it issues to be binding upon the parties. As to **subject-matter jurisdiction**, state courts have general jurisdiction while federal courts have limited jurisdiction. Always begin your rule statement for subject-matter jurisdiction with "Federal courts are courts of limited jurisdiction." Each claim brought in federal court must have an independent basis for jurisdiction. Objections to subject-matter jurisdiction can never be waived.

Subject-matter jurisdiction issues lend themselves well to practicing your essay organization as you always need to address both bases of jurisdiction. Always analyze both bases even if it is clear that one basis does or does not apply. You need to tell the examiner that you considered the other basis and your analysis is that it doesn't apply. First, the federal court has jurisdiction if the claim arises under federal law or is created by state law but depends on a substantial **federal question**, usually a constitutional question. Be clear that this basis of jurisdiction includes the constitution, laws, and treaties of the United States. This basis of jurisdiction is referred to as "federal question jurisdiction." A defense based on a federal question is insufficient to establish federal jurisdiction.

Second, the federal court also has jurisdiction based on **diversity jurisdiction**. This requires complete diversity of citizenship and over $75,000 in controversy. Complete diversity means that no single plaintiff may be a citizen of the same state as any single defendant. An individual's citizenship is determined by domicile. A corporation is a citizen of its state of incorporation and a citizen of a state where its principal place of business is located. A partnership or association is deemed a citizen of every state in which one of its members is a citizen. The plaintiff's view governs the amount in controversy and only the alleged amount governs. A claimant may aggregate claims against a single defendant, but not against multiple defendants. Multiple claimants cannot aggregate claims to meet the $75,000 minimum.

When the plaintiff brings more than one claim, analyze subject-matter jurisdiction for each claim as there must be a jurisdictional basis for each claim. If you find that no subject-matter jurisdiction exists for one claim, then consider **supplemental jurisdiction**. A federal court has discretion to consider a pure state law claim if there is a common nucleus of operative facts between the

---

### Order of Analysis Federal Subject-Matter Jurisdiction

**Overall Rule:** Federal courts are courts of limited jurisdiction.

**General Rule:** Federal courts may only hear cases that involve a federal question or are based on diversity jurisdiction.

> **Rule 1:** Federal courts have jurisdiction over claims arising under the constitution, laws, and treaties of the United States.
>
> > **Apply** federal question jurisdiction to facts.
>
> **Conclude** Issue 1: Federal question jurisdiction?
>
> **Rule 2:** Federal courts have jurisdiction over matters involving diverse citizens, where the amount in controversy is more than $75,000.
>
> > **Rule A:** Complete diversity is required, meaning no plaintiff and defendant can be citizens of the same state.
> >
> > (Note: May need further rule development if a corporation is one of the parties.)
> >
> > > **Apply** complete diversity requirements to facts.
> > >
> > > **Conclude** Sub-issue A: Complete diversity exists?
> >
> > **Rule B:** The amount in controversy must be more than $75,000. A claimant may aggregate claims against a single defendant, but not against multiple defendants. Multiple claimants cannot aggregate claims to meet the $75,000 minimum.
> >
> > > **Apply** amount in controversy requirement to facts.
> > >
> > > **Conclude** Sub-issue B: Amount in controversy exists?
> >
> > **Conclude:** Diversity of jurisdiction?

**Overall conclusion:** Federal subject-matter jurisdiction exists?

---

state law claim and the federal claim. If the federal claim is based on diversity jurisdiction, then only claims involving diverse parties may be added provided they arise from a common nucleus of operative facts, although they do not need to have their own $75,000 in controversy. If one claim is based on a federal question, then a state law claim with non-diverse parties may be brought under supplemental jurisdiction, again provided they arise from a common nucleus of operative facts.

Defendants in state court may **remove** an action to the federal court that geographically embraces the state court if the federal court would have jurisdiction, all defendants consent, and a notice of removal is filed within 30 days of the service of the state court complaint. Notice must be served on all plaintiffs and on the state court. When the basis of subject-matter jurisdiction is diversity of citizenship, no removal is allowed if any defendant is a citizen of the state where the action is pending. When the basis of subject-matter jurisdiction is federal question, this rule does not apply. A defendant cannot remove the claim to federal court if the only federal component is a federal law-based defense.

If federal jurisdiction does not exist, the plaintiff can seek a **remand** back to the state court within 30 days of the filing of the notice of removal.

**Personal jurisdiction** exists if the court has *in personam* jurisdiction over the parties, *in rem* jurisdiction over property that is the subject of the claim, or *quasi in rem* jurisdiction over property that is attached to satisfy judgment in the action. The plaintiff must establish personal jurisdiction over each defendant. Be on the lookout for MBE questions where different defendants may have different bases of personal jurisdiction. Objections to personal jurisdiction must be brought in the first responsive pleading or they will be waived.

*In personam* jurisdiction exists if a person is located within the state by either domicile or service. Domicile exists if the person resides within the state and has expressed the intent to remain there indefinitely. If a defendant is served with process while in the forum state, *in personam* jurisdiction exists even if his presence is temporary and even if his presence is unrelated to the lawsuit. If the defendant's presence in the forum state is solely due to force, fraud, or participation in another judicial proceeding, service may not establish jurisdiction.

*In personam* jurisdiction also exists if the person consents to jurisdiction. Consent can be express, implied, or waived:

* Express consent.
* Implied consent: State has a substantial interest in regulating nonresidents in a particular in-state activity—for example, traffic laws. Driving within a state results in implied consent to personal jurisdiction in that state for traffic violations.
* Waived: Defendant fails to raise the defense of lack of personal jurisdiction in an answer or first responsive pleading. Defendant does not waive jurisdiction if he appears in court to contest jurisdiction.

*In personam* jurisdiction also exists over nonresidents through the operation of a state's long-arm jurisdiction even if they did not consent. Personal jurisdiction exists if the law of the forum grants personal jurisdiction and the law of the forum is constitutional. A long-arm statute provides specific jurisdiction over the defendant who does specific activities enumerated in the statute. Typical provisions include transacting business within the state, entering contracts within the state, and committing a tortious act within the state.

The assertion of personal jurisdiction must also meet constitutional requirements. The issue is whether the defendant engaged in minimum contacts such that it would not offend traditional notions of fair play and substantial justice. The issue then becomes whether the defendant purposely availed itself of the benefits of the forum state.

Personal jurisdiction through *in rem* jurisdiction is based on the parties' interest in a particular piece of property located within the state. Although rarely used, MBE questions may ask about *quasi in rem* jurisdiction. *Quasi in rem* jurisdiction exists in actions involving attachment of real or personal property as a part of the relief requested. A minimum contacts analysis is also required for *quasi in rem* jurisdiction.

**Service of process** is proper if the method of process follows the forum's rules and the method is constitutional. Service is not required for the action to be considered commenced, but must occur within 120 days of the filing of the complaint. Proper methods of service include:

* Abode service
* Waiver
* Agent service
* State methods
* Personal service

A summons is served with a copy of the complaint. If the service of process or the process itself is insufficient, the defendant must raise that defense in its first responsive pleading or those defenses will be waived.

**Venue** operates as a limit on a plaintiff's choice of where to file. Even if a court has subject-matter and personal jurisdiction, the plaintiff must also bring its claim in the proper venue.

Venue is proper:

* where any defendant resides, if all defendants reside in that state;
* in the federal district where a substantial part of the claim arose or where the property is located; or
* where the defendant can be found provided the court has personal jurisdiction, if there is no other district in which the action may otherwise be brought.

If the venue is improper, that is, if the claim does not meet any of these bases, then the remedy is to file a motion to dismiss based on **improper venue** in the first responsive pleading. If not raised then, that defense will be waived.

If a defendant would prefer a different venue, even though the current venue is proper, then the remedy is to file a **motion for transfer**. A motion to transfer is based on the doctrine of *forum non conveniens*. For the convenience of the parties and witnesses and in the interest of justice, a district court may transfer a civil action to any other district court where the action might have been brought. Note that substantial deference is given to the plaintiff's choice of forum.

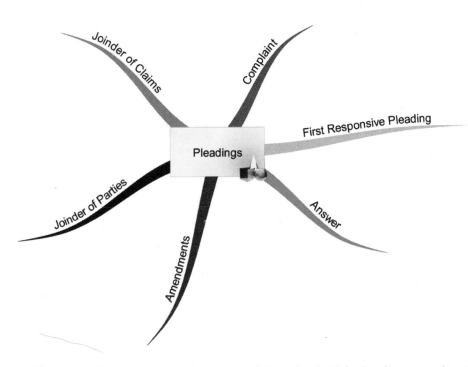

The general requirements for a complaint, the initial **pleading**, are that it must contain sufficient facts to place the adversary on notice of plausible claims. A claim for relief must include a short and plain statement of the jurisdiction, a statement of a claim that would entitle the claimant to relief, and a demand for relief. Legal conclusions in a complaint are disregarded as are "formulaic recitation of elements."[1] A party may set out alternative claims and make inconsistent claims or defenses.

Once served with a complaint, the defendant must file a **responsive motion** or an **answer**. Either a motion or an answer, whichever is filed first, is considered the first responsive pleading. The defendant has 21 days from the date of service of the complaint to file its first responsive pleading. The 21 days includes weekends and holidays. If the twenty-first day falls on a weekend or holiday, the first responsive pleading or answer must be filed on the next business day.

**Rule 12(b) defenses** must be filed within the first responsive pleading. If not, these defenses are waived. Rule 12(b) defenses include:

* Lack of personal jurisdiction
* Insufficient service of process or insufficient process
* Improper venue
* Failure to state a claim
* Failure to join an indispensable party

Rule 12(b) also includes the defense of lack of subject-matter jurisdiction. This defense is never waived. It can be raised at any time and can be raised by the court itself.

If the defendant does not file a motion to dismiss or if its motion to dismiss is denied, it must file an **answer** that must fairly and precisely admit or deny every allegation in the complaint. In addition, the answer must include the previous 12(b) defenses and all **affirmative defenses** or they are waived. The affirmative defenses under Rule 8(c)(1) include:

* accord and satisfaction,
* arbitration and award,
* assumption of risk,
* contributory negligence,
* discharge in bankruptcy,
* duress,
* estoppel,
* failure of consideration,
* fraud,
* illegality,
* injury by fellow servant,
* laches,
* licenses,
* payment,
* release,
* *res judicata*,
* Statute of Frauds,
* statute of limitations, and
* waiver.

The plaintiff may **amend** its complaint once as of right within 21 days of service upon the defendant. After that, the plaintiff must file a leave to amend, which is granted freely by the court when justice requires. The issues

---

1. *Ashcroft v. Iqbal*, 556 U.S. 662, 678 (2009).

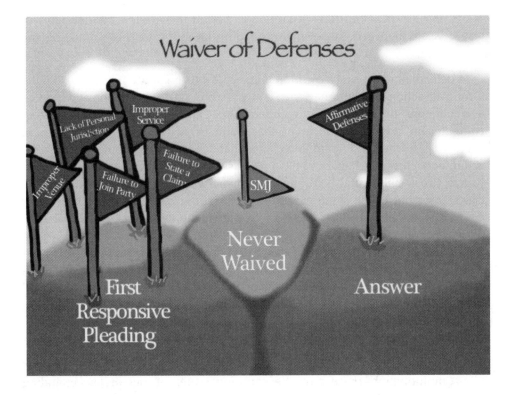

that arise with amending a complaint involve the relation back of amendments to conform to the statute of limitations. If the amendment is a new claim, then it relates back to the date of a timely-filed complaint if the new claim derives from the same transaction or occurrence as the earlier timely-filed complaint. If the amendment is a new party, relation back applies only if the amendment derives from the same transaction or occurrence, and the new party acquired knowledge within 120 days of the earlier timely-filed complaint that but for a mistake in name it would have been sued.

**Joinder of parties** and **joinder of claims** are frequently tested topics. The plaintiff may join parties to the same lawsuit if the claims involving those parties derive from the same transaction or occurrence or at least the same series of common transactions or occurrences. The plaintiff must join indispensable parties where there would be prejudice to any parties' right to a full and fair adjudication, including leaving an existing party subject to a substantial risk of incurring multiple inconsistent obligations.

The plaintiff may join as many claims as they have against a defendant regardless of whether there is any connection between those claims.

Third parties outside of the lawsuit may join a suit and bring claims. These actions are remembered by the three "I's":

- **Impleader**—Defendant may bring in a third party if that party may be liable to Defendant for all or part of Defendant's liability to Plaintiff.
- **Interpleader**—The holder of a common fund may file a lawsuit as a plaintiff and join as defendants all rival claimants to its common fund.
- **Intervention**—A non-party moves to enter into a lawsuit.
  - As of right: Non-party's interest will be adversely affected by the lawsuit, and that right is not protected by the parties.

- Permissive: Court has discretion to permit if there is a commonality of issues between those in the ongoing lawsuit and those affecting the intervener.

A defendant may bring a **counterclaim** against the plaintiff. If it arises from the same transaction or occurrence, then it must be brought in that action and is called a mandatory or compulsory counterclaim. Failure to bring a mandatory counterclaim results in waiver of that claim. A defendant has a permissive counterclaim when it seeks to join claims that do not arise from the same transaction or occurrence. Failure to file a permissive counterclaim does not result in waiver. **Cross-claims** may be brought by any party against any co-party when the claim arises out of the same transaction or occurrence as the original claim or counterclaim. The court has subject-matter jurisdiction under supplemental jurisdiction for compulsory counterclaims and cross-claims if they arise out of the same transaction or occurrence in the absence of an independent basis for federal jurisdiction. If a claim is only a permissive counterclaim, then no supplemental jurisdiction exists because it did not arise out of the same transaction or occurrence and independent grounds for federal jurisdiction must exist.

**Class actions** are actions in which a named plaintiff represents a class of commonly-situated absent plaintiffs. The certification requirements for class actions can be remembered by the acronym CANT:

- **Commonality**—there must be common issues of fact or law including common claims and common injuries.
- **Adequacy**—the named plaintiff and class counsel lawyers must fairly and adequately represent the class.
- **Numbers**—the class must be so numerous that joinder of them all would be impracticable (at least 40).
- **Typicality**—the claims of the named plaintiff are typical of the class.

Additional requirements are predominance and superiority. Common questions must predominate over individual questions with class representation superior to other methods of adjudicating the controversy. Thus, a court is not likely to grant class certification where multiple state laws are involved and individual claims require separate investigation. Constitutional requirements include notice to the class and a chance to opt out if the claim involves money.

**Discovery** includes both mandatory disclosures and the more traditional means of discovery. Mandatory disclosures are required within two weeks of the initial discovery conference. A party has a duty to supplement the mandatory disclosures or be subject to the exclusion of that evidence at trial. The mandatory disclosures are:

- All supporting witnesses
- All supporting documents
- A damages computation
- Relevant insurance coverage

The traditional means of discovery are:

- Depositions: Direct questioning of a party or witness under oath.
- Interrogatories: Written questions that must be answered by another party in writing under oath within 30 days. Only served on parties, not witnesses.
- Request for admissions: Any request that is admitted is deemed established for all purposes in the litigation.

- Production of documents: A request to a party to produce documents or property for inspection and copying.
- Request for physical or mental examination: Only when a person's condition is in controversy. Advance court approval with a showing of "good cause" is required.

The scope of discovery is relevant information that is not privileged and it need not be admissible at trial. Parties can object to the requests for discovery or request a protective order.

One privilege that frequently arises in discovery is the **work-product doctrine**, which covers any material that an attorney or someone at her discretion prepared for litigation and was not in the ordinary course of business. If the material includes an attorney's mental impressions, it is never discoverable. All other forms of work product are discoverable only with a showing of substantial need and undue hardship. Sanctions for refusing to produce discovery can range from not being able to use the withheld information at trial to the striking of a claim to the dismissal of the case.

A party has a constitutional right to a **jury trial** if its claim primarily seeks monetary damages. The party must file a written demand within 14 days of service of the complaint. Each party is entitled to strike potential jurors for cause. Otherwise, each party receives three peremptory challenges that may be used to strike jurors without cause.

**Motions** are a major part of litigation and the practice of law. Focus on four critical motions:

- Summary judgment:
  - Filed within 30 days after close of discovery.
  - May be granted if there are no genuine issues of material fact and the movant is entitled to judgment as a matter of law.
  - Movant must produce evidence to support each element of the cause of action.
  - All inferences are drawn in favor of the non-movant.
- Judgment as matter of law: Formerly called a directed verdict, the motion is made at the close of the opponent's case. The grounds are that there is a legally insufficient evidentiary basis from which a reasonable jury could find for the non-moving party.
- Default judgment: Entered against a defendant who failed to respond to the complaint in a timely manner.
- Post-trial motions:
  - Renewed motion for judgment as a matter of law: Formerly called a judgment notwithstanding the verdict, the motion is made within 28 days of judgment. The basis of the motion is identical to that made at the close of the opponent's case.
  - Motion for new trial: Also made within 28 days, this motion will be granted in the court's discretion if either the errors at trial affected the parties' substantive trial rights or the verdict was against the manifest weight of the evidence.

**Preclusion** means that parties are barred from relitigating claims or issues that they have already fully and fairly litigated to a final judgment on the merits. These doctrines are intended to promote judicial economy and the finality of judgments. In essence, these doctrines mean that once a case has reached a final judgment, that case and its related claims and issues have been decided permanently and are not eligible for relitigation. ***Res judicata*** or claim preclusion means that a claim cannot be relitigated if the claim arises between the same parties or those in privity with them; it arises out of the same transaction or occurrence; and that the court determined the claim on the merits and had proper subject-matter and personal jurisdiction. *Res judicata* is an affirmative defense that is waived if not asserted in an answer.

**Collateral estoppel** or issue preclusion refers to an issue that cannot be relitigated. Collateral estoppel may not be used against someone who was not a party to the previous action. Issue preclusion may be used offensively by one who was not a party to the first action against one who was a party in the earlier suit. Courts are reluctant to permit offensive use of issue preclusion and will look to see if the plaintiff in the second suit could have joined the first action; whether there are procedural opportunities available to the defendant in the second suit that were unavailable in the earlier action; and whether the defendant had incentive to litigate the issue in the first action.

A judgment is **appealable** when it is a final order entered by a lower court. The party seeking to appeal must file its notice of appeal within 30 days from the entry of judgment. A **final judgment** is one that disposes of all issues as to all parties. If it is a partial final order that resolves only some of the claims, but not all of the claims, then an interlocutory appeal can be requested. Both the trial court and the appellate court must find that there is doubt as to a controlling legal issue and that appellate review would advance the litigation.

Within one year of a judgment, a party can file a **motion for relief from a judgment**. The requirements can be remembered by the acronym MEND:

- **Merit**
- **Equity**
- **New** facts
- **Due diligence**

Post-Trial Motion Timing

**EXAM TIP**
Keep careful track of timing when any civil procedure question contains dates or references to time, such as "30 days later." They are there for a reason and are not mere fillers.

## II. MBE STRATEGIES[2]

Civil Procedure was added to the MBE portion of the exam beginning with the February 2015 bar exam. As such, few actual bar questions are available to review for specific strategies.

Based on prior testing areas in essay questions, certain strategies are also likely to be effective on MBE questions.

Subject-matter jurisdiction issues are plentiful and time spent studying these rules will be well worth it. Keep the parties straight, particularly when additional parties and claims are added. Additional parties or claims inevitably result in supplemental jurisdiction issues. Supplemental jurisdiction is likely to apply to compulsory counterclaims; additional parties to a compulsory counterclaim; impleader of third-party defendants for claims of third-party plaintiffs and vice versa, but not for claims by the original plaintiff against the third-party defendants; and multiple plaintiffs joined under Rule 20 for amount in controversy purposes only.

Supplemental jurisdiction does not apply to impleader of third-party defendants for purposes of solving lack of diversity or lack of amount in controversy problems in claims by the original plaintiff against the third-party defendant and Rule 20 joinder of co-plaintiffs or co-defendants for solving lack of complete diversity.

Look for personal jurisdiction issues whenever the defendant is being sued in a state other than her home state.

Certification of class actions requires commonality. Thus, look for plaintiffs suffering different harms. Employment discrimination class actions may suffer this flaw.

A non-movant cannot establish a genuine issue of material fact to defeat summary judgment by relying solely on his own pleadings. But the non-movant is not required to submit additional proof if the movant's own materials establish a genuine issue of material fact.

An interlocutory appeal is more likely allowed for injunctions, either granting or refusing to grant, and collateral orders. Look for collateral order issues with orders granting or denying immunity when dealing with added parties or added claims. A collateral order interlocutory appeal requires that:

- The court has reached a final decision on the matter,
- The matter is separate from the merits of the claim,
- The matter is too important to be denied appellate review entirely, and
- Deferring appeal until entry of final judgment on the merits of the claim would prevent the review from being effective.

Also watch for problems with the timing of motions and of pleadings. For example, did the defendant file its first responsive pleading or answer in time or was it late such that the defendant waived its Rule 12(b) defenses? Did the defendant fail to timely file a post-trial motion or a motion for relief of judgment? What are the consequences of failing to timely file? Was amending the complaint sufficient to trigger the doctrine of relation back?

---

2. Some of these strategies are from Steven L. Emanuel, *Strategies & Tactics for the MBE* 1-24 (6th ed. 2016).

Carefully lay out a timeline of what happened when. This is critical for the first responsive pleading, the answer, post-trial motions, and the notice of appeal, among others. Memorize the time requirements for each. Include those requirements in your mind maps. You could even make a chart of all the time requirements to help you memorize them.

Your mind maps will be more than adequate to help you through both MBE and essay questions.

## III. ESSAY PRACTICE QUESTION[3]

A woman and a man have both lived their entire lives in State A. The man once went to a gun show in State B where he bought a gun. Otherwise, neither the woman nor the man had ever left State A until the following events occurred.

The woman and the man went hunting for wild turkey at a State A game preserve. The man was carrying the gun he had purchased in State B. The man had permanently disabled the gun's safety features to be able to react more quickly to a turkey sighting. The man dropped the gun and it accidentally fired, inflicting a serious chest wound on the woman. The woman was immediately flown to a hospital in neighboring State C, where she underwent surgery.

One week after the shooting accident, the man traveled to State C for business and took the opportunity to visit the woman in the hospital. During the visit, the woman's attorney handed the man the summons and complaint in a suit the woman had initiated against the man in the United States District Court for the District of State C. Two days later, the woman was released from the hospital and returned home to State A where she spent weeks recovering.

The woman's complaint alleges separate claims against the man: 1) a state-law negligence claim and 2) a federal claim under the Federal Gun Safety Act (Safety Act). The Safety Act provides a cause of action for individuals harmed by gun owners who alter the safety features of a gun that has traveled in interstate commerce. The Safety Act caps damages at $100,000 per incident, but does not preempt state causes of action. The woman's complaint seeks damages of $100,000 on the Safety Act claim and $120,000 on the state-law negligence claim. Both sets of damages are sought as compensation for the physical suffering the woman experienced and the medical costs the woman incurred as a result of the shooting.

The man has moved to dismiss the complaint, asserting (a) lack of personal jurisdiction, (b) lack of subject-matter jurisdiction, and (c) improper venue. State C's jurisdictional statutes provide that state courts may exercise personal jurisdiction "to the limits allowed by the United States Constitution."

With respect to each asserted basis for dismissal, should the man's motion to dismiss be granted? Explain.

---

3. The Multistate Bar Examination ("MBE[®]") questions, the Multistate Essay Examination ("MEE[®]") questions, and excerpts from the Multistate Performance Tests ("MPT[®]") have been reprinted by permission from the NCBE[®]. Copyright© by the National Conference of Bar Examiners. All rights reserved.

## IV. MBE PRACTICE QUESTIONS[4]

### Question 1

An entrepreneur from State A decided to sell hot sauce to the public, labeling it "Best Hot Sauce."

A company incorporated in State B and headquartered in State C sued the entrepreneur in federal court in State C. The complaint sought $50,000 in damages and alleged that the entrepreneur's use of the name "Best Hot Sauce" infringed the company's federal trademark. The entrepreneur filed an answer denying the allegations, and the parties began discovery. Six months later, the entrepreneur moved to dismiss for lack of subject-matter jurisdiction.

Should the court grant the entrepreneur's motion?

(A) No, because the company's claim arises under federal law.

(B) No, because the entrepreneur waived the right to challenge subject-matter jurisdiction by not raising the issue initially by motion or in the answer.

(C) Yes, because although the claim arises under federal law, the amount in controversy is not satisfied.

(D) Yes, because although there is diversity, the amount in controversy is not satisfied.

### Question 2

An investor from State A filed an action against his State B stockbroker in federal court in State A. The summons and complaint were served at the stockbroker's office in State B, where the process server handed the documents to the stockbroker's administrative assistant.

The stockbroker has answered the complaint, asserting the defense of improper service of process. Assume that both states' requirements for service of process are identical to the requirements of the Federal Rules of Civil Procedure.

Is the court likely to dismiss the action for improper service of process?

(A) No, because service was made on a person of suitable age found at the stockbroker's place of employment.

(B) No, because the stockbroker waived her claim for improper service of process by asserting it in her answer.

(C) Yes, because an individual defendant may not be served by delivering process to a third party found at the defendant's place of employment.

(D) Yes, because the process of State A courts is not effective in State B.

### Question 3

A truck driver from State A and a bus driver from State B were involved in a collision in State B that injured the truck driver. The truck driver filed a federal diversity action in State B based on negligence, seeking $100,000 in damages from the bus driver.

What law of negligence should the court apply?

(A) The court should apply the federal common law of negligence.

(B) The court should apply the negligence law of State A, the truck driver's state of citizenship.

---

4. *Id.*

(C) The court should consider the negligence law of both State A and State B and apply the law that the court believes most appropriately governs negligence in this action.

(D) The court should determine which state's negligence law a state court in State B would apply and apply that law in this action.

## Question 4

A patent holder brought a patent infringement action in federal court against a licensee of the patent. The patent holder believed that a jury would be more sympathetic to his claims than a judge, and asked his lawyer to obtain a jury trial.

What should the lawyer do to secure the patent holder's right to a jury trial?

(A) File and serve a complaint that includes a jury trial demand.

(B) File and serve a jury trial demand at the close of discovery.

(C) File and serve a jury trial demand within 30 days after the close of the pleadings.

(D) Make a jury trial demand at the initial pretrial conference.

## Question 5

A consumer from State A filed a $100,000 products liability action in federal court against a manufacturer incorporated and with its principal place of business in State B. The consumer claimed that a flaw in the manufacturer's product had resulted in severe injuries to the consumer. In its answer, the manufacturer asserted a third-party complaint against the product designer, also incorporated and with its principal place of business in State B. Believing that the consumer had sued the wrong defendant, the manufacturer claimed both that the designer was solely responsible for the flaw that had led to the consumer's injuries and that the manufacturer was not at fault.

The designer is aware that the manufacturer did not follow all of the designer's specifications when making the product.

Which of the following arguments is most likely to achieve the designer's goal of dismissal of the third-party complaint?

(A) The court does not have subject-matter jurisdiction over the third-party complaint, because both the manufacturer and the designer are citizens of State B.

(B) The manufacturer failed to obtain the court's leave to file the third-party complaint.

(C) The manufacturer's failure to follow the designer's specifications caused the flaw that resulted in the consumer's injuries.

(D) The manufacturer's third-party complaint failed to state a proper third-party claim.

## Question 6

A wholesaler brought a federal diversity action against a large pharmaceutical company for breach of contract. During jury selection, one potential juror stated that five years earlier he had been an employee of the company and still owned several hundred shares of its stock. In response to questioning from the judge, the potential juror stated that he could fairly consider the evidence in the case.

The wholesaler's attorney has asked the judge to strike the potential juror for cause.

Should the judge strike the potential juror for cause?

(A) No, because the potential juror said that he could fairly consider the evidence in the case.

(B) No, because the wholesaler's attorney could use a peremptory challenge to strike the potential juror.

(C) Yes, because other potential jurors still remain available for the jury panel.

(D) Yes, because the potential juror is presumed to be biased because of his relationship to the company.

## Question 7

After being fired, a woman sued her former employer in federal court, alleging that her supervisor had discriminated against her on the basis of her sex. The woman's complaint included a lengthy description of what the supervisor had said and done over the years, quoting his telephone calls and emails to her and her own emails to the supervisor's manager asking for help.

The employer moved for summary judgment, alleging that the woman was a pathological liar who had filed the action and included fictitious documents in revenge for having been fired. Because the woman's attorney was at a lengthy out-of-state trial when the summary-judgment motion was filed, he failed to respond to it. The court therefore granted the motion in a one-line order and entered final judgment. The woman has appealed.

Is the appellate court likely to uphold the trial court's ruling?

(A) No, because the complaint's allegations were detailed and specific.

(B) No, because the employer moved for summary judgment on the basis that the woman was not credible, creating a factual dispute.

(C) Yes, because the woman's failure to respond to the summary-judgment motion means that there was no sworn affidavit to support her allegations and supporting documents.

(D) Yes, because the woman's failure to respond to the summary-judgment motion was a default giving sufficient basis to grant the motion.

## Question 8

A man brought a federal diversity action against his insurance company, alleging that the company had breached its duty under his insurance policy by refusing to pay for his medical expenses resulting from a mountain-biking accident.

At the jury trial, the man presented evidence that he had paid all premiums on the insurance policy and that the policy covered personal-injury-related medical expenses arising from accidents. After he rested his case, the company presented evidence that a provision of the policy excluded payment for injury-related expenses resulting from an insured's "unduly risky" behavior. The company also presented a witness who testified that the accident had occurred in an area where posted signs warned bikers not to enter. The man did not cross-examine the witness.

After resting its case, the company moved for judgment as a matter of law.

Should the court grant the motion?

(A) No, because a motion for judgment as a matter of law must first be made at the close of the plaintiff's case-in-chief.

(B) No, because whether the man's behavior was unduly risky is a question of fact for the jury to resolve.

(C) Yes, because the company's uncontradicted evidence of the man's unduly risky behavior means that no reasonable jury could find that the policy covers his injuries.

(D) Yes, because the man waived his right to rebut the company's evidence by not addressing the "unduly risky" policy provision in his case-in-chief.

## Question 9

A motorcyclist was involved in a collision with a truck. The motorcyclist sued the truck driver in state court for damage to the motorcycle. The jury returned a verdict for the truck driver, and the court entered judgment. The motorcyclist then sued the company that employed the driver and owned the truck in federal court for personal-injury damages, and the company moved to dismiss based on the state-court judgment.

If the court grants the company's motion, what is the likely explanation?

(A) Claim preclusion (res judicata) bars the motorcyclist's action against the company.

(B) Issue preclusion (collateral estoppel) establishes the company's lack of negligence.

(C) The motorcyclist violated the doctrine of election of remedies.

(D) The state-court judgment is the law of the case.

## Question 10

A student at a private university sued the university in federal court for negligence after he fell from scaffolding in a university-owned theater building. At trial, after briefing from both parties, the court permitted the jury to hear testimony that there had been several previous accidents in the same building. The jury found for the student, and the university appealed. One of the university's arguments on appeal is that the testimony about the previous accidents should have been excluded as irrelevant and highly prejudicial.

Which standard of review applies to this argument?

(A) Abuse of discretion.
(B) Clearly erroneous.
(C) De novo.
(D) Harmless error.

# CHAPTER 10

# Mapping MBE Topics—Constitutional Law

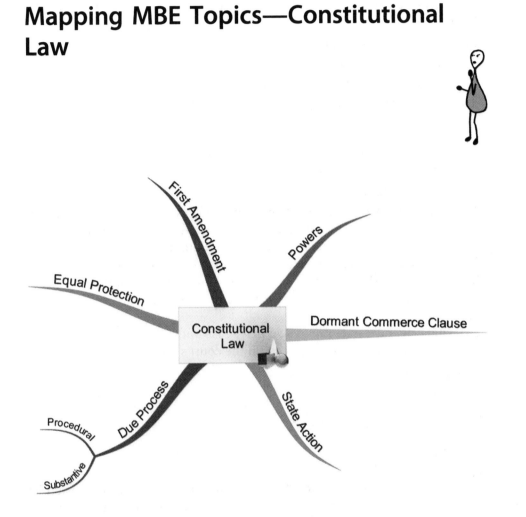

## I. MIND MAP

Constitutional Law affects virtually every area of law. Federal law is "the supreme law of the land" and includes every federal statute, every federal regulation, and every federal treaty. A hierarchy of authority exists such that the Constitution[1] is at the top and all law is below it. This hierarchy of law means that every law must not conflict with the Constitution. In addition, the Constitution sets the parameters for our system of federalism—that is, the co-existence of the federal government with state governments. Specifically, the Constitution sets forth the federal government's powers. The Tenth Amendment provides that powers not

---

1. All references to "Constitution" will be to the federal constitution unless otherwise stated.

delegated to the federal government nor prohibited by the Constitution to the States are reserved to the States.[2]

No need exists to memorize the Constitution word for word for the bar exam. What is needed is to understand the powers of the branches of the federal government, to understand the protections of due process and equal protection, and to achieve a sound understanding of the First Amendment. Use your mind map:

- Powers of Each Branch of Government
- Dormant Commerce Clause
- State Action
- Due Process
  - Procedural Due Process
  - Substantive Due Process
- Equal Protection
- First Amendment

The drafters of the Constitution were concerned with creating a government with unfettered power. Thus, the Constitution limits the power of the federal government. The Constitution authorizes specific **powers** to each branch of government. Actions by each branch are valid only if authorized by the Constitution.

The **judiciary's power** emanates from Article III and from *Marbury v. Madison*,[3] which established judicial review. Under *Marbury*, the Court held that the Constitution is "law" and that the judiciary's province and duty was to declare what the law is.

The judiciary does not have to hear every case under its subject-matter jurisdiction. Certain limitations are placed on the court's jurisdiction:

- Case or controversy
- Mootness
- Ripeness
- Abstention
- Standing
- Political questions

First, jurisdiction is limited to a "**case or controversy**"—a real and substantial dispute that touches the legal relations of parties with adverse interests and that can be resolved by a judicial decree of a conclusive character. The court does not give advisory opinions. Next, if the matter has already been resolved, the case will be dismissed as moot. Ripeness bars consideration of claims before they have fully developed. The court may abstain or refuse to hear a particular case when there are undecided issues of state law presented. Then, the state court resolves the issues of state law first, perhaps making a decision on the constitutional issue unnecessary. This is called abstention. A person litigating a constitutional question must have standing. To prove standing, the litigant must show injury-in-fact, causation, and redressability.

---

2. U.S. Const. amend. X.
3. 5 U.S. (1 Cranch) 137 (1803).

The **executive branch's powers** rest in the president as Chief Executive and Commander-in-Chief. The executive branch's power extends to international affairs. As Chief Executive, the president has appointment power to nominate and appoint ambassadors, justices of the Supreme Court, and all other officers of the United States.[4] The president also has **veto power** over Congress's legislation. The president has ten days in which to act upon legislation. If the president fails to act, the proposed legislation becomes law. The president can pocket veto a bill passed within ten days of the end of the congressional term by not signing it. Congress has the power to override a veto by a two-thirds vote of both houses of Congress. A line-item veto has been held unconstitutional. Only Congress has the power to amend legislation to delete provisions.

Congress can enact legislation that delegates **rulemaking power** to an executive or administrative agency in designated areas. This is an exception to the general rule that the executive branch does not "make law."

Additional powers vested in the executive branch include the **pardon power** and **executive privilege**. As Commander-in-Chief, the president also has the power to deploy military forces, but does not have the power to declare war. In international affairs, the president has the power to make treaties with foreign nations, which require the consent of two-thirds of the Senate before enactment.

Primarily, the **legislature's power** is to make laws. Incidental to that power is the right to conduct investigations and hearings, consider matters upon which legislation may be enacted, and do all other things "necessary and proper" to the enacting of legislation.[5] The Necessary and Proper Clause gives Congress the implied power "to make all Laws which shall be necessary and proper for carrying into Execution the foregoing Powers. . . ."[6]

As the legislative branch, Congress has a host of specific powers:

* Legislative
* Commerce
* Taxing
* Spending
* War and defense
* Investigatory
* Property
* Eminent domain
* Admiralty
* Bankruptcy
* Postal
* Copyright and patent
* Speech and debate
* Civil War amendments

Detailed knowledge of each power is not necessary to achieve the 75% competence you need to pass the bar exam. Focus your efforts on the legislative

---

4. U.S. Const. art. II, § 2.
5. U.S. Const. art. I, § 1.
6. *Id.* § 8.

power, the commerce power, and the taxing power. Eminent domain is addressed under takings in Chapter 14.

The **Commerce Clause** and its later interpretations by the Supreme Court gives Congress the power to regulate:

- channels of interstate commerce, such as highways, waterways, and air traffic;
- instrumentalities of interstate commerce, such as cars, trucks, ships, and airplanes; and
- activities that have a "substantial economic effect" upon interstate commerce.

Under the substantially effects test, Congress must show that the regulated activity is economic in nature and that the regulated activity—when taken cumulatively throughout the nation—has a substantial effect on commerce.

States may regulate local transactions affecting interstate commerce as long as Congress has not enacted legislation. This state power is subject to certain limitations. These limitations are known as the **Dormant Commerce Clause**.

If a state law discriminates on its face between in-state and out-of-state economic actors, the state must show that the regulation serves a compelling state interest, and the regulation is narrowly tailored to serve that interest. If the state law merely incidentally burdens interstate commerce, the state must show that the regulation serves an important state interest and the burden on interstate commerce is not excessive in relation to the interest served.

Congress has the power to lay and **collect taxes**, duties, imposts, and excises.[7] A congressional act purporting to be a tax should be upheld as a valid exercise of the taxing power provided that it does, in fact, raise revenue—an objective standard—or that it was intended to raise revenue—a subjective standard. Congress can use its taxing power to achieve a regulatory effect as long as Congress has the power to regulate the activity taxed.

State taxation of interstate commerce is permissible as long as the tax does not discriminate against or unduly burden interstate commerce. In reviewing a state tax of interstate commerce, courts generally require that:

- there must be a substantial nexus between the activity taxed and the taxing state;
- the tax must be fairly apportioned;
- the tax must not discriminate against interstate commerce; and
- the tax must be fairly related to the services provided by the taxing state.

The **Supremacy Clause** provides that a federal law will supersede any state law with which it is in direct conflict. Thus, the federal law preempts the state law in an area in which the exercise of federal power is constitutional. For example, Congress passed legislation in the 1960s mandating warnings on cigarette packaging. As a result, states cannot demand different warnings as the federal legislation preempts state legislation.

Before analyzing any constitutional violation, you must show that there is government action and not action by a private citizen or entity. This **state action**

---

7. *Id.*

requirement refers to actions by either the federal or state government. This requirement is based on the Fourteenth and Fifteenth Amendments. Therefore, analyzing whether a state action exists is the first step for both MBE and essay questions.

Private actors may be found to be state actors when the private entity is carrying on activities traditionally and exclusively performed by the government or where the government and private entity are so closely related that the action by the private party fairly can be treated as action by the government.

Originally, the **Bill of Rights** applied only to the federal government. The Court has since interpreted the Fourteenth Amendment to apply the Bill of Rights to states by holding that fundamental rights are not privileges and immunities of national citizenship. For an essay question, always include how an amendment applies to the states through the Fourteenth Amendment.

The second portion of the Fourteenth Amendment is the **Due Process Clause**. The Due Process Clause (and the Equal Protection Clause) protects the rights of "persons," not just "citizens." Corporations and aliens are considered "persons." Corporations do not, however, have the privilege against self-incrimination.

The Fifth and Fourteenth Amendments protect against the deprivation of life, liberty, or property without due process of law. Thus, an individual is entitled to certain safeguards that include some form of notice and a meaningful hearing within a reasonable time. This is known as **procedural due process**. Protected liberty interests include freedom from bodily restraints, physical punishment, and commitment to a mental institution. Protected property interests include public education, welfare benefits, retention of driver's license, public employment, prejudgment garnishment, forfeiture of property, and business licensing. Without question, capital punishment is a deprivation of a life interest. As such, rigorous due process protections are employed. The Court has addressed other life interests such as abortion or right-to-die situations under other provisions of the Constitution.

For an economic regulation, **substantive due process** requires a more deferential standard than the standard for fundamental rights regulations. As such, an economic regulation will be upheld if it is rationally related to a legitimate government interest. But when evaluating governmental regulations that affect fundamental rights of personhood, either **strict scrutiny** review or other forms of heightened scrutiny are used. These fundamental rights include the:

- right to travel,
- right to vote, and
- right to privacy.

Privacy rights may be remembered by the acronym CAMPERS:

- **C**ontraceptives
- **A**bortion
- **M**arriage
- **P**rocreation
- Private **E**ducation
- Family **R**elations
- **S**exual relations (meaning private adult consensual activity[8])

---

8. *Lawrence v. Texas*, 539 U.S. 558, 578 (2003) (Kennedy, J.) (holding that private adult consensual activity is a substantive due process liberty right, not a privacy right).

**Strict Scrutiny Applies in Equal Protection Analysis and in Other Contexts**

The guarantee of substantive due process assures that a law will be fair and reasonable, not arbitrary. Use substantive due process review when the law affects the rights of all persons with respect to the specific activity. Use equal protection when a law affects the rights of some persons with respect to a specific activity. A state statute must be involved for equal protection to be implicated.

**Equal protection** uses different standards of review depending upon the classification in the statute. Strict scrutiny puts the burden of persuasion on the government to prove that the measure being challenged is necessary to further a compelling governmental interest. In an equal protection analysis, strict scrutiny applies to suspect classifications—race, alienage, and national origin. In other contexts, strict scrutiny applies to the deprivation of fundamental rights, First Amendment rights, and access to courts.

**Intermediate scrutiny** also places the burden of persuasion on the government to prove that the measure being challenged is substantially related to the achievement of an important governmental interest. "Substantially related" means an exceedingly persuasive justification must be shown. Intermediate scrutiny applies to quasi-suspect classifications—gender and illegitimacy.

> **EXAM TIP**
>
> If a federal statute is used in a question, any response that implicates equal protection is automatically incorrect.

**Rational basis scrutiny** places the burden of persuasion on the plaintiff. The plaintiff must show that the measure being challenged serves no legitimate government interest or is not rationally related to any legitimate interest. Rational relationship means that the law cannot be arbitrary or unreasonable. Rational basis review applies to all classifications not falling under strict or intermediate scrutiny including classifications based on age, poverty, wealth, disability, and the need for necessities of life such as food, shelter, clothing, and medical care. As this is a more deferential standard, rarely does a regulation not meet rational basis scrutiny.

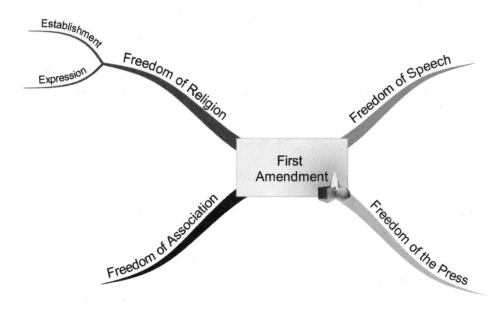

Focus your study of the **First Amendment** on freedom of religion, freedom of speech, freedom of the press, and freedom of association. **Freedom of religion** includes both the establishment of religion and the free exercise of religion. When analyzing an **establishment clause** issue, the first step is whether the law is a sect preference. All sect preference laws are subject to strict scrutiny analysis. Always include this rule in an essay answer. These are easy, low-hanging fruit points and they show the examiners that you know there is a difference between an explicit sect preference statute and one that is not.

If there is no explicit sect preference, then the Court analyzes the legislation or government program under the *Lemon* test:[9]

* The statute must have a secular legislative purpose;
* The principal or primary effect or purpose must neither advance nor inhibit religion; and
* The statute must not foster an excessive government entanglement with religion.

As a general rule, religious activities at public schools violate the Establishment Clause. Most government aid to religious schools is unconstitutional. If the program provides aid to all elementary and secondary school students including those attending parochial schools, however, then the program "passes" the *Lemon* test. Similarly, holiday displays on government property are generally permissible if they do not favor one religion over another.

Under the **Free Exercise Clause** of the First Amendment, religious beliefs are absolutely protected. The government may not punish an individual by denying benefits or imposing burdens based on religious belief.

Under the **Freedom of Speech Clause** of the First Amendment, "Congress shall make no law . . . abridging the freedom of speech. . . ."[10] The government may not censor all categories of speech or engage in content-based

---

9. *Lemon v. Kurtzman*, 403 U.S. 602, 612-13 (1971).
10. U.S. Const. amend. I.

discrimination with some exceptions. Regulations are allowed if they pass strict scrutiny. Exceptions to the ban on government censorship include:

- Conduct-based regulation: If the regulation creates an incidental burden on speech, it is allowed if it furthers an important or substantial government interest unrelated to the suppression of free expression, and the incidental restriction on speech is no greater than is essential to the furtherance of that interest.
- Government as speaker: When the government is the speaker rather than a private actor, the government may discriminate based on the content of the speech.
- Unprotected speech:
  - Speech that advocates violence or unlawful action:
    - Speech "is directed to inciting or producing imminent lawless action and is likely to incite or produce such action."[11]
  - Fighting words:
    - Words likely to incite acts of immediate physical retaliation that are more than annoying or offensive. There must be a genuine likelihood of imminent violence.
  - Hostile audience speech:
    - Speech that elicits an immediate violent response against the speaker by an audience may be grounds for prosecution.
  - Obscene speech—three-part test:
    - An average person applying contemporary community standards would find that the work, taken as a whole, appeals to a prurient interest;
    - The work depicts or describes, in a patently offensive way, sexual conduct specifically defined by state law; and
    - The work, taken as a whole, lacks serious literary, artistic, political, or scientific value.
  - Defamatory speech:
    - Constitutional restrictions on what is considered defamatory speech apply where the plaintiff is either a public official or public figure or where the statement involves a matter of public concern.
    - Then, the plaintiff must prove actual malice; that is, knowledge of falsity or reckless disregard of the truth or falsity of the statement.[12]

Certain categories of speech receive lower levels of protection:

- Commercial speech:
- Still highly protected, but not protected if false or deceptive or if related to unlawful activity. The government can regulate the speech only if the regulation:
  - Serves a substantial governmental interest;
  - Directly advances the substantial governmental interest; and
  - Is not more extensive than is necessary to serve that interest.
  - Sexual speech: Regulation must serve a substantial government interest and leave open reasonable alternative channels of communication.

---

11. *Brandenburg v. Ohio*, 395 U.S. 444, 447 (1969).
12. *New York Times v. Sullivan*, 376 U.S. 254, 280 (1964).

Regulations of time, place, and manner of speech are allowed. These restraints apply to public areas such as streets, sidewalks, and parks. A three-part test is used to determine the constitutionality of such restrictions:

1. Regulation must be content-neutral as to both subject matter and viewpoint,
2. Regulation must be narrowly tailored to serve a significant government interests, and
3. Regulation leaves alternative channels of communication open.

The freedom of speech and **association** bear a close nexus. State action that may curtail or have the effect of curtailing the freedom to associate is subject to the closest scrutiny.

**Freedom of the press** means that the press has no greater freedom to speak than any ordinary member of the general public. The press has no special right of access to government information. Both the public and the press have a right to attend criminal trials unless the judge finds an overriding interest that cannot be accommodated by less restrictive means. Gag orders on the press will almost never be held constitutional as the judge has other alternatives at her disposal.

Generally, radio and television broadcasting can be more closely regulated than the press, due to the limited number of airwaves available. Cable television receives First Amendment protection somewhere between broadcast television and newspapers.

A Constitutional Law essay focused on an amendment is ripe for low-hanging fruit points. Follow each step to set up the rule to be applied.

### Constitutional Law Bill of Rights Analysis Steps

1. Identify the amendment.
2. State how amendment applies to states.
3. Identify the state action.
4. Give the language of the amendment itself.
5. Give the Court's interpretation of that language.

For example, in a takings question where a cable company seeks to lay cable on a private person's property, your rule statement should look like this:

The Fifth Amendment to the U.S. Constitution applies to the states through the Due Process Clause of the Fourteenth Amendment. Although a private company and not the government itself is doing the digging, the government is not shielded as state action is found because a government ordinance authorized the taking.

Under the Fifth Amendment, the government may take private property for public use so long as just compensation is paid to the owner. Any type of physical appropriation can constitute a taking. It does not have to be a physical appropriation of all of the property owner's rights to the property to constitute a taking.

The first paragraph identifies the amendment, showing how the amendment applies to the state and the source of state action. The second paragraph gives the language of the amendment itself and then the Court's interpretation of that language. Don't be tempted to just give the Court's interpretation of the language. Do all five steps of the analysis to show the examiners that you understand the Constitution's interplay with the Court's interpretation so you can rack up the points!

## II. MBE STRATEGIES[13]

About half of the MBE questions will focus on state action, due process, equal protection, takings, and the First Amendment. The other half focuses on the powers of the different branches of government (including judicial review), and the relationship of a nation and its states in a federal system.

Unlike essay questions, answering MBE questions usually does not require you to set up the various provisions of the Constitution. Instead, they focus on the specific application of the provisions and whether each provision applies to

| Constitutional Provisions | | | |
|---|---|---|---|
| **Provision of Constitution** | **Applies to:** | **Source, Prohibition, or Limitation** | **What does provision do?** |
| Commerce Clause | Federal Government | Source | Clause applies to: 1. Channels of interstate commerce; 2. Instrumentalities of interstate commerce; 3. Articles moving in interstate commerce; 4. Activities substantially affecting commerce. What else should be added? |
| Taxing & Spending Clauses | Federal Government | Source | Power to tax and spend for the general welfare. Only place where general welfare is addressed. What else should be added? |
| Contract Clause | States | Prohibition | If a state is acting under a health and safety statute or regulation, the state's statute will trump the Contract Clause. |
| Privileges & Immunities Clause of the Fourteenth Amendment | States | Limitation | ?? |
| "Interstate" Privileges & Immunities Clause of Article IV | States | Limitation | ?? |
| Eleventh Amendment | Individuals | Limitation | ?? |
| Thirteenth Amendment | Federal & State Governments and Individuals | Limitation | ?? |

---

13. Some of these strategies are from Steven L. Emanuel, *Strategies & Tactics for the MBE* 89-104 (6th ed. 2016).

the federal or state government or to individuals. Consider making a chart of the various clauses—whether the clause is a source of power or a prohibition on governmental action and whether the clause applies to the federal or state government or to individuals. Then, expand your chart to include what the provision does. This chart gives you a head start so that you can now fill in the rest of the provisions.

Many MBE questions focus on the validity of a statute. The first step is to determine whether it is a federal or state statute. That, in and of itself, will eliminate answer responses. For a federal statute, look to see if the statute is rationally related to an enumerated power or if it is necessary and proper to effectuate an enumerated power:

- Remember the major enumerated powers: Civil Rights, Elections, Admiralty, Taxation, Eminent domain, Spending/taxing for general welfare, Defense, Interstate commerce, Citizenship, External (foreign) affairs (C-R-E-A-T-E-S D-I-C-E).
- On a Constitutional Law question, only the Constitution is tested. You must leave your understanding of other federal statutes and regulations at the door. Thus, your understanding of the requirements of the Americans with Disabilities Act is irrelevant to a question regarding whether a state can prohibit chair lifts on all stairs in public buildings. Avoid thinking "it's illegal to discriminate."

Use these strategies to analyze federal statutes questions:

- Congress can regulate an activity if the activity is commercial and the activity substantially affects (or is part of a class of activities that substantially affect) interstate commerce. If the activity is noncommercial, use a stricter test to find an "obvious connection" between the activity and interstate commerce.
- Federal regulation of an item that has finished traveling through the stream of commerce might not be permissible.
- If a regulated activity is noncommercial but part of a class of activities that are traditionally commercial and substantially affect interstate commerce, then federal regulation is permissible.
- If the question focuses on a federal statute, do not pick an equal protection answer choice. Instead, if it looks like equal protection, choose an answer choice involving the Fifth Amendment or due process.
- If the answer choice involves the general welfare, only the Taxing and Spending Clause applies.
- There is no federal police power.
- Taxpayers do not generally have standing except in cases alleging both the exercise of congressional taxing/spending authority and a violation of the Establishment Clause of the First Amendment.

State statutes must meet a three-part test:

- The law must be enacted within the state's powers. Police powers are the most common source of state authority including public health, safety, welfare, or morals;
- It must not violate any person's constitutional rights (most common are due process and equal protection); and

- It must not unduly burden interstate commerce.

Use these strategies to analyze state questions:

- Only analyze a state statute under the Commerce Clause when there is no relevant federal regulation. If relevant federal legislation exists, analyze under the Supremacy Clause.
- Congress can expressly authorize state regulation. Under the Tenth Amendment, Congress cannot, however, *require* or "commandeer" the states to act.
- If Congress did not expressly authorize or prohibit state regulation, does a federal regulation preempt state law?
  - Yes, if there is a direct contradiction between the state and federal law.
  - If not, determine whether Congress intended federal law to occupy the field.
- Privileges and Immunities Clause of the Fourteenth Amendment: This "distractor" will almost never be the best answer choice on the MBE.
- "Interstate" Privileges and Immunities Clause of Article IV: could be a legitimate answer choice on the MBE.
- "Overbroad" if it prohibits not only unprotected speech but also some protected speech. "Vague" if so unclearly defined that a reasonable person would have to guess at its meaning.
- Special points regarding freedom of religion:
- Government may only regulate religious practice with secular laws.
- Protected beliefs must be sincerely held religious views, not mere philosophical or political views.
- Watch for MBE questions on aid to private, religious schools; will parallel Supreme Court cases.
- A state court case must have addressed a federal question in order to reach the Supreme Court.
- The Supreme Court will not address a state court decision that rests on adequate and independent state law grounds.
- A purely economic regulation equals no due process or equal protection problem.

Constitutional law is myriad and complex. If you skip it, there is really little to no chance to pass the exam. Don't be intimidated thinking you need to have 100% understood and memorized. Your 75% is just right.

## III. ESSAY PRACTICE QUESTION[14]

State A, a leader in wind energy, recently enacted the "Green Energy Act" ("the Act").

Section 1 of the Act requires that 50% of the electricity sold by utilities in the state come from "environmentally friendly energy sources." Wind energy, which is produced in State A, is classified by the Act as an "environmentally friendly energy source." Natural gas, which is not produced in State A, is not classified by the Act as environmentally friendly. The preamble of the Act contains express findings that the burning of natural gas releases significant quantities of greenhouse gases into the atmosphere and requires the diversion of scarce water resources for use in gas-burning thermoelectric plants.

Section 2 of the Act prohibits the Public Service Commission of State A from approving any new coal-burning power plants in the state, unless it finds that "the construction of the plant is necessary to meet urgent energy needs of this state." A public utility in neighboring State B has applied for a permit to build a coal-burning power plant on property it owns across the border in State A. The Commission has denied the utility's application based on its finding that there is no evidence of any urgent energy needs in State A. The State B utility presented undisputed evidence of severe energy shortages in State B, but the Commission rejected this evidence as irrelevant to the statutory exception.

Section 3 of the Act requires State A, whenever possible, to buy goods and services only from "environmentally friendly vendors located within the state." To qualify as an "environmentally friendly vendor," a firm must meet specified standards concerning energy efficiency, chemical use, and use of recycled materials. A vendor located outside of State A meets all the standards to qualify as an environmentally friendly vendor. The vendor has sought to sell goods and services to State A. The relevant State A agencies have refused to purchase from this vendor, pointing out that the Act requires them to purchase, if possible, only from "environmentally friendly vendors located within the state," of which there are several.

There is no federal statute or regulation relevant to this problem.

Which provisions, if any, of the Green Energy Act unconstitutionally burden or discriminate against interstate commerce? Explain.

## IV. MBE PRACTICE QUESTIONS

### Question 1

In the wake of massive terrorist attacks carried out inside the United States by foreign citizens, Congress declared war on the terrorists' nation of origin. It also passed a statute requiring every alien who is a citizen of the enemy nation to either immediately leave the United States voluntarily or be subject to deportation. An inseverable provision of the new statute provides that the United States

---

14. The Multistate Bar Examination ("MBE®") questions, the Multistate Essay Examination ("MEE®") questions, and excerpts from the Multistate Performance Tests ("MPT®") have been reprinted by permission from the NCBE®. Copyright© by the National Conference of Bar Examiners. All rights reserved.

Supreme Court will have original and exclusive jurisdiction over any action brought to challenge the validity of the statute.

Is the new statute constitutional?

(A) No, because the statute does not fall within the categories of cases specified in Article III as those over which the Supreme Court shall have original jurisdiction.

(B) No, because the statute violates the equal protection component of the Fifth Amendment.

(C) Yes, because among the powers of Congress enumerated in Article I, Section 8, is the power to enact laws governing immigration and naturalization.

(D) Yes, because Article III specifically provides that the jurisdiction of the Supreme Court shall be subject to such exceptions and regulations as Congress shall make.

## Question 2

The United States had long recognized the ruling faction in a foreign country as that country's government, despite an ongoing civil war. Throughout the civil war, the ruling faction controlled the majority of the country's territory, and the United States afforded diplomatic immunity to the ambassador representing the ruling faction.

A newly elected President of the United States decided to recognize a rebel group as the government of the foreign country and notified the ambassador from the ruling faction that she must leave the United States within 10 days. The ambassador filed an action in federal district court for a declaration that the ruling faction was the true government of the foreign country and for an injunction against enforcement of the President's order that she leave the United States. The United States has moved to dismiss the action.

If the court dismisses the action, what will be the most likely reason?

(A) The action involves a nonjusticiable political question.

(B) The action is not ripe.

(C) The action is within the original jurisdiction of the U.S. Supreme Court.

(D) The ambassador does not have standing.

## Question 3

An employer owed an employee $200 in unpaid wages. A law of the state in which the employer and the employee reside and in which the employee works provides that the courts of that state must decide claims for unpaid wages within 10 days of filing.

After the employee filed a claim in state court pursuant to this law, the employer filed a voluntary bankruptcy petition in federal bankruptcy court. In the bankruptcy proceeding, the employer sought to stay further proceedings in the unpaid wages claim on the basis of a federal statute which provides that a person who files a federal bankruptcy petition receives an automatic stay of all proceedings against him or her in all federal and state courts. No other federal laws apply.

In addition to the supremacy clause of Article VI, what is the most obvious constitutional basis for the imposition of a stay of the unpaid wages claim in the state court?

(A) Congress's power to provide for the general welfare.
(B) Congress's power to provide uniform rules of bankruptcy.
(C) Congress's power to regulate the jurisdiction and procedures of the courts.
(D) Congress's power to regulate commerce among the states.

## Question 4

Congress enacted a statute directing U.S. ambassadors to send formal letters to the governments of their host countries, protesting any violations by those governments of international treaties on weapons sales. The President prefers to handle violations by certain countries in a less formal manner and has directed ambassadors not to comply with the statute.

Is the President's action constitutional?

(A) No, because Congress has the power to implement treaties, and therefore the statute is binding on the President.
(B) No, because Congress has the power to regulate commerce with foreign nations, and therefore the statute is binding on the President.
(C) Yes, because Congress has no jurisdiction over matters outside the U.S. borders.
(D) Yes, because the President and his subordinates are the exclusive official representatives of the United States in foreign affairs.

## Question 5

Congress enacted a statute that authorized the construction of a monument commemorating the role of the United States in liberating a particular foreign nation during World War II. Another statute appropriated $3 million for the construction. When the United States became involved in a bitter trade dispute with the foreign nation, the President announced that he was canceling the monument's construction and that he would not spend the appropriated funds. Although the actual reason for the President's decision was the trade dispute, the announcement stated that the reason was an unexpected rise in the federal deficit.

Assume that no other statutes apply.
Is the President's decision constitutional?

(A) No, because the President failed to invoke his foreign affairs powers in his announcement.
(B) No, because the President is obligated to spend funds in accordance with congressional directions.
(C) Yes, because the President is vested with inherent executive power to control federal expenditures.
(D) Yes, because the President's decision is a valid exercise of his foreign affairs powers.

## Question 6

A city ordinance created a three-member zoning board, which is responsible for approving the location of all entertainment venues in the city. In an inseverable provision, the ordinance requires that one member of the board be a representative of the local council of churches.

A minister was appointed to the board to represent the local council of churches. During the minister's tenure, the board denied a company permission to open a nightclub in a particular location solely because it would be so close to an existing church that it might disturb the church's operations. The company has challenged the ordinance and its application in federal court on constitutional grounds.

Is the company likely to prevail?

(A)   No, because the existing church has a right to have its vested property interests protected.

(B)   No, because the minister was only one of three votes and, therefore, could not dictate the decision of the zoning board.

(C)   Yes, because the requirement that the zoning board include a representative of the local council of churches violates the First and Fourteenth Amendments.

(D)   Yes, because, as applied, the ordinance denied the company the equal protection of the laws by irrationally discriminating against its particular type of business.

## Question 7

Congress recently enacted a statute creating a program that made federal loans available to family farmers who had been unable to obtain loans from private lenders. Congress appropriated a fixed sum of money to fund loans made pursuant to the program and gave a designated federal agency discretion to decide which applicants were to receive the loans.

Two weeks after the program was established, a family farmer applied to the agency for a loan. Agency officials promptly reviewed her application and summarily denied it.

The farmer has sued the agency in federal district court, claiming only that the denial of her application without the opportunity for a hearing violated the due process clause of the Fifth Amendment. The farmer claims that she could have proved at such a hearing that without the federal loan it would be necessary for her to sell her farm.

Should the court uphold the agency's decision?

(A)   No, because due process requires federal agencies to provide a hearing before making any factual determination that adversely affects an identified individual on the basis of his or her particular circumstances.

(B)   No, because the denial of a loan may deprive the farmer of an established liberty interest to pursue her chosen occupation.

(C)   Yes, because the applicable statute gives the farmer no legitimate claim of entitlement to receive a loan.

(D)   Yes, because the spending clause of Article I, Section 8, gives Congress plenary power to control the distribution of appropriated funds in any manner it wishes.

## Question 8

A state law provides that only U.S. citizens may serve as jurors in the state courts of that state. A woman who is a lawful resident alien and who has resided in the state for many years was summoned for jury duty in a state court. The woman's name was selected from a list of potential jurors that was compiled from a comprehensive list of local residents. She was disqualified from service solely because she is not a U.S. citizen.

The woman has filed an action for a declaratory judgment that the state law is unconstitutional. Who should prevail in this action?

(A) The state, because a state may limit to U.S. citizens functions that are an integral part of the process of self-government.
(B) The state, because jury service is a privilege, not a right, and therefore it is not a liberty interest protected by the due process clause of the Fourteenth Amendment.
(C) The woman, because the Constitution gives Congress plenary power to make classifications with respect to aliens.
(D) The woman, because the state has not articulated a legitimate reason for prohibiting resident aliens from serving as jurors in the state's courts.

## Question 9

Congress enacted a statute that made it illegal for "any employee, without the consent of his or her employer, to post on the Internet any information concerning the employer." The purpose of the statute was to prevent employees from revealing their employers' trade secrets.

Is the statute constitutional?

(A) No, because it is not narrowly tailored to further a compelling government interest.
(B) No, because it targets a particular medium of communication for special regulation.
(C) Yes, because it leaves open ample alternative channels of communication.
(D) Yes, because it prevents employees from engaging in unethical conduct.

## Question 10

A state law imposed substantial regulations on insurance companies operating within the state with respect to their rates, cash reserves, and financial practices.

A privately owned insurance company operating within the state advertised that it wanted to hire a new data processor. After reviewing applications for that position, the company hired a woman who appeared to be well qualified. The company refused to consider the application of a man who was better qualified than the woman, because he was known to have radical political views.

The man sued the company, alleging only a violation of his federal constitutional right to freedom of expression. Is the man likely to prevail?

(A) No, because hiring decisions are wholly discretionary and thus are not governed by the First Amendment.
(B) No, because the company is not subject to the provisions of the First and Fourteenth Amendments.
(C) Yes, because the company is affected with a public interest.
(D) Yes, because the company is substantially regulated by the state, and thus its employment decisions may fairly be attributed to the state.

## Question 11

In order to foster an environment conducive to learning, a school board enacted a dress code that prohibited all public high school students from wearing in school shorts cut above the knee. Because female students at the school considered it unfashionable to wear shorts cut at or below the knee, they no longer wore shorts to school. On the other hand, male students at the school regularly wore shorts cut at or below the knee because they considered such shorts to be fashionable.

Female students sued to challenge the constitutionality of the dress code on the ground that it denied them the equal protection of the laws.

Should the court uphold the dress code?

(A) No, because the dress code is not necessary to further a compelling state interest.

(B) No, because the dress code is not substantially related to an important state interest.

(C) Yes, because the dress code is narrowly tailored to further an important state interest.

(D) Yes, because the dress code is rationally related to a legitimate state interest.

## Question 12

A company owned a large tract of land that contained coal deposits that the company intended to mine. The company acquired mining equipment and began to plan its mining operations. Just as the company was about to begin mining, Congress enacted a statute that imposed a number of new environmental regulations and land-reclamation requirements on all mining operations within the United States. The statute made the company's planned mining operations economically infeasible. As a result, the company sold the tract of land to a farmer. While the sale price allowed the company to recover its original investment in the land, it did not cover the additional cost of the mining equipment the company had purchased or the profits it had expected to earn from its mining operations on the land.

In an action filed against the appropriate federal official, the company claims that the statute effected a taking of its property for which it is entitled to just compensation in an amount equal to the cost of the mining equipment it purchased and the profits it expected to earn from its mining operations on the land.

Which of the following is the most appropriate result in the action?

(A) The company should prevail on its claims for the cost of the mining equipment and for its lost profits.

(B) The company should prevail on its claim for the cost of the mining equipment, but not for its lost profits.

(C) The company should prevail on its claim for lost profits, but not for the cost of the mining equipment.

(D) The company should not prevail on its claim for the cost of the mining equipment or for its lost profits.

## Question 13

A number of psychotherapists routinely send mailings to victims of car accidents informing the victims of the possibility of developing post-traumatic stress disorder (PTSD) as the result of the accidents, and offering psychotherapy services. Although PTSD is a possible result of a car accident, it is not common.

Many accident victims in a particular state who received the mailings complained that the mailings were disturbing and were an invasion of their privacy. These victims also reported that as a result of the mailings, their regard for psychotherapists and for psychotherapy as a form of treatment had diminished. In response, the state enacted a law prohibiting any licensed psychotherapist from sending mailings that raised the concern of PTSD to any car accident victim in the state until 30 days after the accident. The state justified the law as an effort to address the victims' complaints as well as to protect the reputation of psychotherapy as a form of treatment.

Is this law constitutional?

(A) No, because the law singles out one type of message for prohibition while allowing others.

(B) No, because the mailings provide information to consumers.

(C) Yes, because mailings suggesting the possibility of developing PTSD as the result of an accident are misleading.

(D) Yes, because the law protects the privacy of accident victims and the public regard for psychotherapy without being substantially more restrictive than necessary.

## Question 14

A clerical employee of a city water department was responsible for sending out water bills to customers. His work in this respect had always been satisfactory.

The employee's sister ran in a recent election against the incumbent mayor, but she lost. The employee had supported his sister in the election campaign. After the mayor found out about this, she fired the employee solely because his support for the sister indicated that he was "disloyal" to the mayor. The city's charter provides that "all employees of the city work at the pleasure of the mayor."

Is the mayor's action constitutional?

(A) No, because public employees have a property interest in their employment, which gives them a right to a hearing prior to discharge.

(B) No, because the mayor's action violates the employee's right to freedom of expression and association.

(C) Yes, because the employee has no property interest in his job since the city charter provides that he holds the job "at the pleasure of the mayor."

(D) Yes, because the mayor may require members of her administration to be politically loyal to her.

## Question 15

An environmental organization's stated mission is to support environmental causes. The organization's membership is generally open to the public, but its bylaws permit its officers to refuse to admit anyone to membership who does not adhere to the organization's mission statement.

In a recent state administrative proceeding, the organization opposed plans to begin mining operations in the mountains surrounding a small town. Its opposition prevented the mine from being opened on schedule. In an effort to force the organization to withdraw its opposition, certain residents of the town attended a meeting of the organization and tried to become members, but the officers refused to admit them. The residents sued the organization, claiming that the refusal to admit them was discriminatory and violated a local ordinance that prohibits any organization from discriminating on the basis of an individual's political views. The organization responded that the ordinance is unconstitutional as applied to its membership decisions.

Are the residents likely to prevail in their claim?

(A) No, because the membership policies of a private organization are not state action.

(B) No, because the organization's right to freedom of association allows it to refuse to admit potential members who do not adhere to its mission statement.

(C) Yes, because the action of the officers in refusing to admit the residents as members violates equal protection of the laws.

(D) Yes, because the ordinance serves the compelling interest of protecting the residents' free speech rights.

## Question 16

A fatal virus recently infected poultry in several nations. Some scientific evidence indicates that the virus can be transmitted from poultry to humans.

Poultry farming is a major industry in several U.S. states. In one such state, the legislature has enacted a law imposing a fee of two cents per bird on all poultry farming and processing operations in the state. The purpose of the fee is to pay for a state inspection system to ensure that no poultry raised or processed in the state is infected with the virus.

A company that has poultry processing plants both in the state and in other states has sued to challenge the fee. Is the fee constitutional?

(A) No, because although it attaches only to intrastate activity, in the aggregate, the fee substantially affects interstate commerce.

(B) No, because it places an undue burden on interstate commerce in violation of the negative implications of the commerce clause.

(C) Yes, because it applies only to activities that take place wholly within the state, and it does not unduly burden interstate commerce.

(D) Yes, because it was enacted pursuant to the state's police power, which takes precedence over the negative implications of the commerce clause.

# CHAPTER 11

# Mapping MBE Topics—Contracts

## I. MIND MAP

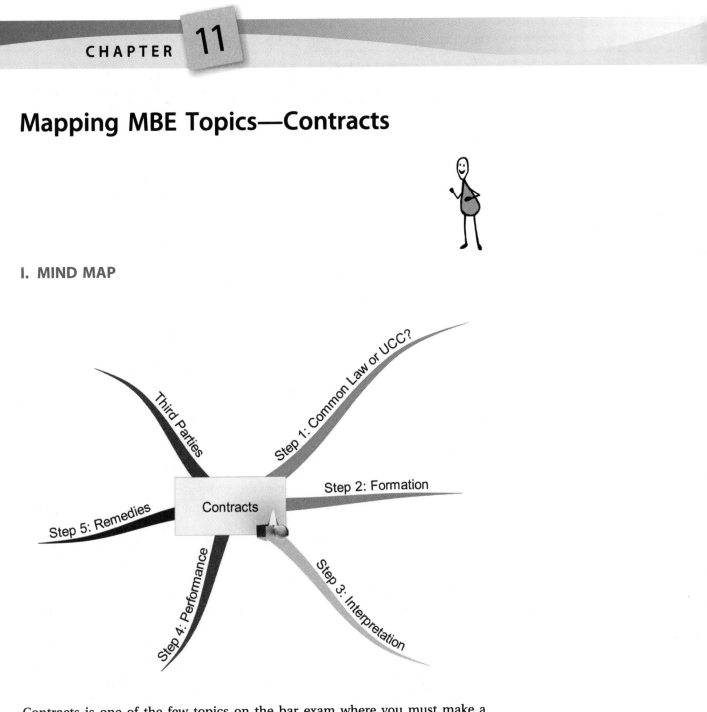

Contracts is one of the few topics on the bar exam where you must make a decision about what law applies before you do any other analysis. Whether an MBE or essay question, your first decision must be whether the common law of contracts applies or whether the Uniform Commercial Code (UCC) Article 2 governing the sale of goods applies. Only then can you move forward with analyzing whether a contract exists, how the contract should be interpreted, whether each party performed its part of the bargain, whether the lack of performance constituted a breach of the contract, how third parties are impacted by the contract, and what remedies exist for the non-breaching party.

Your mind map then begins at contract formation, moving through interpretation and performance, before addressing remedies and third parties:

- UCC or common law?
  - Transaction in goods?
  - Mixed services and goods
  - Merchant?
- Contract formation
  - Offer/acceptance/consideration
  - Statute of Frauds
- Interpretation
  - Parol evidence
  - Warranties
- Performance
  - Conditions
- Remedies
- Third parties
  - Beneficiaries
  - Assignment
  - Delegation

Your analysis of whether the common law of contracts applies or whether the UCC applies is actually an analysis of whether the facts involved a **transaction in goods**. The UCC only applies to a transaction in goods. Without a transaction in goods, the common law of contracts governs.

Real estate and services contracts are governed by common law. Thus, when the fact pattern involves services or real estate, just begin with a simple statement: "Because this is a services contract (or a real estate contract), the common law of contracts governs instead of the UCC." This sentence tells the examiners that you knew this was your first step and that you correctly determined the result.

If not a real estate and services contract, begin your answer with defining a transaction in goods, applying your facts, and concluding that the UCC applies. A transaction in goods is a sale of tangible, personal property. If the contract is a combination of services and the sale of goods, such as when one party sells the goods and agrees to install them, then your analysis determines which part is the most predominant and applies that law to the entire contract.

If you decide that the UCC applies, then you have a second preliminary step: Are one or both parties a merchant? Several rules in Article 2 depend upon whether a party is a merchant. A merchant is "one who regularly deals in goods of the kind sold or who otherwise by his profession holds himself out as having special knowledge or skills as to the practices or goods involved."[1] Apply that definition to both parties.

Now that you know which law applies, you need to be sure a contract has been formed. If the fact pattern states that A and B entered into a valid contract, then you can skip this step. Do not analyze it. You would be wasting your time and the examiners would infer that you could not spot the actual issues.

**EXAM TIP**

Common Law v. UCC? Always the first issue on every Contracts question!

---

1. U.C.C. § 2-104(1).

Analyzing the **formation** of a contract focuses on the existence of mutual assent, consideration, and the absence of any defense to enforcement. Do not just state that a contract requires an offer, acceptance, and consideration. Always include that no defenses to enforcement must also exist.

Understand that there are two types of contracts—bilateral and unilateral. A **bilateral contract** is formed by an exchange of promises. A **unilateral contract** is formed by a promise in exchange for performance.

**Mutual assent** is determined by whether there was an offer and an acceptance of that offer. An **offer** exists when there was intent to enter a contract through a promise or undertaking. The terms of the deal must be definite and certain, and the offer must be communicated to the offeree, giving her actual knowledge of the offer. An offer creates the power of acceptance in the person to whom the offer was made. However, an offer cannot be accepted if it has been terminated. Termination may be by the offeror or the offeree:

* By offeror—revocation
* By offeree
  * Rejection
  * Counteroffer

A **counteroffer** generally terminates the offer and creates a new offer. While mere bargaining is not a counteroffer, a conditional acceptance terminates the offer. The language will have an additional term, such as "provided," or "so long as," etc. If the acceptance does not contain the exact same terms as the offer, then the new terms are treated like a revocation of the original offer and a counteroffer under common law. This is known as the mirror-image rule.

Under the UCC, a change of terms is not a counteroffer and can constitute acceptance unless stated otherwise in one of the forms. This occurs when a buyer places an order and the seller's acceptance form contains different

**EXAM TIP**

An offer, acceptance, consideration, AND no defenses to enforcement are required for a contract. List all four requirements!

**Bilateral v. Unilateral Contract**

terms or the terms are not addressed in the order at all. Under the **battle of the forms**, this nonconforming acceptance is treated as a legally effective acceptance. Unless acceptance is expressly made conditional on assent to the additional or different terms, the nonconforming acceptance creates a valid and binding contract. If the buyer is a consumer, then the additional terms are treated as proposals. If both parties are merchants, additional terms become part of the contract unless the offer expressly limits acceptance to its terms, the offeror objects within a reasonable time, or the additional terms would materially alter the contract. If the terms are different, the knockout rule applies and omits the offeror's original provision and the offeree's differing provision from the resulting contract.

Under both the common law and the UCC, the offeror can control the method of **acceptance** by stating conditions. If the offer is silent as to the method of acceptance, the offeree may indicate its acceptance through starting performance. In a unilateral contract, the offeree must complete the performance for there to be a contract.

Acceptance by letter is valid upon dispatch—that is when the offeree places the letter in the mail. If the offeree changes its mind and sends a later acceptance, then whichever is received first controls.

A legally enforceable contract must also have **consideration**. In most situations, consideration is not an issue in real life. You do need to understand it as it will likely appear on MBE questions. Consideration is a bargained-for exchange. The promise must induce the detriment and the detriment must induce the promise. An act of forbearance by the promisee is sufficient if it gives the promisor a benefit. The detriment and benefit must have legal value. Under the common law, a pre-existing contractual or statutory duty cannot act as consideration for a new promise. New consideration is required. Under the UCC, new consideration is not required to modify a sale of goods contract. Good faith is the test for changes to an existing sale of goods contract.

One substitute for consideration is **promissory estoppel** or detrimental reliance that requires:

1. Promise;
2. Reliance that is reasonable, detrimental, and foreseeable; and
3. Enforcement necessary to avoid injustice.

**Defenses** to the enforcement of a contract include lack of capacity; the Statute of Frauds; illegality; misrepresentation; nondisclosure; duress; unconscionability; and mistake of fact, whether mutual or unilateral. Individuals who lack capacity to contract include individuals under the age of 18; mental incompetents that lack the ability to understand the agreement; and intoxicated persons, if the other party has reason to know.

The **Statute of Frauds** is a heavily tested area on the bar exam. Spend considerable time understanding the doctrine. Five types of contracts fall within the Statute of Frauds:

* Promise to pay the debts of another (suretyship)
* Promise in consideration of marriage
* Service contract not capable of being performed within a year from the time of the contract
* Real estate contracts
* Sale of goods for $500 or more

These contracts must be evidenced by a writing signed by the parties sought to be bound. This does not mean the entire contract must be in writing, only that the party claiming a contract exists must show a writing signed by the defendant where the material terms of the contract are included. The UCC requirement does not look to the material terms, but instead that the writing states it is a contract for the sale of goods and contains the quantity of goods.

When both parties to a contract are mistaken about a material fact, then the contract is voidable by the adversely affected party. This mutual mistake of fact operates as a defense to contract enforcement. If, however, only one party is mistaken about the facts, the mistake does not prevent enforcement of the contract. But if the non-mistaken party knew or had reason to know about the mistake by the other party, the contract is voidable by the mistaken party.

Once the contract is formed, the next issues to address deal with the **interpretation** of the contract terms. Contracts are construed as a whole with a preference given to written or typed provisions using the ordinary meanings of words, and construed against the drafter if there is ambiguity. Two key areas should be considered in dealing with interpretation: gap-filling provisions, such as warranties, and the parol evidence rule.

While parties generally reach explicit agreement on the essential parts of a contract, they often fail to be as explicit as to the details. Gaps result that are subject to more than one interpretation. Contract law supplies terms that govern areas where the contract is silent. The parties can override these terms by being explicit in their agreement. The UCC provides default rules for the sale of goods. One key area is warranties.

Applicants often confuse the different types of **warranties**: an express warranty, an implied warranty of merchantability, and an implied warranty of fitness for a particular purpose. Express warranties are created by the seller. These become part of the agreement if they are the basis of the bargain. The implied

**Express Warranty**

warranty of merchantability is included with every sale of goods. Goods must be fit for their ordinary purposes. Implied warranty of fitness for a particular purpose generally has unusual fact patterns. There must be a direct representation by the seller or the seller's representative that the product fits what the buyer wants. So look for the salesman who picks the product out for a buyer.

A seller can alter these implied warranties by explicitly excluding or modifying language mentioning merchantability. If in writing, it must be conspicuous. If the contract includes an expression such as "as is" or "with all faults" or similar language, that language is sufficient to call the buyer's attention to the exclusion of warranties. Course of dealing, course of performance, or usage of trade may also indicate that the warranty is excluded or modified.

Another gap-filling issue is when the contract is missing terms completely. The UCC provides the missing terms. These missing terms include price, time, and place of delivery. The common law also provides missing terms including price and duration. Both sources of law include an obligation of good faith and fair dealing

Perhaps the most heavily tested contract interpretation topic is the **parol evidence rule**. The parol evidence rule governs whether the meaning of a document can be determined by the negotiations of the parties prior to the written contract. The admissibility of this evidence depends upon the answers to two questions. First, what is the purpose for which the evidence is being introduced? Second, does the evidence relate to a term or contract that is integrated?

**Integration** refers to whether the parties intended the written contract to be the final discussion as to specific terms. The court relies on whether a **merger clause** is included. The merger clause states words to the effect that the writing is the complete and entire agreement of the parties. The court may also look at how detailed the contract is.

**Implied Warranty of Merchantability**

**Implied Warranty of Fitness for a Particular Purpose**

If the purpose of the introduction of extrinsic evidence is to explain or interpret the terms of a written contract, parol evidence is admissible. Some jurisdictions first require a showing that the term is ambiguous. Unless the contract is completely integrated, parol evidence is admissible to supplement the terms of a written contract. The UCC will use usage of trade, course of dealing, and course of performance to supplement terms of the written contract. To contradict the terms of the agreement, parol evidence is admissible unless the contract is fully integrated. The UCC will again use course of dealing or course of performance to qualify the meaning of a term. The parol evidence rule does not bar evidence to prove the written agreement is invalid or unenforceable.

Other interpretation issues involve ambiguity, trade usage, and course of dealing.

A duty to perform is discharged by **performance**, by tender of performance, and by a completed condition subsequent. Performance is also discharged if performance is illegal, impossible, impractical, frustrated, or rescinded. Failure to fulfill a promise constitutes a breach of the contract.

**Conditions** in a contract can be express, implied, or constructive. Conditions can be precedent, concurrent, or subsequent. Constructive conditions are read into the contract by a court; or, if both performances can be performed simultaneously, then each is a constructive condition precedent to each other. If one party's performance will take longer, it is a constructive condition precedent to the other. Failure to fulfill a condition does not necessarily constitute breach of the contract, but may relieve the other party from performance.

**Breach** occurs when there is a failure to perform when under a duty to perform. If a minor breach, it does not relieve the non-breaching party from performance, but that party is entitled to damages. A material breach excuses the non-breaching party from performance and he is entitled to all available remedies.

Under the UCC, if the goods or their delivery fail to conform in any way with the contract, the buyer may reject them, accept them, or just accept certain ones. Buyers cannot reject after already accepting by inspecting and indicating the goods do conform or by failing to inspect. Acceptance may be revoked if the goods are so defective that their value is substantially impaired.

When considering modification issues, carefully consider the pre-existing duty rule under the common law. In essence, a promisor cannot provide consideration where that consideration is a duty the promisor is already obligated to perform. If the parties mutually agree to modify the contract terms, then the pre-existing duty rule is no longer at issue. Under the UCC, the pre-existing duty rule is abolished and an agreement modifying an existing contract needs no consideration. Instead, a good faith test is used.

**Remedies** issues require identifying whether monetary damages or an equitable remedy is available. Under the common law, **monetary damages** range from expectation damages, reliance damages, restitution, and liquidated damages. Under the UCC, the seller's remedies depend on whether the goods have been delivered. A buyer's remedies include damages or specific performance. One key factor is whether the buyer has covered its loss by purchasing replacement goods.

**Equitable remedies** include specific performance, restitution, unjust enrichment, and negative injunctive relief. **Specific performance** is an extraordinary remedy available only when a monetary award would be inadequate to grant relief to the aggrieved party. Specific performance is available for unique objects and real property. Specific performance is usually not available for personal services contracts or contracts requiring ongoing cooperation between the parties. When considering an equitable remedy, the court will consider whether the aggrieved party has clean hands or whether the party has waited too long to seek recovery, a defense called "**laches**."

**Third parties** come into play in three ways: as a beneficiary, through an assignment, or through delegation of the obligation. The issue with **third-party beneficiaries** is whether they have standing to sue the promisor. Incidental beneficiaries are those that benefit from a promisor's performance, but were not intended to benefit. An incidental beneficiary has no standing to enforce the contract.

Intended beneficiaries arise when the promisor's performance was intended to benefit that third party. Intended third-party beneficiaries may enforce the contract against a breaching promisor. They do not, however, have rights against the promisee in the event the performance is not forthcoming. There must be an independent obligation for the promisee to be liable.

An **assignment** is a transfer of a right to receive a performance under a contract. The owner of the right must manifest an intention to make a present transfer of the right. Partial assignments are valid. The assignee may then enforce the contract against the obligor. Certain rights are not assignable: those that substantially change the contract's risks/duties, those that are for future rights to arise under future contracts, and those that are illegal.

A **delegation** occurs when a third party agrees to satisfy a performance obligation owed by one of the parties to a contract. A delegation does not relieve the delegator from his obligations under the contract and the delegator remains liable for its performance unless there has been a **novation**. A novation occurs when the obligee agrees to release the delegator in return for the liability of the delagatee.

Certain duties are not delegable. These include personal performance contracts when the recipient relies on the qualities of the party who is to render the performance. Duties cannot be delegated if the contract prohibits delegation.

Difficulties on contracts questions arise if the applicant does not understand when the UCC and the common law differ. It is useful to make a chart of the specific provisions that differ. When analyzing fact patterns, keep track of the parties' promises. Who promised what to whom? Watch for the details in the question. For example, if a promisor delegates to John with equivalent experience as a contractor or if a promisor delegates to John who is just starting his business—that small difference in facts probably makes the difference in whether the delegation is valid.

## II. MBE STRATEGIES[2]

Common law questions and UCC questions cover most of the same topics. Approximately 50% of the questions will cover formation and performance.

---

2. Some of these strategies are from Steven L. Emanuel, *Strategies & Tactics for the MBE* 161-72 (6th ed. 2016).

Defenses to enforceability, parol evidence and interpretation, remedies, and third-party rights constitute the remaining 50%. Approximately 25% of the total number of questions will be based on Articles 1 and 2 of the UCC.

Chart out the key differences between the UCC and the common law and have them solidly memorized. Particularly look at modification of agreements, irrevocability of offers, and delay in performance. MBE questions frequently focus on those distinctions with one response correctly laying out the UCC response and another response correctly laying out the common law response. If you are not careful about which applies to the fact pattern, you will choose the wrong response.

Use these strategies to analyze contracts questions:

- Consideration is a bargained-for exchange, plus either detriment to the promisee or benefit to the promisor. Key is the bargain. Detriment to the promisee may be surrender of a legal claim.
- Find that a contract exists, wherever possible. Lack of an enforceable contract is a prerequisite to promissory estoppel or quasi contract.
- Determine what interpretation a reasonable person, knowing all that the parties know, would place on the terms. Avoid extraordinary or unusually strict interpretations of contract language.
- If the parties fully address a matter in the contract, the court will not go outside "the four corners" of the contract to use gap-filling provisions.
- When you encounter an oral contract on an MBE question, methodically check it against your memorized list of contracts covered by the Statute of Frauds. You must know when the need for a writing will be excused at common law and under the UCC.
- The parol evidence rule does not bar evidence of defects in contract formation, such as lack of consideration, fraud, and duress.
- Even if a court determines that an agreement is only partially integrated, the written agreement will be considered final as to the terms it does state.
- Only intended beneficiaries have enforceable rights.
- Beneficiary's rights are not enforceable until they vest—parties can modify or rescind before vesting.
- A third-party beneficiary's rights cannot vest until he knows about the contract.
- Meaningless details are relevant! They are there for a reason. If someone is retired, they are not a merchant. If someone is an experienced carpenter, then in all likelihood a duty to perform could be delegated to that person.
- Keep track of third-party beneficiaries and assignees. They are easy to keep track of as a beneficiary is created in the contract and an assignee gains rights later when a party transfers his contract rights to the assignee.

Because of the conflux of UCC and common law rules, contract MBE questions can be difficult. First determine if it is a transaction in goods. Keep track of the parties—offeror v. offeree, merchant v. non-merchant, third-party beneficiary v. assignee. Determine who promised what and then question if the promise was fulfilled. Follow your mind map to then consider at what stage in the contract's life the issue arises. Then you know what rule to apply to determine the correct response.

## III. ESSAY PRACTICE QUESTION[3]

A homeowner and his neighbor live in houses that were built at the same time. The two houses have identical exteriors and are next to each other. The homeowner and his neighbor have not painted their houses in a long time, and the exterior paint on both houses is cracked and peeling. A retiree, who lives across the street from the homeowner and the neighbor, has complained to both of them that the peeling paint on their houses reduces property values in the neighborhood.

Last week, the homeowner contacted a professional housepainter. After some discussion, the painter and the homeowner entered into a written contract, signed by both of them, pursuant to which the painter agreed to paint the homeowner's house within 14 days and the homeowner agreed to pay the painter $6,000 no later than three days after completion of painting. The price was advantageous for the homeowner because, to paint a house of that size, most professional housepainters would have charged at least $8,000.

The day after the homeowner entered into the contract with the painter, he told his neighbor about the great deal he had made. The neighbor then stated that her parents wanted to come to town for a short visit the following month, but that she was reluctant to invite them. "This would be the first time my parents would see my house, but I can't invite them to my house with its peeling paint; I'd be too embarrassed. I'd paint the house now, but I can't afford the going rate for a good paint job."

The homeowner, who was facing cash-flow problems of his own, decided to offer the neighbor a deal that would help them both. The homeowner said that, for $500, the homeowner would allow the neighbor to take over the homeowner's rights under the contract. The homeowner said, "You'll pay me $500 and take the contract from me; the painter will paint your house instead of mine, and when he's done, you'll pay him the $6,000." The neighbor happily agreed to this idea.

The following day, the neighbor paid the homeowner $500 and the homeowner said to her, "The paint deal is now yours." The neighbor then invited her parents for the visit that had been discussed. The neighbor also remembered how annoyed the retiree had been about the condition of her house. Accordingly, she called the retiree and told him about the plans to have her house painted. The retiree responded that it was "about time."

Later that day, the homeowner and the neighbor told the painter about the deal pursuant to which the neighbor had taken over the contract from the homeowner. The painter was unhappy with the news and stated, "You can't change my deal without my consent. I will honor my commitment to paint the house I promised to paint, but I won't paint someone else's house."

---

3. The Multistate Bar Examination ("MBE®") questions, the Multistate Essay Examination ("MEE®") questions, and excerpts from the Multistate Performance Tests ("MPT®") have been reprinted by permission from the NCBE®. Copyright© by the National Conference of Bar Examiners. All rights reserved.

There is no difference in magnitude or difficulty between the work required to paint the homeowner's house and the work required to paint the neighbor's house.

1. If the painter refuses to paint the neighbor's house, would the neighbor succeed in a breach of contract action against the painter? Explain.
2. Assuming that the neighbor would succeed in the breach of contract action against the painter, would the retiree succeed in a breach of contract action? Explain.
3. If the painter paints the neighbor's house and the neighbor does not pay the $6,000 contract price, would the painter succeed in a contract claim against the neighbor? Against the homeowner? Explain.

## IV. MBE PRACTICE QUESTIONS[4]

### Question 1

A restaurant supplier sent a letter to a regular customer offering to sell the customer an industrial freezer for $10,000. Two days later, the customer responded with a letter that stated: "I accept your offer on the condition that you provide me with a warranty that the freezer is merchantable." In response to the customer's letter, the supplier called the customer and stated that the offer was no longer open. The supplier promptly sold the freezer to another buyer for $11,000.

If the customer sues the supplier for breach of contract, is the customer likely to prevail?

(A) No, because the customer's letter added a term, making it a counteroffer.
(B) No, because the subsequent sale to a bona fide purchaser for value cut off the claims of the customer.
(C) Yes, because the customer's letter was an acceptance of the supplier's offer, since the warranty of merchantability was already implied in the sale.
(D) Yes, because the supplier's letter was a firm offer that could not be revoked for a reasonable time.

### Question 2

A seller sent an email to a potential buyer, offering to sell his house to her for $150,000. The buyer immediately responded via email, asking whether the offer included the house's front porch swing. The seller emailed back: "No, it doesn't." The buyer then ordered a front porch swing and emailed back to the seller: "I accept your offer." The seller refused to sell the house to the buyer, claiming that the offer was no longer open.

Is there a contract for the sale of the house?

(A) No, because the buyer's initial email was a counteroffer.
(B) No, because the offer lapsed before the buyer accepted.
(C) Yes, because the buyer relied on the offer by ordering the swing.
(D) Yes, because the buyer's initial email merely asked for information.

---

4. *Id.*

## Question 3

In a telephone conversation, a jewelry maker offered to buy 100 ounces of gold from a precious metals company if delivery could be made within 10 days. The jewelry maker did not specify a price, but the market price for 100 ounces of gold at the time of the conversation was approximately $65,000. Without otherwise responding, the company delivered the gold six days later.

In the meantime, the project for which the jewelry maker planned to use the gold was canceled. The jewelry maker therefore refused to accept delivery of the gold or to pay the $65,000 demanded by the company.

Is there an enforceable contract between the jewelry maker and the company?

(A) No, because the parties did not agree on a price term.

(B) No, because the parties did not put their agreement in writing.

(C) Yes, because the absence of a price term does not defeat the formation of a valid contract for the sale of goods where the parties otherwise intended to form a contract.

(D) Yes, because the company relied on an implied promise to pay when it delivered the gold.

## Question 4

A man sent an email to a friend that stated: "Because you have been a great friend to me, I am going to give you a rare book that I own." The friend replied by an email that said: "Thanks for the rare book. I am going to give you my butterfly collection." The rare book was worth $10,000; the butterfly collection was worth $100. The friend delivered the butterfly collection to the man, but the man refused to deliver the book.

If the friend sues the man to recover the value of the book, how should the court rule?

(A) For the man, because there was no bargained-for exchange to support his promise.

(B) For the man, because the consideration given for his promise was inadequate.

(C) For the friend, because she gave the butterfly collection to the man in reliance on receiving the book.

(D) For the friend, because she conferred a benefit on the man by delivering the butterfly collection.

## Question 5

A farmer who wanted to sell her land received a letter from a developer that stated, "I will pay you $1,100 an acre for your land." The farmer's letter of reply stated, "I accept your offer." Unbeknownst to the farmer, the developer had intended to offer only $1,000 per acre but had mistakenly typed "$1,100." As both parties knew, comparable land in the vicinity had been selling at prices between $1,000 and $1,200 per acre.

Which of the following states the probable legal consequences of the correspondence between the parties?

(A) There is no contract, because the parties attached materially different meanings to the price term.

(B) There is no enforceable contract, because the developer is entitled to rescission due to a mutual mistake as to a basic assumption of the contract.

(C) There is a contract formed at a price of $1,000 per acre.

(D) There is a contract formed at a price of $1,100 per acre.

## Question 6

A buyer and a seller entered into a written contract for the sale of a copy machine, using the same form contract that they had used a number of times in the past. The contract stated that payment was due 30 days after delivery and provided that the writing contained the complete and exclusive statement of the parties' agreement.

On several past occasions, the buyer had taken a 5% discount from the contract price when paying within 10 days of delivery, and the seller had not objected. On this occasion, when the buyer took a 5% discount for paying within 10 days, the seller objected because his profit margin on this particular machine was smaller than on his other machines.

If the seller sues the buyer for breach of contract, may the buyer introduce evidence that the 5% discount was a term of the agreement?

(A) No, because the seller timely objected to the buyer's proposal for different terms.

(B) No, because the writing contained the complete and exclusive agreement of the parties.

(C) Yes, because a modification made in good faith does not require consideration.

(D) Yes, because evidence of course of dealing is admissible even if the writing contains the complete and exclusive agreement of the parties.

## Question 7

A buyer purchased a new car from a dealer under a written contract that provided that the price of the car was $20,000 and that the buyer would receive a "trade-in allowance of $7,000 for the buyer's old car." The old car had recently been damaged in an accident. The contract contained a merger clause stating: "This writing constitutes the entire agreement of the parties, and there are no other understandings or agreements not set forth herein." When the buyer took possession of the new car, she delivered the old car to the dealer. At that time, the dealer claimed that the trade-in allowance included an assignment of the buyer's claim against her insurance company for damage to the old car. The buyer refused to provide the assignment.

The dealer sued the buyer to recover the insurance payment. The dealer has offered evidence that the parties agreed during their negotiations for the new car that the dealer was entitled to the insurance payment.

Should the court admit this evidence?

(A) No, because the dealer's acceptance of the old car bars any additional claim by the dealer.
(B) No, because the merger clause bars any evidence of the parties' prior discussions concerning the trade-in allowance.
(C) Yes, because a merger clause does not bar evidence of fraud.
(D) Yes, because the merger clause does not bar evidence to explain what the parties meant by "trade-in allowance."

## Question 8

A buyer agreed in writing to purchase a car from a seller for $15,000, with the price to be paid on a specified date at the seller's home. The contract provided, and both parties intended, that time was of the essence. Before the specified date, however, the seller sold the car to a third party for $18,000. On the specified date, the buyer arrived at the seller's home prepared to tender payment. The seller was not there, so the buyer called the seller to ask where he was. The seller then told the buyer that he had sold the car to the third party.

If the buyer sues the seller for breach of contract, will the buyer be likely to prevail?

(A) No, because the contractual obligations were discharged on the ground of impossibility.
(B) No, because the buyer did not tender her performance on the specified date.
(C) Yes, because the seller did not inform the buyer of his repudiation.
(D) Yes, because the seller anticipatorily repudiated the contract when he sold the car to the third party.

## Question 9

A mill and a bakery entered into a written contract that obligated the mill to deliver to the bakery 1,000 pounds of flour every Monday for 26 weeks at a specified price per pound. The mill delivered the proper quantity of flour in a timely manner for the first 15 weeks. However, the 16th delivery was tendered on a Tuesday, and amounted to only 800 pounds. The mill told the bakery that the 200-pound shortage would be made up on the delivery due the following Monday. The late delivery and the 200-pound shortage will not significantly disrupt the bakery's operations.

How may the bakery legally respond to the nonconforming tender?

(A) Accept the 800 pounds tendered, but notify the mill that the bakery will cancel the contract if the exact amount is not delivered on the following Monday.
(B) Accept the 800 pounds tendered, but notify the mill that the bakery will deduct from the price any damages for losses due to the nonconforming tender.
(C) Reject the 800 pounds tendered, but notify the mill that the bakery will accept delivery the following Monday if it is conforming.
(D) Reject the 800 pounds tendered, and notify the mill that the bakery is canceling the contract.

## Question 10

A buyer agreed to purchase a seller's house for $250,000 "on condition that the buyer obtain mortgage financing within 30 days." Thirty days later, the buyer told the seller that the buyer would not purchase the house because the buyer had not obtained mortgage financing. The seller asked the buyer where the buyer had tried to obtain mortgage financing, and the buyer responded, "I was busy and didn't have time to seek mortgage financing."

If the seller sues the buyer for breach of contract, is the court likely to find the buyer in breach?

(A) No, because the buyer's performance was subject to a condition that did not occur.

(B) No, because the promise was illusory since the buyer was not obligated to do anything.

(C) Yes, because a promise was implied that the buyer had to make reasonable efforts to obtain mortgage financing.

(D) Yes, because a reasonable interpretation of the agreement is that the buyer had an obligation to purchase the house for $250,000 in 30 days.

## Question 11

A producer contracted to pay an inexperienced performer a specified salary to act in a small role in a play the producer was taking on a six-week road tour. The contract was for the duration of the tour. On the third day of the tour, the performer was hospitalized with a stomach disorder. The producer replaced her in the cast with an experienced actor. One week later, the performer recovered, but the producer refused to allow her to resume her original role for the remainder of the tour.

In an action by the performer against the producer for breach of contract, which of the following, if proved, would be the producer's best defense?

(A) The actor, by general acclaim, was much better in the role than the performer had been.

(B) The actor was the only replacement the producer could find, and the actor would accept nothing less than a contract for the remainder of the six-week tour.

(C) The producer offered to employ the performer as the actor's understudy for the remainder of the six-week tour at the performer's original salary, but the performer declined.

(D) Both the producer and the performer knew that a year earlier the performer had been incapacitated for a short period of time by the same kind of stomach disorder.

## Question 12

An art collector paid a gallery $1,000 to purchase a framed drawing from the gallery's collection. The price included shipping by the gallery to the collector's home. The gallery's owner used inadequate materials to wrap the drawing. The frame broke during shipment and scratched the drawing, reducing the drawing's value to $300. The collector complained to the gallery owner, who told the collector to take the drawing to a specific art restorer to have the drawing repaired. The collector paid the restorer $400 to repair the drawing, but not all of the scratches could be fixed. The drawing, after being repaired, was worth $700. The gallery owner subsequently refused to pay either for the repairs or for the damage to the drawing.

In an action by the collector against the gallery owner for damages, which of the following awards is most likely?

(A) Nothing.
(B) $300.
(C) $400.
(D) $700.

## Question 13

A businesswoman sold her business to a company for $25 million in cash pursuant to a written contract that was signed by both parties. Under the contract, the company agreed to employ the businesswoman for two years as a vice president at a salary of $150,000 per year. After six months, the company, without cause, fired the businesswoman.

Which of the following statements best describes the businesswoman's rights after being fired?

(A) She can recover the promised salary for the remainder of the two years if she remains ready to work.
(B) She can recover the promised salary for the remainder of the two years if no comparable job is reasonably available and she does not take another job.
(C) She can rescind the contract of sale and get back her business upon tender to the company of $25 million.
(D) She can get specific performance of her right to serve as a vice president of the company for two years.

## Question 14

On June 15, a teacher accepted a contract for a one-year position teaching math at a public high school at a salary of $50,000, starting in September. On June 22, the school informed the teacher that, due to a change in its planned math curriculum, it no longer needed a full-time math teacher. The school offered instead to employ the teacher as a part-time academic counselor at a salary of $20,000, starting in September. The teacher refused the school's offer. On June 29, the teacher was offered a one-year position to teach math at a nearby private academy for $47,000, starting in September. The teacher, however, decided to spend the year completing work on a graduate degree in mathematics and declined the academy's offer.

If the teacher sues the school for breach of contract, what is her most likely recovery?

(A) $50,000, the full contract amount.
(B) $30,000, the full contract amount less the amount the teacher could have earned in the counselor position offered by the school.
(C) $3,000, the full contract amount less the amount the teacher could have earned in the teaching position at the academy.
(D) Nothing, because the school notified the teacher of its decision before the teacher had acted in substantial reliance on the contract.

## Question 15

A produce distributor contracted to provide a grocer with eight crates of lettuce at the distributor's listed price. The distributor's shipping clerk mistakenly shipped only seven crates to the grocer. The grocer accepted delivery of the seven crates but immediately notified the distributor that the delivery did not conform to the contract. The distributor's listed price for seven crates of lettuce was 7/8 of its listed price for eight crates. The distributor shipped no more lettuce to the grocer, and the grocer has not yet paid for any of the lettuce.

How much, if anything, is the distributor entitled to collect from the grocer?

(A) Nothing, because the tender of all eight crates was a condition precedent to the grocer's duty to pay.

(B) The reasonable value of the seven crates of lettuce, minus the grocer's damages, if any, for the distributor's failure to deliver the full order.

(C) The listed price for the seven crates of lettuce, minus the grocer's damages, if any, for the distributor's failure to deliver the full order.

(D) The listed price for the seven crates of lettuce.

## Question 16

A seller borrowed $5,000 from a bank. Soon thereafter the seller filed for bankruptcy, having paid nothing on his debt to the bank.

Five years after the debt had been discharged in bankruptcy, the seller contracted to sell certain goods to a buyer for $5,000. The contract provided that the buyer would pay the $5,000 to the bank. The only debt that the seller ever owed the bank is the $5,000 debt that was discharged in bankruptcy. The seller delivered the goods to the buyer, who accepted them.

If the bank becomes aware of the contract between the seller and the buyer, and the buyer refuses to pay anything to the bank, is the bank likely to succeed in an action against the buyer for $5,000?

(A) No, because the buyer's promise to pay the bank was not supported by consideration.

(B) No, because the seller's debt was discharged in bankruptcy.

(C) Yes, because the bank was an intended beneficiary of the contract between the buyer and the seller.

(D) Yes, because no consideration is required to support a promise to pay a debt that has been discharged in bankruptcy.

## Question 17

A builder borrowed $10,000 from a lender to finance a small construction job under a contract with a homeowner. The builder gave the lender a writing that stated, "Any money I receive from the homeowner will be paid immediately to the lender, regardless of any demands from other creditors." The builder died after completing the job but before the homeowner paid. The lender demanded that the homeowner pay the $10,000 due to the builder directly to the lender. The homeowner refused, saying that he would pay directly to the builder's estate everything that he owed the builder.

Is the lender likely to succeed in an action against the homeowner for $10,000?

(A) No, because the builder's death terminated the lender's right to receive payment directly from the homeowner.

(B) No, because the writing the builder gave to the lender did not transfer to the lender the right to receive payment from the homeowner.

(C) Yes, because the builder had manifested an intent that the homeowner pay the $10,000 directly to the lender.

(D) Yes, because the lender is an intended beneficiary of the builder-homeowner contract.

# CHAPTER 12

# Mapping MBE Topics—Criminal Law and Procedure

## I. CRIMINAL LAW

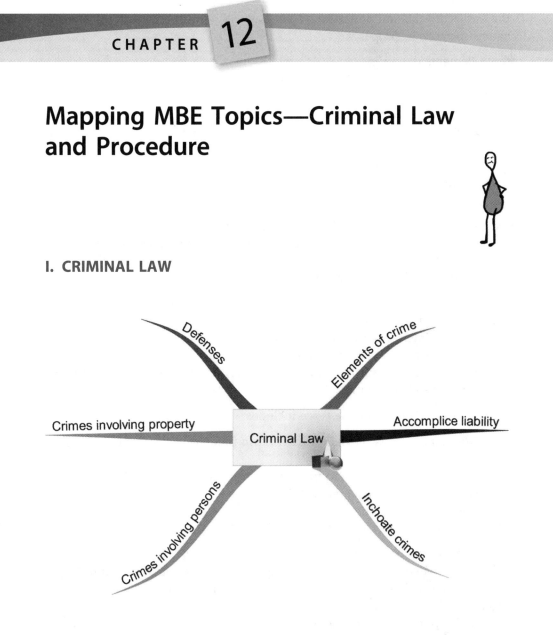

Criminal law is based on three sources of law: common law, the Model Penal Code, and statutory law. If a statute is involved, the examiners will give you the statute. Thus, focus on common law and the Model Penal Code for memorization.

Your mind map focuses first on understanding the common law requirements of a crime before moving to the characteristics of particular crimes. Inchoate crimes are frequently tested, particularly attempt crimes. Understand the basics of each and understand that they can pop up with various offenses against persons or property:

- Elements of a crime
  - *Mens rea*
  - *Actus rea*
- Accomplice liability
- Inchoate crimes
- Offenses against persons
- Offenses against property
- Defenses

**Mens rea** refers to the level of intent required for specific crimes. The *mens rea* must occur simultaneously with the *actus rea*. Divide your memorization into the common law *mens rea* and the Model Penal Code *mens rea*. Under the common law, intent moves from no intent required to purposeful actions. The common law *mens rea* includes:

- Strict liability—no *mens rea* required (statutory rape, public health, and safety regulations).
- General intent—criminal negligence (rape, battery, kidnapping).
- Malice—gross negligence (murder, arson).
- Specific intent—purpose (first-degree murder, assault, inchoate crimes, property-related crimes).

The Model Penal Code *mens rea* includes:

- Negligently—gross deviation from norm in failing to perceive substantial and unjustifiable risk.
- Recklessly—gross deviation from norm in consciously disregarding substantial and unjustifiable risk.
- Knowingly—awareness.
- Purposely—conscious object.

A frequent test area is the intent required for attempt. The examiners want to know that you understand that specific intent is required. Another frequently tested area is **transferred intent**. In essence, the intent to harm a particular individual or object transfers if instead it causes similar harm to another person or object.

The component of **actus rea** includes a physical or external component and either a voluntary act or the omission to act that violates a legal duty. Just like torts, there is generally no legal duty to act or aid. A duty may arise from statute, contract, the relationship between the parties, the assumption of care, or the creation of the peril.

**Accomplice liability** refers to individuals that are accessories to a crime committed by someone else. Under the modern approach, one is liable for someone else's crime if they assisted by aiding, encouraging, or advising and they intended to assist in the commission of the crime.

Under the common law approach, there are four categories to parties to a crime:

- Principal in the first degree—present at scene and commits one element of the crime.

- Principal in the second degree—present at scene, assists but does not commit any element of the crime.
- Accessory before the fact—not at scene, provided assistance beforehand.
- Accessory after the fact—not at scene, provided assistance after crime completed.

The principals are liable for the crimes committed. An accessory before the fact is liable for every crime committed—both planned and all foreseeable crimes. An accessory after the fact is not liable for the crime committed, but is liable for the separate crime of being an accessory after the fact. If someone encourages the crime and then discourages the crime, that person has withdrawn from liability. If an aider then neutralizes the aid, prevents the crime, or notifies the authorities, the aider has withdrawn from liability.

Spend considerable time understanding **inchoate crimes**. These include solicitation, conspiracy, and attempt. All are specific intent crimes. They cannot be committed through mere negligence or recklessness. **Solicitation** means asking or encouraging someone to commit a crime with the intent to commit that crime. Solicitation merges into the completed offense. That the crime was impossible to commit is not a defense.

**Conspiracy** requires an agreement to commit the unlawful act and the specific intent to achieve the object of the agreement. The majority approach, but not under the common law, is that an overt act in furtherance of the conspiracy is required. This can be a minor act. Conspirators are liable for the conspiracy, for the completed target crime, and for any foreseeable crimes by co-conspirators in furtherance of the conspiracy.

Under the common law, a conspirator can withdraw from the conspiracy by notifying co-conspirators in time for them to abandon their plans. They are still liable for the conspiracy and the crime itself, but are no longer liable for further crimes. Under the Model Penal Code, voluntarily withdrawing and thwarting the success of the conspiracy is a defense against the conspiracy itself. Impossibility is not a defense.

Under the common law, **attempt** requires an act with a dangerous propensity towards completion of the crime while the Model Penal Code requires a substantial step beyond mere preparation towards completion of the crime. Both require the specific intent to commit a crime. Attempt merges into the completed target offense. Factual impossibility is not a defense to attempt while legal impossibility is a defense.

Of all the **crimes against persons**, critical to your success on the bar exam is understanding and memorizing **homicide**. Common law murder requires an unlawful killing and "malice aforethought." There are four types of malice. Always analyze all of them. Some questions focus on differentiating these different types of malice. Don't stop when you find one that fits; quickly consider them all:

- Intent to kill.
- Intent to inflict serious bodily injury.
- Gross recklessness (depraved heart).
- Felony murder—killing during course of felony. Intent not required.

Under the common law, felony murder would stand if the killing was done by anyone. Under the modern approach, the killing must be done by the defendant or co-defendant.

**Manslaughter** can be voluntary or involuntary. Voluntary manslaughter is an intentional killing in the heat of passion. Heat of passion requires a sudden and intense reaction with adequate provocation and no cooling off period. Words alone are insufficient. Involuntary manslaughter is either an unlawful killing with negligence or recklessness or a killing during the course of a misdemeanor or a felony not included in felony murder.

The modern approach to homicide includes classifying the murder by degrees. First-degree murder includes the only specific intent homicide—premeditated murder. First-degree felony murder occurs when the felony is enumerated by statute but typically includes rape, burglary, robbery, arson, and kidnapping. Second-degree murder is a catch-all for all other common law murders.

As for **crimes against property**, pay particular attention to the differences between larceny, embezzlement, and false pretenses:

- **Larceny**—taking away another's property by trespass with the intent to permanently deprive the person of their property.
- **Embezzlement**—conversion of property held in trust with the intent to defraud.
- **False pretenses**—taking title to property by misrepresentation with intent to defraud.

The key difference between larceny and embezzlement is that the owner was originally in possession with larceny. With embezzlement, the criminal originally had possession.

**Larceny v. Embezzlement v. False Pretenses**

**Robbery** is larceny by force or threat of force. Thus, analyze the elements of larceny adding the element of "by force" or "threat of force."

Another key crime against property is **burglary**. Under the common law, burglary is the breaking and entering a dwelling of another at night with the intent to commit a felony within the dwelling. Thus, burglary is a specific intent crime. The modern approach expands dwelling to include any structure and is not limited to "at night."

**Defenses** to crimes include insanity, intoxication, infancy, mistake, self-defense, defense of others, defense of property, duress, necessity, and entrapment. For **insanity**, the common law rule is called the M'Naughten rule. Under that rule, mental illness precluded knowing right from wrong or understanding the nature and quality of act. Under the Model Penal Code, mental illness resulted in lack of substantial capacity to appreciate wrongfulness of conduct or to conform conduct to law.

**Involuntary intoxication** is a defense to all elements of a crime. Intoxication is caused by any substance including alcohol, drugs, and medicine. Involuntary intoxication results when the individual is taking the intoxicating substance without knowledge of its nature, under direct duress imposed by another, or pursuant to medical advice while unaware of the substance's intoxicating effect. Involuntary intoxication may be treated as a mental illness in some jurisdictions.

**Voluntary intoxication** is self-induced and results from intentional taking without duress a substance known to be intoxicating. The person need not have intended to become intoxicated. Voluntary intoxication may be a defense to crimes requiring intent or knowledge if the intoxication prevented the accused from formulating the requisite intent. Thus, voluntary intoxication may be a good defense to specific intent crimes, but not for general defense crimes including murder as malice aforethought includes recklessness.

A **mistake of fact** must negate the state of mind. For general intent crimes, the mistake must be reasonable. For specific intent crimes, reasonableness is not required as any mistake of fact is a defense. As strict liability offenses do not require a particular state of mind, mistake of fact is not a defense. **Mistake of law** is not a defense to a crime.

An individual may use non-deadly force in **self-defense** if she reasonably believed the force used was necessary to defend against imminent unlawful force. Deadly force is allowed only when the accused reasonably believes the force used is necessary to defend against imminent unlawful deadly force or serious bodily injury.

Criminal law is a topic that some applicants brush off thinking it is more manageable than others. Don't be mistaken. Keep your focus on the subtle differences between similar crimes and the *mens rea* for each crime. On essays, generally give both the common law and Model Penal Code approach. For example, the *actus rea* required for attempt under the common law is an act with a dangerous propensity towards completion of the crime while under the Model Penal Code the act must be a substantial step in a course of conduct planned to culminate in the commission of the crime. In an attempt essay, analyze both. If a statute is given in either an essay or MBE question, hands down the central issue will focus on that statute. It's not just thrown in as a red herring. It's there for a purpose.

## II. CRIMINAL PROCEDURE

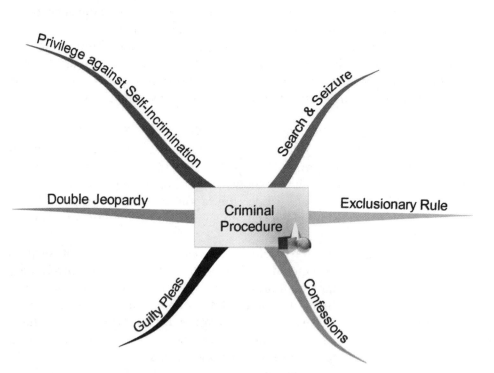

Your mind map for criminal procedure follows the chronological progression of a suspect from evidence gathering and arrest until a guilty plea or conviction:

- Search and seizure
- Exclusionary rule

- Confession
- Guilty pleas
- Double jeopardy
- Privilege against self-incrimination

The Fourth Amendment of the U.S. Constitution provides that people should be free in their persons from unreasonable **searches and seizures**. "Search" is a government intrusion into an area where a person has a reasonable expectation of privacy. "Seizure" is the government exercising control over a person or thing. "Reasonableness" depends upon the circumstances—a valid warrant authorizing that the action is reasonable and an action that is reasonable without a warrant if the evidence is in plain view or another warrant exception makes the search reasonable.

Your analysis needs to follow each step:

- State action?
- Search or seizure?
- Warrant or warrant exception?
- Execution of warrant proper?
- Standing to protest?
- Evidence suppressed?

A **search** is a physical intrusion into a constitutionally protected area to obtain information. The person must have a reasonable expectation of privacy in that area, whether that is a home, an automobile, or a homeless person's sleeping space.

The **seizure** of a person is an **arrest**. Warrants are not required for arrests in public if supported by probable cause. While felonies only require probable cause, misdemeanors require both probable cause and that the misdemeanor was committed in the presence of an officer. Warrants are required for arrests in private, such as the person's home, unless an exception applies. If the person is in someone else's home, then a search warrant and an arrest warrant are necessary.

The seizure of a thing requires a meaningful interference with a possessory interest in the thing.

The only person who can challenge the constitutionality of a search or seizure is the person who was searched or seized. Thus, the accused has no **standing** to assert an unconstitutional search and seizure defense when the search occurred in a friend's home, where the accused has no reasonable expectation of privacy. This is an issue of standing and is a frequent test area.

To have a valid search or seizure, it must be authorized by a valid **warrant** or by a **warrant exception**. To have a valid warrant, there must be:

- Probable cause—fair probability, reasonable grounds, or reasonably trustworthy information sufficient for a prudent person to conclude that:
  - a crime has been or is being committed by the person to be seized, OR
  - there is evidence of criminality in place to be searched. (Note: hearsay and anonymous tips may support probable cause. Test is totality of circumstances.)

**Automobile Searches**

* Particularity—sufficiently definite for police to identify persons, places, or items to be searched or seized with reasonable certainty. Particularity must be on the face of the warrant or an incorporated affidavit.
* Oath or affirmation.
* Detached and neutral magistrate.

The warrant exceptions include:

* Plain view—police may seize an item they see in plain view or can "plain feel" if they have authority to be where they are and the item is connected with criminality.
* Consent—voluntary under totality of circumstances. May not search home over present objection of co-occupant.
* Exigent circumstances—police have reasonable belief to believe delay in obtaining warrant would result in evidence destruction, danger to public/ police, or flight of suspect.
* Automobile search—probable cause that any area of car to be searched (including containers) harbors evidence of criminality.
* Search incident to lawful arrest:
  * Person: contemporaneous search of person, lunge area, and containers for weapons or evidence.
  * Car:
    * no search unless reasonable belief that arrested occupant or recent occupant may access car;
      OR
    * reasonable belief that car contains evidence of crime of arrest (not speeding).

- Home: during the time it takes to complete arrest, may conduct a protective sweep for accomplices in adjoining rooms if reasonable suspicion of danger.
- Inventory—within scope of a reasonable and routine procedure to protect valuables, police, and public, police may inventory contents of possessions at time of booking and automobiles after impoundment.
- *Terry:*
  - Stop: reasonable suspicion that suspect is engaged in criminal activity based on specific and articulate facts. Reasonable suspicion is less than probable cause, but more than a hunch.
  - Frisk: *Terry Stop* plus reasonable suspicion that suspect is armed and dangerous. May not frisk for evidence, only weapons.

The **execution of the warrant** must be reasonable. Before the search, police must knock and announce their presence and purpose before entering the premises unless they have reasonable grounds to believe it would be dangerous or futile. The requirement to knock and announce is also suspended if the police have reasonable grounds to believe evidence would be destroyed. During the search, police may take reasonable steps to secure premises including temporarily detaining individuals at the scene and ordering occupants out of a car.

The **exclusionary rule** is the main sanction against the state for violating an accused's constitutional rights. Any evidence gathered as a result of the state's unconstitutional conduct is inadmissible against the person whose rights were violated unless an exception applies. This rule is known as the "**fruit of the poisonous tree.**" This includes all evidence downstream from the violation. In your analysis, once you have found a constitutional violation, state the exclusionary rule and that the evidence should be excluded. Only then do you address if an exception applies:

- Procedural exceptions:
  - Impeachment purposes
  - Grand jury proceedings
  - Parole revocation hearing
  - Civil proceedings such as immigration
- Doctrinal exceptions:
  - Knock and announce violation
  - Reasonable good faith reliance on facially valid warrant, although later found to be lacking probable cause
  - Clerical errors by court employees in maintaining records such as arrest warrants
  - Isolated negligence by police in maintaining records such as arrest warrants
- Found not to be fruit of the poisonous tree:
  - Independent source for obtaining evidence
  - Inevitable discovery
  - Attenuation

**Confessions** obtained by a state actor may be suppressed if obtained in violation of the Due Process Clause, the Sixth Amendment right to counsel, or the Fifth Amendment *Miranda* doctrine. The test for a due process violation is whether the confession was involuntary because the accused's will was overborne by state coercion.

The Sixth Amendment provides a **right to counsel** after the initiation of adversarial proceedings. The state cannot undermine this right by deliberate elicitation of a confession in the absence of counsel. If formal charges are brought such as an indictment and not a mere arrest, then the right to counsel arises. The test is violated by deliberate elicitation without counsel.

To protect the accused, the Supreme Court has construed the Fifth and Sixth Amendments to require a right to counsel and a **right to silence** when in a custodial interrogation. The state—the police—are required to inform the accused of their rights through *Miranda* **warnings**. When looking at confessions, go through each step of the analysis:

- Custody?
- Interrogation?
- Warnings given?
- Did accused invoke right to counsel? (unequivocally/expressly)
- Did accused waive rights? (voluntary, knowing, and intelligent)

The actual *Miranda* warnings are:

- Right to remain silent;
- Any statements can be used against you;
- Right to counsel before and during questions;
- If you cannot afford a lawyer, one will be appointed for you.

Once invoked, police must scrupulously honor both the right to silence and the right to counsel. If the suspect initiates conversation or a significant amount of time has elapsed, the police can resume interrogation after giving new warnings and receiving a valid waiver. Thus, if the first interrogation was invalid as without warnings and then a valid confession occurs in a second interrogation, that confession will be admissible with proper warnings and proper waiver.

When an accused decides to make a **guilty plea**, the judge must follow the plea-taking colloquy on the record:

- Nature of charge;
- Maximum authorized sentence and any statutory minimum;
- Right to plead not guilty and to have a trial;
- Defendant waiving right to trial.

The accused cannot then withdraw her guilty plea unless:

- Defective plea-taking colloquy;
- Jurisdictional defect;
- Ineffective assistance of counsel; or
- Prosecutor fails to fulfill his side of plea bargain. (Note: Judge is not bound by prosecutor's bargain.)

**Double jeopardy** prohibits a person being put twice in jeopardy of life or limb for the same offense by the same sovereign. Double jeopardy attaches when someone is put "in jeopardy"—when a jury is sworn in, when the first witness is sworn in during a bench trial, or when the judge accepts the plea unconditionally. Double jeopardy does not apply to civil proceedings. Double jeopardy is not implicated when the charges are not the same offense as when each offense has an element that the other does not.

Retrials are permitted if there is a hung jury, a mistrial due to manifest necessity, or a successful appeal.

The Fifth Amendment prohibits compelled testimony in a criminal case. Anyone may invoke the **privilege against self-incrimination** in a custodial interrogation and in any proceeding with testimony under oath. It does not apply to physical evidence or to prior uncompelled communication.

Most of your focus in your Criminal Procedure preparation should be on search and seizure, the exclusionary rule, and confessions. Without a doubt, that is where your 75% lies.

## III. MBE STRATEGIES[1]

The split between Criminal Law questions and Criminal Procedure questions is almost exactly 50/50. The call of the question can range from whether the defendant should be found guilty to best argument questions. Always remember that best argument questions are really not the "best" argument. Only one of the responses is correct both in the result and the reasoning. Any mismatch and the response is incorrect.

A favorite topic is the differences between degrees and types of homicides. Remember, murder does not require intent. The *mens rea* can be satisfied by a "depraved heart"—a disregarding of an unreasonably high risk of harm to human life. In addition, look for any provocation. If the provocation is sufficient to anger this accused and it would provoke a reasonable person to kill, then the charge should be voluntary manslaughter if there was no cooling off and a reasonable person would not have cooled off under these circumstances.

Understand the differences between larceny, robbery, and burglary. These are frequent test topics. Make a chart of the differences to help you encode in your memory.

Memorize the list of warrantless searches allowed. If no warrant is in the fact pattern, go through this list to see if any apply. This type of question is frequently asked and the responses can trick you if they set out the reasoning for a different type of search not implicated by your facts.

Custodial interrogations and confessions are frequent topics. Look for whether the situation is custodial before you decide if the accused's rights were violated.

Use these strategies to analyze criminal law questions:

- Apply statutes verbatim. Criminal law questions frequently include a snippet of a statute. That snippet is loaded with potential issues, particularly concerning *mens rea*.
- Causation is always required for liability. Don't ignore if the defendant's conduct did not cause the victim's injury.
- Victim forgiveness (or settlement) does not negate the crime. Criminal violations are considered wrongs against the state, not against the individual.

---

1. Some of these strategies are from Steven L. Emanuel, *Strategies & Tactics for the MBE* 233-41 (6th ed. 2016).

- Once property is taken with the intent to steal, subsequent return of the property does not negate larceny.
- Categorize the *type* of search first; identifying the correct category will often allow elimination of one or more answer choices applying an inapplicable test.
- A person may object to a search only if she has a legitimate expectation of privacy as to the place being searched; this is a threshold issue.
- MBE questions dealing with witness testimony may state, before the call of the question, "If the jury believes him":
  - Always treat the testimony as fact.
  - Ignore any instinctual belief that the witness is lying.
  - Watch for hidden intent problems.

# IV. ESSAY PRACTICE QUESTION[2]

While on routine patrol, a police officer observed a suspect driving erratically and pulled the suspect's car over to investigate. When he approached the suspect's car, the officer detected a strong odor of marijuana. The officer immediately arrested the suspect for driving under the influence of an intoxicant (DUI). While the officer was standing near the suspect's car placing handcuffs on the suspect, the officer observed burglary tools on the backseat.

The officer seized the burglary tools. He then took the suspect to the county jail, booked him for the DUI, and placed him in a holding cell. Later that day, the officer gave the tools he had found in the suspect's car to a detective who was investigating a number of recent burglaries in the neighborhood where the suspect had been arrested.

At the time of his DUI arrest, the suspect had a six-month-old aggravated assault charge pending against him and was being represented on the assault charge by a lawyer.

Early the next morning, upon learning of her client's arrest, the lawyer went to the jail. She arrived at 9:00 a.m., immediately identified herself to the jailer as the suspect's attorney, and demanded to speak with the suspect. The lawyer also told the jailer that she did not want the suspect questioned unless she was present. The jailer told the lawyer that she would need to wait one hour to see the suspect. After speaking with the lawyer, the jailer did not inform anyone of the lawyer's presence or her demands.

The detective, who had also arrived at the jail at 9:00 a.m., overheard the lawyer's conversation with the jailer. The detective then entered the windowless interview room in the jail where the suspect had been taken 30 minutes earlier. Without informing the suspect of the lawyer's presence or her demands, the detective read to the suspect full and accurate Miranda warnings. The detective then informed the suspect that he wanted to ask about the burglary tools found in his car and the recent burglaries in the neighborhood where he had been arrested. The suspect replied, "I think I want my lawyer here before I talk to you." The detective responded, "That's up to you."

After a few minutes of silence, the suspect said, "Well, unless there is anything else I need to know, let's not waste any time waiting for someone to call my attorney and having her drive here. I probably should keep my mouth shut, but I'm willing to talk to you for a while." The suspect then signed a Miranda waiver form and, after interrogation by the detective, made incriminating statements regarding five burglaries. The interview lasted from 9:15 a.m. to 10:00 a.m.

In addition to the DUI, the suspect has been charged with five counts of burglary.

The lawyer has filed a motion to suppress all statements made by the suspect to the detective in connection with the five burglaries.

The state supreme court follows federal constitutional principles in all cases interpreting a criminal defendant's rights.

---

2. The Multistate Bar Examination ("MBE[®]") questions, the Multistate Essay Examination ("MEE[®]") questions, and excerpts from the Multistate Performance Tests ("MPT[®]") have been reprinted by permission from the NCBE[®]. Copyright© by the National Conference of Bar Examiners. All rights reserved.

1. Did the detective violate the suspect's Sixth Amendment right to counsel when he questioned the suspect in the absence of the lawyer? Explain.
2. Under Miranda, did the suspect effectively invoke his right to counsel? Explain.
3. Was the suspect's waiver of his Miranda rights valid? Explain.

## V. MBE PRACTICE QUESTIONS[3]

### Question 1

A state statute provides: "The sale of an alcoholic beverage to any person under the age of 21 is a misdemeanor."

A woman who was 20 years old, but who looked older and who had a very convincing fake driver's license indicating that she was 24, entered a convenience store, picked up a six-pack of beer, and placed the beer on the counter. The store clerk, after examining the driver's license, rang up the purchase.

Both the clerk and the store owner have been charged with violating the state statute.

If the court finds both the clerk and the store owner guilty, what standard of liability must the court have interpreted the statute to impose?

(A) Strict liability only.
(B) Vicarious liability only.
(C) Both strict and vicarious liability.
(D) Either strict or vicarious liability.

### Question 2

A woman charged with murder has entered a plea of not guilty by reason of insanity. At her trial, in which the questions of guilt and sanity are being tried together, the evidence shows that the woman stalked the victim for several hours before following him to an isolated hiking trail where she shot and killed him. Expert witnesses for the defense have testified that the woman knew that killing was illegal and wrong, but that she suffered from a serious mental illness that left her in the grip of a powerful and irresistible compulsion to kill the victim.

If the jury believes the testimony of the defense experts, under what circumstances could the jury properly acquit the woman of murder?

(A) Only if the jurisdiction follows the M'Naghten test for insanity.
(B) Only if the jurisdiction follows the ALI Model Penal Code test for insanity.
(C) If the jurisdiction follows either the M'Naghten or the ALI Model Penal Code test for insanity.
(D) Even if the jurisdiction has abolished the insanity defense.

---

3. *Id.*

## Question 3

A valid warrant was issued for a woman's arrest. The police learned that a person with the woman's name and physical description lived at a particular address. When police officers went to that address, the house appeared to be unoccupied: the windows and doors were boarded up with plywood, and the lawn had not been mowed for a long time. A neighbor confirmed that the house belonged to the woman but said that the woman had not been there for several months.

The officers knocked repeatedly on the front door and shouted, "Police! Open up!" Receiving no response, they tore the plywood off the door, smashed through the door with a sledgehammer, and entered the house. They found no one inside, but they did find an illegal sawed-off shotgun. Upon her return to the house a few weeks later, the woman was charged with unlawful possession of the shotgun.

The woman has moved to suppress the use of the shotgun as evidence at her trial. Should the court grant the motion?

(A) No, because the officers acted in good faith under the authority of a valid warrant.

(B) No, because the officers did not violate any legitimate expectation of privacy in the house since the woman had abandoned it.

(C) Yes, because the officers entered the house by means of excessive force.

(D) Yes, because the officers had no reason to believe that the woman was in the house.

## Question 4

A woman was subpoenaed to appear before a grand jury. When she arrived, she was taken into the grand jury room to be questioned. She answered preliminary questions about her name and address. She was then asked where she had been at a certain time on a specified night when a murder had occurred. Before answering the question, the woman said that she wanted to consult her attorney, who was waiting outside the grand jury room, and she was allowed to do so. When she returned to the grand jury room, she stated that she refused to answer the question because the answer might incriminate her.

The prosecutor believes that the woman's nephew committed the murder. The nephew has said that he was with the woman at the time of the murder, and the prosecutor believes that this alibi is false. The prosecutor does not believe that the woman is guilty of the murder, either as a principal or as an accomplice, although he does believe that the woman may be guilty of other crimes. The prosecutor wants to compel the woman to answer the question by whatever means will result in the least harm to the prosecution's case.

Which of the following steps should the prosecutor take to get the woman to answer the question?

(A) Request the grand jury to order the woman to answer the question.

(B) Ask the woman's attorney to explain to the woman that the rules of evidence do not apply in grand jury proceedings, and to advise her that she cannot refuse to testify.

(C) Prepare the documents necessary to grant the woman immunity from any future use against her of her grand jury testimony or any evidence derived from it.

(D) Prepare the documents necessary to grant the woman immunity from any future prosecution for any crime she might disclose in the course of her testimony.

## Question 5

A defendant was validly arrested for the murder of a store clerk and was taken to a police station where he was given Miranda warnings. When an interrogator asked the defendant, "Do you understand your Miranda rights, and are you willing to give up those rights and talk to us?" the defendant replied, "Yes." When asked, "Did you kill the clerk?" the defendant replied, "No." When asked, "Where were you on the day the clerk was killed?" the defendant replied, "Maybe I should talk to a lawyer." The interrogator asked, "Are you sure?" and the defendant replied, "I'm not sure." The interrogator then asked, "Why would you want to talk with a lawyer?" and the defendant replied, "Because I killed the clerk. It was an accident, and I think I need a lawyer to defend me." At that point all interrogation ceased. Later, the defendant was formally charged with murdering the clerk.

The defendant has moved to suppress evidence of his statement "I killed the clerk" on the ground that this statement was elicited in violation of his Miranda rights.

Should the defendant's motion be granted?

(A) No, because although the defendant effectively asserted the right to counsel, the question "Why would you want to talk with a lawyer?" did not constitute custodial interrogation.

(B) No, because the defendant did not effectively assert the right to counsel, and his conduct prior to making the statement constituted a valid waiver of his Miranda rights.

(C) Yes, because although the defendant did not effectively assert the right to counsel, his conduct prior to making the statement did not constitute a valid waiver of his Miranda rights.

(D) Yes, because the defendant effectively asserted the right to counsel, and the question "Why would you want to talk with a lawyer?" constituted custodial interrogation.

## Question 6

Two defendants were being tried together in federal court for bank robbery. The prosecutor sought to introduce testimony from the first defendant's prison cellmate. The cellmate would testify that the first defendant had admitted to the cellmate that he and the second defendant had robbed the bank. The prosecutor asked the court to instruct the jury that the cellmate's testimony could be considered only against the first defendant.

Can the cellmate's testimony be admitted in a joint trial over the second defendant's objection?

(A) No, because the first defendant made the statement without Miranda warnings.

(B) No, because the limiting instruction cannot ensure that the jury will not consider the testimony in its deliberations regarding the second defendant.

(C) Yes, because the first defendant's statement was a declaration against penal interest.

(D) Yes, because the limiting instruction sufficiently protects the second defendant.

## Question 7

A prosecutor presented to a federal grand jury the testimony of a witness in order to secure a defendant's indictment for theft of government property. The prosecutor did not disclose to the grand jury that the witness had been convicted four years earlier of perjury. The grand jury returned an indictment, and the defendant pleaded not guilty.

Shortly thereafter, the prosecutor took the case to trial, calling the witness to testify before the jury. The prosecutor did not disclose the witness's prior perjury conviction until the defense was preparing to rest. Defense counsel immediately moved for a mistrial, which the court denied. Instead, the court allowed the defense to recall the witness for the purpose of impeaching him with this conviction, but the witness could not be located. The court then allowed the defense to introduce documentary evidence of the witness's criminal record to the jury before resting its case. The jury convicted the defendant.

The defendant has moved for a new trial, arguing that the prosecutor's failure to disclose the witness's prior conviction in a timely manner violated the defendant's right to due process of law.

If the court grants the defendant's motion, what will be the most likely reason?

(A) The defendant was unable to cross-examine the witness about the conviction.

(B) The prosecutor failed to inform the grand jury of the witness's conviction.

(C) The court found it reasonably probable that the defendant would have been acquitted had the defense had timely access to the information about the witness's conviction.

(D) The court found that the prosecutor had deliberately delayed disclosing the witness's conviction to obtain a strategic advantage.

## Question 8

A state statute divides murder into degrees and defines murder in the first degree as murder committed willfully with premeditation and deliberation. The statute defines murder in the second degree as all other murder at common law and defines voluntary manslaughter as at common law.

A man hated one of his coworkers. Upon learning that the coworker was at a neighbor's house, the man grabbed his gun and went to the neighbor's house hoping to provoke the coworker into attacking him so that he could then shoot the coworker. After arriving at the house, the man insulted the coworker and bragged that he had had sexual relations with the coworker's wife two weeks earlier. This statement was not true, but it enraged the coworker, who grabbed a knife from the kitchen table and ran toward the man. The man then shot and killed the coworker.

What is the most serious homicide offense of which the man could properly be convicted?

(A) Murder in the first degree.
(B) Murder in the second degree.
(C) Voluntary manslaughter, because he provoked the coworker.
(D) No form of criminal homicide, because he acted in self-defense.

## Question 9

A wife decided to kill her husband because she was tired of his infidelity. She managed to obtain some cyanide, a deadly poison. One evening, she poured wine laced with the cyanide into a glass, handed it to her husband, and proposed a loving toast. The husband was so pleased with the toast that he set the glass of wine down on a table, grabbed his wife, and kissed her passionately. After the kiss, the wife changed her mind about killing the husband. She hid the glass of wine behind a lamp on the table, planning to leave it for the maid to clean up. The husband did not drink the wine.

The maid found the glass of wine while cleaning the next day. Rather than throw the wine away, the maid drank it. Shortly thereafter, she fell into a coma and died from cyanide poisoning.

In a common law jurisdiction, of what crime(s), if any, could the wife be found guilty?

(A) Attempted murder of the husband and murder or manslaughter of the maid.
(B) Only attempted murder of the husband.
(C) Only murder or manslaughter of the maid.
(D) No crime.

## Question 10

In a crowded football stadium, a man saw a wallet fall out of a spectator's purse. The man picked up the wallet and found that it contained $100 in cash. Thinking that he could use the money and seeing no one watching, the man put the wallet in the pocket of his coat. Just then, the spectator approached the man and asked if he had seen a missing wallet. The man said no and went home with the wallet.

Of what crime, if any, is the man guilty?

(A) Embezzlement.
(B) False pretenses.
(C) Larceny.
(D) No crime.

## Question 11

A woman went to an art gallery and falsely represented that she was an agent for a museum and wanted to purchase a painting that was hanging in the gallery. The woman and the gallery owner then agreed on a price for the painting to be paid 10 days later, and the woman took the painting. When the gallery failed to receive the payment when due, the owner called the museum and discovered that the woman did not work there. The owner then notified the police.

When interviewed by the police, the woman admitted making the false representation and acquiring the painting, but she said she believed that the painting had been stolen from her by someone who worked in the gallery.

Is the woman guilty of obtaining property by false pretenses?

(A) No, because she believed that the painting belonged to her.

(B) No, because the gallery owner would have sold the painting to anyone who agreed to pay the price.

(C) Yes, because even if her representation was not material, she never intended to pay for the painting.

(D) Yes, because she knowingly made a false representation on which the gallery owner relied.

## Question 12

A woman broke off her engagement to a man but refused to return the engagement ring the man had given her. One night, the man entered the woman's house after midnight to retrieve the ring. Although the woman was not at home, a neighbor saw the man enter the house and called the police. The man unsuccessfully searched for the ring for 10 minutes. As he was walking out the front door, the police arrived and immediately arrested him.

The man has been charged with burglary in a jurisdiction that follows the common law. Which of the following, if proved, would serve as the man's best defense to the charge?

(A) The man knew that the woman kept a key under the doormat and he used the key to enter the house.

(B) The man incorrectly and unreasonably believed that he was legally entitled to the ring.

(C) The man knew that no one was at home when he entered the house.

(D) The man took nothing of value from the house.

## Question 13

A woman wanted to kill a business competitor. She contacted a man who she believed was willing to commit murder for hire and offered him $50,000 to kill the competitor. The man agreed to do so and accepted $25,000 as a down payment. Unbeknownst to the woman, the man was an undercover police officer.

In a jurisdiction that has adopted the unilateral theory of conspiracy, is the woman guilty of conspiracy to murder the business competitor?

(A) No, because the man did not intend to kill the competitor.

(B) No, because it would have been impossible for the woman to kill the competitor by this method.

(C) Yes, because the woman believed that she had an agreement with the man that would bring about the competitor's death.

(D) Yes, because the woman took a substantial step toward bringing about the competitor's death by paying the man $25,000.

## Question 14

A state statute provides as follows: "The maintenance of any ongoing enterprise in the nature of a betting parlor or bookmaking organization is a felony."

A prosecutor has evidence that a woman has been renting an office to a man, that the man has been using the office as a betting parlor within the meaning of the statute, and that the woman is aware of this use.

Which of the following additional pieces of evidence would be most useful to the prosecutor's effort to convict the woman as an accomplice to the man's violation of the statute?

(A) The woman was previously convicted of running a betting parlor herself on the same premises.

(B) The woman charges the man considerably more in rent than she charged the preceding tenant, who used the office for legitimate activities.

(C) The woman has personally placed bets with the man at the office location.

(D) The man has paid the woman the rent in bills that are traceable as the proceeds of gambling activity.

## Question 15

After a defendant was indicted on federal bank fraud charges and released on bail, his attorney filed notice of the defendant's intent to offer an insanity defense. The prosecutor then enlisted the help of a forensic psychologist who was willing to participate in an "undercover" mental examination of the defendant. The psychologist contacted the defendant and pretended to represent an executive personnel agency. She told the defendant about an attractive employment opportunity and invited him to a "preliminary screening interview" to determine his qualifications for the job. As part of the purported screening process, the psychologist gave the defendant psychological tests that enabled her to form a reliable opinion about his mental state at the time of the alleged offense.

What is the strongest basis for a defense objection to the psychologist's testimony regarding the defendant's mental state?

(A) The Fourth Amendment prohibition against unreasonable searches and seizures.

(B) The Fifth Amendment privilege against compelled self-incrimination.

(C) The Sixth Amendment right to the assistance of counsel.

(D) The federal common law privilege for confidential communications between psychotherapist and patient.

## Question 16

A defendant is charged with an offense under a statute that provides as follows: "Any person who, while intoxicated, appears in any public place and manifests a drunken condition by obstreperous or indecent conduct is guilty of a misdemeanor."

At trial, the evidence shows that the defendant was intoxicated when police officers burst into his house and arrested him pursuant to a valid warrant. It was a cold night, and the officers hustled the defendant out of his house without giving him time to get his coat. The defendant became angry and obstreperous when the officers refused to let him go back into the house to retrieve his coat. The officers left him handcuffed outside in the street, waiting for a special squad car to arrive. The arrest warrant was later vacated.

Can the defendant properly be convicted of violating the statute?

(A) No, because the defendant's claim of mistreatment is valid.

(B) No, because the statute requires proof of a voluntary appearance in a public place.

(C) Yes, because the defendant voluntarily became intoxicated.

(D) Yes, because the defendant voluntarily behaved in an obstreperous manner.

## Question 17

A police officer had a hunch, not amounting to probable cause or reasonable suspicion, that a man was a drug dealer. One day while the officer was on highway patrol, her radar gun clocked the man's car at 68 mph in an area where the maximum posted speed limit was 65 mph. The officer's usual practice was not to stop a car unless it was going at least 5 mph over the posted limit, but contrary to her usual practice, she decided to stop the man's car in the hope that she might discover evidence of drug dealing. After she stopped the car and announced that she would be writing a speeding ticket, the officer ordered the man and his passenger to step out of the car. When the passenger stepped out, the officer saw that the passenger had been sitting on a clear bag of what the officer immediately recognized as marijuana. The officer arrested both the man and the passenger for possession of marijuana.

At their joint trial, the man and the passenger claim that their Fourth Amendment rights were violated because the officer improperly (1) stopped the car for speeding as a pretext for investigating a hunch rather than for the stated purpose of issuing a traffic ticket and (2) ordered the passenger to step out of the car even though there was no reason to believe that the passenger was a criminal or dangerous.

Are the man and the passenger correct?

(A) No, as to both the stop of the car and the officer's order that the passenger step out of the car.

(B) No as to the stop of the car, but yes as to the officer's order that the passenger step out of the car.

(C) Yes as to the stop of the car, but no as to the officer's order that the passenger step out of the car.

(D) Yes, as to both the stop of the car and the officer's order that the passenger step out of the car.

# CHAPTER 13

# Mapping MBE Topics—Evidence

## I. MIND MAP

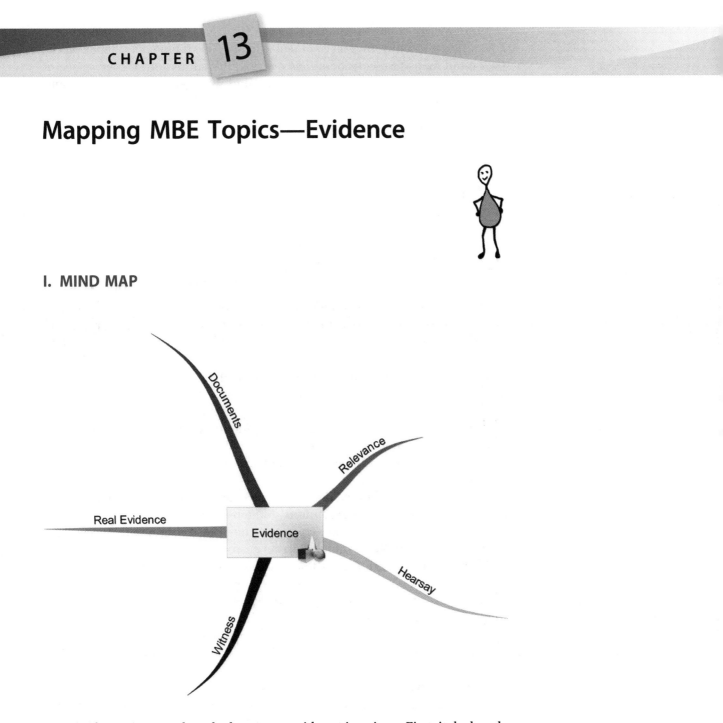

Among the topics tested on the bar exam, evidence is unique. First, it deals only with the admission of proof in a trial of a lawsuit. It does not set out elements of a crime or a civil cause of action. Its focus is solely on whether a document, real evidence, or a witness's testimony should be admitted before a court to consider in deciding whether the elements of a cause of action or crime have been met.

Second, as a result of its sole mission, evidence has little interaction with other areas of the law. While most other topics have some overlap with another topic, evidence does not. Thus, your study focuses on only one source of law—the Federal Rules of Evidence (FRE).

Your mind map begins with the type of evidence. Is the evidence a document, a witness's testimony, or a piece of real evidence? Each type of evidence has its own mind map. Two considerations override the admission of every piece of evidence—relevancy and hearsay. These mind maps are then imbedded into each type of evidence:

- Relevancy
  - Definition
  - Legal relevance
  - Exceptions
  - Character
- Hearsay
  - Definition
  - Nonhearsay
  - Hearsay exceptions—declarant unavailable
  - Hearsay exceptions—declarant availability immaterial

**Relevant evidence** is evidence having any tendency to make the existence of any fact of consequence to the action more probable than it would be without the evidence.[1] Relevant evidence may still be excluded for public policy reasons including **legal relevance**. Under FRE 403, a court has the discretion to exclude relevant evidence if its probative value is substantially outweighed by the danger of unfair prejudice; confusion of the issues; misleading the jury; or by consideration of undue delay, waste of time, or needless presentation of cumulative evidence.[2] Keep in mind that the requirement is unfair prejudice, not just prejudice. The evidence is always prejudicial to the party objecting to the evidence, but that does not mean it rises to the level of unfair prejudice.

Evidence may be admitted that does not relate to the particular event, but is a **prior similar event**. These **exceptions** to the relevancy rule include causation; similar accidents or injuries caused by the same event; and similar acts admissible to prove intent, habit, and industrial custom or routine.

Other exceptions are policy-based. **Liability insurance** may be admissible to prove ownership or control, although it is not admissible to show negligence or ability to pay.[3] Likewise, **subsequent remedial measures** are not admissible to prove negligence, but may be admissible to prove ownership or control, or to prove destruction of evidence.[4] **Settlement offers**[5] and **withdrawn guilty pleas**[6] are also inadmissible, although they may be admissible for other purposes.

**Character evidence** poses special problems and thus is a frequent test topic. Considerations include the purpose for the offer of character evidence and the means of proving character. Your mind map starts with asking whether this is a criminal or civil case. Then, ask whether this is testimony being offered on direct exam or on cross exam. Make a chart to insert the rules.

---

1. Fed. R. Evid. 401.
2. Fed. R. Evid. 403.
3. Fed. R. Evid. 411.
4. Fed. R. Evid. 407.
5. Fed. R. Evid. 408(a).
6. Fed. R. Evid. 410(a).

| CHARACTER EVIDENCE | | |
|---|---|---|
| | **Criminal** | **Civil** |
| Direct Examination | Prosecution cannot initiate. | Generally not admissible.<br><br>Only when character directly at issue: child custody, defamation, etc. |
| Cross-Examination | Party: Defendant can introduce evidence of good character to help prove innocence.<br><br>Party or Witness: Impeachment. | Party or witness: Only for impeachment. |

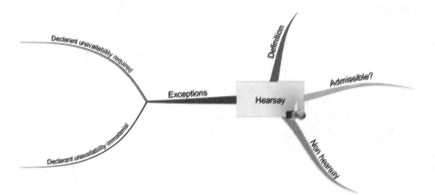

**Hearsay** is another overriding consideration. When dealing with hearsay, you can garner low-hanging fruit points by how you set out the rule. Even if you know from the get-go that the key issue revolves around a hearsay exception, do not jump to the exception. Still give the rule for the admissibility of hearsay evidence including the definition of hearsay. Continue by identifying whether the declarant is a party. Analyze both parts of the definition. Check for double hearsay and then begin your CRAC or IRAC on possible exceptions. For example:

- State rule: "Hearsay is inadmissible without an exception."[7]
- Define hearsay: Hearsay is an out-of-court statement offered to prove the truth of the matter.[8]
- Party? Then, it is an admission of a party-opponent.[9]
- If not a party, analyze both parts of the rule: out-of-court statement and offered for the truth of the matter.

---

7. Fed. R. Evid. 802.
8. Fed. R. Evid. 801(c)(1)-(2).
9. Fed. R. Evid. 801(d)(2)(A).

- Conclude if hearsay.
- Check for double hearsay. Do same analysis for each level of hearsay.
- Exception apply?
  - Declarant unavailability required?
  - Declarant unavailability immaterial?

One way to identify hearsay is to picture the witness on the stand and then identify who is making the actual statement.

**Hearsay with Person as Declarant**

Remember that a document can also be hearsay.

**Hearsay with Document as Declarant**

A regular issue on essay questions is **double or triple hearsay**. Each level of hearsay must be analyzed separately; again, look for documents and individuals.

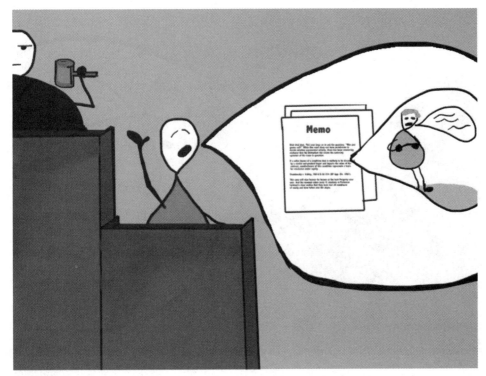

**Double Hearsay with a Document**

**Double Hearsay with a Person**

A twist that can throw some applicants off is **party-admissions**. To avoid that being you, see if the individual making the statement is wearing a party hat.

**Party-Admission**

**EXAM TIP**

Be on the lookout for admissions in any hearsay-within-hearsay scenario. It's an easy trap to have one layer be an admission. Analyze the admission layer of hearsay *and* analyze the other layer of hearsay. Both levels must be admissible before concluding whether the testimony is admissible.

Only after you have determined that it is hearsay and not a party-admission, then address whether a hearsay exception applies. Then, be careful that you also look for admissions in all double and triple hearsay questions.

**Hearsay exceptions** are divided into whether the declarant must be unavailable. Declarant unavailability results from:

* Privilege;
* Refusing to testify;
* Lack of memory;
* Death or physical/mental illness;
* Absent beyond the reach of the court's subpoena power and the proponent of the statement has been unable to procure attendance or testimony.[10]

Focus on the five exceptions that require the declarant to be unavailable:

* Former testimony:[11]
  * Given as a witness at a trial, hearing, or lawful deposition;
  * Offered against a party who had an opportunity and similar motive to develop it by direct, cross, or redirect examination;

---

10. Fed. R. Evid. 804(a).
11. Fed. R. Evid. 804(b)(3).

- Statements against interest:[12]
  - Reasonable person in the declarant's position would have made only if the person believed it to be true;
  - Contrary to declarant's proprietary or pecuniary interest;
  - Supported by corroborating circumstances that clearly indicate its trustworthiness;
- Dying declarations:[13]
  - Statement made by declarant believing that declarant's death was imminent;
  - Statement about its cause or circumstances;
- Statement of personal or family history;[14]
- Statement offered against party procuring declarant's unavailability.[15]

Having this list memorized allows you to quickly eliminate declarant unavailability as an issue for all other possible exceptions.

All other hearsay exceptions do not require declarant unavailability. The most frequently tested of these exceptions include:

- Present state of mind or physical condition:[16]
  - Must be then-existing state of mind or emotional, sensory, or physical condition;
  - Not including a statement of memory or belief;
- Excited utterance:[17]
  - Statement relating to a startling event or condition;
  - Made while under the stress of excitement that it caused;
- Present sense impressions:[18]
  - Statement describing or explaining an event or condition;
  - Made while or immediately after the declarant perceived it;
- Business records:[19]
  - Made at or near the time by someone with knowledge;
  - Kept in the course of a regularly conducted activity of a business or organization;
  - Making the record was a regular practice of that activity;
  - Shown by a custodian's testimony or by certification;
  - Neither the source of information nor the method of preparation indicate a lack of trustworthiness;
- Public records:[20]
  - Record sets out the office's activities;
  - Of a matter observed while under a legal duty to report;
  - Neither the source of information nor other circumstances indicate a lack of trustworthiness;

---

12. Fed. R. Evid. 804(b)(3).
13. Fed. R. Evid. 804(b)(2).
14. Fed. R. Evid. 804(b)(4).
15. Fed. R. Evid. 804(b)(6).
16. Fed. R. Evid. 803(3).
17. Fed. R. Evid. 803(2).
18. Fed. R. Evid. 803(1).
19. Fed. R. Evid. 803(6).
20. Fed. R. Evid. 803(8).

- Past recollection recorded:[21]
  - A record that:
    - is on a matter the witness once knew about but now cannot recall;
    - was made or adopted by the witness when the matter was fresh in the witness's memory; and
    - accurately reflects the witness's knowledge;
  - May be read into evidence;
  - May only be received as an exhibit if offered by an adverse party.

Remember not to jump into analyzing a hearsay exception. Always, always analyze the general rule of hearsay. State first that hearsay is inadmissible without an exception. Then, state and apply the hearsay definition to determine if it actually is hearing, Remember to always check for admissions. And then, analyze the potential hearsay exceptions. You will garner all the low-hanging fruit points.

These two overriding considerations—relevancy and hearsay—apply to both documents and witnesses. Relevancy also applies to real evidence.

The mind map for **documents** is fairly short:

- Relevant?
- Authentication
- Best evidence rule
- Hearsay?

**Authentication** means that the document is what the proponent claims it to be.[22] While a few writings are self-authenticating, most writings require a testimonial sponsor to prove that the writing was made, signed, or adopted by the particular relevant person. One frequent issue is photographs. Photographs must be identified by a witness as both a portrayal of relevant facts and a correct representation of those facts. The witness needs to be familiar with the scene or object depicted. Neither the photographer nor an expert is required.

Self-authenticating documents[23] include:

(OIL CANS)
- **O**fficial publications issued by public authority
- **I**nstruments—negotiable and commercial paper
- **L**abel, tag, or trademark affixed on item in regular course of business
- **C**ertified public documents (by clerk of agency or court that had custody)
- **A**cknowledged documents signed before notary, sworn to truth, content, and execution (except wills)
- **N**ewspapers and periodicals with reasonably wide circulation
- **S**ealed documents (government certified)

The **best evidence rule** only applies to documents. Any multiple choice question that has a response that indicates testimony unrelated to a document is inadmissible as it violates the best evidence rule is incorrect. The best evidence rule requires the "original writing, recording, or photograph, . . . to prove its content. . . ."[24] Thus, the rule applies only if the contents of the writing are at

---

21. Fed. R. Evid. 803(5).
22. Fed. R. Evid. 901(a).
23. Fed. R. Evid. 902.
24. Fed. R. Evid. 1002.

**EXAM TIP**

Sometimes, more than one exception potentially applies. Be sure to analyze all possibilities even if you decide that the requirements of one exception have been met—not all exceptions, just the possible ones. Don't eat all the candy—just the good ones!

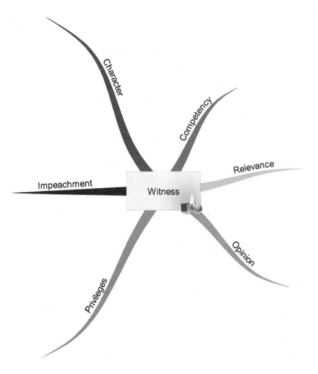

issue. Look for best evidence rule issues with operative or dispositive instruments such as contracts, deeds, and wills.

The mind map for **witnesses** or testimonial evidence is more detailed:

* Competency
* Relevance
* Opinion
  * Lay witness
  * Expert witness
* Character
* Impeachment
* Privileges
* Hearsay

**Competency** has four attributes. A witness must have the capacity to observe, to recollect, to communicate, and to appreciate the obligation to speak truthfully. The FRE requires that the witness have personal knowledge and must declare he will testify truthfully.[25]

Separate **opinion evidence** into lay opinions and expert opinions. **Lay opinion** testimony is generally inadmissible. Lay opinions may be allowed if no better evidence exists. In those situations, the lay opinion must be:

* based on the witness's perception,
* helpful for a clear understanding of a fact at issue, and
* not based on scientific, technical, or other specialized knowledge.[26]

---

25. Fed. R. Evid. 602, 603.
26. Fed. R. Evid. 701.

**Expert opinion** testimony questions are usually not as difficult as actually presenting an expert at trial. The reason is that the examiners must give you sufficient facts to identify the issues, including qualification—an often heated area in trials. One area that is commonly tested is whether expert testimony is needed at all. Another area tested is whether the opinion is supported by a proper factual basis. Memorize all the requirements for expert testimony, but focus on whether the subject matter is appropriate for expert opinion and if the opinion is supported by a proper factual basis for detailed memorization:

- Subject matter appropriate for expert opinion:
  - Scientific knowledge
  - Technical knowledge
  - Other specialized knowledge
- Witness qualifies as expert
- Opinion backed with reasonable certainty
- Opinion supported by a proper factual basis[27]:
  - Personal knowledge
  - Facts made known at trial
  - Facts made known outside of court:
    - Facts need not be admissible in court
    - Of the kind that are reasonably relied upon by experts in the field

On direct examination in a criminal trial, **character** evidence is not allowed to prove conformity with the party's character. It is allowed for other purposes including motive, opportunity, intent, preparation, common scheme or plan, knowledge, identity, absence of mistake or accident. In a civil trial, character evidence is not allowed unless character is at issue, such as child custody. Character evidence issues also arise with impeachment.

The purpose of **impeachment** is to cast an adverse reflection on a witness's truthfulness. Two methods of impeachment are cross-examination and extrinsic evidence, that is by asking the witness directly or by admitting other evidence such as another witness or a document. Impeachment through cross-examination includes prior inconsistent statements, bias or interest, and criminal convictions.

A party need not show a **prior inconsistent statement** to a witness. The party must, on request, show it to an adverse party's attorney. Extrinsic evidence is admissible only if the witness has the opportunity to explain the statement and an adverse party has the opportunity to examine the witness about it or if justice requires. This rule does not apply to admissions by a party opponent under FRE 801(d)(2).

Divide crimes into two categories. First are **crimes involving dishonesty** such as fraud or perjury, whether a felony or misdemeanor. The court has no discretion to exclude these crimes and there is no time limitation on how old the crime is.

The second category is **felonies not involving dishonesty**. Here, the court does have discretion to exclude the conviction. The crime must not be too remote. Generally, if it has been over ten years since the date of conviction or release from confinement imposed for the conviction, the conviction is excluded. Additionally, the court employs a balancing test. For the accused, the government must show the probative value as impeachment is not outweighed by its prejudicial effect. This generally favors exclusion as the standard is just "outweighs" and not "substantially outweighs." For a witness other than

---

27. Fed. R. Evid. 702.

an accused, the balancing test is FRE 403 and requires that the probative value is substantially outweighed by the danger of unfair prejudice. This favors admission. Extrinsic evidence of the crime is permitted.

Extrinsic evidence is most prevalent as an issue when dealing with **prior bad acts**. Most definitely, FRE 608 is a rule to spend significant time understanding. Generally, **interrogation** about prior bad acts is admissible within the court's discretion. The bad act must be probative of truthfulness. **Extrinsic evidence** of bad acts is not permitted. Thus, if the witness denies the act, the cross-examiner cannot refute the testimony by calling other witnesses or by producing other evidence.

Be watchful for another form of extrinsic evidence—**reputation** evidence. A witness may be impeached by showing a poor reputation for truthfulness. This is done by calling another witness from the community where the impeached witness lives or from his business circle. The impeaching witness may also state her personal opinion based on acquaintance, subject to the court's discretion.

Impeachment is not allowed on a collateral matter, but impeachment is allowed of a hearsay declarant.

Like all other forms of evidence, **real evidence** must be relevant. In addition, the object must be authenticated—that it is what its proponent claims it to be. This is accomplished by recognition testimony or chain of custody. A witness may authenticate an object if it has significant features that make it identifiable upon inspection. Otherwise, the proponent must present evidence of the chain of custody of the object and that it has been held in a substantially unbroken chain of possession.

No specific provision of the FRE provides for federal **privileges**. FRE 501 states that privileges are governed by common law. The federal courts have recognized these privileges in states that provide for them and thus should be your focus:

- Attorney-client privilege:
  - Client may refuse to disclose and to prevent any other person from disclosing confidential communications made for the purpose of rendition of professional legal services to the client;
  - Includes the attorney and its representatives;
  - Only the client can waive the privilege.
- Physician, psychotherapist, or social worker-patient privilege:
  - Confidential communications made for the purpose of diagnosis or treatment of the patient's physical, mental, or emotional condition.
- Spousal privilege:
  - Marital communication privilege: Provides that either spouse has a privilege to refuse to disclose and to prevent her spouse from disclosing a confidential communication made between spouses while they were husband and wife.
  - Spousal testimony privilege: A spouse may not be called as a witness by the prosecution against his spouse in a criminal case and may not be compelled to testify against his spouse in any criminal proceeding including those where the spouse is not the defendant.

In sum, focus on the FRE. Always sort out the characters in the scenario. Who are the parties? Who is the witness? Is it a direct examination or a cross-examination? If you aren't sure, is it your client's attorney who is questioning them or is it the opposing party's attorney? Once you have sorted out the players, then focus on the specific evidence. What is being offered into evidence? For what purpose is it being offered? Is this extrinsic evidence? That will get you through all Evidence MBE and essay questions.

## II. MBE STRATEGIES[28]

On MBE questions, one-fourth of the questions are on hearsay, one-fourth are on presentation of evidence, one-third cover relevancy, and the remaining are on privileges, and documents such as writings, recordings, and photographs. Evidence questions tend to be relatively short questions that are also easy to identify. When you read the call of the question and the responses, it will be immediately clear the question is about evidence because the responses will address admissibility. You should easily be able to tell which area of evidence and which rule should be applied before reading the fact pattern. Keep in mind that not only do you need to know whether it is admissible, but you also need to know for what purpose it is being admitted.

Some answer choices are **always** wrong:

* Latin terms that you have never studied or never seen are not correct. You may be fooled into thinking that the term is a correct answer that you just don't know. For example, *res gestae* is a relic from common law evidence. It is not in the Federal Rules of Evidence.
* Testimony on "ultimate issues" is an old rule from the common law. Ignore.
* "Testimony is inadmissible due to its self-serving nature" is always wrong because the self-serving nature goes to credibility, not admissibility.

Other answers require careful consideration:

* Have the exceptions that require unavailability of the declarant memorized. Then, any answer choice that states that the evidence is inadmissible because the declarant is available to testify is easily identified as correct or incorrect.
* Beware of answer choices that state that the witness is not competent to give certain evidence. The answer is usually one of bias, not competence.

Some answer choices look wrong, but may actually be correct:

* Carefully analyze questions that include responses dealing with legal relevance (probative value substantially outweighed by undue prejudice). Legal relevance can be the best choice or can be wrong. Evidence excluded by FRE 403 must be shocking evidence, not merely prejudicial. If all other choices are incorrect, then FRE 403 may be correct.
* Another choice that looks wrong but that may be correct is "inadmissible because it is hearsay not within any exception." Avoid the instinct to try to find a way to make evidence admissible because your gut tells you it should be. Some evidence just isn't admissible.

Evidence is a technical area of the law. Understanding the FRE in detail is essential. Visualize the scene of the courtroom. Who is on the stand and who is doing the questioning? What is the evidence? Witness, document, or real evidence? Follow your mind maps and you will do well.

---

28. Some of these strategies are from Steven L. Emanuel, *Strategies & Tactics for the MBE* 305-14 (6th ed. 2016).

## III. ESSAY PRACTICE QUESTION[29]

A prison inmate has filed a civil rights lawsuit against a guard at the prison, alleging that the guard violated the inmate's constitutional rights during an altercation. The inmate and the guard are the only witnesses to this altercation. They have provided contradictory reports about what occurred.

The trial will be before a jury. The inmate plans to testify at trial. The guard's counsel has moved for leave to impeach the inmate with the following:

(a) Twelve years ago, the inmate was convicted of felony distribution of marijuana. He served a three-year prison sentence, which began immediately after he was convicted. He served his full sentence and was released from prison nine years ago.

(b) Eight years ago, the inmate pleaded guilty to perjury, a misdemeanor punishable by up to one year in jail. He paid a $5,000 fine.

(c) Seven years ago, the inmate was convicted of felony sexual assault of a child and is currently serving a 10-year prison sentence for the crime. The victim was the inmate's daughter, who was 13 years old at the time of the assault.

The inmate's counsel objects to the admission of any evidence related to these three convictions and to any cross-examination based on this evidence.

The guard also plans to testify at trial. The inmate's counsel has moved for leave to impeach the guard with the following:

Last year, the guard applied for a promotion to prison supervisor. The guard submitted a résumé to the state that indicated that he had been awarded a B.A. in Criminal Justice from a local college. An official copy of the guard's academic transcript from that college indicates that the guard dropped out after his first semester and did not receive a degree.

The guard's counsel objects to the admission of this evidence and to any cross-examination based on this evidence.

The transcript and the résumé have been properly authenticated. The trial will be held in a jurisdiction that has adopted all of the Federal Rules of Evidence.

1. What evidence, if any, proffered by the guard to impeach the inmate should be admitted? Explain.

2. What evidence, if any, proffered by the inmate to impeach the guard should be admitted? Explain.

## IV. MBE PRACTICE QUESTIONS[30]

### Question 1

A defendant was tried on multiple counts of bank fraud for a scheme in which he allegedly made withdrawals from the bank accounts of others by using false

---

29. The Multistate Bar Examination ("MBE®") questions, the Multistate Essay Examination ("MEE®") questions, and excerpts from the Multistate Performance Tests ("MPT®") have been reprinted by permission from the NCBE®. Copyright© by the National Conference of Bar Examiners. All rights reserved.

30. *Id.*

identification cards and forging signatures on checks. A codefendant, who had assisted the defendant in 5 of the 75 transactions for which the defendant was being tried, testified that he was present and saw the defendant endorse 5 of the checks. Thereafter, the prosecutor moved for admission of all 75 checks that the defendant had allegedly endorsed, arguing that a comparison by the jury of the signatures on the checks identified by the codefendant with those on the other 70 checks would demonstrate that they were all signed by the defendant.

Should the court permit the proposed comparison of the handwriting specimens by the jury?

(A) No, because such a comparison may be done only by an expert.

(B) No, because such a comparison may be done only by an expert or by a nonexpert who can testify to the genuineness of the handwriting.

(C) Yes, because the jurors are allowed to determine the genuineness of handwriting specimens based on comparison with authenticated specimens

(D) Yes, but only if the court first makes a preliminary finding of authenticity as to the other 70 checks.

## Question 2

A defendant is on trial for knowing possession of a stolen television. The defendant claims that the television was a gift from a friend, who has disappeared. The defendant seeks to testify that he was present when the friend told her neighbor that the television had been given to the friend by her mother.

Is the defendant's testimony about the friend's statement to the neighbor admissible?

(A) No, because the friend's statement is hearsay not within any exception.

(B) No, because the defendant has not presented evidence of circumstances that clearly corroborate the statement.

(C) Yes, as nonhearsay evidence of the defendant's belief that the friend owned the television.

(D) Yes, under the hearsay exception for statements affecting an interest in property.

## Question 3

A plaintiff has brought a civil suit against a defendant for injuries arising out of a fistfight between them. The day after the fight, a police officer talked to the plaintiff, the defendant, and an eyewitness, and made an official police report. At trial, the plaintiff seeks to introduce from the properly authenticated police report a statement attributed to the eyewitness, who is unavailable to testify at trial, that "[the defendant] started the fight."

Should the court admit the statement from the report?

(A) No, unless the entire report is introduced.

(B) No, because it is hearsay not within any exception.

(C) Yes, because it was based on the eyewitness's firsthand knowledge.

(D) Yes, because it is an excerpt from a public record offered in a civil case.

## Question 4

A plaintiff has sued a defendant, alleging that she was run over by a speeding car driven by the defendant. The plaintiff was unconscious after her injury and, accompanied by her husband, was brought to the hospital in an ambulance.

At trial, the plaintiff calls an emergency room physician to testify that when the physician asked the plaintiff's husband if he knew what had happened, the husband, who was upset, replied, "I saw my wife get run over two hours ago by a driver who went right through the intersection without looking."

Is the physician's testimony about the husband's statement admissible?

(A) No, because it relates an opinion.
(B) No, because it is hearsay not within any exception.
(C) Yes, as a statement made for purposes of diagnosis or treatment.
(D) Yes, as an excited utterance.

## Question 5

A plaintiff has sued a defendant for personal injuries the plaintiff suffered when she was bitten as she was trying to feed a rat that was part of the defendant's caged-rat experiment at a science fair. At trial, the plaintiff offers evidence that immediately after the incident the defendant said to her, "I'd like to give you this $100 bill, because I feel so bad about this."

Is the defendant's statement admissible?

(A) No, because it is not relevant to the issue of liability.
(B) No, because it was an offer of compromise.
(C) Yes, as a present sense impression.
(D) Yes, as the statement of a party-opponent.

## Question 6

A defendant is charged with aggravated assault. The physical evidence at trial has shown that the victim was hit with a lead pipe in the back of the head and on the forearms and left in an alley. The medical examiner has testified that the injuries to the victim's forearms appear to have been defensive wounds. The victim has testified that he cannot remember who attacked him with the lead pipe. He would further testify that he remembers only that a passerby found him in the alley, and that he told the passerby that the defendant had hit him with the lead pipe; he then lost consciousness. The defendant objects to this proposed testimony, arguing that it is hearsay and that the victim had no personal knowledge of the identity of the perpetrator.

Is the victim's testimony concerning his previous statement to the passerby admissible?

(A) No, because the prosecutor has failed to show that it is more likely than not that the victim had personal knowledge of the perpetrator's identity.
(B) No, because the victim has no memory of the attack itself and therefore cannot be effectively cross-examined.
(C) Yes, because the victim is subject to cross-examination, and there is sufficient showing of personal knowledge.
(D) Yes, because it is the victim's own out-of-court statement.

## Question 7

A man suffered a broken jaw in a fight with a neighbor that took place when they were both spectators at a soccer match.

If the man sues the neighbor for personal injury damages, which of the following actions must the trial court take if requested by the man?

(A) Prevent the neighbor's principal eyewitness from testifying, upon a showing that six years ago the witness was convicted of perjury and the conviction has not been the subject of a pardon or annulment.
(B) Refuse to let the neighbor cross-examine the man's medical expert on matters not covered on direct examination of the expert.
(C) Exclude nonparty eyewitnesses from the courtroom during the testimony of other witnesses.
(D) Require the production of a writing used before trial to refresh a witness's memory.

## Question 8

A defendant is charged with robbing a bank. The prosecutor has supplied the court with information from accurate sources establishing that the bank is a federally insured institution and that this fact is not subject to reasonable dispute. The prosecutor asks the court to take judicial notice of this fact. The defendant objects.

How should the court proceed?

(A) The court must take judicial notice and instruct the jury that it is required to accept the judicially noticed fact as conclusive.
(B) The court must take judicial notice and instruct the jury that it may, but is not required to, accept the judicially noticed fact as conclusive.
(C) The court may refuse to take judicial notice, because judicial notice may not be taken of essential facts in a criminal case.
(D) The court must refuse to take judicial notice, because whether a bank is federally insured would not be generally known within the court's jurisdiction.

## Question 9

The beneficiary of a decedent's life insurance policy has sued the life insurance company for the proceeds of the policy. At issue is the date when the decedent first experienced the heart problems that led to his death. The decedent's primary care physician has testified at trial that the decedent had a routine checkup on February 15. The physician then identifies a photocopy of a questionnaire, provided by the physician and completed by the decedent on that date, in which the decedent wrote: "Yesterday afternoon I broke into a big sweat and my chest hurt for a while." The beneficiary now offers the photocopy in evidence.

Should the court admit the photocopy?

(A) No, because the original questionnaire has not been shown to be unavailable.
(B) No, because the statement related to past rather than present symptoms.
(C) Yes, as a business record.
(D) Yes, as a statement for the purpose of obtaining medical treatment.

## Question 10

A defendant is charged with mail fraud. At trial, the defendant has not taken the witness stand, but he has called a witness who has testified that the defendant has a reputation for honesty. On cross-examination, the prosecutor seeks to ask the witness, "Didn't you hear that two years ago the defendant was arrested for embezzlement?"

Should the court permit the question?

(A) No, because the defendant has not testified and therefore has not put his character at issue.

(B) No, because the incident was an arrest, not a conviction.

(C) Yes, because it seeks to impeach the credibility of the witness.

(D) Yes, because the earlier arrest for a crime of dishonesty makes the defendant's guilt of the mail fraud more likely.

## Question 11

At a woman's trial for bank robbery, the prosecutor has called a private security guard for the bank who has testified, without objection, that while he was on a coffee break, the woman's brother rushed up to him and said, "Come quickly! My sister is robbing the bank!" The woman now seeks to call a witness to testify that the brother later told the witness, "I got my sister into trouble by telling a security guard that she was robbing the bank, but now I realize I was mistaken." The brother is unavailable to testify.

Is the witness's testimony admissible?

(A) No, because the brother will be afforded no opportunity to explain or deny the later statement.

(B) No, because the prosecutor will be afforded no opportunity to confront the brother.

(C) Yes, because it is substantive proof that the woman did not rob the bank.

(D) Yes, but only as an inconsistent statement to impeach the brother's credibility.

## Question 12

A woman's car was set on fire by vandals. When she submitted a claim of loss for the car to her insurance company, the insurance company refused to pay, asserting that the woman's policy had lapsed due to the nonpayment of her premium. The woman sued the insurance company for breach of contract.

At trial, the woman testified that she had, in a timely manner, placed a stamped, properly addressed envelope containing the premium payment in the outgoing mail bin at her office. The woman's secretary then testified that every afternoon at closing time he takes all outgoing mail in the bin to the post office. The insurance company later called its mail clerk to testify that he opens all incoming mail and that he did not receive the woman's premium payment.

The woman and the insurance company have both moved for a directed verdict. For which party, if either, should the court direct a verdict?

(A) For the insurance company, because neither the woman nor her secretary has any personal knowledge that the envelope was delivered to the post office.

(B) For the insurance company, because the mail clerk's direct testimony negates the woman's circumstantial evidence.

(C) For the woman, because there is a presumption that an envelope properly addressed and stamped was received by the addressee.

(D) For neither the woman nor the insurance company, because under these circumstances the jury is responsible for determining whether the insurance company received the payment.

## Question 13

At a defendant's trial for mail fraud, the defendant calls his wife to testify that she committed the fraud herself without the defendant's knowledge. On cross-examination, the prosecutor asks the wife, "Isn't it true that you have fled your home several times in fear of your husband?"

Is this question proper?

(A) No, because it is leading a witness not shown to be hostile.

(B) No, because its probative value is outweighed by the danger of unfair prejudice to the defendant.

(C) Yes, because by calling his wife, the defendant has waived his privilege to prevent her from testifying against him.

(D) Yes, because it explores the wife's possible motive for testifying falsely.

## Question 14

A driver sued her insurance company on an accident insurance policy covering personal injuries to the driver. The insurance company defended on the ground that the driver's injuries were intentionally self-inflicted and therefore excluded from the policy's coverage.

The driver testified at trial that she had inflicted the injuries, as her negligence had caused the crash in which she was injured, but that she had not done so intentionally. She then called as a witness her treating psychiatrist to give his opinion that the driver had been mentally unbalanced, but not self-destructive, at the time of the crash.

Should the court admit the witness's opinion?

(A) No, because it is a statement about the driver's credibility.

(B) No, because it is an opinion about a mental state that constitutes an element of the defense.

(C) No, because the witness did not first state the basis for his opinion.

(D) Yes, because it is a helpful opinion by a qualified expert.

## Question 15

A plaintiff has brought a products liability action against a defendant, the manufacturer of a sport-utility vehicle that the plaintiff's decedent was driving when she was fatally injured in a rollover accident. The plaintiff claims that a design defect in the vehicle caused it to roll over. The defendant claims that the cause of the accident was the decedent's driving at excessive speed during an ice storm. Eyewitnesses to the accident have given contradictory estimates about the vehicle's speed just before the rollover. It is also disputed whether the decedent was killed instantly.

Which of the following items of offered evidence is the court most likely to admit?

(A) A videotape offered by the defendant of a test conducted by the defendant showing that a sport-utility vehicle of the same model the decedent was driving did not roll over when driven by a professional driver on a dry test track at the top speed testified to by the eyewitnesses.

(B) A videotape offered by the plaintiff of a television news program about sport-utility vehicles that includes footage of accident scenes in which the vehicles had rolled over.

(C) Evidence offered by the defendant that the decedent had received two citations for speeding in the previous three years.

(D) Photographs taken at the accident scene and during the autopsy that would help the plaintiff's medical expert explain to the jury why she concluded that the decedent did not die instantly.

## Question 16

At the start of the trial of a defendant and a codefendant for robbery, the codefendant and her attorney offered to give the prosecutor information about facts that would strengthen the prosecutor's case against the defendant in exchange for leniency toward the codefendant. The prosecutor refused the offer. Shortly thereafter, the codefendant committed suicide.

During the defendant's trial, the prosecutor called the codefendant's attorney and asked him to relate the information that the codefendant had revealed to the attorney.

Is the attorney's testimony admissible?

(A) No, because the codefendant's communications are protected by the attorney-client privilege.

(B) No, because the plea discussion was initiated by the codefendant rather than by the prosecutor.

(C) Yes, because the codefendant intended to disclose the information.

(D) Yes, because the information the codefendant gave to her attorney revealing her knowledge of the crime would be a statement against the codefendant's penal interest.

# CHAPTER 14

# Mapping MBE Topics—Real Property

## I. MIND MAP

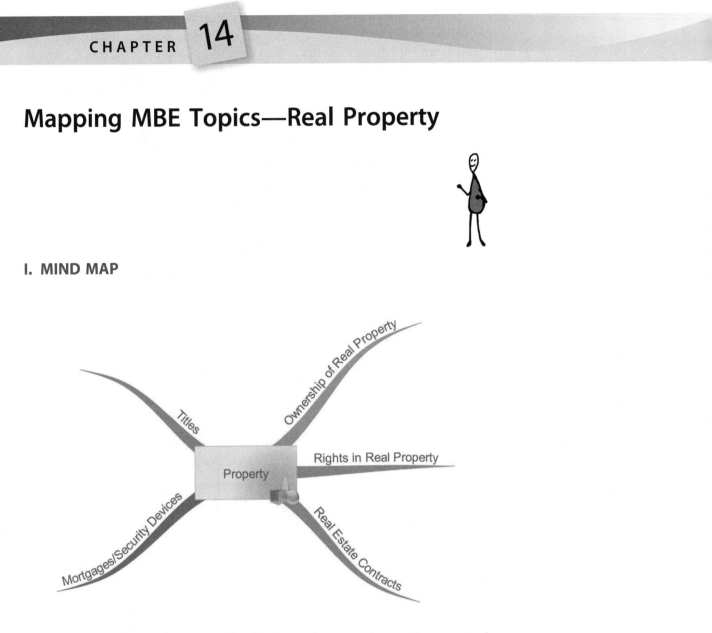

While some mind maps have a predictable format because they can be organized along a chronological series of events, real property is not one of them. Instead, real property considers various interests in land including different ways to achieve ownership, different rights in property, real estate contracts, mortgages, and titles. Your mind map then focuses on these areas.

- Ownership of real property
- Rights in real property
- Real estate contracts
- Mortgages/security devises
- Titles

*Ownership of Real Property.* Ownership covers present estates and future interests, co-tenancy, landlord-tenant law, and special problems such as the Rule Against Perpetuities, and fair housing/discrimination.

Many students shy away from studying **estates and future interests** as the language seems awkward and a bit archaic. Don't give up before you start. Understand present possessory estates first. Then, memorize the future interests that can follow each possessory estate. Only certain future interests follow certain present possessory estates. After you have memorized these pairings, then work towards a deeper understanding.

**Real Property Interests Analysis Steps**

1. Nature and characteristics of the interests of real property.
2. How a particular interest can be created.
3. How to classify the interest.
4. The rights of possession and the rights of the user of the interest.
5. The legal and equitable remedies stemming from that interest.

| PRESENT POSSESSORY ESTATES AND POSSIBLE FUTURE INTERESTS | | | | | |
|---|---|---|---|---|---|
| Words of Purchase | Words of Limitation | Present Possessory Estate | Possible Future Interests | Characteristics of Future Interest | RAP apply? |
| To A | None | Fee Simple Absolute | None | N/A | N/A |
| To A | and her heirs | Fee Simple Absolute | None | N/A | N/A |
| To A | and the heirs of his body | Fee Tail | Same as Life Estate | (Fill in) | (Fill in) |
| To A | for so long as; during; while; until | Fee Simple Determinable | Possibility of Reverter | Created in grantor | No |
| To A | provided; however; however if; but if; on condition that; or in the event that | Fee Simple Subject to a Condition Subsequent | Right of Entry or Power of Termination | Does not automatically terminate the estate; "O may reenter and terminate/retake A's estate" | (Fill in) |
| To A | Same as condition subsequent | Fee Simple subject to Executory Interest | Shifting/Springing executory interest (Power of Termination) | Automatically terminates the estate | Yes |
| To A | for life | Life Estate | Reversion/Remainder (Contingent or Vested) | (Fill in) | Reversion: No Remainder: Yes |
| To A | for life of B | Life Estate | Reversion/Remainder (Contingent or Vested) | (Fill in) | Reversion: No Remainder: Yes |

Both the present possessory estate and the future estate attached to it can be determined by critical reading. Make a chart of the different types of present possessory estates and which future interests may be connected to each estate. Add additional detail to this chart from practice MBE and essay questions for your later memorization.

**Life estates** have some special considerations because they can be made defeasible if the life estate holder breaches certain duties. Because the property is always going to pass to someone else upon the life estate holder's death, the life estate holder must maintain the property:

- Duty to not adversely affect the future interest (waste):
  - Duty to repair and maintain
  - Duty to pay mortgage interest
  - Duty to pay all ordinary taxes
  - Duty to pay the full cost of special assessments if the life of the public improvement is less than the duration of the life tenant's estate. Equitable apportionment is applied to improvements likely to last longer.

The **Rule Against Perpetuities (RAP)** has befuddled many a law student and many a bar applicant. Yet if you follow this analysis, you can work your way through any possible question:

- Identify whether or not the interest is subject to RAP:
  - Interests *not* subject to RAP:
    - Present possessory estates
    - Charitable trusts
    - Resulting trusts
    - Fully vested interests at creation, such as reversionary interests and completely vested remainders
  - Interests subject to RAP:
    - Options to purchase land
    - Powers of appointment
    - Rights of first refusal
    - Interests not fully vested at creation, such as:
      - Remainders subject to open
      - Contingent remainders
      - Executory interests
- Identify the life or lives in being, express or implied.
- Determine whether the interest will for certain either vest **or** fail to vest within 21 years of the life or lives in being.

**Concurrent estates** exist when two or more persons share an interest. Each is called a co-tenant. There are different types of joint estates:

- **Tenancy in Common:** Each co-tenant owns an undivided interest in the whole with no right of survivorship. Presumed form of co-ownership.
  - Possession: Unity of possession—each joint tenant has the right to possess the whole.
  - Transfer: Co-tenant may transfer his interest *inter vivos*.
  - Divisibility: Co-tenant may devise his interest and the interest can descend by intestacy.

- **Joint Tenancy:** Each co-tenant owns an undivided interest in the whole and has a right of survivorship.
  - Four unities required:
    - Unity of time—joint tenants must take at the same time.
    - Unity of title—joint tenants must take by the same instrument.
    - Unity of interest—joint tenants must take equal shares of the same type.
    - Unity of possession—each joint tenant has the right to possess the whole.
  - **Right of survivorship:** At the death of one joint tenant, the interest of the surviving joint tenant absorbs the interest of the deceased joint tenant. Only the last surviving joint tenant has an interest that is devisable.
  - Severed: Joint tenancy severed if one joint tenant conveys his interest voluntarily or involuntarily (creditor forces sale). Tenancy in common then results.
- **Tenancy by the Entirety:** Reserved for married couples. Presumed in some states if conveyance to a married couple. Gives each spouse an undivided interest in the whole and a right of survivorship.

A co-tenant has the right to seek partition of the property either voluntarily or involuntarily. A co-tenant who pays a mortgage or tax may seek contribution from the other co-tenant. A co-tenant does not have a right to seek a contribution or setoff for improvements made to the premises unless the improvements generate increased rents or profits. Then, those costs are recoverable only in a partition suit.

Keep in mind that **restraints on alienation** are usually unenforceable.

Under **landlord-tenant** law, a lease gives the tenant exclusive possession of the premises for a period of time. A lease can be created expressly or implied by conduct of the parties. An implied lease includes when a holdover tenant pays rent and the landlord accepts the rent. There are four types of leases:

- Term of years: definite beginning and end. No notice required to terminate.
- Periodic: set beginning and continues from period to period, such as month to month, without a set termination date until notice is given. Notice must be at the end of period. The required notice is measured by the rent payment clause (one full period), but no longer than six months.
- At will: no fixed duration. Terminates if either party dies; the tenant commits waste; the tenant attempts to assign his interest; the landlord transfers his interest; or the landlord transfers the premises to a third party for a term of years. Most states provide for 30 days' notice.
- Tenancy at Sufferance/Holdover Tenancy: tenant remains in possession of the leased premises after the end of the lease term. The landlord can recover possession and receive the reasonable rental value for the holdover period.

Both the landlord and tenant owe specific duties to each other:

- Duties of tenant:
  - Pay rent
  - Not commit waste

- Repair
- Other duties as contracted
- Duties of landlord:
  - Deliver legal right to possession of premises
  - Water and heat
  - Duties in lease document
  - Quiet enjoyment
  - Implied warranty of habitability

If the tenant fails to pay rent or commits another material breach of the lease, the landlord may seek to evict the tenant and/or to recover damages for the tenant's breach. Under the modern rule, rent acceleration clauses are permitted in leases. A tenant abandons the premises if he vacates the premises without intending to return and fails to pay rent. The landlord may then retake the premises, ignore the abandonment, and continue to hold the tenant liable for rent or reenter and relet the premises. The landlord has a duty to mitigate its damages. Retaliatory eviction in response to tenant's complaints about the landlord is prohibited in most states.

A tenant may seek money damages for the landlord's breach of the lease. A tenant may vacate the premises and terminate the lease if the tenant has been evicted by the landlord, actually or constructively. Statutes in some jurisdictions provide the tenant with additional remedies including withholding rent or repairing the premises and deducting the cost of repair from subsequent rent payments.

An assignment occurs when the tenant transfers to a third person all of his rights in the leased premises. The assignee then comes into privity of estate with the landlord. Thus, when the rent is not paid, the landlord may sue the assignee.

# Assignment

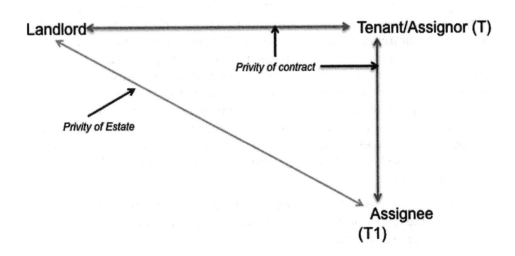

# Sublease

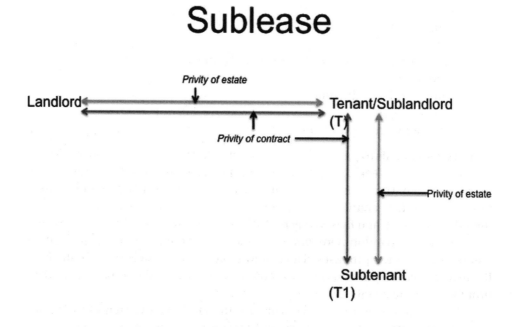

A sublease occurs when the tenant transfers less than all of his rights to a third person. A subtenant does not come into privity of estate with the landlord. Absent an express assumption of the duty to pay rent, the landlord may not sue the subtenant directly.

*Rights in Real Property.* Rights in real property includes easements, profits, and licenses as well as restrictive covenants, fixtures, and zoning.

An **easement** is an interest to use the land of another. Easements may be either affirmative or negative and may be either appurtenant or in gross. Most easements are affirmative, which gives the holder the right to do something on the land of another. A negative easement gives the holder the right to prevent a landowner from doing something on the land. The common law recognizes negative easements regarding light, air, water, and lateral and subjacent support. A writing is always required for a negative easement. An easement appurtenant requires a dominant and servient tenement. An easement in gross is personal in nature, resulting in a servient but not a dominant estate.

Creation of an easement may be created through a writing, by implication, by prescription, or by estoppel. The Statute of Frauds applies to a writing. An affirmative easement may be created by implication either by prior use or by necessity. An affirmative easement may also be created by prescription, which is similar to adverse possession, requiring use of the property that is open and notorious, continuous, exclusive, actual, and non-permissive (hostile). These are the same requirements as adverse possession. Creation of an easement by estoppel requires proof of an act or representation by the owner of the burdened estate in respect to the easement, justifiable reliance on that act or representation by the owner, and damages suffered by the owner of the benefited estate.

Easements can be transferred. An easement may be terminated by any of the following methods:

* End of a time period, if easement is created for a specific term;
* When the holder of the dominant estate releases his interest to the holder of the servient estate;

- When the dominant and servient estates come into common ownership;
- Abandonment;
- Estoppel;
- By prescription; or
- When a governmental body acquires the servient estate through an exercise of the eminent domain power.

Be sure to understand the difference between an easement and a license. A **license** is a privilege, usually to do something on someone else's property. A writing and consideration are not required. Licenses are not transferable unless the licensor intends them to be. Licenses expire upon the death of the licensor or the conveyance of the servient estate. Licenses are revocable at the will of the licensor unless the license is coupled with an interest in personal property that is on the land of another and has a privilege that is incidental to the personal property. Another exception to revocability is an executed license based on estoppel and involving a substantial expenditure of funds in reliance on the promisor's promise to allow the promisee to use the land. This becomes an easement by estoppel.

A **covenant** is a promise that attaches to land. The promise can be to do or to refrain from doing something on his land. A covenant that **runs with the land** is a promise that attaches to land. In contrast to easements, most running covenants are negative in nature. Running covenants include promises to pay rent, condominium common charges, and maintenance fees. These are said to touch and concern the land. Covenants run with the land when there is a writing, intent, horizontal and vertical privity, touch and concern, and notice. Horizontal privity refers to the relationship between the original covenantor and covenantee. This requirement is satisfied by a conveyance of land between the convenantee and covenantor, which occurs by the same deed that includes the covenant. Vertical privity refers to the relationship between an original party to a running covenant and the successor in interest to the original party. The successor steps into the shoes of the original party. A covenant touches and concerns the land when the covenant exercises direct influence on the occupation, use, or enjoyment of the premises.

A court may enforce a covenant as an **equitable servitude** if the plaintiff can establish all the elements for a covenant that runs with the land, but the plaintiff seeks equitable relief. An equitable servitude also exists when the plaintiff cannot establish at law all of the elements, but the plaintiff can demonstrate the relaxed requirements for an equitable servitude. For example, as an equity doctrine, if one of the covenant requirements is not met, a court may impose an equitable servitude such as when the covenant is not in writing. The plaintiff may prove the covenant through part performance or estoppel.

**Zoning** is another restriction on the use of land. The state possesses the power to regulate for the health, safety, and welfare of its citizens. A zoning ordinance may be challenged under the Due Process and Equal Protection Clauses. A zoning ordinance may also be subject to a First Amendment challenge if it regulates billboards or aesthetics.

A **taking** occurs when the government exercises its eminent domain power to take private property. The government may take the entirety of the land in fee simple or take an easement or an interest in the estate of the property. The Takings Clause of the Fifth Amendment, applicable to the states through the

Fourteenth Amendment, provides that private property may not be taken for a public use without just compensation. A *per se* taking occurs when an act by the government results in a permanent occupation of private property. A governmental regulation may constitute a taking if it "goes too far." A court engages in a balancing test considering the economic impact on the property owner, the extent to which the regulation interferes with distinct investment-backed expectations, and the character of the governmental action.

*Real Estate Contracts.* The topic of **real estate contracts** covers real estate brokerage; creation and construction of contracts, including the Statute of Frauds; marketable title; duty to disclose defects; implied warranty of quality; and remedies for breach of a contract to sell real property. Real property contracts fall within the **Statute of Frauds** and require a writing signed by the party to be charged. The writing must include:

- Description of the property
- Description of the parties
- Price
- Any conditions of price or payment agreed upon

All contracts for the sale of real property include an implied promise to convey a **marketable title** to the purchaser at the time for performance (the closing). A marketable title is a title that is reasonably free from doubt in both fact and law. Title is not reasonably free from doubt if it contains any of the following defects:

- Defects in the chain of title, such as adverse possession, defective execution of a deed, or significant variation of the description of the land.
- Encumbrances such as mortgages, liens, easements, leases, and covenants.
  - Be careful: Seller may satisfy a mortgage or lien at closing with the proceeds.
- Encroachment of your improvements onto another's land, or encroachments of another onto your land.
- Zoning and other land use restrictions do not render title unmarketable unless a zoning violation exists.

Remedies for failure to convey a marketable title include rescission, money damages, or specific performance.

Under the traditional rule, covenants in a real estate contract **merge** into the deed at closing. This typically means that a purchaser must sue under the deed's warranties rather than under the sales contract.

The seller has a **duty to disclose** all material latent defects known to the seller that are not readily observable or known to the buyer. Most jurisdictions recognize an implied warranty of quality. This warranty can be called of workmanlike quality, of habitability, of fitness, or of suitability. This runs from a seller/builder to subsequent purchasers.

A seller's **remedies** for a buyer's breach to purchase property include expectation damages, foreseeable consequential damages, reasonable reliance damages, retaining the down payment, or liquidated damages. If willful, punitive damages may be valid. In equity, the seller may seek rescission of the contract if property has increased in value or specific performance if property has decreased in value.

A buyer's remedies for a seller's breach include expectation damages, reliance damages, restitution of the down payment, and punitive damages. In equity, the buyer may seek rescission or specific performance.

*Mortgages/Security Devices.* Security devices include mortgages, deeds of trust, and installment land contracts. A debtor is the mortgagor and gives the mortgage to a lender who is the mortgagee. For a deed of trust, the debtor is the trustor. The trustor gives the deed of trust to a third-party trustee. For an installment land contract, the debtor is the purchaser who signs a contract with the seller/vendor, agreeing to make regular installment payments until the full contract price is paid. Only then will the vendor give a deed transferring legal title to the purchaser.

Jurisdictions are split on the nature of the interests held by the mortgagor and mortgagee. Three mortgage theories are used by different states:

- Title theory: Mortgagee receives legal title to the mortgaged real property and has the right to take possession. The title is subject to a condition subsequent that divests title if the mortgagor repays the loan by the due date. Until then, the mortgagor retains only an equitable interest. This is now the minority rule.
- Lien theory: Mortgagee receives a lien and the mortgagor retains legal and equitable title and possession to the mortgaged property unless and until foreclosure occurs. This is the majority rule.
- Intermediate theory: Mortgagor retains legal title until default occurs. After default, legal title and possession pass to the mortgagee. Limited number of states have adopted.

A mortgagor is not to commit **waste**, if without the mortgagee's consent, the mortgagor or life tenant:

- Fails to pay taxes or governmental assessments;
- Makes physical changes to property that reduces its value;
- Fails to maintain and repair the property in a reasonable manner, except for repair of casualty or acts of third parties not the fault of the mortgagor;
- Fails to comply materially with mortgage covenants respecting the physical care, maintenance, construction, demolition, or insurance against casualty or the property;
- Fails to comply materially with mortgage covenants respecting the physical care, maintenance, construction, demolition, or insurance against casualty of the property or improvements on it; or
- Retains rents to which the mortgagee has a right of possession.

Two types of questions involving mortgages regularly arise. The first concerns the sale of property encumbered by a mortgage. The second concerns multiple mortgages on the same property. Typically, unless the mortgagor is paying off the mortgage with the proceeds of a sale, a mortgagor must receive consent from a mortgagee before transferring property encumbered by a mortgage because of "due on sale" clauses. A key distinction to understand is the difference between **assuming** an existing mortgage on property and taking property **"subject to"** an existing mortgage.

Assuming an existing mortgage means the mortgage is transferred from the mortgagor/grantor to the grantee. The grantee assumes the mortgage via an agreement and must pay off the grantor's debt to the mortgagee. Absent a later modification agreement between the grantee and mortgagee that removes the mortgagor/grantor from the dispute, the mortgagor/grantor remains on the hook for a default. Thus, when a default occurs, the mortgagee may:

- Foreclose on the real property;
- Sue grantee on the debt as the grantee is primarily liable; or
- Sue mortgagor/grantor on the debt as secondarily liable.
  - Mortgagor/grantor could then seek reimbursement from the grantee personally.

Taking property "subject to" an existing mortgage also begins with a pre-existing mortgage on the property that is transferred from the mortgagor/grantor to the grantee. The difference is that the grantee does not sign an assumption agreement and so does not assume the existing mortgage, but takes the property "subject to the mortgage." In this case, the mortgagor/grantor remains on the hook to the mortgagee, but the grantee is not on the hook to the mortgagee. Thus, when a default occurs, the mortgagee may:

- Foreclose on the real property now owned by the grantee; or
- Sue the mortgagor/grantor on the debt.
  - Could then foreclose on the property, but may not successfully pursue a personal action against the grantee.

The second topic that occurs regularly in relation to mortgages is **multiple mortgages** on the same property. Priority is determined by chronological order of recording. Every mortgagee may redeem "up" by paying off and acquiring any mortgages of higher priority. For example, mortgagee 2 could "redeem" from mortgagee 1, and mortgagor then owes both mortgages to mortgagee 2. In addition, a mortgagee can foreclose "down," thereby wiping out mortgages and other interests of lower priority. A foreclosure sale wipes out all later mortgages—those coming later in time than the mortgage being foreclosed—but does not wipe out prior mortgages.

*Titles.* Titles in real property include adverse possession, transfer by deed, transfer by operation of law and by will, and recording acts.

A favorite topic of bar examiners is **adverse possession**, particularly boundary disputes. Check for each requirement using the acronym OCEAN:

- **O**pen and notorious
- **C**ontinuous possession for the statutory period
- **E**xclusive
- **A**ctual
- **N**on-permissive (hostile)

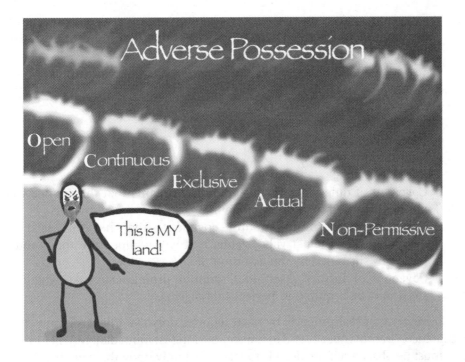

An adverse possessor must possess the premises for the requisite time period. The specific timing requirements are set out by state statute. If the adverse possessor has not been in possession for the full statutory possession, he may still meet the time period by tacking his period of possession onto that period of possession of another possessor if the possessors are in privity of estate. Privity of estate exists when there has been a voluntary transfer of possession from the first adverse possessor to the second adverse possessor, such as by deed. The statutory period may also be tolled if the owner has a disability at the time the adverse possessor enters.

There are three types of deeds. In a **general warranty deed**, the grantor warrants that no title defects exist in the chain of title. In a **special warranty deed**, the grantor warrants that no title defects occurred during his ownership of the property, but does not warrant against title defects that occurred prior to his ownership. In a **quitclaim deed**, the grantor provides no warrants. The grantee takes whatever interest the grantor had.

A general or special warranty deed contains a series of covenants, divided into present and future covenants. Present covenants are broken, if at all, only at the time of conveyance, and a grantee has a limited time to make a claim. Present covenants do not generally run with the land to remote grantees. Future covenants may be broken after the time of conveyance and do run with the land to subsequent purchasers. Remember these points about covenants:

* Present covenants:
    * Covenant of seisin—grantor owns and possesses the estate granted. Existence of an encumbrance does not breach the covenant.
    * Covenant of right to convey—grantor has the right to convey the property. This differs from the covenant of seisin as a trustee may be seised of the fee but barred from conveying the property by the trust document.

- Covenant against encumbrances—grantor promises that there are no encumbrances. No third person has a right that diminishes the value or limits the use of the land granted, including:
  - mortgage and judgment liens,
  - taxes,
  - leases,
  - water rights,
  - easements, and
  - restrictions on use.
- Future covenants:
  - Covenant of quiet enjoyment—grantor covenants that the grantee will not be disturbed by a superior claim.
  - Covenant of warranty—grantor covenants that he will assist in defending title against valid claims and will compensate the grantee for losses sustained by the assertion of superior title.
  - Covenant of further assurances—grantor promises to take whatever steps may be required to perfect title defects.

Conveyance of real property by deed requires donative intent, delivery, and acceptance. Grantor must intend to transfer the interest immediately. Will formalities must be observed if the deed is to take effect only upon the grantor's death. Delivery is usually accomplished by the physical act of handing the deed over to someone else. Mere words including a declaration of intent and relinquishment of control can accomplish delivery. A presumption of delivery arises if:

- the deed is later found in the grantee's possession;
- the deed is properly executed and recorded; or
- the deed contains an attestation clause that attests to delivery.

Handing the deed to an agent does not constitute delivery until the agent delivers the deed to the grantee or grantee's agent. That triggers the doctrine of relation back as long as the grantor relinquishes all control over the deed. When delivery is accomplished through the agent, delivery relates back to the date the grantor handed the deed to the agent.

When there are conflicting descriptions of the property contained in the deed, rules of construction determine which description prevails. The order of superiority relies first on natural deed descriptions:

- Natural monuments
- Artificial monuments
- Courses and angles
- Distances
- Name and quantity

**Recording** a deed is not required to validate the transfer of title. Recording becomes important when two or more parties claim that the owner has conveyed or mortgaged the property to them and their relative priority is at issue. Title based on adverse possession is not recordable until title has been quieted. Because adverse possession is a nondocumented title, it is not recordable and is not made invalid by a *bona fide purchaser*. Other nondocumented interests include prescriptive easements, implied easements, and boundary adjustments by acquiescence or by oral agreement.

There are three types of recording statutes: race, notice, and race-notice. Under the **race statute**, the person who records first prevails. Under a **notice statute**, an unrecorded conveyance is invalid against a subsequent *bona fide* purchaser for value and without notice. To prevail under a notice statute, a claimant must prove:

* The claimant took subsequent in time to another person claiming ownership;
* The claimant was a *bona fide* purchaser for value; and
* The claimant took the property without actual, constructive, or inquiry notice.

Constructive notice exists if the other party's deed is recorded in the proper chain of title in the record books. Inquiry notice exists if the appearance of the property is such that the claimant should have asked more questions about the property's title. A quitclaim deed gives rise to inquiry notice.

**Notice Recording Statute**

Under a **race-notice statute**, an unrecorded conveyance is invalid against a subsequent *bona fide* purchaser for value who takes without notice and records first. To prevail under a race-notice statute, the claimant must prove:

* The claimant took subsequent in time to another person claiming ownership;
* The claimant was a *bona fide* purchaser for value;
* The claimant took the property without actual, constructive, or inquiry notice; and
* The claimant recorded first.

The **shelter rule** provides protection for a subsequent purchaser who does not satisfy the applicable recording statute. Under the shelter rule, a person who is a successor in interest to a person protected by the recording statute is also protected.

**Race-Notice Recording Statute**

## II. MBE STRATEGIES[1]

Property questions tend to have the longest fact patterns. They are complicated and require careful reading. As you work through the fact patterns, keep in mind a couple of things as you sort through the parties and each interest in the property.

*Bona fide* purchaser status does not matter between the original parties to a transaction and is only relevant if subsequent purchasers are involved. Most of these fact patterns involve recording statutes.

Marketable title is a frequent topic on the MBE. Remember that marketable title is implied in every real estate sales contract; but once the deed takes effect, the terms of the deed control.

Another popular topic is the difference between real covenants and equitable servitudes. Keep track of notice.

Know the differences between recording statutes. Pure race statutes do not come up very often on the MBE. The other two types of recording statutes are distinguishable by one point: whether the subsequent *bona fide* purchaser is protected before he records his own interest. Under a pure notice statute, the *bona fide* purchaser is protected from the moment of conveyance. Under a race-notice statute, he is not protected until he records his interest.

---

1. Some of these strategies are from Steven L. Emanuel, *Strategies & Tactics for the MBE* 375-383-276 (6th ed. 2016).

Use these strategies for analyzing property questions:

- Questions asking for the answer choice that is "most likely to succeed": Determine which answer choice most closely addresses the greatest obstacle to success in the case; the answer choice containing a point that is extremely difficult to prove is likely the incorrect answer where another answer would also resolve the case but be easier to prove.
- Questions asking for the "most important point" or "which of the following is the best comment concerning the conflicting claims of A and B": Look for the answer choice that will determine who will prevail in the case, and determine the pivotal fact, if possible.
- Beware of constitutional answers: Answer choices voiding a zoning ordinance or covenant on constitutional grounds are likely to be incorrect unless the restriction is far outside the realm of standard restrictions; eliminate all property law answer choices first.
- In "class gift" problems, always check first to see if the gift is an *inter vivos* conveyance or a conveyance by a will. Why does it matter? There are no RAP problems with a class of grandchildren when the conveyance is by a will because the grantor/testator is deceased and cannot have additional children.
- In Rule Against Perpetuities problems, see if you can think of *any* scenario that won't satisfy the Rule.

Give future interests a chance before you punt the topic. Keep track of the language including the words of conveyance and any words of limitation. Identify the present possessory interest and remember which future interests can follow from that interest.

## III. ESSAY PRACTICE QUESTION[2]

Seventeen years ago, a property owner granted a sewer-line easement to a private sewer company. The easement allowed the company to build, maintain, and use an underground sewer line in a designated sector of the owner's three-acre tract. The easement was properly recorded with the local registrar of deeds.

Fifteen years ago, a man having no title or other interest in the owner's three-acre tract wrongfully entered the tract, built a cabin, and planted a vegetable garden. The garden was directly over the sewer line constructed pursuant to the easement the owner had granted to the sewer company. The cabin and garden occupied half an acre of the three-acre tract. The man moved into the cabin immediately after its completion and remained in continuous and exclusive possession of the cabin and garden until his death. However, he did not use the remaining two and one-half acres of the three-acre tract in any way.

Eight years ago, the man died. Under the man's duly probated will, he bequeathed to his sister "all real property in which I have or may have an interest at the time of my death." The man's sister took possession of the cabin and garden immediately after the man's death and remained in exclusive and continuous possession of them for one year, but she, too, did not use the remaining two and one-half acres of the tract.

Seven years ago, the man's sister executed and delivered to a buyer a general warranty deed stating that it conveyed the entire three-acre tract to the buyer. The deed contained all six title covenants. Since this transaction, the buyer has continuously occupied the cabin and garden but has not used the remaining two and one-half acres.

A state statute provides that "any action to recover the possession of real property must be brought within 10 years after the cause of action accrues."

Last month, the property owner sued the buyer to recover possession of the three-acre tract.

1. Did the buyer acquire title to the three-acre tract or any portion of it? Explain.
2. Assuming that the buyer did not acquire title to the entire three-acre tract, can the buyer recover damages from the sister who sold him the three-acre tract? Explain.
3. Assuming that the buyer acquired title to the entire three-acre tract or the portion above the sewer-line easement, can the buyer compel the sewer company to remove the sewer line under the garden? Explain.

## IV. MBE PRACTICE QUESTIONS[3]

### Question 1

A man obtained a bank loan secured by a mortgage on an office building that he owned. After several years, the man conveyed the office building to a woman,

---

2. The Multistate Bar Examination ("MBE®") questions, the Multistate Essay Examination ("MEE®") questions, and excerpts from the Multistate Performance Tests ("MPT®") have been reprinted by permission from the NCBE®. Copyright© by the National Conference of Bar Examiners. All rights reserved.

3. *Id.*

who took title subject to the mortgage. The deed to the woman was not recorded. The woman took immediate possession of the building and made the mortgage payments for several years.

Subsequently, the woman stopped making payments on the mortgage loan, and the bank eventually commenced foreclosure proceedings in which the man and the woman were both named parties. At the foreclosure sale, a third party purchased the building for less than the outstanding balance on the mortgage loan. The bank then sought to collect the deficiency from the woman.

Is the bank entitled to collect the deficiency from the woman?

(A) No, because the woman did not record the deed from the man.

(B) No, because the woman is not personally liable on the loan.

(C) Yes, because the woman took immediate possession of the building when she bought it from the man.

(D) Yes, because the woman was a party to the foreclosure proceeding.

## Question 2

A credit card company obtained and properly filed a judgment against a man after he failed to pay a $10,000 debt. A statute in the jurisdiction provides as follows: "Any judgment properly filed shall, for 10 years from filing, be a lien on the real property then owned or subsequently acquired by any person against whom the judgment is rendered."

Two years later, the man purchased land for $200,000. He made a down payment of $20,000 and borrowed the remaining $180,000 from a bank. The bank loan was secured by a mortgage on the land. Immediately after the closing, the deed to the man was recorded first, and the bank's mortgage was recorded second.

Five months later, the man defaulted on the mortgage loan and the bank initiated judicial foreclosure proceedings. After receiving notice of the proceedings, the credit card company filed a motion to have its judgment lien declared to be the first lien on the land.

Is the credit card company's motion likely to be granted?

(A) No, because the bank's mortgage secured a loan used to purchase the land.

(B) No, because the man's down payment exceeded the amount of his debt to the credit card company.

(C) Yes, because the bank had constructive notice of the judgment lien.

(D) Yes, because the bank is a third-party lender and not the seller of the land.

## Question 3

A husband and wife acquired land as common law joint tenants with right of survivorship. One year later, without his wife's knowledge, the husband executed a will devising the land to his best friend. The husband subsequently died.

Is the wife now the sole owner of the land?

(A) No, because a joint tenant has the unilateral right to end a joint tenancy without the consent of the other joint tenant.

(B) No, because the wife's interest in the husband's undivided 50% ownership in the land adeemed.

(C)  Yes, because of the doctrine of after-acquired title, or estoppel by deed.

(D)  Yes, because the devise to the friend did not sever the joint tenancy.

## Question 4

A landlord leased a building to a tenant for a 10-year term. Two years after the term began, the tenant subleased the building to a sublessee for a 5-year term. Under the terms of the sublease, the sublessee agreed to make monthly rent payments to the tenant.

Although the sublessee made timely rent payments to the tenant, the tenant did not forward four of those payments to the landlord. The tenant has left the jurisdiction and cannot be found. The landlord has sued the sublessee for the unpaid rent.

There is no applicable statute.

If the court rules that the sublessee is not liable to the landlord for the unpaid rent, what will be the most likely reason?

(A)  A sublessee is responsible to the landlord only as a surety for unpaid rent owed by the tenant.

(B)  The sublease constitutes a novation of the original lease.

(C)  The sublessee is not in privity of estate or contract with the landlord.

(D)  The sublessee's rent payments to the tenant fully discharged the sublessee's obligation to pay rent to the landlord.

## Question 5

A woman who owned a house executed a deed purporting to convey the house to her son and his wife. The language of the deed was sufficient to create a common law joint tenancy with right of survivorship, which is unmodified by statute in the jurisdiction. The woman mailed the deed to the son with a letter saying: "Because I intend you and your wife to have my house after my death, I am enclosing a deed to the house. However, I intend to live in the house for the rest of my life, so don't record the deed until I die. The deed will be effective at my death."

The son put the deed in his desk. The wife discovered the deed and recorded it without the son's knowledge. Subsequently, the son and the wife separated, and the wife, without telling anyone, conveyed her interest in the house to a friend who immediately reconveyed it to the wife.

The woman learned that the son and the wife had separated and also learned what had happened to the deed to the house. The woman then brought an appropriate action against the son and the wife to obtain a declaration that the woman was still the owner of the house and an order canceling of record the woman's deed and the subsequent deeds.

If the court determines that the woman owns the house in fee simple, what will be the likely explanation?

(A)  The deed was not delivered.

(B)  The wife's conduct entitles the woman to equitable relief.

(C)  The woman expressly reserved a life estate.

(D)  The woman received no consideration for her deed.

## Question 6

A woman borrowed $100,000 from a bank and executed a promissory note to the bank in that amount. As security for repayment of the loan, the woman's brother gave the bank a mortgage on a tract of land solely owned by him. The brother did not sign the promissory note.

The woman subsequently defaulted on the loan, and after acceleration, the bank instituted foreclosure proceedings on the brother's land. The brother filed a timely objection to the foreclosure.

Will the bank succeed in foreclosing on the tract of land?

(A) No, because the bank has an equitable mortgage rather than a legal mortgage.

(B) No, because a mortgage from the brother is invalid without a mortgage debt owed by him.

(C) Yes, because the bank has a valid mortgage.

(D) Yes, because the bank is a surety for the brother's mortgage.

## Question 7

A mother executed a will devising vacant land to her son. The mother showed the will to her son.

Thereafter, the son purported to convey the land to a friend by a warranty deed that contained no exceptions. The friend paid value for the land and promptly recorded the deed without having first conducted any title search. The friend never took possession of the land.

The mother later died, and the will devising the land to her son was duly admitted to probate.

Thereafter, the friend conducted a title search for the land and asked the son for a new deed. The son refused, because the value of the land had doubled, but he offered to refund the purchase price to the friend.

The friend has sued to quiet title to the land. Is the friend likely to prevail?

(A) No, because the friend failed to conduct a title search before purchasing the land.

(B) No, because the son had no interest in the land at the time of conveyance.

(C) Yes, because of the doctrine of estoppel by deed.

(D) Yes, because the deed was recorded.

## Question 8

A woman inherited a house from a distant relative. The woman had never visited the house, which was located in another state, and did not want to own it. Upon learning this, a man who lived next door to the house called the woman and asked to buy the house. The woman agreed, provided that the house was sold "as is." The man agreed, and the woman conveyed the house to the man by a warranty deed.

The man had purchased the house for investment purposes, intending to rent it out while continuing to live next door. After the sale, the man started to renovate the house and discovered serious termite damage. The man sued the woman for breach of contract.

There are no applicable statutes. How should the court rule?

(A)  For the woman, because the man planned to change the use of the house for investment purposes.
(B)  For the woman, because she sold the house "as is."
(C)  For the man, because of the doctrine of caveat emptor.
(D)  For the man, because he received a warranty deed.

## Question 9

A man owned a large tract of land that had frontage on a public highway. The land had no access to any other road.

Fifteen years ago, the man conveyed the rear half of the land to a woman and at the same time conveyed an express easement to the woman that provided access from her land across his retained land to the public highway.

The woman used the easement until she reconveyed the land back to the man 10 years ago. The deed to the man made no reference to the easement.

Five years ago, the man again conveyed the rear half of the land, this time to an investor in a deed that made no reference to any easement to the public highway.

Recently, the man told the investor that he could no longer cross the man's land for access to the public highway. A neighbor has told the investor that he can use her land for access to another public road "for a price."

The investor has sued the man for the right to cross the man's land to the public highway.

For whom will the court likely decide?

(A)  The investor, because an easement will be implied.
(B)  The investor, because the man is estopped by his grant of an easement to the woman.
(C)  The man, because the express easement was terminated by the reconveyance.
(D)  The man, because the investor can reasonably acquire another means of access to a public road.

## Question 10

Two friends planned to incorporate a business together and agreed that they would own all of the corporation's stock in equal proportion.

A businesswoman conveyed land by a warranty deed to "the corporation and its successors and assigns." The deed was recorded.

Thereafter, the friends had a disagreement. No papers were ever filed to incorporate the business. There is no applicable statute.

Who owns the land?

(A)  The businesswoman, because the deed was a warranty deed.
(B)  The businesswoman, because the deed was void.
(C)  The two friends as tenants in common, because they intended to own the corporation's stock in equal proportion.
(D)  The two friends as tenants in common, because they were the intended sole shareholders.

## Question 11

A landlord leased a building to a tenant for a term of six years. The lease complied with the statute of frauds and was not recorded. During the lease term, the tenant sent an email to the landlord that stated: "I hereby offer to purchase for $250,000 the building that I am now occupying under a six-year lease with you." The tenant's name was placed below the word "signed" on the message.

In response, the landlord emailed the tenant: "That's fine. We'll close in 60 days." The landlord's name was placed below the word "signed" on the reply message.

Sixty days later, the landlord refused to tender the deed to the building when the tenant tendered the $250,000 purchase price. The tenant has sued for specific performance.

Who is likely to prevail?

(A) The landlord, because formation of an enforceable contract to convey the building could not occur until after the lease term expired.

(B) The landlord, because the landlord's email response did not contain a sufficient signature under the statute of frauds.

(C) The tenant, because the email messages constitute an insufficient attornment of the lease.

(D) The tenant, because the email messages constitute a sufficient memorandum under the statute of frauds.

## Question 12

A tenant leased a commercial property from a landlord for a 12-year term. The property included a large store and a parking lot. At the start of the lease period, the tenant took possession and with the landlord's oral consent installed counters, display cases, shelving, and special lighting. Both parties complied with all lease terms.

The lease is set to expire next month. Two weeks ago, when the landlord contacted the tenant about a possible lease renewal, she learned that the tenant had decided not to renew the lease, and that the tenant planned to remove all of the above-listed items on or before the lease termination date. The landlord claimed that all the items had become part of the real estate and had to remain on the premises. The tenant asserted his right and intention to remove all the items.

Both the lease and the statutes of the jurisdiction are silent on the matter in dispute. At the time the landlord consented and the tenant installed the items, nothing was said about the tenant's right to retain or remove the items.

The landlord has sued the tenant to enjoin his removal of the items. How is the court likely to rule?

(A) For the landlord, because the items have become part of the landlord's real estate.

(B) For the landlord as to items bolted or otherwise attached to the premises, and for the tenant as to items not attached to the premises other than by weight.

(C) For the tenant, provided that the tenant reasonably restores the premises to the prior condition or pays for the cost of restoration.

(D) For the tenant, because all of the items may be removed as trade fixtures without any obligation to restore the premises.

## Question 13

For 22 years, the land records have shown a man as the owner of an 80-acre farm. The man has never physically occupied the land.

Nineteen years ago, a woman entered the farm. The character and duration of the woman's possession of the farm caused her to become the owner of the farm under the adverse possession law of the jurisdiction.

Three years ago, when the woman was not present, a neighbor took over possession of the farm. The neighbor repaired fences, put up "no trespassing" signs, and did some plowing. When the woman returned, she found the neighbor in possession of the farm. The neighbor vigorously rejected the woman's claimed right to possession and threatened force. The woman withdrew.

The woman then went to the man and told him of the history of activity on the farm. The woman orally told the man that she had been wrong to try to take his farm. She expressly waived any claim she had to the land. The man thanked her.

Last month, unsure of the effect of her conversation with the man, the woman executed a deed purporting to convey the farm to her son. The son promptly recorded the deed.

The period of time to acquire title by adverse possession in the jurisdiction is 10 years. Who now owns the farm?

(A) The man, because the woman's later words and actions released title to the man.

(B) The neighbor, because the neighbor succeeded to the woman's adverse possession title by privity of possession.

(C) The son, because he succeeded to the woman's adverse possession title by privity of conveyance.

(D) The woman, because she must bring a quiet title action to establish her title to the farm before she can convey the farm to her son.

## Question 14

In the most recent deed in the chain of title to a tract of land, a man conveyed the land as follows: "To my niece and her heirs and assigns in fee simple until my niece's daughter marries, and then to my niece's daughter and her heirs and assigns in fee simple."

There is no applicable statute, and the common law Rule Against Perpetuities has not been modified in the jurisdiction. Which of the following is the most accurate statement concerning the title to the land?

(A) The niece has a life estate and the daughter has a contingent remainder.

(B) The niece has a fee simple and the daughter has no interest, because after the grant of a fee simple there can be no gift over.

(C) The niece has a fee simple and the daughter has no interest, because she might not marry within 21 years after the date of the deed.

(D) The niece has a defeasible fee simple determinable and the daughter has an executory interest.

## Question 15

A businessman executed a promissory note for $200,000 to a bank, secured by a mortgage on commercial real estate owned by the businessman. The promissory note stated that the businessman was not personally liable for the mortgage debt.

One week later, a finance company obtained a judgment against the businessman for $50,000 and filed the judgment in the county where the real estate was located. At the time the judgment was filed, the finance company had no actual notice of the bank's mortgage.

Two weeks after that filing, the bank recorded its mortgage on the businessman's real estate.

The recording act of the jurisdiction provides: "Unless the same be recorded according to law, no conveyance or mortgage of real property shall be good against subsequent purchasers for value and without notice or against judgment creditors without notice."

The finance company sued to enforce its judgment lien against the businessman's real estate. The bank intervened in the action, contending that the judgment lien was a second lien on the real estate and that its mortgage was a first lien.

Is the bank's contention correct?

(A) No, because the judgment lien was recorded before the mortgage, and the finance company had no actual notice of the mortgage.

(B) No, because the businessman was not personally liable for the mortgage debt, and the mortgage was therefore void.

(C) Yes, because a mortgage prior in time has priority over a subsequent judgment lien.

(D) Yes, because the recording of a mortgage relates back to the date of execution of the mortgage note.

## Question 16

A seller conveyed residential land to a buyer by a warranty deed that contained no exceptions and recited that the full consideration had been paid. To finance the purchase, the buyer borrowed 80% of the necessary funds from a bank. The seller agreed to finance 15% of the purchase price, and the buyer agreed to provide cash for the remaining 5%.

At the closing, the buyer signed a promissory note to the seller for 15% of the purchase price but did not execute a mortgage. The bank knew of the loan made by the seller and of the promissory note executed by the buyer to the seller. The buyer also signed a note to the bank, secured by a mortgage, for the 80% advanced by the bank.

The buyer has now defaulted on both loans. There are no applicable statutes.

Which loan has priority?

(A) The bank's loan, because the seller can finance a part of the purchase price only by use of an installment land contract.

(B) The bank's loan, because it was secured by a purchase-money mortgage.

(C) The seller's loan, because a promissory note to a seller has priority over a bank loan for residential property.

(D) The seller's loan, because the bank knew that the seller had an equitable vendor's lien.

## Question 17

A seller and a buyer signed a contract for the sale of vacant land. The contract was silent concerning the quality of title, but the seller agreed in the contract to convey the land to the buyer by a warranty deed without any exceptions.

When the buyer conducted a title search for the land, she learned that the applicable zoning did not allow for her planned commercial use. She also discovered that there was a recorded restrictive covenant limiting the use of the land to residential use.

The buyer no longer wants to purchase the land. Must the buyer purchase the land?

(A) No, because the restrictive covenant renders the title unmarketable.

(B) No, because the zoning places a cloud on the title.

(C) Yes, because the buyer would receive a warranty deed without any exceptions.

(D) Yes, because the contract was silent regarding the quality of the title.

# CHAPTER 15

# Mapping MBE Topics—Torts

## I. MIND MAP

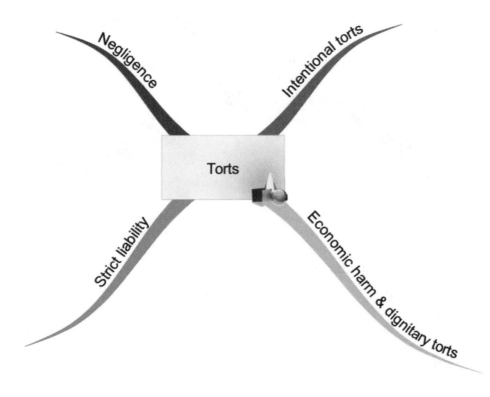

Torts questions are answered by the law of general applicability. Applicants are instructed to make several assumptions:

- No statutes apply unless specified.
- The jurisdiction has survival actions and claims for wrongful death are allowed.

- Pure comparative fault applies.
- Joint and several liability applies.

Torts can be divided into four major categories. The torts in each category share common characteristics and similar defenses. Map each category separately to visualize the common characteristics. The four categories are:

- Intentional torts
- Harm to economic/dignitary interests
- Strict liability
- Negligence

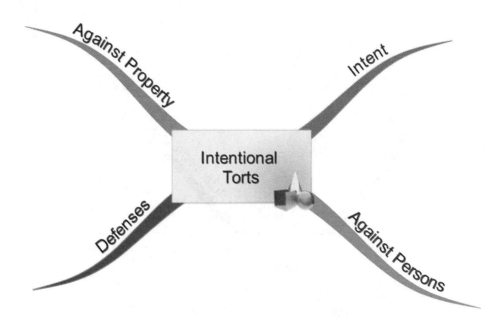

Liability for an **intentional tort** requires:

- a voluntary act,
- intent,
- the elements of a prima facie claim for that tort,
- causation,
- harm, and
- lack of a privilege or defense.

**Intent** is established if the defendant either desires that his act will cause the harmful result or knows with a substantial certainty that the result will follow. Children and mentally incompetent persons can be held liable for an intentional tort if the required intent is met. In certain situations, the defendant intends to commit one tort, but commits a different tort against that person or another person. The defendant's intent is transferred to the second tort. This **transferred intent** is limited to certain torts:

- Assault
- Battery

- False imprisonment
- Trespass to land
- Trespass to chattels

After mapping intent, then map the intentional torts by three sections: torts against persons, torts against property, and defenses.

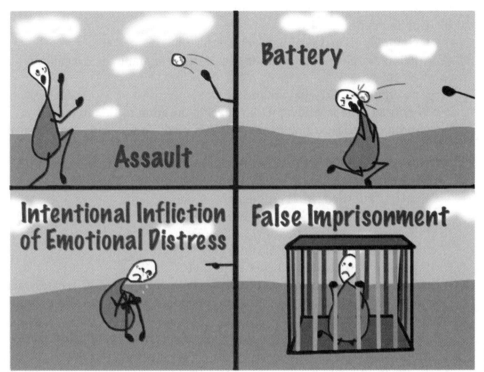

**Intentional Torts Against Persons**

Torts against persons include:

- **Assault:** Plaintiff experiences a reasonable apprehension of an immediate harmful or offensive contact.
  - Apparent ability is all that is required. That defendant could not have committed the harmful or offensive contact does not defeat liability.
  - Harmful or offensive contact exists if a reasonable person would regard it as offensive.
    - Exaggerated fears are not actionable unless the defendant knew about that fear and used it to put plaintiff in apprehension.
    - Fear is not required, only an apprehension of a harmful or offensive contact.
  - Words alone are insufficient. Some overt act is required.
  - Actual damages not required; can recover nominal damages.
- **Battery:** Harmful or offensive contact with the victim or something closely connected with the victim.
  - Reasonable person standard.
  - Includes anything connected to the victim's person.

* Direct touching not required for the tortfeasor or the victim.
* Includes setting in motion a force that brings about the harmful or offensive contact (throwing a baseball).
* Apprehension is not required.
* Lack of consent.
* **False imprisonment:** Intentional act that causes a plaintiff to be confined or restrained to a bounded area against plaintiff's will and the plaintiff knows of the confinement or is injured.
  * Confinement includes:
    * confining by physical barriers,
    * failing to release the plaintiff where the defendant has a legal duty to do so, or
    * asserting invalid legal authority.
  * Very brief time is sufficient. No specific duration of time required.
  * No duty to resist if defendant makes a credible threat to use physical force.
  * Not confined if there is a reasonable means of escape that plaintiff is actually aware exists.
  * Requires knowledge of confinement or actual harm.
  * Defense: Shopkeeper's privilege requires detention that is:
    * in a reasonable manner,
    * for a reasonable period of time, and
    * based on a reasonable belief as to theft.
* **Intentional infliction of emotional distress:** Intentional or reckless act amounting to extreme and outrageous conduct that causes the plaintiff severe mental distress.
  * Reckless conduct is sufficient if defendant acts in deliberate disregard of a high degree of probability that emotional distress will follow.
  * Extreme and outrageous conduct is beyond the bounds of decency. Conduct a civilized society would not tolerate.
  * Mental distress must be severe and substantial. More than a reasonable person could be expected to endure.

Torts against property include:

* **Trespass to land:** Tortfeasor's intentional act is a physical invasion of property.
  * Intentional entry is all that is required. No intent to cause harm required.
  * Mistake is not a defense. Need not know they are trespassing.
  * Plaintiff must be in actual possession or have the right to immediate possession of that land. Note: not ownership.
  * Satisfied if plaintiff causes a third person to enter onto plaintiff's land or remains upon the plaintiff's land when under a legal duty to leave.
  * Plaintiff's land includes the area both above and below the surface.
  * Liable for nominal damages and actual harm.
* **Trespass to chattels:** Intentional act that interferes with the plaintiff's chattel, causing harm.
  * Chattel means tangible personal property or intangible property that has a physical representation.
  * Mistake is not a defense.

**EXAM TIP**

Be leery of concluding that intentional infliction of emotional distress exists. Raise the issue of a possible cause of action wherever the facts justify, but be careful of concluding that the elements are met. It must be outrageous conduct.

- Interference includes dispossession or intermeddling.
- More serious interference may amount to conversion.
- **Conversion:** Intentional act that causes the destruction or serious interference with the plaintiff's chattel.
  - Interference is more serious than trespass to chattel and includes
    - a greater use of the chattel and
    - a longer period of interference.
  - Mistake is not a defense.
  - Plaintiff entitled to fair market value at the time of conversion plus consequential damages, or replevin.
  - Defendant's offer to return the chattel does not alleviate the conversion.

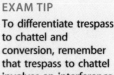

**EXAM TIP**

To differentiate trespass to chattel and conversion, remember that trespass to chattel involves an interference with the plaintiff's right of possession while conversion raises the interference to a serious enough level that warrants the defendant paying the full value of the chattel.

**Intentional Torts Against Property**

**Defenses** to intentional torts include self-defense, defense of others, defense of property, necessity, and consent. **Self-defense** means a defendant may use force reasonably necessary to protect against injury when he reasonably believes he is being or is about to be attacked. The defendant cannot be the initial aggressor and reasonable mistakes as to the danger are allowed. Look for when a duty to retreat may be imposed. The same considerations apply to the **defense of others** defense.

**Defense of property** requires the defendant to request the plaintiff to stop or leave unless it would be futile. Defendant may not use deadly force.

**Necessity** requires that injuring plaintiff's property was reasonably necessary to avoid a substantially greater harm to the public, to the defendant, or to save the defendant's more valuable property. A reasonable person standard is used.

**Consent** can be express or implied, and defendant will still be liable if he exceeds the scope of the consent.

When you have an intentional torts essay question that asks which claims can be brought or which claims will be successful, give the defenses that apply as well. Don't stop with one intentional tort if more than one may apply. Raise all the intentional torts that potentially apply, even if your conclusion is that the plaintiff will not be successful. Likewise, don't stop with one defense if more than one potentially applies.

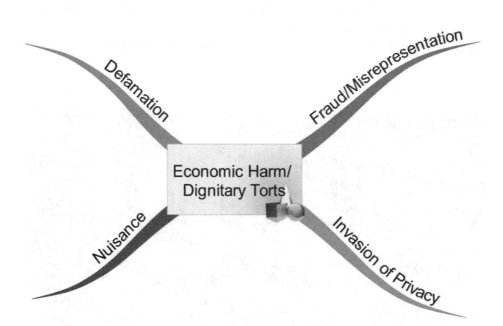

After you have read the call of the question and the fact pattern and decided that no intentional torts issues are raised, then consider **economic harm and dignitary torts**. These torts include defamation, fraud/misrepresentation, invasion of privacy, and nuisance.

**Defamation** is a defamatory message of or concerning the plaintiff that is communicated to a third person and damages the plaintiff's reputation:

- Elements:
  - Defamatory message: Message lowers a plaintiff in the community's esteem or discourages a third person from associating with him.
  - Of or concerning the plaintiff.
  - Publication: A third person received the defamatory message and understood it to be about the plaintiff.
  - Harm to reputation.
- Types:
  - Libel is the written form of defamation.
  - Slander is defamation not preserved in permanent form, including the spoken word.

- Slander *per se*:
  - Commission of a crime.
  - Allegations of a loathsome disease.
  - Imputes improper conduct of business or profession.
  - Serious sexual misconduct.
- Damages:
  - General damages: No proof of actual damages required.
  - Pecuniary or special damages: Quantifiable monetary losses.
    - Plaintiff must prove unless slander *per se*
  - Punitive damages: Need additional showing of malice.
- Defenses:
  - Truth: Historical defense. Now, plaintiff must prove falsity of claim in *prima facie* case.
  - Privileges:
    - Absolute:
      - Defendant may not be held liable for an otherwise defamatory statement as a matter of law.
      - Applies to legislator, participant in judicial proceeding, policy-making officials, and spouses.
      - Defendant has burden of proving privilege.
    - Qualified: Defendant is not held liable for an otherwise defamatory message unless he loses the protection of the privilege.
      - Applies to communications of a matter of interest to the recipient.
      - Defendant has burden of proving privilege.
      - Privilege does not apply or is lost if:
        - the matter is outside the scope of the privilege (includes matters not relevant to the interests protected by the privilege), or
        - defendant acts out of malice (defendant's primary motive was something other than furthering the interest that justified the privilege).
  - Consent
- Constitutional considerations: The U.S. Supreme Court has modified the standards of common law defamation as applied to the nature of the plaintiff and the subject matter of the defamatory statement. *New York Times v. Sullivan*, 376 U.S. 254 (1964).
  - Malice is required: knowing falsity or recklessness as to truth or falsity.
  - Nature of the plaintiff:
    - Public official.
    - Public figure: A person who has achieved pervasive fame or notoriety or as to specific limited issues.
  - Subject matter of the controversy:
    - Matter of public concern.
  - Required for presumed or punitive damages.

## Order of Analysis Defamation

1. **Rule:** Defamatory message of or concerning the plaintiff published to a third person that harms the plaintiff's reputation.
   **Apply** defamation definition to facts.
   **Conclude:** Defamation?
2. **Rule:** Malice required for public official, public figure, or matter of public concern (only if facts support).
   **Define** malice: Knowing falsity or reckless disregard for truth or falsity.
   **Apply** malice to facts.
   **Conclude:** Malice?
3. **Rule:** Damages
   **Apply** damages rules to facts.
   **Conclude:** Available damages?
4. **Rule:** Defenses—truth, privilege, consent.
   **Apply** defenses to facts.
   a. outside scope of privilege or
   b. malice.
   **Conclude:** Defense exists?
   **Conclude:** Liable for defamation?

**EXAM TIP**

Defamation questions almost always include a qualified privilege defense. Look for it!

**Misrepresentation** or fraud is an intentional assertion of a material false fact that a plaintiff justifiably relied upon and that causes damages to the plaintiff:

- Misstatement of fact, not an opinion unless rendered by someone with superior skill:
  - False, affirmative statement
  - Active concealment
  - Omissions of fact/failure to disclose
- Scienter/malice; statement was made:
  - Knowing it was false, or
  - With reckless disregard as to its truth or falsity
- Intent to induce reliance
- Justifiable reliance; reasonable person standard
- Causation/damages

In a commercial setting, the scienter element can drop to negligence.

**Invasion of Privacy** is actually four separate torts:

- Appropriation of the plaintiff's name or picture: Unauthorized use of the plaintiff's identity or likeness for the defendant's commercial advantage.
- Intrusion on the plaintiff's affairs/seclusion: Defendant unreasonably intrudes into the plaintiff's seclusion:
  - Physical or non-physical intrusion.
  - Must be highly objectionable to a reasonable person.
  - Refers to the plaintiff's physical solitude and the privacy of personal affairs or concerns. The plaintiff must have a reasonable expectation of privacy.
- Publication of facts placing plaintiff in a false light: Defendant publishes matters that portray a plaintiff in a false light.

- Attributing to the plaintiff views he does not hold or actions he did not take.
- Reasonable person would find offensive.
- Must be communicated to a substantial number of people.
- Public disclosure of private facts about the plaintiff: Defendant unreasonably discloses private facts about a plaintiff to the public.
  - Needs to be highly offensive to a reasonable person and not of legitimate public concern.
  - Must be publication to the public.
  - Does not apply if publication is newsworthy.

Both consent and privilege defenses apply to all invasion of privacy torts; truth only applies as a defense to portrayal in a false light.

**Types of Invasion of Privacy Torts**

The last economic/dignitary tort is **nuisance**. Nuisance can be public or private. A public nuisance is an unreasonable interference with a right common to the general public. The court will consider:

- whether the conduct involves a significant interference with the public health, safety, peace, comfort, or convenience;
- whether the conduct is proscribed by a statute, ordinance, or regulation; and
- whether the conduct is of a continuing nature or has produced a permanent or long-lasting effect.

An individual cannot recover personally for public nuisance unless the individual suffers a harm of a kind different from that suffered by other members of the public.

Private nuisance is an activity or thing that substantially and unreasonably interferes with the plaintiff's use and enjoyment of the land. The interference must be substantial including offensive, inconvenient, or annoying to an average person in the community. The interference must be unreasonable.

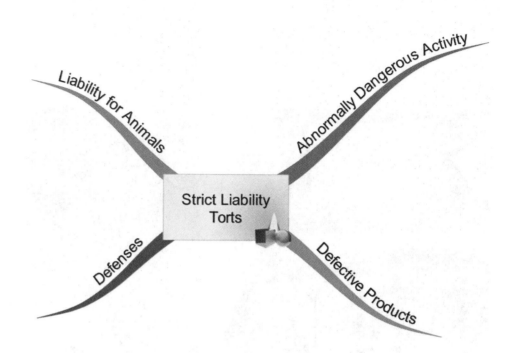

The next area of torts to analyze is **strict liability**. In strict liability, a defendant is liable for injuring a plaintiff whether or not the defendant exercised due care. For these activities, the policy of the law is to impose liability regardless of how carefully the defendant conducted himself.

Strict liability has three common law bases:

- Abnormally dangerous activity
- Wild animals
- Products liability

Strict liability can also be grounded in a statute. When that occurs, the bar examiners will give you the actual statute. Thus, when you see a statute embedded in the facts of a torts question, think strict liability!

To establish a prima facie case for strict liability, the plaintiff must prove:

- The nature of the defendant's activity imposes an absolute duty to make safe;
- The dangerous aspect of the activity is the actual and proximate cause of the plaintiff's injury; and
- The plaintiff suffered damage to person or property.

**Strict Liability: Abnormally Dangerous Activity, Wild Animals, and Products**

An **abnormally dangerous activity** must create a foreseeable risk of serious harm even with the exercise of reasonable care, and must be an activity that is not a matter of common usage. While driving a vehicle is dangerous, it is a matter of common usage. Moreover, if reasonable care is used, it is not abnormally dangerous.

Liability for animals depends upon the nature of the animal. Injury by a **wild animal** will almost always result in strict liability even if the defendant claims it is "domesticated." Likewise, the owner is strictly liable for damages when his animal trespasses, if it is reasonably foreseeable. Strict liability for domesticated animals typically arises by statute and is dependent on the owner's knowledge. The examiners will have to give you a statute if the issue is strict liability for domesticated animals.

**Products liability** is not a separate theory of strict liability. Thus, you do not do an analysis of strict liability and an additional analysis of products liability. It is one analysis, but it requires consideration of proof unique to products:

- Defect:
  - Manufacturing defect: Product was dangerous beyond the expectation of the ordinary consumer because of a departure from its intended design.
  - Food products treated same way—consumer expectations standard.
- Design defect: Plaintiff must show a reasonable alternative design that is a less dangerous modification or alteration and was economically feasible:
  - Warning defect: While adequate warnings insulate a defendant, inadequate warnings result in liability.

- Seller must anticipate reasonably foreseeable misuses of the product.
- No requirement of contractual privity.
- Reasonable alternative design must exist at the time of the original design. Later improvements, so-called "state of the art," do not constitute a reasonable alternative design.
- Control: Defect must have existed at the time the product left that defendant's control.
- Changes: Product must reach the user without substantial change in the condition in which it was supplied.
- Business: Only commercial suppliers can be held liable. Casual sellers are not liable.
- Causation: Both actual cause and proximate cause required.
- Damages: Compensatory and punitive damages available. Most states deny recovery under strict liability when the sole claim is for economic loss.

Additional theories of recovery are also possible when a person is injured by a product. Intentional conduct, negligence, and breach of warranties claims can also be brought. Defenses to strict liability claims include comparative fault and assumption of risk.

Once you have decided that no intentional torts and economic or dignitary torts are evoked by your fact pattern and the fact pattern does not involve abnormally dangerous activity, wild animals, or a product, then the theory to analyze is **negligence**. Negligence accounts for over half of the Torts essay questions in whole or in part.

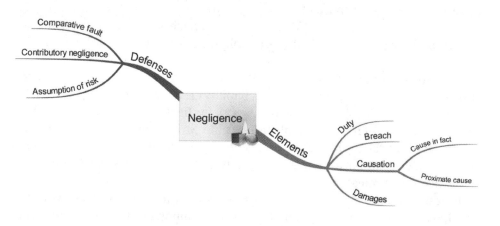

You probably have had the basic rule for negligence memorized since the first semester of law school: duty, breach, causation, and damages. For the bar exam, stating the rule in such a simple manner is insufficient. You must establish each element in more detail. Most of the time, each element will require its own CRAC. Occasionally, only one CRAC is appropriate.

The first part of your analysis is whether a **duty** exists. Include the appropriate additional rules when they are raised by the facts. Do not rule dump all of them. To analyze whether a duty exists, consider:

- Defendant must meet a certain standard of conduct for the protection of others against unreasonable risk.

- When action is taken, a duty of care is owed to all foreseeable plaintiffs.
- No affirmative duty to act exists.
  - Exceptions resulting in an affirmative duty:
    - innkeepers
    - common carriers
    - special relationships

**Defendants with Affirmative Duty to Act: Innkeepers, Common Carriers, Professionals, Parents**

- One can assume a duty to act. Besides standard of care, also liable if leaves plaintiff in worse condition.
  - Remember, assume no statute.
  - Fact pattern may give you a statute.
  - In an essay, include "if jurisdiction has a Good Samaritan statute, it would govern and relieve liability under certain conditions."
- No duty to control others.
  - Exception: special relationship.
  - Parents have a duty to exercise reasonable care to control their child if they know or have reason to know of the necessity and have the ability to control their child.
  - Masters have duty to control servants while acting within the scope of employment.
  - Masters have a duty of care in hiring employees. Look for knowledge of a servant's prior bad acts.
- Negligent infliction of emotional distress.
  - Plaintiff must be in zone of danger.
    - Suffered a physical manifestation.
    - Exceptions to zone of danger and physical manifestation: Negligent death notice and mishandling of corpse.

* Bystander.
  * Located near the scene of the accident.
  * Suffered severe emotional distress from the sensory and contemporaneous observation of scene.
  * Had a close personal relationship with victim.
* Possessors of Land.
  * Invitee: Duty to prevent injuries and duty to discover dangerous conditions.
  * Licensee: Duty to exercise reasonable care and to warn of dangerous conditions.
  * Trespasser:
    * Unknown trespassers: No duty of care.
    * Known trespassers: Jurisdictions take different approaches.
    * Children: Heightened standard of care as to artificial conditions.

The second part of your duty analysis is determining the **standard of care**. A defendant's conduct is measured against a reasonable, ordinary, prudent person. By utilizing a reasonable person, the standard is an objective one. A higher standard of care is imposed on professionals. The standard also varies depending upon the relationship between the parties such as bailor/bailee, owners/occupiers of land, and landlord/tenant. A child's conduct is held to the standard of care of a reasonable child of the same age, education, intelligence, and experience. Some jurisdictions divide by age: For ages 6 and below it is conclusively presumed that they are incapable of negligence; for ages 7 through 13 there is a rebuttable presumption of no negligence; and for ages 14 and up there is a rebuttable presumption of capability for negligence.

Next, **breach** occurs when the defendant's conduct falls short of the standard of care. Two special situations should be considered. The first is **negligence *per se***. When a statute provides for a criminal penalty, that statute's specific duty replaces the common law duty. The plaintiff must prove that he was in the class intended to be protected by the statute, the harm suffered is the particular harm that the statute was designed to prevent, and the standards of conduct are clearly defined.

The second situation is ***res ipsa loquitur***. *Res ipsa* applies based on the particular injury. It is a circumstantial evidence doctrine. The accident that caused the injury would not normally occur unless someone was negligent, and the negligence is attributable to the defendant. When a jet crashes into a mountain on a clear day and there are no survivors to tell what happened, *res ispa* applies as, whether it was a mechanical error or pilot error, the airline is still responsible.

The third element of negligence is **causation**. Always address both actual cause and legal cause. **Actual cause** is also called cause-in-fact. But for the defendant's actions, the plaintiff's injury would not have occurred. Or, the defendant's actions were a significant factor in bringing about the injury. When two or more defendants have been negligent, but uncertainty exists about which one caused the injury, the burden of proof shifts to the plaintiff to prove that harm has been caused by one of them. The burden then shifts back to the defendants to show their negligence was not the actual cause.

**EXAM TIP**

When a statute appears in a torts fact pattern, issue will be either negligence *per se* or strict liability.

**EXAM TIP**

If you know what caused the injury, then *res ispa* does not apply. It only applies when the instrument of injury is in the defendant's sole control. *Res ispa* cannot apply to more than one defendant.

The plaintiff must also prove that the defendant's actions were the **proximate or legal cause** of her injury. The test is based on foreseeability and is actually a limitation on liability in that every actual cause case does not rise to legal cause. Defendants are liable for the normal incidents within the increased risk caused by their acts. As duty arises only to foreseeable plaintiffs who are within the zone of danger, proximate cause requires that the risk also be foreseeable. An exception to the foreseeable risk doctrine is the **eggshell plaintiff**. Defendants take the full consequence for a plaintiff's injuries, even if the injuries are more severe than they would have been with a normal person.

If there is an uninterrupted chain of events between a defendant's negligent act and the plaintiff's injury, then it is a **direct cause** case. Defendant is liable for all foreseeable harmful results. An **indirect cause** case is one where a force came into motion after the defendant's act and combined with the negligent act to cause the plaintiff's injury. The intervening force may break the chain of causation between the initial act and the ultimate injury.

**Foreseeable intervening acts** do not cut off a defendant's liability. These include subsequent medical malpractice, negligence of rescuers, and subsequent accidents. The key is again foreseeability. **Unforeseeable intervening acts** do cut off liability. Such superseding causes may include naturally occurring phenomena, criminal acts of third persons (unless foreseeable), intentional torts of third persons, or extraordinary forms of negligent conduct by the third person.

The element of **damages** means actual harm or injury. Unlike some intentional torts, a plaintiff cannot recover nominal damages. Plaintiff is compensated for all past, present, and prospective damages including economic

**EXAM TIP**

The alternative liability theory applies only when you know both defendants are negligent. It does not apply if one or both are **not** negligent.

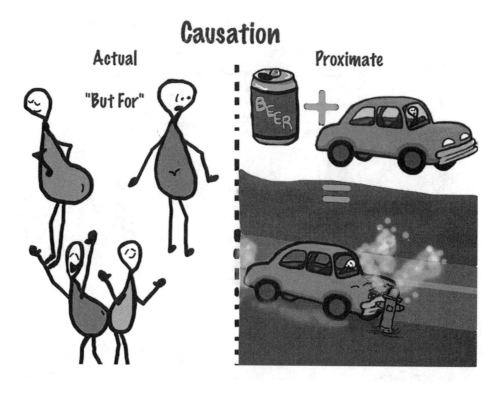

damages, such as medical expenses and lost earnings, and noneconomic damages, such as pain and suffering. Punitive damages may be recoverable if defendant's actions were wanton and willful, reckless, or malicious.

**Defenses** include contributory fault, comparative fault, and assumption of risk. The examiners tell applicants to assume that pure comparative fault applies in the jurisdiction of the case. Thus, detail regarding contributory fault is generally not needed. Instead, spend your time on comparative fault and assumption of the risk. **Comparative fault** means that the plaintiff's conduct contributed to her injury and is compared to defendant's negligence. Damages are reduced accordingly. Comparative fault does not apply to intentional torts.

**Assumption of risk** requires that the plaintiff must have known of the risk and still voluntarily proceeded with the action. Essentially, assumption of risk means that the plaintiff consented to the defendant's actions. Assumption of the risk can be express or implied.

In addition to these elements, issues arise when two or more tortious acts combine to cause an indivisible injury. When this occurs, each defendant is liable for the entirety of plaintiff's damages—the doctrine of **joint and several liability**. If plaintiff recovers in full from one defendant, then there is satisfaction and she cannot also recover from the second defendant. The rule of contribution allows the tortfeasor that paid to seek recovery for the amount that was more than his share from the other defendant. This occurs when the fault is apportioned, as is the case with pure comparative fault.

## II. MBE STRATEGIES[1]

Approximately one-half of the MBE Torts questions will be on negligence. The rest will consist of questions on all other torts. Thus, first read the call of the question. The responses may concern only one cause of action. Other questions will consider different causes of action. Go through your mind map on the other torts to determine if any apply. If none apply, then it's a negligence question.

The most common call of the question on an MBE Torts question asks whether the plaintiff will prevail. You must first determine the nature of the claim. Then, determine the elements of the claim. Then, determine if any defenses to the claim arise. Then, you must apply each rule to the facts. The response will give you a snippet of the reasoning, but the first and second snippets could be on defenses while the third and fourth snippets are on the elements. Do not get tripped up. Only one of the answer choices is correct. Look at each one in isolation to determine if it is an accurate conclusion with accurate reasoning. Similarly, questions asking for the "best claim" or "best defense" will also have only one successful claim or defense.

Use these strategies to analyze Torts questions:

- Questions where the type of claim is identified that ask what the plaintiff will need to prove: Only one answer choice will supply the correct level of proof, and others will overstate or understate the required proof.
- Actual Causation: There can be more than one cause in fact. The defendant need only be a substantial factor in causing the plaintiff's damages.
- Legal Causation: Try ignoring every actor except the defendant and the plaintiff—were the plaintiff's injuries within the risk created by the defendant's act? If yes, proximate cause is established.
- Intervening causes only relieve the defendant of liability if the results of the intervening causes are unforeseeable.
- Plaintiff is free to pick his defendant.
- Negligence "shortcut"—If the defendant's conduct is reasonable, the defendant cannot be negligent.

Truth is a defense for defamation, but is not a defense to any of the invasion of privacy torts. Everything a defendant states may well be true, but she is still liable because she disclosed private facts or intruded on the plaintiff's seclusion.

Do not ignore Torts questions in your MBE practice because you think they may be "easier" than the other topics. The differences between the answer responses are actually quite subtle. Only practice followed by autopsying your answers will get you to the level of competency you need.

---

1. Some of these strategies are from Steven L. Emanuel, *Strategies & Tactics for the MBE* 441-49 (6th ed. 2016).

## III. ESSAY PRACTICE QUESTION[2]

Six months ago, a man visited his family physician, a general practitioner, for a routine examination. Based on blood tests, the physician told the man that his cholesterol level was somewhat elevated. The physician offered to prescribe a drug that lowers cholesterol, but the man stated that he did not want to start taking drugs because he preferred to try dietary change and "natural remedies" first. The physician told the man that natural remedies are not as reliable as prescription drugs and urged the man to come back in three months for another blood test. The physician also told the man about a recent research report showing that an herbal tea made from a particular herb can reduce cholesterol levels.

The man purchased the herbal tea at a health-food store and began to drink it. The man also began a cholesterol-lowering diet.

Three months ago, the man returned to his physician and underwent another blood test; the test showed that the man's cholesterol level had declined considerably. However, the test also showed that the man had an elevated white blood cell count. The man's test results were consistent with several different infections and some types of cancer. Over the next two weeks, the physician had the man undergo more tests. These tests showed that the man's liver was inflamed but did not reveal the reason. The physician then referred the man to a medical specialist who had expertise in liver diseases. In the meantime, the man continued to drink the herbal tea.

Two weeks ago, just before the man's scheduled consultation with the specialist, the man heard a news bulletin announcing that government investigators had found that the type of herbal tea that the man had been drinking was contaminated with a highly toxic pesticide. The investigation took place after liver specialists at a major medical center realized that several patients with inflamed livers and elevated white blood cell counts, like the man, were all drinking the same type of herbal tea and the specialists reported this fact to the local health department.

All commercially grown herbs used for this tea come from Country X, and are tested for pesticide residues at harvest by exporters that sell the herb in bulk to the five U.S. companies that process, package, and sell the herbal tea to retailers. U.S. investigators believe that the pesticide contamination occurred in one or more export warehouses in Country X where bulk herbs are briefly stored before sale by exporters, but they cannot determine how the contamination occurred or what bulk shipments were sent to the five U.S. companies. The companies that purchase the bulk herbs do not have any control over these warehouses, and there have been no prior incidents of pesticide contamination. The investigators have concluded that the U.S. companies that process, package, and sell the herbal tea were not negligent in failing to discover the contamination.

Packages of tea sold by different companies varied substantially in pesticide concentration and toxicity, and some packages had no contaminants. Further investigation has established that the levels of contamination and toxicity in the herbal tea marketed by the five different U.S. companies were not consistent.

---

2. The Multistate Bar Examination ("MBE®") questions, the Multistate Essay Examination ("MEE®") questions, and excerpts from the Multistate Performance Tests ("MPT®") have been reprinted by permission from the NCBE®. Copyright © by the National Conference of Bar Examiners. All rights reserved.

The man purchased all his herbal tea from the same health-food store. The man is sure that he purchased several different brands of the herbal tea at the store, but he cannot establish which brands. The store sells all five brands of the herbal tea currently marketed in the United States.

The man has suffered permanent liver damage and has sued to recover damages for his injuries. It is undisputed that the man's liver damage was caused by his herbal tea consumption. The man's action is not preempted by any federal statute or regulation.

1. Is the physician liable to the man under tort law? Explain.
2. Are any or all of the five U.S. companies that processed, packaged, and sold the herbal tea to the health-food store liable to the man under tort law? Explain.
3. Is the health-food store liable to the man under tort law? Explain.

## IV. MBE PRACTICE QUESTIONS[3]

### Question 1

An assistant to a famous writer surreptitiously observed the writer as the writer typed her private password into her personal computer in order to access her email. On several subsequent occasions in the writer's absence, the assistant read the writer's email messages and printed out selections from them.

The assistant later quit his job and earned a considerable amount of money by leaking information to the media that he had learned from reading the writer's email messages. All of the information published about the writer as a result of the assistant's conduct was true and concerned matters of public interest.

The writer's secretary had seen the assistant reading the writer's emails and printing out selections, and she has told the writer what she saw. The writer now wishes to sue the assistant for damages. At trial, the writer can show that the media leaks could have come only from someone reading her email.

Can the writer recover damages from the assistant?

(A) No, because the assistant was an invitee on the premises.
(B) No, because the published information resulting from the assistant's conduct was true and concerned matters of public interest.
(C) Yes, because the assistant invaded the writer's privacy.
(D) Yes, because the published information resulting from the assistant's conduct constituted publication of private facts concerning the writer.

### Question 2

A man sued his neighbor for defamation based on the following facts:

The neighbor told a friend that the man had set fire to a house in the neighborhood. The friend, who knew the man well, did not believe the neighbor's allegation, which was in fact false. The friend told the man about the neighbor's allegation. The man was very upset by the allegation, but neither the man nor the neighbor nor the friend communicated the allegation to anyone else.

---

3. *Id.*

Should the man prevail in his lawsuit?

(A) No, because the friend did not believe what the neighbor had said.
(B) No, because the man cannot prove that he suffered pecuniary loss.
(C) Yes, because the man was very upset at hearing what the neighbor had said.
(D) Yes, because the neighbor communicated to the friend the false accusation that the man had committed a serious crime.

## Question 3

A manufacturing plant emitted a faint noise even though the owner had installed state-of-the-art sound dampeners. The plant operated only on weekdays and only during daylight hours. A homeowner who lived near the plant worked a night shift and could not sleep when he arrived home because of the noise from the plant. The other residents in the area did not notice the noise.

Does the homeowner have a viable nuisance claim against the owner of the plant?

(A) No, because the homeowner is unusually sensitive to noise during the day.
(B) No, because the plant operates only during the day.
(C) Yes, because the noise is heard beyond the boundaries of the plant.
(D) Yes, because the operation of the plant interferes with the homeowner's quiet use and enjoyment of his property.

## Question 4

Toxic materials being transported by truck from a manufacturer's plant to a warehouse leaked from the truck onto the street a few miles from the plant. A driver lost control of his car when he hit the puddle of spilled toxic materials on the street, and he was injured when his car hit a stop sign.

In an action for damages by the driver against the manufacturer based on strict liability, is the driver likely to prevail?

(A) No, because the driver's loss of control was an intervening cause.
(B) No, because the driver's injury did not result from the toxicity of the materials.
(C) Yes, because the manufacturer is strictly liable for leaks of its toxic materials.
(D) Yes, because the leak occurred near the manufacturer's plant.

## Question 5

A man and his friend, who were both adults, went to a party. The man and the friend had many drinks at the party and became legally intoxicated. They decided to play a game of chance called "Russian roulette" using a gun loaded with one bullet. As part of the game, the man pointed the gun at the friend and, on her command, pulled the trigger. The man shot the friend in the shoulder.

The friend has brought a negligence action against the man. Traditional defenses based on plaintiff's conduct apply. What is likely to be the dispositive issue in this case?

(A) Whether the game constituted a joint venture.
(B) Whether the friend could validly consent to the game.
(C) Whether the friend was also negligent.
(D) Whether the man was legally intoxicated when he began playing the game.

## Question 6

A woman signed up for a bowling class. Before allowing the woman to bowl, the instructor required her to sign a waiver explicitly stating that she assumed all risk of injuries that she might suffer in connection with the class, including injuries due to negligence or any other fault. After she signed the waiver, the woman was injured when the instructor negligently dropped a bowling ball on the woman's foot.

The woman brought a negligence action against the instructor. The instructor has filed a motion for summary judgment based on the waiver.

What is the woman's best argument in opposition to the instructor's motion?

(A) Bowling is an inherently dangerous activity.

(B) In circumstances like these, it is against public policy to enforce agreements that insulate people from the consequences of their own negligence.

(C) It was unreasonable to require the woman to sign the waiver before she was allowed to bowl.

(D) When she signed the form, the woman could not foresee that the instructor would drop a bowling ball on her foot.

## Question 7

A pedestrian was crossing a street in a crosswalk when a woman walking just ahead of him was hit by a truck. The pedestrian, who had jumped out of the way of the truck, administered CPR to the woman, who was a stranger. The woman bled profusely, and the pedestrian was covered in blood. The woman died in the ambulance on the way to the hospital. The pedestrian became very depressed immediately after the incident and developed physical symptoms as a result of his emotional distress.

The pedestrian has brought an action against the driver of the truck for negligent infliction of emotional distress. In her defense, the driver asserts that she should not be held liable, because the pedestrian's emotional distress and resulting physical symptoms are not compensable.

What is the strongest argument that the pedestrian can make in response to the driver's defense?

(A) The pedestrian saw the driver hit the woman.

(B) The pedestrian was acting as a Good Samaritan.

(C) The pedestrian was covered in the woman's blood and developed physical symptoms as a result of his emotional distress.

(D) The pedestrian was in the zone of danger.

## Question 8

Upon the recommendation of her child's pediatrician, a mother purchased a vaporizer for her child, who had been suffering from respiratory congestion. The vaporizer consisted of a gallon-size glass jar, which held water to be heated until it became steam, and a metal heating unit into which the jar fit. The jar was covered by a plastic cap with an opening to allow the steam to escape. At the time the vaporizer was manufactured and sold, there was no safer alternative design.

The booklet that accompanied the vaporizer read: "This product is safe, spill proof, and practically foolproof. It shuts off automatically when the water is gone." The booklet had a picture of a vaporizer sending steam over a baby's crib.

The mother used the vaporizer whenever the child was suffering from congestion. She placed the vaporizer on the floor near the child's bed.

One night, the child got out of bed to get a drink of water and tripped over the cord of the vaporizer as she crossed the room. The top of the vaporizer separated from the base, and boiling water from the jar spilled on the child when the vaporizer tipped over. The child suffered serious burns as a consequence.

The child's representative brought an action for damages against the manufacturer of the vaporizer. The manufacturer moved to dismiss after the representative presented the evidence above.

Should the manufacturer's motion be granted?

(A) No, because a jury could find that the manufacturer expressly represented that the vaporizer was spill proof.
(B) No, because the vaporizer caused a serious injury to the child.
(C) Yes, because it should have been obvious to the mother that the water in the jar would become boiling hot.
(D) Yes, because there was no safer alternative design.

## Question 9

A man was admitted to a hospital after complaining of persistent severe headaches. While he was there, hospital staff failed to diagnose his condition, and he was discharged. Two days later, the man died of a massive brain hemorrhage due to a congenital defect in an artery.

The man's wife has brought a wrongful death action against the hospital. The wife offers expert testimony that the man would have had a "reasonable chance" (not greater than 50%) of surviving the hemorrhage if he had been given appropriate medical care at the hospital.

In what type of jurisdiction would the wife's suit most likely be successful?

(A) A jurisdiction that applies traditional common law rules concerning burden of proof.
(B) A jurisdiction that allows recovery based on strict liability.
(C) A jurisdiction that allows recovery for the loss of the chance of survival.
(D) A jurisdiction that recognizes loss of spousal consortium.

## Question 10

A mother purchased an expensive television from an appliance store for her adult son. Two years after the purchase, a fire started in the son's living room in the middle of the night. The fire department concluded that the fire had started in the television. No other facts are known.

The son sued the appliance store for negligence. The store has moved for summary judgment. Should the court grant the store's motion?

(A) No, because televisions do not catch fire in the absence of negligence.
(B) No, because the store sold the television.
(C) Yes, because the son is not in privity with the store.
(D) Yes, because there is no evidence of negligence on the part of the store.

## Question 11

A shopper was riding on an escalator in a department store when the escalator stopped abruptly. The shopper lost her balance and fell down the escalator steps, sustaining injuries. Although the escalator had been regularly maintained by an independent contractor, the store's obligation to provide safe conditions for its invitees was nondelegable. The shopper has brought an action against the store for damages, and the above facts are the only facts in evidence.

The store has moved for a directed verdict. Should the court grant the motion?

(A) No, because the finder of fact could infer that the escalator malfunction was due to negligence.

(B) No, because the store is strictly liable for the shopper's injuries.

(C) Yes, because an independent contractor maintained the escalator.

(D) Yes, because the shopper has not produced evidence of negligence.

## Question 12

A 14-year-old girl of low intelligence received her parents' permission to drive their car. She had had very little experience driving a car and did not have a driver's license. Although she did the best she could, she lost control of the car and hit a pedestrian.

The pedestrian has brought a negligence action against the girl. Is the pedestrian likely to prevail?

(A) No, because only the girl's parents are subject to liability.

(B) No, because the girl was acting reasonably for a 14-year-old of low intelligence and little driving experience.

(C) Yes, because the girl was engaging in an adult activity.

(D) Yes, because the girl was not old enough to obtain a driver's license.

## Question 13

A firstborn child was examined as an infant by a doctor who was a specialist in the diagnosis of speech and hearing impairments. Although the doctor should have concluded that the infant was totally deaf due to a hereditary condition, the doctor negligently concluded that the infant's hearing was normal. After the diagnosis, but before they learned that the infant was in fact deaf, the parents conceived a second child who also suffered total deafness due to the hereditary condition.

The parents claim that they would not have conceived the second child had they known of the high probability of the hereditary condition. They have sought the advice of their attorney regarding which negligence action against the doctor is most likely to succeed.

What sort of action against the doctor should the attorney recommend?

(A) A medical malpractice action seeking damages on the second child's behalf for expenses related to his deafness, on the ground that the doctor's negligence caused him to be born deaf.

(B) A wrongful birth action by the parents for expenses they have incurred due to the second child's deafness, on the ground that but for the doctor's negligence, they would not have conceived the second child.

(C) A wrongful life action by the parents for expenses for the entire period of the second child's life, on the ground that but for the doctor's negligence, the second child would not have been born.

(D) A wrongful life action on the second child's behalf for expenses for the entire period of his life, on the ground that but for the doctor's negligence, he would not have been born.

## Question 14

A boater, caught in a sudden storm and reasonably fearing that her boat would capsize, drove the boat up to a pier, exited the boat, and tied the boat to the pier. The pier was clearly marked with "NO TRESPASSING" signs. The owner of the pier ran up to the boater and told her that the boat could not remain tied to the pier. The boater offered to pay the owner for the use of the pier. Regardless, over the boater's protest, the owner untied the boat and pushed it away from the pier. The boat was lost at sea.

Is the boater likely to prevail in an action against the owner to recover the value of the boat?

(A) No, because the owner told the boater that she could not tie the boat to the pier.

(B) No, because there was a possibility that the boat would not be damaged by the storm.

(G) Yes, because the boater offered to pay the owner for the use of the pier.

(D) Yes, because the boater was privileged to enter the owner's property to save her boat.

## Question 15

Unaware that a lawyer was in the county courthouse library late on a Friday afternoon, when it was unusual for anyone to be using the library, a clerk locked the library door and left. The lawyer found herself locked in when she tried to leave the library at 7 p.m. It was midnight before the lawyer's family could find out where she was and get her out. The lawyer was very annoyed by her detention but was not otherwise harmed by it.

Does the lawyer have a viable claim for false imprisonment against the clerk?

(A) No, because it was unusual for anyone to be using the library late on a Friday afternoon.

(B) No, because the clerk did not intend to confine the lawyer.

(C) Yes, because the clerk should have checked to make sure no one was in the library before the clerk locked the door.

(D) Yes, because the lawyer was aware of being confined.

## Question 16

A man tied his dog to a bike rack in front of a store and left the dog there while he went inside to shop. The dog was usually friendly and placid.

A five-year-old child started to tease the dog by pulling gently on its ears and tail. When the man emerged from the store and saw what the child was doing to the dog, he became extremely upset.

Does the man have a viable claim against the child for trespass to chattels?

(A) No, because the child did not injure the dog.
(B) No, because the child was too young to form the requisite intent.
(C) Yes, because the child touched the dog without the man's consent.
(D) Yes, because the child's acts caused the man extreme distress.

## Question 17

A mother and her six-year-old child were on a walk when the mother stopped to talk with an elderly neighbor. Because the child resented having his mother's attention diverted by the neighbor, the child angrily threw himself against the neighbor and knocked her to the ground. The neighbor suffered a broken wrist as a result of the fall.

In an action for battery by the neighbor against the child, what is the strongest argument for liability?

(A) The child intended to throw himself against the neighbor.
(B) The child was old enough to appreciate that causing a fall could inflict serious injury.
(C) The child was old enough to appreciate the riskiness of his conduct.
(D) The child was not justified in his anger.

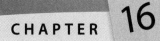

# CHAPTER 16

# Mapping Business Topics

## I. AGENCY/PARTNERSHIP

Although the NCBE considers Agency and Partnership one topic, consider them as separate topics for your preparation. Usually, your question will center on one or the other.

### A. Agency

#### 1. Mind Map

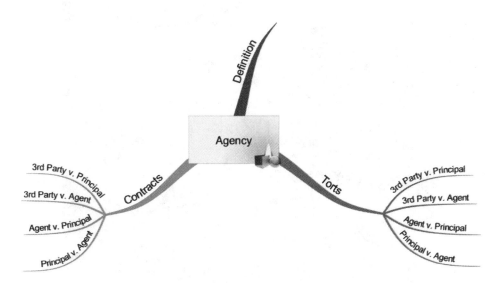

Your mind map for Agency consists of two questions:

* Who is suing whom?
* Tort or Contract?

Asking just those two questions covers almost all of Agency. Agency involves only three types of people—an agent, a principal, and a third party. By first identifying the parties involved, you immediately narrow the possible rules. Is it the principal suing the agent? Is it a third party suing the principal? Is it the third

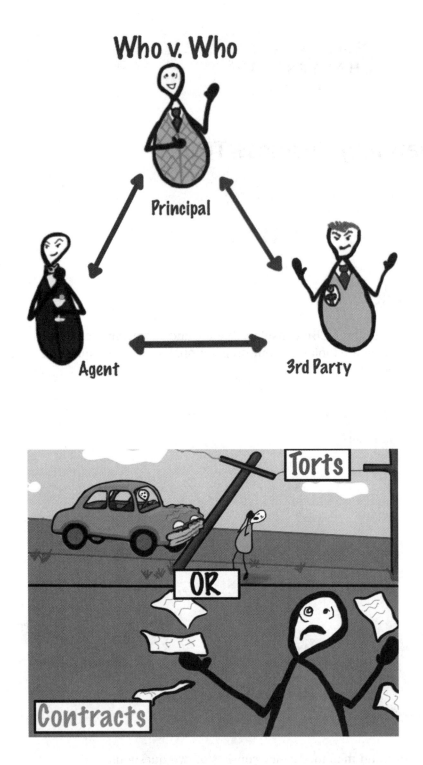

**First Question to Ask**

**Second Question to Ask**

party suing the agent? What frequently happens in agency essay questions is that the issues look at different setups. The first issue may be third party v. principal while the second issue is principal v. agent. Identifying the parties starts your analysis on the correct path.

The second question is whether the party is being sued in tort or contract. That differentiation then helps you lay out the specific rules that apply to each conflict.

For example, in order to hold a principal liable to a third party for an agent's actions in contract, the agent must have authority to enter the agreement. That authority comes from actual authority, apparent authority, or ratification. And, voilá! The rules are quickly recalled and off you go! If instead the answers to the two questions set up whether a principal is liable to a third party for an agent's tort, your analysis would be based on *respondeat superior* or the rules for liability for an independent contractor's tort.

The only two issues not covered with the two-question mind map are determining whether the **agency relationship** exists in the first place and determining whether the servant is an **independent contractor or an employee**. The employer versus independent contractor distinction is relevant only for determining tort liability. The rules for both issues are relatively straightforward:

* Creating an agency relationship: One person, a principal, assents to another person, an agent, to act on the principal's behalf. The agent must also assent to act.
* Independent contractor or employee?
* The employer has no right to control the details of the performance of the independent contractor. Factors considered include:
  * Distinct occupation or business
  * Work customarily done under a principal's supervision
  * Skill required in the agent's occupation
  * Who supplies the tools and place of performance
  * Length of time the agent is engaged by the principal
  * Whether agent is paid by the job or by the hour
  * Intent of the parties
  * Whether the principal is in business
* The employer has the right to control the details of the conduct of its employee as to the result and the means to the result.

**Tort Liability**

* Third party v. principal:
  * Agent is **employee:**
    * *Respondeat superior:* Doctrine imposes vicarious liability upon a principal for the torts his agent commits in the **scope of employment**.
      * Agent performs tasks assigned by the employer or engages in a course of conduct subject to employer's control.
      * Serves employer's purposes.
      * Employer is not liable if the employee substantially deviates from the authorized route (frolic).
        * Employee can return to the scope of the employment after a frolic.
      * Employer is still liable for slight deviations (detour).
    * Employer's liability is in addition to the agent's liability.
    * Employer and employee are jointly and severally liable.
    * Strict liability doctrine, so no defenses.
  * Agent is **independent contractor:**
    * General rule: No liability.
    * Exceptions:
      * Inherently dangerous activities: nature and circumstances of the work to be performed are such that injury to others will probably result unless precautions are taken.

- Nondelegable duty.
- Loaned agent.
- Negligent selection of contractor.
- Third party v. agent:
  - Individuals are always liable for their own torts.
- Principal v. agent:
  - Agents are liable for breach of their duties to the principal (COLA).
    - Duty of **C**are.
    - Duty of **O**bedience.
    - Duty of **L**oyalty.
      - No self-dealing.
      - May not usurp a business opportunity belonging to the principal.
      - Duty not to compete.
      - No dual agency.
    - Duty to **A**ccount.
- Agent v. principal:
  - Individuals are always liable for their own torts.

**Contract Liability**

- Third party v. principal:
  - An agent acting within the scope of his **authority** may bind his principal in contract.
  - Types of authority:
    - **Actual:** Manifestation of the principal to the agent that the agent acts for the benefit of the principal in a particular way and that the principal agrees to be bound by the agent's actions.
      - Express: Principal directly requests the agent to act.
      - Implied:
        - Authority to accomplish the principal's express request; or
        - Things the agent believes the principal wishes him to do based on his reasonable understanding of the principal's expressed request.
    - **Apparent:** The agent is "cloaked" with authority.
      - Third party reasonably believes the agent has authority to act on behalf of the principal, and
      - Belief is based on the principal's representations made to the third party.
    - **Ratification:** Principal grants retroactive authority for his agent's earlier unauthorized actions.
      - Ratified act must be one that the principal could have authorized at the time of the act.
      - Once ratified, an act has the same effect as if it were originally done with authority.

**EXAM TIP**

Apparent authority is a favorite of the bar examiners. Always address any cloaking of authority!

In your answer, be sure to address each type of authority—giving the rule for each type of authority and applying each rule to the facts. Do not stop even if you find authority out of the gate. Analyze each type to gather all the low-hanging fruit points. These work best as separate CRACs.

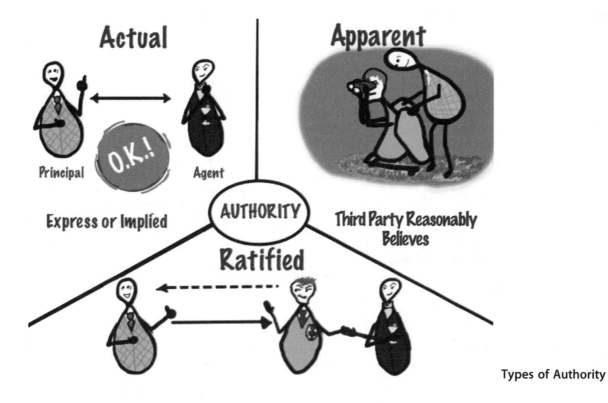

Types of Authority

**Contract Liability (cont.)**

- Third party v. agent:
  - Disclosed v. undisclosed principal:
    - Fully disclosed principal: Agent is not liable in contract.
    - Undisclosed principal: Agent is personally liable in contract.
    - Partially disclosed principal: Agent is personally liable in contract.
      - When the third party learns the identity of the principal, the third party must elect to go after either the agent or principal, but not both.
  - Breach of warranty of authority: Agent acts beyond her authority on behalf of a principal. Agent is personally liable.
- Principal v. agent: Contract liability based on the terms of their contract.
  - Would be highly unusual to be a test area as examiners would have to give you the contract terms.
- Agent v. principal: Contractual duties owed to agents.
  - Compensate—per the agency contract.
  - Indemnify—for reasonably incurred legal liabilities.
  - Reimburse—for reasonably incurred expenses.
  - Cooperate:
    - Principal may not interfere with the agent's performance.
    - Principal must affirmatively aid where reasonably required to do so.

| AGENCY CHART | | | |
|---|---|---|---|
| Is this a principal-agent relationship? Rule: | | | |
| | **Tort** | | **Contract** |
| Third Party v. Principal | Independent Contractor<br>• Employer has no right to control performance. | Employee<br>• Employer has right to control performance.<br>Factors? | Authority:<br>• Actual<br>  • Express<br>  • Implied<br>• Apparent<br>• Ratification<br>Same rules if principal seeks to hold a third party to a contract. |
| | No liability unless:<br>• Inherently dangerous activities<br>• Loaned agents<br>• Nondelegable duty<br>• Negligent selection of contractor | *Respondeat superior:* Scope of employment | |
| Third Party v. Agent | Individuals are liable for their own torts. | | Undisclosed principal<br>or<br>Breach of warranty of authority |
| Principal v. Agent | • Care<br>• Obedience<br>• Loyalty<br>  • Not to compete<br>  • Not to be a dual agent<br>• Account | | Terms of their contract<br>(Probably never tested as they would have to give you the contract, but tort questions are tested.) |
| Agent v. Principal | Individuals are liable for their own torts. | | Compensate<br>Indemnify<br>Reimburse<br>Cooperate |

Organizing your memorization materials around the two-question mind map works on either a graphical map or a simple chart. Take this chart and add more detail to the rules as you autopsy your practice questions.

### 2. Essay Practice Question[1]

Able is in the business of buying and selling rare coins. She buys coins for her inventory mostly at sales conducted by auction houses. Able uses the services of "purchasers," who attend the sales and bid for coins to be added to her inventory. Each of the purchasers sign an agreement, the form of which is reproduced below:

#### PURCHASER AGREEMENT

The undersigned ("Purchaser") agrees to act on behalf of Able ("Able") as an independent contractor purchaser of rare coins. Purchaser shall attend sales specified by Able and bid on coins from a confidential listing supplied by Able (the "Buy List"), at a price not to exceed the amount shown on the Buy List. Purchaser shall not submit any bid until Able has given telephonic approval for the specific bid.

Purchaser shall contract in the name of Purchaser for such coins, without disclosing the identity of Able. Funds for authorized purchases shall be supplied by wire transfer upon Purchaser's request.

Purchaser shall be compensated for travel expenses at the lesser of (i) Purchaser's actual costs in attending such sales, or (ii) a per diem of $150. Purchaser shall also receive a quarterly bonus equal to 25% of the savings affected by Purchaser on coins purchased during each quarter for less than the authorized prices set forth on the Buy List.

This arrangement may be terminated upon notice by either Purchaser or Able.

Baker signed a purchaser agreement. Baker thereafter attended several sales on Able's behalf. At the first sale, Baker located coins on the Buy List. After calling Able for authorization, Baker contracted to buy the coins in his name at prices less than the Buy List prices. Able wired funds allowing Baker to consummate the transaction.

Baker subsequently learned from the other purchasers that, although they have all been informed of the standard policy requiring them to get prior approval, they never call Able for authorization. If a coin is on the Buy List, they buy it if they can get it at or under the Buy List price. None of the other purchasers has ever had a problem getting the funds from Able to complete a purchase. Able has refused to forward the money only when the sale price has exceeded the Buy List price. After learning this information, Baker began purchasing coins at prices below the Buy List prices without Able's prior authorization. Able always supplied Baker with funds to cover these purchases, despite the lack of Able's prior approval.

Last Saturday, Baker attended an auction and found a U.S. 1913 Leaping Liberty quarter in mint, uncirculated condition. The price shown on the current Buy List for a 1913 Leaping Liberty quarter is $50,000. Without calling Able, Baker contracted to buy the coin for $30,000, and now claims a bonus of $5,000 (25% of the difference between the $50,000 Buy List price and the $30,000 contract price).

---

1. The Multistate Bar Examination ("MBE®") questions, the Multistate Essay Examination ("MEE®") questions, and excerpts from the Multistate Performance Tests ("MPT®") have been reprinted by permission from the NCBE®. Copyright© by the National Conference of Bar Examiners. All rights reserved.

It turns out that the Buy List was in error. The entry should have read "1913 Leaping Liberty Quarter, mint, uncirculated condition: $20,000."

Able refused to wire the funds to close the transaction.

What is the legal relationship between Able and Baker, and, in light of that relationship, what are the liabilities of Able and Baker to the third-party seller and to one another? Explain.

## B. Partnership

### 1. Mind Map

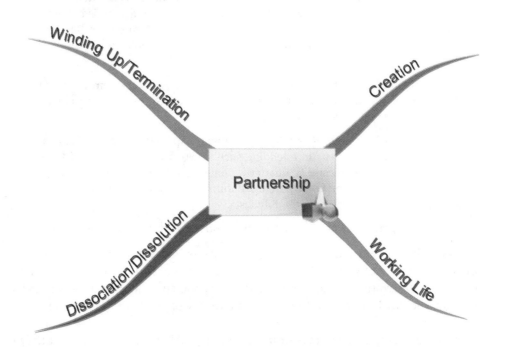

Think about Partnership as a living entity. It has a beginning, a life in the middle, and an end. Thus, the mind map follows that life:

- Creation
- Working life
- Dissociation/dissolution
- Winding up/termination

*Creation.* Partnership questions may tell you "Bob and Sam had a valid partnership agreement to. . . ." That one sentence tells you loads. First, it is a partnership question. Second, because it already states there is a valid partnership agreement, you will not have *any* issues regarding **creation**! You can leap frog over this part of your mind map.

Instead, if the problem states that Bob and Sam started a business, you will need to consider both partnership and corporations. The rest of the fact pattern and the call of the question will let you know if the question is partnership or corporations. The facts will lead you down either the partnership path or the corporations path. Corporations' questions will require some facts that address filing Articles of Incorporation or facts that reference the name of the business as including "Inc." If those facts are missing, then it is a partnership question. This type of problem automatically requires you to go through **creation** of a partnership.

First define a partnership: an association of two or more persons to carry on as co-owners a business for profit. Then, address the aspects of general partnership creation. Apply to your facts. You have two possible results. First, the parties agreed to work together on a handshake, shared profits, yet put nothing in writing. That would be a general partnership. Second, the parties agreed to work together, shared profits, and put everything in writing. That would also be a general partnership. But then another issue arises. Is this a limited partnership? Address the additional requirements for a limited partnership and apply to your facts.

Reach your conclusion: no partnership, general partnership, or limited partnership:

- **General partnership:** an association of two or more persons to carry on as co-owners a business for profit.
  - No writing required.
  - No statutory formalities required.
  - Types:
    - For a specific undertaking.
    - For a term.
    - At will.
  - Key test: intent of the parties, no matter what it is called.
  - Sharing of profits is *prima facie* evidence of a partnership.
- **Limited partnership:**
  - Types of partners:
    - General partners: manage the business and are personally liable without limitation for partnership obligations.

- Limited partners: contribute capital and share in profits, but take no part in the control or management of the business, and whose liability is limited to their contributions.
  - Formation:
    - Filing a certificate of limited partnership with the Secretary of State.
    - Must have at least one general partner and at least one limited partner.

*Working Life.* Once a partnership is created, the business of the partnership begins. This part of your mind map deals with issues such as who can bind the partnership in contract, who receives remuneration, the partnership's liability in torts to third parties, and whether the partnership or the individual partners are liable for any judgment. In addition, a frequent question concerns what happens when a new partner joins the partnership, both in relation to liability for contracts and for torts. Issues within the working life branch include:

- Partners' powers:
  - Every partner is an agent of the partnership for the purpose of its business.
  - Authority:
    - Express.
    - Apparent: based on the nature and course of business.
    - Restrictions: Third party must know about restrictions on authority or the partnership will be bound.
    - Partner who acted without authority may be liable for breach of the partnership agreement.
- Remuneration: Partners are not entitled unless specified in the partnership agreement.
- Liability:
  - All partners are jointly and severally liable for all obligations of the partnership.
  - Each partner is individually liable for the entire amount of the partnership's obligation.
  - Partner is entitled to indemnification by the partnership for any payments he makes on the partnership's behalf.
  - Partner may seek contribution from other partners if he pays more than his share of liability.
  - Retiring partner remains liable on all obligations incurred before retirement.
  - Incoming partner is not personally liable for any partnership obligation incurred prior to her admission as a partner.

*Dissociation and Dissolution.* Now, one of the partners wants out of the partnership. This triggers the last two parts of the mind map. **Dissociation** refers generally to a partner's separation from the partnership including death, withdrawal, bankruptcy, or expulsion. The partnership is technically still alive at that point as the law wants businesses to continue.

Once a partner wants out, the next question is whether he has a right to dissociate. Generally, a partner always has a right to dissociate. That does not mean, however, that he may not be liable to the partnership for wrongful dissociation.

After a partner dissociates from the partnership, the next issue is whether the partnership is dissolved. Usually on the bar exam, very few partners are involved—sometimes only two. On the exam partnerships tend to be on a handshake and thus more frequently dissolve. Thus, the dissociation of a partner inevitably means a race immediately to **dissolution** of the partnership. The partnership continues after dissolution only for the purposes of winding up the business.

*Winding Up.* Every dissolved partnership must go through **winding up** before the partnership is **terminated**. Winding up includes reducing the partnership assets to cash and then distributing that cash to the entitled parties.

There may be an issue as to whether a specific asset is actually partnership property or whether it is the individual partner's property:

- Partnership property:
  - Originally brought in—part of capital of partnership.
    - May contrarily contend in agreement.
  - Subsequently acquired.
  - Purchased with partnership funds.
- Partner's individual property:
  - Intent evidenced that any property originally brought in was not to be partnership property.
  - Partners have a contrary intention from the applicable law.

Once that is decided, the assets are sold and the cash distributed in a specific order:

- Costs of the sale
- Outside creditors
- Inside creditors
- Capital contributions
- Profits

Winding Up ~ Profits

Winding Up ~ Losses

Issues arise when assets are insufficient to cover the partnership's obligations. Partners must contribute the amount necessary to cover liabilities. If a partner fails to contribute, the other partners must make up the difference and then seek contribution from that partner.

Watch for "advances" given by a partner to keep a failing business afloat. These are not capital contributions, but an inside creditor loan. If the cash comes up short and doesn't cover everything, add up the loans and capital contributions. Subtract from the available cash. Then divide the losses equally between the partners. If math is not your strong suit, then describe what needs to be done and make an attempt. Don't worry about getting the math correct. You will get the points for having described the process accurately.

### 2. Essay Practice Question[2]

Four years ago, a man and a woman properly formed a partnership to own and manage a multi-million-dollar apartment complex. They qualified the partnership as a limited liability partnership (LLP). The complex required a good deal of maintenance, and they anticipated regular borrowings of up to $25,000 to cover maintenance expenses as is customary in this industry.

While the partnership agreement contained no limitations on the authority of the partners to act for LLP, two months after LLP was formed the man and the woman agreed that neither partner would have authority to incur indebtedness on behalf of LLP in excess of $10,000 without the consent of the other partner. They then signed a statement of partnership authority describing this limitation, but this statement was never filed.

Over the next two years, the man regularly borrowed amounts from LLP's bank to cover the complex's ordinary maintenance expenses. The amounts borrowed ranged from $5,000 to $9,000, and the man did not ask for the woman's consent when he entered into these loans on behalf of LLP.

Earlier this year, the man, without the woman's knowledge, asked the bank to loan $25,000 to LLP. The man told the bank's loan officer that the funds would be used for ordinary maintenance of the apartment complex. This amount, though greater than LLP's previous borrowings from the bank for maintenance, was in line with loans made by the bank for maintenance to other similar apartment complexes.

When the loan officer asked the man if he had authority to borrow the money on behalf of LLP, the man handed the loan officer a copy of the partnership agreement. The man, however, did not give the officer a copy of the statement of partnership authority, nor did he tell the loan officer that it existed. The bank had no actual knowledge of the limitation on the man's authority to obtain the loan on behalf of LLP.

Without contacting the woman, the bank loaned $25,000 to LLP. The loan agreement was signed only by the man and the bank's loan officer. The woman, though she had knowledge of the earlier borrowings from the bank, had no knowledge of this loan.

The man then used the $25,000 to pay his personal gambling debts. LLP has not made any payments to the bank on the loan.

---

2. *Id.*

1. Is LLP liable to the bank on the loan? Explain.
2. Is the woman personally liable to the bank on the loan? Explain.
3. Is the man liable for breaching his fiduciary duties and, if so, to whom is he liable? Explain.

## II. CORPORATIONS

### A. Mind Map

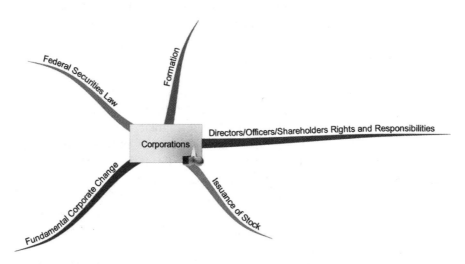

Like a partnership, think of a corporation as a living entity with a beginning, a life in the middle, and an end. Unlike a partnership, a corporation usually involves more people and has more formalities and structure in its formation. As such, the people involved have more responsibilities and distinctions than just general partner or limited partner. As a result, our mind map becomes a bit more complicated. Most of the bar exam questions will deal with small, closely-held corporations rather than large or publicly-traded corporations. The branches of your mind map are:

* Formation
* Directors, officers, and shareholders' rights and responsibilities
* Issuance of stock
* Fundamental corporate change
* Federal securities law

*Formation.* First, look to see if there is a promoter liability issue. Promoters act on behalf of the corporation prior to its formation. Then, understand what is required to form a corporation, which includes understanding the difference between a *de facto* corporation and a *de jure* corporation. Alternative forms of corporations may be tested including closely-held corporations, professional corporations, and limited liability companies. Formation issues can include:

* Commencement: Corporate entity begins at the filing of the Articles of Incorporation with the Secretary of State's office.

- **Promoter liability:**
  - Promoter: person who causes a corporation to be formed, organized, and financed.
    - Usually they become shareholders, officers, and directors of the new corporation.
  - Promoters are personally liable as the corporation's agent on pre-incorporation contracts entered on the corporation's behalf.
    - Contract can specifically disclaim a promoter's personal liability.
    - Personal liability continues until a novation—the corporation adopts the contract and all parties agree that the promoter will be discharged from the contract.
  - Corporation is not liable on any pre-incorporation agreements unless it assumes liability by its own act after the Articles of Incorporation are filed.
    - Can be express or implied.
- Defective incorporation:
  - **De jure corporation:** organized in compliance with the statute but failed to comply with a statutory provision.
  - **De facto corporation:** statutory compliance is insufficient for *de jure* status. Formed if:
    - Good faith, colorable attempt to comply; and
    - Corporate principals, in good faith, acted as if they were a corporation.
  - **Corporation by Estoppel:**
    - Creditor who has always dealt with the principals as if they were a corporation is estopped from later alleging that the corporation is defective.
    - Defendant who has held himself out as a corporation cannot avoid liability by claiming there is no corporation.
- **Limited Liability Companies (LLC):**
  - Treated like a corporation for limited liability purposes in protecting its members, managers, and agents from liability for the obligations of the company, but if properly organized, it has the attributes of a partnership for federal income tax purposes.
  - Formed through filing articles of organization with the secretary of state with at least one member.
  - Members can be added with the consent of all other members, unless the operating agreement provides otherwise.
  - Control lies with the members in proportion to their equity in the LLC at the time a vote is taken—**member-managed**.
    - Each member in a member-managed LLC has:
      - Equal rights in the management and conduct of the company's activities.
      - Authority to bind the LLC in contracts for carrying on the ordinary business of the company unless the member lacks authority to do so and the other party to the contract has notice that the member lacks such authority.
    - Matters outside the ordinary course of the company's activities require the consent of all members.
  - Members may agree to appoint one or more managers to operate the business—**manager-managed**.

- Managers owe the duties or care and loyalty similar to those owed by directors to a corporation.
- If not stated in operating agreement, LLC presumed to be member-managed.
- A member's withdrawal results in dissociation. Withdrawing member loses:
  - the right to participate in the LLC, and
  - the right to distributions only if and when made by the continuing members.
- Disassociation does not result in dissolution of the LLC. Dissolution requires the consent of all the members.

*Directors, Officers, and Shareholders' Rights and Responsibilities.* Three types of people are involved in corporations. Individuals can be directors, officers, or shareholders. Indeed, an individual could be all three. Keep track of which role the individual was playing when taking a specific action. Ask yourself—which hat was the individual wearing at that time?

Points to remember about shareholders, directors, and officers:

- **Shareholders:**
  - No personal liability for the corporation's debts.
  - Exception: Challenger can **pierce the corporate veil**.
    - Court disregards corporate entity and holds shareholders liable.
    - Challenger goes against the corporation and corporate assets first and then goes against the shareholders and their assets.
    - Grounds:
      - Alter ego:
        - Corporation has no existence of its own.
        - Corporate form used fraudulently for improper purpose.

First Question to Ask

- Injury or unjust loss resulted.
    - Inadequate capitalization:
        - Not sufficient alone if corporate formalities observed.
    - Failure to comply with corporate formalities:
        - Only those active in corporate management are held liable.
    - Corporate veil more likely pierced for a tort action.
- Shareholders are personally liable for any tort they commit, such as fraud.
- Meetings:
    - Annual.
    - Special: requires written notice stating the place, date, hour, and purpose of the meeting no less than 10 and no more than 60 days prior to the meeting.
        - Notice may be waived in writing before or after the meeting.
    - Quorum: majority of the shares entitled to vote.
- **Voting agreements:** contracts to ensure shareholders will vote in concert with regard to issues designated by the agreement:
    - Often used to ensure election of certain directors.
- **Voting trusts:** involves the transfer of legal title to a trustee who votes the shares according to the trust terms.
- **Shareholder derivative suit:** Shareholder sues on behalf of the corporation to redress a wrong when the corporation fails to enforce its right.
    - Must be a shareholder at the time of the transaction.
    - Must make a demand upon the corporation unless futile.
- Majority shareholders owe fiduciary duty to refrain from exercising control to obtain a benefit not shared proportionately with minority shareholders.
- **Directors:**
    - Directors manage the corporation.
    - Directors are protected from liability by the **Business Judgment Rule:** rebuttable presumption that directors are honest, well-meaning, and acting through informed decisions.
    - Directors are fiduciaries of the corporation.
    - Duties:
        - Duty of care: to act in good faith in the honest belief that one is acting in the best interests of the corporation on an informed basis.
        - Duty of loyalty: must not promote own interests in a manner injurious to the corporation.
            - **Conflict of interest** is inherent when director has a personal or financial interest in the transaction:
                - Business dealings with the corporation.
                - Usurping corporate opportunity.
                - Competing with corporation.
            - Transaction is voidable by the corporation unless:
                - Material facts of conflict were fully disclosed, or
                - Transaction is fair.
            - Rebuttable presumption of conflict of interest.
    - Indemnification: Corporation must indemnify a director who was successful in the defense of any proceeding to which he was a party because he was a director.

> **EXAM TIP**
>
> Be careful concerning notice of director and shareholder meetings. Attendance at a meeting constitutes waiver of a notice defect. "Attendance" does not require physical presence, but includes using a device where the person can hear everyone.

- *Ultra Vires*: Board of directors is not permitted to undertake action that is beyond the corporation's authority. Corporation cannot be obliged to undertake a contract or activity that is beyond the scope of its powers.
- **Officers:**
  - Same duties as directors.
  - Agents of the corporation.
  - Hired by the directors and can be removed by the directors.

*Issuance of Stock.* Every corporation must authorize and issue at least one class of common stock and may authorize one or more classes of preferred stock:

- Any unissued stock may be issued by the vote of the shareholders or by the vote of the directors.
- Judgment of board of directors is conclusive as to the value of consideration received for shares.
- Shareholders' **preemptive rights:** right of existing shareholders to acquire unissued shares in the corporation in proportion to their holdings of the original shares when the corporation seeks to issue additional stock:
  - Not automatic.
  - Must be in Articles of Incorporation.
- **Dividends:** A distribution by a corporation to its shareholders of cash or property of the corporation:
  - Shareholder has no inherent right to be paid a dividend.
  - Board of directors has discretion to decide whether and when to declare a dividend.
- Voting: Unless the Articles of Incorporation state otherwise, each share is entitled to one vote.

*Fundamental Corporate Change.* A significant number of bar exam questions focus on fundamental corporate change. First, define when a fundamental corporate change is attempted: sale of all or substantially all of the corporation's assets. Then, go through every step to be sure all procedures were followed:

- Notice to directors to hold meeting.
- Board enters resolution to hold a special meeting of shareholders.
- Notice of special meeting is sent to shareholders. This notice has specific requirements:
  - Written.
  - States place, date, hour, and purpose of meeting.
  - No less than 10 and no more than 60 days prior to the meeting.
  - Notice can be waived.
- Approval by a majority of all shares entitled to vote and by a majority of each voting group adversely affected by the change.
- Possibility of dissenting shareholders' **right of appraisal:** Shareholder who objects to the action is entitled to an appraisal and payment for his stock.
  - Dissenting shareholder must file a written objection to the proposed action before the shareholders' vote.
  - Dissenter must not vote his shares in favor of the proposed action.
  - If corporation and dissenter fail to agree as to the value of the stock, the court makes a determination of value.
- File notice with the state.

Be especially careful about meetings. Usually it is a closely-held corporation in which some of the directors/shareholders meet and push through a change. Be sure to identify whether they are meeting as directors or shareholders. There may be only one meeting. Thus, going through each step of what is necessary for a fundamental corporate change will garner mega points.

*Federal Securities Law.* Occasionally, questions will have issues regarding federal securities law. Include in your mind map the elements of a section 10(b) action of the Securities Exchange Act of 1934 and a section 16(b) action regarding short-swing trading profits:

- Section 10(b) action of the Securities Exchange Act of 1934 (applies to all corporations):
- Available causes of action:
  - Against those who made misrepresentations in connection with the purchase of securities
  - Against those who traded in the stock while under a duty either to disclose or to abstain from trading until the inside information is disclosed
- Elements:
  - A misrepresentation of a material fact
  - Knowledge by the defendant of the misrepresentation or reckless disregard of the truth
  - Scienter (intent to deceive, manipulate, or defraud)
  - Reliance of the plaintiff
  - Damages
- Section 16(b) action: recovery of short-swing profits (applies only to publicly-traded companies):
  - Prevent unfair use of information and internal manipulation of price
  - Profit recoverable

- Requires two transactions in stock
- Strict liability offense
- Damages

## B. Essay Practice Question[3]

The board of directors of a commercial real estate development corporation consists of the corporation's chief executive officer (CEO) and three other directors, who are executives at various other firms.

The corporation owns a commercial office tower, the value of which is approximately 10 percent of the corporation's total holdings. The corporation uses one floor of the tower as its corporate headquarters, but it wants to vacate that floor as soon as it locates suitable replacement space.

Two years ago, the board obtained an independent appraisal of the tower, which indicated a fair market value of between $12 and $15 million. After considering that appraisal, the board authorized the corporation's CEO to seek a purchaser for the tower.

The CEO immediately showed the tower to several sophisticated real estate investors and received offers ranging from $8 million to $13 million. The CEO decided that these offers were insufficient, and after he reported back to the board, no further action to sell the tower was taken.

Two months ago, the CEO and the other three directors of the corporation formed a limited liability company (LLC) in which each holds a 25 percent ownership interest.

One month ago, the corporation's board unanimously authorized the corporation's sale of the tower to LLC for $12 million. The minutes of the board's meeting at which the tower sale was authorized reflect that the meeting lasted for 10 minutes and that the only document reviewed by the corporation's directors was the two-year-old appraisal of the tower.

The minutes of the board's meeting further state that the transaction was to be carried out with "a friendly company so that the corporation will have time to relocate to a new headquarters" and that the board "authorized the transaction because the $12 million price is toward the high end of the range of offers received in the past from sophisticated real estate investors and is within the range of fair market values listed in the appraisal."

After the board's authorization of the tower sale, the corporation entered into a contract to sell the tower to LLC. The board did not seek shareholder approval of the transaction.

A non-director shareholder of the corporation is upset with the board's decision authorizing the sale of the tower to LLC. The shareholder believes that the corporation could have obtained a higher price for the tower.

1. Does the business judgment rule apply to the board's decision to have the corporation sell the tower to LLC? Explain.
2. Did the directors breach their fiduciary duties by authorizing the tower sale? Explain.

---

3. *Id.*

# CHAPTER 17

# Mapping Trusts and Estates

The NCBE combines the topics of Decedents' Estates, Trusts, and Future Interests. Future Interests are studied as part of Property for the MBE. That mind map is in Chapter 14.

## I. DECEDENTS' ESTATES

### A. Mind Map

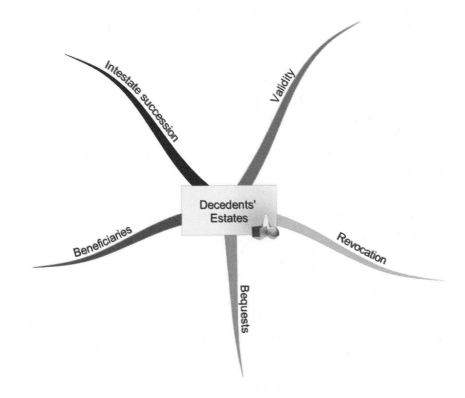

A will is a document that takes effect on the death of the testator. If properly executed, a will disposes of the person's property, but need not do so. The mind map for Decedents' Estates considers the life of a will in the sense of studying its creation and then studying later events such as changes in the testator's intent, changes in the property owned by the testator, or changes in beneficiaries. Lastly, the mind map considers intestate succession that applies not only to circumstances where there is no will, but also where the will is not properly executed and no substitute will exists. Intestate succession also applies when changes in beneficiaries result in no named person receiving the residue of the will.

- Validity
- Revocation
- Bequests
- Beneficiaries
- Intestate succession

Many topics have the same first step: Is _____ valid? You have already seen this step in Contracts, Partnership, and Corporations. Now, you will see it in Decedents' Estates, Trusts, and Family Law. Here, the examiners want to know if the will was **valid**, that is, was it properly executed by an individual with capacity. Start your analysis with the requirements of execution. If the facts state Testator executed a valid will or give another indicia of validity, then skip this step. There would be no points for that analysis. The graders would decide that you could not spot the true issues, and you would waste time that should have been spent on the true issues.

Each state has its own statutes for **will execution**. If the statutory requirements are not met, the will is void and not just voidable. That is, the will cannot be admitted to probate at all even if no one objects. The most common formalities include:

- Will must be in writing: Most states recognize a holographic will—that is, a will entirely in the testator's handwriting and no attesting witnesses.
- Testator's signature: may be by any mark. Testator can direct another person to sign for him in his presence.
- Two attesting witnesses.
- Testator must sign or acknowledge a previous signature in each witness's presence.
- Witnesses sign in testator's presence.

Some states' additional requirements include:

- Testator's signature must be at end of will.
- Testator much publish the will—declare to the witnesses that this document is intended to be the testator's will.
- Witnesses must sign in the presence of each other.

If the testator's writing was in contemplation of a future writing, then the writing is not a valid will. For example, the testator writes a letter to her attorney spelling out her bequests and beneficiaries and asks the attorney to change or prepare her will. If the testator dies before the new will is executed, the court will not accept the letter as a holographic will.

A **codicil** is a later testamentary instrument that amends or alters the prior will. A codicil must be executed in the same manner as a will. Some states will accept an amendment through incorporation by reference such as a list of personal property if the will manifests intent to incorporate the document.

**Will contests** focus on a defective execution, a testator's lack of capacity, or a revocation. Lack of capacity arises with issues of mental capacity, undue influence, and fraud. **Mental capacity** to execute a will is a lower standard than capacity required to contract. Mental capacity requires:

- Testator must be 18 years old or older at date of execution of will;
- Testator understands the nature of the act;
- Testator understands the nature and extent of his property;
- Beneficiaries are the natural objects of his bounty; and
- Testator understands the nature of the disposition he is making.

A will contest based on the will being obtained through the **exercise of undue influence** requires:

- Influence exerted on testator;
- Effect of influence overpowers the testator's mind and free will; and
- Product of influence was a will not being executed but for the influence.

Look for situations where a presumption of undue influence arises such as the existence of a confidential or fiduciary relationship between the testator and the beneficiary; the beneficiary participated in some way in procuring or drafting the will; and the will's provisions appear to be unnatural and favor the beneficiary who allegedly exercised undue influence.

**Fraud** could be fraud in the factum or fraud in the inducement. Fraud in the factum would involve a misrepresentation as to the nature of the contents of the will. Fraud in the inducement would be a misrepresentation as to facts that would influence the testator's motivation to make a will in the first place.

A **no-contest clause** attempts to disqualify anyone contesting the will from taking under it. Most states hold that the clause is ineffectual if the person affected had reasonable cause to contest the will. The no-contest clause will be enforceable if the will contest is unsuccessful and no probable cause existed.

Several considerations arise when analyzing **revocation** of a will:

- Types of revocation:
  - Methods:
    - Operation of law:
      - Testator divorces after making a will—all provisions in favor of the ex-spouse become ineffective for all purposes, unless the provisions were intended to survive the divorce.
      - Surviving spouse married testator after testator executed the will. Surviving spouse entitled to the value of the share she would have received if the testator had died intestate.
    - Written instrument: executing a subsequent will or codicil.
    - Physical Act: burning, tearing, canceling, obliterating, or destroying the will or any part of it.
  - Partial revocation is allowed under the Uniform Probate Code.
  - Dependent relative revocation: Testator revokes an old will with the intention that a newly executed will replaces it. If new will is not made or is invalid, some jurisdictions will admit the revoked will to probate. Need evidence of testator's intent.
- Presumptions.
- Revival after revocation.

**Dependent relative revocation** appears frequently as part of an essay question. This is an equity doctrine where a court may disregard a revocation. Look for dependent relative revocation when the testator revokes based on a mistake of law or fact where the testator would have made a different bequest but for the mistaken belief.

**Presumptions** arise when the will is found after a testator's death, but is mutilated. There must be some extrinsic evidence to show testator's intent. A prior will is **revived** upon undergoing all formalities of making a will or by codicil. Otherwise the previous will is revived only if it is evident from the circumstances of the revocation of the subsequent will or the testator's contemporary declarations that the testator intended the previous will to take effect as executed.

Issues with **beneficiaries** arise when a beneficiary dies prior to the testator or when a child of the testator is not included as a beneficiary. When a beneficiary dies prior to the testator, that person's gift **lapses**, or fails. It does not automatically pass to that person's heirs, but falls into the residue. For example, a wife predeceases her husband. She has a child from a prior relationship. Husband then dies. Husband's gift to wife under the will does not pass to the stepchild and instead becomes part of the residue. If the gift was the residue, there is generally no residue of residue. Modern statutes provide that the residuary beneficiaries who survive the testator take the deceased beneficiary's share of the residuary estate.

Most states have an **anti-lapse statute**. This statute operates to save the gift when the predeceased beneficiary was in a specified degree of relationship to the testator and left descendants. Some states require the beneficiary and the beneficiary's descendant to be a descendant of the testator. Thus, a stepchild would not receive the gift. However, the Uniform Probate Code extends the statute's application to the testator's stepchild, a grandparent, or a descendant of the testator's grandparent.

If a beneficiary participates in any fashion in the willful and unlawful killing of the testator, that beneficiary receives nothing under a will according to **Slayer Act** statutes.

If a testator fails to provide in his will for any of his children born or adopted after the execution of the will, the **omitted after-born** or after-adopted child may receive a share of the decedent's estate unless the omission was intentional or the testator has provided for the child outside of the will.

A **simultaneous death** occurs when two or more persons, one of whom is the beneficiary of the other, die under circumstances where there is insufficient evidence to determine which party survived the other. Under the Uniform Probate Code, a person who cannot be established to have survived the decedent by 120 hours is deemed to have predeceased the decedent.

A person may **disclaim** an interest in property under a will. In order to be effective, a disclaimer must:

- Be in writing or other record;
- Declare the disclaimer;
- Describe the interest or power disclaimed;
- Be signed by the disclaiming party; and
- Be delivered or filed.

**Bequests** under a will are subject to ademption, satisfaction, advancement, and a spouse's elective share. The first step to determine a beneficiary's right to specific property is to classify the type of bequest:

- **Specific bequest** or specific devise: gift of a specific article or other property, which is identified and distinguished from all other things of the same kind and is satisfied only by delivery of the particular thing.
  - Use of the word "my"—"my car" versus "a car."
- **General legacy:** payable out of the general assets of the decedent's estate and not in any separated or distinguished fund from other things of the same kind.
- **Demonstrative bequest:** bequest of a certain sum to be paid out of a particular fund.
  - "100 shares of stock" v. "my 100 shares of stock," which would be a specific bequest.
  - Beneficiary is entitled to value of the 100 shares of stock out of the general estate if the particular fund is not in existence at the testator's death.

The doctrine of **ademption** applies to specific bequests that are not in the testator's estate at the time of death. The gift is considered "adeemed" and other property is not substituted. Ademption does not apply to general or demonstrative legacies. Modern statutes have modified the common law doctrine with various exceptions including casualty insurance proceeds, condemnation awards, and property sold by a guardian such that the property is not adeemed.

**Satisfaction** occurs when a gift has been satisfied by an *inter vivos* transfer from the testator to the beneficiary subsequent to the will's execution. The testator must provide for the satisfaction in the will or a contemporaneous writing or the devisee acknowledges in writing. An **advancement** is a lifetime gift made to an heir with the intent that the gift be applied against the heir's share of the estate. Lifetime gifts are presumed not to be an advancement unless intended as such.

Surviving spouses are protected from disinheritance by **elective share** statutes. These statutes give the spouse an election to take a statutory share in lieu of taking under the will. Under most statutes, the amount is one-third of the net probate estate if the decedent is survived by issue and one-half if the decedent is not survived by descendants.

If no will exists or a will is found invalid, then the decedent's property passes under the state's **intestate succession** statutes. If there are no surviving descendants, the spouse takes the entire estate. A surviving spouse takes one-third or one-half of the estate if there are surviving descendants. The descendants take the remainder of the estate.

Two different schemes are used by states:

- Majority rule—per capita with representation
- Modern trend—per capita at each generational level

Under a per capita with representation scheme, the property is divided into equal shares at the first generational level with living heirs. Each person at that level takes a share. If that person is deceased, her share passes to her issue by right of representation. That is, her share is divided between her own children. Under this scheme, the grandchildren receive different amounts based on whether they have siblings.

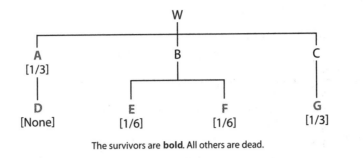

The survivors are **bold**. All others are dead.

**Per Capita with Representation**

Under a per capita at each generational level, the first split is the same. But instead of an heir's children dividing only that share, all takers with deceased parents at that generational level divide the shares equally. Under this scheme, the grandchildren take equal shares.

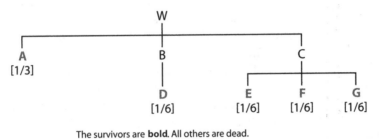

The survivors are **bold**. All others are dead.

**Per Capita at Each Generational Level**

Parents, siblings, and other collateral kin never inherit if the decedent is survived by children or more remote descendants such as grandchildren and great-grandchildren. If there is no spouse or descendants, then parents take the estate followed by siblings and then their descendants.

When faced with an intestate succession question, best to make your own generational graph to be sure not to confuse who is who.

The bar examiners also include **durable powers of attorney** ("POA") as a topic of Trusts and Estates. A POA empowers a designated agent to make health care decisions for the principal in the event of the principal's incapacity. Unless it states otherwise, a designated agent is empowered to make health care decisions for the principal whenever the principal lacks capacity. The power is not limited to a particular illness or a particular time period. Health care decisions includes decisions to withhold or withdraw treatment. The agent is to make decisions for the principal in the principal's best interest considering the principal's personal values to the extent known by the agent. An agent who acts in good faith is not liable for civil or criminal liability.

## B. Essay Practice Question[1]

A husband and wife were married in 2005.

In 2009, the husband transferred $600,000 of his money to a revocable trust. Under the terms of the properly executed trust instrument, upon the husband's death all trust assets would pass to his alma mater, University.

In 2012, the husband properly executed a will, prepared by his attorney based on the husband's oral instructions. Under the will, the husband bequeathed $5,000 to his best friend and the balance of his estate "to my wife, regardless of whether we have children." The husband failed to mention the revocable trust to his attorney during the preparation of this will, and the attorney did not ask the husband whether he had made any significant transfers in prior years.

In 2013, the husband and wife had a daughter.

In 2014, the husband was killed in an automobile accident. After his death, the wife found the husband's will and the revocable trust instrument on his desk. On the first page of the will, beginning in the left-hand margin and extending over the words setting forth the bequests to the husband's best friend and his wife, were the following words: "This will makes no sense, as most of my assets are in the trust for University and neither my wife nor my daughter seems adequately provided for. Estate plan should be changed. Call lawyer to fix." The statement was indisputably in the husband's handwriting. The wife also found a voice message on the phone from the husband's lawyer, which said, "Calling back. I understand you have concerns about your will."

The husband is survived by his wife, their daughter, and the husband's best friend. The assets in the revocable trust are now worth $900,000. The husband's probate estate is worth $300,000. He owed no debts at his death.

All the foregoing events occurred in State A, which is not a community property state. State A has enacted all of the customary probate statutes, but of particular relevance to the wife are the following:

(i) If a decedent dies intestate survived by a spouse and issue, the decedent's surviving spouse takes one-half of the estate and the decedent's surviving issue take the other half.

(ii) A revocable trust created by a decedent during the decedent's marriage is deemed illusory and the decedent's surviving spouse is entitled to receive one-half of the trust's assets.

1. How should the assets of the husband's probate estate be distributed? Explain.

2. How should the assets of the revocable trust be distributed? Explain.

---

1. The Multistate Bar Examination ("MBE®") questions, the Multistate Essay Examination ("MEE®") questions, and excerpts from the Multistate Performance Tests ("MPT®") have been reprinted by permission from the NCBE®. Copyright© by the National Conference of Bar Examiners. All rights reserved.

## II. TRUSTS

### A. Mind Map

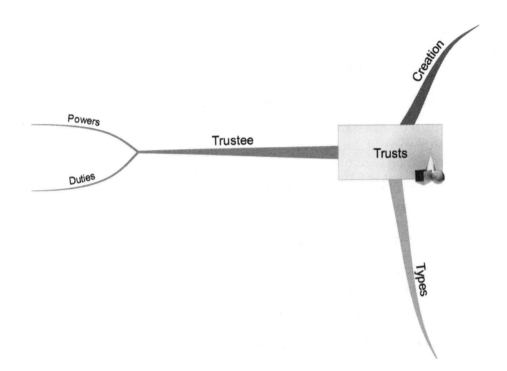

A trust is a fiduciary relationship where the trustee holds legal title to property with a duty to manage, invest, safeguard, and administer the trust assets and income for the benefit of designated beneficiaries, who hold equitable title. Although shorter than other mind maps, the trusts mind map focuses on the three main issues that arise in essay questions:

- Creation
- Classification
- Trustee's powers and duties

Just like Decedents' Estates, your inquiry begins with whether or not this is a valid trust. If the facts indicate in any manner that the grantee executed a valid trust, then you can skip this first step of **creation**. Otherwise, go through each element of creating a valid trust:

- Settlor's capacity: Analyze similar to a testator's capacity to form a will.
- Intent: Present intent to create a trust now, not in the future. No particular words required, not even "trust"; just a manifestation of intent to create a trust.
- Trustee: Must have mental capacity to administer the trust. Cannot be a minor or a mentally incompetent person. Corporations are allowed to be trustees. State statutes may impose additional requirements on corporations as trustees. A settlor can create a trust naming herself as trustee.
- Res—trust property: Settlor places title to the trust property and delivers to the trustee by

* an *inter vivos* transfer, or
* a testamentary trust (Testator can direct the executor of his will to distribute property to a trustee).
* Identifiable beneficiary: Except for charitable trusts, trust must have definite or ascertainable beneficiaries. Beneficiaries are equitable owners of trust property.
* Proper purpose: virtually any purpose except an illegal purpose, a purpose that violates the Rule Against Perpetuities, or a purpose contrary to public policy.
* Statute of Frauds and Statute of Wills, if necessary.

A trust terminates automatically at the end of the trust term. A trust also terminates when all the purposes of the trust have been accomplished.

**Modification** of a trust depends upon which party seeks the modification:

* Settlor: can revoke or amend a trust unless the terms state it is **irrevocable**.
* Beneficiaries:
  * Modification conflicts with a material purpose of the trust: settlor's consent is required.
  * Modification does not conflict with a material purpose of the trust: settlor's consent is not required.
  * If all the beneficiaries do not agree, a court may modify or terminate a trust when
    * the trust could have been modified if all beneficiaries had consented, and
    * the interests of any nonconsenting beneficiaries will be adequately protected.
* Trustee: can terminate a trust when the property's value is less than $50,000 and the amount is insufficient to justify the cost of administration.

Two special trust provisions warrant notice. Both **spendthrift provisions** and **discretionary provisions** appear on essay questions. A beneficiary's equitable interest in the property is freely transferable. A frequent scenario is one in which a beneficiary's creditor seeks to reach the property in appropriate proceedings. A creditor can only reach the beneficiary's interest and not the trust property itself. In order to avoid this scenario, a settlor may include a spendthrift provision in the trust.

A **spendthrift provision** means that the beneficiary cannot voluntarily or involuntarily transfer his interests. This provision does not apply if the income has already been paid to the beneficiary. Once in the beneficiary's hands, it is no longer protected by the trust's provisions and is fully owned by the beneficiary. Creditors can then reach the beneficiary's income from the trust. A spendthrift clause does not protect against a claim by the government or a claim for child support or spousal maintenance or for necessary supplies or services rendered to a beneficiary. A settlor is not allowed to create its own spendthrift trust to avoid creditors' claims. Note that a trustee's creditor cannot reach trust property as the trust "owns" the property, not the trustee.

A trust may contain **discretionary provisions**. These vest additional power in the trustee to decide when to distribute income of the trust. If the beneficiary's interest stems from a discretionary provision, then the beneficiary has no "right" to income until the trustee distributes the income. The trustee's decision is subject to an abuse of discretion review.

Trusts may be **classified** as an express trust, a charitable trust, a constructive trust, or a resulting trust:

- Express trusts arise from the intention of the property owner:
  - Private express trusts: comprise most of the trusts established by individuals.
  - Charitable trusts: resemble private express trusts but have some significant, distinguishing characteristics.
- Implied trusts arise by operation of law:
  - Resulting trusts: places property in the hands of rightful owners when circumstances require it, even though there has not been any wrongdoing on anyone's part.
  - Constructive trusts: deprive a wrongdoer from retaining improperly obtained property.

An **express trust** may be created by:

- An *inter vivos* trust created by a declaration of trust by the property owner, stating the trustee holds the property as trustee in trust.
- An *inter vivos* trust created by transfer of property during settlor's lifetime.
- A testamentary trust created by a will. In addition, "pour over" provisions in a will are allowed. Pour over provisions direct the transfer of property into a trust established either by the testator during his lifetime or by another person rather than creating a brand-new trust.

Spendthrift Clause

**Charitable trusts** have distinctive rules because of their substantial benefit to society. Charitable trusts are liberally construed to effectuate the purpose of the settlor:

- Indefinite beneficiaries:
  - But—trust cannot be restricted to a small group of people even if the benefits are payable for charitable purposes like education or health.
- Charitable purpose:
  - Categories:
    - Relief of poverty
    - Advancement of education
    - Advancement of religion
    - Promotion of health
    - Performance of governmental and municipal purposes (parks and recreation)
    - Other purposes beneficial to the community
  - Purpose can be broad.
  - Objective must be to benefit the public, although settlor can have a selfish reason such as reducing personal tax burden.
- Rule Against Perpetuities: limited application to charitable trusts.
  - Trust may have a perpetual existence.
  - If preceded by a noncharitable estate, the charitable interest must vest within the period of time proscribed by the RAP.
- *Cy pres* **doctrine** applies: When designated charity is not in existence at settlor's death, the court may redirect the trust to a purpose as near as possible to the charitable endeavor designated by the settlor.
- Termination: If the charitable trust cannot be performed as intended and the requirements for *cy pres* are not met, the charitable trust terminates and a resulting trust in favor of the settlor's estate results.

**Constructive trusts** are an equitable remedy in cases involving wrongful conduct and unjust enrichment. The trustee's duty is to convey the property to the person who owned it but for the wrongful conduct. A constructive trust may arise from theft, conversion, fraud, duress, or other situations requiring an equitable remedy such as breach of fiduciary duty.

A **resulting trust** arises upon the failure of an express trust, from a purchase money resulting trust or from an incomplete disposition of trust assets. The beneficiary is the one responsible for supplying the trust property, and the trustee holds title, but did not give consideration for the trust property.

The examiners frequently focus on the **trustee's powers and duties**. A trustee's powers originate in the terms of the trust together with the powers appropriate to achieve the proper investment, management, and distribution of the trust property.

A **trustee's powers** include the power to:

- settle or abandon trust claims;
- exercise all rights and powers an unmarried individual has over his own property;
- borrow money;
- sell or lease trust assets;
- apportion trust income; and
- incur reasonable expenses necessary to maintain trust property.

Matters within the trustee's discretion are not subject to attack unless she has abused her discretion in undertaking the conduct in question. If the trustee has absolute discretion, then her actions are improper only if undertaken in bad faith.

A trustee has specific fiduciary **duties:**

- Duty of loyalty and good faith:
  - No self-dealing, unless trust permits specific acts
  - No personal benefit other than official compensation
  - No apparent conflict of interest
  - Keep trust assets segregated from personal assets
- Duty to preserve trust property and make it productive:
  - Objective standard of care unless superior skills warrant a higher standard of care
  - Prudent investor rule governs:
    - Trustee is permitted to invest trust assets as would a prudent investor, considering both the interests of life beneficiaries and remaindermen. Thus, the trustee must consider both the investment's ability to produce a reasonable rate of income and the safety of the principal.
    - Trustee must seek to diversify the investments.
    - Standard is reasonable care, skill, and caution.
    - Some states maintain a "legal list" approach of approved types of investments.
  - Duty to dispose of wasting or non-productive assets
  - Duty to maintain accounting of transactions
  - Duty to enforce claims and defend trust from attack

Assets and expenses received by the trustee must be allocated to either principal or income of the trust. Why? One beneficiary may have a life interest in the trust principal, while another beneficiary is to receive the income from the trust. Income is usually attributed to income, while assets are principal. The problem arises with receipts of a mixed nature. Likewise, certain expenses benefit both the principal and income.

Because a trustee stands in a fiduciary relationship with the beneficiaries, trustees incur **liability** to the beneficiaries when duties are breached. When addressing an issue of whether a trustee violated a duty, ask first whether the trustee was authorized to perform the act. Then, ask whether the trustee performed to the required standard of care. Remedies available include compelling the trustee to convey property back to the trust, recovering profits made by the trustee, returning appreciation or profits from commingled funds, punitive damages, and removal as trustee.

Trustees may incur liability to third parties through performance of their duties. In certain situations, a trustee can obtain indemnification from the trust. The trustee cannot then be personally at fault. A trustee is entitled to indemnification where the tort was a normal incident to an activity in which the trustee was properly engaged on behalf of the trust, the tort is based on strict liability, or liability is based upon *respondeat superior* principles and the trustee did not make an improper delegation of discretionary functions to an agent or violate his duty to exercise reasonable care in the selection and supervision of the agent. A trustee is not personally liable on a contract properly entered into in the trustee's fiduciary capacity in the course of administering the trust if the trustee in the contract disclosed the fiduciary capacity.

Trusts may be an area that you did not take in law school, and you may not have had personal experience in the area. Parts of trusts law are extremely complicated. Those parts are in that 25% that you do not need to push yourself to know. Keep to the mind map and you can pass a Trusts essay.

## B. Essay Practice Question[2]

In 1995, a man and his friend created a corporation. The man owned 55% of the stock, and the friend owned 45% of the stock. When the man died in 2005, he left all of his stock in the corporation to his wife.

In 2009, the wife died. Under her duly probated will, the wife bequeathed the stock her husband had left her to a testamentary trust and named her husband's friend as trustee. Under the wife's will, the trustee was required to distribute all trust income to the wife's son "for so long as he shall live or until such time as he shall marry" and, upon the son's death or marriage, to distribute the trust principal to a designated charity. The stock, valued at $500,000 at the wife's death, comprised the only asset of this trust.

In 2013, after the stock's value had risen to $1.5 million, the trustee's lawyer properly advised the trustee to sell the stock in order to comply with the state's prudent investor act. Because of this advice, the trustee decided to sell the stock. However, instead of testing the market for potential buyers, the trustee purchased the stock himself for $1.2 million. Thereafter, on behalf of the trust, the trustee invested the $1.2 million sales proceeds in a balanced portfolio of

---

2. *Id.*

five mutual funds (including both stocks and bonds) with strong growth and current income potential.

Recently, both the son and the charity discovered the trustee's sale of the stock to himself and his reinvestment of the proceeds from the stock's sale. They learned that, due to general economic conditions, the stock in the corporation that had been purchased by the trustee for $1.2 million had declined in value to $450,000 and the value of the trust's mutual-fund portfolio had declined from $1.2 million to $1 million. Both the son and the charity have threatened to sue the trustee.

The son has also decided that he wants to get married and has notified the trustee that he believes the trust provision terminating his income interest upon marriage is invalid.

1. Would the son's interest in the trust terminate upon the son's marriage? Explain.
2. Did the trustee breach any duties by buying the trust's stock and, if yes, what remedies are available to the trust beneficiaries if they sue the trustee? Explain.
3. Did the trustee breach any duties in acquiring and retaining the portfolio of mutual funds and, if yes, what remedies are available to the trust beneficiaries if they sue the trustee? Explain.

# CHAPTER 18

# Mapping Family Law

## I. MIND MAP

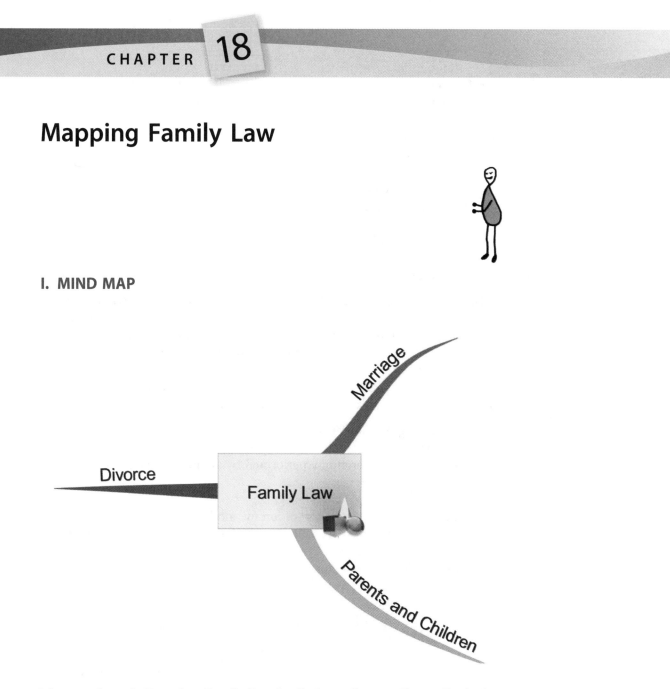

Many students believe that Family Law is all about divorce. The reality is that Family Law covers all parts of personal relationships between adults and between parents and children. Family law contains principles of contract law and property law, with a side of torts, evidence, and criminal law. The issues can range from a property dispute between unmarried cohabitants to determining which court has jurisdiction over a child's custody in a divorce. The starting point is establishing a marriage, but the end is not divorce, as issues arise between the parties years later. Family law covers:

- Marriage
  - Establishing marriage
    - Procedural requirements of formal marriage
    - Common law marriage

- Limitations on marriage
- Annulment
- Antenuptial agreements
- Divorce
  - Child custody
  - Visitation
  - Money issues
    - Child support
    - Maintenance
    - Property division
- Parents and children
  - Establishing parenthood
  - Nonmarital children
  - Termination of parental rights
  - Adoption

Issues regarding **marriage** focus on establishing marriage and antenuptial agreements, also called pre-nuptial agreements. The legal effects of the marital relationship are not heavily tested. This includes interspousal immunity, liability for debts, necessaries of a needy spouse, domestic violence, and postnuptial property agreements.

**Establishing marriage** includes addressing the procedural requirements, common law marriage, and the limitations on marriage:

- Procedural requirements of formal marriage:
  - License
  - Solemnization: ceremony performed by an authorized official
- Common law marriage:
  - Only a minority of states recognize
  - Issue still relevant for recognition by another state
    - Second state must recognize a valid marriage from another state
    - Basis—Full Faith and Credit Clause of the Constitution
  - Requirements—state-specific:
    - Consent
    - Cohabitation
    - Holding out as husband and wife
    - Legal capacity
- Limitations on marriage:
  - Age: parental consent required if under 18. State may require court approval if under 16 and prohibit marriage under 14.
  - Not closely-related
  - Capacity:
    - Mental capacity: must understand the nature of the marriage contract
    - Lack of consent: intoxication
  - Fraud
  - Prior marriage still in force

A **putative spouse** is one who entered into a ceremonial marriage and had a good faith belief in the validity of the marriage. The spouse later discovers that the marriage is void or voidable. In some states, a putative spouse acquires the rights conferred upon a legal spouse, including inheritance, property rights, and right to maintenance. In other states, the court will use equitable remedies.

| DISTINGUISHING INFORMAL RELATIONSHIPS | | |
|---|---|---|
| **Type of Relationship** | **State of Mind** | **Effect** |
| Common law marriage | Entered with present ability and intent | Creates full marital rights |
| Putative spouse | Believes they are legally married because there was a ceremony, but unaware of impediment to marriage | May have equitable spousal inheritance rights, but rights of property division and support are same as annulment |
| Unmarried partners | Know they are not married | May have statutory, contractual, or equitable rights that vary by state |

**Unmarried partners** have no legally recognized status unless they meet the requirements for common law marriage or are a putative spouse. Most states will recognize express and implied contracts between the partners concerning support and property, as long as there is consideration other than their sexual relationship. States will also utilize equitable remedies such as *quantum meruit.*

If the validity of a marriage is in doubt in any context from probate to divorce, a party may seek a judgment declaring the marriage invalid. This process is seeking an **annulment**. Most states distinguish between marriages that are void and marriages that are voidable. A void marriage has no legal effect. A voidable marriage is valid unless an aggrieved party obtains an annulment or ratifies the marriage. If one of the parties of a voidable marriage dies, the marriage's validity cannot be attacked by any person—a third party lacks standing to challenge the marriage.

| VOID v. VOIDABLE MARRIAGES | |
|---|---|
| **Grounds** | **Result** |
| Bigamy | Void |
| Closely-related (incest) | Void |
| Under age | Voidable |
| Impotence | Voidable |
| Temporary incapacity (intoxication, duress, fraud) | Voidable |
| Mental incompetence | Voidable |

**Antenuptial agreements**, often called pre-nuptial agreements, are contracts. The consideration is the entry into marriage. The Statute of Frauds applies. The validity requirements are state-specific. Most states have adopted standards regarding basic contract formation, procedural fairness, and substantively fair terms. Particularly look at procedural fairness. Was execution of the agreement voluntary or under duress? Was there full financial disclosure?

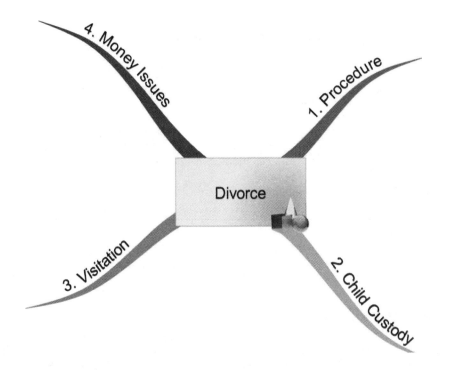

Only **divorce** terminates a legal marriage. Remember, an annulment is a declaration that a marriage is invalid. No common law divorce exists. Parties to a common law marriage must seek a divorce decree from a court. Divorce or dissolution issues focus on four categories:

- Procedure
- Child custody
- Visitation
- Money issues
  - Child support
  - Maintenance
  - Property division

Most states only have **no-fault grounds** for divorce—the marriage is irretrievably broken. Some states have retained fault grounds, such as adultery and desertion. A court has **jurisdiction** to enter a divorce decree if one of the parties is domiciled in that jurisdiction. Personal jurisdiction is not required as a divorce is considered an *in rem* action. Spousal support, child support, and property rights require personal jurisdiction over both parties. Thus, a court can grant a divorce, but not decide any other issues without personal jurisdiction.

Jurisdiction for child custody and visitation is governed by the Uniform Child Custody Jurisdiction and Enforcement Act ("UCCJEA"). The UCCJEA focuses on the home state of the child—the state in which the child lived with a parent for at least six consecutive months prior to the commencement of the proceeding. The home state maintains jurisdiction not only to grant the original order, but also to modify it. Thus, even though the child has moved to another state, the home state maintains jurisdiction.

When faced with a family law issue involving any type of divorce, the next issue to address is **child custody**. A court's decree regarding custody affects all other issues. Custody can mean legal custody, which is decision-making power,

**Children and Money**

or physical custody, where the child resides. If both parents are granted custody, it can be joint legal custody (parents share decision making, but child resides with one parent) or joint physical custody (parents share decision making and child divides time between each parent's home, although does not need to be equal time) or both. Some states have a preference for joint custody. Others do not award it unless the parents expressly agree.

Child custody is determined by the **best interest of the child** standard. Courts consider several factors in determining the child's best interest:

- Wishes of the parents and child
- Interaction and interrelationship of the child with parents, siblings, and others
- Child's adjustment to home, school, and community
- The mental and physical health of the individuals involved

A child's preference is generally not considered until over the age of 12. The judge would then question the child in chambers. A preference may be given to a primary caregiver—the one most involved in the child's day-to-day life. Preference may also be given to the "friendly parent"; that is, the parent willing to cooperate and facilitate the child's relationship with the other parent.

Child custody awards are always modifiable. The standard is a substantial and material change in circumstances such that the child's best interests would be better served by a change in custody. Custody modifications usually require a certain amount of time to elapse. On the exam, an applicant may go down the wrong path if they do not realize the issues involved a modification instead of the original order. Watch for language such as "four years later." That's a signal that it probably involves a modification.

# Original or Modification?

Months or Years Later...

**Relocation** is one of the most difficult custody modification issues. One parent wishes to relocate to another state to better his or her situation and the situation for the child. Yet it will mean a separation from the other parent and will make it more difficult to maintain frequent, in-person contact. Courts will use a balancing test as to the impact on visitation versus the benefits of the move. The overall trend is to be lenient to the needs of the parent with whom the child primarily lives. If the motivation to move is vindictive, the court will generally not permit the child to move.

**Visitation** or parenting plans are granted to the **noncustodial parent** unless visitation is detrimental to the best interests of the child. While a court may limit visitation if a parent engages in actions that amount to misconduct that might injure the child, absolute denial of visitation is rare. Failure to pay child support does not entitle the custodial parent the right to deny visitation to the noncustodial parent.

State statutes vary widely in granting visitation to **third parties**, such as grandparents. The best interest standard still applies and usually may not override the wishes of a fit parent. Usually, these statutes are limited to situations when the grandparents' child has died or the child's parents have divorced. Some statutes are broader and include siblings, stepparents, or a parent's former same-sex partner. Other statutes are broader still and allow visitation when the family is intact; that is, there has been no death or divorce. These statutes are constitutionally limited. As long as a parent is fit, that parent's determination as to the appropriateness of third-party visitation must be given "special weight." The judge may not override a fit parent's decision to deny a third-party visitation, even if she feels visitation would be in the best interests of the child.

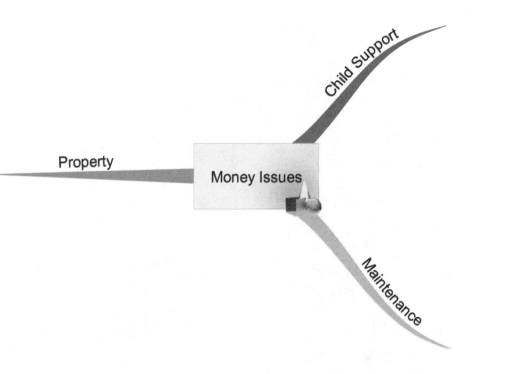

Therefore, with both custody and visitation issues, keep in mind that fit parents' wishes regarding their children are not overridden in favor of third parties. Be leery of concluding that a third party should have custody over a fit parent. For example, a stepfather has raised the child with the biological mother, but never adopted the child. The stepfather has no right to visitation in a divorce unless a statute provides for stepparent visitation.

**Money issues** are child support, spousal maintenance, and property division. Both parents equally share a duty to support their child. The amount of any **child support** award is determined by state guidelines. The guidelines use a formula based upon the parents' income, the age of the child, and the number of children supported. Because of this formula, you will never need to determine an actual monetary amount for child support. The formula sets a presumptive amount. This can be rebutted with a showing that a variation is in order. Remember, denial of visitation cannot be used as a punishment for failure to pay child support.

Child support is modifiable based upon a substantial change in circumstances. Most states have presumptions set in their guidelines for increases. Child support terminates upon the child's death or emancipation (usually 18 years of age).

A frequent issue with child support deals with parents who have lost income. If it is a voluntary reduction in pay, the court will impute income to the parent. What would the parent be making if employed in a job suitable to the parent's experience and education? This same concept will arise in determining the income of a homemaker.

Spousal **maintenance**, formerly called alimony, is awarded to ensure an adequate income stream for spouses whose economic dependency has

resulted from the marital relationship. Different types of maintenance can be awarded:

- Periodic maintenance: a certain amount of money paid at set intervals, usually monthly. Obligation ends at the recipient's death, remarriage, or a court-ordered modification.
- Lump sum maintenance: fixed amount of money, although may be paid in installments. The award is not modifiable.
- Rehabilitative maintenance: awarded for a limited period of time to support the recipient in receiving education or training to be employable and self-supporting.
- Reimbursement maintenance: awarded if the recipient spouse made contributions in the marriage to the other spouse's education, training, or increased earning capacity.

The amount is based on factors including:

- standard of living established during the marriage,
- duration of marriage,
- age and health of both parties,
- financial resources of both parties,
- contribution of each party to the marriage,
- time needed to obtain education or training to enable either party to find appropriate employment, and
- ability of payor spouse to meet her needs while paying support.

Maintenance terminates upon the spouse's death or remarriage. Modification requires a substantial and continuing change in circumstances. Some states will consider cohabitation as a factor in a modification.

For **property division**, the court follows three steps: classify the property, value the assets, and divide the property. First, the court classifies the property as either separate property or marital property:

- Separate property: all property owned before the marriage, property acquired after the dissolution, and property acquired by gift or inheritance during the marriage.
- Marital property: earnings from both parties and appreciation of marital property. Property acquired after the marriage is presumed to be marital property.

One issue that arises is mixed property. Mixed property includes commingled property, transmuted separate property, and improvement of separate property. Commingled property is when separate property becomes marital property because it is inextricably mingled with marital property or with the separate property of the other spouse. If the property can be traced back to its origins, it retains its nature as separate property.

Mixed property also includes transmuted property. If separate property is treated in a way that evidences an intention for the property to be marital property, it is transmuted into marital property. Separate property can be improved with marital funds. The property maintains its nature as separate property, but the marital estate is reimbursed for the value added to the separate property.

Specific property interests that arise:

- Marital residence:
  - Difficulties arise if the house was purchased prior to the marriage but marital funds were used to pay off the mortgage or build equity.
  - Difficulties also arise if a spouse's separate funds are used to make improvements or build equity; then, a gift to the marital estate is presumed but can be rebutted.
  - If a spouse's labor increases the value of the other spouse's separate property, the increase is marital.
  - **Source of funds** rule is used to apportion the value of the property between separate and marital efforts and funds.
  - Appreciation in the value of the property is apportioned in the same manner.
- Pensions:
  - Subject to equitable distribution if accumulated during the marriage.
  - Vested or nonvested.
  - Premarital and post-separation increases or contributions are usually not deemed marital property.
  - A **qualified domestic relations order (QDRO)** recognizes the right of the alternate payee to receive all or a portion of the retirement benefits that would otherwise be payable to the spouse.
- Stock options: presumed to be marital property.
- Professional degrees and licenses:
  - Most states hold they are not a property interest subject to equitable distribution.
  - May be considered in the division of other marital property or in a maintenance or reimbursement award.
- Professional practice and goodwill:
  - A professional practice or corporation is subject to disposition as a marital asset.

- Enterprise goodwill—transferable with the business.
- Personal goodwill—generated solely by the reputation and professional expertise of the owner-spouse and not divisible.

Valuation of assets is usually not tested. Valuation disputes require expert witnesses to appraise the property. Instead, the examiners will give you a dollar amount.

States take one of three different approaches to **property division:**

- Community property approach: All property acquired during marriage is deemed owned one-half by each spouse. Each keeps separate property and the remainder is divided.
- Equitable division of all property approach: All property owned, whether marital or separate, is divided between each spouse.
- Equitable division of all marital property approach: Spouses keep separate property that includes property owned prior to the marriage, gifts, or inheritance and the remainder is divided.

Under the equitable division approaches, courts look to factors to decide how to divide. Note that the division does not have to be equal, but equitable. Courts consider:

- Age, education, and earning capacity
- Duration of marriage
- Standard of living enjoyed during marriage
- Present income
- Source of funds for acquisition of property
- Health
- Assets, debt, and liabilities of parties
- Parties' needs
- Child custody
- Contribution as a homemaker
- Evidence of dissipation

The court's order dividing property is a final judgment and is not modifiable. For example, if the parties omitted property from the division, the party would not seek modification of the divorce degree but would have to follow the civil procedure rules for reopening a judgment.

**Analysis Order for Divorce Issues**

- Jurisdiction over each issue
- Original order or modification?
- Child custody
- Visitation
- Money issues
  - Child support
  - Maintenance
  - Property division

The issues involved with **parents and children** include establishing parent-hood, nonmarital children, termination of parental rights, and adoption.

Establishing maternity usually is fairly straightforward for obvious reasons. With the advent of surrogacy and assisted reproduction methods, motherhood may now need to be established through adjudication.

Establishing paternity is more complicated:

- Presumption of marital paternity: A child born and conceived by a woman while she is married is presumed to be the child of her husband.
  - Presumption is rebuttable by clear and convincing evidence.
  - Many states allow DNA evidence within a few years of the child's birth.
- Putative fathers: an alleged father when the child has a presumed father:
  - State statutes dictate time limits on when an unmarried father can establish his paternity.
  - Time limits are imposed to resolve the issue without subjecting the child to a long period of unsettled circumstances.
  - Additional presumptions under the Uniform Parentage Act:
    - Parents married after the child's birth and the man voluntarily asserted his paternity.
    - Parents resided in the same household for the first two years of the child's life and the man openly held out the child as his own.

Suits to establish paternity may be brought by the mother, the child, or the state. The statute of limitations encompasses the child's minority.

A "**nonmarital child**" is a child born to an unmarried woman. Nonmarital children have the same right to support and government benefits as marital children. A nonmarital child has the same right of inheritance from its mother as a marital child. The state may require that paternity has been proven during the life of the alleged father in order to inherit from him.

**Termination of parental rights** occurs through emancipation of the child, voluntary relinquishment of parental rights, and involuntary termination of parental rights:

- Emancipation
  - Age of majority set by statute
  - Financial independence and maturity are considerations
  - Minor who marries before the age of majority
- Voluntary relinquishment of parental rights
- Involuntary relinquishment of parental rights
  - Due process concerns
    - Notice
    - Hearing
  - Considerations
    - Abandonment
    - Neglect
    - Abuse

**Adoption** questions involve jurisdiction, consent, and the consequences of adopting a child. The UCCJEA excludes adoption from its provisions. Thus, each state's statutes govern jurisdiction within the state. The biological parents must consent to the adoption by the adopting parents. Consent is not required if the biological parents' rights have been terminated or they have abandoned the child, which is defined by state statute. A committed father is entitled to due process, if he chooses to protest the adoption. Some states have statutes that grant fathers a veto right in any possible adoption. After the adoption, the adoptive parents have all the legal rights and responsibilities with their child as if they were the biological parents.

## II. ESSAY PRACTICE QUESTION[1]

Eight years ago, a woman and a man began living together. The woman worked as an investment banker, and the man worked part-time as a bartender while he struggled to write his first novel. The couple lived in a condominium that the woman had purchased shortly before the man moved in. The woman had purchased the condominium for $300,000 using her own money and had taken title in her own name.

Four years ago, the woman and the man were married at City Hall. One week before the wedding, the woman presented the man with a proposed premarital agreement and an asset list. The asset list correctly stated that the woman owned the condominium, then worth $350,000, and a brokerage account, then worth $500,000. The agreement specified that, in the event of divorce, each spouse would be entitled to retain "all assets which he or she then owns, whether or not those assets are acquired during the marriage." The man was surprised when the woman gave him the agreement to sign, and he contacted a lawyer friend for advice. The lawyer urged the man not to sign the agreement. Nonetheless, the man signed the agreement, telling the woman, "I'm a little hurt, but I guess I understand that you want to keep what you earn." The woman signed the agreement as well.

After their wedding, the woman and the man continued to live in the woman's condominium and to work at the jobs each held before the marriage. The man also continued to work on his novel.

Six months ago, the man's novel was accepted by a publisher. The novel will be released next spring. The publisher has estimated that the royalties may total as much as $200,000 over the next five years.

Two months ago, the woman and the man separated. The woman remained in the condominium, now worth $400,000 as a result of market appreciation. The woman's brokerage account, worth $500,000 when she and the man married, is now worth $1,000,000 as a result of market appreciation and additional investments that the woman made with employment bonuses she received during the marriage. The woman has made no withdrawals from this account.

One month ago, the woman won, but has not yet received, a $5 million lottery jackpot.

One week ago, the man filed for divorce. In the man's divorce petition, he asks the court to invalidate the premarital agreement and seeks half of all assets owned by the woman, i.e., the woman's brokerage account, her condominium, and her right to the lottery payment. The man owns no assets except for personal effects and the book contract under which he will receive future royalties based on sales of his novel.

This jurisdiction has adopted the Uniform Premarital Agreement Act, which in relevant part provides that "the party against whom enforcement [of the premarital agreement] is sought must prove (1) involuntariness or (2) *both* that 'the agreement was unconscionable when it was executed' *and* that he or she did not

---

1. The Multistate Bar Examination ("MBE[®]") questions, the Multistate Essay Examination ("MEE[®]") questions, and excerpts from the Multistate Performance Tests ("MPT[®]") have been reprinted by permission from the NCBE[®]. Copyright© by the National Conference of Bar Examiners. All rights reserved.

receive or waive a 'fair and reasonable' disclosure and 'did not have or reasonably could not have had . . . an adequate knowledge' of the other's assets and obligations."

The jurisdiction's divorce law requires "equitable distribution" of all marital (community) assets and prohibits the division of separate assets.

1. Is the premarital agreement enforceable? Explain.
2. Assuming that the agreement is unenforceable, what assets are subject to division in the divorce action, and what factors should a court consider in distributing those assets? Explain.

# CHAPTER 19

# Mapping Secured Transactions

The Uniform Commercial Code (UCC) is intimidating at first glance. Fortunately, Article 9 Secured Transactions lends itself well to mind mapping. If followed, this system results in at least 75% of the issues and rules involved.

## I. MIND MAP

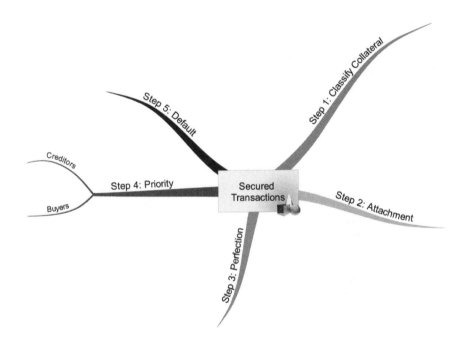

First, always begin your answer with "Under Article 9 of the Uniform Commercial Code, . . ." You do not need to remember UCC section numbers.

Secured Transactions (ST) focuses on creditors. A **secured transaction** is created when a debtor seeks a loan and the entity giving the loan takes a special property interest—a **security interest**—in a specific piece of the debtor's property—the **collateral**—to insure repayment of the loan. Debtors have few rights under Article 9. In a secured transaction question, debtors always don't pay their debts. Occasionally an issue that relates to the debtor's interests arises when the sale of the collateral does not follow UCC requirements. When you see only one creditor, think default.

For the most part, the issues on ST essay questions relate to which creditor has priority over the collateral in order to sell it and apply the proceeds to its loan. Thus, the issues center on the creation of the secured interest and how a creditor has priority over other creditors.

### Keys to a High ST Score

- More than one creditor → almost always!
- Debtor doesn't pay → always!
- Go through each analytical step with each creditor for each piece of collateral, keeping in mind each loan that creditor made.
- Determine each creditor's status.
- Only then can you apply the correct priority rule.

Our mind map then focuses on laying out the analytical steps you must address for each creditor for each piece of collateral, keeping in mind each loan that creditor made to that debtor:

- Classify collateral
- Attachment
  - Security interest created
  - Debtor had rights in the collateral
  - Creditor gave value
- Perfection
- Priority
- Default

The first two steps of your analysis, classification and attachment, deal with whether the creditor has actually created a security interest. If a creditor has not created a security interest, it is at the end of the line when that collateral is sold. Creditors always want to be secured and want to be first in line. The first step then is to classify the **collateral**. This step is first because some later rules vary depending upon the classification. These classifications include:

- Consumer goods
- Business use:
  - Inventory: goods that are used up or sold
  - Farm products: crops, livestock, etc.
  - Equipment: machinery, office equipment
- Intangibles: negotiable instruments, investment property, deposit accounts
- Chattel paper: written promise to pay and security interest in goods
- Fixtures: personal property adhered to real property
- Proceeds

In addition, a creditor can include property the debtor has yet to own if it includes an **after-acquired property clause** in a security agreement.

The same type of personal property is not always the same type of collateral. For example, an office desk is business equipment when used in a business's office. But the same desk is inventory at the office supply store and a consumer good if a customer takes it home for personal use.

The next step, **attachment**, is one some applicants skip in their essay instead of garnering all the low-hanging fruit points they can get by meticulously going through each step of attachment with each creditor on each collateral for each loan. Indeed, attachment is a key concept for scoring well. Attaching a security interest to collateral gives the creditor rights against the debtor on that collateral. And, every single essay requires an attachment analysis. Without it, no security interest is even created.

The concept of attachment starts with creating the security interest itself and then affixing the security interest to the collateral.

A mnemonic to remember the creation of a security interest is **CAP**. A creditor can create a security interest by having **control** of an intangible, by having an authenticated security **agreement** creating the security interest, or by taking **possession** of the collateral.

But the security interest just created is worthless if it is not affixed to specific collateral. To affix the security interest to the collateral, the debtor must also have had rights in the collateral and the creditor must have given value. If the security interest never attaches to the collateral, then the creditor remains unsecured and the creditor cannot claim that specific property to sell.

Use the mnemonic ARV to remember the requirements to attach a security interest to collateral:

*ARV*
* **A**uthenticated security agreement/possession/control
  * **C**ontrol: used for intangibles
  * **A**uthenticated security **a**greement
  * **P**ossession
* Debtor had **R**ights in the collateral.
* Secured party gave **V**alue in exchange for a security interest.

**Creating a Security Interest**

Once the security interest has attached to the collateral, the secured creditor must tell the rest of the world that it has a security interest in this specific collateral in order to claim priority over other creditors. This notice is called **perfection**. The security interest must be perfected in the specific collateral.

Methods of perfection:

- File financing statement
- Automatic

- Temporary
- Possession
- Control

Not all five types of perfection apply to all types of collateral. For example, possession cannot work on intangibles as there is nothing to possess. Have you noticed that possession of collateral and control of collateral keep popping up? Possession or control of collateral not only creates a security interest, but they also operate as perfection.

The most common way to perfect a security interest is to file a **financing statement** with the Secretary of State's office where the collateral is located. This gives actual notice to those who look at the financing statement and constructive notice to all others.

---

**Possession of collateral and control of collateral are a triple threat! They operate to:**

- create a security interest,
- satisfy one step of attachment, and
- perfect the security interest.

---

**Automatic perfection** arises with a special kind of security interest called a **Purchase Money Security Interest** (PMSI). A PMSI is created when:

- Seller sells goods to a buyer on credit
  OR
- Lender lends the purchaser money to buy specific goods

Perfection of a Security Interest

| | | | Creditor #1 | | | Creditor #2 | | |
|---|---|---|---|---|---|---|---|---|
| | | | Original | Proceeds? | After-Acquired? | Original | Proceeds? | After-Acquired? |
| **Decides If S E C U R E D** | Classify Collateral | 1. Tangible (CIFE) Consumer Goods Inventory Farm Products Equipment 2. Intangible 3. Proceeds | | | | | | |
| | Attachment (**ARV**) | **A**uthenticated Security Agreement (Can be by **P**ossession, **A**greement, or **C**ontrol) **PAC** | | | | | | |
| | | Debtor has **R**ights in collateral | | | | | | |
| | | Creditor has given **V**alue | | | | | | |
| | Perfection | Filed Financing Statement **OR** | | | | | | |
| | | Possession **OR** | | | | | | |
| | | Control | | | | | | |
| | | Possible **PMSI**? (Automatic if consumer goods; 20 days temporary perfection if not) | | | | | | |

**SECURED TRANSACTIONS ANALYSIS CHART**
**Is creditor secured and perfected for this property with this loan?**

This security interest is given special status because the lender or seller has directly given value for a particular purchase. PMSI creditors who properly perfect are given priority over all other perfected secured creditors—a super-priority.

If the PMSI is for the purchase of consumer goods, perfection is automatic. The creditor does not need to do anything except for two situations: for motor vehicles, where the security interest must be noted on the vehicle's title, and for fixtures that require filing in the Recorder of Deeds office.

Not all PMSIs have automatic perfection. If the PMSI purchase is collateral other than consumer goods, the security interest is **temporarily perfected** for 20 days. If the creditor files a financing statement within the 20 days, its priority relates back and continues. If the creditor perfects over 20 days, it loses its PMSI status, although it still is a perfected secured creditor. If the creditor does not perfect, it is an unperfected secured creditor.

Remember to go through classification, attachment, and perfection with each creditor for each piece of collateral and each loan. Determine each creditor's status on each collateral. For example, Bank has a security interest in Machine One and gave Debtor a $100,000 loan. Debtor then acquires Machine Two. Does Bank's security interest cover Machine Two? Let's say it does, and then Bank gives a second loan to debtor for $50,000. Does the security interest apply to the second loan? Then, our second creditor is Finance. Finance gave Debtor a loan of $75,000 to purchase Machine Two. The call of the question is who has priority over Machine Two. You would need to analyze Finance's interest with one loan on one machine. You would then need to analyze Bank's first loan and whether it covers Machine Two and then analyze whether the second loan also covers Machine Two.

> **EXAM TIP**
>
> PMSI issues are ripe for picking! Remember, only security interests in consumer goods have automatic perfection. Everything else requires the creditor to perfect within 20 days. If it does not perfect, it loses super-priority. If you classify the collateral first and remember this distinction, you will have it nailed.

---

### Creditor's Status

- Perfected secured party
- Unperfected secured party
- Unsecured party

---

Use this chart while doing practice essays to get used to analyzing creditors' interests separately and to analyze each collateral and loan for each creditor separately.

Once you have identified each creditor as a perfected secured creditor, an unperfected secured creditor, or an unsecured creditor, you need to apply the correct **priority** rule to the conflicting interests. Be sure to keep track of the dates each event occurs. Constructing a timeline can help.

---

### Priority Rules for Creditors

PMSI Perfected Secured Creditor = **Wins over all other creditors**
Perfected Secured Creditor v. Perfected Secured Creditor = **First to File or Perfect**
Perfected Secured Creditor v. Unperfected Secured Creditor = **Perfected Secured Creditor**
Unperfected Secured Creditor v. Unperfected Secured Creditor = **First to Attach**
Secured creditor (whether or not perfected) v. Unsecured Creditor = **Secured Creditor**

---

EXAM TIP

**1st to Perfect v. 1st to Attach**

While perfection of a security interest relates back to the date of the filing, attachment does not occur until the last event and does not relate back.

Pay particular attention to the rule for a dispute between two perfected secured creditors. The rule is the **first to file or perfect**. "Perfect" means the creditor has already created the security interest, attached the security interest, *and* perfected its interest. "File" means it has filed a financing statement. The creditor need do nothing else at first. It's like calling "dibs" to hold your place in line. The creditor who just files is holding its place in line. It keeps its place in line as long as it completes the requirements of creating and attaching its security interest. Its interest then relates back to the original filing date. Thus, even if a second creditor comes along and perfects fulfilling all three steps first, the first creditor has priority.

THIS RULE IS THE NUMBER ONE BAR TRAP! This rule is tested frequently and absolutely must be understood and recognized on an essay.

A note concerning two other types of entities that may usurp a secured party's place in line: buyers and lien creditors. The general rule is that a secured interest stays attached to the collateral despite a sale to a buyer. There are three primary exceptions: when the creditor consents, when the buyer is in the ordinary course of business, and when a buyer purchases a consumer good from another consumer (garage sale exception).

A buyer in the ordinary course of business (BIOC) purchases the goods from a seller who sells goods as part of its regular business. A buyer of consumer goods who, in a resale, purchases consumer goods with an automatically perfected PMSI takes free of the creditor's security interest. If, however, the creditor does file, then the security interest remains attached.

**Buyers**

Discount store shopping = BIOC
Car purchase from car dealer = BIOC (but if purchase on credit, buyer has given its creditor its own security interest)
Car purchase from neighbor = Not BIOC (unless neighbor in car selling business)
Garage sale purchase = Not BIOC, but possible buyer of consumer goods

A lien creditor is not a secured creditor. The lien creditor acquires a lien on the collateral through a court judgment. If the lien creditor has levied on the collateral before a security interest is perfected, then the lien creditor has priority except for a PMSI creditor.

The last step of your analysis is to look for any issues related to **default**. Default is defined by the security agreement between the parties. Thus, whether a default has occurred will be given to you. Upon default, the creditor can take two steps. It usually does both, although depending upon the collateral and the amount of the remaining debt it may decide to take only one of the steps.

* Creditor can sue upon the debt
  OR
* Take possession of the property

Possession can occur by an action for replevin or by self-help repossession. Yes, the repo man. Self-help repossession is allowed as long as there is no breach of the peace. Do not rely on any reality television show for defining breach of the peace! If in doubt, give the reasoning on both sides.

After default, the debtor has a right to redeem the debt. The debtor must pay the entire debt plus attorney fees and costs. It is then entitled to keep the collateral.

Any sale of the collateral upon default must be commercially reasonable.

* Is a public or private sale required or allowed?
* Has notice been given to all parties?
  * Notice not required if:
    * property can be sold on a recognized market, such as the stock market, or
    * the collateral is perishable (that is, the collateral's value is threatened to decline prior to sale; think of a truck full of lettuce to get the picture).
* Has secured party made an effort to get the best price?

Following the sale, the proceeds are distributed in a set order. If the sale proceeds don't cover the debt and costs, the debtor is still liable for the remainder—a deficiency judgment. If the creditor does not follow the proper procedure after default, it may forfeit the right to receive a deficiency judgment. The distribution order is:

* Costs of sale
* First secured party's debt
* Any other secured party's debt in priority order
* Surplus to debtor (very rare)

Five tricky issues arise in secured transactions questions. The file or perfect rule is the most common. PMSI issues are second. The remaining traps are after-acquired property, future advances, and proceeds. Understand the rules for these five issues and the fact patterns that trigger the issues and you are well on your way to a high score on a secured transactions essay.

### Beware of Bar Traps

* File OR Perfect
* Purchase Money Security Interest
* After-acquired property
* Proceeds
* Future advances

**After-acquired property clauses** are one of the reasons that you *must* analyze each creditor's interest by analyzing attachment and perfection. After-acquired property issues arise when a creditor's initial security agreement includes a clause that covers future acquisitions of property. The security interest attaches the moment the debtor acquires an interest in the new collateral. An after-acquired property clause is not needed for inventory or proceeds. After-acquired property clauses are tricky because typically a second or

**After-Acquired Property**

**Future Advances**

third creditor pops up between the first creditor's first acquisition of the security interest and the debtor's acquisition of the second collateral. If you lay the groundwork of attachment and perfection, you garner most of the points for the question, even if you are incorrect on who would ultimately prevail.

Likewise, a **future advance** clause refers to events that happen after the initial security agreement. Here, the creditor loans additional money and the original security interest secures the loan. The second loan is covered only if the original security agreement includes a future advances clause. Look for it when the debtor gets additional money from the same creditor. The same tricky circumstances arise as with after-acquired property—a second creditor jumps in and loans money to the debtor. If the first creditor did not include a future advance clause, then it must get a new security agreement from the debtor. This security agreement will relate back to the original filing. Just keep track of attachment and perfection of each piece of collateral and each loan and you'll get the points.

The last tricky issue regards **proceeds**. Proceeds occur when the original collateral is sold. Whatever the debtor receives from the sale is proceeds, including cash, negotiable instruments, and chattel paper. Proceeds are temporarily perfected for 20 days. That perfection continues if the proceeds are identifiable cash proceeds or the financing statement for the proceeds would be filed in the same office as the original collateral. If it's in a different office, then another filing (possession or control) must occur.

Follow the mind map, analyze each creditor separately on each piece of collateral and on each loan, and you will garner most of the points available on a secured transaction question.

## II. ESSAY PRACTICE QUESTION[1]

Two years ago, a retailer of home electronic equipment borrowed $5 million from a finance company. The loan agreement, signed by both parties, provided that the retailer granted the finance company a security interest in all of the retailer's present and future inventory to secure the retailer's obligation to repay the loan. On the same day that it made the loan, the finance company filed in the appropriate state filing office a properly completed financing statement reflecting this transaction.

Six months ago, a buyer purchased a home entertainment system from the retailer for a total price of $7,000. The buyer paid $1,000 as a down payment on the system and agreed to make 12 additional monthly payments of $500 each. The buyer signed a "credit purchase agreement" memorializing the financial arrangement with the retailer and providing that the retailer would "retain title" to the entertainment system until the buyer's obligation to the retailer was paid in full. The buyer then returned home with her new home entertainment system. The buyer had no knowledge of the retailer's agreement with the finance company and acted in good faith in acquiring the home entertainment system. The retailer did not file a financing statement with respect to this transaction.

Two months ago, the buyer decided that she could no longer afford her monthly $500 payments for the home entertainment system. She contacted her friend, who had often expressed interest in acquiring a home entertainment system. After a brief discussion, the friend agreed to buy the home entertainment system from the buyer for $4,000 if the friend could pay the price 90 days later, when he anticipated receiving a bonus at work. The buyer accepted the friend's

---

1. The Multistate Bar Examination ("MBE®") questions, the Multistate Essay Examination ("MEE®") questions, and excerpts from the Multistate Performance Tests ("MPT®") have been reprinted by permission from the NCBE®. Copyright© by the National Conference of Bar Examiners. All rights reserved.

proposal, and the friend gave the buyer a check for $4,000. The buyer promised to hold the $4,000 check for 90 days before depositing it. The friend took the entertainment system and began using it at his own home. The friend had no knowledge of the buyer's agreement with the retailer or of the retailer's agreement with the finance company.

The retailer is in financial distress and has missed a payment owed to the finance company. Meanwhile, since the friend bought the home entertainment system from the buyer, the buyer has not made any of her monthly payments to the retailer.

1. Does the finance company have an interest in the home entertainment system? Explain.
2. Does the retailer have an interest in the home entertainment system? Explain.
3. Does the retailer have an interest in the $4,000 check? Explain.

# CHAPTER 20

# Mapping Conflict of Laws

Conflict of Laws is no longer a stand-alone topic; that is, you will not have a question that only involves Conflict of Laws. Instead, Conflict of Laws issues will be embedded into other MEE topic areas. The most frequent inclusion is in Civil Procedure, Contracts, Decedents' Estates, and Family Law. The Conflicts portion of a question may well be over 50% of the points allowed. Thus, spend some time on Conflicts, but not as much time as you would on other topics that stand alone and are routinely tested.

## I. MIND MAP

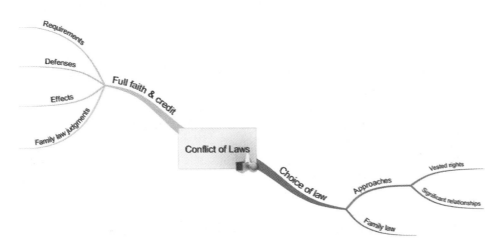

Conflict of Laws centers around two main issues:

* Recognition of another state's judgment
* Choice of law in an ongoing suit

### A. Recognition of Another State's Judgment

Whether a judgment in one state is recognized by another state is governed by the **Full Faith and Credit Clause** of the Constitution: "Full faith and credit shall be given in each state to the public acts, records, and judicial proceedings of every state."[1] A federal statute provides that this clause is extended to federal courts requiring recognition of judgments between state and federal courts and between federal courts. Three considerations arise:

* Requirements met?
* Any defenses?
* Effects of recognition

Analyze **each requirement** of the Full Faith and Credit Clause separately:

* There must be proper jurisdiction:
  * Subject-matter and personal jurisdiction.
  * If jurisdiction was fully and fairly litigated in the original action, the defendant cannot have that determination relitigated in the recognizing state.
  * Why? The litigated issue of jurisdiction has already been determined. That determination is subject to full faith and credit itself.
* Judgment must be on the merits:
  * Must involve the substance of the plaintiff's claim.
  * Includes default judgments.
* Judgment must be final: No further action by the rendering court is needed to resolve the litigation.

**EXAM TIP**

Default judgments are a popular twist in Conflict of Laws questions. A default judgment means that the defendant did not appear in the original action. The court still renders judgment on the merits.

**Defenses** to full faith and credit include penal judgments, extrinsic fraud, and inconsistent judgments. The public policy exception is no longer recognized. Thus, even if the first action in the rendering state could not have been brought under the recognizing state's law as it was against that state's public policy, the recognizing state is required to enforce it.

The **effects** of applying full faith and credit are *res judicata* and enforcement of the judgment. *Res judicata* operates the same in the recognizing state as it does in the rendering state. Because both parties and those in privity with those parties are bound, the recognizing court can enforce the judgment against them. Parties in privity include beneficiaries, holders of future interests, successors in interest, and all persons represented in a class action.

A special note about **family law** judgments. Full faith and credit applies to divorce judgments as long as one of the spouses is domiciled in the rendering state. Domicile is determined by physical presence and intent to be domiciled.

Meanwhile, **child custody** is governed by reciprocal statutes adopted by all 50 states. The Uniform Child Custody Jurisdiction and Enforcement Act determines which state is the "home state" of the child and all other states must give full faith and credit to that judgment. The home state retains jurisdiction and no other court may modify that order unless the rendering court has no remaining significant connection with the child or any parties in the dispute.

## B. Choice of Law

Deciding what law applies to an ongoing case when two or more potential jurisdictions' laws apply is determined by the choice of law approach used by the forum trying the case. Questions may ask you to analyze the issue under each

---

1. U.S. Const. art. IV, §1.

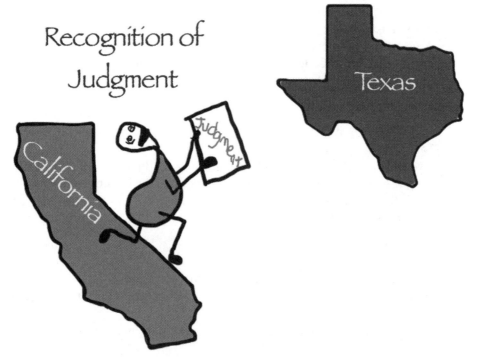

**Full Faith and Credit**

approach or to analyze under a single approach. The approaches to focus upon are:

- Vested-Rights Approach of the First Restatement:
  - Traditional approach.
  - Forum state must apply the law of the state in which the rights of the parties "vest"—where the act or relationship giving rise to the cause of action occurred or was created.
  - Forum applies its own procedural rules, although applying a foreign state's substantive law.
    - Particularly relevant for statute of limitations.
      - Traditional approach viewed as procedural.
      - More modern approach views as substantive.
  - Characterization as procedural or substantive determined by the forum state's law.
- Most Significant-Relationship Approach of the Second Restatement:
  - Modern approach.
  - All circumstances considered to determine which state has the most significant relationship to each issue raised.
  - *Depeçage*: choice of law depends upon the issue involved:
    - Different factors for different topics of law.
    - Different law may apply in one cause of action as determined by each issue.
  - Public policy considerations.
    - the needs of the interstate and international systems to further harmony and facilitate commerce;
    - the relevant policies of the forum;
    - the relevant policies of other interested states;

* protection of justified expectations;
* the basic policies underlying the particular field of law;
* certainty, predictability, and uniformity of result; and
* the ease in the determination and application of the law to be applied.

Special rules may exist under each approach for specific topics.

### 1. Torts

The vested-rights approach looks to the law of the place of the wrong. In essence, the place where the last event giving rise to the injury occurred.

The significant-relationship approach looks at which state has the most significant relationship to both the occurrence and the parties. Factors considered include:

* place of the injury;
* place where the conduct causing the injury occurred;
* the domicile, residence, nationality, place of incorporation, and place of business of the parties; and
* the place where the relationship between the parties is centered.

### 2. Contracts

If the parties choose to include a clause in their contract that expressly sets forth the governing law, a court will apply that law. If the contract does not specify which law applies, the traditional approach would look to the place where the contract was made or performed.

Displeased with the often mechanical application of the traditional approach, the modern approach considers:

* the place of contracting;
* the place of negotiation of the contract;
* the place of performance;
* the location of the subject matter of the contract; and
* the domicile, residence, nationality, place of incorporation, and place of business of the parties.

### 3. Property

If the issue is the interpretation of a real estate contract, then the contract choice-of-law rules apply. If the cause of action focuses on a property interest, then the first step is to characterize the property as immovable or movable:

* Immovable: closely connected with or related to land:
  * Law of the *situs* governs.
  * Includes mortgages, validity of a deed, capacity of a grantor, and liens.
* Movable: all other property interests, including personal property:
  * Law of the *situs* at the time of the relevant transaction governs.
  * Security interests and sale of goods governed by the Uniform Commercial Code.
  * Intangible: law of the representative instrument governs. If no instrument, then the law of the place of transfer.

### 4. Corporations

Look to the law of the state of incorporation regarding issues of the existence of a corporation and issues related to its structure, including the authority and liability of directors and the rights of shareholders.

### 5. Family Law

Choice of law in an action that must determine the validity of a marriage can range from a probate action, a property dispute, or a dissolution of marriage. A marriage is generally valid if the state where celebrated considers it a valid marriage. An exception is if the marriage violates a prohibitory rule of the domicile of one of the parties. Choice of law relating to the grounds for divorce is governed by the plaintiff's domicile. Remember, a divorce may be entered even if there is no personal service or domicile of the other party as the divorce itself needs only subject-matter jurisdiction. The other party may attack a finding of domicile of the procuring party. For a judgment to pay money or transfer property, personal jurisdiction is required.

Choice of law also arises in a family law essay when child custody is in dispute and the parties live in different states. The Uniform Child Custody Jurisdiction and Enforcement Act looks to the "home state" of the child—the state in which the child lived with a parent or person acting as a parent for at least six consecutive months before the commencement of the proceeding. If the child has no home state, then a court has jurisdiction if the child and at least one parent has a significant connection with the state and substantial evidence is available in the state concerning the child's welfare.

The home state has exclusive continuing jurisdiction as long as the child or the child's parent continues to reside in the state or the child has a significant connection with the state and substantial evidence exists regarding the child's welfare in that state.

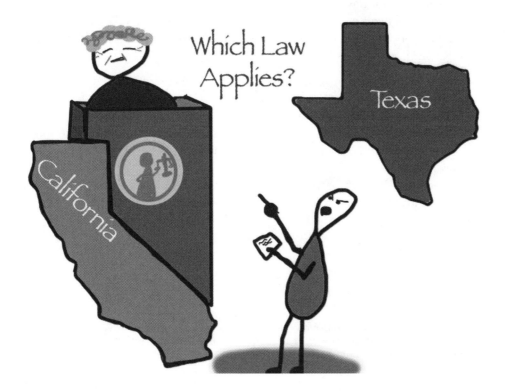

## II. ESSAY PRACTICE QUESTION[2]

Note: This question combines Conflict of Laws with Family Law

Dave and Meg lived in State A. Three years ago, they began dating. Two years ago, Meg became pregnant with their child. Shortly thereafter, Dave and Meg discussed marriage. Dave told Meg, "Perhaps we should get married if we're going to have a child." Meg told Dave, "I am committed to marrying you, but I want a real wedding, and we can't afford that now." Meg proposed that Dave move in with her so that "we can save money to get married." Dave agreed and began living in Meg's rented apartment. Meg did not tell her landlord about Dave. She did tell her family and friends that "Dave, my fiancé, has moved in."

Fifteen months ago, Meg gave birth to Child. Meg and Dave agreed that Child's birth certificate would identify Dave as Child's father. Meg and Dave sent birth announcements to friends and relatives noting the birth of "our son, Child." After Child's birth, Meg quit work. Dave took on a second job in order to support Meg and Child.

Five months ago, Meg took Child and abruptly left Dave. Dave hired a private investigator to find Meg and Child. The investigator recently discovered that they are living in State B with Husband, whom Meg married three months ago. The investigator also discovered that Meg and Husband have filed a petition to terminate Dave's parental rights and authorize Husband's adoption of Child.

State B permits a mother or a married father to veto the adoption of his or her child unless he or she "has willfully refused to support said child for a period of one or more years."

State B permits an unmarried father to veto the adoption of his child only if he (a) "has consistently supported such child" and (b) "has maintained a residential relationship with such child for at least 9 of the 12 months immediately preceding the filing of an adoption petition."

State B does not have a putative father registry.

State A recognizes common law marriage. State B does not. Both State A and State B have adopted the Uniform Child Custody Jurisdiction and Enforcement Act (UCCJEA).

1. Will State B recognize a common law marriage contracted in State A? Explain.
2. Did Dave and Meg enter into a common law marriage in State A? Explain.
3. Assuming that Dave is an unmarried father, can State B constitutionally grant Meg and Husband's adoption petition over Dave's opposition? Explain.
4. Does the UCCJEA permit State B to terminate Dave's parental rights or issue an order awarding custody of Child to Meg? Explain.

---

2. The Multistate Bar Examination ("MBE[®]") questions, the Multistate Essay Examination ("MEE[®]") questions, and excerpts from the Multistate Performance Tests ("MPT[®]") have been reprinted by permission from the NCBE[®]. Copyright© by the National Conference of Bar Examiners. All rights reserved.

# Essay Score Sheets and MBE Practice Analyses

## I. Chapter 9  CIVIL PROCEDURE

### ESSAY SCORE SHEET

| Stated | Implied | |
|---|---|---|
| | | **Point One (25%) Personal jurisdiction** |
| _____ | _____ | **Conclusion:** Personal service of process on the man while he was voluntarily present in State C is sufficient to warrant the U.S. District Court's exercise of personal jurisdiction over the man. |
| _____ | _____ | **Rule:** Federal Rule of Civil Procedure 4(k)(1)(A) provides that a federal court can take personal jurisdiction over a defendant "who is subject to the jurisdiction of a court of general jurisdiction in the state where the district court is located." |
| _____ | _____ | Thus, the U.S. District Court's jurisdiction over the man in this action depends on whether the state courts of State C would take jurisdiction over the man under the circumstances of the case. |
| _____ | _____ | **Application/Conclusion:** State C courts generally will take jurisdiction over a defendant whenever the U.S. Constitution permits them to do so. |
| _____ | _____ | **Rule:** The court's exercise of such "transient jurisdiction," *i.e.*, jurisdiction based on physical presence alone, is generally consistent with due process. |
| _____ | _____ | "The Due Process Clause of the Fourteenth Amendment generally permits a state court to exercise jurisdiction over a defendant if he is served with process while voluntarily present in the forum State." |
| _____ | _____ | **Application:** Here, |
| _____ | _____ | The man was personally served with process while he was voluntarily present in State C. |
| _____ | _____ | The man was physically present in State C when he was served with process, and his presence in State C was voluntary. |
| _____ | _____ | Furthermore, given that transient jurisdiction has long been the rule in American courts, the man was on notice that his presence within State C could, upon service, subject him to personal jurisdiction. |
| _____ | _____ | Moreover, by traveling to State C, the man availed himself of various benefits provided by State C, such as the benefits of "police, fire, and emergency medical" protection; access to the state's transportation system; and "fruits of the State's economy." |
| _____ | _____ | At the same time, the burden on the man of defending the suit in neighboring State C is insubstantial in light of modern communication and transportation and the man's demonstrated ability to travel to State C. |

*continued on next page*

| Stated | Implied | |
|--------|---------|---|
| _____ | _____ | **Conclusion:** Thus, the man's motion to dismiss for lack of personal jurisdiction should be denied. |
| | | [NOTE: Although no facts suggest that the Federal Gun Safety Act has special rules related to service of process and personal jurisdiction, some examinees may mention that possibility.] |
| | | **Point Two (a) (15%) Subject-matter jurisdiction: Federal question** |
| _____ | _____ | **Conclusion:** The U.S. District Court has federal-question jurisdiction over the woman's Safety Act claim. |
| _____ | _____ | **Rule:** Federal courts are courts of limited jurisdiction. Under 28 U.S.C. § 1331, district courts may exercise subject-matter jurisdiction over "all civil actions arising under the Constitution, laws, or treaties of the United States." |
| _____ | _____ | As a general rule, causes of action that are created by federal law qualify for federal-question jurisdiction while those created by state law do not. |
| _____ | _____ | **Application:** In this case, the allegations of the woman's well-pleaded complaint state a Safety Act claim that is created by federal law. |
| _____ | _____ | **Conclusion:** As a result, federal-question jurisdiction exists over the woman's Safety Act claim. |
| | | **Point Two (b) (35%) Subject-matter jurisdiction: Diversity of citizenship** |
| _____ | _____ | **Conclusion:** The U.S. District Court does not have diversity jurisdiction over the state-law negligence claim, but it may nonetheless hear the claim pursuant to its supplemental jurisdiction. |
| _____ | _____ | **Rule:** Federal courts also have subject-matter jurisdiction over state law claims under diversity of citizenship jurisdiction. |
| _____ | _____ | Diversity jurisdiction requires the parties be citizens of different states and the amount in controversy be over $75,000. |
| _____ | _____ | State citizenship for individual U.S. citizens is determined by their domicile: the true, fixed, permanent home to which the individual intends to return when absent. |
| _____ | _____ | **Application:** The woman and the man are both domiciled in (and therefore citizens of) State A, where they have lived their entire lives, and where they both currently live. |
| _____ | _____ | While the woman was convalescing in a hospital in State C when the suit was brought, the woman exhibited no intent to change domicile, and she returned to State A upon her release from the hospital. |
| _____ | _____ | **Conclusion:** Because both parties are State A citizens, the fundamental requirement for diversity jurisdiction is not met. |
| _____ | _____ | **Rule:** However, a district court may exercise supplemental jurisdiction over claims that form part of the same "case or controversy under Article III" as claims over which the district court has original jurisdiction. |
| _____ | _____ | Claims are part of the same case or controversy if they arise from a common nucleus of operative facts. |
| _____ | _____ | **Application:** Here, |

*continued on next page*

| Stated | Implied | |
|---|---|---|
| _____ | _____ | The woman's Safety Act and negligence claims arise from a common nucleus of operative facts: the man's disabling of his gun's safety features and the resulting accidental shooting of the woman. |
| _____ | _____ | **Conclusion:** As a result, the U.S. District Court could exercise supplemental jurisdiction over the woman's state-law negligence claim. |
| _____ | _____ | **Rule:** Although a court has power to exercise supplemental jurisdiction, it need not do so in all cases. A "district court[] may decline to exercise supplemental jurisdiction" under certain conditions, including when "the claim [over which the court has only supplemental jurisdiction] substantially predominates over the claim . . . over which the district court has original jurisdiction." |
| _____ | _____ | **Application:** Here, |
| _____ | _____ | The woman's negligence claim substantially predominates over the federal-question claim because the damages sought on the woman's negligence claim are larger than the damages sought on the woman's federal claim. |
| _____ | _____ | Nonetheless, the U.S. District Court is unlikely to dismiss the negligence claim given the factual and evidentiary overlap in the two claims and the resulting efficiency of resolving them together. |
| _____ | _____ | **Conclusion:** In short, the U.S. District Court has federal-question jurisdiction over the woman's Safety Act claim and possesses supplemental jurisdiction over the woman's state-law negligence claim. |
| _____ | _____ | As a result, the man's motion to dismiss for lack of subject-matter jurisdiction should be denied. |
| | | **Point Three (25%) Venue** |
| _____ | _____ | **Conclusion:** Venue is not appropriate in the U.S. District Court for the District of State C because the man does not reside in State C, the events giving rise to the woman's claims did not occur there, and there is another district (in State A) where venue would have been proper. |
| _____ | _____ | **Rule:** Venue is appropriate "in (1) a judicial district in which any defendant resides, if all defendants are residents of the State in which the district is located, (2) a judicial district in which a substantial part of the events or omissions giving rise to the claim occurred, . . . or (3) if there is no district in which an action may otherwise be brought . . . , any judicial district in which any defendant is subject to the court's personal jurisdiction with respect to such action." |
| _____ | _____ | **Application:** Here, |
| _____ | _____ | The man does not reside in the district of State C, so venue cannot be based on § 1391(b)(1). |
| _____ | _____ | State C also does not qualify as an appropriate venue because it is not "a judicial district in which a substantial part of the events or omissions giving rise to the claim occurred." |
| _____ | _____ | The events giving rise to the woman's claims were the disabling of the gun's safety features and the accidental shooting—both of which occurred in State A. |
| _____ | _____ | One might argue that a substantial part of the events giving rise to the claim occurred in State C because the woman received medical treatment there and, as a result, it was in State C that the woman experienced much of the harm (physical suffering and medical expenses) for which she seeks to recover damages. |

*continued on next page*

| Stated | Implied | |
|--------|---------|---|
| _____ | _____ | However, most courts that have considered this statutory language in the context of personal injury torts have concluded that venue is proper in the district where the defendant's tortious acts occurred, but not in a district that is connected to the incident only because the plaintiff received medical treatment there. |
| _____ | _____ | Nor would venue be appropriate in State C on the § 1391(b)(3) grounds that the man was found there at the time of service. |
| _____ | _____ | Although the man was in State C at the time of service, § 1391(b)(3) is a backup provision that applies only when no other district qualifies as an appropriate venue. |
| _____ | _____ | Here, the man resides in State A and the acts giving rise to the cause of action occurred there. |
| _____ | _____ | Accordingly, a relevant district in that state would qualify as an appropriate venue under either § 1391(b)(1) or § 1391(b)(2). |
| _____ | _____ | **Conclusion:** Thus, the man's motion to dismiss for improper venue should be granted. |

## MBE PRACTICE ANALYSIS[1]

### Question 1

An entrepreneur from State A decided to sell hot sauce to the public, labeling it "Best Hot Sauce."

A company incorporated in State B and head-quartered in State C sued the entrepreneur in federal court in State C. The complaint sought $50,000 in damages and alleged that the entrepreneur's use of the name "Best Hot Sauce" infringed the company's federal trademark. The entrepreneur filed an answer denying the allegations, and the parties began discovery. Six months later, the entrepreneur moved to dismiss for lack of subject-matter jurisdiction.

Should the court grant the entrepreneur's motion?

(A) No, because the company's claim arises under federal law.

**Correct.** The claim asserts federal trademark infringement, and therefore it arises under federal law. Subject-matter jurisdiction is proper under 28 U.S.C. § 1331 as a general federal-question action. That statute requires no minimum amount in controversy, so the amount the company seeks is irrelevant.

(B) No, because the entrepreneur waived the right to challenge subject-matter jurisdiction by not raising the issue initially by motion or in the answer.

**Incorrect.** Under Federal Rule 12(h)(3), subject-matter jurisdiction cannot be waived and the court can determine at any time that it lacks subject-matter jurisdiction. Therefore, the fact that the entrepreneur delayed six months before raising the lack of subject-matter jurisdiction is immaterial and the court will not deny his motion on that basis.

(C) Yes, because although the claim arises under federal law, the amount in controversy is not satisfied.

**Incorrect.** There is no amount-in-controversy requirement for actions that arise under federal law.

1. The Multistate Bar Examination ("MBE®") questions, the Multistate Essay Examination ("MEE®") questions, and excerpts from the Multistate Performance Tests ("MPT®") have been reprinted by permission from the NCBE®. Copyright© by the National Conference of Bar Examiners. All rights reserved.

(D) Yes, because although there is diversity, the amount in controversy is not satisfied.

**Incorrect.** Although diversity jurisdiction requires an amount in controversy of $75,000 or more, when diverse parties are litigating a federal claim, the action is treated for jurisdictional purposes as a federal-question action, not a diversity action. The claim here asserts federal trademark infringement and therefore it arises under federal law. The fact that the action does not meet all the requirements for diversity jurisdiction is irrelevant.

### Question 2

An investor from State A filed an action against his State B stockbroker in federal court in State A. The summons and complaint were served at the stockbroker's office in State B, where the process server handed the documents to the stockbroker's administrative assistant.

The stockbroker has answered the complaint, asserting the defense of improper service of process. Assume that both states' requirements for service of process are identical to the requirements of the Federal Rules of Civil Procedure.

Is the court likely to dismiss the action for improper service of process?

(A) No, because service was made on a person of suitable age found at the stockbroker's place of employment.

**Incorrect.** Federal Rule 4(e)(2) governs service on individual defendants and authorizes service on a person of "suitable age and discretion" only when service is made at the defendant's "dwelling or usual place of abode," not at the defendant's workplace.

(B) No, because the stockbroker waived her claim for improper service of process by asserting it in her answer.

**Incorrect.** Federal Rule 12(b) provides that every defense to a claim for relief, including insufficient service of process, must be asserted either in the responsive pleading (answer) or by motion. Therefore, the stockbroker did not waive her claim for improper service by asserting it in her answer.

(C) Yes, because an individual defendant may not be served by delivering process to a third party found at the defendant's place of employment.

**Correct.** Federal Rule 4(e)(2) provides that an individual defendant may be served by delivering a copy of the summons and complaint to an agent authorized by appointment or by law to receive service of process on behalf of the defendant. No facts suggest that the administrative assistant was a designated agent of the stockbroker, and the Rules provide no general authority to serve process on third parties at a defendant's place of employment.

**(D)** Yes, because the process of State A courts is not effective in State B.
**Incorrect.** Federal Rule 4(k)(1)(A) makes clear that the process of the federal courts may exceed state boundaries. Therefore, the process of the federal courts in State A can be effective in State B so long as the stockbroker is subject to jurisdiction in State A.

## Question 3

A truck driver from State A and a bus driver from State B were involved in a collision in State B that injured the truck driver. The truck driver filed a federal diversity action in State B based on negligence, seeking $100,000 in damages from the bus driver.

What law of negligence should the court apply?

**(A)** The court should apply the federal common law of negligence.
**Incorrect.** There is no federal common law of negligence, and the federal courts are prohibited from creating general federal common law. Rather, they must adhere to state law in substantive matters.

**(B)** The court should apply the negligence law of State A, the truck driver's state of citizenship.
**Incorrect.** The court cannot simply select the law of the truck driver's state of citizenship as the governing law. In *Klaxon Co. v. Stentor Elec. Mfg. Co.*, 313 U.S. 487 (1941), the Court made clear that in a federal diversity action a court must look to the choice-of-law rules of the state in which it sits to determine which of two competing states' laws should be applied to the action before it.

**(C)** The court should consider the negligence law of both State A and State B and apply the law that the court believes most appropriately governs negligence in this action.
**Incorrect.** If the court were to review both states' laws and select the one it found most appropriate, it effectively would be developing its own federal choice-of-law rules. This would violate both *Erie R.R. v. Tompkins*, 304 U.S. 64 (1938) and *Klaxon Co. v. Stentor Elec. Mfg. Co.*, 313 U.S. 487 (1941). In *Klaxon*, the Court made clear that

in a federal diversity action a court must look to the choice-of-law rules of the state in which it sits to determine which of two competing states' laws should be applied to the action before it.

**(D)** The court should determine which state's negligence law a state court in State B would apply and apply that law in this action.
**Correct.** In *Klaxon Co. v. Stentor Elec. Mfg. Co.*, 313 U.S. 487 (1941), the Court made clear that in a federal diversity action a court must look to the choice-of-law rules of the state in which it sits to determine which of two competing states' laws should be applied to the action before it.

## Question 4

A patent holder brought a patent infringement action in federal court against a licensee of the patent. The patent holder believed that a jury would be more sympathetic to his claims than a judge, and asked his lawyer to obtain a jury trial.

What should the lawyer do to secure the patent holder's right to a jury trial?

**(A)** File and serve a complaint that includes a jury trial demand.
**Correct.** Federal Rule 38(b)(1) provides specifically that a jury trial demand may be included in a pleading. Therefore, including it in a properly filed and served complaint secures the right.

**(B)** File and serve a jury trial demand at the close of discovery.
**Incorrect.** Under Federal Rule 38(b)(1), a jury trial demand must be served no later than 14 days after service of the last pleading directed to the issue on which a jury is sought. The close of discovery will be much later than 14 days after the pleadings have closed.

**(C)** File and serve a jury trial demand within 30 days after the close of the pleadings.
**Incorrect.** Under Federal Rule 38(b)(1), a jury trial demand must be served no later than 14 days after service of the last pleading directed to the issue on which a jury is sought.

**(D)** Make a jury trial demand at the initial pretrial conference.
**Incorrect.** Under Federal Rule 38(b)(1), a jury trial demand must be served no later than 14 days after service of the last pleading directed to the issue on which a jury is sought. The initial pretrial conference likely will

not be scheduled until weeks after the pleadings have closed. Therefore, making the demand at the initial pretrial conference is too late.

## Question 5

A consumer from State A filed a $100,000 products liability action in federal court against a manufacturer incorporated and with its principal place of business in State B. The consumer claimed that a flaw in the manufacturer's product had resulted in severe injuries to the consumer. In its answer, the manufacturer asserted a third-party complaint against the product designer, also incorporated and with its principal place of business in State B. Believing that the consumer had sued the wrong defendant, the manufacturer claimed both that the designer was solely responsible for the flaw that had led to the consumer's injuries and that the manufacturer was not at fault.

The designer is aware that the manufacturer did not follow all of the designer's specifications when making the product.

Which of the following arguments is most likely to achieve the designer's goal of dismissal of the third-party complaint?

(A) The court does not have subject-matter jurisdiction over the third-party complaint, because both the manufacturer and the designer are citizens of State B.

**Incorrect.** Third-party claims fall within the court's supplemental jurisdiction, so there is no need to have diversity between the manufacturer and the designer. This is because the manufacturer's claim is so closely related to the consumer's main claim that it is part of the same case or controversy. Both claims rest on whether there was a product defect and who is responsible for any defect.

(B) The manufacturer failed to obtain the court's leave to file the third-party complaint.

**Incorrect.** Under Federal Rule 14(a)(1), a defendant is required to seek leave to file a third-party complaint only if it seeks to add the claim more than 14 days after serving its original answer. Because the manufacturer inserted its third-party claim in its answer, there was no need for it to seek leave.

(C) The manufacturer's failure to follow the designer's specifications caused the flaw that resulted in the consumer's injuries.

**Incorrect.** The assertion that the manufacturer's failure to follow the specifications caused the flaw is a factual allegation that goes to the merits of the dispute. A motion to dismiss does not resolve factual allegations but instead seeks to determine whether, if taken as true, the factual allegations are sufficient to state a claim for relief as a matter of law.

(D) The manufacturer's third-party complaint failed to state a proper third-party claim.

**Correct.** Under Federal Rule 14(a)(1), a defendant may serve a third-party claim only on a nonparty "who is or may be liable to it for all or part of the claim against it." This means that the basis of the claim must be derivative liability (e.g., indemnification or contribution). In order to satisfy the Rule, the manufacturer cannot simply allege that the consumer sued the wrong defendant.

## Question 6

A wholesaler brought a federal diversity action against a large pharmaceutical company for breach of contract. During jury selection, one potential juror stated that five years earlier he had been an employee of the company and still owned several hundred shares of its stock. In response to questioning from the judge, the potential juror stated that he could fairly consider the evidence in the case.

The wholesaler's attorney has asked the judge to strike the potential juror for cause.

Should the judge strike the potential juror for cause?

(A) No, because the potential juror said that he could fairly consider the evidence in the case.

**Incorrect.** In deciding how to rule, the judge may take into account the fact that the potential juror said that he could fairly consider the evidence in the case. However, the juror's statement is not determinative and, standing alone, is not sufficient for the judge to refuse to strike the juror for cause.

(B) No, because the wholesaler's attorney could use a peremptory challenge to strike the potential juror.

**Incorrect.** Peremptory challenges allow an attorney to disqualify a potential juror because the juror has displayed an attitude or characteristic that is unfavorable to the attorney's client but that does not rise to the level of bias or a relationship to one of the litigants that would be grounds for a challenge for cause. Therefore, the fact that the wholesaler has peremptory challenges remaining is irrelevant. If the court finds that the wholesaler's attorney has met the objective standard for disqualification for cause, it must exclude the potential juror.

**(C)** Yes, because other potential jurors still remain available for the jury panel.

**Incorrect.** The fact that other potential jurors remain available is irrelevant to how the judge should rule. A challenge for cause requires the court's objective determination as to whether the potential juror meets the statutory qualifications for jury duty. In making this determination, the court will consider only a potential juror's relationship to one of the litigants or evidence of bias or prejudice regarding one of the litigants.

**(D)** Yes, because the potential juror is presumed to be biased because of his relationship to the company.

**Correct.** Stock ownership, or having worked for or having a spouse who works or worked for one of the litigants, has been found to create a presumption of bias that merits striking a potential juror for cause.

## Question 7

After being fired, a woman sued her former employer in federal court, alleging that her supervisor had discriminated against her on the basis of her sex. The woman's complaint included a lengthy description of what the supervisor had said and done over the years, quoting his telephone calls and emails to her and her own emails to the supervisor's manager asking for help.

The employer moved for summary judgment, alleging that the woman was a pathological liar who had filed the action and included fictitious documents in revenge for having been fired. Because the woman's attorney was at a lengthy out-of-state trial when the summary-judgment motion was filed, he failed to respond to it. The court therefore granted the motion in a one-line order and entered final judgment. The woman has appealed.

Is the appellate court likely to uphold the trial court's ruling?

**(A)** No, because the complaint's allegations were detailed and specific.

**Incorrect.** The fact that the complaint's allegations were detailed and specific does not automatically prevent the court from entering summary judgment. The question is whether, taking into account those allegations, as well as the allegations the employer raised in its summary-judgment motion, there remains no genuine dispute of any material fact such that the employer is entitled to judgment as a matter of law. By challenging the woman's credibility in its motion, the employer disputed all the facts and evidence she had laid out in her complaint.

**(B)** No, because the employer moved for summary judgment on the basis that the woman was not credible, creating a factual dispute.

**Correct.** The standard for summary judgment is whether there is no genuine dispute as to any material fact such that the moving party is entitled to judgment as a matter of law. By challenging the woman's credibility in its motion, the employer disputed all the facts and evidence she had laid out in her complaint. Therefore, the motion did not meet the standard for summary judgment, and the trial court should be reversed.

**(C)** Yes, because the woman's failure to respond to the summary-judgment motion means that there was no sworn affidavit to support her allegations and supporting documents.

**Incorrect.** Although the woman failed to respond, that is not in itself a basis for summary judgment. The court may grant summary judgment only if the employer's motion and supporting materials show that the employer is entitled to that relief. The standard for summary judgment is whether there is no genuine dispute as to any material fact such that the moving party is entitled to judgment as a matter of law. By challenging the woman's credibility in its motion, the employer disputed all the facts and evidence she had laid out in her complaint.

**(D)** Yes, because the woman's failure to respond to the summary-judgment motion was a default giving sufficient basis to grant the motion.

**Incorrect.** The woman's failure to respond does not act as a default by which the court can automatically enter summary judgment. The employer has the burden to show that the summary-judgment standard is met—that there is no genuine dispute as to any material fact such that it is entitled to judgment as a matter of law. Only if the employer satisfies that burden will the burden then shift to the woman to introduce arguments or evidence showing that a genuine dispute of material fact does exist.

## Question 8

A man brought a federal diversity action against his insurance company, alleging that the company had breached its duty under his insurance policy by refusing to pay for his medical expenses resulting from a mountain-biking accident.

At the jury trial, the man presented evidence that he had paid all premiums on the insurance policy and that the policy covered personal-injury-related medical expenses arising from accidents. After he rested his case, the company presented evidence that a provision of the policy excluded payment for injury-related expenses resulting from an insured's "unduly risky" behavior. The company also presented a witness who testified that the accident had occurred in an area where posted signs warned bikers not to enter. The man did not cross-examine the witness.

After resting its case, the company moved for judgment as a matter of law.

Should the court grant the motion?

(A) No, because a motion for judgment as a matter of law must first be made at the close of the plaintiff's case-in-chief.
**Incorrect.** A motion for judgment as a matter of law may be made at any time before the court submits the case to the jury.

(B) No, because whether the man's behavior was unduly risky is a question of fact for the jury to resolve.
**Correct.** Because a motion for judgment as a matter of law takes the case away from the jury, it can be granted only if the court determines that the evidence is legally insufficient to allow the jury to decide the case. The jury here must determine the meaning of the warning signs and whether the signs alone establish that the man's behavior was unduly risky. A reasonable jury might conclude that the warning signs were designed to keep bikers out of the area for reasons other than risk, given no additional evidence as to why the signs were posted or of other events in which harm occurred to those ignoring the signs.

(C) Yes, because the company's uncontradicted evidence of the man's unduly risky behavior means that no reasonable jury could find that the policy covers his injuries.
**Incorrect.** The fact that the man did not introduce any evidence to contradict the testimony about the warning signs does not in itself establish that the man's behavior was "unduly risky." The jury must determine the meaning of the warning signs and whether the signs alone establish that the man's behavior was unduly risky. A reasonable jury might conclude that the warning signs were designed to keep bikers out of the area for reasons other than risk, given no additional evidence as to why the signs were posted or of other events in which harm occurred to those ignoring the signs. Therefore, the testimony, standing alone, does not establish that a reasonable jury could determine that the company had met its burden to prove that the area was actually dangerous.

(D) Yes, because the man waived his right to rebut the company's evidence by not addressing the "unduly risky" policy provision in his case-in-chief.
**Incorrect.** The company properly raised, as a defense to the man's claim, the issue of whether the man's behavior was unduly risky and excluded from coverage. Therefore, the man had no obligation to raise the issue of the warning signs in his case-in-chief, but could decide either to rebut the issue on cross-examination or remain silent, as he did, and allow the jury to determine whether the testimony was sufficient to satisfy the company's burden of proof.

## Question 9

A motorcyclist was involved in a collision with a truck. The motorcyclist sued the truck driver in state court for damage to the motorcycle. The jury returned a verdict for the truck driver, and the court entered judgment. The motorcyclist then sued the company that employed the driver and owned the truck in federal court for personal-injury damages, and the company moved to dismiss based on the state-court judgment.

If the court grants the company's motion, what is the likely explanation?

(A) Claim preclusion (res judicata) bars the motorcyclist's action against the company.
**Correct.** Claim preclusion prevents a claimant from splitting his cause of action; when the claimant loses a judgment, all possible grounds for relief arising out of the same transaction or occurrence are barred in future litigation between the same parties. Because the motorcyclist's personal-injury and property-damage claims arise out of the same accident, they are part of the same cause of action and he should have brought them in one action. Although claim

preclusion typically operates to prevent relitigation between the same parties, it also operates in favor of entities that are in privity with the parties. Here, because the company is in privity with the truck driver (based on the employer-employee relationship), the company cannot be found liable for his acts if he is not found liable. Therefore, the first judgment extinguishes the claim against the company as well.

(B) Issue preclusion (collateral estoppel) establishes the company's lack of negligence.

**Incorrect.** It is true that the same negligence issue that was presented against the truck driver is being presented in the action against the company and that that issue was actually litigated in the first action—two requirements for the application of issue preclusion. However, the jury's general verdict for the truck driver does not necessarily establish that he was free from negligence. It may instead reflect the jury's conclusion that the motorcyclist was more negligent than the truck driver. This may prevent the application of issue preclusion. In addition, the court is not likely to base its ruling on issue preclusion because that defense will be utilized only if claim preclusion is unavailable.

(C) The motorcyclist violated the doctrine of election of remedies.

**Incorrect.** The election-of-remedies doctrine was a pleading limitation at common law and under some early codes that prevented a plaintiff from presenting alternative or inconsistent claims when the plaintiff had a choice among inconsistent remedies. For example, a plaintiff who was fraudulently induced to enter into a contract had to elect either to sue under the contract for damages or to disaffirm the contract and seek rescission. The Federal Rules reject this doctrine and allow for alternative and inconsistent allegations in a complaint. Even if the doctrine were applicable, it would be inapposite here because there is no inconsistency between the motorcyclist's claims for personal-injury and property damages, and the question presented is one addressed to preclusion, not pleading.

(D) The state-court judgment is the law of the case.

**Incorrect.** Law of the case prevents redetermination of issues that are decided in a case but that recur in later stages of the same case. For example, issues decided on appeal are binding on the trial court if the case is remanded to the trial court for further action. While there was only one accident here, there are two separate actions, one in the state court and one in the

federal court. Therefore, the law-of-the-case doctrine is inapplicable.

## Question 10

A student at a private university sued the university in federal court for negligence after he fell from scaffolding in a university-owned theater building. At trial, after briefing from both parties, the court permitted the jury to hear testimony that there had been several previous accidents in the same building. The jury found for the student, and the university appealed. One of the university's arguments on appeal is that the testimony about the previous accidents should have been excluded as irrelevant and highly prejudicial.

Which standard of review applies to this argument?

(A) Abuse of discretion.

**Correct.** A determination as to whether evidence is irrelevant or highly prejudicial and should be excluded is within the trial court's discretion because it requires an understanding of the entire case and the factual context in which the evidence is being offered. Therefore, it is reviewed on appeal using an abuse-of-discretion standard.

(B) Clearly erroneous.

**Incorrect.** An appellate court applies the clearly erroneous standard when reviewing findings of fact made by the trial court in a bench trial. Therefore, the standard does not apply to judicial rulings on the admissibility of evidence in a jury trial.

(C) De novo.

**Incorrect.** An appellate court applies the de novo standard to trial court rulings on pure issues of law. Because an evidentiary ruling involves the application of legal standards to facts—*i.e.*, relevance and prejudice as related to the facts in the case—it is not a ruling on a pure issue of law and therefore not subject to de novo review.

(D) Harmless error.

**Incorrect.** An appellate court applies the harmless-error standard when it determines that a trial court's erroneous admission of evidence did not affect any party's substantial rights. It is a conclusion an appellate court reaches after reviewing and determining the impact of an erroneous evidentiary ruling, not the standard of review that the court applies to determine whether it was erroneous to admit the evidence in the first instance.

## II. Chapter 10 CONSTITUTIONAL LAW

### ESSAY SCORE SHEET

| Stated | Implied | |
|--------|---------|---|
| _____ | _____ | Even when Congress has not acted, the Commerce Clause of the United States Constitution imposes by negative implication a limitation on state laws that discriminate against or unduly burden interstate commerce. |
| | | **Point One (40%) Facial Discrimination/Practical Effect** |
| _____ | _____ | **Conclusion:** Section 1 of the Act, which requires utilities to use environmentally friendly energy sources, is probably valid given that it is not facially discriminatory against out-of-state energy producers and its discriminatory impact is not in the market being regulated (generation of electricity), but instead affects another market (natural gas production). |
| _____ | _____ | Further, the law appears to satisfy the *Pike* balancing test, given that its burdens on interstate commerce are not clearly excessive in light of the putative in-state benefits. |
| _____ | _____ | **Rule:** State laws that discriminate against out-of-state commerce in favor of in-state commerce—either on their face or in practical effect—are subject to strict scrutiny and thus a nearly per se rule of invalidity. |
| _____ | _____ | Even if not discriminatory, state laws that affect interstate commerce can also be invalidated if the burden on interstate commerce is clearly excessive in relation to the putative in-state benefits. |
| _____ | _____ | **Application:** Here, |
| _____ | _____ | Section 1 is not facially discriminatory because it applies equally to in-state and out-of-state utilities, and it does not impede the import or export of electricity. |
| _____ | _____ | The law's incidental effect of favoring an in-state industry (wind) at the expense of an out-of-state industry (natural gas production) probably does not trigger strict scrutiny. |
| _____ | _____ | Utilities may meet the requirement that 50% of their electricity come from environmentally friendly energy sources by acquiring electricity from out-of-state wind or other environmentally friendly energy sources; natural gas does not qualify as an environmentally friendly energy source regardless of where it is produced. |
| _____ | _____ | **Transition:** Section 1, however, may be discriminatory in practical effect because it favors an in-state industry (wind) over an out-of-state industry (natural gas). |
| _____ | _____ | **Rule:** If the discriminatory impact is in a market different from the one regulated by the state, the state law is not discriminatory. |
| _____ | _____ | **Application:** Here, |
| _____ | _____ | The discriminatory impact of Section 1 is felt in a market (natural gas production) different from the one being regulated (generation of electricity). |
| _____ | _____ | Although evidence of protectionist motives (such as statements in the legislative history) might be relevant to whether the law is discriminatory in practical effect, the facts do not suggest any such motive. |
| _____ | _____ | Further, Section 1 does not appear to burden interstate commerce in ways that are clearly excessive in relation to the putative in-state benefits. |

*continued on next page*

| Stated | Implied | |
|--------|---------|---|
| \_\_\_\_\_ | \_\_\_\_\_ | Conversely, the findings of the legislature indicate that the law's goal is to promote environmentally friendly energy sources, which could reduce air pollution and generate other significant local benefits (e.g., less use of water in electricity production). |
| | | **Point Two (35%) Nonresidents** |
| \_\_\_\_\_ | \_\_\_\_\_ | **Conclusion:** Section 2 of the Act, as applied by the Public Service Commission, is likely unconstitutional because it discriminates against out-of-state consumers by preventing the export of electricity from new coal-burning power plants. |
| \_\_\_\_\_ | \_\_\_\_\_ | Although the environmental purposes of the law are legitimate, the law is not narrowly tailored to meet them. |
| \_\_\_\_\_ | \_\_\_\_\_ | **Rule:** A state law or administrative decision that explicitly discriminates against nonresidents violates the Commerce Clause unless it is narrowly tailored to meet a legitimate, nonprotectionist purpose. |
| \_\_\_\_\_ | \_\_\_\_\_ | **Application:** Here, |
| \_\_\_\_\_ | \_\_\_\_\_ | Section 2 of the Act, and the Public Service Commission's denial of a permit for an out-of-state utility's coal-burning power plant, are discriminatory on their face. |
| \_\_\_\_\_ | \_\_\_\_\_ | While a general ban on the construction of coal-burning power plants would not be discriminatory because it would treat resident and nonresident producers and consumers alike, the State A law creates an exception for the urgent energy needs of state residents only. |
| \_\_\_\_\_ | \_\_\_\_\_ | Thus, the law treats in-state electricity consumers more favorably than out-of-state consumers and effectively bans the export of electricity from new in-state coal-burning plants. |
| \_\_\_\_\_ | \_\_\_\_\_ | The permit denial here discriminates against out-of-state consumers. If the application had been for the sale of electricity to meet the urgent needs of consumers in State A, the application could have been approved. |
| \_\_\_\_\_ | \_\_\_\_\_ | Instead, it was denied because the State B utility only identified the urgent needs of consumers in State B. |
| \_\_\_\_\_ | \_\_\_\_\_ | **Rule:** In particular, a law is not narrowly tailored if there are less discriminatory alternative means to accomplish the state's purpose. |
| \_\_\_\_\_ | \_\_\_\_\_ | **Application/Conclusion:** Thus, although reducing air pollution from coal-burning plants (the apparent reason for Section 2) may be a legitimate, nonprotectionist purpose, the law is not narrowly tailored. |
| \_\_\_\_\_ | \_\_\_\_\_ | There are less discriminatory alternatives that would better accomplish the state's objectives, such as (1) strict environmental regulation of all in-state coal-burning power plants, (2) an across-the-board ban on all in-state coal-burning power plants (without any exception), and (3) an exception for such plants for urgent energy needs that does not discriminate against out-of-state consumers. |
| | | **Point Three (25%) Market participant** |
| \_\_\_\_\_ | \_\_\_\_\_ | **Conclusion:** Section 3, even though it discriminates against out-of-state vendors by requiring the state to prefer in-state vendors, is a valid exercise of the state's role as a "market participant." |

*continued on next page*

| Stated | Implied | |
|--------|---------|---|
| _____ | _____ | **Rule:** The state may discriminate in favor of residents when buying or selling goods and services because the state is acting as a "market participant" rather than as a regulator of an economic activity. |
| _____ | _____ | Thus, State A may limit its purchases to vendors in the state. |
| _____ | _____ | **Conclusion:** Therefore even though the out-of-state vendor meets all of State A's requirements for an "environmentally friendly" vendor, State A is still entitled to favor in-state vendors over the out-of-state vendor. |

## MBE PRACTICE ANALYSIS[2]

### Question 1

In the wake of massive terrorist attacks carried out inside the United States by foreign citizens, Congress declared war on the terrorists' nation of origin. It also passed a statute requiring every alien who is a citizen of the enemy nation to either immediately leave the United States voluntarily or be subject to deportation. An inseverable provision of the new statute provides that the United States Supreme Court will have original and exclusive jurisdiction over any action brought to challenge the validity of the statute.

Is the new statute constitutional?

(A) No, because the statute does not fall within the categories of cases specified in Article III as those over which the Supreme Court shall have original jurisdiction.

**Correct.** Article III of the Constitution provides that the U.S. Supreme Court has original jurisdiction over cases involving foreign ambassadors, cases involving other public ministers and consuls of foreign countries, and cases in which a state is a party. The Supreme Court has held that Congress cannot give the Court original jurisdiction over any other type of case. The statute at issue is unconstitutional because it purports to give the Court original jurisdiction over cases that are not among those provided for in Article III.

(B) No, because the statute violates the equal protection component of the Fifth Amendment.

**Incorrect.** The U.S. Supreme Court has held that statutes that create classifications on the basis of alienage do not violate equal protection requirements if the classification is rationally related to a legitimate government interest. This is not a demanding burden of justification. The deportation requirement at issue would be rationally related to protecting national security during wartime.

The statute at issue is unconstitutional, however, because it purports to give the Supreme Court original jurisdiction over cases that are not among those provided for in Article III. Article III of the Constitution provides that the Supreme Court has original jurisdiction over cases involving foreign ambassadors, cases involving other public ministers and consuls of foreign countries, and cases in which a state is a party. The Supreme Court has held that Congress cannot give the Court original jurisdiction over any other type of case.

(C) Yes, because among the powers of Congress enumerated in Article I, Section 8, is the power to enact laws governing immigration and naturalization.

**Incorrect.** Although Congress has broad power to control immigration and naturalization, the statute at issue violates Article III of the Constitution because it purports to give the U.S. Supreme Court original jurisdiction over cases that are not among those provided for in Article III. Article III of the Constitution provides that the Supreme Court has original jurisdiction over cases involving foreign ambassadors, cases involving other public ministers and consuls of foreign countries, and cases in which a state is a party. The Supreme Court has held that Congress cannot give the Court original jurisdiction over any other type of case.

(D) Yes, because Article III specifically provides that the jurisdiction of the Supreme Court shall be subject to such exceptions and regulations as Congress shall make.

**Incorrect.** Article III gives Congress the power to make exceptions to and regulations of the appellate jurisdiction of the U.S. Supreme Court, but the Supreme Court has ruled that Congress cannot give the Court original jurisdiction over cases other than those provided for in Article III. Article III provides that the Supreme Court has original jurisdiction over cases involving foreign ambassadors, cases involving other public ministers and consuls of foreign countries, and cases in which a state is a party. The statute at issue is unconstitutional because it purports to give the Court original jurisdiction over cases that are not among those provided for in Article III.

### Question 2

The United States had long recognized the ruling faction in a foreign country as that country's government, despite an ongoing civil war. Throughout the civil war, the ruling faction controlled the majority of the country's territory, and the United States afforded diplomatic immunity to the ambassador representing the ruling faction.

---

2. *Id.*

A newly elected President of the United States decided to recognize a rebel group as the government of the foreign country and notified the ambassador from the ruling faction that she must leave the United States within 10 days. The ambassador filed an action in federal district court for a declaration that the ruling faction was the true government of the foreign country and for an injunction against enforcement of the President's order that she leave the United States. The United States has moved to dismiss the action.

If the court dismisses the action, what will be the most likely reason?

(A) The action involves a nonjusticiable political question.

**Correct.** The action likely satisfies the political question doctrine and therefore should be dismissed as nonjusticiable. The President's Article II power to receive foreign ambassadors is likely a textually demonstrable commitment by the Constitution of exclusive authority to recognize foreign governments. Moreover, Article II provides no judicially manageable standards by which a court could review the constitutionality of a President's decision on whether to recognize a foreign government. Finally, because the action involves the President's administration of foreign affairs, the prudential elements of the political question doctrine also indicate that the court should dismiss the action as nonjusticiable.

(B) The action is not ripe.

**Incorrect.** The action is ripe for adjudication even though the ambassador may remain in the United States for 10 days. The ambassador has suffered immediate harm because she no longer represents the foreign country in the United States, she has lost her diplomatic immunity, and she is facing expulsion within a very short period of time. Also, the constitutional issues are fit for review without waiting for the ambassador's expulsion.

The reason the action should be dismissed is that it likely is nonjusticiable under the political question doctrine. The President's Article II power to receive foreign ambassadors is likely a textually demonstrable commitment by the Constitution of exclusive authority to recognize foreign governments. Moreover, Article II provides no judicially manageable standards by which a court could review the constitutionality of a President's decision on whether to recognize a foreign government. Finally, because the action involves the President's administration of foreign affairs, the

prudential elements of the political question doctrine also indicate that the court should dismiss the action as nonjusticiable.

(C) The action is within the original jurisdiction of the U.S. Supreme Court.

**Incorrect.** Although Article III of the Constitution provides that the Supreme Court has original jurisdiction over actions involving ambassadors, federal district courts also may exercise original jurisdiction over actions within the Supreme Court's original jurisdiction.

The reason the action should be dismissed is that it likely is nonjusticiable under the political question doctrine. The President's Article II power to receive foreign ambassadors is likely a textually demonstrable commitment by the Constitution of exclusive authority to recognize foreign governments. Moreover, Article II provides no judicially manageable standards by which a court could review the constitutionality of a President's decision on whether to recognize a foreign government. Finally, because the action involves the President's administration of foreign affairs, the prudential elements of the political question doctrine also indicate that the court should dismiss the action as nonjusticiable.

(D) The ambassador does not have standing.

**Incorrect.** The ambassador has standing, because she has been injured by the President's decision that her faction is no longer the government of her country, her injury is fairly traceable to this decision, and the injury is likely redressable by a court order invalidating the decision.

The reason the action should be dismissed is that it likely is nonjusticiable under the political question doctrine. The President's Article II power to receive foreign ambassadors is likely a textually demonstrable commitment by the Constitution of exclusive authority to recognize foreign governments. Moreover, Article II provides no judicially manageable standards by which a court could review the constitutionality of a President's decision on whether to recognize a foreign government. Finally, because the action involves the President's administration of foreign affairs, the prudential elements of the political question doctrine also indicate that the court should dismiss the action as nonjusticiable.

## Question 3

An employer owed an employee $200 in unpaid wages. A law of the state in which the employer and the employee reside and in which the employee works provides that the courts of that state must decide claims for unpaid wages within 10 days of filing.

After the employee filed a claim in state court pursuant to this law, the employer filed a voluntary bankruptcy petition in federal bankruptcy court. In the bankruptcy proceeding, the employer sought to stay further proceedings in the unpaid wages claim on the basis of a federal statute which provides that a person who files a federal bankruptcy petition receives an automatic stay of all proceedings against him or her in all federal and state courts. No other federal laws apply.

In addition to the supremacy clause of Article VI, what is the most obvious constitutional basis for the imposition of a stay of the unpaid wages claim in the state court?

(A) Congress's power to provide for the general welfare.

**Incorrect.** Congress's power to provide for the general welfare authorizes only taxing and spending laws. Because the statute requiring the imposition of a stay of the unpaid wages claim concerns neither taxing nor spending, it is not authorized by the general welfare clause.

Congress's power to provide uniform rules of bankruptcy offers the most obvious constitutional basis for a federal statute requiring a stay of court proceedings against a person who has filed a federal bankruptcy petition.

(B) Congress's power to provide uniform rules of bankruptcy.

**Correct.** Congress's power to provide uniform rules of bankruptcy offers the most obvious constitutional basis for a federal statute requiring a stay of court proceedings against a person who has filed a federal bankruptcy petition.

(C) Congress's power to regulate the jurisdiction and procedures of the courts.

**Incorrect.** The constitutional provisions that give Congress the power to regulate the jurisdiction and procedures of federal courts do not authorize Congress to regulate state courts.

Congress's power to provide uniform rules of bankruptcy offers the most obvious constitutional basis for a federal statute requiring a stay of court proceedings against a person who has filed a federal bankruptcy petition.

(D) Congress's power to regulate commerce among the states.

**Incorrect.** A federal statute providing for a stay of court proceedings against a person who has filed a federal bankruptcy petition is not authorized by the commerce clause, because it is not a regulation of the channels or instrumentalities of interstate commerce, nor does it regulate an economic or commercial activity.

Congress's power to provide uniform rules of bankruptcy offers the most obvious constitutional basis for a federal statute requiring a stay of court proceedings against a person who has filed a federal bankruptcy petition.

## Question 4

Congress enacted a statute directing U.S. ambassadors to send formal letters to the governments of their host countries, protesting any violations by those governments of international treaties on weapons sales. The President prefers to handle violations by certain countries in a less formal manner and has directed ambassadors not to comply with the statute.

Is the President's action constitutional?

(A) No, because Congress has the power to implement treaties, and therefore the statute is binding on the President.

**Incorrect.** Although Congress has the power, under the necessary and proper clause, to enact legislation in support of treaties, the President's action is constitutional, because the U.S. Supreme Court has ruled that the President alone has the authority to represent the United States in foreign affairs. Because the statute intrudes on that authority, it is unconstitutional and has no effect.

(B) No, because Congress has the power to regulate commerce with foreign nations, and therefore the statute is binding on the President.

**Incorrect.** Congress has the power to regulate commerce with foreign nations, but this statute does not concern commercial relationships between the United States and foreign nations. The President's action is constitutional, because the U.S. Supreme Court has ruled that the President alone has the authority to represent the United States in foreign affairs. Because the statute intrudes on that authority, it is unconstitutional and has no effect.

(C) Yes, because Congress has no jurisdiction over matters outside the U.S. borders.

**Incorrect.** Article I of the Constitution gives Congress several powers concerning matters outside the U.S. borders, including the power to declare war and the power to regulate commerce with foreign nations. However, because the U.S. Supreme Court has ruled that the President alone has the authority to represent the United States in foreign affairs, the President's action is constitutional. Because the statute intrudes on the President's authority, it is unconstitutional and has no effect.

(D) Yes, because the President and his subordinates are the exclusive official representatives of the United States in foreign affairs.

**Correct.** The President's action is constitutional, because the U.S. Supreme Court has ruled that the President alone has the authority to represent the United States in foreign affairs. Because the statute intrudes on the President's authority, it is unconstitutional and has no effect.

## Question 5

Congress enacted a statute that authorized the construction of a monument commemorating the role of the United States in liberating a particular foreign nation during World War II. Another statute appropriated $3 million for the construction. When the United States became involved in a bitter trade dispute with the foreign nation, the President announced that he was canceling the monument's construction and that he would not spend the appropriated funds. Although the actual reason for the President's decision was the trade dispute, the announcement stated that the reason was an unexpected rise in the federal deficit.

Assume that no other statutes apply.

Is the President's decision constitutional?

(A) No, because the President failed to invoke his foreign affairs powers in his announcement.

**Incorrect.** The constitutionality of the President's decision does not depend on whether he invoked a constitutional power to support the decision. While it is correct that the decision is unconstitutional, it is so because Article II of the Constitution obligates the President to take care that the laws are faithfully executed. Because the appropriations statute is a valid exercise of Congress's spending power, the President must abide by the requirements of the statute.

(B) No, because the President is obligated to spend funds in accordance with congressional directions.

**Correct.** The President's decision is unconstitutional, because Article II of the Constitution obligates the President to take care that the laws are faithfully executed. Because the appropriations statute is a valid exercise of Congress's spending power, the President must abide by the requirements of the statute.

(C) Yes, because the President is vested with inherent executive power to control federal expenditures.

**Incorrect.** The Constitution does not give the President power to control federal expenditures by refusing to authorize spending directed by Congress. The President's decision is unconstitutional, because Article II of the Constitution obligates the President to take care that the laws are faithfully executed. Because the appropriations statute is a valid exercise of Congress's spending power, the President must abide by the requirements of the statute.

(D) Yes, because the President's decision is a valid exercise of his foreign affairs powers.

**Incorrect.** The President's foreign affairs powers do not justify his refusal to authorize spending directed by Congress. The President's decision is unconstitutional, because Article II of the Constitution obligates the President to take care that the laws are faithfully executed. Because the appropriations statute is a valid exercise of Congress's spending power, the President must abide by the requirements of the statute.

## Question 6

A city ordinance created a three-member zoning board, which is responsible for approving the location of all entertainment venues in the city. In an inseverable provision, the ordinance requires that one member of the board be a representative of the local council of churches.

A minister was appointed to the board to represent the local council of churches. During the minister's tenure, the board denied a company permission to open a nightclub in a particular location solely because it would be so close to an existing church that it might disturb the church's operations. The company has challenged the ordinance and its application in federal court on constitutional grounds.

Is the company likely to prevail?

(A) No, because the existing church has a right to have its vested property interests protected.

**Incorrect.** While it is true that churches have a right to protect their property interests, the ordinance is an unconstitutional means of affording that protection. The U.S. Supreme Court has held that the establishment clause of the First Amendment does not permit important, discretionary governmental powers, such as the power to make zoning decisions, to be delegated to or shared with religious institutions. Therefore, the requirement that the zoning board include a representative of the local council of churches violates the establishment clause.

**(B)** No, because the minister was only one of three votes and, therefore, could not dictate the decision of the zoning board.

**Incorrect.** The fact that the representative of the local council of churches does not control the decisions of the zoning board is not dispositive. The U.S. Supreme Court has held that the establishment clause of the First Amendment does not permit important, discretionary governmental powers, such as the power to make zoning decisions, to be delegated to or shared with religious institutions. Therefore, the requirement that the zoning board include a representative of the local council of churches violates the establishment clause.

**(C)** Yes, because the requirement that the zoning board include a representative of the local council of churches violates the First and Fourteenth Amendments.

**Correct.** The U.S. Supreme Court has held that the establishment clause of the First Amendment does not permit important, discretionary governmental powers, such as the power to make zoning decisions, to be delegated to or shared with religious institutions. Therefore, the requirement that the zoning board include a representative of the local council of churches violates the establishment clause.

**(D)** Yes, because, as applied, the ordinance denied the company the equal protection of the laws by irrationally discriminating against its particular type of business.

**Incorrect.** The U.S. Supreme Court has held that cities have a legitimate interest in protecting churches from the disturbances associated with land uses such as nightclubs. Therefore, the decision of the zoning board to deny the company's preferred location of its nightclub near a church did not violate the equal protection clause of the Fourteenth Amendment.

However, the U.S. Supreme Court has also held that the establishment clause of the First Amendment does not permit important, discretionary governmental powers, such as the power to make zoning decisions, to be delegated to or shared with religious institutions. Therefore, the requirement that the zoning board include a representative of the local council of churches violates the establishment clause.

## Question 7

Congress recently enacted a statute creating a program that made federal loans available to family farmers who had been unable to obtain loans from private lenders. Congress appropriated a fixed sum of money to fund loans made pursuant to the program and gave a designated federal agency discretion to decide which applicants were to receive the loans.

Two weeks after the program was established, a family farmer applied to the agency for a loan. Agency officials promptly reviewed her application and summarily denied it.

The farmer has sued the agency in federal district court, claiming only that the denial of her application without the opportunity for a hearing violated the due process clause of the Fifth Amendment. The farmer claims that she could have proved at such a hearing that without the federal loan it would be necessary for her to sell her farm.

Should the court uphold the agency's decision?

**(A)** No, because due process requires federal agencies to provide a hearing before making any factual determination that adversely affects an identified individual on the basis of his or her particular circumstances.

**Incorrect.** The due process clause obligates agencies to provide an individual with an opportunity for a hearing only when the agency makes an adjudicatory decision that deprives the individual of a property or liberty interest that is protected by the clause. The court should uphold the agency's decision, because the due process clause does not require the government to provide the farmer an opportunity for an administrative hearing on her loan application. The farmer had no legitimate claim of entitlement to a loan, because the statute gave the agency discretion to decide which applicants were to receive the loans. The agency's denial of the farmer's application therefore did not deprive her of a property or liberty interest protected by the due process clause.

(B) No, because the denial of a loan may deprive the farmer of an established liberty interest to pursue her chosen occupation.

**Incorrect.** The farmer's decision to pursue her chosen occupation does not qualify as a liberty interest protected by the due process clause. The court should uphold the agency's decision, because the due process clause does not require the government to provide the farmer an opportunity for an administrative hearing on her loan application. The farmer had no legitimate claim of entitlement to a loan, because the statute gave the agency discretion to decide which applicants were to receive the loans. The agency's denial of the farmer's loan application therefore did not deprive her of a property or liberty interest protected by the due process clause.

(C) Yes, because the applicable statute gives the farmer no legitimate claim of entitlement to receive a loan.

**Correct.** The court should uphold the agency's decision, because the due process clause does not require the government to provide the farmer an opportunity for an administrative hearing on her loan application. The farmer had no legitimate claim of entitlement to a loan, because the statute gave the agency discretion to decide which applicants were to receive the loans. The agency's denial of the farmer's application therefore did not deprive her of a property or liberty interest protected by the due process clause.

(D) Yes, because the spending clause of Article I, Section 8, gives Congress plenary power to control the distribution of appropriated funds in any manner it wishes.

**Incorrect.** Although Congress has broad authority to control the distribution of appropriated funds, that authority is subject to many constitutional limitations on the legislative power, including the due process clause of the Fifth Amendment. While the court should uphold the agency's decision, it should do so because the due process clause does not require the government to provide the farmer an opportunity for an administrative hearing on her loan application. The farmer had no legitimate claim of entitlement to a loan, because the statute gave the agency discretion to decide which applicants were to receive the loans. The agency's denial of the farmer's application therefore did not deprive her of a property or liberty interest protected by the due process clause.

**Question 8**

A state law provides that only U.S. citizens may serve as jurors in the state courts of that state. A woman who is a lawful resident alien and who has resided in the state for many years was summoned for jury duty in a state court. The woman's name was selected from a list of potential jurors that was compiled from a comprehensive list of local residents. She was disqualified from service solely because she is not a U.S. citizen.

The woman has filed an action for a declaratory judgment that the state law is unconstitutional. Who should prevail in this action?

(A) The state, because a state may limit to U.S. citizens functions that are an integral part of the process of self-government.

**Correct.** The state should prevail, because the law excluding aliens from jury service is rationally related to the state's legitimate interest in ensuring that only citizens perform functions that are central to self-government. Although strict scrutiny generally applies to state laws that discriminate against aliens, rational basis scrutiny is appropriate when alienage classifications restrict the right to participate in functions that are central to self-government, such as voting, running for office, or serving on a jury.

(B) The state, because jury service is a privilege, not a right, and therefore it is not a liberty interest protected by the due process clause of the Fourteenth Amendment.

**Incorrect.** Application of the due process clause no longer turns on whether the individual interest involved is a right or a privilege. In any event, the woman's constitutional challenge to the state law should be based on the equal protection clause rather than on the due process clause. While the state should prevail, it is because the law excluding aliens from jury service is rationally related to the state's legitimate interest in ensuring that only citizens perform functions that are central to self-government. Although strict scrutiny generally applies to state laws that discriminate against aliens, rational basis scrutiny is appropriate when alienage classifications restrict the right to participate in functions that are central to self-government, such as voting, running for office, or serving on a jury.

(C) The woman, because the Constitution gives Congress plenary power to make classifications with respect to aliens.

**Incorrect.** Although the Constitution gives Congress plenary power to control immigration, states may exercise their police powers to regulate the conduct of aliens within their borders unless the regulation is preempted by federal law or otherwise violates the Constitution. While strict scrutiny generally applies to state laws that discriminate against aliens, rational basis scrutiny is appropriate when alienage classifications restrict the right to participate in functions that are central to self-government, such as voting, running for office, or serving on a jury. The state should prevail here, because the law excluding aliens from jury service is rationally related to the state's legitimate interest in ensuring that only citizens perform functions that are central to self-government.

**(D)** The woman, because the state has not articulated a legitimate reason for prohibiting resident aliens from serving as jurors in the state's courts.

**Incorrect.** The state should prevail, because the law excluding aliens from jury service is rationally related to the state's legitimate interest in ensuring that only citizens perform functions that are central to self-government. Although strict scrutiny generally applies to state laws that discriminate against aliens, rational basis scrutiny is appropriate when alienage classifications restrict the right to participate in functions that are central to self-government, such as voting, running for office, or serving on a jury.

## Question 9

Congress enacted a statute that made it illegal for "any employee, without the consent of his or her employer, to post on the Internet any information concerning the employer." The purpose of the statute was to prevent employees from revealing their employers' trade secrets.

Is the statute constitutional?

**(A)** No, because it is not narrowly tailored to further a compelling government interest.

**Correct.** The statute violates the freedom of speech protected by the First Amendment. The statute targets speech based on its content, because it prohibits employees from posting only "information concerning the employer" on the Internet. Because the statute is a content-based restriction on speech, it is subject to strict judicial scrutiny. Speech restrictions rarely survive strict scrutiny; the government must prove that the restriction is necessary to further a compelling

government interest. Even if the government's interest in preventing employees from revealing trade secrets were deemed compelling, Congress could enact legislation utilizing less speech-restrictive means to protect trade secrets.

**(B)** No, because it targets a particular medium of communication for special regulation.

**Incorrect.** The statute does target one medium of communication—Internet postings—and this focus may cause a court to look more closely at the restriction when evaluating its constitutionality. However, a statute does not violate the First Amendment simply because it targets a particular medium. In this case, the statute violates the freedom of speech protected by the First Amendment because it targets speech based on its content; it prohibits employees from posting only "information concerning the employer" on the Internet. Because the statute is a content-based restriction on speech, it is subject to strict judicial scrutiny. Speech restrictions rarely survive strict scrutiny; the government must prove that the restriction is necessary to further a compelling government interest. Even if the government's interest in preventing employees from revealing trade secrets were deemed compelling, Congress could enact legislation utilizing less speech-restrictive means to protect trade secrets.

**(C)** Yes, because it leaves open ample alternative channels of communication.

**Incorrect.** The statute leaves open channels of communication other than the Internet, but this fact does not save the statute. The availability of ample alternative channels of communication is an element of the First Amendment test for evaluating speech restrictions that are content-neutral, but it is not as important with respect to content-based restrictions. In this case, the statute violates the freedom of speech protected by the First Amendment because it targets speech based on its content; it prohibits employees from posting only "information concerning the employer" on the Internet. Because the statute is a content-based restriction on speech, it is subject to strict judicial scrutiny. Speech restrictions rarely survive strict scrutiny; the government must prove that the restriction is necessary to further a compelling government interest. Even if the government's interest in preventing employees from revealing trade secrets were deemed compelling, Congress could enact legislation utilizing less speech-restrictive means to protect trade secrets.

**(D)** Yes, because it prevents employees from engaging in unethical conduct.

**Incorrect.** The statute may prevent employees from engaging in unethical conduct, but this fact does not save the statute. The statute violates the freedom of speech protected by the First Amendment because it targets speech based on its content; it prohibits employees from posting only "information concerning the employer" on the Internet. Because the statute is a content-based restriction on speech, it is subject to strict judicial scrutiny. Speech restrictions rarely survive strict scrutiny; the government must prove that the restriction is necessary to further a compelling government interest. Even if the government's interest in preventing employees from revealing trade secrets were deemed compelling, Congress could enact legislation utilizing less speech-restrictive means to protect trade secrets.

## Question 10

A state law imposed substantial regulations on insurance companies operating within the state with respect to their rates, cash reserves, and financial practices.

A privately owned insurance company operating within the state advertised that it wanted to hire a new data processor. After reviewing applications for that position, the company hired a woman who appeared to be well qualified. The company refused to consider the application of a man who was better qualified than the woman, because he was known to have radical political views.

The man sued the company, alleging only a violation of his federal constitutional right to freedom of expression. Is the man likely to prevail?

**(A)** No, because hiring decisions are wholly discretionary and thus are not governed by the First Amendment.

**Incorrect.** The First Amendment applies to discretionary decisions of governments and government officials. The man is unlikely to prevail, but it is because the First and Fourteenth Amendments generally apply only to the actions of governments and government officials, not to the actions of privately owned companies such as the insurance company.

**(B)** No, because the company is not subject to the provisions of the First and Fourteenth Amendments.

**Correct.** The man is unlikely to prevail, because the First and Fourteenth Amendments generally apply

only to the actions of governments and government officials, not to the actions of privately owned companies such as the insurance company.

**(C)** Yes, because the company is affected with a public interest.

**Incorrect.** The question whether the First and Fourteenth Amendments apply to the actions of a privately owned company does not turn on whether the company is affected with a public interest. The man is unlikely to prevail, because the First and Fourteenth Amendments generally apply only to the actions of governments and government officials, not to the actions of privately owned companies such as the insurance company.

**(D)** Yes, because the company is substantially regulated by the state, and thus its employment decisions may fairly be attributed to the state.

**Incorrect.** The fact that the company is substantially regulated by the state does not make the company's actions subject to the First and Fourteenth Amendments. The man is unlikely to prevail, because the First and Fourteenth Amendments generally apply only to the actions of governments and government officials, not to the actions of privately owned companies such as the insurance company.

## Question 11

In order to foster an environment conducive to learning, a school board enacted a dress code that prohibited all public high school students from wearing in school shorts cut above the knee. Because female students at the school considered it unfashionable to wear shorts cut at or below the knee, they no longer wore shorts to school. On the other hand, male students at the school regularly wore shorts cut at or below the knee because they considered such shorts to be fashionable.

Female students sued to challenge the constitutionality of the dress code on the ground that it denied them the equal protection of the laws.

Should the court uphold the dress code?

**(A)** No, because the dress code is not necessary to further a compelling state interest.

**Incorrect.** The court should uphold the dress code, because the code is rationally related to the state's legitimate interest in fostering a proper educational environment. The dress code should not trigger heightened judicial scrutiny, because there are no facts to suggest that the purpose of the code is to discriminate against female students.

**(B)** No, because the dress code is not substantially related to an important state interest.
**Incorrect.** The court should uphold the dress code, because the code is rationally related to the state's legitimate interest in fostering a proper educational environment. The dress code should not trigger heightened judicial scrutiny, because there are no facts to suggest that the purpose of the code is to discriminate against female students.

**(C)** Yes, because the dress code is narrowly tailored to further an important state interest.
**Incorrect.** While the court should uphold the dress code, it should do so because the code is rationally related to the state's legitimate interest in fostering a proper educational environment. The dress code should not trigger heightened judicial scrutiny, because there are no facts to suggest that the purpose of the code is to discriminate against female students.

**(D)** Yes, because the dress code is rationally related to a legitimate state interest.
**Correct.** The court should uphold the dress code, because the code is rationally related to the state's legitimate interest in fostering a proper educational environment. The dress code should not trigger heightened judicial scrutiny, because there are no facts to suggest that the purpose of the code is to discriminate against female students.

## Question 12

A company owned a large tract of land that contained coal deposits that the company intended to mine. The company acquired mining equipment and began to plan its mining operations. Just as the company was about to begin mining, Congress enacted a statute that imposed a number of new environmental regulations and land-reclamation requirements on all mining operations within the United States. The statute made the company's planned mining operations economically infeasible. As a result, the company sold the tract of land to a farmer. While the sale price allowed the company to recover its original investment in the land, it did not cover the additional cost of the mining equipment the company had purchased or the profits it had expected to earn from its mining operations on the land.

In an action filed against the appropriate federal official, the company claims that the statute effected a taking of its property for which it is entitled to just compensation in an amount equal to the cost of the mining equipment it purchased and the profits it expected to earn from its mining operations on the land.

Which of the following is the most appropriate result in the action?

**(A)** The company should prevail on its claims for the cost of the mining equipment and for its lost profits.
**Incorrect.** The company should not prevail on any aspect of its claim for just compensation. The statute did not effect a taking of the company's land or of the mining equipment, because the new regulations did not deny all economically viable use of the land. The company recovered its original investment in the land by selling it to the farmer, and the land is economically viable as farmland. The company may sell the mining equipment or use it for mining on other land. Finally, the profits the company expected to earn from its mining operations do not constitute a property interest subject to the takings clause.

**(B)** The company should prevail on its claim for the cost of the mining equipment, but not for its lost profits.
**Incorrect.** The company should not prevail on any aspect of its claim for just compensation. The statute did not affect a taking of the company's land or of the mining equipment, because the new regulations did not deny all economically viable use of the land. The company recovered its original investment in the land by selling it to the farmer, and the land is economically viable as farmland. The company may sell the mining equipment or use it for mining on other land. Finally, the profits the company expected to earn from its mining operations do not constitute a property interest subject to the takings clause.

**(C)** The company should prevail on its claim for lost profits, but not for the cost of the mining equipment.
**Incorrect.** The company should not prevail on any aspect of its claim for just compensation. The statute did not affect a taking of the company's land or of the mining equipment, because the new regulations did not deny all economically viable use of the land. The company recovered its original investment in the

land by selling it to the farmer, and the land is economically viable as farmland. The company may sell the mining equipment or use it for mining on other land. Finally, the profits the company expected to earn from its mining operations do not constitute a property interest subject to the takings clause.

(D) The company should not prevail on its claim for the cost of the mining equipment or for its lost profits.

**Correct.** The company should not prevail on any aspect of its claim for just compensation. The statute did not affect a taking of the company's land or of the mining equipment, because the new regulations did not deny all economically viable use of the land. The company recovered its original investment in the land by selling it to the farmer, and the land is economically viable as farmland. The company may sell the mining equipment or use it for mining on other land. Finally, the profits the company expected to earn from its mining operations do not constitute a property interest subject to the takings clause.

## Question 13

A number of psychotherapists routinely send mailings to victims of car accidents informing the victims of the possibility of developing post-traumatic stress disorder (PTSD) as the result of the accidents, and offering psychotherapy services. Although PTSD is a possible result of a car accident, it is not common.

Many accident victims in a particular state who received the mailings complained that the mailings were disturbing and were an invasion of their privacy. These victims also reported that as a result of the mailings, their regard for psychotherapists and for psychotherapy as a form of treatment had diminished. In response, the state enacted a law prohibiting any licensed psychotherapist from sending mailings that raised the concern of PTSD to any car accident victim in the state until 30 days after the accident. The state justified the law as an effort to address the victims' complaints as well as to protect the reputation of psychotherapy as a form of treatment.

Is this law constitutional?

(A) No, because the law singles out one type of message for prohibition while allowing others.

**Incorrect.** It is true that the law singles out one type of message for prohibition while allowing other types. Such content-based restrictions on speech typically are subjected to strict judicial scrutiny and are invalidated. This law, however, is subject to a less exacting form of judicial scrutiny because it restricts commercial speech.

The law is constitutional, because it satisfies the First Amendment standards for government restrictions on commercial speech. The mailings qualify as commercial speech, because they advertise services provided by the psychotherapists. A restriction on commercial speech is subject to a form of intermediate judicial scrutiny, requiring the government to show that the restriction directly advances an important government interest and that the restriction is not substantially more extensive than necessary to protect that interest. The law here satisfies that standard; the 30-day waiting period for the psychotherapists' mailings narrowly serves the government's substantial interests in protecting both the privacy of accident victims and the public regard for psychotherapy.

(B) No, because the mailings provide information to consumers.

**Incorrect.** The fact that the mailings provide information to consumers entitles the mailings to First Amendment protection. However, because the mailings advertise the services of psychotherapists, they contain commercial speech and therefore are entitled to less constitutional protection than other forms of speech.

The law is constitutional, because it satisfies the First Amendment standards for government restrictions on commercial speech. A restriction on commercial speech is subject to a form of intermediate judicial scrutiny, requiring the government to show that the restriction directly advances an important government interest and that the restriction is not substantially more extensive than necessary to protect that interest. The law here satisfies that standard; the 30-day waiting period for the psychotherapists' mailings narrowly serves the government's substantial interests in protecting both the privacy of accident victims and the public regard for psychotherapy.

(C) Yes, because mailings suggesting the possibility of developing PTSD as the result of an accident are misleading.

**Incorrect.** Misleading commercial speech is not protected by the First Amendment, and governments therefore are free to restrict such speech. The mailings in this case are not misleading, however, because the facts state that "PTSD is a possible result" of car accidents.

The law is constitutional, because it satisfies the First Amendment standards for government restrictions on commercial speech. The mailings qualify as commercial speech because they advertise services provided by the psychotherapists. A restriction on commercial speech is subject to a form of intermediate judicial scrutiny, requiring the government to show that the restriction directly advances an important government interest and that the restriction is not substantially more extensive than necessary to protect that interest. The law here satisfies that standard; the 30-day waiting period for the psychotherapists' mailings narrowly serves the government's substantial interests in protecting both the privacy of accident victims and the public regard for psychotherapy.

**(D)** Yes, because the law protects the privacy of accident victims and the public regard for psychotherapy without being substantially more restrictive than necessary.

**Correct.** The law is constitutional, because it satisfies the First Amendment standards for government restrictions on commercial speech. The mailings contain commercial speech, because they advertise services provided by the psychotherapists. A restriction on commercial speech is subject to a form of intermediate judicial scrutiny, requiring the government to show that the restriction directly advances an important government interest and that the restriction is not substantially more extensive than necessary to protect that interest. The law here satisfies that standard; the 30-day waiting period for the psychotherapists' mailings narrowly serves the government's substantial interests in protecting both the privacy of accident victims and the public regard for psychotherapy.

## Question 14

A clerical employee of a city water department was responsible for sending out water bills to customers. His work in this respect had always been satisfactory.

The employee's sister ran in a recent election against the incumbent mayor, but she lost. The employee had supported his sister in the election campaign. After the mayor found out about this, she fired the employee solely because his support for the sister indicated that he was "disloyal" to the mayor. The city's charter provides that "all employees of the city work at the pleasure of the mayor."

Is the mayor's action constitutional?

**(A)** No, because public employees have a property interest in their employment, which gives them a right to a hearing prior to discharge.

**Incorrect.** A public employee has a property interest in his or her employment if the employee can be fired only for cause. Because the city's charter provides that "all employees of the city work at the pleasure of the mayor," the clerical employee does not have a property interest in his employment.

Nevertheless, the mayor's action is unconstitutional, because it violates the employee's right to freedom of expression and association protected by the First Amendment. The U.S. Supreme Court has held that the government may not fire an employee because of the employee's political views or affiliations unless certain political views or affiliations are required for the effective performance of the employee's job. The political views or affiliations of a clerical employee of a city water department are not relevant to the employee's job, and thus the employee may not be fired because of them.

**(B)** No, because the mayor's action violates the employee's right to freedom of expression and association.

**Correct.** The mayor's action is unconstitutional, because it violates the employee's right to freedom of expression and association protected by the First Amendment. The U.S. Supreme Court has held that the government may not fire an employee because of the employee's political views or affiliations unless certain political views or affiliations are required for the effective performance of the employee's job. The political views or affiliations of a clerical employee of a city water department are not relevant to the employee's job, and thus the employee may not be fired because of them.

**(C)** Yes, because the employee has no property interest in his job since the city charter provides that he holds the job "at the pleasure of the mayor."

**Incorrect.** It is true that the employee has no property interest in his job, and therefore he is not entitled to the constitutional protections of procedural due process. Nevertheless, the mayor's action is unconstitutional, because it violates the employee's right to freedom of expression and association protected by the First Amendment. The U.S. Supreme Court has held that the government may not fire an employee because of the employee's political views or affiliations unless certain political views or affiliations are required for the effective performance of the employee's job. The political views or affiliations of a clerical employee of a city water department are not relevant to the employee's job, and thus the employee may not be fired because of them.

**(D) Yes, because the mayor may require members of her administration to be politically loyal to her.**
**Incorrect.** The mayor may require members of her administration to be politically loyal to her only if political loyalty is required for the effective performance of the job in question. The U.S. Supreme Court has held that the government may not fire an employee because of the employee's political views or affiliations unless certain political views or affiliations are required for the effective performance of the employee's job. The political views or affiliations of a clerical employee of a city water department are not relevant to the employee's job, and thus the employee may not be fired because of them. The mayor's action is unconstitutional, because it violates the employee's right to freedom of expression and association protected by the First Amendment.

## Question 15

An environmental organization's stated mission is to support environmental causes. The organization's membership is generally open to the public, but its bylaws permit its officers to refuse to admit anyone to membership who does not adhere to the organization's mission statement.

In a recent state administrative proceeding, the organization opposed plans to begin mining operations in the mountains surrounding a small town. Its opposition prevented the mine from being opened on schedule. In an effort to force the organization to withdraw its opposition, certain residents of the town attended a meeting of the organization and tried to become members, but the officers refused to admit them. The residents sued the organization, claiming that the refusal to admit them was discriminatory and violated a local ordinance that prohibits any organization from discriminating on the basis of an individual's political views. The organization responded that the ordinance is unconstitutional as applied to its membership decisions.

Are the residents likely to prevail in their claim?

**(A) No, because the membership policies of a private organization are not state action.**

**Incorrect.** It is true that the membership policies of a private organization are not state action. The local ordinance on which the residents base their suit is state action, however, and it is subject to the requirements of the First Amendment.

The residents are not likely to prevail in their claim, because it would violate the environmental organization's First Amendment right to freedom of association if the state were to force the organization to accept the residents as members. The U.S. Supreme Court has held that the forced inclusion of an unwanted person in a group violates the group's freedom of association if including that person would significantly affect the group's ability to express its viewpoints. The freedom of association entitles the environmental organization to refuse membership to the residents, because admitting them would effect a change in the organization's viewpoint on the mining operations.

**(B) No, because the organization's right to freedom of association allows it to refuse to admit potential members who do not adhere to its mission statement.**
**Correct.** The residents are not likely to prevail in their claim, because it would violate the environmental organization's First Amendment right to freedom of association if the state were to force the organization to accept the residents as members. The U.S. Supreme Court has held that the forced inclusion of an unwanted person in a group violates the group's freedom of association if including that person would significantly affect the group's ability to express its viewpoints. The freedom of association entitles the environmental organization to refuse membership to the residents, because admitting them would effect a change in the organization's viewpoint on the mining operations.

**(C) Yes, because the action of the officers in refusing to admit the residents as members violates equal protection of the laws.**
**Incorrect.** The action of the officers in refusing to admit the residents as members is not subject to the equal protection clause, because the environmental organization is a private entity, and therefore the conduct of the organization's officers does not constitute state action.

The residents are not likely to prevail in their claim, because it would violate the environmental organization's First Amendment right to freedom of association if the state were to force the organization to accept the residents as members. The U.S. Supreme

Court has held that the forced inclusion of an unwanted person in a group violates the group's freedom of association if including that person would significantly affect the group's ability to express its viewpoints. The freedom of association entitles the environmental organization to refuse membership to the residents, because admitting them would effect a change in the organization's viewpoint on the mining operations.

(D) Yes, because the ordinance serves the compelling interest of protecting the residents' free speech rights.

**Incorrect.** The U.S. Supreme Court has held that even statutes that support compelling interests do not justify the severe burden on an organization's freedom of association that would result from forcing an organization to accept members who would significantly affect the organization's ability to express its viewpoints. The residents are not likely to prevail in their claim, because it would violate the environmental organization's First Amendment right to freedom of association if the state were to force the organization to accept the residents as members. The U.S. Supreme Court has held that the forced inclusion of an unwanted person in a group violates the group's freedom of association if including that person would significantly affect the group's ability to express its viewpoints. The freedom of association entitles the environmental organization to refuse membership to the residents, because admitting them would effect a change in the organization's viewpoint on the mining operations.

## Question 16

A fatal virus recently infected poultry in several nations. Some scientific evidence indicates that the virus can be transmitted from poultry to humans.

Poultry farming is a major industry in several U.S. states. In one such state, the legislature has enacted a law imposing a fee of two cents per bird on all poultry farming and processing operations in the state. The purpose of the fee is to pay for a state inspection system to ensure that no poultry raised or processed in the state is infected with the virus.

A company that has poultry processing plants both in the state and in other states has sued to challenge the fee. Is the fee constitutional?

(A) No, because although it attaches only to intrastate activity, in the aggregate, the fee substantially affects interstate commerce.

**Incorrect.** Having a substantial effect on interstate commerce does not make the fee unconstitutional. The fee in this case is constitutional, because it does not violate the negative implications of the commerce clause: it does not discriminate against interstate commerce, and its burden on interstate commerce is not clearly excessive in relation to the legitimate public health benefit the inspection system will bring to the state.

(B) No, because it places an undue burden on interstate commerce in violation of the negative implications of the commerce clause.

**Incorrect.** The fee does not violate the negative implications of the commerce clause, because it does not discriminate against interstate commerce, and its burden on interstate commerce is not clearly excessive in relation to the legitimate public health benefit the inspection system will bring to the state. The fee is therefore constitutional.

(C) Yes, because it applies only to activities that take place wholly within the state, and it does not unduly burden interstate commerce.

**Correct.** The fee does not violate the negative implications of the commerce clause, because it does not discriminate against interstate commerce, and its burden on interstate commerce is not clearly excessive in relation to the legitimate public health benefit the inspection system will bring to the state.

(D) Yes, because it was enacted pursuant to the state's police power, which takes precedence over the negative implications of the commerce clause.

**Incorrect.** The fee was enacted pursuant to the state's police power, but the supremacy clause of the Constitution prohibits state laws that violate federal constitutional limits on state authority. The fee is constitutional, nonetheless, because it does not violate the negative implications of the commerce clause: it does not discriminate against interstate commerce, and its burden on interstate commerce is not clearly excessive in relation to the legitimate public health benefit the inspection system will bring to the state.

## III. Chapter 11 CONTRACTS

### ESSAY SCORE SHEET

| Stated | Implied | |
|---|---|---|
| _____ | _____ | **Point One (45%) Assignment**<br><br>**Conclusion:** The homeowner's rights against the painter are assignable. |
| _____ | _____ | **Rule for when assignment is precluded:** While contract rights are generally assignable, a contract is not assignable if the assignment (i) would materially change the duty of the obligor (here, the painter), (ii) would materially increase the burden or risk imposed on the obligor, (iii) would materially impair the obligor's chance of obtaining return performance or materially reduce the value of that return performance to the obligor, (iv) is forbidden by statute or precluded by public policy, or (v) is validly precluded by contract. |
| _____ | _____ | **Application:** Here, |
| _____ | _____ | No statute or public policy would forbid or preclude the assignment, and no contractual provision prohibiting assignment exists. |
| _____ | _____ | There is no difference in magnitude or difficulty between the work required to paint the homeowner's house and the work required to paint the neighbor's house, the assignment from the homeowner to the neighbor does not materially increase the painter's duty or risk. |
| _____ | _____ | The exterior of the neighbor's house is identical to the exterior of the homeowner's house, both are peeling, and the labor to paint each house would be comparable in magnitude and difficulty. |
| _____ | _____ | Moreover, the neighbor's house is next door to the homeowner's house, so no additional travel burden would be placed on the painter by painting the neighbor's house rather than the homeowner's house. |
| _____ | _____ | **Conclusion:** Thus, a court would likely conclude that the assignment from the homeowner to the neighbor would neither materially change the painter's duty nor materially increase the burden imposed on the painter. |
| _____ | _____ | There is no indication under these facts that the assignment would materially impair the painter's chance of obtaining return performance (the agreed $6,000 payment), or materially reduce the value of the contract to the painter. |
| _____ | _____ | None of these factors is present here, particularly in light of the fact that the assignor (here, the homeowner) remains liable to pay the painter if the painter fulfills his obligation and the assignee (here, the neighbor) will be liable as well. |
| _____ | _____ | **Rule on creating an assignment:** All that is generally necessary for an effective assignment is (a) that the assignor manifest his or her intent to transfer the right to the assignee, without reserving any right to confirm or nullify the transfer, and (b) that the assignee manifest assent to the assignment. |
| _____ | _____ | No particular form is required for the assignment. With minor exceptions not relevant here, the relevant manifestations of assent may be made either orally or in writing. |

*continued on next page*

| Stated | Implied | |
|--------|---------|---|
| _____ | _____ | **Application:** Here, |
| _____ | _____ | Both conditions are satisfied by the conversation between the homeowner and the neighbor. No action or manifestation of assent is required from the obligor. |
| _____ | _____ | **Conclusion:** If the painter does not paint the neighbor's house, the neighbor has a cause of action against the painter. |
| | | [NOTE: Some examinees might argue against assignability of the contract because there are inevitable differences between the paint jobs, such as the relative ease of dealing with the homeowners. If well-reasoned, such analysis should receive credit.] |
| | | **Point Two (20%) Third-party beneficiary** |
| _____ | _____ | **Overall/Conclusion:** The retiree is neither an assignee of the contract nor a third-party beneficiary of the painter's promise; accordingly, the retiree cannot enforce the painter's obligations. |
| _____ | _____ | **Conclusion:** The retiree has no cause of action for the painter's breach as an assignee. |
| _____ | _____ | **Application/Conclusion:** The homeowner's rights under the contract have been assigned to the neighbor, not to the retiree; therefore, the retiree may not enforce the contract as an assignee. |
| _____ | _____ | **Conclusion:** Moreover, the retiree does not qualify as a third-party beneficiary who can enforce the contract. |
| _____ | _____ | **Rule:** Contract law distinguishes between "incidental" beneficiaries and "intended" beneficiaries, and only the latter can enforce a promise of which he or she is not the promisee. |
| _____ | _____ | **Application:** While the retiree would benefit from the painter's performance of his obligations, he is not an intended beneficiary. |
| _____ | _____ | Nothing indicates that benefitting him was in the contemplation of any of the parties when the contract was entered into. |
| | | **Point Three (35%) Delegation** |
| _____ | _____ | **Conclusion:** The painter's right to be paid for the completed paint job is enforceable against the delegatee (the neighbor) and also against the original/delegator (the homeowner). |
| _____ | _____ | The transaction between the homeowner and the neighbor is not only an assignment to the neighbor of the homeowner's rights against the painter, but also a delegation to the neighbor of the homeowner's obligation to the painter. |
| _____ | _____ | **Rule:** An assignment includes a delegation of the assignor's unperformed duties under the contract. |
| _____ | _____ | **Application:** Here, |
| _____ | _____ | The neighbor assented to the homeowner's idea of the neighbor paying the painter. |
| _____ | _____ | **Conclusion:** As a result, if the painter completes the paint job and is not paid in accordance with the terms of the contract, then he has a cause of action against |

*continued on next page*

| Stated | Implied | |
|--------|---------|---|
| | | the neighbor, even though the neighbor was not a party to the original contract. |
| _____ | _____ | The homeowner's delegation to the neighbor of the duty to pay the painter does not, however, relieve the homeowner of that payment responsibility in the absence of the painter's agreement to the discharge of the homeowner. |
| _____ | _____ | As a result, if the painter is not paid in accordance with the terms of the contract, then the painter retains a cause of action against the homeowner as well. |

## MBE PRACTICE ANALYSIS[3]

### Question 1

A restaurant supplier sent a letter to a regular customer offering to sell the customer an industrial freezer for $10,000. Two days later, the customer responded with a letter that stated: "I accept your offer on the condition that you provide me with a warranty that the freezer is merchantable." In response to the customer's letter, the supplier called the customer and stated that the offer was no longer open. The supplier promptly sold the freezer to another buyer for $11,000.

If the customer sues the supplier for breach of contract, is the customer likely to prevail?

(A) No, because the customer's letter added a term, making it a counteroffer.
**Incorrect.** It is true that a purported acceptance that is conditioned on an offeror's assent to a term additional to or different from the terms contained in an offer is a counteroffer. In this case, however, the customer's letter constituted an acceptance rather than a counteroffer. Under UCC § 2-314, a warranty of merchantability is implied in every contract for the sale of a good by a seller who is a merchant with respect to goods of that kind. Therefore, the condition contained in the customer's letter merely stated a term that was already implied in the sale. A contract arose when the customer mailed its letter accepting the offer. Accordingly, the supplier's attempted revocation of its offer was ineffective, and its sale of the freezer to the third party breached its contract with the customer.

(B) No, because the subsequent sale to a bona fide purchaser for value cut off the claims of the customer.
**Incorrect.** Under some circumstances, the sale of goods to a bona fide purchaser may cut off the claims of other parties. In this case, however, the dispositive issue is whether the customer's letter in response to the supplier's offer constituted an acceptance or a counteroffer. Under UCC § 2-314, a warranty of merchantability is implied in every contract for the sale of a good by a seller who is a merchant with respect to goods of that kind. Therefore, the condition contained in the customer's letter merely stated a term that was

already implied in the sale. A contract arose when the customer mailed its letter accepting the offer. Accordingly, the supplier's attempted revocation of its offer was ineffective, and its sale of the freezer to the third party breached its contract with the customer.

(C) Yes, because the customer's letter was an acceptance of the supplier's offer, since the warranty of merchantability was already implied in the sale.
**Correct.** It is true that a purported acceptance that is conditioned on an offeror's assent to a term additional to or different from the terms contained in an offer is a counteroffer. In this case, however, the customer's letter constituted an acceptance rather than a counteroffer. Under UCC § 2-314, a warranty of merchantability is implied in every contract for the sale of a good by a seller who is a merchant with respect to goods of that kind. Therefore, the condition contained in the customer's letter merely stated a term that was already implied in the sale. A contract arose when the customer mailed its letter accepting the offer. Accordingly, the supplier's attempted revocation of its offer was ineffective, and its sale of the freezer to the third party breached its contract with the customer.

(D) Yes, because the supplier's letter was a firm offer that could not be revoked for a reasonable time.
**Incorrect.** The supplier's letter did not create a firm offer because it failed to give assurance that the offer would be held open, a principal requirement of a firm offer under UCC § 2-205. The dispositive issue here is whether the customer's response to the supplier's offer constituted an acceptance or a counteroffer. Under UCC § 2-314, a warranty of merchantability is implied in every contract for the sale of a good by a seller who is a merchant with respect to goods of that kind. Therefore, the condition contained in the customer's letter merely stated a term that was already implied in the sale. A contract arose when the customer mailed its letter accepting the offer. Accordingly, the supplier's attempted revocation of its offer was ineffective, and its sale of the freezer to the third party breached its contract with the customer.

### Question 2

A seller sent an email to a potential buyer, offering to sell his house to her for $150,000. The buyer immediately responded via email, asking whether the offer included the house's front porch swing. The seller emailed back: "No, it doesn't." The

---

3. *Id.*

buyer then ordered a front porch swing and emailed back to the seller: "I accept your offer." The seller refused to sell the house to the buyer, claiming that the offer was no longer open.

Is there a contract for the sale of the house?

(A) No, because the buyer's initial email was a counteroffer.

**Incorrect.** A reply to an offer that merely requests information regarding the offer constitutes an inquiry rather than a counteroffer. The buyer's response asking whether the seller intended to include the front porch swing in his offer was an inquiry rather than a counteroffer. The buyer's subsequent email stating "I accept your offer" was an acceptance that created a contract between the parties. Therefore, the seller's attempted revocation of his offer was ineffective.

(B) No, because the offer lapsed before the buyer accepted.

**Incorrect.** An offeree's power of acceptance may terminate due to a lapse of time when the offeree fails to accept the offer within the time stated in the offer or within a reasonable time. In this case, the offer did not include an express time limitation. Therefore, the buyer could accept within a reasonable period of time. The email exchanges between the buyer and the seller demonstrate that the buyer accepted the seller's offer within a reasonable time period. The dispositive issue here is whether the buyer's reply to the seller's offer constituted an acceptance or a counteroffer.

A reply to an offer that merely requests information regarding the offer constitutes an inquiry rather than a counteroffer. The buyer's response asking whether the seller intended to include the front porch swing in his offer was an inquiry rather than a counteroffer. The buyer's subsequent email stating "I accept your offer" was an acceptance that created a contract between the parties. Therefore, the seller's attempted revocation of his offer was ineffective.

(C) Yes, because the buyer relied on the offer by ordering the swing.

**Incorrect.** An offeree's reliance on an offer can create a binding option contract that precludes an offeror from revoking its offer. In this case, however, there is no indication that the buyer's purchase of the swing was the type of act performed in substantial reliance on the offer that the seller reasonably could have expected at the time he communicated his offer. The dispositive issue here is whether the buyer's reply to the seller's offer constituted an acceptance or a counteroffer.

A reply to an offer that merely requests information regarding the offer constitutes an inquiry rather than a counteroffer. The buyer's response asking whether the seller intended to include the front porch swing in his offer was an inquiry rather than a counteroffer. The buyer's subsequent email stating "I accept your offer" was an acceptance that created a contract between the parties. Therefore, the seller's attempted revocation of his offer was ineffective.

(D) Yes, because the buyer's initial email merely asked for information.

**Correct.** A reply to an offer that merely requests information regarding the offer constitutes an inquiry rather than a counteroffer. The buyer's response asking whether the seller intended to include the front porch swing in his offer was an inquiry rather than a counteroffer. The buyer's subsequent email stating "I accept your offer" was an acceptance that created a contract between the parties. Therefore, the seller's attempted revocation of his offer was ineffective.

## Question 3

In a telephone conversation, a jewelry maker offered to buy 100 ounces of gold from a precious metals company if delivery could be made within 10 days. The jewelry maker did not specify a price, but the market price for 100 ounces of gold at the time of the conversation was approximately $65,000. Without otherwise responding, the company delivered the gold six days later.

In the meantime, the project for which the jewelry maker planned to use the gold was canceled. The jewelry maker therefore refused to accept delivery of the gold or to pay the $65,000 demanded by the company.

Is there an enforceable contract between the jewelry maker and the company?

(A) No, because the parties did not agree on a price term.

**Incorrect.** Under UCC § 2-305, a contract may be enforceable in the absence of a price term so long as the parties otherwise intended to enter into a contract. In this case, the dispositive issue is whether the parties' oral agreement is enforceable. Under UCC § 2-201(1), a contract for the sale of goods for a price of $500 or more is not enforceable unless there is a writing indicating the contract that is signed by the party against whom enforcement is sought. In this case, the absence of such a writing signed by the jewelry maker renders the parties' oral agreement unenforceable. An exception to the writing requirement arises when a seller delivers goods that are accepted by the buyer, but in this case, the jewelry maker did not accept the gold.

**(B)** No, because the parties did not put their agreement in writing.

**Correct.** The parties failed to comply with the writing requirement of UCC § 2-201(1). Under that section, a contract for the sale of goods for a price of $500 or more is not enforceable unless there is a writing indicating a contract of sale that is signed by the party against whom enforcement is sought. In this case, the absence of such a writing signed by the jewelry maker renders the parties' oral agreement unenforceable. An exception to the writing requirement arises when a seller delivers goods that are accepted by the buyer, but in this case, the jewelry maker did not accept the gold.

**(C)** Yes, because the absence of a price term does not defeat the formation of a valid contract for the sale of goods where the parties otherwise intended to form a contract.

**Incorrect.** Under UCC § 2-305, a contract may be enforceable in the absence of a price term so long as the parties otherwise intended to enter into a contract. In this case, however, the dispositive issue is whether the parties' oral agreement is enforceable. Under UCC § 2-201(1), a contract for the sale of goods for a price of $500 or more is not enforceable unless there is a writing indicating the contract that is signed by the party against whom enforcement is sought. The absence of such a writing signed by the jewelry maker renders the parties' oral agreement unenforceable. An exception to the writing requirement arises when a seller delivers goods that are accepted by the buyer. In this case, however, the jewelry maker did not accept the gold.

**(D)** Yes, because the company relied on an implied promise to pay when it delivered the gold.

**Incorrect.** The dispositive issue in this case is whether the parties' oral agreement is enforceable. Under UCC § 2-201(1), a contract for the sale of goods for a price of $500 or more is not enforceable unless there is a writing indicating the contract that is signed by the party against whom enforcement is sought. The absence of such a writing signed by the jewelry maker renders the parties' oral agreement unenforceable. An exception to the writing requirement arises when a seller delivers goods that are accepted by the buyer. In this case, however, the jewelry maker did not accept the gold.

## Question 4

A man sent an email to a friend that stated: "Because you have been a great friend to me, I am going to give you a rare book that I own." The friend replied by an email that said: "Thanks for the rare book. I am going to give you my butterfly collection." The rare book was worth $10,000; the butterfly collection was worth $100. The friend delivered the butterfly collection to the man, but the man refused to deliver the book.

If the friend sues the man to recover the value of the book, how should the court rule?

**(A)** For the man, because there was no bargained-for exchange to support his promise.

**Correct.** To constitute consideration, a return promise must be bargained for. A return promise is bargained for when it is sought by the promisor in exchange for his promise and is given by the promisee in exchange for that promise. Because the man's promise to give the rare book to the friend did not seek a return promise or performance, the friend's promise to give the man her butterfly collection did not constitute consideration for the man's promise. Accordingly, no contract arose between the parties, and the court should rule in favor of the man.

**(B)** For the man, because the consideration given for his promise was inadequate.

**Incorrect.** Instead of giving inadequate consideration, the friend gave no consideration at all. To constitute consideration, a return promise must be bargained for. A return promise is bargained for when it is sought by the promisor in exchange for his promise and is given by the promisee in exchange for that promise. Because the man's promise to give the rare book to the friend did not seek a return promise or performance, the friend's promise to give the man her butterfly collection did not constitute consideration for the man's promise. Accordingly, no contract arose between the parties, and the court should rule in favor of the man.

**(C)** For the friend, because she gave the butterfly collection to the man in reliance on receiving the book.

**Incorrect.** Although it is true that a promisee's reliance may provide the basis for the enforcement of a promise in the absence of consideration, that principle is inapplicable here. The man's promise failed to induce reliance by the friend of the type that the man reasonably might have expected when he promised to give her the rare book. In addition, this is not a case in which injustice could only be avoided by the enforcement of the man's promise. The dispositive issue here is whether the friend's promise to give her butterfly collection to the man constituted consideration for the man's promise. Because the man's promise to give the rare book to the friend did not seek a return promise or performance, the friend's promise did not constitute consideration for the man's promise. Accordingly, no contract arose between the parties, and the court should rule in favor of the man.

**(D)** For the friend, because she conferred a benefit on the man by delivering the butterfly collection. **Incorrect.** The fact that a promisee confers a benefit on a promisor does not create an enforceable obligation on the part of the promisor. The dispositive issue here is whether the friend's promise to give her butterfly collection to the man constituted consideration for the man's promise. Because the man's promise to give the rare book to the friend did not seek a return promise or performance, the friend's promise did not constitute consideration for the man's promise. Accordingly, no contract arose between the parties, and the court should rule in favor of the man.

## Question 5

A farmer who wanted to sell her land received a letter from a developer that stated, "I will pay you $1,100 an acre for your land." The farmer's letter of reply stated, "I accept your offer." Unbeknownst to the farmer, the developer had intended to offer only $1,000 per acre but had mistakenly typed "$1,100." As both parties knew, comparable land in the vicinity had been selling at prices between $1,000 and $1,200 per acre.

Which of the following states the probable legal consequences of the correspondence between the parties?

**(A)** There is no contract, because the parties attached materially different meanings to the price term. **Incorrect.** There is a general rule that contract formation may be defeated, under some circumstances, where parties attach materially different meanings to a material term. That rule, however, is inapplicable here where the critical issue relates to the developer's intent, as manifested by his conduct, and the impact of the farmer's lack of knowledge of the developer's mistake. An enforceable

contract requires mutual assent as determined by the parties' objective, rather than subjective, manifestations of that assent. Here, given the parties' knowledge of the price of comparable land, the developer's offer created a reasonable understanding that the developer would purchase the land for $1,100 per acre. Moreover, because the farmer neither knew nor had reason to know that the developer intended to purchase the land for only $1,000 per acre, the developer will be bound to purchase it for $1,100 per acre. Accordingly, the parties' conduct gave rise to a contract formed at $1,100 per acre when the farmer accepted the developer's offer.

**(B)** There is no enforceable contract, because the developer is entitled to rescission due to a mutual mistake as to a basic assumption of the contract. **Incorrect.** While a mutual mistake may give rise to an action for rescission, there was no mutual mistake in this case. The critical issue here relates to the developer's intent as manifested by his conduct, and the impact of the farmer's lack of knowledge of the developer's mistake. An enforceable contract requires mutual assent as determined by the parties' objective, rather than subjective, manifestations of assent. Given the parties' knowledge of the price of comparable land, the developer's offer created a reasonable understanding that the developer would purchase the land for $1,100 per acre. Moreover, because the farmer neither knew nor had reason to know that the developer intended to purchase the land for only $1,000 per acre, the developer will be bound to purchase it for $1,100 per acre. Accordingly, the parties' conduct gave rise to a contract formed at $1,100 per acre when the farmer accepted the developer's offer.

**(C)** There is a contract formed at a price of $1,000 per acre. **Incorrect.** An enforceable contract requires mutual assent as determined by the parties' objective, rather than subjective, manifestations of assent. Given the parties' knowledge of the price of comparable land, the developer's offer created a reasonable understanding that the developer would purchase the land for $1,100 per acre. Moreover, because the farmer neither knew nor had reason to know that the developer intended to purchase the land for only $1,000 per acre, the developer will be bound to purchase it for $1,100 per acre. Accordingly, the parties' conduct gave rise to a contract formed at $1,100 per acre when the farmer accepted the developer's offer.

(D) There is a contract formed at a price of $1,100 per acre.

**Correct.** An enforceable contract requires mutual assent as determined by the parties' objective, rather than subjective, manifestations of assent. Given the parties' knowledge of the price of comparable land, the developer's offer created a reasonable understanding that the developer would purchase the land for $1,100 per acre. Moreover, because the farmer neither knew nor had reason to know that the developer intended to purchase the land for only $1,000 per acre, the developer will be bound to purchase it for $1,100 per acre. Accordingly, the parties' conduct gave rise to a contract formed at $1,100 per acre when the farmer accepted the developer's offer.

## Question 6

A buyer and a seller entered into a written contract for the sale of a copy machine, using the same form contract that they had used a number of times in the past. The contract stated that payment was due 30 days after delivery and provided that the writing contained the complete and exclusive statement of the parties' agreement.

On several past occasions, the buyer had taken a 5% discount from the contract price when paying within 10 days of delivery, and the seller had not objected. On this occasion, when the buyer took a 5% discount for paying within 10 days, the seller objected because his profit margin on this particular machine was smaller than on his other machines.

If the seller sues the buyer for breach of contract, may the buyer introduce evidence that the 5% discount was a term of the agreement?

(A) No, because the seller timely objected to the buyer's proposal for different terms.

**Incorrect.** Under UCC § 1-303(b), course of dealing is defined as "a sequence of conduct concerning previous transactions between the parties to a particular transaction. . . ." In this case, on several past occasions the buyer had taken a 5% discount without objection from the seller, thus establishing a course of dealing. Given the course of dealing between the parties, the seller's objection to the 5% discount, after the buyer had acted in accordance with the course of dealing, was ineffective. Under the UCC's parol evidence rule, course-of-dealing evidence is admissible to explain or supplement a final written agreement.

(B) No, because the writing contained the complete and exclusive agreement of the parties.

**Incorrect.** Under UCC § 1-303(b), course of dealing is defined as "a sequence of conduct concerning previous transactions between the parties to a particular transaction. . . ." In this case, on several past occasions the buyer had taken a 5% discount without objection from the seller, thus establishing a course of dealing. Under the UCC's parol evidence rule, course-of-dealing evidence is admissible to explain or supplement a final written agreement even if the parties intended the agreement to be complete and exclusive. Accordingly, the course-of-dealing evidence is admissible.

(C) Yes, because a modification made in good faith does not require consideration.

**Incorrect.** UCC Article 2 contains a general rule that a good-faith modification does not require consideration to be enforceable. However, the enforceability of a modification is not at issue here. The issue here is whether the UCC's parol evidence rule will preclude the admissibility of evidence of course of dealing. The facts indicate that in the parties' previous contracts the buyer had taken a 5% discount without objection from the seller. This conduct amounted to a course of dealing that is defined under UCC § 1-303(b) as "a sequence of conduct concerning previous transactions between the parties to a particular transaction. . . ." Because the UCC's parol evidence rule explicitly allows for the admission of course-of-dealing evidence to explain or supplement a final written agreement, the evidence is admissible.

(D) Yes, because evidence of course of dealing is admissible even if the writing contains the complete and exclusive agreement of the parties.

**Correct.** Under UCC § 1-303(b), course of dealing is defined as "a sequence of conduct concerning previous transactions between the parties to a particular transaction. . . ." In this case, on several past occasions the buyer had taken a 5% discount without objection from the seller, thus establishing a course of dealing. Under the UCC's parol evidence rule, course-of-dealing evidence is admissible to explain or supplement a final written agreement even if the parties intended the agreement to be complete and exclusive. Accordingly, the course-of-dealing evidence is admissible.

## Question 7

A buyer purchased a new car from a dealer under a written contract that provided that the price of the car was $20,000 and that the buyer would receive a "trade-in allowance of $7,000 for the buyer's old car." The old car had recently been damaged in an accident. The contract contained a merger clause stating: "This writing constitutes the entire agreement of the parties, and there are no other understandings or agreements not set forth herein." When the buyer took possession of the new car, she delivered the old car to the dealer. At that time, the dealer claimed that the trade-in allowance included an assignment of the buyer's claim against her insurance company for damage to the old car. The buyer refused to provide the assignment.

The dealer sued the buyer to recover the insurance payment. The dealer has offered evidence that the parties agreed during their negotiations for the new car that the dealer was entitled to the insurance payment.

Should the court admit this evidence?

(A) No, because the dealer's acceptance of the old car bars any additional claim by the dealer.

**Incorrect.** A buyer's mere acceptance of goods does not waive its potential claims against a seller. The dispositive issue here is whether the parol evidence rule will allow the proffered evidence. Under that rule, a merger clause does not conclusively determine that an agreement is completely integrated. Moreover, a finding that an agreement is completely integrated does not necessarily bar the admission of extrinsic evidence. Although extrinsic evidence is inadmissible to supplement or contradict the express terms of a completely integrated agreement, such evidence is admissible to explain the terms of an agreement. In this case, evidence of the parties' discussions during their negotiations is admissible to aid in explaining whether they intended "trade-in allowance" to include an assignment of the buyer's claim against her insurance company.

(B) No, because the merger clause bars any evidence of the parties' prior discussions concerning the trade-in allowance.

**Incorrect.** Under the UCC's parol evidence rule, a merger clause does not conclusively determine that an agreement is completely integrated. Moreover, a finding that an agreement is completely integrated does not necessarily bar the admission of extrinsic evidence. Although extrinsic evidence is inadmissible to supplement or contradict the express terms of a completely integrated agreement, such evidence is

admissible to explain the terms of an agreement. In this case, evidence of the parties' discussions during their negotiations is admissible to aid in explaining whether they intended "trade-in allowance" to include an assignment of the buyer's claim against her insurance company.

(C) Yes, because a merger clause does not bar evidence of fraud.

**Incorrect.** The UCC's parol evidence rule allows the introduction of extrinsic evidence to establish fraud even if an agreement is completely integrated. Because there is no indication of fraud in this case, the fraud exception is irrelevant. The dispositive issue here is whether the parol evidence rule will allow the proffered evidence. Under that rule, a merger clause does not conclusively determine that an agreement is completely integrated. Moreover, a finding that an agreement is completely integrated does not necessarily bar the admission of extrinsic evidence. Although extrinsic evidence is inadmissible to supplement or contradict the express terms of a completely integrated agreement, such evidence is admissible to explain the terms of an agreement. In this case, evidence of the parties' discussions during their negotiations is admissible to aid in explaining whether they intended "trade-in allowance" to include an assignment of the buyer's claim against her insurance company.

(D) Yes, because the merger clause does not bar evidence to explain what the parties meant by "trade-in allowance."

**Correct.** Under the UCC's parol evidence rule, a merger clause does not conclusively establish that an agreement is completely integrated. Moreover, a finding that an agreement is completely integrated does not necessarily bar the admission of extrinsic evidence. Although extrinsic evidence is inadmissible to supplement or contradict the express terms of a completely integrated agreement, such evidence is admissible to explain the terms of an agreement. In this case, evidence of the parties' discussions during their negotiations is admissible to aid in explaining what amount they intended for the trade-in and whether they intended "trade-in allowance" to include an assignment of the buyer's claim against her insurance company.

## Question 8

A buyer agreed in writing to purchase a car from a seller for $15,000, with the price to be paid on a specified date at the seller's home. The contract provided, and both parties intended, that time was of the essence. Before the specified date, however, the seller sold the car to a third party for $18,000. On the specified date, the buyer arrived at the seller's home prepared to tender payment. The seller was not there, so the buyer called the seller to ask where he was. The seller then told the buyer that he had sold the car to the third party.

If the buyer sues the seller for breach of contract, will the buyer be likely to prevail?

**(A)** No, because the contractual obligations were discharged on the ground of impossibility.

**Incorrect.** While the seller's sale of the car to the third party rendered it impossible for the seller to sell the car to the buyer, such conduct does not meet the standard to establish impossibility as a legal defense for nonperformance. Under UCC Article 2, a seller's tender of delivery of goods and a buyer's tender of payment are concurrent conditions of exchange. Therefore, the buyer and the seller were obligated to simultaneously tender their respective performances. However, because the seller breached by anticipatory repudiation, the buyer's performance obligation was discharged. Accordingly, the buyer has a claim for breach of contract, even though she did not tender performance.

**(B)** No, because the buyer did not tender her performance on the specified date.

**Incorrect.** The facts demonstrate that the seller repudiated the contract by selling the car to the third party. Under UCC Article 2, a seller's tender of delivery of goods and a buyer's tender of payment are concurrent conditions of exchange. Therefore, the buyer and the seller were obligated to simultaneously tender their respective performances. However, because the seller breached by anticipatory repudiation, the buyer's performance obligation was discharged. Accordingly, the buyer has a claim for breach of contract, even though she did not tender performance.

**(C)** Yes, because seller did not inform the buyer of his repudiation.

**Incorrect.** An anticipatory repudiation can be either express or implied. It is express if the repudiating party informs the other party of his intention not to perform. It is implied if the repudiating party puts it out of his power to perform. Here, there was an implied

repudiation when the seller sold the car to the third party. The fact that the seller did not inform the buyer of his repudiation is irrelevant to the buyer's claim.

**(D)** Yes, because the seller anticipatorily repudiated the contract when he sold the car to the third party.

**Correct.** The seller's sale of the car to the third party was an anticipatory repudiation that gave the buyer an immediate claim for breach of contract. Under UCC Article 2, a seller's tender of delivery of goods and a buyer's tender of payment are concurrent conditions of exchange. Therefore, the buyer and the seller were obligated to simultaneously tender their respective performances. However, because the seller breached by anticipatory repudiation, the buyer's performance obligation was discharged. Accordingly, the buyer has a claim for breach of contract, even though she did not tender performance.

## Question 9

A mill and a bakery entered into a written contract that obligated the mill to deliver to the bakery 1,000 pounds of flour every Monday for 26 weeks at a specified price per pound. The mill delivered the proper quantity of flour in a timely manner for the first 15 weeks. However, the 16th delivery was tendered on a Tuesday, and amounted to only 800 pounds. The mill told the bakery that the 200-pound shortage would be made up on the delivery due the following Monday. The late delivery and the 200-pound shortage will not significantly disrupt the bakery's operations.

How may the bakery legally respond to the nonconforming tender?

**(A)** Accept the 800 pounds tendered, but notify the mill that the bakery will cancel the contract if the exact amount is not delivered on the following Monday.

**Incorrect.** Because the contract authorizes the delivery of flour in separate lots to be separately accepted, the parties entered into an installment contract. UCC § 2-612 adopts a "substantial impairment" standard for determining whether a buyer can reject a particular installment or cancel the entire contract. A buyer can reject an installment if a nonconformity substantially impairs that installment and the nonconformity cannot be cured. A buyer can cancel the contract only when the nonconformity with respect to one or more install-ments substantially impairs the value of the whole con-tract. Here, the mill's tender of less than the contracted-for quantity did not amount to a nonconformity that substantially impaired the value of either the 16th installment or the whole contract. The mill's proposed cure, the delivery of the remaining 200 pounds on the following Monday, is sufficient given that the late deliv-ery and the shortage will not significantly disrupt the bakery's business. Accordingly, not only must the bak-ery accept the delivery of the tendered 800 pounds of flour, it also must accept the remaining 200 pounds that the mill proposes to deliver on the following Monday.

**(B)** Accept the 800 pounds tendered, but notify the mill that the bakery will deduct from the price any damages for losses due to the nonconforming tender.
**Correct.** Because the contract authorizes the delivery of flour in separate lots to be separately accepted, the parties entered into an installment contract. UCC § 2-612 adopts a "substantial impairment" standard for determining whether a buyer can reject a particular installment or cancel the entire contract. A buyer can reject an installment if a nonconformity substantially impairs that installment and the nonconformity cannot be cured. Here the mill's tender of less than the con-tracted-for quantity did not amount to a nonconformity that substantially impaired either the value of the 16th installment or the whole contract. The mill's proposed cure, the delivery of the remaining 200 pounds on the following Monday, is sufficient given that the late deliv-ery and the shortage will not significantly disrupt the bakery's business. Accordingly, the bakery must accept the delivery of the tendered 800 pounds of flour but may deduct from the price any damages for losses resulting from the late delivery.

**(C)** Reject the 800 pounds tendered, but notify the mill that the bakery will accept delivery the following Monday if it is conforming.
**Incorrect.** Because the contract authorizes the delivery of flour in separate lots to be separately accepted, the parties entered into an installment contract. UCC § 2-612 adopts a "substantial impairment" standard for determining whether a buyer can reject a particular installment or cancel the entire contract. A buyer can reject an installment if a nonconformity substantially impairs that installment and the nonconformity cannot be cured. Here the mill's tender of less than the con-tracted-for quantity did not amount to a nonconformity that substantially impaired either the value of the 16th

installment or the whole contract. The mill's proposed cure, the delivery of the remaining 200 pounds on the following Monday, is sufficient given that the late deliv-ery and the shortage will not significantly disrupt the bakery's business. Accordingly, not only must the bak-ery accept the delivery of the tendered 800 pounds of flour, it also must accept the remaining 200 pounds that the mill proposes to deliver on the following Monday.

**(D)** Reject the 800 pounds tendered, and notify the mill that the bakery is canceling the contract.
**Incorrect.** Because the contract authorizes the delivery of flour in separate lots to be separately accepted, the parties entered into an installment contract. UCC § 2-612 adopts a "substantial impairment" standard for determining whether a buyer can reject a particular installment or cancel the entire contract. A buyer can reject an installment if a nonconformity substantially impairs that installment and the nonconformity cannot be cured. Additionally, a buyer can cancel the contract only when the nonconformity with respect to one or more installments substantially impairs the value of the whole contract. Here, the mill's tender of less than the contracted-for quantity did not amount to a nonconfor-mity that substantially impaired the value of the 16th installment or the whole contract. The mill's proposed cure, the delivery of the remaining 200 pounds on the following Monday, is sufficient given that the late deliv-ery and the shortage will not significantly disrupt the bakery's business. Accordingly, the buyer has no right to reject the tender or to cancel the contract.

### Question 10

A buyer agreed to purchase a seller's house for $250,000 "on condition that the buyer obtain mortgage financing within 30 days." Thirty days later, the buyer told the seller that the buyer would not purchase the house because the buyer had not obtained mortgage financing. The seller asked the buyer where the buyer had tried to obtain mortgage financing, and the buyer responded, "I was busy and didn't have time to seek mortgage financing."

If the seller sues the buyer for breach of contract, is the court likely to find the buyer in breach?

**(A)** No, because the buyer's performance was subject to a condition that did not occur.
**Incorrect.** A performance that is subject to an express condition cannot become due unless the condition

occurs or its non-occurrence is excused. However, the duty of good faith, which is implied in every contract, imposed an obligation on the buyer to make reasonable efforts to secure mortgage financing. Because the buyer made no such efforts, the non-occurrence of the condition to the buyer's obligation to purchase the house—the buyer's securing financing—was excused. Accordingly, the court is likely to find that the buyer is in breach.

**(B)** No, because the promise was illusory since the buyer was not obligated to do anything.

**Incorrect.** The duty of good faith, which is implied in every contract, imposed an obligation on the buyer to make reasonable efforts to secure mortgage financing. Accordingly, the buyer's promise to secure financing was not illusory. A performance that is subject to an express condition cannot become due unless the condition occurs or its non-occurrence is excused. In this case, the non-occurrence of the condition to the buyer's obligation to perform was excused, because the buyer failed to make reasonable efforts to secure mortgage financing. Therefore, the court is likely to find that the buyer is in breach.

**(C)** Yes, because a promise was implied that the buyer had to make reasonable efforts to obtain mortgage financing.

**Correct.** A performance that is subject to an express condition cannot become due unless the condition occurs or its non-occurrence is excused. However, the duty of good faith, which is implied in every contract, imposed an obligation on the buyer to make reasonable efforts to secure mortgage financing. Because the buyer made no such efforts, the non-occurrence of the condition to the buyer's obligation to purchase the house—the buyer's securing financing—was excused. Accordingly, the court is likely to find that the buyer is in breach.

**(D)** Yes, because a reasonable interpretation of the agreement is that the buyer had an obligation to purchase the house for $250,000 in 30 days.

**Incorrect.** The contract explicitly stated that the buyer's obligation to perform was expressly conditioned on the buyer obtaining mortgage financing. A performance that is subject to an express condition cannot become due unless the condition occurs or its non-occurrence is excused. However, the duty of good faith, which is implied in every contract, imposed an obligation on the buyer to make reasonable efforts to secure mortgage financing. Because the buyer made no such efforts, the

non-occurrence of the condition to the buyer's obligation to purchase the house—the buyer's securing financing—was excused. Accordingly, the court is likely to find that the buyer is in breach.

## Question 11

A producer contracted to pay an inexperienced performer a specified salary to act in a small role in a play the producer was taking on a six-week road tour. The contract was for the duration of the tour. On the third day of the tour, the performer was hospitalized with a stomach disorder. The producer replaced her in the cast with an experienced actor. One week later, the performer recovered, but the producer refused to allow her to resume her original role for the remainder of the tour.

In an action by the performer against the producer for breach of contract, which of the following, if proved, would be the producer's best defense?

**(A)** The actor, by general acclaim, was much better in the role than the performer had been.

**Incorrect.** After the performer became ill, the temporary impracticability doctrine excused the performer's contractual obligation and also gave the producer the right to suspend his performance obligation during the period that the performer's illness prevented her from acting. The critical issue here is whether the producer also had the right to cancel the contract. Circumstances that would give the producer the right to cancel include the degree of uncertainty relating to the nature and duration of the performer's illness and the extent to which a delay in making substitute arrangements would have prevented the producer from continuing the tour. The relative quality of the actor's performance is not a circumstance that would give the producer the right to cancel the performer's contract.

**(B)** The actor was the only replacement the producer could find, and the actor would accept nothing less than a contract for the remainder of the six-week tour.

**Correct.** After the performer became ill, the temporary impracticability doctrine excused the performer's contractual obligation and also gave the producer the right to suspend his performance obligation during the period that the performer's illness prevented her from acting. The critical issue here is whether the producer also had the right to cancel the contract. Circumstances that would give the producer the right to cancel the contract include the degree of uncertainty relating to the nature and duration of the performer's illness and the extent to which a delay in making substitute arrangements would have prevented the producer from continuing the tour. The unwillingness of the actor, the only replacement available, to take a contract for less than the remainder of the six-week tour and the uncertainty surrounding when the performer might return to work would have discharged the producer's performance obligations and justified his cancellation of the contract with the performer.

(C) The producer offered to employ the performer as the actor's understudy for the remainder of the six-week tour at the performer's original salary, but the performer declined.

**Incorrect.** After the performer became ill, the temporary impracticability doctrine excused the performer's contractual obligation and also gave the producer the right to suspend his performance obligation during the period that the performer's illness prevented her from acting. The critical issue here is whether the producer also had the right to cancel the contract. Circumstances that would give the producer the right to cancel include the degree of uncertainty relating to the nature and duration of the performer's illness and the extent to which a delay in making substitute arrangements would have prevented the producer from continuing the tour. Because the producer had the right to cancel the contract, his action in offering the performer a job as understudy is irrelevant.

(D) Both the producer and the performer knew that a year earlier the performer had been incapacitated for a short period of time by the same kind of stomach disorder.

**Incorrect.** After the performer became ill, the temporary impracticability doctrine excused the performer's contractual obligation and also gave the producer the right to suspend his performance obligation during the period that the performer's illness prevented her from acting. The critical issue here is whether the producer also had the right to cancel the contract. Circumstances that would give the producer the right to cancel include the degree of uncertainty relating to the nature and duration of the performer's illness and the extent to which a delay in making substitute arrangements would have prevented the producer from continuing the tour. A history of having been ill for a short time would not justify the producer's cancellation of the contract. In fact, the short period of time that the performer had been incapacitated a year earlier from the same illness would weaken the producer's defense.

## Question 12

An art collector paid a gallery $1,000 to purchase a framed drawing from the gallery's collection. The price included shipping by the gallery to the collector's home. The gallery's owner used inadequate materials to wrap the drawing. The frame broke during shipment and scratched the drawing, reducing the drawing's value to $300. The collector complained to the gallery owner, who told the collector to take the drawing to a specific art restorer to have the drawing repaired. The collector paid the restorer $400 to repair the drawing, but not all of the scratches could be fixed. The drawing, after being repaired, was worth $700. The gallery owner subsequently refused to pay either for the repairs or for the damage to the drawing.

In an action by the collector against the gallery owner for damages, which of the following awards is most likely?

(A) Nothing.

**Incorrect.** The gallery's use of inadequate materials to wrap the drawing constituted a breach of warranty. Therefore, the collector is entitled to be placed in the position he would have been in but for the gallery's breach. Awarding the collector nothing would violate the expectation damages principle. Under UCC § 2-714(2), the generally applicable standard for measuring the collector's resulting damages would be the difference between the value of the drawing as accepted and the value of the drawing if it had been as warranted. Repair costs often are used to determine this difference in value, but when repairs fail to restore the goods to their value as warranted, an adjustment is required. The collector is entitled to recover the repair costs ($400) plus the difference between the value of the drawing if it had been as warranted and its value after the repairs ($1,000 − $700 = $300). Accordingly, the collector should recover $700.

(B) $300.

**Incorrect.** The gallery's use of inadequate materials to wrap the drawing constituted a breach of warranty. Therefore, the collector is entitled to be placed in the position he would have been in but for the gallery's breach. Awarding the collector $300 would violate the expectation damages principle. Under UCC § 2-714(2), the generally applicable standard for measuring the collector's resulting damages would be the difference between the value of the drawing as accepted and the value of the drawing if it had been as warranted. Repair costs often are used to determine this difference in value, but when repairs fail to restore the goods to their value as warranted, an adjustment is required. The collector is entitled to recover the repair costs ($400) plus the difference between the value of the drawing if it had been as warranted and its value after the repairs ($1,000 − $700 = $300). Accordingly, the collector should recover $700.

**(C) $400.**
**Incorrect.** The gallery's use of inadequate materials to wrap the drawing constituted a breach of warranty. Therefore, the collector is entitled to be placed in the position he would have been in but for the gallery's breach. Awarding the collector $400 would violate the expectation damages principle. Under UCC § 2-714(2), the generally applicable standard for measuring the collector's resulting damages would be the difference between the value of the drawing as accepted and the value of the drawing if it had been as warranted. Repair costs often are used to determine this difference in value, but when repairs fail to restore the goods to their value as warranted, an adjustment is required. The collector is entitled to recover the repair costs ($400) plus the difference between the value of the drawing if it had been as warranted and its value after the repairs ($1,000 − $700 = $300). Accordingly, the collector should recover $700.

**(D) $700.**
**Correct.** The gallery's use of inadequate materials to wrap the drawing constituted a breach of warranty. Therefore, the collector is entitled to be placed in the position he would have been in but for the gallery's breach. Under UCC § 2-714(2), the generally applicable standard for measuring the collector's resulting damages would be the difference between the value of the drawing as accepted and the value of the drawing if it had been as warranted. Repair costs often are used to determine this difference in value, but when repairs fail to restore the goods to their value as warranted, a further adjustment is required. Here the repairs failed to restore the drawing to its value as warranted. Therefore, the collector is entitled to recover the repair costs ($400) plus the difference between the value of the drawing if it had been as warranted

and its value after the repairs ($1,000 − $700 = $300). Accordingly, the collector should recover $700.

## Question 13

A businesswoman sold her business to a company for $25 million in cash pursuant to a written contract that was signed by both parties. Under the contract, the company agreed to employ the businesswoman for two years as a vice president at a salary of $150,000 per year. After six months, the company, without cause, fired the businesswoman.

Which of the following statements best describes the businesswoman's rights after being fired?

**(A)** She can recover the promised salary for the remainder of the two years if she remains ready to work.
**Incorrect.** The company's unjustified termination of the businesswoman's employment constituted a breach of contract entitling the businesswoman to recover monetary damages. However, a wrongfully discharged employee is expected to mitigate damages by making reasonable efforts to seek comparable employment. In this case, to avoid a reduction in her damages, the businesswoman is required to do more than remain ready to work. Her recovery will be reduced by the compensation she earned or could have earned if she had made reasonable efforts to secure comparable employment.

**(B)** She can recover the promised salary for the remainder of the two years if no comparable job is reasonably available and she does not take another job.
**Correct.** The company's unjustified termination of the businesswoman's employment constituted a breach of contract entitling the businesswoman to recover monetary damages. A wrongfully discharged employee is expected to mitigate damages by making reasonable efforts to seek comparable employment. However, if no comparable employment is reasonably available and the businesswoman does not take another job, the businesswoman is entitled to recover the promised salary for the remainder of the two years.

**(C)** She can rescind the contract of sale and get back her business upon tender to the company of $25 million.
**Incorrect.** The company's unjustified termination of the businesswoman's employment was probably not

a material breach of contract. It represented only a small part of a large contract and can easily be remedied by an award of damages. But even if the breach was material, a court would likely employ the concept of divisibility to preclude the businesswoman from rescinding the contract of sale. As stated in Restatement (Second) of Contracts § 240, a contract is divisible where "the performances to be exchanged under an exchange of promises can be apportioned into corresponding pairs of part performances so that the parts of each pair are properly regarded as agreed equivalents." Here, the agreed equivalents would be the sale of the business and the corresponding $25 million purchase price, and the businesswoman's promise to work for the company and the corresponding yearly salary of $150,000. Applying this concept, the businesswoman would be able to recover damages for the company's breach of its promise to employ her, but she would not be permitted to rescind the contract of sale.

**(D)** She can get specific performance of her right to serve as a vice president of the company for two years.

**Incorrect.** The company's unjustified termination of the businesswoman's employment constituted a breach of contract entitling the businesswoman to recover monetary damages. The general rule is that employers cannot obtain specific performance requiring an employee who has breached a personal services contract to work for the employer. It is also true generally that courts refuse to grant specific performance of an employment contract against a breaching employer. Consequently, the businesswoman's recovery will consist of the unpaid salary under the contract, reduced by the compensation she earned or could have earned if she had made reasonable efforts to secure comparable employment.

## Question 14

On June 15, a teacher accepted a contract for a one-year position teaching math at a public high school at a salary of $50,000, starting in September. On June 22, the school informed the teacher that, due to a change in its planned math curriculum, it no longer needed a full-time math teacher. The school offered instead to employ the teacher as a part-time academic counselor at a salary of $20,000, starting in September. The teacher refused the school's offer. On June 29, the teacher was offered a one-year position to teach math at a

nearby private academy for $47,000, starting in September. The teacher, however, decided to spend the year completing work on a graduate degree in mathematics and declined the academy's offer.

If the teacher sues the school for breach of contract, what is her most likely recovery?

**(A)** $50,000, the full contract amount.
**Incorrect.** The teacher is entitled to recover damages that will place her in the position she would have been in but for the school's breach. However, an injured party is expected to make reasonable efforts to mitigate the loss resulting from the other party's breach. In the case of a wrongfully discharged employee, the employee is expected to accept an offer of comparable employment. If the employee fails or refuses to do so, the employee's recovery is reduced by the amount of the loss that the employee could have avoided by accepting comparable employment. Here, the teacher's damages of $50,000 should be reduced by the $47,000 she would have earned if she had accepted the comparable teaching position at the private academy. Therefore, the teacher is entitled to recover $3,000 from the school.

**(B)** $30,000, the full contract amount less the amount the teacher could have earned in the counselor position offered by the school.
**Incorrect.** The teacher is entitled to recover damages that will place her in the position she would have been in but for the school's breach. However, an injured party is expected to make reasonable efforts to mitigate the loss resulting from the other party's breach. In the case of a wrongfully discharged employee, the employee is expected to accept an offer of comparable employment. If the employee fails or refuses to do so, the employee's recovery is reduced by the amount of the loss that the employee could have avoided by accepting comparable employment. Because it is unlikely that a court would consider the counseling position to be comparable employment, the teacher's damages should not be reduced by the $20,000 she would have earned if she had accepted that position. On the other hand, her damages of $50,000 should be reduced by the $47,000 she would have earned if she had accepted the comparable teaching position at the private academy. Therefore, the teacher is entitled to recover $3,000 from the school.

**(C)** $3,000, the full contract amount less the amount the teacher could have earned in the teaching position at the academy.

**Correct.** The teacher is entitled to recover damages that will place her in the position she would have been in but for the school's breach. However, an injured party is expected to make reasonable efforts to mitigate the loss resulting from the other party's breach. In the case of a wrongfully discharged employee, the employee is expected to accept an offer of comparable employment. If the employee fails or refuses to do so, the employee's recovery is reduced by the amount of the loss that the employee could have avoided by accepting comparable employment. Here, the teacher's damages of $50,000 should be reduced by the $47,000 she would have earned if she had accepted the comparable teaching position at the private academy. Therefore, the teacher is entitled to recover $3,000 from the school.

**(D)** Nothing, because the school notified the teacher of its decision before the teacher had acted in substantial reliance on the contract.

**Incorrect.** The teacher and the school entered into an enforceable contract, and the school's unjustified nonperformance constituted a breach of contract. The teacher is therefore entitled to recover damages that will place her in the position she would have been in but for the breach and need not show reliance in order to recover. However, while she is entitled to damages from the breach, an injured party is expected to make reasonable efforts to mitigate the loss resulting from the other party's breach. In the case of a wrongfully discharged employee, the employee is expected to accept an offer of comparable employment. If the employee fails or refuses to do so, the employee's recovery is reduced by the amount of the loss that the employee could have avoided by accepting comparable employment. Here, the teacher's damages of $50,000 should be reduced by the $47,000 she would have earned if she had accepted the comparable teaching position at the private academy. Therefore, the teacher is entitled to recover $3,000 from the school.

### Question 15

A produce distributor contracted to provide a grocer with eight crates of lettuce at the distributor's listed price. The distributor's shipping clerk mistakenly shipped only seven crates to the grocer. The grocer accepted delivery of the seven crates but immediately notified the distributor that the delivery did not conform to the contract. The distributor's listed price for seven crates of lettuce was 7/8 of its listed price for eight crates. The distributor shipped no more lettuce to the grocer, and the grocer has not yet paid for any of the lettuce.

How much, if anything, is the distributor entitled to collect from the grocer?

**(A)** Nothing, because the tender of all eight crates was a condition precedent to the grocer's duty to pay.

**Incorrect.** The distributor's nonconforming shipment constituted both an acceptance of the grocer's offer to purchase and a breach of the parties' contract. With respect to a nonconforming tender, UCC § 2-601 allows a buyer to accept the whole, reject the whole, or partially accept or reject commercial units. A buyer who accepts a tender of goods, whether conforming or nonconforming, becomes obligated to pay the seller the contract price of the goods. Accordingly, the grocer's acceptance of the nonconforming shipment obligated it to pay the distributor's listed price for the seven crates, reduced by any damages for losses resulting from the nonconforming shipment.

**(B)** The reasonable value of the seven crates of lettuce, minus the grocer's damages, if any, for the distributor's failure to deliver the full order.

**Incorrect.** The distributor's nonconforming shipment constituted both an acceptance of the grocer's offer to purchase and a breach of the parties' contract. With respect to a nonconforming tender, UCC § 2-601 allows a buyer to accept the whole, reject the whole, or partially accept or reject commercial units. A buyer who accepts a tender of goods, whether conforming or nonconforming, becomes obligated to pay the seller the contract price of the goods. Accordingly, the grocer's acceptance of the nonconforming shipment obligated it to pay the distributor's listed price for, rather than the reasonable value of, the seven crates of lettuce. The price paid by the grocer will be reduced by any damages for losses resulting from the nonconforming shipment.

**(C)** The listed price for the seven crates of lettuce, minus the grocer's damages, if any, for the distributor's failure to deliver the full order.

**Correct.** The distributor's nonconforming shipment constituted both an acceptance of the grocer's offer to purchase and a breach of the parties' contract. With respect to a nonconforming tender, UCC § 2-601 allows a buyer to accept the whole, reject the whole, or partially accept or reject commercial units. A buyer who accepts a tender of goods, whether conforming or nonconforming, becomes obligated to pay the seller the contract price of the goods. Accordingly, the grocer's acceptance of the nonconforming shipment obligated it to pay the distributor's listed price for the seven crates, reduced by any damages for losses resulting from the nonconforming shipment.

(D) The listed price for the seven crates of lettuce.
**Incorrect.** The distributor's nonconforming shipment constituted both an acceptance of the grocer's offer to purchase and a breach of the parties' contract. With respect to a nonconforming tender, UCC § 2-601 allows a buyer to accept the whole, reject the whole, or partially accept or reject commercial units. A buyer who accepts a tender of goods, whether conforming or nonconforming, becomes obligated to pay the seller the contract price of the goods. Accordingly, the grocer's acceptance of the nonconforming shipment obligated it to pay the distributor's listed price for the seven crates. However, that price should be reduced by any damages for losses resulting from the nonconforming shipment.

## Question 16

A seller borrowed $5,000 from a bank. Soon thereafter the seller filed for bankruptcy, having paid nothing on his debt to the bank.

Five years after the debt had been discharged in bankruptcy, the seller contracted to sell certain goods to a buyer for $5,000. The contract provided that the buyer would pay the $5,000 to the bank. The only debt that the seller ever owed the bank is the $5,000 debt that was discharged in bankruptcy. The seller delivered the goods to the buyer, who accepted them.

If the bank becomes aware of the contract between the seller and the buyer, and the buyer refuses to pay anything to the bank, is the bank likely to succeed in an action against the buyer for $5,000?

(A) No, because the buyer's promise to pay the bank was not supported by consideration.
**Incorrect.** The buyer and the seller entered into a bargained-for exchange for the sale and purchase of goods. Thus their agreement was supported by consideration. Moreover, a promisee (the seller) can intend that a third party be the beneficiary of the performance the promisee expects to receive from a promisor (the

buyer). Because the parties' agreement provided that the buyer would pay to the bank the $5,000 that the buyer had promised to pay for the goods, the bank was an intended beneficiary of the enforceable agreement between the seller and the buyer, and the buyer is obligated to pay the bank.

(B) No, because the seller's debt was discharged in bankruptcy.
**Incorrect.** The bank was an intended beneficiary of the contract between the buyer and the seller, and the fact of discharge is irrelevant. The seller and the buyer entered into a bargained-for exchange for the sale and purchase of goods. Because their agreement provided that the buyer would pay to the bank the $5,000 that the buyer had promised to pay for the goods, the bank was an intended beneficiary of the enforceable agreement between the seller and the buyer, and the buyer is obligated to pay the bank.

(C) Yes, because the bank was an intended beneficiary of the contract between the buyer and the seller.
**Correct.** The buyer and the seller entered into a bargained-for exchange for the sale and purchase of goods. Because their agreement provided that the buyer would pay to the bank the $5,000 that the buyer had promised to pay for the goods, the bank was an intended beneficiary of the enforceable agreement between the seller and the buyer, and the buyer is obligated to pay the bank.

(D) Yes, because no consideration is required to support a promise to pay a debt that has been discharged in bankruptcy.
**Incorrect.** It is true that a promise by a debtor to pay a debt that has been discharged in bankruptcy requires no consideration to be enforceable. In this case, however, the discharge of the seller's debt is irrelevant. Here, the seller and the buyer entered into a bargained-for exchange for the sale and purchase of goods. Because their agreement provided that the buyer would pay to the bank the $5,000 that the buyer had promised to pay for the goods, the bank was an intended beneficiary of the enforceable agreement between the seller and the buyer, and the buyer is obligated to pay the bank.

## Question 17

A builder borrowed $10,000 from a lender to finance a small construction job under a contract with a homeowner. The builder gave the lender a writing that stated, "Any money I receive from the homeowner will be paid immediately to the lender, regardless of any demands from other creditors." The builder died after completing the job but before the homeowner paid. The lender demanded that the homeowner pay the $10,000 due to the builder directly to the lender. The homeowner refused, saying that he would pay directly to the builder's estate everything that he owed the builder.

Is the lender likely to succeed in an action against the homeowner for $10,000?

**(A)** No, because the builder's death terminated the lender's right to receive payment directly from the homeowner.

**Incorrect.** The builder never gave the lender a valid assignment. An assignment arises when the holder of a right, an obligee, manifests the intent to make a present transfer of that right to another, the assignee. An assignment is to be distinguished from a promise to do something in the future, such as the payment of money. Here, the writing in which the builder promised to pay the lender the $10,000 he received from the homeowner did not transfer to the lender the right to receive payment directly from the homeowner, and thus it did not create an assignment.

**(B)** No, because the writing the builder gave to the lender did not transfer to the lender the right to receive payment from the homeowner.

**Correct.** An assignment arises when the holder of a right, an obligee, manifests the intent to make a present transfer of that right to another, the assignee. Upon an assignment, the assignor's rights are extinguished and transferred to the assignee. An assignment is to be distinguished from a promise to do something in the future, such as the payment of money. Here, the writing in which the builder promised to pay the lender the $10,000 he received from the homeowner did not transfer to the

lender the right to receive payment directly from the homeowner, and thus it did not create an assignment.

**(C)** Yes, because the builder had manifested an intent that the homeowner pay the $10,000 directly to the lender.

**Incorrect.** It may have been the builder's subjective intent to have the homeowner pay the $10,000 directly to the lender if the builder died, but more was required in order for the lender to have the right to receive that direct payment. The dispositive issue here is whether the builder gave the lender a valid assignment. An assignment arises when the holder of a right, an obligee, manifests the intent to make a present transfer of that right to another, the assignee. An assignment is to be distinguished from a promise to do something in the future, such as the payment of money. Here, the writing in which the builder promised to pay to the lender the $10,000 he received from the homeowner did not transfer to the lender the right to receive payment directly from the homeowner, and thus it did not create an assignment.

**(D)** Yes, because the lender is an intended beneficiary of the builder-homeowner contract.

**Incorrect.** Because any rights that may have been granted to the lender were not created by the contract between the builder and the homeowner, the lender did not acquire third-party beneficiary status. The dispositive issue here is whether the builder gave the lender a valid assignment. An assignment arises when the holder of a right, an obligee, manifests the intent to make a present transfer of that right to another, the assignee. An assignment is to be distinguished from a promise to do something in the future, such as the payment of money. Here, the writing in which the builder promised to pay to the lender the $10,000 he received from the homeowner did not transfer to the lender the right to receive payment directly from the homeowner, and thus it did not create an assignment.

## IV. Chapter 12 CRIMINAL LAW AND PROCEDURE

### ESSAY SCORE SHEET

| Stated | Implied | |
|---|---|---|
| | | **Point One (35%) Right to Counsel for Unrelated Charges** |
| ____ | ____ | **Conclusion:** The suspect's Sixth Amendment right to counsel was not violated because the right does not attach on new charges until formal adversarial judicial proceedings have commenced on those charges. |
| ____ | ____ | **Rule:** The Sixth Amendment, as applied to the states through the Fourteenth Amendment, provides that "[i]n all criminal prosecutions, the accused shall enjoy the right . . . to have the Assistance of Counsel for his defense." |
| ____ | ____ | The right to counsel does not attach with respect to particular charges until formal adversarial judicial proceedings have commenced—whether by way of formal charge, preliminary hearing, indictment, information, or arraignment (or in some states, arrest warrant). |
| ____ | ____ | Once a suspect's Sixth Amendment right to counsel has attached, any attempts to "deliberately elicit" statements from him in the absence of his attorney violate the Sixth Amendment. |
| ____ | ____ | The Sixth Amendment right to counsel is charge- or offense-specific. Representation by counsel in one prosecution does not, in itself, guarantee counsel for uncharged offenses. |
| ____ | ____ | **Application:** Here, |
| ____ | ____ | The suspect's Sixth Amendment right to counsel had attached only for the pending aggravated assault charge. |
| ____ | ____ | The suspect's right to counsel for the aggravated assault case did not guarantee counsel for the five unrelated and uncharged burglaries that were the subject of the detective's interrogation. |
| ____ | ____ | **Conclusion:** Thus, because formal adversarial judicial proceedings against the suspect for the uncharged burglaries had not begun, he had no Sixth Amendment right to counsel. |
| ____ | ____ | Finally, the detective's failure to inform the suspect of the lawyer's presence and demands to speak with him does not implicate the suspect's Sixth Amendment right to counsel, which had not yet attached. |
| | | **Point Two (30%) Invocation of Right to Counsel** |
| ____ | ____ | **Conclusion:** The suspect did not effectively invoke his right to counsel under Miranda because his statement was not unambiguous. |
| ____ | ____ | **Rule:** A suspect subject to custodial interrogation has a right to consult with counsel and to have an attorney present during questioning. |
| ____ | ____ | When a suspect invokes his right to counsel during an interrogation, law enforcement must immediately cease all questioning. |
| ____ | ____ | Custodial interrogation cannot be reinitiated unless and until the suspect has been re-advised of his Miranda rights, has provided a knowing and voluntary waiver, *and* (1) counsel is present and (2) the suspect himself initiated further communication with the police, (3) (if the suspect was released from custody after the initial interrogation) at least 14 days have passed. |

*continued on next page*

| Stated | Implied | |
|---|---|---|
| _____ | _____ | To invoke the right to counsel, a suspect's request must be "unambiguous." |
| _____ | _____ | This means that the suspect must articulate the desire for counsel sufficiently clearly that a reasonable officer would understand the statement to be a request for counsel. |
| _____ | _____ | If the request is ambiguous, the police are not required to stop the interrogation. |
| _____ | _____ | **Application:** Here, |
| _____ | _____ | The suspect's statement, "I think I want my lawyer here before I talk to you," was not an unambiguous request for counsel. |
| _____ | _____ | The most reasonable interpretation of this statement is that the suspect *might* be invoking his right to counsel. |
| _____ | _____ | **Conclusion:** Under these circumstances, the detective was not required to cease the custodial interrogation of the suspect. |
| _____ | _____ | Nor was the detective required to clarify or ask follow-up questions to determine whether the suspect in fact wanted an attorney. |
| | | **Point Three (35%) Waiver of Right to Counsel** |
| _____ | _____ | **Conclusion:** The suspect's waiver of his Miranda rights was knowing, intelligent, and voluntary despite the fact that he was never told of the lawyer's presence in the jail or of the lawyer's demands. |
| _____ | _____ | **Rule:** A valid waiver of Miranda rights must be "voluntary"—i.e., the product of a free or deliberate choice rather than intimidation, coercion, or deception. |
| _____ | _____ | In addition, the waiver must be knowing and intelligent. |
| _____ | _____ | That is, it "must have been made with a full awareness of both the nature of the right being abandoned and the consequences of the decision to abandon it." |
| _____ | _____ | **Application:** Here, |
| _____ | _____ | The suspect signed a Miranda waiver form after receiving proper warnings. |
| _____ | _____ | There is no evidence "that the police resorted to physical or psychological pressure to elicit the statements." |
| _____ | _____ | The entire interview lasted only 45 minutes. |
| _____ | _____ | **Transition/Issue:** The only issue is whether the suspect knowingly and intelligently waived his Miranda rights despite the fact that the detective did not tell the suspect about the lawyer's presence and her demands. |
| _____ | _____ | **Rule:** "Events occurring outside of the presence of the suspect and entirely unknown to him surely can have no bearing on the capacity to comprehend and knowingly relinquish a constitutional right." |
| _____ | _____ | If the suspect "knew that he could stand mute and request a lawyer, and . . . was aware of the State's intention to use his statements to secure a conviction," then the waiver is valid regardless of the information withheld. |
| _____ | _____ | **Application:** Here, |
| _____ | _____ | The suspect was correctly informed of his rights. His comments demonstrate that he understood that he could have a lawyer present if he desired (*i.e.*, wondering whether he should call his attorney) and that he understood that there might be consequences to |

*continued on next page*

| Stated | Implied | |
|--------|---------|---|
| | | speaking with the detective ("I probably should keep my mouth shut, but I'm willing to talk to you for a while."). |
| _____ | _____ | His comment, "[L]et's not waste any time waiting for someone to call my attorney and having her drive here," along with his signature on the Miranda waiver form, show that his waiver was valid under the constitutional standard. |
| _____ | _____ | That the detective did not tell the suspect about the lawyer's presence and demands has no bearing on the validity of the suspect's waiver because "such conduct is only relevant to the constitutional validity of a waiver if it deprives a defendant of knowledge essential to his ability to understand the nature of his rights and the consequences of abandoning them." |
| _____ | _____ | The Supreme Court has specifically declined to adopt a rule requiring that law enforcement tell a suspect of an attorney's efforts to contact him. |
| | | [NOTE: An examinee might also recognize that this general rule is further supported by the Supreme Court's decision in *Florida v. Powell*, 559 U.S. 50 (2010), approving state Miranda warnings that do not explicitly warn suspects that they have a right to have counsel present during custodial interrogation.] |

# MBE PRACTICE ANALYSIS[4]

## Question 1

A state statute provides: "The sale of an alcoholic beverage to any person under the age of 21 is a misdemeanor."

A woman who was 20 years old, but who looked older and who had a very convincing fake driver's license indicating that she was 24, entered a convenience store, picked up a six-pack of beer, and placed the beer on the counter. The store clerk, after examining the driver's license, rang up the purchase.

Both the clerk and the store owner have been charged with violating the state statute.

If the court finds both the clerk and the store owner guilty, what standard of liability must the court have interpreted the statute to impose?

(A) Strict liability only.
**Incorrect.** The court must have applied strict liability to convict the clerk (who did not act knowingly, and arguably not even negligently), but must have applied vicarious liability to convict the store owner for the sale by the clerk.

(B) Vicarious liability only.
**Incorrect.** The court must have applied vicarious liability to convict the store owner for the sale by the clerk, but must have applied strict liability to convict the clerk (who did not act knowingly, and arguably not even negligently).

(C) Both strict and vicarious liability.
**Correct.** The court must have applied strict liability to convict the clerk (who did not act knowingly, and arguably not even negligently) and vicarious liability to convict the store owner for the sale by the clerk.

(D) Either strict or vicarious liability.
**Incorrect.** The court must have applied strict liability to convict the clerk (who did not act knowingly, and arguably not even negligently) and vicarious liability to convict the store owner for the sale by the clerk.

## Question 2

A woman charged with murder has entered a plea of not guilty by reason of insanity. At her trial, in which the questions of guilt and sanity are being tried together, the evidence shows that the woman stalked the victim for several hours before following him to an isolated hiking trail where she shot and killed him. Expert witnesses for the defense have testified that the woman knew that killing was illegal and wrong, but that she suffered from a serious mental illness that left her in the grip of a powerful and irresistible compulsion to kill the victim.

If the jury believes the testimony of the defense experts, under what circumstances could the jury properly acquit the woman of murder?

(A) Only if the jurisdiction follows the M'Naghten test for insanity.
**Incorrect.** The jury could not find the woman to be legally insane under the M'Naghten test, which requires either that she did not know the nature and quality of the act she was committing or that she did not know the difference between right and wrong.

(B) Only if the jurisdiction follows the ALI Model Penal Code test for insanity.
**Correct.** The jury could find the woman to be legally insane under the ALI Model Penal Code test, because she could not conform her conduct to the requirements of the law.

(C) If the jurisdiction follows either the M'Naghten or the ALI Model Penal Code test for insanity.
**Incorrect.** The jury could not find the woman to be legally insane under the M'Naghten test, which requires either that she did not know the nature and quality of the act she was committing or that she did not know the difference between right and wrong. The jury could find the woman to be legally insane under the ALI Model Penal Code test, because she could not conform her conduct to the requirements of the law.

(D) Even if the jurisdiction has abolished the insanity defense.
**Incorrect.** The woman committed all the elements of murder and can be excused from responsibility only if she meets a recognized defense of insanity.

## Question 3

A valid warrant was issued for a woman's arrest. The police learned that a person with the woman's name and physical description lived at a particular address. When police officers went to that address, the house appeared to be unoccupied: the windows and doors were boarded up with plywood, and the

---

4. *Id.*

lawn had not been mowed for a long time. A neighbor confirmed that the house belonged to the woman but said that the woman had not been there for several months.

The officers knocked repeatedly on the front door and shouted, "Police! Open up!" Receiving no response, they tore the plywood off the door, smashed through the door with a sledgehammer, and entered the house. They found no one inside, but they did find an illegal sawed-off shotgun. Upon her return to the house a few weeks later, the woman was charged with unlawful possession of the shotgun.

The woman has moved to suppress the use of the shotgun as evidence at her trial. Should the court grant the motion?

(A) No, because the officers acted in good faith under the authority of a valid warrant.

**Incorrect.** Under the Fourth Amendment, the arrest warrant would have authorized forcible entry only if the officers had reason to believe that the woman was at home at the time of the entry. Here, the officers knew that the woman was not at home.

(B) No, because the officers did not violate any legitimate expectation of privacy in the house since the woman had abandoned it.

**Incorrect.** The facts here are legally insufficient to suggest that the woman had abandoned any reasonable expectation of privacy in the house.

(C) Yes, because the officers entered the house by means of excessive force.

**Incorrect.** Under the Fourth Amendment, the arrest warrant would have authorized forcible entry if the officers had reason to believe that the woman was at home at the time of the entry. Here, however, the officers knew that the woman was not at home.

(D) Yes, because the officers had no reason to believe that the woman was in the house.

**Correct.** Under the Fourth Amendment, the arrest warrant would have authorized forcible entry only if the officers had reason to believe that the woman was at home at the time of the entry. Here, the officers knew that the woman was not at home.

## Question 4

A woman was subpoenaed to appear before a grand jury. When she arrived, she was taken into the grand jury room to be questioned. She answered preliminary questions about her name and address. She was then asked where she had been at a certain time on a specified night when a murder had occurred. Before answering the question, the woman said that she wanted to consult her attorney, who was waiting outside the grand jury room, and she was allowed to do so. When she returned to the grand jury room, she stated that she refused to answer the question because the answer might incriminate her.

The prosecutor believes that the woman's nephew committed the murder. The nephew has said that he was with the woman at the time of the murder, and the prosecutor believes that this alibi is false. The prosecutor does not believe that the woman is guilty of the murder, either as a principal or as an accomplice, although he does believe that the woman may be guilty of other crimes. The prosecutor wants to compel the woman to answer the question by whatever means will result in the least harm to the prosecution's case.

Which of the following steps should the prosecutor take to get the woman to answer the question?

(A) Request the grand jury to order the woman to answer the question.

**Incorrect.** The woman cannot be compelled to provide potentially incriminating testimony unless she is granted use and derivative-use immunity.

(B) Ask the woman's attorney to explain to the woman that the rules of evidence do not apply in grand jury proceedings, and to advise her that she cannot refuse to testify.

**Incorrect.** While the rules of evidence do not apply before grand juries, a witness cannot be compelled to provide potentially incriminating testimony unless the witness is granted use and derivative-use immunity.

(C) Prepare the documents necessary to grant the woman immunity from any future use against her of her grand jury testimony or any evidence derived from it.

**Correct.** A witness cannot be compelled to provide potentially incriminating testimony unless the witness is granted use and derivative-use immunity.

(D) Prepare the documents necessary to grant the woman immunity from any future prosecution for any crime she might disclose in the course of her testimony.

**Incorrect.** A witness cannot be compelled to provide potentially incriminating testimony unless the witness is granted use and derivative-use immunity, but the witness need not be granted transactional immunity.

## Question 5

A defendant was validly arrested for the murder of a store clerk and was taken to a police station where he was given Miranda warnings. When an interrogator asked the defendant, "Do you understand your Miranda rights, and are you willing to give up those rights and talk to us?" the defendant replied, "Yes." When asked, "Did you kill the clerk?" the defendant replied, "No." When asked, "Where were you on the day the clerk was killed?" the defendant replied, "Maybe I should talk to a lawyer." The interrogator asked, "Are you sure?" and the defendant replied, "I'm not sure." The interrogator then asked, "Why would you want to talk with a lawyer?" and the defendant replied, "Because I killed the clerk. It was an accident, and I think I need a lawyer to defend me." At that point all interrogation ceased. Later, the defendant was formally charged with murdering the clerk.

The defendant has moved to suppress evidence of his statement "I killed the clerk" on the ground that this statement was elicited in violation of his Miranda rights.

Should the defendant's motion be granted?

(A) No, because although the defendant effectively asserted the right to counsel, the question "Why would you want to talk with a lawyer?" did not constitute custodial interrogation.
**Incorrect.** The defendant did not effectively assert his right to counsel, because such an assertion must be unambiguous. The defendant's statement "Maybe I should talk to a lawyer" is not an unambiguous request for counsel.

(B) No, because the defendant did not effectively assert the right to counsel, and his conduct prior to making the statement constituted a valid waiver of his Miranda rights.
**Correct.** The defendant did not effectively assert his right to counsel, because such an assertion must be unambiguous. The defendant's statement "Maybe I should talk to a lawyer" is not an unambiguous request for counsel. In addition, the defendant had unequivocally waived his Miranda rights prior to making this statement.

(C) Yes, because although the defendant did not effectively assert the right to counsel, his conduct prior to making the statement did not constitute a valid waiver of his Miranda rights.
**Incorrect.** The defendant unequivocally waived his Miranda rights, and his statement "Maybe I should talk to a lawyer" did not affect the validity of that waiver.

(D) Yes, because the defendant effectively asserted the right to counsel, and the question "Why would you want to talk with a lawyer?" constituted custodial interrogation.
**Incorrect.** The defendant did not effectively assert his right to counsel, because such an assertion must be unambiguous. The defendant's statement "Maybe I should talk to a lawyer" is not an unambiguous request for counsel.

## Question 6

Two defendants were being tried together in federal court for bank robbery. The prosecutor sought to introduce testimony from the first defendant's prison cellmate. The cellmate would testify that the first defendant had admitted to the cellmate that he and the second defendant had robbed the bank. The prosecutor asked the court to instruct the jury that the cellmate's testimony could be considered only against the first defendant.

Can the cellmate's testimony be admitted in a joint trial over the second defendant's objection?

(A) No, because the first defendant made the statement without Miranda warnings.
**Incorrect.** Miranda warnings were not required, because the first defendant was not compelled by a known law enforcement agent to make the statement, and in any event the second defendant could not assert Miranda rights belonging to the first defendant.

(B) No, because the limiting instruction cannot ensure that the jury will not consider the testimony in its deliberations regarding the second defendant.
**Correct.** The limiting instruction is constitutionally insufficient to avoid the risk that the jury will consider the incriminating statement against the second defendant, who has no opportunity at trial to confront the first defendant.

(C) Yes, because the first defendant's statement was a declaration against penal interest.

**Incorrect.** The first defendant's statement incriminating the second defendant could not, under the Sixth Amendment confrontation clause, be considered against the second defendant on a theory that it constitutes a declaration against penal interest.

(D) Yes, because the limiting instruction sufficiently protects the second defendant.

**Incorrect.** The limiting instruction is constitutionally insufficient to avoid the risk that the jury will consider the incriminating statement against the second defendant, who has no opportunity at trial to confront the first defendant.

## Question 7

A prosecutor presented to a federal grand jury the testimony of a witness in order to secure a defendant's indictment for theft of government property. The prosecutor did not disclose to the grand jury that the witness had been convicted four years earlier of perjury. The grand jury returned an indictment, and the defendant pleaded not guilty.

Shortly thereafter, the prosecutor took the case to trial, calling the witness to testify before the jury. The prosecutor did not disclose the witness's prior perjury conviction until the defense was preparing to rest. Defense counsel immediately moved for a mistrial, which the court denied. Instead, the court allowed the defense to recall the witness for the purpose of impeaching him with this conviction, but the witness could not be located. The court then allowed the defense to introduce documentary evidence of the witness's criminal record to the jury before resting its case. The jury convicted the defendant.

The defendant has moved for a new trial, arguing that the prosecutor's failure to disclose the witness's prior conviction in a timely manner violated the defendant's right to due process of law.

If the court grants the defendant's motion, what will be the most likely reason?

(A) The defendant was unable to cross-examine the witness about the conviction.

**Incorrect.** The court did not limit the defendant's right to cross-examine the witness. Rather, the constitutional violation, if any, was the prosecutor's untimely disclosure of impeachment information that would have created a reasonable probability of a different outcome had it been disclosed earlier.

(B) The prosecutor failed to inform the grand jury of the witness's conviction.

**Incorrect.** The prosecutor is not required to present a grand jury with evidence favorable to a defendant. Rather, the constitutional violation, if any, was the prosecutor's untimely disclosure of impeachment information that would have created a reasonable probability of a different outcome had it been disclosed earlier.

(C) The court found it reasonably probable that the defendant would have been acquitted had the defense had timely access to the information about the witness's conviction.

**Correct.** The untimely disclosure of evidence favorable to the defense (including impeachment information) violates the Constitution if the evidence would have created a reasonable probability of a different outcome had it been disclosed earlier.

(D) The court found that the prosecutor had deliberately delayed disclosing the witness's conviction to obtain a strategic advantage.

**Incorrect.** The prosecutor's motive is not an element of a constitutional claim involving untimely disclosure of evidence favorable to the defense (including impeachment information). Rather, such untimely disclosure would violate the Constitution only if the evidence would have created a reasonable probability of a different outcome had it been disclosed earlier.

## Question 8

A state statute divides murder into degrees and defines murder in the first degree as murder committed willfully with premeditation and deliberation. The statute defines murder in the second degree as all other murder at common law and defines voluntary manslaughter as at common law.

A man hated one of his coworkers. Upon learning that the coworker was at a neighbor's house, the man grabbed his gun and went to the neighbor's house hoping to provoke the coworker into attacking him so that he could then shoot the coworker. After arriving at the house, the man insulted the coworker and bragged that he had had sexual relations with the coworker's wife two weeks earlier. This statement was not true, but it enraged the coworker, who grabbed a knife from the kitchen table and ran toward the man. The man then shot and killed the coworker.

What is the most serious homicide offense of which the man could properly be convicted?

**(A)** Murder in the first degree.

**Correct.** The killing was committed willfully with premeditation and deliberation. The killing cannot be justified as having been in self-defense, because the man was the clear aggressor who intentionally provoked the coworker so that he could shoot and kill him.

**(B)** Murder in the second degree.

**Incorrect.** Murder in the second degree is not the most serious homicide offense of which the man could properly be convicted. The man is guilty of first-degree murder, because he committed the killing willfully with premeditation and deliberation. The killing cannot be justified as having been in self-defense, because the man intentionally provoked the coworker so that he could shoot and kill him.

**(C)** Voluntary manslaughter, because he provoked the coworker.

**Incorrect.** Voluntary manslaughter is not the most serious homicide offense of which the man could properly be convicted, because he was not acting in the heat of passion when he killed the coworker. The man is guilty of first-degree murder, because he committed the killing willfully with premeditation and deliberation, and the killing cannot be justified as having been in self-defense.

**(D)** No form of criminal homicide, because he acted in self-defense.

**Incorrect.** The killing cannot be justified as having been in self-defense, because the man intentionally provoked the coworker so that he could shoot and kill him. The man is guilty of first-degree murder, because he committed the killing willfully with premeditation and deliberation.

## Question 9

A wife decided to kill her husband because she was tired of his infidelity. She managed to obtain some cyanide, a deadly poison. One evening, she poured wine laced with the cyanide into a glass, handed it to her husband, and proposed a loving toast. The husband was so pleased with the toast that he set the glass of wine down on a table, grabbed his wife, and kissed her passionately. After the kiss, the wife changed her mind about killing the husband. She hid the glass of wine behind a lamp on the table, planning to leave it for the maid to clean up. The husband did not drink the wine.

The maid found the glass of wine while cleaning the next day. Rather than throw the wine away, the maid drank it. Shortly thereafter, she fell into a coma and died from cyanide poisoning.

In a common law jurisdiction, of what crime(s), if any, could the wife be found guilty?

**(A)** Attempted murder of the husband and murder or manslaughter of the maid.

**Correct.** As to the husband, the wife intended to murder him and took a substantial step to carry out that murder; the husband would have been killed had he drunk the wine. As to the maid, a trier of fact could view the wife's conduct as depraved-heart recklessness (which would make her guilty of murder) or at the very least as criminal negligence (which would make her guilty of manslaughter).

**(B)** Only attempted murder of the husband.

**Incorrect.** The woman could be found guilty of attempted murder of the husband, because she intended to murder him and took a substantial step to carry out that murder; the husband would have been killed had he drunk the wine. However, the wife could also be found guilty of murder or manslaughter of the maid. As to the maid, a trier of fact could view the wife's conduct as depraved-heart recklessness (which would make her guilty of murder) or at the very least as criminal negligence (which would make her guilty of manslaughter).

**(C)** Only murder or manslaughter of the maid.

**Incorrect.** The wife could be found guilty of murder or manslaughter of the maid, because a trier of fact could view the wife's conduct as depraved-heart recklessness (which would make her guilty of murder) or at the very least as criminal negligence (which would make her guilty of manslaughter). However, the wife could also be found guilty of attempted murder of the husband. As to the husband, she intended to murder him and took a substantial step to carry out that murder; the husband would have been killed had he drunk the wine.

**(D)** No crime.

**Incorrect.** The wife could be found guilty of attempted murder of the husband and murder or manslaughter of the maid. As to the husband, the wife intended to murder him and took a substantial step to carry out that murder; the husband would have been killed had he drunk the wine. As to the maid, a trier of fact could view the wife's conduct as depraved-heart recklessness (which would make her guilty of murder) or at the very least as criminal negligence (which would make her guilty of manslaughter).

## Question 10

In a crowded football stadium, a man saw a wallet fall out of a spectator's purse. The man picked up the wallet and found that it contained $100 in cash. Thinking that he could use the money and seeing no one watching, the man put the wallet in the pocket of his coat. Just then, the spectator approached the man and asked if he had seen a missing wallet. The man said no and went home with the wallet.

Of what crime, if any, is the man guilty?

(A) Embezzlement.

**Incorrect.** The initial taking of the wallet was a trespass, because the man knew that the wallet belonged to the spectator and he intended to convert the wallet to his own use in permanent deprivation of the spectator's right. Accordingly, and because the spectator never entrusted the man with the wallet, the man is guilty of larceny rather than embezzlement.

(B) False pretenses.

**Incorrect.** The initial taking of the wallet was a trespass, because the man knew that the wallet belonged to the spectator and he intended to convert the wallet to his own use in permanent deprivation of the spectator's right. Accordingly, and because the man never obtained title to the wallet, he is guilty of larceny rather than false pretenses.

(C) Larceny.

**Correct.** The initial taking of the wallet was a trespass, because the man knew that the wallet belonged to the spectator and he intended to convert the wallet to his own use in permanent deprivation of the spectator's right. Accordingly, the man is guilty of larceny.

(D) No crime.

**Incorrect.** The initial taking of the wallet was a trespass, because the man knew that the wallet belonged to the spectator and he intended to convert the wallet to his own use in permanent deprivation of the spectator's right. Accordingly, the man is guilty of larceny.

## Question 11

A woman went to an art gallery and falsely represented that she was an agent for a museum and wanted to purchase a painting that was hanging in the gallery. The woman and the gallery owner then agreed on a price for the painting to be paid 10 days later, and the woman took the painting. When the gallery failed to receive the payment when due, the owner called the museum and discovered that the woman did not work there. The owner then notified the police.

When interviewed by the police, the woman admitted making the false representation and acquiring the painting, but she said she believed that the painting had been stolen from her by someone who worked in the gallery.

Is the woman guilty of obtaining property by false pretenses?

(A) No, because she believed that the painting belonged to her.

**Correct.** The crime of false pretenses, like other theft crimes, requires the intent to steal. The woman cannot properly be found guilty of obtaining property by false pretenses, because she made the false statements to obtain property that she subjectively believed belonged to her.

(B) No, because the gallery owner would have sold the painting to anyone who agreed to pay the price.

**Incorrect.** This fact does not excuse the woman for knowingly making false statements to obtain property that she would not otherwise have been able to obtain. The reason the woman cannot properly be found guilty of obtaining property by false pretenses is that she lacked the requisite intent to steal; she made the false statements to obtain property that she subjectively believed belonged to her.

(C) Yes, because even if her representation was not material, she never intended to pay for the painting.

**Incorrect.** In some jurisdictions, a false pretenses conviction can be based on a promise to make payment in the future if the promisor had no present intent to make the future payment. But the promisor must have the intent to steal the property. The woman cannot properly be found guilty of obtaining property by false pretenses, because she lacked the requisite intent to steal; she made the false statements to obtain property that she subjectively believed belonged to her.

(D) Yes, because she knowingly made a false representation on which the gallery owner relied.

**Incorrect.** Even assuming that the woman otherwise could be convicted of false pretenses, false pretenses requires the intent to steal required for other theft crimes. Accordingly, the woman cannot properly be found guilty of obtaining property by false pretenses, because she made the false statements to obtain property that she subjectively believed belonged to her.

## Question 12

A woman broke off her engagement to a man but refused to return the engagement ring the man had given her. One night, the man entered the woman's house after midnight to retrieve the ring. Although the woman was not at home, a neighbor saw the man enter the house and called the police. The man unsuccessfully searched for the ring for 10 minutes. As he was walking out the front door, the police arrived and immediately arrested him.

The man has been charged with burglary in a jurisdiction that follows the common law. Which of the following, if proved, would serve as the man's best defense to the charge?

(A) The man knew that the woman kept a key under the doormat and he used the key to enter the house.
**Incorrect.** This fact does not provide a defense to burglary, because the man still broke into and entered the house without the woman's consent. Instead, the man's subjective belief that he was entitled to the ring (even if that belief was incorrect and unreasonable) negates the intent required for the underlying felony of larceny.

(B) The man incorrectly and unreasonably believed that he was legally entitled to the ring.
**Correct.** The crime of burglary requires that the breaking and entering of the dwelling have been done with the intent to commit an underlying felony (in most cases, larceny). The man's subjective belief that he was entitled to the ring (even if that belief was incorrect and unreasonable) negates the intent required for the underlying felony of larceny.

(C) The man knew that no one was at home when he entered the house.
**Incorrect.** This fact does not provide a defense, because the crime of burglary does not require that the dwelling be occupied at the time of the breaking and entering. Instead, the man's subjective belief that he was entitled to the ring (even if that belief was incorrect and unreasonable) negates the intent required for the underlying felony of larceny.

(D) The man took nothing of value from the house.
**Incorrect.** This fact does not provide a defense, because burglary requires that the person breaking and entering intend to commit a felony, not that the person be successful in committing the felony. Instead, the man's subjective belief that he was entitled to the ring (even if that belief was incorrect and unreasonable) negates the intent required for the underlying felony of larceny.

## Question 13

A woman wanted to kill a business competitor. She contacted a man who she believed was willing to commit murder for hire and offered him $50,000 to kill the competitor. The man agreed to do so and accepted $25,000 as a down payment. Unbeknownst to the woman, the man was an undercover police officer.

In a jurisdiction that has adopted the unilateral theory of conspiracy, is the woman guilty of conspiracy to murder the business competitor?

(A) No, because the man did not intend to kill the competitor.
**Incorrect.** In jurisdictions that recognize unilateral conspiracies, it is enough that one person agree with another person to commit a crime (and in some jurisdictions, that an overt act in furtherance of that agreement be committed). It is no defense to unilateral conspiracy that the other person was feigning agreement or acting in an undercover capacity. Therefore, the man's lack of intent does not make the woman any less guilty.

(B) No, because it would have been impossible for the woman to kill the competitor by this method.
**Incorrect.** In jurisdictions that recognize unilateral conspiracies, it is enough that one person agree with another person to commit a crime (and in some jurisdictions, that an overt act in furtherance of that agreement be committed). It is no defense to unilateral conspiracy that the other person was feigning agreement or acting in an undercover capacity. Therefore, the woman cannot prevail on any impossibility defense.

(C) Yes, because the woman believed that she had an agreement with the man that would bring about the competitor's death.
**Correct.** In jurisdictions that recognize unilateral conspiracies, it is enough that one person agree with

another person to commit a crime (and in some jurisdictions, that an overt act in furtherance of that agreement be committed). It is no defense to unilateral conspiracy that the other person was feigning agreement or acting in an undercover capacity. Here, the woman agreed to commit a crime and she committed an overt act in furtherance of that agreement when she paid the man $25,000. She therefore is guilty of conspiracy in a jurisdiction that recognizes unilateral conspiracies.

(D) Yes, because the woman took a substantial step toward bringing about the competitor's death by paying the man $25,000.
**Incorrect.** The woman is guilty, but not because she took a substantial step, which is a concept relevant under the Model Penal Code to attempt rather than conspiracy. The woman is guilty of conspiracy because in jurisdictions that recognize unilateral conspiracies, it is enough that one person agree with another person to commit a crime (and in some jurisdictions, that an overt act in furtherance of that agreement be committed). It is no defense to unilateral conspiracy that the other person was feigning agreement or acting in an undercover capacity.

## Question 14

A state statute provides as follows: "The maintenance of any ongoing enterprise in the nature of a betting parlor or bookmaking organization is a felony."

A prosecutor has evidence that a woman has been renting an office to a man, that the man has been using the office as a betting parlor within the meaning of the statute, and that the woman is aware of this use.

Which of the following additional pieces of evidence would be most useful to the prosecutor's effort to convict the woman as an accomplice to the man's violation of the statute?

(A) The woman was previously convicted of running a betting parlor herself on the same premises.
**Incorrect.** The woman's prior conviction would not necessarily show that she has a personal stake in the continuing success of the man's criminal venture (and thus an intent to aid in that venture).

(B) The woman charges the man considerably more in rent than she charged the preceding tenant, who used the office for legitimate activities.

**Correct.** Showing that the woman benefits from the gambling would indicate her personal stake in the continuing success of the man's criminal venture (and thus her intent to aid in that venture).

(C) The woman has personally placed bets with the man at the office location.
**Incorrect.** Showing that the woman has placed bets would confirm that she knows that the premises are being used for gambling. However, it would not necessarily show that she has a personal stake in the continuing success of the man's criminal venture (and thus an intent to aid in that venture).

(D) The man has paid the woman the rent in bills that are traceable as the proceeds of gambling activity.
**Incorrect.** The source of the rent payments, assuming that the rent is not above the market price for the premises, would not necessarily show that the woman has a personal stake in the continuing success of the man's criminal venture (and thus an intent to aid in that venture).

## Question 15

After a defendant was indicted on federal bank fraud charges and released on bail, his attorney filed notice of the defendant's intent to offer an insanity defense. The prosecutor then enlisted the help of a forensic psychologist who was willing to participate in an "undercover" mental examination of the defendant. The psychologist contacted the defendant and pretended to represent an executive personnel agency. She told the defendant about an attractive employment opportunity and invited him to a "preliminary screening interview" to determine his qualifications for the job. As part of the purported screening process, the psychologist gave the defendant psychological tests that enabled her to form a reliable opinion about his mental state at the time of the alleged offense.

What is the strongest basis for a defense objection to the psychologist's testimony regarding the defendant's mental state?

(A) The Fourth Amendment prohibition against unreasonable searches and seizures.
**Incorrect.** The Fourth Amendment does not prevent the government from using deception to obtain incriminating admissions.

**(B)** The Fifth Amendment privilege against compelled self-incrimination.

**Incorrect.** The Fifth Amendment privilege protects against compelled self-incrimination, not against the use of deception to obtain a suspect's voluntary admissions.

**(C)** The Sixth Amendment right to the assistance of counsel.

**Correct.** After a defendant is indicted, the right to counsel attaches, and authorities may not use deception to deliberately elicit statements related to the crime from the defendant without the representation of counsel.

**(D)** The federal common law privilege for confidential communications between psychotherapist and patient.

**Incorrect.** While there is such a federal common law privilege for communications intended to be kept confidential for the purpose of obtaining psychiatric services, the facts in this case do not support the privilege.

## Question 16

A defendant is charged with an offense under a statute that provides as follows: "Any person who, while intoxicated, appears in any public place and manifests a drunken condition by obstreperous or indecent conduct is guilty of a misdemeanor."

At trial, the evidence shows that the defendant was intoxicated when police officers burst into his house and arrested him pursuant to a valid warrant. It was a cold night, and the officers hustled the defendant out of his house without giving him time to get his coat. The defendant became angry and obstreperous when the officers refused to let him go back into the house to retrieve his coat. The officers left him handcuffed outside in the street, waiting for a special squad car to arrive. The arrest warrant was later vacated.

Can the defendant properly be convicted of violating the statute?

**(A)** No, because the defendant's claim of mistreatment is valid.

**Incorrect.** The defendant cannot properly be convicted, regardless of whether his claim is valid, because of the general legal rule that a person is not guilty of a crime unless the act constituting the crime was committed voluntarily. This rule precludes the defendant's

conviction, because he did not voluntarily appear in a public place.

**(B)** No, because the statute requires proof of a voluntary appearance in a public place.

**Correct.** The general legal rule is that a person is not guilty of a crime unless the act constituting the crime was committed voluntarily. This rule precludes the defendant's conviction, because he did not voluntarily appear in a public place.

**(C)** Yes, because the defendant voluntarily became intoxicated.

**Incorrect.** The general legal rule is that a person is not guilty of a crime unless the act constituting the crime was committed voluntarily. This rule precludes the defendant's conviction because, while the defendant voluntarily became intoxicated, he did not voluntarily appear in a public place.

**(D)** Yes, because the defendant voluntarily behaved in an obstreperous manner.

**Incorrect.** The general legal rule is that a person is not guilty of a crime unless the act constituting the crime was committed voluntarily. This rule precludes the defendant's conviction because, while the defendant voluntarily behaved obstreperously, he did not voluntarily appear in a public place.

## Question 17

A police officer had a hunch, not amounting to probable cause or reasonable suspicion, that a man was a drug dealer. One day while the officer was on highway patrol, her radar gun clocked the man's car at 68 mph in an area where the maximum posted speed limit was 65 mph. The officer's usual practice was not to stop a car unless it was going at least 5 mph over the posted limit, but contrary to her usual practice, she decided to stop the man's car in the hope that she might discover evidence of drug dealing. After she stopped the car and announced that she would be writing a speeding ticket, the officer ordered the man and his passenger to step out of the car. When the passenger stepped out, the officer saw that the passenger had been sitting on a clear bag of what the officer immediately recognized as marijuana. The officer arrested both the man and the passenger for possession of marijuana.

At their joint trial, the man and the passenger claim that their Fourth Amendment rights were violated because the officer improperly (1) stopped the car for speeding as a pretext for investigating a hunch rather than for the stated purpose of issuing a traffic ticket and (2) ordered the passenger to step out of the car even though there was no reason to believe that the passenger was a criminal or dangerous.

Are the man and the passenger correct?

(A) No, as to both the stop of the car and the officer's order that the passenger step out of the car.
**Correct.** The stop of the car was constitutional, because it was objectively justifiable (regardless of the officer's subjective motivation), and both the driver and any passengers may be ordered to step out of a car during a lawful traffic stop.

(B) No as to the stop of the car, but yes as to the officer's order that the passenger step out of the car.
**Incorrect.** It is correct that the stop of the car was constitutional, because it was objectively justifiable (regardless of the officer's subjective motivation). However, it is also correct that both the driver and any passengers may be ordered to step out of a car during a lawful traffic stop.

(C) Yes as to the stop of the car, but no as to the officer's order that the passenger step out of the car.
**Incorrect.** It is correct that both the driver and any passengers may be ordered to step out of a car during a lawful traffic stop. However, it is also correct that the stop of the car here was constitutional, because it was objectively justifiable (regardless of the officer's subjective motivation).

(D) Yes, as to both the stop of the car and the officer's order that the passenger step out of the car.
**Incorrect.** The stop of the car was constitutional, because it was objectively justifiable (regardless of the officer's subjective motivation), and both the driver and any passengers may be ordered to step out of the car during a lawful traffic stop.

## V. Chapter 13 EVIDENCE

## ESSAY SCORE SHEET

| Stated | Implied | |
|---|---|---|
| | | **Point One (10%) Impeachment by Criminal Convictions** |
| _____ | _____ | **Rule:** The Federal Rules of Evidence permit impeachment of witnesses with evidence of prior convictions. |
| _____ | _____ | Whether convictions should be admitted to impeach generally depends on the nature of the crime, the amount of time that has passed, and (only in criminal cases) whether the "witness" is the defendant. |
| _____ | _____ | Under Rule 609(a), evidence of prior convictions may be admitted for the purpose of "attacking a witness's character for truthfulness." |
| _____ | _____ | There are two basic types of convictions that can be admitted for the purpose of impeachment: |
| _____ | _____ | (1) convictions for crimes "punishable by death or by imprisonment for more than one year" (which generally correlates to "felonies"); and |
| _____ | _____ | (2) convictions "for any crimes regardless of the punishment . . . if the court can readily determine that establishing the elements of the crime required proving—or the witness's admitting—a dishonest act or false statement." |
| _____ | _____ | Pursuant to Rule 609(a)(1), in civil cases, the admission of evidence of a felony conviction is "subject to Rule 403 [which says that a court may exclude relevant evidence if its probative value is substantially outweighed by other factors]." |
| _____ | _____ | However, Rule 403 does not protect the witness against admission of prior convictions involving dishonesty—which *must* be admitted by the court. |
| _____ | _____ | Finally, Federal Rule of Evidence 609(b) contains the presumption that a conviction that is more than 10 years old, or where more than 10 years has passed since the witness's release from confinement (whichever is later), should *not* be admitted unless "its probative value, supported by specific facts and circumstances, substantially outweighs its prejudicial effect" and the proponent has provided the adverse party with reasonable written notice. |
| | | **Point One (a) (25%) Twelve-year-old Felony Conviction** |
| _____ | _____ | **Conclusion:** The court should admit evidence of the inmate's 12-year-old felony marijuana distribution conviction. |
| _____ | _____ | **Application:** Here, |
| _____ | _____ | The inmate's conviction for marijuana distribution was for a felony punishable by imprisonment for more than one year. |
| _____ | _____ | Moreover, although the conviction was 12 years ago, the 10-year time limit of Rule 609(b) is not exceeded because that time limit runs from the date of either "the witness's conviction or release from confinement for it, whichever is later." |
| _____ | _____ | Because the inmate served three years in prison, he was released from confinement nine years ago. |
| _____ | _____ | **Transition:** However, the admission of felony convictions to impeach a witness in a civil case is subject to Rule 403. |

*continued on next page*

| Stated | Implied | |
|--------|---------|---|
| ___ | ___ | **Rule:** Neither Rule 609(a) nor the advisory committee notes specify which factors courts should consider when balancing the probative value of a conviction against the dangers identified in Rule 403 (which include (1) unfair prejudice, (2) confusion of the issues, (3) misleading the jury, (4) waste of time or undue delay, and (5) needless presentation of cumulative evidence). |
| ___ | ___ | **Application:** Here, |
| ___ | ___ | Credibility is very important because the evidence consists primarily of the testimony of the disputing parties and there were no other eyewitnesses to the altercation. |
| ___ | ___ | This enhances the probative value of any evidence bearing on the inmate's credibility. |
| ___ | ___ | A court is likely to conclude that the inmate's prior felony drug conviction is relevant to his credibility. |
| ___ | ___ | Although the probative value of any conviction diminishes with age, the inmate's ongoing problems with the law suggest that he has continued (and even escalated) his criminal behavior over the past nine years. |
| ___ | ___ | **Conclusion:** The court should admit this evidence because its probative value is not substantially outweighed by any Rule 403 concerns. |
| ___ | ___ | Specifically, any prejudice to the inmate would be slight because the conviction is unrelated to the altercation at issue and the conviction was not for a heinous crime that might inflame the jury. |
| | | [NOTE: Whether an examinee identifies the jury instruction as containing a "conclusive" or "mandatory" presumption is less important than the examinee's analysis of the constitutional infirmities.] |
| | | **Point One (b) (15%) Eight-year-old Misdemeanor Conviction** |
| ___ | ___ | **Conclusion:** The court must admit evidence of the inmate's eight-year-old misdemeanor conviction because perjury is a crime of dishonesty. |
| ___ | ___ | **Rule:** Rule 609(a)(2) provides that evidence of a criminal conviction "must be admitted if the court can readily determine that establishing the elements of the crime required proving—or the witness's admitting—a dishonest act or false statement." |
| ___ | ___ | **Application:** The inmate's conviction for perjury would have necessarily required proving that the inmate engaged in an act of dishonesty. |
| ___ | ___ | **Conclusion:** This conviction occurred within the past 10 years, so it "*must* be admitted" because, in contrast to Rule 609(a)(1), admission under Rule 609(a)(2) is mandatory and not subject to Rule 403. |
| | | **Point One (c) (20%) Seven-year-old Sexual Assault Conviction** |
| ___ | ___ | **Conclusion:** The court should exclude evidence of the inmate's seven-year-old felony sexual assault conviction because the probative value of this evidence is substantially outweighed by the danger of unfair prejudice. |
| ___ | ___ | In the alternative, the details of the prior conviction could be excluded. |
| ___ | ___ | **Rule:** The inmate's conviction for felony sexual assault was seven years ago, and he has not yet been released from incarceration, so Rule 609(a) but not 609(b) is applicable here. |

*continued on next page*

| Stated | Implied | |
|---|---|---|
| _____ | _____ | **Application:** This conviction is therefore admissible to impeach the inmate, unless its probative value is substantially outweighed by the danger of unfair prejudice or any other Rule 403 concern. |
| _____ | _____ | **Rule:** Sex crimes are generally *not* considered relevant to credibility, so the probative value of this conviction is relatively low. |
| _____ | _____ | Moreover, the heinous nature of the inmate's crime (sexual assault on his daughter) makes the danger of unfair prejudice to the inmate very high. |
| _____ | _____ | **Conclusion:** Thus, the court should exclude evidence of the conviction because it was for a heinous offense that is likely to inflame the jury and it has little bearing on credibility. |
| _____ | _____ | As an alternative to excluding this evidence, the judge could minimize the unfair prejudice to the inmate by permitting limited cross-examination but refusing to allow specific questions about the nature of the inmate's conviction. |
| _____ | _____ | For example, a court could limit cross-examination to the fact that the inmate was convicted of a "felony" or perhaps that he was convicted of a "sexual assault" without identifying the victim. |
| _____ | _____ | However, because evidence of the inmate's prior convictions can be admitted solely for the purpose of enabling the jury to assess his credibility and because his two earlier convictions should have already been admitted, the court should exclude all evidence of the felony sexual assault conviction. |
| | | **Point Two (a) (15%) Bad Acts—Résumé** |
| _____ | _____ | **Conclusion:** The court should permit the inmate's counsel to cross-examine the guard regarding the false statement in his résumé because the guard's misconduct bears on his truthfulness. |
| _____ | _____ | **Rule:** Rule 608(b) allows witnesses to be cross-examined about specific instances of prior non-conviction misconduct probative of untruthfulness "in order to attack . . . the witness's character for truthfulness." |
| _____ | _____ | The court's decision to allow cross-examination about the guard's prior dishonest behavior depends on the probative value of such evidence balanced against the danger of unfair prejudice to the guard or any other Rule 403 concern. |
| _____ | _____ | **Application:** Here, |
| _____ | _____ | The guard's false statement on his résumé that he obtained a degree in Criminal Justice is highly probative of his untruthfulness because it grossly misrepresents his actual academic record, was made recently, and was made with the intent to deceive. |
| _____ | _____ | **Conclusion:** Because the probative value of this evidence is very strong and is not substantially outweighed by any Rule 403 concerns, cross-examination of the guard on this topic should be permitted. |
| _____ | _____ | The court may also consider it fair to permit this cross-examination of the guard on these matters, assuming that one or more of the inmate's prior convictions have been admitted to impeach his credibility. |
| | | **Point Two (b) (15%) Bad Acts—Non-Conviction Misconduct** |
| _____ | _____ | **Conclusion:** The court should exclude extrinsic evidence of the guard's non-conviction misconduct, even if the guard denies wrongdoing or refuses to answer questions about the matter. |

*continued on next page*

| Stated | Implied | |
|--------|---------|---|
| _____ | _____ | **Rule:** Although Rule 608(b) allows cross-examination about specific instances of prior misconduct probative of untruthfulness, "extrinsic evidence" offered to prove such misconduct is not admissible. |
| _____ | _____ | The rationale for this rule is that allowing the introduction of extrinsic evidence of prior misconduct by witnesses, when these acts are relevant *only* to the witnesses' truthfulness and not to the main issues in the case, would create too great a risk of confusing the jury and unduly delaying the trial. |
| _____ | _____ | The court does not have discretion to admit this extrinsic evidence. |
| _____ | _____ | **Application:** Here, |
| _____ | _____ | The inmate's counsel may cross-examine the guard about the false statement on his résumé. |
| _____ | _____ | However, the inmate's counsel must accept the guard's response. |
| _____ | _____ | Even if the guard denies wrongdoing or refuses to answer questions about the matter, the inmate's counsel cannot introduce the guard's résumé or the transcript from the local college to prove the guard's misconduct. |

## MBE PRACTICE ANALYSIS[5]

### Question 1

A defendant was tried on multiple counts of bank fraud for a scheme in which he allegedly made withdrawals from the bank accounts of others by using false identification cards and forging signatures on checks. A codefendant, who had assisted the defendant in 5 of the 75 transactions for which the defendant was being tried, testified that he was present and saw the defendant endorse 5 of the checks. Thereafter, the prosecutor moved for admission of all 75 checks that the defendant had allegedly endorsed, arguing that a comparison by the jury of the signatures on the checks identified by the codefendant with those on the other 70 checks would demonstrate that they were all signed by the defendant.

Should the court permit the proposed comparison of the handwriting specimens by the jury?

(A) No, because such a comparison may be done only by an expert.
**Incorrect.** Rule 901(b) sets forth examples that satisfy the requirement that evidence must be authentic. While having an expert opinion on handwriting is sufficient, it is not required. Rule 901(b)(3) allows a "comparison with an authenticated specimen by an expert witness or the trier of fact." (Emphasis added).

(B) No, because such a comparison may be done only by an expert or by a nonexpert who can testify to the genuineness of the handwriting.
**Incorrect.** Rule 901(b)(3) allows authenticity to be established either by an expert witness or by the trier of fact. Therefore this answer is wrong because it is not necessary to authenticate evidence through an expert or a comparison by a nonexpert witness.

(C) Yes, because the jurors are allowed to determine the genuineness of handwriting specimens based on comparison with authenticated specimens.
**Correct.** Rule 901(b)(3) allows the jury to determine the genuineness of evidence by comparison with other authenticated specimens. Because five specimens have been properly authenticated by a witness with personal knowledge, the rule permits the jury to compare the remaining specimens with those five.

(D) Yes, but only if the court first makes a preliminary finding of authenticity as to the other 70 checks.
**Incorrect.** What Rule 901 requires is that some specimens have been found to be genuine. This has been accomplished by the testimony of a witness with personal knowledge of the five checks. After that condition is met, nothing in Rule 901 requires the judge to make a preliminary finding of authenticity as to the remainder. The rule specifically permits the jury to make the determination.

### Question 2

A defendant is on trial for knowing possession of a stolen television. The defendant claims that the television was a gift from a friend, who has disappeared. The defendant seeks to testify that he was present when the friend told her neighbor that the television had been given to the friend by her mother.

Is the defendant's testimony about the friend's statement to the neighbor admissible?

(A) No, because the friend's statement is hearsay not within any exception.
**Incorrect.** The statement would be hearsay if it were offered to prove that the friend actually owned the television. But the defendant is offering the friend's statement as evidence that the defendant thought that the friend owned the television (i.e., that it had not been stolen). Because the defendant is charged with knowing possession of a stolen television, his state of mind is relevant. If the defendant had heard the friend say that the television was hers, that evidence would be relevant to the defendant's state of mind regardless of the truth of the statement. Therefore, the friend's out-of-court statement is not hearsay and is admissible.

(B) No, because the defendant has not presented evidence of circumstances that clearly corroborate the statement.
**Incorrect.** There is no requirement that a statement offered to prove its effect on the person who heard it must be corroborated. In this case, the defendant is offering the friend's statement as evidence that the defendant thought that the friend owned the television (i.e., that it had not been stolen). Because the defendant is charged with knowing possession of a stolen television, his state of mind is relevant. If the defendant had heard the friend say that the television was hers, that evidence would be relevant to the defendant's state of

---

5. *Id.*

mind regardless of whether it was corroborated. Because the statement is not being offered for its truth, it is not hearsay and is admissible.

(C) Yes, as nonhearsay evidence of the defendant's belief that the friend owned the television.
**Correct.** The defendant is offering the friend's statement as evidence that the defendant thought that the friend owned the television (i.e., that it had not been stolen). Because the defendant is charged with knowing possession of a stolen television, his state of mind is relevant. If the defendant had heard the friend say that the television was hers, that evidence would be relevant to the defendant's state of mind regardless of the truth of the statement. Therefore, the friend's out-of-court statement is not hearsay.

(D) Yes, under the hearsay exception for statements affecting an interest in property.
**Incorrect.** The statement is offered for a nonhearsay purpose, so there is no need to find an applicable hearsay exception. The defendant is offering the friend's statement as evidence that the defendant thought that the friend owned the television (i.e., that it had not been stolen). Because the defendant is charged with knowing possession of a stolen television, his state of mind is relevant. If the defendant had heard the friend say that the television was hers, that evidence would be relevant to the defendant's state of mind regardless of the truth of the statement. Therefore, the friend's out-of-court statement is not hearsay.

Moreover, if an exception were required, the exception for statements affecting an interest in property would not be applicable, because that exception requires that the statement be contained in a document. Here the statement was oral.

## Question 3

A plaintiff has brought a civil suit against a defendant for injuries arising out of a fistfight between them. The day after the fight, a police officer talked to the plaintiff, the defendant, and an eyewitness, and made an official police report. At trial, the plaintiff seeks to introduce from the properly authenticated police report a statement attributed to the eyewitness, who is unavailable to testify at trial, that "[the defendant] started the fight."

Should the court admit the statement from the report?

(A) No, unless the entire report is introduced.
**Incorrect.** The statement is inadmissible hearsay even if the entire report is introduced; the eyewitness's statement is hearsay within the hearsay report. The report itself could be admissible as a business or public record, but the hearsay within it is admissible only if it satisfies a separate hearsay exception or if it can be shown that the eyewitness had a business or public duty to report the information accurately. The eyewitness had no such duty, and no other hearsay exception applies.

(B) No, because it is hearsay not within any exception.
**Correct.** The eyewitness's statement is hearsay within the hearsay report. The report itself could be admissible as a business or public record, but the hearsay within it is admissible only if it satisfies a separate hearsay exception or if it can be shown that the eyewitness had a business or public duty to report the information accurately. The eyewitness had no such duty. The eyewitness's statement is also not a present sense impression, because it was made the day after the fight, and no other hearsay exception applies.

(C) Yes, because it was based on the eyewitness's firsthand knowledge.
**Incorrect.** The fact that the eyewitness purports to have personal knowledge does not solve the hearsay problem, which arises because the eyewitness might not have told the truth about the event he purportedly saw and is not subject to cross-examination about it. The eyewitness's statement is hearsay within the hearsay report. The report itself could be admissible as a business or public record, but the hearsay within it is admissible only if it satisfies a separate hearsay exception or if it can be shown that the eyewitness had a business or public duty to report the information accurately. The eyewitness had no such duty, and no other hearsay exception applies.

(D) Yes, because it is an excerpt from a public record offered in a civil case.
**Incorrect.** The eyewitness's statement is hearsay within the hearsay report. The report itself could be admissible as a business or public record, but the hearsay within it is admissible only if it satisfies a separate hearsay exception or if it can be shown that the eyewitness had a business or public duty to report the information accurately. The eyewitness had no such duty, and no other hearsay exception applies.

## Question 4

A plaintiff has sued a defendant, alleging that she was run over by a speeding car driven by the defendant. The plaintiff was unconscious after her injury and, accompanied by her husband, was brought to the hospital in an ambulance.

At trial, the plaintiff calls an emergency room physician to testify that when the physician asked the plaintiff's husband if he knew what had happened, the husband, who was upset, replied, "I saw my wife get run over two hours ago by a driver who went right through the intersection without looking."

Is the physician's testimony about the husband's statement admissible?

(A) No, because it relates an opinion.

**Incorrect.** An out-of-court statement is not inadmissible simply because it contains an opinion. Statements of opinion by out-of-court declarants may be admitted if they qualify under a hearsay exception and otherwise satisfy the rules governing opinion testimony of in-court witnesses. This statement, however, is hearsay not within any exception and is inadmissible.

(B) No, because it is hearsay not within any exception.

**Correct.** The statement is offered to prove liability for the accident. As such, it is not a statement made for purposes of diagnosis or treatment. Moreover, the statement was made two hours after the accident, so it is very unlikely that the husband (who was not himself an accident victim) was under a continuous state of excitement between the time of the accident and the time he made the statement. Therefore, the statement is not admissible as an excited utterance, and no other hearsay exception applies.

(C) Yes, as a statement made for purposes of diagnosis or treatment.

**Incorrect.** The husband's statement is making an accusation of fault for the accident. Such a statement is not pertinent to the diagnosis or treatment of the plaintiff, as is required by the hearsay exception. No other hearsay exception applies, so the statement is inadmissible.

(D) Yes, as an excited utterance.

**Incorrect.** In order for this statement to be admissible as an excited utterance, the declarant must have been under a continuous state of excitement between the time of the event and the time of the statement. Here, the husband made the statement two hours after the accident, so it is very unlikely that the husband (who was not himself an accident victim) was under a continuous state of excitement between the time of the accident and the time he made the statement. Therefore, the statement is not admissible as an excited utterance, and no other hearsay exception applies, so the statement is inadmissible.

## Question 5

A plaintiff has sued a defendant for personal injuries the plaintiff suffered when she was bitten as she was trying to feed a rat that was part of the defendant's caged-rat experiment at a science fair. At trial, the plaintiff offers evidence that immediately after the incident the defendant said to her, "I'd like to give you this $100 bill, because I feel so bad about this."

Is the defendant's statement admissible?

(A) No, because it is not relevant to the issue of liability.

**Incorrect.** The defendant's statement of contrition and offer of compensation clearly have a tendency to prove that he is liable, and a tendency is all that is required for the evidence to be relevant under Rule 401. The statement is admissible as the statement of a party-opponent.

(B) No, because it was an offer of compromise.

**Incorrect.** The statement would not be excluded under Rule 408, which excludes statements that are made to settle a claim, because that rule applies only when the statement is made as a compromise to a disputed claim. Here, at the time the defendant made the statement, he was not contesting that he was at fault. Therefore, there was no disputed claim, and the statement is admissible as the statement of a party-opponent.

(C) Yes, as a present sense impression.

**Incorrect.** The exception to the hearsay rule for present sense impressions covers a statement describing or explaining an event or condition made during or immediately after the event or condition. The defendant's statement is just an expression of contrition and not an attempt to explain any event or condition. However, the statement is admissible as the statement of a party-opponent.

(D) Yes, as the statement of a party-opponent.

**Correct.** An out-of-court statement by a party that is relevant to his or her liability is admissible under the exception to the hearsay rule for statements of a party-opponent. One might think that the statement would be excluded because of Rule 408, which excludes statements that are made to settle a claim. But that rule is inapplicable, because it applies only when the statement is made to compromise a disputed claim. Here, at the time the defendant made the statement, he was not contesting that he was at fault. Therefore, there was no disputed claim.

## Question 6

A defendant is charged with aggravated assault. The physical evidence at trial has shown that the victim was hit with a lead pipe in the back of the head and on the forearms and left in an alley. The medical examiner has testified that the injuries to the victim's forearms appear to have been defensive wounds. The victim has testified that he cannot remember who attacked him with the lead pipe. He would further testify that he remembers only that a passerby found him in the alley, and that he told the passerby that the defendant had hit him with the lead pipe; he then lost consciousness. The defendant objects to this proposed testimony, arguing that it is hearsay and that the victim had no personal knowledge of the identity of the perpetrator.

Is the victim's testimony concerning his previous statement to the passerby admissible?

(A) No, because the prosecutor has failed to show that it is more likely than not that the victim had personal knowledge of the perpetrator's identity.
**Incorrect.** The standard for personal knowledge under Rule 602 is whether a reasonable juror could find that the witness is speaking on the basis of personal knowledge. This standard is referred to as "prima facie" proof and is significantly easier to satisfy than "more likely than not."

(B) No, because the victim has no memory of the attack itself and therefore cannot be effectively cross-examined.
**Incorrect.** The U.S. Supreme Court held in *United States v. Owens* that a declarant-witness is subject to cross-examination within the meaning of the hearsay exception for prior identifications even if the witness lacks memory of the prior identification.

(C) Yes, because the victim is subject to cross-examination, and there is sufficient showing of personal knowledge.
**Correct.** The U.S. Supreme Court held in *United States v. Owens* that a declarant-witness is subject to cross-examination within the meaning of the hearsay exception for prior identifications even if the witness lacks all memory of the prior identification. As to personal knowledge, the evidence of defensive wounds is more than sufficient to persuade a reasonable juror that the victim saw his attacker.

(D) Yes, because it is the victim's own out-of-court statement.
**Incorrect.** The rule against hearsay applies to any out-of-court statement admitted for its truth, including earlier statements of trial witnesses. In this case, however, there is a hearsay exception for prior identifications when the declarant is testifying and subject to cross-examination.

## Question 7

A man suffered a broken jaw in a fight with a neighbor that took place when they were both spectators at a soccer match.

If the man sues the neighbor for personal injury damages, which of the following actions must the trial court take if requested by the man?

(A) Prevent the neighbor's principal eyewitness from testifying, upon a showing that six years ago the witness was convicted of perjury and the conviction has not been the subject of a pardon or annulment.
**Incorrect.** A witness can never be excluded from testifying simply because there is impeachment evidence that could be used against that witness. Under Rule 601, all witnesses are presumed to be competent. The man can use this evidence to impeach the witness when the witness testifies.

(B) Refuse to let the neighbor cross-examine the man's medical expert on matters not covered on direct examination of the expert.
**Incorrect.** The trial court is not required to prohibit a cross-examiner from asking questions unrelated to the direct examination. Rule 611(b) states that the court "may allow inquiry into additional matters."

(C) Exclude nonparty eyewitnesses from the courtroom during the testimony of other witnesses.
**Correct.** Rule 615 provides that if a party moves to exclude prospective witnesses before they testify, "the court must order witnesses excluded so they cannot hear other witnesses' testimony."

(D) Require the production of a writing used before trial to refresh a witness's memory.

**Incorrect.** Under Rule 612, the trial court has discretion to order a party to produce for the adversary a writing used before trial to refresh the memory of a witness called by the party, but the court is not required to do so.

## Question 8

A defendant is charged with robbing a bank. The prosecutor has supplied the court with information from accurate sources establishing that the bank is a federally insured institution and that this fact is not subject to reasonable dispute. The prosecutor asks the court to take judicial notice of this fact. The defendant objects.

How should the court proceed?

(A) The court must take judicial notice and instruct the jury that it is required to accept the judicially noticed fact as conclusive.

**Incorrect.** In criminal cases, the trial judge may not instruct the jury to accept a judicially noticed fact as conclusive. To do so would impermissibly limit the defendant's right to a jury trial. The court must take judicial notice of a fact if the court is supplied with the necessary information to indicate that the fact is not subject to reasonable dispute. However, Rule 201(f) provides that in a criminal case, "the court must instruct the jury that it may or may not accept the noticed fact as conclusive."

(B) The court must take judicial notice and instruct the jury that it may, but is not required to, accept the judicially noticed fact as conclusive.

**Correct.** The court must take judicial notice of a fact if the court is supplied with the necessary information to indicate that the fact is not subject to reasonable dispute. Rule 201(f) provides that in a criminal case, "the court must instruct the jury that it may or may not accept the noticed fact as conclusive."

(C) The court may refuse to take judicial notice, because judicial notice may not be taken of essential facts in a criminal case.

**Incorrect.** The court must take judicial notice of a fact if the court is supplied with the necessary information to indicate that the fact is not subject to reasonable dispute. Here the facts indicate that the court has been supplied with the necessary information. However, Rule 201(f) provides that in a criminal case, "the court must instruct the jury that it may or may not accept the noticed fact as conclusive."

(D) The court must refuse to take judicial notice, because whether a bank is federally insured would not be generally known within the court's jurisdiction.

**Incorrect.** Whether a bank is federally insured is a fact that would be generally known within the jurisdiction. Even if it were not, however, under Rule 201(b) judicial notice must be taken if the indisputability of a fact "can be accurately and readily determined from sources whose accuracy cannot be questioned." The facts here so provide. However, Rule 201(f) provides that in a criminal case, "the court must instruct the jury that it may or may not accept the noticed fact as conclusive."

## Question 9

The beneficiary of a decedent's life insurance policy has sued the life insurance company for the proceeds of the policy. At issue is the date when the decedent first experienced the heart problems that led to his death. The decedent's primary care physician has testified at trial that the decedent had a routine checkup on February 15. The physician then identifies a photocopy of a questionnaire, provided by the physician and completed by the decedent on that date, in which the decedent wrote: "Yesterday afternoon I broke into a big sweat and my chest hurt for a while." The beneficiary now offers the photocopy in evidence.

Should the court admit the photocopy?

(A) No, because the original questionnaire has not been shown to be unavailable.

**Incorrect.** This answer refers to the best evidence rule. Under the best evidence rule, a copy of a document is as admissible as the original unless a genuine question is raised about the authenticity of the original or the circumstances make it unfair to admit the copy. No such question or circumstances are present here. The photocopy should be admitted as a statement for the purpose of obtaining medical treatment.

(B) No, because the statement related to past rather than present symptoms.

**Incorrect.** Statements of medical history can be admitted under the hearsay exception in Rule 803(4) if they are pertinent to diagnosis or treatment, regardless of whether the statements relate to past or present symptoms. The decedent's statement clearly qualifies under this hearsay exception.

**(C)** Yes, as a business record.

**Incorrect.** For a recorded statement to be admissible as a business record under Rule 803(6), the business record must be kept in the course of a regularly conducted activity and it must be a regular practice of the business to make the record. Here, the record was made by the decedent, not by the physician, and there is no indication that the decedent regularly prepared such records. However, the photocopy should be admitted as a statement for the purpose of obtaining medical treatment.

**(D)** Yes, as a statement for the purpose of obtaining medical treatment.

**Correct.** The decedent's statement of his medical history was made for the purpose of diagnosis and treatment, and it is clearly pertinent to the physician's diagnosis and treatment. Therefore, it is admissible under Rule 803(4).

## Question 10

A defendant is charged with mail fraud. At trial, the defendant has not taken the witness stand, but he has called a witness who has testified that the defendant has a reputation for honesty. On cross-examination, the prosecutor seeks to ask the witness, "Didn't you hear that two years ago the defendant was arrested for embezzlement?"

Should the court permit the question?

**(A)** No, because the defendant has not testified and therefore has not put his character at issue.

**Incorrect.** When a defendant calls a witness to testify to the defendant's reputation for character, the prosecutor is permitted to test the character witness's knowledge of the defendant's reputation. The fact that the defendant has not put his character at issue is irrelevant.

**(B)** No, because the incident was an arrest, not a conviction.

**Incorrect.** For purposes of testing the witness's knowledge of the defendant's reputation for honesty, the bad act need not have resulted in a conviction. An arrest is sufficient to have an impact on the community's view of the defendant's honesty.

**(C)** Yes, because it seeks to impeach the credibility of the witness.

**Correct.** The witness has testified that she knows about the defendant's reputation. The prosecutor has the right to test the basis and adequacy of that knowledge, as well as the nature of the community itself. If the witness answers that she had not heard about the arrest, that admission could indicate that she is not very knowledgeable about the defendant's reputation in the community, because such an arrest would likely have a negative effect on that reputation. If the witness says that she had heard about the arrest, a negative inference could be raised about the community itself and its view of what it is to be an honest person.

**(D)** Yes, because the earlier arrest for a crime of dishonesty makes the defendant's guilt of the mail fraud more likely.

**Incorrect.** The prosecutor is not allowed to use a bad act to show that the defendant has a propensity to commit a similar bad act. Rule 404 limits the use of character evidence to prove conduct in accordance with a character trait. However, the prosecutor has the right to attempt to impeach the witness's credibility by testing the basis and adequacy of her knowledge of the defendant's reputation, so the question should be permitted.

## Question 11

At a woman's trial for bank robbery, the prosecutor has called a private security guard for the bank who has testified, without objection, that while he was on a coffee break, the woman's brother rushed up to him and said, "Come quickly! My sister is robbing the bank!" The woman now seeks to call a witness to testify that the brother later told the witness, "I got my sister into trouble by telling a security guard that she was robbing the bank, but now I realize I was mistaken." The brother is unavailable to testify.

Is the witness's testimony admissible?

**(A)** No, because the brother will be afforded no opportunity to explain or deny the later statement.

**Incorrect.** What is being offered here is an inconsistent statement of a hearsay declarant. The goal is to impeach that declarant's credibility. The brother's original statement would have been admitted as an excited utterance under the Rule 803(2) hearsay exception. While it is ordinarily true that a witness impeached with a prior inconsistent statement must be given an opportunity to explain or deny the statement, that opportunity is not available when a hearsay declarant is not produced at trial. Rule 806 provides that the ordinary requirement of a "fair opportunity to explain or deny" is not applicable to hearsay declarants who are being impeached with prior inconsistent statements.

**(B)** No, because the prosecutor will be afforded no opportunity to confront the brother.

**Incorrect.** A prosecutor has no right to confrontation; only a criminal defendant has that right. In any case, here it is the prosecutor who offered the statement that the brother made at the time of the crime, so the prosecutor cannot argue a lack of opportunity to confront the brother.

**(C)** Yes, because it is substantive proof that the woman did not rob the bank.

**Incorrect.** The statement later made by the brother was an out-of-court statement, and if offered for its truth, it is hearsay. There is no applicable hearsay exception.

**(D)** Yes, but only as an inconsistent statement to impeach the brother's credibility.

**Correct.** It is ordinarily true that a witness impeached with a prior inconsistent statement must be given an opportunity to explain or deny the statement. That is not possible, however, when a hearsay declarant is not produced at trial. Therefore Rule 806 provides that the ordinary requirement of a "fair opportunity to explain or deny" is not applicable to hearsay declarants who are being impeached with prior inconsistent statements. The inconsistent statement is probative of the brother's credibility, and Rule 806 permits such impeachment.

## Question 12

A woman's car was set on fire by vandals. When she submitted a claim of loss for the car to her insurance company, the insurance company refused to pay, asserting that the woman's policy had lapsed due to the nonpayment of her premium. The woman sued the insurance company for breach of contract.

At trial, the woman testified that she had, in a timely manner, placed a stamped, properly addressed envelope containing the premium payment in the outgoing mail bin at her office. The woman's secretary then testified that every afternoon at closing time he takes all outgoing mail in the bin to the post office. The insurance company later called its mail clerk to testify that he opens all incoming mail and that he did not receive the woman's premium payment.

The woman and the insurance company have both moved for a directed verdict. For which party, if either, should the court direct a verdict?

**(A)** For the insurance company, because neither the woman nor her secretary has any personal knowledge that the envelope was delivered to the post office.

**Incorrect.** Under Rule 301, the rule on presumptions, the woman has presented sufficient evidence that the envelope containing the premium payment was mailed. The rule does not require that the woman have personal knowledge that the envelope reached the post office. The insurance company then has the burden of producing evidence to rebut the presumption that the envelope was received. Because the insurance company has produced such evidence, the presumption is taken out of the case and it is up to the fact finder to determine whether the insurance company received the payment.

**(B)** For the insurance company, because the mail clerk's direct testimony negates the woman's circumstantial evidence.

**Incorrect.** Under Rule 301, once the woman provides evidence that the envelope containing the premium payment was mailed, the insurance company has the burden of producing evidence sufficient to rebut the presumption that the envelope was received. That does not mean, however, that if the insurance company does provide such evidence it is entitled to a directed verdict. Instead, the presumption is taken out of the case and it is up to the fact finder to determine whether the insurance company received the payment.

**(C)** For the woman, because there is a presumption that an envelope properly addressed and stamped was received by the addressee.

**Incorrect.** It is true that the woman's evidence has triggered the presumption that the envelope containing the premium payment was received. But under Rule 301, the insurance company then has the burden of producing enough evidence to rebut the presumption. Here the insurance company has done so. Consequently, the presumption is taken out of the case and it is up to the fact finder to determine whether the insurance company received the payment. Therefore, it would be error to grant a directed verdict for the woman.

**(D)** For neither the woman nor the insurance company, because under these circumstances the jury is responsible for determining whether the insurance company received the payment.

**Correct.** The woman has presented sufficient evidence to trigger the presumption that her payment was received. The insurance company has presented sufficient evidence to rebut that presumption. Consequently, the presumption is taken out of the case and it is up to the fact finder to determine whether the insurance company received the payment. Therefore, it would be error to grant a directed verdict for either the woman or the insurance company.

## Question 13

At a defendant's trial for mail fraud, the defendant calls his wife to testify that she committed the fraud herself without the defendant's knowledge. On cross-examination, the prosecutor asks the wife, "Isn't it true that you have fled your home several times in fear of your husband?"

Is this question proper?

(A) No, because it is leading a witness not shown to be hostile.
**Incorrect.** Leading questions are generally permitted on cross-examination, and the question is proper because it explores the wife's possible motive for testifying falsely.

(B) No, because its probative value is outweighed by the danger of unfair prejudice to the defendant.
**Incorrect.** This answer applies the wrong balancing test. Under Rule 403, evidence that is probative is admissible unless its probative value is substantially outweighed by the risk of unfair prejudice. That test favors admitting probative evidence. It is not the case, therefore, that the prejudicial effect must simply outweigh the probative value for the evidence to be excluded. The question is proper because it explores the wife's possible motive for testifying falsely.

(C) Yes, because by calling his wife, the defendant has waived his privilege to prevent her from testifying against him.
**Incorrect.** The defendant does not have a privilege to prevent his wife from testifying against him. The privilege against adverse spousal testimony is held by the wife, as the witness, not by the defendant. The question is proper, however, because it explores the wife's possible motive for testifying falsely.

(D) Yes, because it explores the wife's possible motive for testifying falsely.
**Correct.** A cross-examiner is entitled to question in such a way as to raise inferences about the motive of a witness to testify falsely. Here, the question raises an inference that the wife is in fear of her husband and is therefore taking the blame for her husband's crime.

## Question 14

A driver sued her insurance company on an accident insurance policy covering personal injuries to the driver. The insurance company defended on the ground that the driver's injuries were intentionally self-inflicted and therefore excluded from the policy's coverage.

The driver testified at trial that she had inflicted the injuries, as her negligence had caused the crash in which she was injured, but that she had not done so intentionally. She then called as a witness her treating psychiatrist to give his opinion that the driver had been mentally unbalanced, but not self-destructive, at the time of the crash.

Should the court admit the witness's opinion?

(A) No, because it is a statement about the driver's credibility.
**Incorrect.** The witness is not offering to testify that the driver is telling the truth. (If the witness were to do so, the testimony would be inadmissible, because credibility is a question for the jury to assess.) The witness is offering to testify only to the driver's pertinent mental state, which is permissible in a civil case such as this.

(B) No, because it is an opinion about a mental state that constitutes an element of the defense.
**Incorrect.** Rule 704(b), which prohibits an expert from testifying that a criminal defendant had or did not have the requisite mental state to commit the crime charged, is applicable to criminal cases only. There is no absolute bar to such testimony in a civil case such as this.

(C) No, because the witness did not first state the basis for his opinion.
**Incorrect.** Under Rule 705, an expert may state an opinion "without first testifying to the underlying facts or data."

(D) Yes, because it is a helpful opinion by a qualified expert.
**Correct.** The witness's opinion helps the jury understand a relevant mental state. The standard for qualification of an expert is not high; a psychiatrist is qualified to testify to a person's mental state.

## Question 15

A plaintiff has brought a products liability action against a defendant, the manufacturer of a sport-utility vehicle that the plaintiff's decedent was driving when she was fatally injured in a rollover accident. The plaintiff claims that a design defect in the vehicle caused it to roll over. The defendant claims that the cause of the accident was the decedent's driving at excessive speed during an ice storm. Eyewitnesses to the accident have given contradictory estimates about the vehicle's speed just before the rollover. It is also disputed whether the decedent was killed instantly.

Which of the following items of offered evidence is the court most likely to admit?

(A) A videotape offered by the defendant of a test conducted by the defendant showing that a sport-utility vehicle of the same model the decedent was driving did not roll over when driven by a professional driver on a dry test track at the top speed testified to by the eyewitnesses.

**Incorrect.** In order for product demonstrations to be admissible under Rule 403 to prove how an accident happened, the conditions must be substantially similar to the conditions at the time in question. This test was conducted on a dry track with a professional driver. Even if the court admits this evidence in its discretion, the question calls for the evidence that the court is most likely to admit. This evidence is not it.

(B) A videotape offered by the plaintiff of a television news program about sport-utility vehicles that includes footage of accident scenes in which the vehicles had rolled over.

**Incorrect.** This evidence is not very probative, because it shows sport-utility vehicles in general, not necessarily the model used by the decedent, and there is no indication that the conditions in the accident scenes were in any way similar to the conditions in question. Under Rule 403, the probative value of this evidence is likely to be substantially outweighed by its prejudicial effect and risk of jury confusion. Even if the court admits this evidence in its discretion, the question calls for the evidence that the court is most likely to admit. This evidence is not it.

(C) Evidence offered by the defendant that the decedent had received two citations for speeding in the previous three years.

**Incorrect.** This evidence would not be admissible, because it is attempting to show that the decedent had a propensity to drive too fast, to create the inference that the decedent was driving too fast at the time

in question. Under Rule 404, proof of character in order to show conduct consistent with that character is inadmissible in civil cases.

(D) Photographs taken at the accident scene and during the autopsy that would help the plaintiff's medical expert explain to the jury why she concluded that the decedent did not die instantly.

**Correct.** This evidence is most likely to be admitted. If these photographs are offered to illustrate the expert's testimony, the jury can be instructed to use the evidence only for that purpose. Moreover, this evidence is not as prejudicial or potentially confusing to the jury as the evidence in options (A) and (B), while the evidence in option (C) is inadmissible.

## Question 16

At the start of the trial of a defendant and a codefendant for robbery, the codefendant and her attorney offered to give the prosecutor information about facts that would strengthen the prosecutor's case against the defendant in exchange for leniency toward the codefendant. The prosecutor refused the offer. Shortly thereafter, the codefendant committed suicide.

During the defendant's trial, the prosecutor called the codefendant's attorney and asked him to relate the information that the codefendant had revealed to the attorney.

Is the attorney's testimony admissible?

(A) No, because the codefendant's communications are protected by the attorney-client privilege.

**Correct.** The prosecutor is asking for confidential communications between the codefendant and her attorney, which is privileged information. If the codefendant had actually provided information to the prosecutor, the privilege would have been waived as to any communications previously made to her attorney. However, the codefendant did not disclose any confidential communications.

(B) No, because the plea discussion was initiated by the codefendant rather than by the prosecutor.

**Incorrect.** The prosecutor is asking for confidential communications between the codefendant and her attorney, which is privileged information, and it makes no difference who initiated the plea discussion. The question is whether the codefendant waived the privilege by offering information to the prosecutor, which she did not. Because the codefendant did not actually disclose any confidential communications to the prosecutor, there was no waiver.

(C) Yes, because the codefendant intended to disclose the information.
**Incorrect.** The prosecutor is asking for confidential communications between the codefendant and her attorney, which is privileged information. If the codefendant had actually provided information to the prosecutor, the privilege would have been waived as to any communications previously made to her attorney. However, the codefendant did not disclose any confidential communications, and whether she intended to disclose the information is irrelevant.

(D) Yes, because the information the codefendant gave to her attorney revealing her knowledge of the crime would be a statement against the codefendant's penal interest.
**Incorrect.** A declaration against interest is one that tends to expose the declarant to criminal liability. Any statement to the attorney could not have subjected the codefendant to a risk of criminal liability, because the statement was privileged.

## VI. Chapter 14 REAL PROPERTY

## ESSAY SCORE SHEET

| Stated | Implied | |
|---|---|---|
| _____ | _____ | **Point One (a) (35%) Adverse Possession of One-Half Acre**<br><br>**Conclusion:** The acts of possession of the man, his sister, and the buyer were sufficient to acquire title by adverse possession to the one-half acre actually possessed by them. |
| _____ | _____ | **Rule:** To acquire title by adverse possession, the possession must be (1) actual, (2) open and notorious, (3) exclusive, (4) continuous, and (5) hostile and under claim of right. |
| _____ | _____ | **Application:** Here, |
| _____ | _____ | All of these requirements were satisfied as to the one-half acre on which the cabin was built and the garden planted. The possession of the man, his sister, and the buyer was exclusive and continuous, satisfying these two requirements of the test. |
| _____ | _____ | **Rule:** To be actual, acts of possession must be consistent with how a reasonable owner of land would have used it if in possession. |
| _____ | _____ | **Application:** Here, the acts of possession included building and occupying a cabin as well as planting, harvesting, and maintaining a garden. |
| _____ | _____ | These acts are consistent with how a reasonable owner would have used the one-half acre. |
| _____ | _____ | **Rule:** To be open and notorious, the acts of possession must be such that they would have put an owner on notice of the adverse possession had the owner inspected the land. |
| _____ | _____ | **Application:** Here, the cabin and garden occupied a half acre and were visible. |
| _____ | _____ | When the owner acquired the land, it was vacant. |
| _____ | _____ | Had the owner inspected, he would have determined that someone else was in possession. |
| _____ | _____ | **Rule:** Hostility and claim of right are present when a possessor is on the land without the owner's permission. |
| _____ | _____ | Some courts do hold that to acquire title by adverse possession, the possessor must have a good-faith belief that she has a good title to the land; others hold that the possessor must believe that she does not have a good title to the land. |
| _____ | _____ | But most courts and scholars reject these contradictory "subjective hostility" tests. |
| _____ | _____ | Thus, in the vast majority of jurisdictions the fact that the man, his sister, and the buyer were on the tract of land without the permission of the owner would suffice to satisfy the hostility and claim of right requirement. |
| _____ | _____ | **Application/Conclusion:** Thus, the man, his sister, and the buyer satisfied the requirements for acquiring title by adverse possession as to the one-half-acre portion of the three-acre tract that they actually possessed. |
| _____ | _____ | **Point One (b) (20%) Accrual and Privity**<br><br>**Conclusion:** Although neither the man, nor his sister, nor the buyer individually possessed the property for the statutory 10-year period, their periods of possession can be aggregated because they were all in privity with one another. Thus, the 10-year statute has run, and the buyer has acquired title to the one-half acre. |

*continued on next page*

| Stated | Implied | |
|---|---|---|
| _____ | _____ | **Rule:** The period during which possession must endure to create title by adverse possession is determined by statute. |
| _____ | _____ | A cause of action to recover possession of real property "accrues" when a wrongful act of possession occurs. |
| _____ | _____ | **Application:** Here, |
| _____ | _____ | The local statute provides that "any action to recover the possession of real property must be brought within 10 years after the cause of action accrues." |
| _____ | _____ | The initial cause of action thus accrued when the man wrongfully entered a portion of the three-acre tract 15 years ago. |
| _____ | _____ | The man possessed the property for seven years, the man's sister possessed it for one year, and the buyer possessed it for seven years. |
| _____ | _____ | **Conclusion:** None of these individual periods of possession equals the 10-year statutory period. |
| _____ | _____ | **Rule:** When multiple adverse possessors are in "privity" with one another, the period of their respective possessions can be aggregated for the purpose of determining whether the statutory period has run against the holder of the cause of action. |
| _____ | _____ | In this context, privity denotes a relationship between possessors arising because of a voluntary transfer between them, descent under the laws of intestacy, or testamentary succession as the result of a bequest. |
| _____ | _____ | **Application:** Here, |
| _____ | _____ | The man and his sister were in privity as a result of testamentary succession, namely the bequest in the man's will of all real property "in which I have or may have an interest" to his sister. |
| _____ | _____ | The sister and the buyer were also in privity because of the voluntary transfer between them. |
| _____ | _____ | **Conclusion:** Thus, because the 10-year statutory period has elapsed, the buyer has acquired title by adverse possession to the one-half-acre portion of the three-acre tract that he, the sister, and the man actually possessed. |
| | | **Point One (c) (15%) Adverse Possession of 2.5 Acres** |
| _____ | _____ | **Conclusion:** The buyer did not acquire title to the unpossessed two and one-half acres because he did not possess or use that portion of the tract. |
| _____ | _____ | The buyer acquired title by adverse possession only to the portion of the tract for which he met all requirements of the five-prong test. |
| _____ | _____ | Because the man, his sister, and the buyer never possessed (or even used) any of the two and one-half acres beyond the garden, the buyer cannot claim title by adverse possession to those acres. |
| _____ | _____ | **Rule:** The doctrine of constructive adverse possession does not alter this result. |
| _____ | _____ | Under this doctrine, if a possessor enters under color of title (*i.e.*, an instrument creating the possibility of a title in the grantee who enters under the instrument) and the possessor takes possession of only a portion of the land described in the instrument, the possessor's possession is deemed to constructively extend to the portion of the described land. |

*continued on next page*

| Stated | Implied | |
|--------|---------|---|
| _____ _____ _____ | _____ _____ _____ | **Application:** Here, <br><br> Neither the man nor his sister entered under color of title. <br><br> Although the buyer did enter with a deed and, arguably, color of title, his constructive possession endured only seven years, short of the statutory period in which the legal title holder may regain possession. |
| _____ _____ _____ _____ | _____ _____ _____ _____ | **Point Two (15%) Breach of Warranties** <br><br> **Conclusion:** The buyer is entitled to damages from the sister because the sister did not convey title to the three-acre tract by a general warranty deed. <br><br> **Rule:** A warranty deed includes numerous covenants. Two of them—the covenant of seisin and the right to convey—are essentially the same, and they guarantee that the seller owns the conveyed land. <br><br> **Application:** Here, the sister did not own the three-acre tract when she purported to convey it to the buyer by a general warranty deed. <br><br> **Conclusion:** Thus, she was in breach of the covenant of seisin and the right to convey, and the buyer is entitled to damages for that breach. <br><br> [NOTE: Some examinees may confuse the warranty issue with the concept of marketable title. It is true that the man's sister did not have a marketable title when she conveyed to the buyer because her adverse possession claim was clearly subject to the risk of litigation. Nonetheless the buyer agreed to go forward with the transfer, and the sister gave the buyer a warranty deed. Had she given the buyer a quitclaim deed, no warranties would have been breached. While the deed also includes a covenant of quiet enjoyment and a covenant of warranty, no facts suggest that these have been breached here, as the buyer has not been evicted.] |
| _____ _____ _____ _____ _____ | _____ _____ _____ _____ _____ | **Point Three (15%) Adverse Possession and Easement** <br><br> **Conclusion:** The buyer cannot compel the company to remove the sewer line from under the garden because he took subject to the sewer-line easement and probably did not interfere with that easement. <br><br> **Rule:** Where an adverse possessor acquires title by adverse possession, the nature of the acquired title is no greater than the title of the holder of the cause of action who was barred by the running of the statute of limitations. <br><br> **Application:** Here, <br><br> The owner's title was subject to the properly recorded sewer-line easement at the time the man wrongfully entered the land. <br><br> **Rule:** Adversely possessing the easement occurs when the adverse possessor interferes with the rights of the owner. <br><br> **Application:** There is nothing in the facts, however, suggesting that planting and maintaining a garden interfered with the sewer company's access to the sewer line. |

*continued on next page*

| Stated | Implied | |
|---|---|---|
| _____ | _____ | **Conclusion:** In the absence of such interference, the company has no cause of action against the possessors, in which case the buyer acquired the owner's title only—a title subject to the sewer-line easement. <br><br> [NOTE: Examinees who make a plausible argument that possession of the garden *did* interfere with the easement *should* conclude that the buyer could compel the sewer company to remove the sewer line. In that case, its failure to do so within the 10-year statutory period would result in the buyer acquiring a title that is superior to both the owner and the sewer company.] |

## MBE PRACTICE ANALYSIS[6]

### Question 1

A man obtained a bank loan secured by a mortgage on an office building that he owned. After several years, the man conveyed the office building to a woman, who took title subject to the mortgage. The deed to the woman was not recorded. The woman took immediate possession of the building and made the mortgage payments for several years.

Subsequently, the woman stopped making payments on the mortgage loan, and the bank eventually commenced foreclosure proceedings in which the man and the woman were both named parties. At the foreclosure sale, a third party purchased the building for less than the outstanding balance on the mortgage loan. The bank then sought to collect the deficiency from the woman.

Is the bank entitled to collect the deficiency from the woman?

(A) No, because the woman did not record the deed from the man.
**Incorrect.** The woman took title to the office building subject to the mortgage debt, which means that the debt was to be satisfied out of the building. The building is the principal, and the man, as transferor, is the only party liable for any deficiency. This situation can be contrasted with one in which a buyer expressly assumes the mortgage debt. In that case, the buyer would be primarily liable for any deficiency and the seller, absent a release by the mortgagee, would be secondarily liable. Recording the deed would give the bank constructive notice of the transfer but would have no effect on the collection of the deficiency.

(B) No, because the woman is not personally liable on the loan.
**Correct.** The woman took title to the office building subject to the mortgage but did not assume the mortgage debt. The debt is to be satisfied out of the building. The building is the principal, and the man, as transferor, is the only party liable for any deficiency. This situation can be contrasted with one in which a buyer expressly assumes the mortgage debt. In that case, the buyer would be primarily liable for any

deficiency and the seller, absent a release by the mortgagee, would be secondarily liable.

(C) Yes, because the woman took immediate possession of the building when she bought it from the man.
**Incorrect.** The woman took title to the building subject to the mortgage. Her title to the building allowed her to take possession of the building, but her possession has no effect on the payment of any deficiency judgment. Taking title to the building subject to the mortgage means that the debt is to be satisfied out of the building. The building is the principal, and the man, as transferor, is the only party liable for any deficiency. This situation can be contrasted with one in which a buyer expressly assumes the mortgage debt. In that case, the buyer would be primarily liable for any deficiency and the seller, absent a release by the mortgagee, would be secondarily liable.

(D) Yes, because the woman was a party to the foreclosure proceeding.
**Incorrect.** Because the woman took title to the building subject to the mortgage debt, she was a necessary party to the foreclosure proceeding. However, the fact that she took title to the building subject to the mortgage means that the debt is to be satisfied out of the building. The building is the principal, and the man, as transferor, is the only party liable for any deficiency. This situation can be contrasted with one in which a buyer expressly assumes the mortgage debt. In that case, the buyer would be primarily liable for any deficiency and the seller, absent a release by the mortgagee, would be secondarily liable.

### Question 2

A credit card company obtained and properly filed a judgment against a man after he failed to pay a $10,000 debt. A statute in the jurisdiction provides as follows: "Any judgment properly filed shall, for 10 years from filing, be a lien on the real property then owned or subsequently acquired by any person against whom the judgment is rendered."

Two years later, the man purchased land for $200,000. He made a down payment of $20,000 and borrowed the remaining $180,000 from a bank. The bank loan was secured by a mortgage on the land. Immediately after the closing, the deed to the man was recorded first, and the bank's mortgage was recorded second.

---

6. *Id.*

Five months later, the man defaulted on the mortgage loan and the bank initiated judicial foreclosure proceedings. After receiving notice of the proceedings, the credit card company filed a motion to have its judgment lien declared to be the first lien on the land.

Is the credit card company's motion likely to be granted?

(A) No, because the bank's mortgage secured a loan used to purchase the land.

**Correct.** The bank's mortgage is a purchase-money mortgage, meaning that the funds the bank advanced were used to purchase the land. A purchase-money mortgage executed at the same time as the purchase of the real property encumbered takes precedence over any other claim or lien, including a previously filed judgment lien. Therefore, the bank's purchase-money mortgage takes precedence over the credit card company's judgment lien.

(B) No, because the man's down payment exceeded the amount of his debt to the credit card company.

**Incorrect.** The relative amounts of the down payment and the credit card debt are irrelevant. The bank's mortgage is a purchase-money mortgage, meaning that the funds the bank advanced were used to purchase the land. A purchase-money mortgage executed at the same time as the purchase of the real property encumbered takes precedence over any other claim or lien, including a previously filed judgment lien.

(C) Yes, because the bank had constructive notice of the judgment lien.

**Incorrect.** It is true that the judgment lien was properly filed and thus provided the bank with constructive notice of the lien. The bank's mortgage, however, is a purchase-money mortgage, meaning that the funds the bank advanced were used to purchase the land. A purchase-money mortgage executed at the same time as the purchase of the real property encumbered takes precedence over any other claim, including a previously filed judgment lien.

(D) Yes, because the bank is a third-party lender and not the seller of the land.

**Incorrect.** The bank's mortgage is a purchase-money mortgage, meaning that the funds the bank advanced were used to purchase the land. A purchase-money mortgage may be granted by a seller, by a third party, or both. A purchase-money mortgage executed at the same time as the purchase

of the real property encumbered takes precedence over any other claim, including a previously filed judgment lien. Therefore, the bank's purchase-money mortgage takes precedence over the credit card company's judgment lien.

**Question 3**

A husband and wife acquired land as common law joint tenants with right of survivorship. One year later, without his wife's knowledge, the husband executed a will devising the land to his best friend. The husband subsequently died.

Is the wife now the sole owner of the land?

(A) No, because a joint tenant has the unilateral right to end a joint tenancy without the consent of the other joint tenant.

**Incorrect.** As a general rule, a joint tenant's interest is freely alienable during his or her lifetime without the consent of the other joint tenant. However, a joint tenant's interest cannot be devised in a will. In this case, on the death of the husband, the wife's interest in the joint tenancy immediately swelled and she became the sole owner of the land as the surviving joint tenant.

(B) No, because the wife's interest in the husband's undivided 50% ownership in the land adeemed.

**Incorrect.** The doctrine of ademption applies only when an individual dies testate and attempts to devise land that the testator no longer owns. Although as a general rule a joint tenant's interest is freely alienable during his or her lifetime without the consent of the other joint tenant, that interest cannot be devised in a will. In this case, on the death of the husband, the wife's interest in the joint tenancy immediately swelled and she became the sole owner of the land as the surviving joint tenant.

(C) Yes, because of the doctrine of after-acquired title, or by estoppel by deed.

**Incorrect.** The doctrine of after-acquired title, or estoppel by deed, applies when an individual attempts to convey title (usually by warranty deed) at a time when the individual does not have title to the land but later acquires title to the land. Although as a general rule a joint tenant's interest is freely alienable during his or her lifetime without the consent of the other joint tenant, that interest cannot be devised in a will. In this case, on the death of the husband, the wife's interest in the joint tenancy immediately swelled and she became the sole owner of the land as the surviving joint tenant.

(D) Yes, because the devise to the friend did not sever the joint tenancy.

**Correct.** Although as a general rule a joint tenant's interest is freely alienable during his or her lifetime without the consent of the other joint tenant, that interest cannot be devised in a will. In this case, on the death of the husband, the wife's interest in the joint tenancy immediately swelled and she became the sole owner of the land as the surviving joint tenant.

## Question 4

A landlord leased a building to a tenant for a 10-year term. Two years after the term began, the tenant subleased the building to a sublessee for a 5-year term. Under the terms of the sublease, the sublessee agreed to make monthly rent payments to the tenant.

Although the sublessee made timely rent payments to the tenant, the tenant did not forward four of those payments to the landlord. The tenant has left the jurisdiction and cannot be found. The landlord has sued the sublessee for the unpaid rent.

There is no applicable statute.

If the court rules that the sublessee is not liable to the landlord for the unpaid rent, what will be the most likely reason?

(A) A sublessee is responsible to the landlord only as a surety for unpaid rent owed by the tenant.

**Incorrect.** In a sublease, the tenant transfers a right of possession for a time shorter than the balance of the leasehold. Therefore, the sublessee and the tenant are in privity of estate with each other, but only the tenant remains in privity of estate with the landlord. There also is no privity of contract between the sublessee and the landlord, because the sublessee made no promise, either to the landlord or to the tenant, to pay rent to the landlord. Lacking privity, the sublessee is not liable to the landlord for the rent and also is not a surety for the tenant.

(B) The sublease constitutes a novation of the original lease.

**Incorrect.** A novation occurs when a tenant seeks to avoid future liability for rent after an assignment and the landlord agrees to release the tenant from such liability. An assignment occurs when the tenant transfers the entire period of time remaining on the lease agreement. Here, the tenant only transferred a portion of the

remaining time on the lease agreement, and the tenant did not seek a release or novation from the landlord.

(C) The sublessee is not in privity of estate or contract with the landlord.

**Correct.** In a sublease, the tenant transfers a right of possession for a time shorter than the balance of the leasehold. Therefore, the sublessee and the tenant are in privity of estate with each other, but only the tenant remains in privity of estate with the landlord. There also is no privity of contract between the sublessee and the landlord, because the sublessee made no promise, either to the landlord or to the tenant, to pay rent to the landlord. Lacking privity, the sublessee is not liable to the landlord for the rent. Although privity may not be required under an equitable servitude theory, a finding for the sublessee would mean that the court did not use such a theory.

(D) The sublessee's rent payments to the tenant fully discharged the sublessee's obligation to pay rent to the landlord.

**Incorrect.** The sublessee had no obligation to pay rent to the landlord. In a sublease, the tenant transfers a right of possession for a time shorter than the balance of the leasehold. Therefore, the sublessee and the tenant are in privity of estate with each other, but only the tenant remains in privity of estate with the landlord. There also is no privity of contract between the sublessee and the landlord, because the sublessee made no promise, either to the landlord or to the tenant, to pay rent to the landlord. Lacking privity, a sublessee is not liable to the landlord for the rent. Although privity may not be required under an equitable servitude theory, a finding for the sublessee would mean that the court did not use such a theory.

## Question 5

A woman who owned a house executed a deed purporting to convey the house to her son and his wife. The language of the deed was sufficient to create a common law joint tenancy with right of survivorship, which is unmodified by statute in the jurisdiction. The woman mailed the deed to the son with a letter saying: "Because I intend you and your wife to have my house after my death, I am enclosing a deed to the house. However, I intend to live in the house for the rest of my life, so don't record the deed until I die. The deed will be effective at my death."

The son put the deed in his desk. The wife discovered the deed and recorded it without the son's knowledge. Subsequently, the son and the wife separated, and the wife, without telling anyone, conveyed her interest in the house to a friend who immediately reconveyed it to the wife.

The woman learned that the son and the wife had separated and also learned what had happened to the deed to the house. The woman then brought an appropriate action against the son and the wife to obtain a declaration that the woman was still the owner of the house and an order canceling of record the woman's deed and the subsequent deeds.

If the court determines that the woman owns the house in fee simple, what will be the likely explanation?

**(A)** The deed was not delivered.

**Correct.** To be valid, a deed must be properly executed and delivered. Delivery is a question of the grantor's intent. In this case, the woman did not intend the deed to be effective until her death. An intent to have a transfer be effective at the grantor's death is valid in a will but not in a deed unless the deed expressly reserves a life estate, which this deed did not do. The woman remained in possession of the house and intended to retain title to the house until her death. The deed was not delivered, so she owns the house in fee simple.

**(B)** The wife's conduct entitles the woman to equitable relief.

**Incorrect.** The wife's conduct may have been inappropriate, but it is not relevant to whether the woman properly delivered the deed to the son and the wife. To be valid, a deed must be properly executed and delivered. Delivery is a question of the grantor's intent. In this case, the woman did not intend the deed to be effective until her death. An intent to have a transfer be effective at the grantor's death is valid in a will but not in a deed unless the deed expressly reserves a life estate, which this deed did not do. The woman remained in possession of the house and intended to retain title to the house until her death. The deed was not delivered, so she owns the house in fee simple.

**(C)** The woman expressly reserved a life estate.

**Incorrect.** The woman did not expressly reserve a life estate, and she remained in possession of the house. To be valid, a deed must be properly executed and delivered. Delivery is a question of the grantor's intent. In this case, the woman did not intend the deed to be effective until her death. An intent to have a transfer be effective at the grantor's death is valid in a will but not in

a deed unless the deed expressly reserves a life estate, which this deed did not do. The woman remained in possession of the house and intended to retain title to the house until her death. The deed was not delivered, so she owns the house in fee simple.

**(D)** The woman received no consideration for her deed.

**Incorrect.** A grantor may convey property for no consideration. To be valid, however, a deed must be properly executed and delivered. Delivery is a question of the grantor's intent. In this case, the woman did not intend the deed to be effective until her death. An intent to have a transfer be effective at the grantor's death is valid in a will but not in a deed unless the deed expressly reserves a life estate, which this deed did not do. The woman remained in possession of the house, and the deed was not delivered, so she owns the house in fee simple.

## Question 6

A woman borrowed $100,000 from a bank and executed a promissory note to the bank in that amount. As security for repayment of the loan, the woman's brother gave the bank a mortgage on a tract of land solely owned by him. The brother did not sign the promissory note.

The woman subsequently defaulted on the loan, and after acceleration, the bank instituted foreclosure proceedings on the brother's land. The brother filed a timely objection to the foreclosure.

Will the bank succeed in foreclosing on the tract of land?

**(A)** No, because the bank has an equitable mortgage rather than a legal mortgage.

**Incorrect.** A mortgage is security for the performance of an act. The performance may be by the mortgagor or by some other person. Therefore, the mortgage granted by the brother to secure the debt of the woman is valid, and the bank may foreclose on it.

**(B)** No, because a mortgage from the brother is invalid without a mortgage debt owed by him.

**Incorrect.** A mortgage is security for the performance of an act. The performance may be by the mortgagor or by some other person. Therefore, the mortgage granted by the brother to secure the debt of the woman is valid, and the bank may foreclose on it.

**(C)** Yes, because the bank has a valid mortgage.

**Correct.** A mortgage is security for the performance of an act. The performance may be by the mortgagor or by some other person. The mortgage granted by the brother to secure the debt of the woman is valid even though the woman also has personal liability on the debt.

(D) Yes, because the bank is a surety for the brother's mortgage.

**Incorrect.** The bank is the mortgagee under the mortgage and not a surety. The bank may foreclose on the mortgage, however, because the mortgage is valid and the debt is in default. A mortgage is security for the performance of an act. The performance may be by the mortgagor or by some other person.

## Question 7

A mother executed a will devising vacant land to her son. The mother showed the will to her son.

Thereafter, the son purported to convey the land to a friend by a warranty deed that contained no exceptions. The friend paid value for the land and promptly recorded the deed without having first conducted any title search. The friend never took possession of the land.

The mother later died, and the will devising the land to her son was duly admitted to probate.

Thereafter, the friend conducted a title search for the land and asked the son for a new deed. The son refused, because the value of the land had doubled, but he offered to refund the purchase price to the friend.

The friend has sued to quiet title to the land. Is the friend likely to prevail?

(A) No, because the friend failed to conduct a title search before purchasing the land.

**Incorrect.** A buyer may want to search the title before purchasing land to determine if title is as called for in the contract, but such a search is not required. The doctrine of estoppel by deed (sometimes referred to as after-acquired title) provides that even if the grantor has no title to the land at the time the deed is delivered, title automatically passes to the grantee when title is so acquired, provided that the grantor asserts the quality of title conveyed in the deed. In this case, the son conveyed to the friend by a warranty deed with no exceptions.

(B) No, because the son had no interest in the land at the time of conveyance.

**Incorrect.** It is true that the son had no interest in the land at the time of conveyance. The doctrine of estoppel

by deed (sometimes referred to as after-acquired title), however, provides that in such a case title automatically passes to the grantee when the title is so acquired, provided that the grantor asserts the quality of title conveyed in the deed. In this case, the son conveyed to the friend by a warranty deed with no exceptions.

(C) Yes, because of the doctrine of estoppel by deed.

**Correct.** The doctrine of estoppel by deed (sometimes referred to as after-acquired title) provides that even if the grantor has no title to the land at the time the deed is delivered, the title automatically passes to the grantee when title is so acquired, provided that the grantor asserts the quality of title conveyed in the deed. In this case, the son conveyed to the friend by a warranty deed with no exceptions.

(D) Yes, because the deed was recorded.

**Incorrect.** Recording has no effect on title in this case. The doctrine of estoppel by deed (sometimes referred to as after-acquired title) provides that even if the grantor has no title to the land at the time the deed is delivered, the title automatically passes to the grantee when title is so acquired, provided that the grantor asserts the quality of title conveyed in the deed. In this case, the son conveyed to the friend by a warranty deed with no exceptions. It is irrelevant to the doctrine of estoppel by deed whether the deed was recorded or not.

## Question 8

A woman inherited a house from a distant relative. The woman had never visited the house, which was located in another state, and did not want to own it. Upon learning this, a man who lived next door to the house called the woman and asked to buy the house. The woman agreed, provided that the house was sold "as is." The man agreed, and the woman conveyed the house to the man by a warranty deed.

The man had purchased the house for investment purposes, intending to rent it out while continuing to live next door. After the sale, the man started to renovate the house and discovered serious termite damage. The man sued the woman for breach of contract.

There are no applicable statutes. How should the court rule?

(A) For the woman, because the man planned to change the use of the house for investment purposes.

**Incorrect.** The man's proposed change of use was not known to the woman, nor was it stated in the contract. His planned change to the use of the house is irrelevant to the outcome of the case. The woman should prevail, but it is because she sold the house "as is."

**(B) For the woman, because she sold the house "as is."**
**Correct.** A seller may disclaim any duty to disclose defects if the disclaimer is sufficiently clear and specific. In this case, the contract specifically noted that the house was being sold "as is." The woman made no misrepresentations regarding the condition of the house. There are no statutes that might require an owner-occupier to disclose known defects, and in any case the woman inherited the house and had never visited or lived in it. In addition, this is not the sale of a new house by a builder/seller, which may impose a warranty of habitability.

**(C) For the man, because of the doctrine of caveat emptor.**
**Incorrect.** The doctrine of caveat emptor states that the buyer accepts the property in its current condition. Therefore, the caveat emptor doctrine would not protect the man as the buyer. In fact, a seller may disclaim any duty to disclose defects if the disclaimer is sufficiently clear and specific. In this case, the contract specifically noted that the house was being sold "as is," and therefore the woman should prevail.

**(D) For the man, because he received a warranty deed.**
**Incorrect.** A warranty deed provides remedies for breaches of title matters. Termite damage affects the physical quality of the property, not title to the property. A seller may disclaim any duty to disclose physical defects if the disclaimer is sufficiently clear and specific. In this case, the contract specifically noted that the house was being sold "as is," and therefore the woman should prevail.

## Question 9

A man owned a large tract of land that had frontage on a public highway. The land had no access to any other road.

Fifteen years ago, the man conveyed the rear half of the land to a woman and at the same time conveyed an express easement to the woman that provided access from her land across his retained land to the public highway.

The woman used the easement until she reconveyed the land back to the man 10 years ago. The deed to the man made no reference to the easement.

Five years ago, the man again conveyed the rear half of the land, this time to an investor in a deed that made no reference to any easement to the public highway.

Recently, the man told the investor that he could no longer cross the man's land for access to the public highway. A neighbor has told the investor that he can use her land for access to another public road "for a price."

The investor has sued the man for the right to cross the man's land to the public highway.

For whom will the court likely decide?

**(A) The investor, because an easement will be implied.**
**Correct.** The express easement granted to the woman was terminated by merger when she reconveyed her land to the man, who again became the common owner of both tracts. The man then conveyed the rear half of the land to the investor, whose land is now landlocked. An easement by necessity is implied for the benefit of the landlocked parcel at the moment of severance of the common ownership.

**(B) The investor, because the man is estopped by his grant of an easement to the woman.**
**Incorrect.** The investor will likely prevail, but not for this reason. The express easement conveyed to the woman was terminated by merger when she reconveyed her land to the man. The man, as the common owner of both tracts of land, then conveyed the rear half of the land to the investor, whose land is now landlocked. An easement by necessity is implied for the benefit of the landlocked parcel at the moment of severance of the common ownership.

**(C) The man, because the express easement was terminated by the reconveyance.**
**Incorrect.** It is true that the express easement granted to the woman was terminated by merger when she reconveyed her land to the man. But the man, as the common owner of both tracts of land, then conveyed the rear half to the investor, whose land is now landlocked. An easement by necessity for the benefit of the landlocked parcel is implied at the moment of severance of the common ownership.

**(D)** The man, because the investor can reasonably acquire another means of access to a public road.

**Incorrect.** The express easement granted to the woman terminated by merger when she reconveyed her land to the man. The man, as the common owner of both tracts of land, then conveyed the rear half to the investor, whose land is now landlocked. An easement by necessity for the benefit of the landlocked parcel is implied at the moment of severance of the common ownership. The fact that the neighbor has offered to sell the investor a right of access is irrelevant.

## Question 10

Two friends planned to incorporate a business together and agreed that they would own all of the corporation's stock in equal proportion.

A businesswoman conveyed land by a warranty deed to "the corporation and its successors and assigns." The deed was recorded.

Thereafter, the friends had a disagreement. No papers were ever filed to incorporate the business. There is no applicable statute.

Who owns the land?

**(A)** The businesswoman, because the deed was a warranty deed.

**Incorrect.** The businesswoman owns the land, but she does so because the deed was void. To be valid, a deed must be properly executed and delivered. A deed to a nonexistent grantee, such as a corporation that has not yet been legally formed, is void. It does not matter whether the deed is a warranty, quitclaim, or special warranty deed. At the time the businesswoman attempted to convey the land to the corporation, the corporation had not yet been legally formed, so the deed was void.

**(B)** The businesswoman, because the deed was void.

**Correct.** To be valid, a deed must be properly executed and delivered. A deed to a nonexistent grantee, such as a corporation that has not yet been legally formed, is void. At the time the businesswoman attempted to convey the land to the corporation, the corporation had not yet been legally formed, so the deed was void.

**(C)** The two friends as tenants in common, because they intended to own the corporation's stock in equal proportion.

**Incorrect.** To be valid, a deed must be properly executed and delivered. A deed to a nonexistent grantee, such as a corporation that has not yet been legally formed, is void and thus conveys no title. It is irrelevant that the two friends intended to own the corporation's stock in equal proportion.

**(D)** The two friends as tenants in common, because they were the intended sole shareholders.

**Incorrect.** To be valid, a deed must be properly executed and delivered. A deed to a nonexistent grantee, such as a corporation that has not yet been legally formed, is void and thus conveys no title. It is irrelevant that the two friends intended to be the sole shareholders. At the time the businesswoman attempted to convey the land to the corporation, the corporation had not yet been legally formed, so the deed was void.

## Question 11

A landlord leased a building to a tenant for a term of six years. The lease complied with the statute of frauds and was not recorded. During the lease term, the tenant sent an email to the landlord that stated: "I hereby offer to purchase for $250,000 the building that I am now occupying under a six-year lease with you." The tenant's name was placed below the word "signed" on the message.

In response, the landlord emailed the tenant: "That's fine. We'll close in 60 days." The landlord's name was placed below the word "signed" on the reply message.

Sixty days later, the landlord refused to tender the deed to the building when the tenant tendered the $250,000 purchase price. The tenant has sued for specific performance.

Who is likely to prevail?

**(A)** The landlord, because formation of an enforceable contract to convey the building could not occur until after the lease term expired.

**Incorrect.** A contract to convey the building could be made during the lease term or thereafter. The email exchange satisfied the statute of frauds, the contract was valid, and the tenant is entitled to specific performance.

**(B)** The landlord, because the landlord's email response did not contain a sufficient signature under the statute of frauds.

**Incorrect.** The statute of frauds does require a signature by the party against whom enforcement is sought. However, courts are liberal regarding the nature of a signature; it need only reflect an intent to authenticate the writing. Both the tenant's and the landlord's names were placed below the word "signed," which adequately reflected their desire to be bound. The other requirements of the statute of frauds were also met: the writings identified the parties and the property, expressed an intent to buy and sell, and contained a price term.

(C) The tenant, because the email messages constitute an insufficient attornment of the lease.

**Incorrect.** Attornment is not an issue in this case, because it is the tenant who wants to purchase the property. The tenant is likely to prevail, but it is because there was a valid contract of sale. The exchange of emails satisfies the statute of frauds, because the writings identified the parties and the property, expressed an intent to buy and sell, and contained a price term and adequate signatures.

(D) The tenant, because the email messages constitute a sufficient memorandum under the statute of frauds.

**Correct.** The statute of frauds requires a contract for the sale of land to identify the parties, contain a description of the land, evidence an intent to buy and sell, recite (usually) a price term, and be signed by the party against whom enforcement is sought. The email messages here fulfill those requirements. Courts are liberal regarding the nature of a signature; it need only reflect an intent to authenticate the writing. Both the tenant's and the landlord's names were placed below the word "signed," which adequately reflected their desire to be bound.

### Question 12

A tenant leased a commercial property from a landlord for a 12-year term. The property included a large store and a parking lot. At the start of the lease period, the tenant took possession and with the landlord's oral consent installed counters, display cases, shelving, and special lighting. Both parties complied with all lease terms.

The lease is set to expire next month. Two weeks ago, when the landlord contacted the tenant about a possible lease renewal, she learned that the tenant had decided not to renew the lease, and that the tenant planned to remove all of the above-listed items on or before the lease termination date. The landlord claimed that all the items had become part of the real estate and had to remain on the premises. The tenant asserted his right and intention to remove all the items.

Both the lease and the statutes of the jurisdiction are silent on the matter in dispute. At the time the landlord consented and the tenant installed the items, nothing was said about the tenant's right to retain or remove the items.

The landlord has sued the tenant to enjoin his removal of the items. How is the court likely to rule?

(A) For the landlord, because the items have become part of the landlord's real estate.

**Incorrect.** This is a commercial lease, and the tenant has been using the items in his business. Therefore, even if the items have become fixtures, they are trade fixtures, which may be removed by the tenant before the end of the lease term unless very substantial damage would be done by the removal. It is unlikely that the removal of these items will cause substantial damage; if so, however, the tenant must either restore the premises or pay the cost of restoration.

(B) For the landlord as to items bolted or otherwise attached to the premises, and for the tenant as to items not attached to the premises other than by weight.

**Incorrect.** This is a commercial lease, and the tenant has been using the items in his business. Therefore, even if the items have become fixtures, they are trade fixtures, which may be removed by the tenant before the end of the lease term unless very substantial damage would be done by the removal. It is unlikely that the removal of these items will cause substantial damage; if so, however, the tenant must either restore the premises or pay the cost of restoration. Whether an item is bolted or otherwise attached to the premises is only a factor in determining if it is a fixture.

(C) For the tenant, provided that the tenant reasonably restores the premises to the prior condition or pays for the cost of restoration.

**Correct.** This is a commercial lease, and the tenant has been using the items in his business. Therefore, the items are trade fixtures, and the tenant may remove them before the end of the lease term unless very substantial damage would be done by the removal. It is unlikely that the removal of these items will cause substantial damage; if so, however, the tenant must either restore the premises or pay the cost of restoration.

**(D)** For the tenant, because all of the items may be removed as trade fixtures without any obligation to restore the premises.

**Incorrect.** The tenant may be obligated to restore the premises. This is a commercial lease, and the tenant has been using the items in his business. Therefore, the items are trade fixtures, and the tenant may remove them before the end of the lease term unless very substantial damage would be done by the removal. It is unlikely that the removal of these items will cause substantial damage; if so, however, the tenant must either restore the premises or pay the cost of restoration.

## Question 13

For 22 years, the land records have shown a man as the owner of an 80-acre farm. The man has never physically occupied the land.

Nineteen years ago, a woman entered the farm. The character and duration of the woman's possession of the farm caused her to become the owner of the farm under the adverse possession law of the jurisdiction.

Three years ago, when the woman was not present, a neighbor took over possession of the farm. The neighbor repaired fences, put up "no trespassing" signs, and did some plowing. When the woman returned, she found the neighbor in possession of the farm. The neighbor vigorously rejected the woman's claimed right to possession and threatened force. The woman withdrew.

The woman then went to the man and told him of the history of activity on the farm. The woman orally told the man that she had been wrong to try to take his farm. She expressly waived any claim she had to the land. The man thanked her.

Last month, unsure of the effect of her conversation with the man, the woman executed a deed purporting to convey the farm to her son. The son promptly recorded the deed.

The period of time to acquire title by adverse possession in the jurisdiction is 10 years. Who now owns the farm?

**(A)** The man, because the woman's later words and actions released title to the man.

**Incorrect.** The woman acquired her title to the farm by adverse possession. The woman's title was an original title and did not derive from the man's title. The statute of frauds requires that any conveyance of real property be in writing. Therefore, the woman's oral statement was insufficient to release the title to the man, and the woman validly conveyed the farm to her son.

**(B)** The neighbor, because the neighbor succeeded to the woman's adverse possession title by privity of possession.

**Incorrect.** The woman acquired title to the farm by adverse possession. The woman's title was an original title and did not derive from the man's title. The neighbor's actions may have started the statute of limitations running on his adverse possession of the farm, but he has been in possession of the farm for only three years. In addition, the neighbor was never in privity with the woman.

**(C)** The son, because he succeeded to the woman's adverse possession title by privity of conveyance.

**Correct.** The woman acquired title to the farm by adverse possession. The woman's title was an original title and did not derive from the man's title. The statute of frauds requires that the conveyance of the farm be in writing. Therefore, the woman's oral statement was insufficient to release the title to the man, and the woman validly conveyed the farm to her son.

**(D)** The woman, because she must bring a quiet title action to establish her title to the farm before she can convey the farm to her son.

**Incorrect.** The woman acquired title to the farm by adverse possession. The woman's title was an original title and did not derive from the man's title. The statute of frauds requires that any conveyance of real property be in writing. Therefore, the woman's oral statement was insufficient to release the title to the man. Having established title to the farm by adverse possession, there is no requirement that the woman sue to establish title. Therefore, she could convey the farm to her son.

## Question 14

In the most recent deed in the chain of title to a tract of land, a man conveyed the land as follows: "To my niece and her heirs and assigns in fee simple until my niece's daughter marries, and then to my niece's daughter and her heirs and assigns in fee simple."

There is no applicable statute, and the common law Rule Against Perpetuities has not been modified in the jurisdiction. Which of the following is the most accurate statement concerning the title to the land?

**(A)** The niece has a life estate and the daughter has a contingent remainder.

**Incorrect.** The gift to the niece was to the niece "and her heirs and assigns," thereby creating a fee estate rather than a life estate. The fee simple estate was made defeasible by the addition of the words of limitation "until my niece's daughter marries." A remainder interest may follow a life estate; however, a remainder does not follow a fee simple estate. A future interest created in a grantee following a defeasible estate is an executory interest. The executory interest in this case does not violate the Rule Against Perpetuities, because it will be known within the lifetime of the validating lives—the niece and the niece's daughter—whether the condition of marriage has occurred.

**(B)** The niece has a fee simple and the daughter has no interest, because after the grant of a fee simple there can be no gift over.

**Incorrect.** The niece was given a defeasible fee simple. A limitation may be expressly attached to a fee simple estate. The express limitation attached to the grant was "until my niece's daughter marries." A future interest held by a grantee following a defeasible estate is an executory interest. The executory interest in this case does not violate the common law Rule Against Perpetuities, because it will be known within the lifetime of the validating lives—the niece and the niece's daughter—whether the condition of marriage has occurred.

**(C)** The niece has a fee simple and the daughter has no interest, because she might not marry within 21 years after the date of the deed.

**Incorrect.** The niece was granted a defeasible fee simple. The express limitation was the marriage of the niece's daughter. If the limitation occurs, the estate transfers automatically to the niece's daughter. The future interest held by a grantee following a defeasible estate is an executory interest. Executory interests are subject to the common law Rule Against Perpetuities; however, the niece and the niece's daughter are both validating lives and the condition of the marriage either will or will not occur during their lifetimes. The additional 21 years after the death of all validating lives is not needed, and the rule is not violated.

**(D)** The niece has a defeasible fee simple determinable and the daughter has an executory interest.

**Correct.** The niece has a defeasible fee simple because of the limitation placed on the estate by the words "until my niece's daughter marries." If the niece's daughter marries, the estate in the niece will end automatically and will pass to the holder of the future interest (the niece's daughter). The future interest given to the daughter, a grantee, is an executory interest. The executory interest in this case does not violate the common law Rule Against Perpetuities, because it will be known within the lifetime of the validating lives—the niece and the niece's daughter—whether the condition of marriage has occurred.

## Question 15

A businessman executed a promissory note for $200,000 to a bank, secured by a mortgage on commercial real estate owned by the businessman. The promissory note stated that the businessman was not personally liable for the mortgage debt.

One week later, a finance company obtained a judgment against the businessman for $50,000 and filed the judgment in the county where the real estate was located. At the time the judgment was filed, the finance company had no actual notice of the bank's mortgage.

Two weeks after that filing, the bank recorded its mortgage on the businessman's real estate.

The recording act of the jurisdiction provides: "Unless the same be recorded according to law, no conveyance or mortgage of real property shall be good against subsequent purchasers for value and without notice or against judgment creditors without notice."

The finance company sued to enforce its judgment lien against the businessman's real estate. The bank intervened in the action, contending that the judgment lien was a second lien on the real estate and that its mortgage was a first lien.

Is the bank's contention correct?

**(A)** No, because the judgment lien was recorded before the mortgage, and the finance company had no actual notice of the mortgage.

**Correct.** The judgment lien was recorded first in a jurisdiction that expressly protects judgment creditors without notice. The finance company had no actual notice of the mortgage and had no constructive notice because the mortgage was not recorded until two weeks after the judgment was filed. The bank's mortgage was not a purchase-money mortgage, which would have given it priority.

**(B)** No, because the businessman was not personally liable for the mortgage debt, and the mortgage was therefore void.
**Incorrect.** The fact that the businessman was not personally liable for the mortgage debt is irrelevant and does not make the mortgage void. The judgment was recorded first in a jurisdiction that expressly protects judgment creditors without notice. The finance company had no actual notice of the mortgage and had no constructive notice because the mortgage was not recorded until two weeks after the judgment was filed. The bank's mortgage was not a purchase-money mortgage, which would have given it priority.

**(C)** Yes, because a mortgage prior in time has priority over a subsequent judgment lien.
**Incorrect.** The judgment was recorded first in a jurisdiction that expressly protects judgment creditors without notice. The finance company had no actual notice of the mortgage and had no constructive notice because the mortgage was not recorded until two weeks after the judgment was filed. The bank's mortgage was not a purchase-money mortgage, which would have given it priority. Priority is determined under these facts by the order of filing.

**(D)** Yes, because the recording of a mortgage relates back to the date of execution of the mortgage note.
**Incorrect.** The recording of a mortgage does not relate back to the date of execution of the mortgage note. The mortgage gives constructive notice as of the date of its recording. Therefore, at the time the judgment was recorded, the finance company had neither actual nor constructive notice of the mortgage and is protected under the jurisdiction's recording act. The bank's mortgage was not a purchase-money mortgage, which would have given it priority.

## Question 16

A seller conveyed residential land to a buyer by a warranty deed that contained no exceptions and recited that the full consideration had been paid.

To finance the purchase, the buyer borrowed 80% of the necessary funds from a bank. The seller agreed to finance 15% of the purchase price, and the buyer agreed to provide cash for the remaining 5%.

At the closing, the buyer signed a promissory note to the seller for 15% of the purchase price but did not execute a mortgage. The bank knew of the loan made by the seller and of the promissory note executed by the buyer to the seller. The buyer also signed a note to the bank, secured by a mortgage, for the 80% advanced by the bank.

The buyer has now defaulted on both loans. There are no applicable statutes.

Which loan has priority?

**(A)** The bank's loan, because the seller can finance a part of the purchase price only by use of an installment land contract.
**Incorrect.** A seller may finance the purchase of property in a number of ways, including by an installment land contract, by securing the note with a purchase-money mortgage, or by an equitable vendor's lien. However, the seller did not secure the note with a mortgage, nor was an installment land contract used. The seller may have had an equitable vendor's lien for the unpaid purchase price, but the deed recites that the full consideration was paid. Therefore, the bank's purchase-money mortgage takes priority over the seller's unsecured loan and any implied equitable vendor's lien even if the bank knew of the vendor's lien.

**(B)** The bank's loan, because it was secured by a purchase-money mortgage.
**Correct.** The bank has a purchase-money mortgage, because the loan proceeds were used to help purchase the land. A purchase-money mortgage, executed at the same time as the deed to the land, takes precedence over any other lien that attaches to the property. The seller's loan could also have been secured by a purchase-money mortgage, but it was not; the buyer signed an unsecured note to the seller. The seller also may have had an equitable vendor's lien for the unpaid purchase price, but the deed recites that the full consideration was paid. Therefore, the bank's purchase-money mortgage takes priority over the seller's unsecured loan and any implied equitable vendor's lien even if the bank knew of the vendor's lien.

**(C)** The seller's loan, because a promissory note to a seller has priority over a bank loan for residential property.

**Incorrect.** The seller's promissory note could have been secured by a mortgage, but it was not. The seller may have had an equitable vendor's lien for the unpaid purchase price, but the deed recites that the full consideration was paid. Therefore, the bank's purchase-money mortgage takes priority over the seller's unsecured loan and any implied equitable vendor's lien even if the bank knew of the vendor's lien.

**(D)** The seller's loan, because the bank knew that the seller had an equitable vendor's lien.

**Incorrect.** The seller may have had an equitable vendor's lien for the unpaid purchase price, but the deed recites that the full consideration was paid. Therefore, the bank's purchase-money mortgage takes precedence over the seller's unsecured loan as well as any implied equitable vendor's lien, and it is irrelevant that the bank knew of the vendor's lien.

## Question 17

A seller and a buyer signed a contract for the sale of vacant land. The contract was silent concerning the quality of title, but the seller agreed in the contract to convey the land to the buyer by a warranty deed without any exceptions.

When the buyer conducted a title search for the land, she learned that the applicable zoning did not allow for her planned commercial use. She also discovered that there was a recorded restrictive covenant limiting the use of the land to residential use.

The buyer no longer wants to purchase the land. Must the buyer purchase the land?

**(A)** No, because the restrictive covenant renders the title unmarketable.

**Correct.** Unless the contract provides to the contrary, the law will imply that the seller will provide the buyer with a marketable title on the date of closing. A marketable title is not a perfect title but is a title a

court will force an unwilling buyer to purchase. A right held in the land by a third party, such as the right to enforce a restrictive covenant, renders the title unmarketable, and the buyer need not purchase the land.

**(B)** No, because the zoning places a cloud on the title.

**Incorrect.** Although in some cases an existing violation of a zoning code may render title unmarketable, the mere existence of a zoning code does not render the title unmarketable or place a cloud on the title. Unless the contract provides to the contrary, the law will imply that the seller will provide the buyer with a marketable title on the date of closing. A right held in the land by a third party, such as the right to enforce a restrictive covenant, renders the title unmarketable, and the buyer need not purchase the land.

**(C)** Yes, because the buyer would receive a warranty deed without any exceptions.

**Incorrect.** Unless the contract provides to the contrary, the law will imply that the seller will provide the buyer with a marketable title on the date of closing. However, after a buyer accepts the deed, the doctrine of merger prevents the buyer from raising the issue of marketability of title, and the buyer's remedy regarding title issues, if any, will be based on the deed.

**(D)** Yes, because the contract was silent regarding the quality of the title.

**Incorrect.** Unless the contract provides to the contrary, the law will imply that the seller will provide the buyer with a marketable title on the date of closing. This contract was silent on the quality of title and therefore a marketable title will be implied. A marketable title is not a perfect title but is a title a court will require an unwilling buyer to purchase. A right held in the land by a third party, such as the right to enforce a restrictive covenant, renders the title unmarketable, and the buyer need not purchase the land.

## VII. Chapter 15 TORTS

## ESSAY SCORE SHEET

| Stated | Implied | |
|---|---|---|
| | | **Point One (25%) Negligence of Physician** |
| _____ | _____ | **Conclusion:** Because the physician did not fail to comply with the standard of care, the physician would not be liable for the man's injury. |
| _____ | _____ | **Rule:** A medical doctor is liable to a patient only when the evidence shows that he has failed to comply with the standard of care for the relevant specialty and medical community and his failure causes the patient's injury. |
| _____ | _____ | In assessing whether a doctor has met this test, most courts compare the doctor's conduct to national standards rather than those that prevail in his or her locality. |
| _____ | _____ | **Application:** Here, |
| _____ | _____ | There are two possible negligence claims against the physician. |
| _____ | _____ | One claim is that the physician was negligent in suggesting that drinking the herbal tea might lower his cholesterol. |
| _____ | _____ | Next, in his follow-up visit, the physician was negligent in failing to determine that his symptoms were due to the herbal tea if the man could establish that the delay in diagnosis worsened his medical condition. |
| _____ | _____ | There is no indication that the physician failed to comply with the standard of care by suggesting that this type of herbal tea lowered cholesterol levels. |
| _____ | _____ | There is no indication that the physician was aware that this type of herbal tea would be contaminated with toxic pesticides. |
| _____ | _____ | Moreover, there is no indication that complying with the standard of care for general practitioners would have required him to be aware of such contamination. |
| _____ | _____ | The physician advised the man that a prescription drug was the most reliable method of lowering cholesterol levels and told the man to come back for another test in three months. |
| _____ | _____ | The physician only mentioned the herbal tea when the man refused a prescription drug in favor of "natural" methods and dietary change and did so because of a recent research report. Indeed, the herbal tea may have played a role in lowering the man's cholesterol. |
| _____ | _____ | With respect to the physician's failure to correctly diagnose the source of the man's symptoms, the physician responded to the man's elevated white blood cell count promptly and ordered additional tests. |
| _____ | _____ | After these tests revealed a liver inflammation, the physician promptly referred the man to a specialist. |
| _____ | _____ | More importantly, even liver specialists were able to determine the link between the herbal tea and symptoms like the man's only when they had a cluster of patients with similar symptoms and discovered that all of the patients were drinking the same herbal tea. |
| _____ | _____ | **Conclusion:** Thus, the physician may not be found liable to the man. |

*continued on next page*

| Stated | Implied | |
|---|---|---|
| | | **Point Two (a) (20%) Strict Liability and Breach of Warranty of Processor** |
| _____ | _____ | **Rule:** The producer of goods that cause injury to a person may be liable to the injured person in tort if the seller was negligent, if the goods were defective, or if they did not satisfy the implied warranty of merchantability. |
| _____ | _____ | "One who sells any product in a defective condition unreasonably dangerous to the user or consumer . . . is subject to liability for physical harm thereby caused . . . ." |
| _____ | _____ | Products that fail to meet the producer's own specifications are typically described as having a "manufacturing" defect. |
| _____ | _____ | In order to recover for injuries sustained because of a manufacturing defect, a plaintiff need not show that the producer was negligent. |
| _____ | _____ | A producer is strictly liable whenever "the product departs from its intended design even though all possible care was exercised in the preparation and marketing of the product . . . ." |
| _____ | _____ | In the case of food products, the presence of a harmful ingredient is generally considered a manufacturing defect "if a reasonable consumer would not expect the food product to contain that ingredient." |
| _____ | _____ | **Application:** Here, |
| _____ | _____ | The herbal tea that the man consumed falls into the manufacturing defect category even though it is not a manufactured product in the traditional sense because a reasonable consumer would expect the herbal tea to be free of contamination when processed and packaged. |
| _____ | _____ | Given the severe harm caused to consumers by the pesticide residue, its presence clearly rendered the product unreasonably dangerous. |
| _____ | _____ | **Conclusion:** Thus, the processor selling tea with this defect would be liable in tort for resulting injuries. |
| _____ | _____ | **Conclusion:** The man could also rely on the implied warranty of merchantability to establish the U.S. companies' liability. |
| _____ | _____ | **Rule:** Because the sale of the herbal tea by the producers is a sale of goods, it is governed by Article 2 of the Uniform Commercial Code. |
| _____ | _____ | An implied warranty of merchantability exists in goods sold by merchants. |
| _____ | _____ | A merchant is a person who deals in goods of the kind or otherwise holds himself out as having skill or judgment peculiar to the goods or practices involved. |
| _____ | _____ | **Application:** The producers are "merchant(s)" with respect to those goods, so the contract of sale included an implied warranty of merchantability. |
| _____ | _____ | **Conclusion:** There is no evidence that this warranty was excluded or modified in any of the contracts under which those companies sold herbal tea. As a result, an implied warranty of merchantability exists. |
| _____ | _____ | **Rule:** To be merchantable, goods must, *inter alia*, be "fit for the ordinary purposes for which such goods are used." |
| _____ | _____ | **Application:** Here, |
| _____ | _____ | Clearly, the contaminated herbal tea was not fit for the ordinary purpose for which the herbal tea is used. |

*continued on next page*

| Stated | Implied | |
|--------|---------|---|
| _____ | _____ | **Conclusion:** Thus, the producers breached the implied warranty of merchantability and are liable for that breach. |
| _____ | _____ | **Conclusion:** Under both warranty theory and strict products liability, the producers may not rely on the fact that the contamination took place before the herbal tea came into their hands to evade liability. |
| _____ | _____ | **Rule:** In a warranty action, the only issue is whether the herbal tea was merchantable. How it came to be unmerchantable is irrelevant. |
| _____ | _____ | In a strict products liability action, the issue is whether the product was defective. |
| _____ | _____ | Thus, the man could recover against a producer of the herbal tea without proof of negligence *if* he could show that any given producer sold the product that caused his injury. |
| | | [NOTE #1: In some states, privity requirements may be applied to prevent the man from recovering from a seller with whom he is not in privity. However, in many states, privity rules have been relaxed or modified sufficiently to permit a remote purchaser like the man to assert an implied warranty claim against the seller of a food product.] |
| | | [NOTE #2: Some examinees might note that complete analysis of the warranty claim requires knowledge of whether the relevant contract effectively disclaimed the warranty of merchantability. However, this would not affect the tort liability claim.] |
| | | **Point Two (b) (35%) Causation** |
| _____ | _____ | **Conclusion:** Because the man consumed several brands of the herbal tea, he cannot show which producer of the herbal tea supplied the product that caused his injury, and none of the doctrines that permit a plaintiff to meet the causation requirement without direct proof of causation are available here. |
| _____ | _____ | **Rule:** Like all tort plaintiffs, the plaintiff in a products liability action must establish that the defendant caused his injury. |
| _____ | _____ | **Application:** Had the man consumed only one brand of the herbal tea, causation might be established by showing the link between the tea's toxicity and the man's symptoms. |
| _____ | _____ | However, the man drank the herbal tea produced by more than one producer, and he cannot link any particular defendant's product to his injury. |
| _____ | _____ | **Transition:** Several doctrines would permit the jury to find a defendant liable when the plaintiff cannot directly meet the causation requirement. |
| _____ | _____ | However, none of these doctrines would help the man to establish causation here. |
| _____ | _____ | **Rule:** The "market share" liability doctrine permits the jury to apportion damages based on the market shares of manufacturers of a defective product. |
| _____ | _____ | But virtually all courts have held that this doctrine is available only if the manufacturers' defective products are fungible in relation to their capacity to cause harm. |
| _____ | _____ | **Application:** Here, |
| _____ | _____ | The man cannot make such a showing that the pesticide-contaminated herbal tea caused the man's injury and the facts specify that the contamination was not uniform. |
| _____ | _____ | Some packages were heavily contaminated and some not at all. |
| _____ | _____ | **Conclusion:** Thus, market-share liability is unavailable. |

*continued on next page*

| Stated | Implied | |
|--------|---------|---|
| _____ | _____ | **Rule:** The "alternative liability" doctrine permits a jury to find two defendants liable when **each** was negligent and **either** could have caused the plaintiff's injuries. |
| _____ | _____ | **Application/Conclusion:** Here, there are five defendants, and there is no evidence that all producers were negligent. |
| _____ | _____ | **Rule:** The "joint venture" or "joint enterprise" doctrine allows the jury to impute one defendant's tortious conduct to other defendants who are engaged in a common project or enterprise and who have made an explicit or implied agreement to engage in tortious conduct. |
| _____ | _____ | **Application/Conclusion:** Here, no evidence exists that the producers had any control over the warehouses in which the pesticide contamination originated, let alone that they collaborated in tortious conduct. |
| _____ | _____ | **Overall Conclusion:** In sum, none of the producers could be held liable for the man's injury because no evidence links a particular producer to that injury and no exception to this requirement applies. |
| | | **Point Three (20%) Strict Liability of Retailer** |
| _____ | _____ | **Conclusion:** The health-food store from which the man bought the contaminated herbal tea may be found strictly liable in tort even though the store did not produce the tea. |
| _____ | _____ | **Rule:** Strict products liability applies to all commercial sellers; even a retailer who had no control over the design and manufacture of a product may be found strictly liable if that retailer sells a defective product. |
| _____ | _____ | **Application/Conclusion:** Because the health-food store is a commercial seller, it may be found liable to the man for the defective herbal tea that the man purchased there. |
| _____ | _____ | **Rule/Conclusion:** The man could also recover on an implied warranty theory against the health-food store in all jurisdictions because he was in privity with the store. |
| _____ | _____ | **Rule:** Just as with the herbal tea producers, the man has the burden of showing causation. |
| _____ | _____ | **Application:** But the facts specify that the man purchased *all* the herbal tea he consumed from the same health-food store. |
| _____ | _____ | The identification problem that makes causation impossible to establish with respect to the producers thus does not arise with respect to the health-food store. |
| _____ | _____ | **Conclusion:** Thus the health-food store may be found liable for the man's injury because it sold a defective product that caused the man's injury. |
| _____ | _____ | Some states have statutes that exclude strict liability in tort for retailers who sell products in closed packages. |

# MBE PRACTICE ANALYSIS[7]

## Question 1

An assistant to a famous writer surreptitiously observed the writer as the writer typed her private password into her personal computer in order to access her email. On several subsequent occasions in the writer's absence, the assistant read the writer's email messages and printed out selections from them.

The assistant later quit his job and earned a considerable amount of money by leaking information to the media that he had learned from reading the writer's email messages. All of the information published about the writer as a result of the assistant's conduct was true and concerned matters of public interest.

The writer's secretary had seen the assistant reading the writer's emails and printing out selections, and she has told the writer what she saw. The writer now wishes to sue the assistant for damages. At trial, the writer can show that the media leaks could have come only from someone reading her email.

Can the writer recover damages from the assistant?

(A) No, because the assistant was an invitee on the premises.
**Incorrect.** The assistant exceeded the scope of any invitation, whether through his employment as an assistant or through the invitation to work on the premises. The writer did not leave the emails exposed so that others might see them. An invitation to enter premises does not normally include permission to access personal email, especially when the email account is password-protected.

(B) No, because the published information resulting from the assistant's conduct was true and concerned matters of public interest.
**Incorrect.** Truth is a common law defense to defamation but not to invasion of privacy. In some circumstances, the First Amendment or a common law defense based on the public interest in the material disclosed can provide a defense to an action for disclosure of private matters. However, even if these defenses were applicable to the disclosure aspect of this case, they would not provide a defense to the privacy action

based on intrusion. A news-gathering purpose does not provide general immunity from tort law.

(C) Yes, because the assistant invaded the writer's privacy.
**Correct.** By accessing the writer's email, the assistant was intruding upon her privacy. "Intrusion upon seclusion" is one category of the tort of invasion of privacy that is recognized in many states. The assistant did not have permission to access the emails, and the writer did not leave the emails exposed so that others might see them.

(D) Yes, because the published information resulting from the assistant's conduct constituted publication of private facts concerning the writer.
**Incorrect.** The most appropriate privacy action here would be for "intrusion" rather than for "public disclosure of embarrassing private facts," in part because there is no indication that the facts published were embarrassing to the writer. Publication is irrelevant to whether a cause of action for intrusion has been established. By accessing the writer's email, the assistant was intruding upon her privacy. "Intrusion upon seclusion" is one category of the tort of invasion of privacy that is recognized in many states. The assistant did not have permission to access the emails, and the writer did not leave the emails exposed so that others might see them.

## Question 2

A man sued his neighbor for defamation based on the following facts:

The neighbor told a friend that the man had set fire to a house in the neighborhood. The friend, who knew the man well, did not believe the neighbor's allegation, which was in fact false. The friend told the man about the neighbor's allegation. The man was very upset by the allegation, but neither the man nor the neighbor nor the friend communicated the allegation to anyone else.

Should the man prevail in his lawsuit?

(A) No, because the friend did not believe what the neighbor had said.
**Incorrect.** A successful defamation action does not depend on whether a third party actually believed the defamatory statement. It is enough that the defamatory statement was communicated to a third party.

(B) No, because the man cannot prove that he suffered pecuniary loss.

---

7. *Id.*

**Incorrect.** The statement was spoken rather than written, so the rules of slander apply. Often an action in slander requires that pecuniary loss be shown, but there is no such requirement where the statement accuses the plaintiff of engaging in serious criminal conduct. Arson is a crime of moral turpitude, so the neighbor's statement falls within the exception.

(C) Yes, because the man was very upset at hearing what the neighbor had said.

**Incorrect.** Proof of emotional distress is not required to establish a cause of action for defamation, whether the action is in libel or slander. The man should prevail, but it is because the defamatory statement was communicated to a third party. Here, the statement was spoken rather than written, so the rules of slander apply. Often an action in slander requires that pecuniary loss be shown, but there is no such requirement where the statement accuses the plaintiff of engaging in serious criminal conduct. Arson is a crime of moral turpitude, so the neighbor's statement falls within the exception, and special harm need not be shown.

(D) Yes, because the neighbor communicated to the friend the false accusation that the man had committed a serious crime.

**Correct.** The core of a defamation action is the communication of a defamatory statement about the plaintiff to a third party. Here, the statement was spoken rather than written, so the rules of slander apply. Often an action in slander requires that pecuniary loss be shown, but there is no such requirement where the statement accuses the plaintiff of engaging in serious criminal conduct. Arson is a crime of moral turpitude, so the neighbor's statement falls within the exception, and special harm need not be shown.

## Question 3

A manufacturing plant emitted a faint noise even though the owner had installed state-of-the-art sound dampeners. The plant operated only on weekdays and only during daylight hours. A homeowner who lived near the plant worked a night shift and could not sleep when he arrived home because of the noise from the plant. The other residents in the area did not notice the noise.

Does the homeowner have a viable nuisance claim against the owner of the plant?

(A) No, because the homeowner is unusually sensitive to noise during the day.

**Correct.** A landowner is liable for nuisance only when his invasion of another's use and enjoyment is both substantial and unreasonable. Under the norms of the area, the plant owner is not imposing an unreasonable degree of noise upon his neighbors. An unusually noise-sensitive neighbor will not be permitted to block the plant owner's use of his own land.

(B) No, because the plant operates only during the day.

**Incorrect.** If the noise were too loud given the normal expectations of residents in the area, it could still constitute a nuisance even if limited to daylight hours. The homeowner does not have a valid nuisance claim, but it is because he is unusually sensitive to noise during the day.

(C) Yes, because the noise is heard beyond the boundaries of the plant.

**Incorrect.** Recovery in nuisance requires evidence of substantial and unreasonable interference with the plaintiff's use and enjoyment of his own land. Merely showing that a noise can be heard beyond the boundaries of the defendant's land is not enough to establish a nuisance, especially when the noise can be heard only by an unusually noise-sensitive person.

(D) Yes, because the operation of the plant interferes with the homeowner's quiet use and enjoyment of his property.

**Incorrect.** It is not enough to demonstrate interference with quiet use and enjoyment. The interference also must be shown to be both substantial and unreasonable. The noise emitted by the plant interferes only with one unusually noise-sensitive neighbor, so it is unlikely to be found to be unreasonable.

## Question 4

Toxic materials being transported by truck from a manufacturer's plant to a warehouse leaked from the truck onto the street a few miles from the plant. A driver lost control of his car when he hit the puddle of spilled toxic materials on the street, and he was injured when his car hit a stop sign.

In an action for damages by the driver against the manufacturer based on strict liability, is the driver likely to prevail?

(A) No, because the driver's loss of control was an intervening cause.

**Incorrect.** The driver's loss of control was not intentional, nor was it either unforeseeable or unusual. For that reason, it should raise no proximate cause problem.

(B) No, because the driver's injury did not result from the toxicity of the materials.

**Correct.** Strict liability in this situation would be based on the abnormally dangerous nature of the toxic materials. But a successful strict liability action requires that the risk that materializes be the same risk that led courts to label the activity "abnormally dangerous" in the first place. Here, the toxicity of the materials did not contribute to the driver's injury, so his only cause of action would be in negligence.

(C) Yes, because the manufacturer is strictly liable for leaks of its toxic materials.

**Incorrect.** Strict liability in this situation would be based on the abnormally dangerous nature of the toxic materials. But a successful strict liability action requires that the risk that materializes be the same risk that led courts to label the activity "abnormally dangerous" in the first place. Here, the toxicity of the materials did not contribute to the driver's injury, so his only cause of action would be in negligence.

(D) Yes, because the leak occurred near the manufacturer's plant.

**Incorrect.** The manufacturer would be strictly liable for injuries caused by its toxic materials regardless of where the leak occurred, so long as the manufacturer could be said to be responsible for the leak. However, in this situation the toxicity of the materials did not contribute to the driver's injury, so his only cause of action would be in negligence.

### Question 5

A man and his friend, who were both adults, went to a party. The man and the friend had many drinks at the party and became legally intoxicated. They decided to play a game of chance called "Russian roulette" using a gun loaded with one bullet. As part of the game, the man pointed the gun at the friend and, on her command, pulled the trigger. The man shot the friend in the shoulder.

The friend has brought a negligence action against the man. Traditional defenses based on plaintiff's conduct apply. What is likely to be the dispositive issue in this case?

(A) Whether the game constituted a joint venture.

**Incorrect.** The fact that the man and the friend might have been engaged in a joint venture would be relevant if the action were being brought by a third party who was not part of the venture but who had been injured as a consequence of their activities. It is irrelevant to a suit among participants in a joint venture unless it indicates an assumption of risk.

(B) Whether the friend could validly consent to the game.

**Incorrect.** It is likely that consent to this activity would be routinely found to be against public policy, although the consequences of such a determination would vary from state to state. But consent is a defense more appropriately raised in an intentional tort case, not a case for negligence. There is no indication that the friend consented to any negligence, and in any case she was too intoxicated to give a valid consent.

(C) Whether the friend was also negligent.

**Correct.** Contributory negligence is an appropriate defense to a negligence action, and here both parties seem to have been acting unreasonably in exactly the same way. Whether the argument is put in the form of the friend's carelessness in engaging in the activity or in her unreasonable assumption of risk, many states would now evaluate the defense under comparative negligence principles.

(D) Whether the man was legally intoxicated when he began playing the game.

**Incorrect.** The man's intoxication would not insulate him from liability to those he injured while in that state. He would still be held to the "reasonably prudent person" standard.

### Question 6

A woman signed up for a bowling class. Before allowing the woman to bowl, the instructor required her to sign a waiver explicitly stating that she assumed all risk of injuries that she might suffer in connection with the class, including injuries due to negligence or any other fault. After she signed the waiver, the woman was injured when the instructor negligently dropped a bowling ball on the woman's foot.

The woman brought a negligence action against the instructor. The instructor has filed a motion for summary judgment based on the waiver.

What is the woman's best argument in opposition to the instructor's motion?

**(A)** Bowling is an inherently dangerous activity.
**Incorrect.** Bowling is not inherently dangerous; virtually no one is seriously injured while bowling. Even if bowling were inherently dangerous, that characterization would support an argument for permitting recreational participants who appreciate the risks of the activity to assume the risks by signing a waiver rather than constituting a reason for ignoring the waiver.

**(B)** In circumstances like these, it is against public policy to enforce agreements that insulate people from the consequences of their own negligence.
**Correct.** Waivers are most easily justified when an activity poses inherent risks that are familiar to the participants and cannot be entirely eliminated without removing the pleasure from the activity. The risk that materialized here is not inherent to bowling but could arise whenever someone is careless while holding a heavy object. A court might find that it is against public policy to permit individuals or businesses to insulate themselves from the deterrent incentives provided by the threat of negligence liability. For that reason, the court might find that the waiver did not present the woman with a fair choice and could hold the waiver ineffective.

**(C)** It was unreasonable to require the woman to sign the waiver before she was allowed to bowl.
**Incorrect.** Although the court might find that the waiver did not present the woman with a fair choice and therefore hold the waiver to be no bar when the harm was due to the instructor's negligence, asking the woman to sign the waiver was not in itself negligent or unreasonable. For example, the waiver might have barred recovery against the instructor if the woman were injured by the negligence of another class participant, or the court might have decided that the waiver was not inconsistent with public policy given the recreational nature of the activity.

**(D)** When she signed the form, the woman could not foresee that the instructor would drop a bowling ball on her foot.
**Incorrect.** Pre-injury waivers are often enforced despite the fact that the precise injury that materializes is virtually never foreseen with a high level of specificity at the time of the signing of the waiver. The problem here is that the risk that materialized was not inherent to the enjoyment of bowling.

## Question 7

A pedestrian was crossing a street in a crosswalk when a woman walking just ahead of him was hit by a truck. The pedestrian, who had jumped out of the way of the truck, administered CPR to the woman, who was a stranger. The woman bled profusely, and the pedestrian was covered in blood. The woman died in the ambulance on the way to the hospital. The pedestrian became very depressed immediately after the incident and developed physical symptoms as a result of his emotional distress.

The pedestrian has brought an action against the driver of the truck for negligent infliction of emotional distress. In her defense, the driver asserts that she should not be held liable, because the pedestrian's emotional distress and resulting physical symptoms are not compensable.

What is the strongest argument that the pedestrian can make in response to the driver's defense?

**(A)** The pedestrian saw the driver hit the woman.
**Incorrect.** Most states allow plaintiffs to recover damages for the emotional distress of seeing another person injured or killed by a negligent driver, but they usually require that there be a close relationship between the plaintiff and the injured person before recovery is allowed.

**(B)** The pedestrian was acting as a Good Samaritan.
**Incorrect.** Normally, the fact that someone chooses to come to the aid of another neither insulates that person from liability for his or her own negligence nor provides that person with a cause of action for the pure emotional distress suffered as a consequence of providing the aid.

**(C)** The pedestrian was covered in the woman's blood and developed physical symptoms as a result of his emotional distress.
**Incorrect.** The negligent driver did not herself touch or impact the pedestrian, so the fact that the pedestrian became covered in blood and ultimately suffered physical symptoms as a result of emotional distress is not alone sufficient to support a claim for damages.

**(D)** The pedestrian was in the zone of danger.
**Correct.** Because the pedestrian was in the path of the truck, he was under a direct physical threat from the driver's negligence. He could recover for the emotional distress that he suffered as a result of his fear for his own safety, and many courts would also allow him to recover

for all other emotional distress that he suffered in connection with the event.

## Question 8

Upon the recommendation of her child's pediatrician, a mother purchased a vaporizer for her child, who had been suffering from respiratory congestion. The vaporizer consisted of a gallon-size glass jar, which held water to be heated until it became steam, and a metal heating unit into which the jar fit. The jar was covered by a plastic cap with an opening to allow the steam to escape. At the time the vaporizer was manufactured and sold, there was no safer alternative design.

The booklet that accompanied the vaporizer read: "This product is safe, spill-proof, and practically foolproof. It shuts off automatically when the water is gone." The booklet had a picture of a vaporizer sending steam over a baby's crib.

The mother used the vaporizer whenever the child was suffering from congestion. She placed the vaporizer on the floor near the child's bed.

One night, the child got out of bed to get a drink of water and tripped over the cord of the vaporizer as she crossed the room. The top of the vaporizer separated from the base, and boiling water from the jar spilled on the child when the vaporizer tipped over. The child suffered serious burns as a consequence.

The child's representative brought an action for damages against the manufacturer of the vaporizer. The manufacturer moved to dismiss after the representative presented the evidence above.

Should the manufacturer's motion be granted?

(A) No, because a jury could find that the manufacturer expressly represented that the vaporizer was spill proof.
**Correct.** The vaporizer may not have been "defective," in that there was no reasonable alternative design, but the express promise by the manufacturer that it was "safe" and "spill-proof," especially when combined with the manufacturer's picture suggesting that it was safe to place the vaporizer near a child's bed, could be the basis of recovery on the ground of misrepresentation.

(B) No, because the vaporizer caused a serious injury to the child.
**Incorrect.** The fact that a product poses a danger to a user or a bystander will not support the manufacturer's liability in the absence of negligence, defect, or misrepresentation. The manufacturer's motion should not be granted, but it is because the express promise by the manufacturer that the vaporizer was "safe" and "spill-proof," especially when combined with the manufacturer's picture suggesting that it was safe to place the vaporizer near a child's bed, could be the basis of recovery on the ground of misrepresentation.

(C) Yes, because it should have been obvious to the mother that the water in the jar would become boiling hot.
**Incorrect.** The mother could be found to have reasonably relied upon the manufacturer's express promise that the vaporizer was "safe" and "spill-proof," especially when those words were combined with the manufacturer's picture suggesting that it was safe to place the vaporizer near a child's bed. The mother could have believed that the boiling water posed no danger if it could not be spilled. She would have an action against the manufacturer for misrepresentation.

(D) Yes, because there was no safer alternative design.
**Incorrect.** The fact finder may conclude that the vaporizer could not be found to be "defective" because there was no reasonable alternative design, but the manufacturer's express promise that the vaporizer was "safe" and "spill-proof," combined with the manufacturer's picture suggesting that it was safe to place the vaporizer near a child's bed, could still be the basis of recovery on the ground of misrepresentation.

## Question 9

A man was admitted to a hospital after complaining of persistent severe headaches. While he was there, hospital staff failed to diagnose his condition, and he was discharged. Two days later, the man died of a massive brain hemorrhage due to a congenital defect in an artery.

The man's wife has brought a wrongful death action against the hospital. The wife offers expert testimony that the man would have had a "reasonable chance" (not greater than 50%) of surviving the hemorrhage if he had been given appropriate medical care at the hospital.

In what type of jurisdiction would the wife's suit most likely be successful?

(A) A jurisdiction that applies traditional common law rules concerning burden of proof.

**Incorrect.** If traditional common law rules concerning burden of proof were applied, the wife would be required to prove that reasonable action on the part of the hospital (presumably a correct diagnosis) would, more likely than not, have led to the man's survival. Here, however, the wife cannot establish that the chances of the man's survival would have been greater than 50% even if he had been given appropriate medical care. Therefore, the wife could not carry her burden of proof on the issue of cause in fact in such a jurisdiction.

(B) A jurisdiction that allows recovery based on strict liability.

**Incorrect.** Cause in fact is a necessary element of a plaintiff's case in strict liability as well as in negligence. Under either theory, the wife must establish that reasonable action on the part of the hospital (presumably a correct diagnosis) would, more likely than not, have led to the man's survival. Here, however, the wife cannot establish that the chances of the man's survival were greater than 50% even if he had been given appropriate medical care. Therefore, the wife could not carry her burden of proof on the issue of cause in fact in such a jurisdiction.

(C) A jurisdiction that allows recovery for the loss of the chance of survival.

**Correct.** Jurisdictions that allow recovery for the loss of the chance of survival have created an exception to the traditional common law rules for establishing cause in fact. Under the traditional rules, the wife would be required to prove that reasonable action on the part of the hospital (presumably a correct diagnosis) would, more likely than not, have led to the man's survival. Here, the wife cannot establish that the chances of the man's survival would have been greater than 50% even if he had been given appropriate medical care. A jurisdiction that allows recovery for loss of the chance of survival, however, would allow the wife to recover for the reduction in her husband's chance of surviving that was caused by the failure to properly diagnose.

(D) A jurisdiction that recognizes loss of spousal consortium.

**Incorrect.** Cause in fact is a necessary element of a plaintiff's case for loss of spousal consortium, as well as in cases in which a plaintiff is suing for personal injury. In a loss of consortium action, the wife must establish that the hospital's negligence was the cause of her husband's death. Traditional rules of proof regarding causation would require that the wife prove that reasonable action on the part of the hospital (presumably a correct diagnosis) would, more likely than not, have led to her husband's survival. Here, the wife cannot establish that the chances of her husband's survival would have been greater than 50% even if he had been given appropriate medical care. Therefore, the wife could not carry her burden of proof on the issue of cause in fact in such a jurisdiction and she could not recover for loss of spousal consortium.

**Question 10**

A mother purchased an expensive television from an appliance store for her adult son. Two years after the purchase, a fire started in the son's living room in the middle of the night. The fire department concluded that the fire had started in the television. No other facts are known.

The son sued the appliance store for negligence. The store has moved for summary judgment. Should the court grant the store's motion?

(A) No, because televisions do not catch fire in the absence of negligence.

**Incorrect.** Even if it were true that televisions do not catch fire in the absence of negligence, the fact that this television did is insufficient to establish that the store acted negligently. This is not an appropriate case for res ipsa loquitur, because the manufacturer, rather than the store, may have been negligent or the negligence may have occurred after the sale (for example, during a repair or while the television was being used by the son). Because the son cannot establish the store's negligence, the court should grant the store's motion.

(B) No, because the store sold the television.

**Incorrect.** The son sued the store for negligence, not for strict liability. To recover on a negligence claim, the son must establish that the store itself was negligent. If the son had sued under strict liability, he would have had to establish that the television was defective at the time it was sold to his mother. Because the son cannot establish the store's negligence, the court should grant the store's motion.

(C) Yes, because the son is not in privity with the store.

**Incorrect.** A lack of privity is not a barrier to negligence claims based on malfunctioning products. Anyone foreseeably put at risk by a defective product and actually injured by the product's defective condition can sue for negligence. The court should grant the store's motion, but it is because the son cannot establish that the store was the negligent actor.

**(D)** Yes, because there is no evidence of negligence on the part of the store.

**Correct.** The son is suing in negligence, not in strict liability. To make out a prima facie case in negligence, the son must introduce evidence that the store was negligent. However, the son has not pointed to any negligent action or omission by the store. This is not an appropriate case for res ipsa loquitur, because the manufacturer, rather than the store, may have been negligent or the negligence may have occurred after the sale (for example, during a repair or while the television was being used by the son).

## Question 11

A shopper was riding on an escalator in a department store when the escalator stopped abruptly. The shopper lost her balance and fell down the escalator steps, sustaining injuries. Although the escalator had been regularly maintained by an independent contractor, the store's obligation to provide safe conditions for its invitees was nondelegable. The shopper has brought an action against the store for damages, and the above facts are the only facts in evidence.

The store has moved for a directed verdict. Should the court grant the motion?

**(A)** No, because the finder of fact could infer that the escalator malfunction was due to negligence.

**Correct.** There is enough evidence here to support an inference of negligence on the part of the store or the contractor. A jury could find that the malfunction was due to the negligent installation, maintenance, or operation of the escalator; the store would be responsible for all these possible causes under the nondelegable duty doctrine.

**(B)** No, because the store is strictly liable for the shopper's injuries.

**Incorrect.** Landowners and occupiers are not strictly liable even for injuries to their business invitees. The court should not grant the motion, but it is because the fact finder could infer negligence on the part of the store or the contractor, and the store's obligation to provide safe conditions was nondelegable.

**(C)** Yes, because an independent contractor maintained the escalator.

**Incorrect.** Even if the malfunction were due to the negligence of the independent contractor, the store would also be responsible under the nondelegable duty doctrine. These facts illustrate a common situation in which that doctrine is applied: the defendant owns a building and invites the public to enter the building for the defendant's financial benefit. There is enough evidence here to support an inference of negligence on the part of the store or the contractor. A jury could find that the malfunction was due to the negligent installation, maintenance, or operation of the escalator; the store would be responsible for all these possible causes under the nondelegable duty doctrine.

**(D)** Yes, because the shopper has not produced evidence of negligence.

**Incorrect.** There is enough evidence here to support an inference of negligence on the part of the store or the contractor. A jury could find that the malfunction was due to the negligent installation, maintenance, or operation of the escalator; the store would be responsible for all these possible causes under the nondelegable duty doctrine.

## Question 12

A 14-year-old girl of low intelligence received her parents' permission to drive their car. She had had very little experience driving a car and did not have a driver's license. Although she did the best she could, she lost control of the car and hit a pedestrian.

The pedestrian has brought a negligence action against the girl.

Is the pedestrian likely to prevail?

**(A)** No, because only the girl's parents are subject to liability.

**Incorrect.** The parents and the girl may both be liable. The girl was engaging in a dangerous activity that is characteristically undertaken by adults, so she will be held to the adult standard of care and can be sued for the injuries caused by her negligent driving.

**(B)** No, because the girl was acting reasonably for a 14-year-old of low intelligence and little driving experience.

**Incorrect.** The girl was engaging in a dangerous activity that is characteristically undertaken by adults, so she will be held to the adult standard of care. No adjustment will be made to that standard to reflect her low intelligence and lack of experience. Her low intelligence and her inexperience put others at risk, and she will be held to the standard of a reasonably prudent driver even if she is not capable of reasonable prudence.

(C) Yes, because the girl was engaging in an adult activity.
**Correct.** The girl was engaging in a dangerous activity that is characteristically undertaken by adults, so she will be held to the adult standard of care. No adjustment will be made to that standard to reflect her low intelligence and lack of experience. Her low intelligence and her inexperience put others at risk, and she will be held to the standard of a reasonably prudent driver even if she is not capable of reasonable prudence.

(D) Yes, because the girl was not old enough to obtain a driver's license.
**Incorrect.** In the absence of a statute setting a different standard, the girl's failure to obtain a license ordinarily would not be evidence that she was actually negligent at the time of the accident. The pedestrian would have to prove actual negligence, which should be easy given that the girl lost control of the car and given the fact that the girl will be held to an adult standard of care because she was engaging in an activity that is characteristically undertaken by adults.

## Question 13

A firstborn child was examined as an infant by a doctor who was a specialist in the diagnosis of speech and hearing impairments. Although the doctor should have concluded that the infant was totally deaf due to a hereditary condition, the doctor negligently concluded that the infant's hearing was normal. After the diagnosis, but before they learned that the infant was in fact deaf, the parents conceived a second child who also suffered total deafness due to the hereditary condition.

The parents claim that they would not have conceived the second child had they known of the high probability of the hereditary condition. They have sought the advice of their attorney regarding which negligence action against the doctor is most likely to succeed.

What sort of action against the doctor should the attorney recommend?

(A) A medical malpractice action seeking damages on the second child's behalf for expenses related to his deafness, on the ground that the doctor's negligence caused him to be born deaf.
**Incorrect.** The parents assert that they would not have conceived a second child had the doctor properly diagnosed the first child's deafness. Under that theory, the second child would never have been born had the doctor acted properly. Most courts are unwilling to say that it is worse to be born deaf than to never be born at all. Where that approach is taken, the second child has suffered no injury under this theory.

(B) A wrongful birth action by the parents for expenses they have incurred due to the second child's deafness, on the ground that but for the doctor's negligence, they would not have conceived the second child.
**Correct.** This cause of action will be permitted in many states. The parents sought an accurate assessment of their first child, which the doctor failed to provide. Unaware of the hereditary condition, the parents conceived a second child and incurred unexpected expenses that could have been avoided had the doctor acted properly. The parents can recover only for the additional expenses related to the child's deafness.

(C) A wrongful life action by the parents for expenses for the entire period of the second child's life, on the ground that but for the doctor's negligence, the second child would not have been born.
**Incorrect.** A wrongful life action would be brought by a child who would not have been born. An action by the parents based on advice that would have avoided a conception of a child is a wrongful birth action. Also, most courts would not permit the parents to recover all of the expenses for the second child's life even in a proper action, but only those additional expenses attributable to the child's disability.

(D) A wrongful life action on the second child's behalf for expenses for the entire period of his life, on the ground that but for the doctor's negligence, he would not have been born.
**Incorrect.** Most states reject this claim, and of the few states that do permit it, some would limit recovery to the special damages attributable to the disability. The parents' wrongful birth action is more likely to be successful in almost all jurisdictions.

## Question 14

A boater, caught in a sudden storm and reasonably fearing that her boat would capsize, drove the boat up to a pier, exited the boat, and tied the boat to the pier. The pier was clearly marked with "NO TRESPASSING" signs. The owner of the pier ran up to the boater and told her that the boat could not remain tied to the pier. The boater offered to pay the owner for the use of the pier. Regardless, over the boater's protest, the owner untied the boat and pushed it away from the pier. The boat was lost at sea.

Is the boater likely to prevail in an action against the owner to recover the value of the boat?

(A) No, because the owner told the boater that she could not tie the boat to the pier.

**Incorrect.** The boater was privileged to trespass on the owner's property under the doctrine of private necessity, because the boater's property was at risk. Because the boater's intrusion onto the pier was privileged, the owner had no right to exclude her or her boat from the pier. In telling the boater that she could not tie the boat to the pier, the owner was asserting a right that he did not possess. When the owner untied the boat, he committed an unprivileged trespass upon the boater's property, so the owner must pay for the loss of the boat.

(B) No, because there was a possibility that the boat would not be damaged by the storm.

**Incorrect.** The boater was privileged to trespass on the owner's property under the doctrine of private necessity, because her property was at risk. In order to establish that privilege, the boater need not establish that harm to the boat was inevitable, but only that her actions were reasonable given the circumstances. Because the boater's intrusion onto the pier was privileged, the owner had no right to exclude her or her boat from the pier. When the owner untied the boat, he committed an unprivileged trespass upon the boater's property, so the owner must pay for the loss of the boat.

(C) Yes, because the boater offered to pay the owner for the use of the pier.

**Incorrect.** The boater is likely to prevail, but it is because the boater was privileged to trespass on the owner's property under the doctrine of private necessity. Because the boater's property was at risk, her intrusion onto the pier was privileged, and the owner had no right to exclude her or her boat from the pier. Whether or not the boater offered to pay the owner is irrelevant to the privilege of private necessity. When the owner untied the boat, he committed an unprivileged trespass upon the boater's property, so the owner must pay for the loss of the boat.

(D) Yes, because the boater was privileged to enter the owner's property to save her boat.

**Correct.** The boater was privileged to trespass on the owner's property under the doctrine of private necessity, because the boater's property was at risk. Because the boater's intrusion onto the pier was privileged, the owner had no right to exclude her or her boat from the pier. When the owner untied the boat, he committed an unprivileged trespass upon the boater's property, so the owner must pay for the loss of the boat.

## Question 15

Unaware that a lawyer was in the county courthouse library late on a Friday afternoon, when it was unusual for anyone to be using the library, a clerk locked the library door and left. The lawyer found herself locked in when she tried to leave the library at 7 p.m. It was midnight before the lawyer's family could find out where she was and get her out. The lawyer was very annoyed by her detention but was not otherwise harmed by it.

Does the lawyer have a viable claim for false imprisonment against the clerk?

(A) No, because it was unusual for anyone to be using the library late on a Friday afternoon.

**Incorrect.** The fact that it was unusual for anyone to be using the library at the time the clerk locked the door might lead a fact finder to conclude that the clerk was not negligent in failing to detect the lawyer. However, because false imprisonment is an intentional tort, the reasonableness of the clerk's conduct is irrelevant. If the clerk had intended to lock the lawyer in the library, the lawyer would have a claim for false imprisonment even if it was unusual for anyone to be using the library at the time. Under these facts, however, the clerk did not intend to lock the lawyer in the library, so the lawyer does not have a viable claim for false imprisonment.

(B) No, because the clerk did not intend to confine the lawyer.

**Correct.** Intent to confine the claimant (or to commit some other intentional tort) is essential to establishing liability for false imprisonment. There is no evidence that the clerk had such an intent.

(C) Yes, because the clerk should have checked to make sure no one was in the library before the clerk locked the door.

**Incorrect.** Whether a reasonable person in the clerk's position would have checked before locking the door is irrelevant to a claim for false imprisonment. False imprisonment is an intentional tort requiring intent to confine the claimant (or to commit some other intentional tort). What a reasonable person would have done is relevant to a negligence claim, but not to a false imprisonment claim.

(D) Yes, because the lawyer was aware of being confined.

**Incorrect.** In cases involving false imprisonment, courts often hold that the plaintiff must have been aware of the confinement at the time of the imprisonment or else must have sustained actual harm. It is also essential, however, that the defendant have had an intent to confine the plaintiff (or to commit some other intentional tort). If the clerk had had such an intent, the lawyer's awareness that she was confined might have completed the prima facie case, but the clerk had no such intent.

## Question 16

A man tied his dog to a bike rack in front of a store and left the dog there while he went inside to shop. The dog was usually friendly and placid.

A five-year-old child started to tease the dog by pulling gently on its ears and tail. When the man emerged from the store and saw what the child was doing to the dog, he became extremely upset.

Does the man have a viable claim against the child for trespass to chattels?

(A) No, because the child did not injure the dog.

**Correct.** Trespass to chattels requires that the plaintiff show actual harm to or deprivation of the use of the chattel for a substantial time. Here the child's acts caused emotional distress to the man, but the acts did not result in harm to the man's material interest in the dog.

(B) No, because the child was too young to form the requisite intent.

**Incorrect.** Even a small child can commit an intentional tort, such as trespass to chattels, so long as the child is old enough to form an intent to touch. But trespass to chattels requires that the plaintiff show actual harm to

or deprivation of the use of the chattel for a substantial time. Here the child's acts caused emotional distress to the man, but the acts did not result in harm to the man's material interest in the dog.

(C) Yes, because the child touched the dog without the man's consent.

**Incorrect.** Trespass to chattels requires that the plaintiff show actual harm to or deprivation of the use of the chattel for a substantial time. Here the child's acts caused emotional distress to the man (because they were without his consent), but the acts did not result in harm to the man's material interest in the dog.

(D) Yes, because the child's acts caused the man extreme distress.

**Incorrect.** Trespass to chattels requires that the plaintiff show actual harm to or deprivation of the use of the chattel for a substantial time. Here the child's acts caused emotional distress to the man, but the acts did not result in harm to the man's material interest in the dog.

## Question 17

A mother and her six-year-old child were on a walk when the mother stopped to talk with an elderly neighbor. Because the child resented having his mother's attention diverted by the neighbor, the child angrily threw himself against the neighbor and knocked her to the ground. The neighbor suffered a broken wrist as a result of the fall.

In an action for battery by the neighbor against the child, what is the strongest argument for liability?

(A) The child intended to throw himself against the neighbor.

**Correct.** To recover on a claim for battery, it is sufficient for the neighbor to show that the child intended to touch the neighbor in a way that would be considered harmful or offensive, even though the child may have been too young to understand that what he was doing was wrong or to appreciate that the neighbor might be unusually vulnerable to injury.

(B) The child was old enough to appreciate that causing a fall could inflict serious injury.

**Incorrect.** Proof of intent to cause injury or knowledge that injury may result is not necessary to recover on a claim of battery. Instead, it is sufficient that the child intended to touch the neighbor in a way that would be considered harmful or offensive, even though the child may have been too young to understand that what he was doing was wrong or to appreciate that the neighbor might be unusually vulnerable to injury.

**(C) The child was old enough to appreciate the riskiness of his conduct.**
**Incorrect.** Whether the child was old enough to appreciate the riskiness of his conduct is irrelevant to the neighbor's battery claim. It is sufficient that the child intended to touch the neighbor in a way that would be considered harmful or offensive, even though the child may have been too young to understand that what he was doing was wrong. Whether a child is old enough to appreciate a given risk would be relevant in a negligence action, but not in an action for battery.

**(D) The child was not justified in his anger.**
**Incorrect.** It is sufficient that the child intended to touch the neighbor in a way that would be considered harmful or offensive, whether or not the child was justifiably angry. The motive for a defendant's actions may be relevant to an affirmative defense in some situations, but even justified anger is not a defense to an intentional tort.

## VIII. Chapter 16  MAPPING BUSINESS TOPICS

**Agency Essay**

## SCORE SHEET

| Stated | Implied | |
|---|---|---|
| | | **Legal Relationship Between Able and Baker** |
| _____ | _____ | **Conclusion:** Baker is the agent of Able. |
| _____ | _____ | Under agency law, |
| _____ | _____ | **Rule:** An agency is a consensual relationship that arises when one person (the "principal") manifests an intention that another person (the "agent") shall act on the principal's behalf. |
| _____ | _____ | In order to form an agency, both the principal and the agent must **consent** to the relationship. |
| _____ | _____ | Both must have **capacity**; the principal needs contractual capacity, while the agent must have only minimal mental capacity. |
| _____ | _____ | In most cases, a writing is not required, although a writing does exist in this case. No other formalities are required. |
| _____ | _____ | **Application:** Here, |
| _____ | _____ | Able and Baker appear to have consented to an agency relationship by virtue of the signed purchaser agreement—Able did not agree to purchase coins **from Baker** (*i.e.*, the agreement did not Baker a supplier). |
| _____ | _____ | Able asked Baker to purchase coins from others **on Able's behalf.** |
| _____ | _____ | **Conclusion:** Since nothing indicates that either party was incompetent, an agency relationship was created. |
| _____ | _____ | **Independent Contractor or Employee?** |
| _____ | _____ | **Conclusion:** According to the purchaser agreement, Baker is an independent contractor rather than an employee, but the parties' determination is not necessarily binding. |
| _____ | _____ | **Rule:** The single most important factor in determining whether Baker is an employee or an independent contractor is whether Able, as principal, has the right to control the manner and method in which Baker does his job. |
| _____ | _____ | An employee is subject to the supervision of the principal in the details of the employee's work, whereas an independent contractor follows his own discretion. |
| _____ | _____ | **Application:** Here, |
| _____ | _____ | The purchaser agreement requires Baker to attend sales specified by Able, to bid on coins from a listing supplied by Able, to not exceed the price given by Able, and to not submit a bid without Able's approval. |
| _____ | _____ | **Conclusion:** The lack of discretion allowed to Baker in purchasing the coins for Able indicates that Baker is subject to Able's supervision and therefore is Able's employee. |
| _____ | _____ | The right to control overrides even the purchaser agreement's characterization of Baker as an independent contractor. |

*continued on next page*

| Stated | Implied | |
|---|---|---|
| _____ | _____ | **Transition:** However, the independent contractor/employee distinction does not affect Able's liability here; the distinction is important only in cases of **tort** liability, and the issue here is one of **contractual** liability. |
| | | **Liability of Able and Baker to Third-Party Seller** |
| _____ | _____ | **Conclusion:** Able and Baker are both liable to the seller on the contract to purchase the Leaping Liberty quarter. |
| _____ | _____ | At issue is whether the agent had authority to enter the transaction and under what circumstances an agent and undisclosed principal are liable for such transaction. |
| _____ | _____ | First, it is necessary to determine whether Baker was authorized to enter into the contract to purchase the coin. |
| _____ | _____ | **Rule:** There are three types of authority on which Baker could attempt to rely: **actual, apparent, and ratification.** |
| _____ | _____ | Actual authority is that which the agent reasonably believes he has based on the dealings between himself and the principal. |
| _____ | _____ | Apparent authority arises when the principal "holds out" another as having certain authority, causing the third party to believe that authority exists. |
| _____ | _____ | Ratification is authority given by the principal by acceptance of a transaction after the transaction has taken place. |
| _____ | _____ | **Sub-Rule on actual authority:** There are two types of actual authority: express and implied. |
| _____ | _____ | Express authority is that specifically contained in the communication from the principal to the agent that grants authority. |
| _____ | _____ | Implied authority is that which the agent reasonably believes he has based on the actions of the principal. |
| _____ | _____ | **Application:** Here, |
| _____ | _____ | Baker certainly has actual express authority, pursuant to the purchaser agreement, to enter into contracts to purchase coins on behalf of Able. |
| _____ | _____ | That authority is subject to certain **limiting instructions**, e.g., that Baker receive approval of a bid before submitting it, and that Baker not exceed the price on the Buy List. |
| _____ | _____ | **Conclusion:** However, because Able has failed to object to a series of prior transactions in which Baker made bids without calling Able, Baker has **implied authority** by acquiescence to submit the bid on the quarter without Able's approval. |
| | | [NOTE: The examine may also analyze apparent authority and ratification. Additional credit may be given if analyss is well reasoned.] |
| | | **Issue:** The next question is whether Able, Baker, or both are liable on the contract. |
| _____ | _____ | **Rule:** Generally, both the principal and the agent are liable on a contract entered into by an authorized agent on behalf of an undisclosed principal (_i.e._, a principal whose existence and identity are unknown to the third party). |
| _____ | _____ | **Application:** Because Baker was authorized and Able was unknown to the third-party seller as required by the purchaser agreement, both would be liable to the seller. |

_continued on next page_

| Stated | Implied | |
|--------|---------|---|
| _____ | _____ | **Conclusion:** Able would be liable as the principal, and Baker would be liable as if he were actually a party to the contract, because the third party dealt with Baker as if Baker were purchasing the coin on his own behalf, rather than as an agent for someone else. |
| | | **Able's and Baker's Liability to Each Other** |
| _____ | _____ | **Conclusion:** Baker is entitled to recover his commission and the expenses he incurred in purchasing the quarter for Able. |
| _____ | _____ | At issue is the principal's duty to compensate and reimburse an agent for expenses or losses in discharging the agent's duties. |
| _____ | _____ | **Rule:** The principal owes the agent a duty to indemnify him for any legal liability *reasonably* incurred by the agent in acting for the principal, unless the liability was due to the agent's own fault. |
| _____ | _____ | **Application:** Baker had authority to purchase the quarter despite his failure to telephone Able for approval. |
| _____ | _____ | Able would argue that Baker was not authorized to bid in excess of the value of the quarter; however, the agency agreement specifically provided that the price could not exceed that "*shown* on the Buy List." |
| _____ | _____ | Baker acted within these instructions. |
| _____ | _____ | Able could hardly escape her obligation to indemnify Baker based on an error in a list that Able herself provided. |
| _____ | _____ | **Conclusion:** Therefore, Able must reimburse Baker for the entire amount of the purchase price. |
| _____ | _____ | **Conclusion:** Able also has a duty to compensate Baker for the 25% quarterly bonus, pursuant to the purchaser agreement. |
| _____ | _____ | **Rule:** A principal owes the agent a duty to compensate the agent reasonably for his services unless the agent has agreed to act gratuitously. |
| _____ | _____ | Where the agent has breached his fiduciary duty, the principal may refuse to pay the agent for compensation attributable to the particular transaction in question. |
| _____ | _____ | **Application/Conclusion:** Baker is not in breach. |
| _____ | _____ | As a result, Able is liable to Baker for the $5,000 Baker is claiming under the purchaser agreement. |

**Partnership Essay**

## SCORE SHEET

| Stated | Implied | |
|--------|---------|---|
| | | **Point One (30%) LLP's Liability to Bank** |
| _____ | _____ | **Conclusion:** LLP is liable to the bank on the loan because the man, as a partner of LLP, had apparent authority. |
| _____ | _____ | **Rule:** Even if a partner lacks actual authority, a limited liability partnership can be bound by the acts of a partner, "including the execution of an instrument in the partnership name," if the partner was "apparently carrying on in the ordinary course the partnership business or business of the kind carried on by the partnership. . . ." |
| _____ | _____ | **Application:** Here, |
| _____ | _____ | From the bank's perspective, the man acting as a partner had apparent authority to incur the debt because borrowing $25,000 to pay for ordinary maintenance expenses of a multi-million-dollar apartment complex was entirely consistent with LLP's ordinary business. |
| _____ | _____ | The partners anticipated the need for such loans when they formed the LLP, the LLP had previously borrowed from the bank for such maintenance expenses, and the bank had previously made similar loans to other apartment complexes. |
| _____ | _____ | **Rule:** Apparent authority did not exist, however, if the bank had actual knowledge that the man lacked authority. |
| _____ | _____ | A third party is bound by a limitation of authority only if that party "knew or had notice that the partner lacked authority." |
| _____ | _____ | **Application:** Here, |
| _____ | _____ | No facts suggest that the bank had notice or knowledge of the limitation on authority. |
| _____ | _____ | The bank asked the man if he had authority and the man, in response, gave the bank a copy of the partnership agreement containing no limits on his authority. |
| _____ | _____ | The man did not give the bank a copy of the statement of partnership authority evidencing the man's lack of actual authority. Nor did the bank have knowledge of this statement, which was never filed. |
| | | [NOTE: If an examinee concludes that borrowing $25,000 was not in the ordinary course of business, then the examinee must conclude that there was no apparent authority either.] |
| | | **Point Two (30%) Woman's Liability toBank** |
| _____ | _____ | **Conclusion:** The woman is not personally liable to the bank on its claim under the loan agreement. |
| _____ | _____ | **Rule:** A partner in a LLP has limited liability for any partnership debts. RUPA provides that a partner in a limited liability partnership is not liable for partnership obligations "solely by reason of being or acting as a partner." |
| _____ | _____ | **Application:** The loan obligation arises out of contract, and thus the woman would not be liable for it unless there were some basis for asserting liability against her other than her being a partner. |
| _____ | _____ | **Rule:** Partners can become liable, however, for partnership obligations based on their own personal misconduct. |

*continued on next page*

| Stated | Implied | |
|---|---|---|
| _____ _____ | _____ _____ | **Application:** Here,<br><br>There is no indication of fraudulent or inequitable conduct by the woman that would justify liability for personal misconduct or piercing the entity veil.<br><br>[NOTE: Under some statutes, though not RUPA, partners in a limited liability partnership may also become liable for "the negligence, wrongful acts or misconduct of any person under the partner's direct supervision and control." Under this type of statute, the bank may argue that the woman failed to supervise the man when he entered into the loan without authority. There is nothing, however, to suggest that the man warranted supervision or that the woman was negligent for not supervising the man. In a partnership, each partner is deemed to be the co-equal of the other partners, and no partner is under the control of the other partners. *See* RUPA § 401(h) ("Each partner has equal rights in the management and conduct of the partnership's business").] |
| _____<br><br>_____<br><br>_____<br><br>_____<br><br>_____<br><br>_____<br><br>_____ | _____<br><br>_____<br><br>_____<br><br>_____<br><br>_____<br><br>_____<br><br>_____ | **Point Three (a) (20%) Man's Liability to Partnership**<br><br>**Conclusion:** By improperly obtaining the bank loan and then misappropriating the loan proceeds, the man breached his fiduciary duty of loyalty and his duty of care.<br><br>**Rule:** Under RUPA, a partner owes to the partnership and the other partners the duties of loyalty and care. RUPA § 409(a).<br><br>Partners are liable for damages to the partnership and co-partners for breach of these duties.<br><br>Claims for breach of duties by partners in a limited liability partnership are not subject to the rule of limited liability applicable to claims by outside parties.<br><br>The fiduciary duty of loyalty includes the obligation to refrain from appropriating partnership assets for personal use.<br><br>**Application:** The man breached this duty by misappropriating the proceeds of the loan the bank made to the partnership.<br><br>**Rule:** The duty of care, which is remediable in damages, includes a duty not to engage in intentional misconduct and knowing violations of law.<br><br>**Application:** The man breached this duty by not mentioning or providing the loan officer with the statement of partnership authority, which limited his ability to borrow more than $10,000 without the other partner's consent.<br><br>[NOTE: RUPA, as revised in 2013, treats a partner's duty of loyalty as a fiduciary duty, the breach of which gives rise to a full range of legal and equitable remedies. On the other hand, the revision does not refer to a partner's duty of care as a fiduciary duty, because "the duty of care applies in many non-fiduciary situations." Thus, an examinee who refers to the duty of care as a fiduciary duty in the context of this question should receive full credit.] |
| _____<br><br><br><br>_____<br><br>_____ | _____<br><br><br><br>_____<br><br>_____ | **Point Three (b) (20%) Direct Action Against Man**<br><br>**Conclusion:** The woman (or the partnership) can bring a direct action against the man for breaching his duties of loyalty and care. The woman can also bring an accounting action seeking to have the man pay damages to the partnership for his loyalty breach.<br><br>**Rule:** The duties of loyalty and care run to both "the partnership and the other partners."<br><br>Thus, the partnership can maintain an action against a partner for violating his fiduciary duties to the partnership and thus causing harm to the partnership. |

*continued on next page*

| Stated | Implied | |
|---|---|---|
| _____ | _____ | In addition, a partner can maintain an action against another partner, with or without an accounting, to enforce the partner's rights under the Partnership Act, including an action for violations of duties. |
| _____ | _____ | **Application:** Here, |
| _____ | _____ | The woman can bring a direct action seeking to have the man make her whole for any losses to her caused by his misconduct that breached his duties of loyalty and care. |
| _____ | _____ | She can also bring an accounting action to have the man account to the partnership for the money he took from the partnership. |
| _____ | _____ | Although the partnership could seek damages for these breaches as well, in this two-person partnership it is unlikely that the man would agree to have the partnership sue him. |
| | | [NOTE: Some examinees might conclude that the woman can bring a direct action only for the man's care breach, and the woman would have to pursue an accounting action with respect to the loyalty breach. Although this seems to have been the approach of RUPA (1997), this approach was abandoned in the 2013 revisions to ensure that partners can bring direct claims to protect their interests. *See* Comments to RUPA §§ 409, 410(b). Finally, some examinees might point out that derivative actions are not permitted on behalf of a partnership. This analysis does not affect the conclusion that the woman can bring a direct action against the man for breaching his duties of loyalty and care, given that both of these duties run to both "the partnership and the other partners." *See* RUPA § 409(a).] |

**Corporations Essay Score Sheet**

## SCORE SHEET

| Stated | Implied | |
|---|---|---|
| | | **Point One (20%) Directors' Conflicting Interests Transaction** |
| _____ | _____ | **Conclusion:** The sale of the tower was a "director's conflicting interest transaction" (or director self-dealing) because the directors of the corporation had adverse financial interests as owners of LLC. |
| _____ | _____ | The corporation's directors were on both sides of the transaction, both authorizing it for the corporation and standing to gain from it as owners of LLC. |
| _____ | _____ | **Rule:** A "director's conflicting interest transaction" is one effected by the corporation "respecting which . . . the director had knowledge and a material financial interest." |
| _____ | _____ | **Application:** Here, |
| _____ | _____ | The sale of the tower meets this definition of director self-dealing and is subject to special scrutiny. |
| _____ | _____ | The directors' financial interest in the transaction is clearly "material." |
| _____ | _____ | Each director's one-fourth ownership of LLC is likely to have impaired his or her objectivity in considering the transaction. |
| _____ | _____ | In addition, all the directors were aware that the transaction was with their LLC. |
| _____ | _____ | **Conclusion:** The sale of the tower would qualify as a "director's conflicting interest transaction" given that it was a transaction with the corporation and one in which the directors had a direct or indirect interest. |
| _____ | _____ | The conflict of interest is indirect because the directors of the corporation have a "material financial interest" in the other party, here the new LLC. |
| | | **Point Two (30%) Business Judgment Rule** |
| _____ | _____ | **Conclusion:** The board's authorization of the sale of the tower is not protected by the business judgment rule because the transaction was not authorized by a majority of informed, disinterested directors. |
| _____ | _____ | **Rule:** A director's conflicting interest transaction (that is, a director self-dealing transaction) is not absolutely prohibited. |
| _____ | _____ | Instead, modern corporate law permits such transactions—with the consequence that the business judgment rule applies if, after full disclosure of all relevant facts, qualified directors authorized the transaction. |
| _____ | _____ | If, however, the self-dealing transaction is not shown to have been properly authorized, the business judgment rule does not apply and the transaction must be shown to have been fair to the corporation. |
| _____ | _____ | **Application:** Here, |
| _____ | _____ | The MBCA safe harbor for proper board authorization does not apply. |
| _____ | _____ | There was no authorization of the sale of the tower by qualified directors—that is, by directors who did not have an interest in the transaction. |

*continued on next page*

| Stated | Implied | |
|---|---|---|
| _____ | _____ | The only directors who authorized the transaction were those who had a conflict of interest. |
| _____ | _____ | **Conclusion:** Thus, the presumption of the business judgment rule that the directors were informed and acted in good faith is not available because each of the directors had a material conflicting interest in the sale of the tower. |
| | | [NOTE: Approval or ratification of the transaction by qualified shareholders, after full disclosure of all relevant facts, would in some jurisdictions remove the transaction from further judicial review and in others subject it only to review for waste. But here there was no such approval or ratification.] |
| | | **Point Three (30%) Duty of Loyalty** |
| _____ | _____ | **Conclusion:** The directors likely breached their duty of loyalty because it is unlikely they could show that the transaction was substantively and procedurally fair to the corporation. |
| _____ | _____ | **Rule:** The directors can satisfy their fiduciary duty of loyalty by showing that "the transaction, judged according to the circumstances at the relevant time, was fair to the corporation." |
| _____ | _____ | The directors have the burden to show that the transaction as a whole was fair in terms of "fair price" and "fair dealing." |
| _____ | _____ | This means courts will inquire into (1) whether the transaction price was comparable to what might have been obtained in an arm's-length transaction, given the consideration received by the corporation, and (2) whether the process followed by the directors in reaching their decision was appropriate. |
| _____ | _____ | A breach of the directors' duty to deal fairly with the corporation can result in personal liability. |
| _____ | _____ | **Application:** Here, |
| _____ | _____ | The directors may argue that the $12 million price paid by LLC for the tower made the transaction substantively fair because the price was within the range of offers ($8 to $13 million) received by the corporation when the tower was offered for sale two years before. |
| _____ | _____ | Additionally, the directors may argue that even if the sale was not at the highest valuation received by the corporation for the tower, the sale gave the corporation non-economic advantages by enabling it to "have time to relocate to a new headquarters." |
| _____ | _____ | Finally, the directors may argue that the transaction was procedurally fair because information about the value of the tower was already known to them and there was no reason to make further inquiries. |
| _____ | _____ | It is unlikely, however, that the directors' arguments would meet their burden to show the transaction's fairness. |
| _____ | _____ | As to substantive fairness, the offers and appraisal relied on by the directors occurred two years before the sale to LLC, and the $12 million sales price is less than the $13 million offer that the CEO had rejected as insufficient. |
| _____ | _____ | As to procedural fairness, the directors did not conduct a new market test or seek other purchasers. The process of the board's decision was flawed: the meeting was conducted in 10 minutes, there was no discussion of whether market circumstances had changed since the two-year-old appraisal or whether to seek another appraisal, and there was no consideration of looking for other purchasers or conducting another market test. |

*continued on next page*

| Stated | Implied | |
|--------|---------|---|
| _____ | _____ | Finally, the directors did not consider whether another buyer other than LLC would be willing to accommodate the corporation's need for time to locate and move to new headquarters. |
| _____ | _____ | **Point Four (20%) Duty of Care**<br><br>**Conclusion:** The directors likely breached their fiduciary duty of care in authorizing the sale of the tower because they did not become adequately informed prior to their decision. |
| _____ | _____ | **Rule:** Under the MBCA, a director is called on to exercise "the care that a person in a like position would reasonably believe appropriate under similar circumstances" in "becoming informed in connection with their decision-making function." |
| _____ | _____ | A director may be liable for harm to the corporation from a board decision where it is proven that the director was "not informed to an extent the director reasonably believed appropriate in the circumstances." |
| _____ | _____ | Normally, "the party attacking a board decision as uninformed must rebut the presumption that its business judgment was an informed one." |
| _____ | _____ | **Application:** But here the presumption of the business judgment rule does not apply, given that the directors were each financially interested in the transaction. |
| _____ | _____ | A strong case can be made that the directors were grossly negligent in informing themselves about the sale of the tower to LLC, and thus that they breached their fiduciary duty of care. |
| _____ | _____ | The directors decided to sell the tower at a board meeting that lasted 10 minutes; the only document they reviewed was a two-year-old appraisal; they did not discuss whether market circumstances had changed since the appraisal; they did not seek another appraisal; they did not consider looking for other purchasers, including an accommodating purchaser, or conducting another market test; and they did not discuss how the CEO had conducted the earlier market test.<br><br>[NOTE: For the shareholder to recover money damages based on a claim that the directors breached their duty of care, the shareholder would have to prove that the corporation was harmed by a sales price that was below market and that the sales price was proximately caused by the directors' failure to become adequately informed. *See* MBCA §8.31(b)(1). These showings, however, are not elements of whether the directors breached their duty of care.] |

## IX. Chapter 17  MAPPING TRUSTS AND ESTATES

**Decedents' Estates**

### SCORE SHEET

| Stated | Implied | |
|---|---|---|
| | | **Point One (55%) Revocation** |
| _____ | _____ | **Conclusion:** The husband's will was not revoked because there is no evidence that he intended to revoke the will when he wrote on it. |
| _____ | _____ | **Rule:** A will may be revoked by the execution of a new will or by some physical act, such as cancellation or other writings on the will, if the testator (or someone acting at the testator's direction) performs the physical act with the intent to revoke the will. |
| _____ | _____ | The burden of proof to establish that a validly executed will has been revoked is upon the party seeking to revoke the will. |
| _____ | _____ | **Application:** Here, |
| _____ | _____ | That burden cannot be met. |
| _____ | _____ | The husband's handwritten statement on the will does not show an intent to revoke the will. |
| _____ | _____ | Instead, it suggests that he wanted to re-evaluate his overall estate plan in light of the fact that a large portion of his assets were held in the revocable trust and that he did not believe that either his wife or his daughter was adequately provided for. |
| _____ | _____ | The phrases "estate plan should be changed" and "call lawyer to fix" show intent to do something *in the future* after consultation with his attorney, not to revoke the will now. |
| _____ | _____ | In addition, the discovery of the documents found on the husband's desk, his sudden death, and the voice message on his phone from his lawyer suggest that the husband had only recently discovered the problem and called his lawyer to work it out, not that he had revoked his will. |
| _____ | _____ | **Conclusion:** Thus, because the will was not revoked, the friend should take $5,000 under the husband's will and his wife should take $295,000, the balance of the probate estate (possibly increased by assets from the trust (*see* Point Three) but subject to the daughter's claim, if any (*see* Point Two)). |
| | | [NOTE: Alternatively, the markings on the will might be construed as evidencing an intent to revoke the will. The husband appears to have recognized that the will made no sense in light of his family circumstances. The markings state that the plan should be changed and that the husband will take steps to make that change by calling his lawyer which, in fact, he did. Thus, so the argument goes, the will was revoked by cancellation. If the will was revoked, then the husband died intestate and half the estate would pass to the wife and half to the daughter under the intestacy law of the state.] |
| | | [NOTE: The argument claiming that there was an intent to revoke is not as strong as the argument in favor of no revocation because of the language of futurity in those markings.] |

*continued on next page*

| Stated | Implied | |
|--------|---------|---|
| | | **Point Two (15%) Pretermitted Child** |
| _____ | _____ | **Conclusion:** Most likely the husband's daughter is not entitled to a pretermitted child's share. |
| _____ | _____ | The phrase in the will "regardless of whether we have children" suggests that the husband wanted the wife to take even if they had children, thus evidencing his intent that the pretermitted child statute not apply. |
| _____ | _____ | **Rule:** Most states have "pretermitted child" statutes aimed at ensuring that children born after the execution of a will are not inadvertently disinherited. |
| _____ | _____ | Many of these statutes provide that, under certain circumstances, a child born to a testator after the testator's will is executed is entitled to whatever share of the testator's estate the child would have received if the testator had died intestate. |
| _____ | _____ | In states with such statutes, bequests in favor of an afterborn child's other parent are irrelevant. |
| _____ | _____ | However, a testator can avoid the consequences of such a statute if the will evidences intent to do so. |
| _____ | _____ | **Application:** Here, |
| _____ | _____ | That seems to be the husband's intent as evidenced by the phrase "regardless of whether we have children." |
| _____ | _____ | **Rule:** In other states, an afterborn child is denied a share of the decedent parent's estate if the decedent parent bequeathed all or substantially all of his estate to the child's other parent. |
| _____ | _____ | **Conclusion:** In states that follow the UPC approach, the daughter would not be entitled to any share of the husband's estate because her mother (the wife) is entitled to substantially all of the husband's estate. |
| | | [NOTE: Regardless of how examinees conclude Point One, there were enough signals in the question to have prompted discussion of this issue even if they concluded that the will had been revoked.] |
| | | **Point Three (30%) Trust** |
| _____ | _____ | **Conclusion:** The wife is entitled to take one-half of the revocable trust under the state statute. Either the wife, as residuary legatee under the husband's will, or University, as remainderman of the trust, is entitled to the other half. |
| _____ | _____ | **Rule:** Under the law of the state, the wife is entitled to a one-half share of the revocable trust created by the husband because the trust was in existence during the marriage. |
| _____ | _____ | This leaves open the question of who is entitled to the balance of the trust's assets. |
| _____ | _____ | **Application:** Under the statute, the trust is characterized as "illusory." |
| _____ | _____ | This characterization is ambiguous regarding whether it is just illusory as to the wife or illusory for all purposes. |
| _____ | _____ | If the former, then the wife is entitled to her half share, as that share only is illusory, and the balance of the trust (not deemed illusory) should pass to University, as the designated remainderman. |

*continued on next page*

| Stated | Implied | |
|---|---|---|
| \_\_\_\_\_ | \_\_\_\_\_ | On the other hand, if a court deems the trust illusory for all purposes, then the trust is void and the trust assets are distributed to the wife as residuary legatee of the husband's estate, assuming that the will is valid. |
| \_\_\_\_\_ | \_\_\_\_\_ | If, however, the will is invalid, the trust assets pass equally to the wife and her daughter as intestate property. |

**Trusts**

## SCORE SHEET

| Stated | Implied | |
|--------|---------|---|
| | | **Point One (30%) Restraint on Marriage** |
| _____ | _____ | **Conclusion:** The son's income interest in the trust would not terminate upon his marriage because the condition against marriage is void as a matter of public policy. |
| _____ | _____ | **Rule:** Provisions of trusts that violate public policy are void. |
| _____ | _____ | Trust provisions that restrain a first marriage have generally been held to violate public policy. Thus, because the son's income interest would terminate upon his marriage, no matter what the circumstances of that marriage, the provision is void and the son's income interest continues. |
| _____ | _____ | A restraint on marriage might be upheld if the trustee's motive was merely to provide support for a beneficiary while the beneficiary is single. |
| _____ | _____ | **Application:** Here, |
| _____ | _____ | No facts support that motive. |
| _____ | _____ | **Conclusion:** Because this is a mandatory income payout trust, the trust income is payable to the son without regard to his support needs. |
| | | **Point Two (35%) Duty of Loyalty** |
| _____ | _____ | **Conclusion:** The trustee breached his duty of loyalty by purchasing stock from the trust, an act of self-dealing. |
| _____ | _____ | In such a case, trust beneficiaries may obtain an order setting aside the transaction or seek damages based on the difference between the purchased assets' fair market value at the time of purchase and the sales price paid by the trustee. |
| _____ | _____ | **Rule:** A trustee owes a fiduciary duty of loyalty to a trust; self-dealing, such as a purchase of trust assets by the trustee in his individual capacity, violates this obligation. |
| _____ | _____ | Under the "no further inquiry" rule, there is no need to inquire into the motivation for the self-dealing transaction or even its fairness. |
| _____ | _____ | Any trust beneficiary can cause a self-dealing purchase by a trustee to be set aside or obtain a damages award. |
| _____ | _____ | If a beneficiary elects to set aside the transaction, the trust property purchased by the trustee is returned to the trust and the amount the trustee paid for the property is refunded by the trust. |
| _____ | _____ | If a beneficiary seeks damages, those damages are based on the difference in the fair market value of the trust assets at the time of the self-dealing transaction and the amount paid by the trustee. |
| _____ | _____ | Where the assets purchased by the trustee have declined in value since the self-dealing transaction, trust beneficiaries are likely to seek damages instead of setting aside the transaction. |

*continued on next page*

| Stated | Implied | |
|--------|---------|---|
| _____ | _____ | **Application:** Here, |
| _____ | _____ | The beneficiaries should elect to seek damages from the trustee, not rescission. |
| _____ | _____ | First, with rescission, the trustee would return the shares to the trust, and the trust would have to refund the purchase price to the trustee. |
| _____ | _____ | This would leave the trust with assets worth only $450,000. |
| _____ | _____ | Furthermore, because of the market declines, the trust assets are currently worth only $1,000,000; thus the trust doesn't have sufficient assets to refund the purchase price. |
| _____ | _____ | On the other hand, by seeking damages, the trust would collect $300,000, representing the difference between the value of the shares when purchased by the trustee ($1,500,000) and the purchase price ($1,200,000), leaving the trust with $1,300,000 in assets. |
| _____ | _____ | The trustee also breached his duty of care when selling the stock because of his failure to test the market. |
| | | **Point Three (35%) Prudent Investment Duty** |
| _____ | _____ | **Conclusion:** No facts suggest that the trustee breached any prudent investment duty with respect to the selection and management of the investments he made. |
| _____ | _____ | **Rule:** A trustee has a duty to invest trust assets in a prudent manner. |
| _____ | _____ | One of the hallmarks of prudent investing is diversification. |
| _____ | _____ | A balanced portfolio reduces aggregate risk by investing in different investment categories. |
| _____ | _____ | Diversification thus is strong evidence of prudent investing. |
| _____ | _____ | The trustee should consider the purposes, terms, distribution requirements, and other circumstances affecting the trust. |
| _____ | _____ | The prudent investor rule applies to both investment and management decisions. |
| _____ | _____ | Management includes monitoring; thus, the trustee has a duty to monitor investments prudently made to assure that retention of those investments remains prudent. |
| _____ | _____ | If retention is not prudent, the trustee should sell the imprudent investments and reinvest the proceeds in prudent investments. |
| _____ | _____ | A trustee, however, is not liable for declines in value due to a downturn resulting from general economic conditions. |
| _____ | _____ | **Application:** Here, |
| _____ | _____ | The trustee's investment of the sale proceeds seems to satisfy the diversification requirement. |
| _____ | _____ | The trustee selected a balanced group of mutual funds; the portfolio included both stock and bond funds; it contained both growth and income funds. |
| _____ | _____ | The trustee also appears to have considered the needs of both the income beneficiary and remainderman; growth funds are aimed at achieving principal appreciation and income funds at producing current income. |
| _____ | _____ | The funds' decline in value during a period of general economic decline—when most types of investments may well have fallen in value—does not evidence lack of prudence, and there are no facts to show any failure to monitor the portfolio. |

## X. Chapter 18 MAPPING FAMILY LAW

## SCORE SHEET

| Stated | Implied | |
|---|---|---|
| | | **Point One (35%) Validity of Premarital Agreement** |
| _____ | _____ | **Conclusion:** Because the woman fully disclosed her assets, and the facts do not support a finding that the man signed the agreement involuntarily, the agreement is likely enforceable. |
| _____ | _____ | **Rule:** Under the UPAA, a premarital agreement entered into after full disclosure of assets and obligations is binding unless it was entered into involuntarily. |
| _____ | _____ | In all states, the enforceability of such an agreement turns on three factors: voluntariness, fairness, and disclosure. |
| _____ | _____ | In many states, an agreement is unenforceable if the party against whom enforcement is sought succeeds in showing _either_ involuntariness, unfairness, or lack of adequate disclosure. |
| _____ | _____ | However, under the UPAA, which has been adopted in 25 states and the state in which this question is set, the party against whom enforcement is sought must prove (1) involuntariness or (2) _both_ that "the agreement was unconscionable when it was executed" _and_ that he or she did not receive or waive a "fair and reasonable" disclosure and "did not have or reasonably could not have had . . . an adequate knowledge" of the other's assets and obligations. |
| _____ | _____ | Thus, a court may not refuse to enforce a premarital agreement based on substantive unfairness unless it also finds lack of adequate disclosure or knowledge. |
| _____ | _____ | **Application:** Here, |
| _____ | _____ | The man cannot show inadequate disclosure because the woman gave him an accurate asset list with the agreement. |
| _____ | _____ | **Rule:** In considering whether a premarital agreement was voluntarily executed, courts look to whether there was fraud, duress, or coercion. |
| _____ | _____ | One party's insistence on signing the agreement as a condition of the marriage does not, of itself, render the agreement involuntary, but there is no consensus on what additional facts are sufficient to establish involuntariness. |
| _____ | _____ | In analyzing whether an agreement signed very close to the wedding is voluntary, courts have looked at a wide range of factors, including the difficulty of conferring with independent counsel, other reasons for proceeding with the marriage (for example, a preexisting pregnancy), and financial losses and embarrassment arising from cancellation of the wedding. |
| _____ | _____ | **Application:** Here, |
| _____ | _____ | The woman presented the agreement to the man only a week before the wedding. |
| _____ | _____ | But the man had time to confer with independent counsel, and he did so. |
| _____ | _____ | The man ultimately rejected the advice of the lawyer he consulted. |
| _____ | _____ | The man and the woman were married at City Hall, and there are no facts suggesting any hardship that the man would have suffered from canceling or postponing the ceremony. |

_continued on next page_

| Stated | Implied | |
|---|---|---|
| _____ | _____ | **Conclusion:** Therefore, it is unlikely that the man can establish involuntariness. |
| _____ | _____ | Under the UPAA, the premarital agreement thus is likely enforceable. |
| | | **Point Two (a) (50%) Marital v. Separate Property** |
| _____ | _____ | **Conclusion:** The woman's condominium is separate and nondivisible; the woman's lottery winnings are marital and divisible; and some portion of the woman's brokerage account and at least some of the man's royalties are also marital and divisible. |
| _____ | _____ | **Rule:** Assets acquired before marriage or by inheritance are separate, not marital, property. In most jurisdictions, separate property is not subject to division at divorce. |
| _____ | _____ | However, significant spousal effort during the marriage that adds value to a separate asset does create divisible marital property. |
| _____ | _____ | In all states (whether community property or common law jurisdictions), a divorce court may divide marital (community) property without regard to title. |
| _____ | _____ | An asset is marital if it was acquired during the marriage by any means other than a gift, descent, or devise. |
| _____ | _____ | In the majority of states, marital property continues to accrue until a final divorce decree is entered. |
| _____ | _____ | In some states, however, marital property ceases to accrue after the date of permanent separation or the date of divorce filing. |
| _____ | _____ | However, expectancies created during the marriage are still marital even if payment will not be received until after the marriage ends. |
| _____ | _____ | Even contingent expectancies such as unvested pension rights are subject to division at divorce if they were acquired through spousal effort during the marriage. |
| _____ | _____ | An asset that is initially separate property may be partially transformed into divisible marital property if marital funds or significant effort by the owner-spouse enhance its value or build equity. |
| _____ | _____ | In the vast majority of states, the appreciation of separate assets during the marriage does not create marital property. |
| _____ | _____ | In this and the vast majority of jurisdictions, a divorce court may not divide separate property. |
| _____ | _____ | In a minority of jurisdictions—so-called "hotchpot" jurisdictions—the court may divide all assets, whenever or however acquired; a few states permit the division of separate property in special circumstances, such as hardship. |
| _____ | _____ | **Application:** Here, |
| _____ | _____ | **Lottery Award:** Unless the woman and the man live in a state in which marital property ceases to accrue after separation, the woman's lottery award is marital property because the woman purchased the winning ticket before the man filed for divorce. |
| _____ | _____ | It does not matter that the woman may not receive any winnings before the divorce filing. |

*continued on next page*

| Stated | Implied | |
|---|---|---|
| _____ | _____ | **Condominium:** The entire value of the woman's condominium is separate property because she purchased the condominium outright before marriage, and its increased value is due entirely to market forces, not spousal efforts or marital funds. |
| _____ | _____ | **Brokerage Account:** Some portion of the woman's brokerage account is divisible marital property because the woman contributed her employment bonuses during the marriage to that account; only the portion attributable to investments the woman made before marriage remains separate. |
| _____ | _____ | **Royalties:** Some, if not all, of the royalties the man will receive in the future are divisible marital property despite the fact that the man began the novel before marriage. |
| _____ | _____ | **Rule:** Significant spousal effort during marriage that enhances the value of a separate asset creates marital property. |
| _____ | _____ | The man worked at paid employment only part-time throughout the marriage in order to work on the novel. The facts do not specify how much the man worked on the novel during the marriage. |
| _____ | _____ | If the man completed a significant portion of the novel during the marriage, the value of the novel would be apportioned into separate and marital components. It is irrelevant that the royalties will not be received until after the marriage ends. |
| | | [NOTE: The above analysis applies in both common law and community property jurisdictions. Although the rules governing asset management and distribution at death vary depending on whether the jurisdiction is a common law or community property state, today, all states disregard title in defining the pool of assets available for divorce. Indeed, the marital property rules applicable in common law states are sometimes referred to as "deferred" community property.] |
| | | **Point Two (b) (15%) Division of Property** |
| _____ | _____ | **Rule:** In dividing marital assets, divorce courts look at contribution (monetary and nonmonetary), need, and marital duration. |
| _____ | _____ | In an equitable distribution state, courts have broad authority to divide property fairly. |
| _____ | _____ | Typically, either by statute or by case law, courts are given a list of relevant, non-exclusive factors to consider. |
| _____ | _____ | Relevant factors usually include the duration of the marriage; indicators of each spouse's future needs (including age, health, resources, and occupational opportunities); and contributions of the parties to the marriage and the acquisition of assets. |
| _____ | _____ | **Application:** Here, |
| _____ | _____ | The marriage was short, the man is the needier spouse, and the woman made greater financial contributions to the marriage, contributions which may have enabled the man to complete his novel. |
| _____ | _____ | The woman appears to have made much larger financial contributions to the marriage than the man, and she appears to be better off now than the man because of her occupation as an investment banker and her lottery winnings. |
| _____ | _____ | The couple has no children, so the man has made no significant nonfinancial contributions as a parent; there are also no facts to suggest that he has made significant nonfinancial contributions as a homemaker. Instead, the woman's support freed the man to work on his novel. |

*continued on next page*

| Stated | Implied | |
|---|---|---|
| _____ | _____ | The broad discretion given courts to distribute property equitably often makes it impossible to predict with certainty how a court will divide marital property. [NOTE: An examinee may appropriately note that the uncertain value of the man's expected royalties may play a role in determining how a property award should be fashioned. With a pension of uncertain value to be paid in the future, courts often order payment of a specified percentage of pension payments when those payments are actually made instead of requiring the title-holding spouse to compensate the other spouse at the time of divorce.] |

## XI. Chapter 19 MAPPING SECURED TRANSACTIONS

### SCORE SHEET

| Stated | Implied | |
|---|---|---|
| ⎯⎯ | ⎯⎯ | **Point One (40%) Finance Company's Security Interest** |
| ⎯⎯ | ⎯⎯ | **Overall Conclusion:** The buyer obtained the home entertainment system free of the finance company's perfected security interest because the buyer was a buyer in the ordinary course of business. |
| ⎯⎯ | ⎯⎯ | Because the buyer owned the home entertainment system free of the security interest, the buyer's sale to the friend was free of that interest. |
| ⎯⎯ | ⎯⎯ | **The finance company's status:** The finance company had an enforceable, attached security interest in all of the retailer's inventory, including the home entertainment system later sold to the buyer. |
| ⎯⎯ | ⎯⎯ | **Rule:** A creditor can enforce a security interest against a debtor only if the security interest is attached to the collateral. |
| ⎯⎯ | ⎯⎯ | Attachment requires that (1) the debtor give the creditor an authenticated security agreement granting a security interest or the creditor has possession of the collateral or the creditor has control of the collateral; (2) the debtor had rights in the collateral; and (3) the creditor gave value. |
| ⎯⎯ | ⎯⎯ | **Application:** Here, |
| ⎯⎯ | ⎯⎯ | All three elements of enforceability and attachment under UCC § 9-203 were satisfied: value was given (the loan), the debtor (the retailer) had rights in the inventory, and the debtor (the retailer) authenticated a security agreement containing a description of the collateral. |
| ⎯⎯ | ⎯⎯ | **Rule:** A security interest may be perfected by filing a financing statement in the appropriate office. |
| ⎯⎯ | ⎯⎯ | **Application:** Moreover, the finance company's security interest was perfected by the filing of the financing statement. |
| ⎯⎯ | ⎯⎯ | **Conclusion on the finance company's status:** Thus, the finance company was a perfected secured creditor. |
| ⎯⎯ | ⎯⎯ | **Buyer—Rule:** As a general rule, a security interest continues notwithstanding the sale of collateral. |
| ⎯⎯ | ⎯⎯ | An exception to this rule is a "buyer in ordinary course of business" (BIOCOB) who takes free of a security interest created by its seller even if the security interest was perfected. |
| ⎯⎯ | ⎯⎯ | A BIOCOB is a buyer who purchases goods in the regular course of business from someone in the business of selling goods of the kind. |
| ⎯⎯ | ⎯⎯ | **Application:** Here, |
| ⎯⎯ | ⎯⎯ | The buyer appears to have bought the home entertainment system in good faith and in the ordinary course from a person in the business of selling goods of the kind (the retailer) without knowledge that the sale to her violated the rights of a third party. |
| ⎯⎯ | ⎯⎯ | Under these facts, the buyer was a BIOCOB. |
| ⎯⎯ | ⎯⎯ | **Conclusion on buyer:** Because the buyer was a BIOCOB, she acquired the home entertainment system free of the finance company's security interest. |

*continued on next page*

| Stated | Implied | |
|---|---|---|
| _____ | _____ | **Friend—Rule:** Under the "shelter principle," once the buyer acquired the home entertainment system free of the finance company's security interest, any subsequent transfer of the system by the buyer to someone else was also free of the finance company's security interest. |
| _____ | _____ | **Application/Conclusion on friend:** Accordingly, when the friend acquired the home entertainment system from the buyer, it was free of the finance company's security interest. |
| | | **Point Two (40%) Retailer's Security Interest** |
| _____ | _____ | **Conclusion:** The retailer's retention of title to the home entertainment system in the credit sale to the buyer was a security interest in the system. |
| _____ | _____ | While the security interest was automatically perfected, the friend acquired the system free of the retailer's security interest. |
| _____ | _____ | **Rule:** Article 9 governs any transaction *regardless of form* that creates a security interest in personal property by contract. [Substance over form.] |
| _____ | _____ | **Application:** Here, |
| _____ | _____ | While the agreement between the retailer and the buyer indicated that the retailer was retaining title to the home entertainment system, the substance-over-form rules of secured transactions law indicate that the retailer's interest was not ownership but, rather, a security interest. |
| _____ | _____ | All the elements of attachment and enforceability of this security interest were satisfied. |
| _____ | _____ | **Conclusion on attachment:** The retailer has an enforceable security interest against the debtor. |
| _____ | _____ | **Conclusion on perfection:** The retailer's security interest was perfected even though the retailer did not file a financing statement. |
| _____ | _____ | This is because the retailer's security interest was a "purchase-money security interest" (PMSI) in "consumer goods." |
| _____ | _____ | **Rule:** A purchase-money security interest exists when a seller sells goods to a buyer on credit or when a lender lends the purchase money to buy specific goods and is retained by the seller to secure payment of the remainder of the sales price. |
| _____ | _____ | "Consumer goods" are used primarily for personal, family, or household purposes. |
| _____ | _____ | **Conclusion:** The retailer has a PMSI in the home entertainment system. |
| _____ | _____ | **Rule:** A purchase-money security interest in consumer goods perfects automatically upon attachment without the filing of a financing statement. |
| _____ | _____ | **Application/Conclusion:** Therefore, the retailer's security interest in the home entertainment system was a perfected security interest while the system was owned by the buyer. |
| _____ | _____ | **Rule:** As a general rule, a security interest continues notwithstanding the sale of collateral. |
| _____ | _____ | **Application:** Thus, under this general rule, the retailer's security interest in the home entertainment system would continue after the buyer's sale of the system to the friend. |
| _____ | _____ | **Rule:** But this general rule is subject to several exceptions. |

*continued on next page*

| Stated | Implied | |
|--------|---------|---|
| _____ | _____ | The consumer-to-consumer exception provides that a buyer who purchases goods that were used for personal, family, or household purposes before the sale and the subsequent purchaser use the goods in the same manner after the sale, and the buyer acquired the goods for value, without knowledge of the security interest, and before a financing statement was filed with respect to that security interest takes free of the original creditor's security interest. |
| _____ | _____ | **Application:** In this case, the friend acquired the system free of the retailer's security interest under the consumer-to-consumer exception because the home entertainment system was used solely for personal, family, or household purposes both before and after the sale. |
| | | **Point Three (20%) Proceeds** |
| _____ | _____ | **Conclusion:** Because the retailer had a perfected security interest in the home entertainment system at the time of its sale to the friend, the retailer obtained a security interest in the $4,000 check as proceeds from the sale of the system; the security interest in the check was perfected for 20 days and remained perfected thereafter because the check constituted "cash proceeds." |
| _____ | _____ | **Rule:** When collateral is disposed of, a secured party automatically obtains a security interest in identifiable proceeds of the collateral. |
| _____ | _____ | **Application:** Accordingly, when the home entertainment system was sold by the buyer to the friend, and the buyer received the check in return, the check constituted proceeds of the home entertainment system and the retailer (which had a security interest in the system) thereby obtained a security interest in the check. |
| _____ | _____ | **Rule:** When a security interest in the collateral had been perfected, the security interest in proceeds is perfected as well. |
| _____ | _____ | That perfection ceases after 20 days, however, unless an exception applies (home office, cash proceeds, or consent). |
| _____ | _____ | **Application:** In this case, because the check was "cash proceeds," perfection continued. |
| _____ | _____ | **Conclusion:** Thus, the retailer's security interest in the check was continuously perfected after the sale of the system to the friend. |

## XII. Chapter 20  MAPPING CONFLICT OF LAWS

### SCORE SHEET

| Stated | Implied | |
|---|---|---|
| | | **Issue 1: Recognition of Marriage** |
| _____ | _____ | A common law marriage that is valid where contracted is also valid in a state that does not permit common law marriage. |
| _____ | _____ | **Rule:** Under accepted conflict-of-laws principles, |
| _____ | _____ | A marriage valid under the law of the place in which it was contracted is valid elsewhere unless it violates a strong public policy of the state which has the most significant relationship with the spouses and the marriage. |
| _____ | _____ | If a man and woman were domiciled in a state that permits common law marriage and their conduct met the requirements of that state's law for establishing such a marriage, recognition of the marriage does not violate a strong public policy. |
| _____ | _____ | A common law marriage, once established, is the equivalent of a ceremonial marriage. |
| _____ | _____ | **Application/Conclusion:** Thus, if Dave and Meg entered into a valid common law marriage in State A, it would be recognized by a State B court. |
| | | **Issue 2: Common Law Marriage** |
| _____ | _____ | Dave and Meg did not enter into a common law marriage. |
| _____ | _____ | **Rule:** Under family law, |
| _____ | _____ | To establish a common law marriage, the proponent must show: |
| _____ | _____ | (1) capacity to enter a marital contract, |
| _____ | _____ | (2) a present agreement that the two parties are married, |
| _____ | _____ | (3) cohabitation, and |
| _____ | _____ | (4) "holding out" a marital relationship to the community. |
| _____ | _____ | **Application:** Here, |
| _____ | _____ | The evidence clearly establishes capacity and cohabitation. It also suggests an agreement to *become* married. |
| _____ | _____ | However, a common law marriage requires a *present* marriage agreement. |
| _____ | _____ | If Dave and Meg made any marriage agreement, it was an agreement to be married *in the future:* |
| _____ | _____ | Meg told Dave that she was "committed to marrying him," but "wanted a real wedding, and we can't afford that now;" Meg also proposed that Dave move in with her so that "we can save money to get married." |
| _____ | _____ | There is also no evidence that Dave and Meg held themselves out as a married couple. Although Meg said to friends and family that Dave was her fiancé, a fiancé is an intended spouse, not a current marriage partner. |

*continued on next page*

| Stated | Implied | |
|--------|---------|---|
| _____ | _____ | **Conclusion:** Thus, Dave and Meg did not enter into a valid common law marriage, and Dave would be categorized as an unmarried father under State B's adoption-consent statute. |
| | | **Issue 3: Constitutionality of Adoption Statute:** |
| _____ | _____ | State B is constitutionally prohibited from permitting the child's adoption without his consent. |
| _____ | _____ | **Rule:** An unwed father must demonstrate a full commitment to the responsibilities of parenthood by participating in the rearing of his child. |
| _____ | _____ | Then, his interest in personal contact with his child acquires substantial protection under the Fourteenth Amendment Due Process Clause. |
| _____ | _____ | **Application:** Here, |
| _____ | _____ | Dave is a committed father who consistently held himself out as a parent, who resided with his child and who provided support for his child and the child's mother. |
| _____ | _____ | **Conclusion on commitment:** Thus, Dave has a strong argument that State B is constitutionally precluded from permitting his child's adoption without his consent. |
| _____ | _____ | **Rule on constitutionality:** A committed father is entitled to a hearing to demonstrate his parental fitness before his parental rights may be terminated. |
| _____ | _____ | Rule conflict as to whether an unmarried father has a right to veto an adoption by another man. |
| _____ | _____ | **Application:** Dave has demonstrated the kind of commitment that should trigger protection under the Fourteenth Amendment. |
| _____ | _____ | Dave held himself out as Child's father; he consented to be identified as Child's father on Child's birth certificate and sent birth announcements identifying himself as Child's father. |
| _____ | _____ | Dave lived with Child and Child's mother and provided support to them. |
| _____ | _____ | After Child's birth, Dave was the only family breadwinner and held down two jobs in order to provide for Meg and Child. |
| _____ | _____ | He also had volunteered to marry Meg and thus would have been a marital father had Meg agreed. Dave is also blameless for his failure to satisfy the statutory veto requirements; Dave would have lived with Child and Meg for the relevant nine-month period but for Meg's abrupt and unannounced departure from their home. |
| _____ | _____ | **Conclusion on constitutionality of adoption-consent statute:** It is likely that Dave would prevail. |
| _____ | _____ | **Rule:** Adoption-consent statutes that would deny a veto right to a father who has done everything in his power to establish a full relationship with his child are unconstitutional as applied in such a case. |
| _____ | _____ | Under federal law, a voluntary acknowledgment of paternity is binding if unchallenged by the named father within 60 days. |
| _____ | _____ | State B does not provide unmarried fathers with a putative father registry, and Dave thus had no way of obtaining notice of an adoption proceeding. |
| _____ | _____ | **Application:** Here, Dave established his paternity by voluntarily acknowledging Child and causing his name to be placed on Child's birth certificate. |

*continued on next page*

| Stated | Implied | |
|--------|---------|---|
| _____ | _____ | **Conclusion:** Thus, State B's adoption consent statute appears to be unconstitutional as applied to Dave, a committed parent who has fully participated in the rearing of his child. |
| | | **Issue 4: Choice of Law for Child Custody:** |
| _____ | _____ | Because State A has been Child's home state within the past six months and Dave, a parent continues to live in State A, State B does not have jurisdiction to terminate Dave's parental rights or to make an initial child-custody determination respecting Child. |
| _____ | _____ | Under the Uniform Child Custody Jurisdiction and Enforcement Act, a child's "home state" has exclusive jurisdiction to issue an initial custody decree. |
| _____ | _____ | A "home state" is a state where the child has lived with "a parent, or a person acting as a parent, for at least six consecutive months immediately before the commencement of a child-custody proceeding." |
| _____ | _____ | A "child-custody proceeding" includes a proceeding for termination of parental rights. |
| _____ | _____ | A home state continues to have exclusive jurisdiction to issue an initial custody order even if the child is absent from the state when a custody petition is brought, so long as no more than six months has elapsed since the child's departure from the jurisdiction and a parent or person acting as a parent continues to live in the home state. |
| _____ | _____ | Physical presence of, or personal jurisdiction over, a party or a child is not necessary to make a child-custody determination. |
| _____ | _____ | **Application:** Here, Meg took Child from the family home in State A only five months ago, and Dave still lives in State A. |
| _____ | _____ | **Conclusion:** Thus, State A has exclusive jurisdiction to issue an initial custody decree and also to terminate parental rights. State B lacks jurisdiction to do either. |
| | | (Note: The UCCJEA does not apply to adoption proceedings, but termination of a parent's rights is typically a precondition for an adoption. Thus, as a practicality, the UCCJEA should preclude a State B court from granting petition for Husband's adoption of Child.) |